The Functional Mind

Readings in Evolutionary Psychology

DOUGLAS T. KENRICK

Arizona State University

CAROL L. LUCE

Arizona State University

Boston   New York   San Francisco
Mexico City   Montreal   Toronto   London   Madrid   Munich   Paris
Hong Kong   Singapore   Tokyo   Cape Town   Sydney

Executive Editor: Karon Bowers
Editorial Assistant: Carolyn Mulloy
Marketing Manager: Taryn Wahlquist
Production Editor: Michelle Limoges
Editorial-Production Service: Communicáto, Ltd.
Text Design/Composition: Denise Hoffman
Composition and Prepress Buyer: Linda Cox
Manufacturing Buyer: JoAnne Sweeney
Cover Designer: Kristina Mose-Libon

For related titles and support materials, visit our online catalog at www.ablongman.com.

Between the time Website information is gathered and then published, it is not unusual for some sites to have closed. Also, the transcription of URLs can result in typographical errors. The publisher would appreciate notification where these errors occur so that they may be corrected in subsequent editions.

Library of Congress Cataloging-in-Publication Data

The functional mind : readings in evolutionary psychology / [edited by] Douglas T. Kenrick, Carol L. Luce.
    p. cm.
    Includes bibliographical references.
    ISBN 0-205-34409-7
    1. Evolutionary psychology. I. Kenrick, Douglas T. II. Luce, Carol L.

BF698.95.R43 2004
155.7—dc21

                 2003056336

Printed in the United States of America

10 9 8 7 6 5 4 3 2 1   CS   09 08 07 06 05 04 03

Contents

Introduction: The Evolution Revolution

The evolutionary perspective on psychology has the power to fundamentally change how you understand yourself, your fellow humans, and your relationship to the birds, the bees, and your pet dog. Getting a good grasp on this perspective is like turning on a light inside your head: It is both illuminating and exciting. And once people get it—that is, once they understand how to think in evolutionary terms—they never turn back.

Some people are wary when they first encounter the evolutionary perspective on human psychology. Although most educated people now accept Charles Darwin's theory of natural selection as an explanation of the giraffe's long neck, the peacock's multicolored feathers, and the killer whale's streamlined shape, many are still uncomfortable applying the same logic to the human experiences of love, creativity, and family relationships. Yet the readings presented in this book demonstrate how the evolutionary perspective can shed the same light on human thought and behavior as it has on the behaviors of other species, from earthworms to chimpanzees. Indeed, we challenge any skeptical student to read this collection with an open mind and *not* emerge with a new level of understanding of human behavior.

One reason for making the effort to understand evolutionary psychology is the power it provides for organizing a host of otherwise disconnected findings. Psychology's domain ranges from neural firings to word recognition, motor development, fear conditioning, attraction between strangers, and group decision making. One of the common complaints of psychologists, however, has been the lack of a conceptual map—a cohesive paradigm to organize this broad field of topics. Indeed, one of our colleagues, psychologist Peter Killeen, once lamented that psychology needed "its own Charles Darwin"—a grand theorist to pull together all its isolated findings. Killeen was surprised to hear biologist Charles Wolff respond that psychology already had such a person. "Who?" asked Killeen. Wolff's response was a thought-provoking one: "Charles Darwin."

Although evolutionary theory has served quite well to integrate the myriad facts about living organisms, its benefits for psychology have not always been well understood. But all that has begun to change during the last few decades, as the evidence for an evolutionary approach to psychology has continued to mount. This evidence comes from a diverse array of findings:

■ *Cross-cultural findings.* Viewed through standard ethnocentric lenses, our eyes are drawn to the strange and unusual, the ways in which *they* are different from *us*. But beneath the sometimes colorful differences, ours is one species, and our neighbors the world over share certain important ways of behaving, thinking, and feeling (e.g., Daly & Wilson, 1988b; Ekman & Friesen, 1971; Kenrick & Keefe, 1992).

■ *Cross-species comparisons.* Findings from different animal species reveal that our species, although unique in some ways, also shares many behavioral and psychological mechanisms with other species. Comparative research has revealed powerful principles—such as inclusive fitness, differential parental investment, and sexual selection—that can help explain many of the patterns found in animal behavior (Gould & Gould, 1989; Trivers, 1985). Functional analyses have proven essential to understanding why some animals but not others see in color while others do not see at all, why some have dominance hierarchies, and why some have females that are more colorful and competitive than males (Alcock, 2001; Williams, 1996). As the readings in this book demonstrate, such analyses are now being fruitfully applied to human behavior (e.g., Daly & Wilson, 1988a; Pinker, 2003).

■ *Behavior genetic research.* Although evolutionary psychologists are more interested in studying how organisms adapt to the natural environment than in exploring the specific mechanics by which genes affect biochemical development, the evolutionary position does rest on the assumption that genetic predispositions can be passed from one generation to the next. Such an assumption was at odds with the so-called blank-slate model once popular in psychology. However, research from studies of twins and adoptees has completely overturned the blank-slate model and suggested that behavioral, affective, and cognitive capacities and predispositions are indeed passed from one generation to the next (Plomin, DeFries, McClearn, & Rutter, 1997; Rowe, 1994).

■ *Cognitive psychology and artificial intelligence.* One long-held misconception is that adopting an evolutionary perspective requires embracing a doctrine of blind instincts as well. However, several decades of research in cognitive science has made it feasible to talk about inner "programs" for intelligent and flexible behavior that emerge in appropriate contexts (Barkow, Cosmides, & Tooby, 1992; Pinker, 1997).

Part of the appeal of an evolutionary perspective is its strength as an integrative glue for the scattered field of psychology. But a good theory does more than organize existing knowledge. It also suggests new places for researchers to look. Emboldened by new findings, psychologists have begun to consider how adopting an evolutionary perspective can enhance their research into processes ranging from physiology and sensation to perception and learning and to complex problem solving and group behavior. This collection of readings is a celebration of the fruits of those endeavors.

Selection of Readings

In researching readings for this collection, we were both humbled and delighted: humbled by the sheer magnitude of insights and empirical discoveries that have flowed from this endeavor and delighted at the abundance of riches from which to choose. We were reminded of the experience of being an undergraduate student and looking at the university's delicious menu of course offerings, only to be disappointed by being unable to consume them *all* in the upcoming semester. In the end, the student settles on a small selection of all those curiosity-inspiring courses, as we have settled on a small selection of intriguing readings on evolutionary psychology.

Our selection of readings was driven by several criteria:

■ *We wanted to represent the whole field of psychology.* A great deal of work has been done on social behavior, perhaps because mate choice and intrasexual competition are so central to natural selection. In addition to this work, however, we wanted to introduce students to the less sensational but equally important applications of evolutionary thinking to other fundamental areas of research in the field: sensation, perception, psychophysiology, learning, memory, cognition, motivation, emotion, language, nonverbal communication, psychopathology, personality, and development.

- *We wanted to expose students to the fundamental principles of evolutionary psychology.* There is a set of core evolutionary concepts to which every student of behavior ought to be exposed, including natural selection, sexual selection, parental investment, kin selection, and life-history theory. A number of readings were chosen because they give particularly clear accounts of one or more of these central theoretical ideas.

- *We wanted to include readings that would be reasonably accessible.* If students enjoy what they read, they will be more motivated to stretch their minds—to learn new concepts and new ways of thinking about problems. Hence, the teacher's task is often to meet students halfway—to offer material that is interesting enough to motivate the intellectual climb to a higher altitude. We have tried to choose articles that cover the important and sometimes challenging new ideas of evolutionary psychology but that do so in a relatively straightforward and reader-friendly way.

- *We favored shorter articles that emphasize empirical findings over longer theoretical treatises.* Psychology's strength comes from its relentless pursuit of new empirical discoveries. Research findings are often like parables: memorable cases that serve to illustrate and support broader abstract principles. Although we did include a few review-type papers and articles, we included a slightly larger sampling of readings featuring original empirical results.

- *We leaned toward the "psychology" side of evolutionary psychology.* Evolutionary psychology is an interdisciplinary venture, with tributaries in evolutionary biology, ethology, anthropology, and other disciplines. Other collections of readings deal nicely with basic biological theory, with animal behavior, and with cross-cultural findings (e.g., Betzig, 1997; Caplan, 1978; Sherman & Alcock, 1993). The contributors to the present volume include scientists from several disciplines, using different research methodologies, but these readings feature a relatively larger sampling of experimental studies by psychologists.

Organization of Readings

We arranged the readings into the following eleven sections:

Motivation and Emotion. The collection opens with a pair of thought-provoking articles on human motivation and emotion. We begin here to underscore the fact that evolutionary psychology is about so-called hot cognition and functional behavior. Unlike the traditional content-free reductionist approach to psychology, which begins by asking how a single neuron fires, the adaptationist approach begins with questions about why we do what we do, think what we think, and worry about what we worry about.

In the first reading, "The Evolution of Happiness," David Buss (2000) reviews research addressing why people feel happiness in some situations and misery in others. Buss suggests that a more positive psychology would strive to understand the evolved mechanisms related to mating bonds, friendship, kinship, and cooperative coalitions. In the second reading, "Hunger, Eating, and Ill Health," physiological psychologist John Pinel and his colleagues Sunaina Assanand and Darrin Lehman (2000) review evidence to support an evolutionary explanation for the epidemic of obesity in modern urban society and to suggest a connection with eating disorders such as anorexia nervosa.

Psychopathology. A consideration of psychopathology follows naturally from the articles on motivation and emotion; thus, the next pair of readings offer a set of evolutionary models of disordered thought and behavior. We placed these articles early in the book because students' fascination with this topic is the ideal hook to interest them in the more basic research topics.

In "Psychoactive Drug Use in Evolutionary Perspective," the first reading in this section, Randolph Nesse joins with Kent Berridge (1997) to suggest that psychoactive drugs "hijack" the evolved brain mechanisms designed to inform us of when we have done something that promotes our fitness. In the second reading, "Evolutionary Social Psychology and Family Homicide," Martin Daly and Margo Wilson (1988a) deal with a particularly nasty form of human pathology, family homicide, reviewing data to suggest that even this maximally disordered behavior can be better understood through the functionalist lens of an evolutionary perspective.

Sensation, Perception, and Physiology. Natural selection shapes not only internal motivational states but also the mechanisms for collecting information from the outside world. Bats, who hunt at night, have poor vision but hearing so advanced that they perceive a sonogram of the midnight world. Bees, who navigate by sunlight, perceive ultraviolet light even on cloudy days. And hawks, who hunt from high in the sky, see with several times the acuity of humans with cones that pick up two additional regions of the visual spectrum.

In an essay called "Hawk-Eyed," from *The Birder's Handbook,* biologists Paul Ehrlich, David Dobkin, and Darryl Wheye (1988) elegantly and succinctly explain how a comparative evolutionary perspective can help us understand the commonality between visual mechanisms in humans and birds. This essay is followed by a classic study, "Natural Categories," by Eleanor Rosch (1973). She demonstrates that even in the absence of words describing different colors, members of a stone-age tribe from New Guinea seem to perceive the same colors as those individuals who colored in the letters "ROY G. BIV" using giant boxes of distinctly labeled crayons.

Learning. In dismissing the theory of mindless instincts, ethologists such as Niko Tinbergen and Konrad Lorenz demonstrated exquisitely functional interactions between learning experiences and innate predispositions. The first reading in this section, "Biological Boundaries of Learning: The Sauce-Bérnaise Syndrome," is an essay by Martin Seligman and Joanne Hager (1972a) that helped catapult the evolutionary perspective on behavior into the limelight. They review some of the mounting evidence against the *tabula rasa* view of learning—evidence originally gathered into their classic edited volume on the biological boundaries of learning (Seligman &

Hager, 1972b). "Illness-Induced Aversions in Rat and Quail: Relative Salience of Visual and Gustatory Cues," the second selection, was one of the articles in that volume. In it, Hardy Wilcoxon, William Dragoin, and Paul Kral (1971) report that quail, which use vision to locate food, condition nausea more easily to visual cues than to taste, whereas rats, who normally use taste and smell to locate food, show the opposite pattern.

Memory and Cognition. Does an evolutionary perspective apply only to simple conditioned responses and sensory processes? No more so than it applies only to simple organisms such as earthworms and planarians. Every reliably replicating feature of every living organism—from a simple sensory neuron to a large, complex human brain—is designed to facilitate its bearer's survival and reproductive success.

The first reading in this section, "The Hunter-Gatherer Theory of Spatial Sex Differences: Proximate Factors Mediating the Female Advantage in Recall of Object Arrays," by Marion Eals and Irwin Silverman (1994), offers an interesting evolutionary hypothesis and some supportive data about human spatial cognition. Evolved biases in human problem solving are the focus of the second article, "Cross-Cultural Evidence of Cognitive Adaptations for Social Exchange among the Shiwiar of Ecuadorian Amazonia," by Lawrence Sugiyama, John Tooby, and Leda Cosmides (2002). And in the third article, "Error Management Theory: A New Perspective on Biases in Cross-Sex Mind Reading," Martie Haselton and David Buss (2000) consider human attributional biases in the light of evolutionary considerations.

Language and Nonverbal Behavior. Among the functions embodied in our large brain are the capacities to communicate using nonverbal cues and complex language. Charles Darwin (1872) collected some of the first data to support his adaptationist theory of human emotional expression, and a century later, Paul Ekman and Wallace Friesen (1971) found additional support for that theory. In their article "Constants across Cultures in the Face and Emotion," they describe the ability of Neolithic hunter-gatherers from New Guinea to easily recognize emotions expressed by modern Americans. In the second reading, "Language as an Adaptation to the Cognitive Niche," Steven Pinker (2003) presents logical and empirical evidence supporting his argument that complex language is a naturally selected human capacity exquisitely designed for sharing useful information. Finally, in "Nonverbal Courtship Patterns in Women," Monica Moore (1985) examines a form of communication by which human females attract potential mates: nonverbal courtship displays.

Aggression. Part of differential reproduction is competition within and between groups. In their article "Competitiveness, Risk Taking, and Violence: The Young Male Syndrome" (1985), Margo Wilson and Martin Daly examine fascinating data on status-linked homicides and various risky behaviors by young males in light of evolutionary assumptions about a connection between male competition and sexual selection. In "A Few Good Men: Evolutionary Psychology and Female Adolescent Aggression," Anne Campbell (1995) examines the possible adaptive significance of age-linked violence in women.

Prosocial Behavior. It wasn't all tooth-and-claw competition for our ancestors; they probably got at least as much mileage out of cooperating with one another. One of the motors driving cooperation between group members is inclusive fitness. In the first reading in this section, "Nepotism and the Evolution of Alarm Calls," Paul Sherman (1977) presents data demonstrating that prosocial behavior in ground squirrels, as in humans, is much more likely when the recipients are genetic relatives. This is followed by an interesting article on conflict resolution, "Primates—A Natural Heritage of Conflict Resolution," by Frans de Waal (2000). De Waal describes how chimpanzees living in the same group kiss and make up after fighting.

Mate Selection. At the center of the game of evolution is differential reproduction. A trip to almost any park on a spring day will reveal several species of birds displaying their plumage and chirping loudly to attract mates. The park visitor with a pair of binoculars would notice two things: First, the males and the females play this game differently, and second, some of them are better at it than others. Likewise for human beings.

The first article in this section is Joseph Shepher's (1971) classic "Mate Selection among Second Generation Kibbutz Adolescents and Adults: Incest Avoidance and Negative Imprinting," which presents thought-provoking findings from a study of 2,769 marriages involving second-generation kibbutz residents who were raised from birth in close contact with unrelated members of the opposite sex. The puzzling data, which show no cases of intragroup marriage among these podmates, violate one of the basic maxims of social psychology but make sense in light of an adaptionist framework. The other article in this section, "Evolution, Traits, and the Stages of Human Courtship: Qualifying the Parental Investment Model," by Douglas Kenrick, Edward Sadalla, Gary Groth, and Melanie Trost (1990), presents data suggesting that men and women differ most when considering short-term sexual partners and least when considering marriage partners.

Mating Relationships. For some species, including most other mammals, courtship is over within minutes of mate selection. Humans, of course, do not just copulate to reproduce; they become involved in relationships—some short term, some lifelong. The three readings in this section explore these relationships from different perspectives.

In the first reading, "Sociosexuality and Romantic Partner Choice," Jeffry Simpson and Steven Gangestad (1992) explore individual differences in the preferences for exclusive monogamous versus more unrestricted relationships. In the second reading, "Sex Differences in Jealousy: Evolution, Physiology, and Psychology," David Buss and colleagues Randy Larsen, Drew Westen, and Jennifer Semmelroth (1992) examine sex differences in jealousy in light of the different reproductive resources each sex stands to lose if his or her partner is unfaithful. The third reading in this section, "Evolution and Social Cognition: Contrast Effects as a Function of Sex, Dominance, and Physical Attractiveness," by Douglas Kenrick, Steven Neuberg, Kristin Zierk, and Jacquelyn Krones (1994), presents an experimental study of men's and women's reactions to their own mates after viewing alternatives who are either attractive and/or socially dominant. The results suggest that an evolutionary perspective can help us understand ongoing cognitions about our current mating relationships.

Child Development and Family Relations.   The human family was probably one of the keys to our ancestors' success, and that family takes a form that sets us apart from 95 percent of the other mammals. In the first reading, "What Is a Good Mother? Adaptive Variation in Maternal Behavior of Primates," comparative psychologist Lynn Fairbanks (1993) discusses her research on vervet monkey mothers. Fairbanks notes that maternal investment of care is not a constant but varies in adaptive ways, depending on the social context. The second reading, "Evolution and Developmental Sex Differences," by developmental psychologist David Geary (1999), is a nice review of Darwin's concept of sexual selection and its relevance to human development. The fact that boys reach puberty later than girls do, for instance, is a clue that fits with other evidence about the evolved design of our species. Catherine Salmon and Martin Daly (1996) report data on the importance of kin relations, even among modern, urban North Americans, in the final reading, "On the Importance of Kin Relations to Canadian Women and Men."

These readings were selected to demonstrate the range of application of evolutionary principles in exploring all the domains of behavior. They demonstrate, at a minimum, that an evolutionary perspective can raise interesting questions, lead us to look in new places, and help us see our connections with other humans and other living organisms. Yet the most exciting revelation is this: Most of the work is yet to be done, and most of the discoveries on this frontier have yet to be made.

Acknowledgments

The authors would like to thank those individuals who reviewed an early draft of this text for Allyn & Bacon: Clinton Chaptman, Occidental College; Steve Gangestad, University of New Mexico, and Michael Mills, Loyola Marymount. The authors also thank David Lundberg Kenrick for his assistance.

References

Alcock, J. (2001). *The triumph of sociobiology.* New York: Oxford University Press.
Barkow, J., Cosmides, L., & Tooby, J. (Eds.). (1992). *The adapted mind: Evolutionary psychology and the generation of culture.* New York: Oxford University Press.
Betzig, L. (1997). *Human nature: A critical reader.* New York: Oxford University Press.
Buss, D. M. (2000). The evolution of happiness. *American Psychologist, 55,* 15–23.
Buss, D. M., Larsen, R. J., Westen, D., & Semmelroth, J. (1992). Sex differences in jealousy: Evolution, physiology, and psychology. *Psychological Science, 3,* 251–255.
Campbell, A. (1995). A few good men: Evolutionary psychology and female adolescent aggression. *Ethology and Sociobiology, 16,* 99–123.
Caplan, A. L. (1978). *The sociobiology debate: Readings on ethical and scientific issues.* New York: Harper & Row.
Daly, M., & Wilson, M. (1988a). Evolutionary social psychology and family homicide. *Science, 242,* 519–524.
Daly, M., & Wilson, M. (1988b). *Homicide.* New York: Aldine de Gruyter.
de Waal, F. B. M. (2000). Primates—A natural heritage of conflict resolution. *Science, 289,* 586–590.
Eals, M., & Silverman, I. (1994). The hunter-gatherer theory of spatial sex differences: Proximate factors mediating the female advantage in recall of object arrays. *Ethology and Sociobiology, 15,* 95–105.
Ehrlich, P. R., Dobkin, D. S., & Wheye, D. (1988). Hawk-eyed. In *The birder's handbook: A field guide to the natural history of North American birds.* New York: Simon & Schuster.
Ekman, P., & Friesen, W. V. (1971). Constants across cultures in the face and emotion. *Journal of Personality and Social Psychology, 17,* 124–129.

Fairbanks, L. A. (1993). What is a good mother? Adaptive variation in maternal behavior of primates. *Current Directions in Psychological Science, 2,* 179–183.

Geary, D. C. (1999). Evolution and developmental sex differences. *Current Directions in Psychological Science, 8,* 115–119.

Gould, J. L., & Gould, C. L. (1989). *Sexual selection.* New York: Scientific American Library.

Haselton, M. G., & Buss, D. M. (2000). Error management theory: A new perspective on biases in cross-sex mind reading. *Journal of Personality and Social Psychology, 78,* 81–91.

Kenrick, D. T., & Keefe, R. C. (1992). Age preferences in mates reflect sex differences in human reproductive strategies. *Behavioral and Brain Sciences, 15,* 75–133.

Kenrick, D. T., Neuberg, S. L., Zierk, K. L., & Krones, J. M. (1994). Evolution and social cognition: Contrast effects as a function of sex, dominance, and physical attractiveness. *Personality and Social Psychology Bulletin, 20,* 210–217.

Kenrick, D. T., Sadalla, E. K., Groth, G., & Trost, M. R. (1990). Evolution, traits, and the stages of human courtship: Qualifying the parental investment model. *Journal of Personality, 58,* 97–117.

Moore, M. M. (1985). Nonverbal courtship patterns in women. *Ethology and Sociobiology, 6,* 237–247.

Nesse, R. M., & Berridge, K. C. (1997). Psychoactive drug use in evolutionary perspective. *Science, 278,* 63–66.

Pinel, J. P. J., Assanand, S., & Lehman, D. R. (2000). Hunger, eating, and ill health. *American Psychologist, 55,* 1105–1116.

Pinker, S. (1997). *How the mind works.* New York: Norton.

Pinker, S. (2000). Language as an adaptation to the cognitive niche. In *Language evolution: Reports from the research frontier,* edited by M. Christiansen & S. Kirby. New York: Oxford University Press.

Plomin, R., DeFries, J. C., McClearn, G. E., & Rutter, M. (1997). *Behavioral genetics.* 3rd ed. New York: W. H. Freeman.

Rosch, E. H. (1973). Natural categories. *Cognitive Psychology, 4,* 328–350.

Rowe, D. C. (1994). *The limits of family influence: Genes, experience, and behavior.* New York: Guilford.

Salmon, C. A., & Daly, M. (1996). On the importance of kin relations to Canadian women and men. *Ethology and Sociobiology, 17,* 289–297.

Seligman, M. E. P., & Hager, J. L. (August 1972a). Biological boundaries of learning: The sauce-bérnaise syndrome. *Psychology Today,* pp. 59–61, 84–87.

Seligman, M. E. P., & Hager, J. L. (1972b). *Biological boundaries of learning.* New York: Appleton-Century-Crofts.

Shepher, J. (1971). Mate selection among second generation kibbutz adolescents and adults: Incest avoidance and negative imprinting. *Archives of Sexual Behavior, 1,* 293–307.

Sherman, P. W. (1977). Nepotism and the evolution of alarm calls. *Science, 197,* 1246–1253.

Sherman, P. W., & Alcock, J. (1993). *Exploring animal behavior: Readings from American Scientist.* Sunderland, MA: Sinauer.

Simpson, J. A., & Gangestad, S. W. (1992). Sociosexuality and romantic partner choice. *Journal of Personality, 60,* 31–51.

Sugiyama, L. S., Tooby, J., & Cosmides, L. (2002). Cross-cultural evidence of cognitive adaptations for social exchange among the Shiwiar of Ecuadorian Amazonia. *Proceedings of the National Academy of Sciences, 99,* 11537–11542.

Trivers, R. L. (1985). *Social evolution.* Menlo Park, CA: Benjamin/Cummings.

Wilcoxon, H. C., Dragoin, W. B., & Kral, P. A. (1971). Illness-induced aversions in rat and quail: Relative salience of visual and gustatory cues. *Science, 171,* 826–828.

Williams, G. C. (1996). *Plan and purpose in nature.* London: Weidenfeld & Nicolson.

Wilson, M., & Daly, M. (1985). Competitiveness, risk taking, and violence: The young male syndrome. *Ethology and Sociobiology, 6,* 59–73.

The Evolution of Happiness

DAVID M. BUSS

*An evolutionary perspective offers novel insights into some major obstacles to
achieving happiness. Impediments include large discrepancies between modern and
ancestral environments, the existence of evolved mechanisms "designed" to produce
subjective distress, and the fact that evolution by selection has produced competitive
mechanisms that function to benefit one person at the expense of others. On the positive side, people also possess evolved mechanisms that produce deep sources of happiness: those for mating bonds, deep friendship, close kinship, and cooperative
coalitions. Understanding these psychological mechanisms—the selective processes
that designed them, their evolved functions, and the contexts governing their activation—offers the best hope for holding some evolved mechanisms in check and selectively activating others to produce an overall increment in human happiness.*

Happiness is a common goal toward which people strive, but for many it
remains frustratingly out of reach. An evolutionary psychological perspective offers unique insights into some vexing barriers to achieving happiness and consequently into creating conditions for improving the quality of human life. These insights are based on a deeper understanding of the human mind, how the selective
process designed it, and the nature of the evolved functions of its component parts.

Current mechanisms of mind are the end products of a selective process, a sieve
through which features passed because they contributed, either directly or indirectly,
to reproductive success. All living humans are evolutionary success stories. They each
have inherited the mechanisms of mind and body that led to their ancestors' achieve-
ments in producing descendants. If any one of their ancestors had failed along the way
to survive, mate, reproduce, and solve a host of tributary adaptive problems, they
would not have become ancestors. As their descendants, people hold in their possession magical keys—the adaptive mechanisms that led to their ancestors' success.

What evolved psychological mechanisms do humans possess, how are they designed, and what functions were they designed to carry out? At this point in evolutionary psychological science, psychologists can provide only a few provisional answers.
This article offers several reflections on these issues, grounded in recent conceptual
and empirical advances, with the explicit acknowledgment of their tentative and in-
terim nature. The article starts by examining some impediments to happiness and then
offers suggestions for how these obstacles might be overcome.

D. M. Buss, "The evolution of happiness," *American Psychologist, 55* (2000): 15–23. Copyright ©
2000 by the American Psychological Association. Reprinted with permission.

BARRIERS TO IMPROVING QUALITY OF LIFE

An evolutionary analysis leads to several key insights about barriers that must be overcome to improve the quality of human life. These include discrepancies between modern and ancestral environments, evolved mechanisms that lead to subjective distress, and the fact that selection has produced competitive mechanisms.

Discrepancies between Modern and Ancestral Environments

Modern living has brought a bounty of benefits to present day humans. Medical technology has reduced infant mortality in many parts of the world to a fraction of what it undoubtedly was in ancestral times. People have the tools to prevent many diseases that afflicted their Stone Age forebears and to ameliorate the distressing symptoms of many others. The psychological pain of depression and anxiety can be reduced with lithium, Prozac, and other psychotropic drugs. Modern technology gives people the power to prevent the pain inflicted by extremes of cold and heat, food shortages, some parasites, most predators, and other Darwinian (1859) "hostile forces of nature." In many ways, people live in astonishing comfort compared with their ancestors.

At the same time, modern environments have produced a variety of ills, many unanticipated and only now being discovered. Although people have the tools and technology to combat food shortages, they now vastly overconsume quantities of animal fat and processed sugars in ways that lead to clogged arteries, heart disease, diabetes, and other medical ailments (Nesse & Williams, 1994; Symons, 1987). Depletion of the ozone layer may lead to skin cancer at rates that were unlikely to have afflicted their ancestors. The ability to synthesize drugs has led to heroin addiction, cocaine abuse, and addiction to a variety of prescription drugs.

Evolutionary psychological analysis suggests several other ways in which modern psychological environments cause damage. Consider the estimate that humans evolved in the context of small groups, consisting of perhaps 50 to 200 individuals (Dunbar, 1993). Modern humans, in contrast, typically live in a massive urban metropolis surrounded by thousands or millions of other humans. Ancestral humans may have had a dozen or two potential mates to choose from. Modern humans, in contrast, are surrounded by thousands of potential mates. They are bombarded by media images of attractive models on a scale that has no historical precedent and that may lead to unreasonable expectations about the quality and quantity of available mates. Ancestral humans lived in extended kin networks, surrounded by genetic relatives such as uncles and aunts, nephews and nieces, cousins and grandparents. Modern humans typically live in isolated nuclear families often devoid of extended kin. Ancestral humans relied on their friends and relatives to seek justice, to correct social wrongs, to deal with violence inflicted on them from others. Modern humans rely on hired police and a legal system whose labyrinth makes the horror of Kafka's *The Trial* look like a tea party.[1] It is reasonable to speculate that these large discrepancies between ancestral and modern environments create unanticipated psychological problems and reduce the quality of life.

Some empirical evidence supports this proposition. The modern barrage of attractive images of other humans provides an instructive example. The evolutionary psychologist Doug Kenrick and his colleagues have provided evidence that these images may create psychological and social problems. In a series of studies on contrast effects, they discovered that men exposed to multiple images of attractive women subsequently rated their commitment to their regular partner as lower, compared with men exposed to average looking women (Kenrick, Gutierres, & Goldberg, 1989; Kenrick, Neuberg, Zierk, & Krones, 1994). Women exposed to multiple images of dominant, high-status men showed a similar decrement in commitment to and love of their regular partner, compared with women exposed repeatedly to less dominant men. These sex-linked contrast effects were precisely predicted by Kenrick's evolutionary psychological framework.

Repeated exposures apparently affect self-concept as well. Women subjected to successive images of other women who are unusually attractive subsequently feel less attractive themselves, showing a decrease in self-esteem (Gutierres, Kenrick, & Partch, 1999). Men exposed to descriptions of highly dominant and influential men show an analogous diminution in self-concept. These effects are sex-linked in ways precisely predicted by evolutionary psychological hypotheses. The effects suggest that the discrepancy between modern and ancestral environments in exposure to media images may lead to dissatisfactions with current partners and reductions in self-esteem. They may interfere with the quality of close relationships and hence with the quality of life.

A second example is more speculative. Depression is one of the most common psychological maladies of modern humans, and it afflicts roughly twice as many women as men (Nolen-Hoeksema, 1987). There is some evidence that rates of depression are increasing in modern life. Five studies comprised of 39,000 individuals living in five different areas of the world revealed that young people are more likely than older people to have experienced at least one major episode of depression (Nesse & Williams, 1994, p. 220). Moreover, the incidence of depression appears to be higher in more economically developed cultures (Nesse & Williams, 1994). Why would rates of depression be rising in modern environments, despite the greater abundance of creature comforts and the presence of technological solutions to former ancestral maladies of life?

Nesse and Williams (1994) offer one hypothesis:

> Mass communications, especially television and movies, effectively make us all one competitive group even as they destroy our more intimate social networks. . . . In the ancestral environment you would have had a good chance at being the best at something. Even if you were not the best, your group would likely value your skills. Now we all compete with those who are the best in the world. Watching these successful people on television arouses envy. Envy probably was useful to motivate our ancestors to strive for what others could obtain. Now few of us can achieve the goals envy sets for us, and none of us can attain the fantasy lives we see on television. (Nesse & Williams, 1994, p. 220).

According to this analysis, the increase in depression stems from self-perceived failures resulting in erroneous comparisons between people's lives and the lives they see depicted so glamorously in the media.

A related explanation of an increase in depression invokes the fact that modern living conditions of relative anonymity and isolated nuclear families deprive people of the intimate social support that would have characterized ancestral social conditions (Nesse & Williams, 1994, p. 221). In modern America, for example, kin members often scatter in the pursuit of better jobs and promotions, yielding a social mobility that removes the social support of extended kin and makes social bonds more transient. If psychological well-being is linked with having deep intimate contacts, being a valued member of an enduring social group, and being enmeshed in a network of extended kin, then the conditions of modern living seem designed to interfere with human happiness.

These are just a few examples that suggest that some discrepancies between modern and ancestral conditions impede a high quality of life. Other possibilities include the lack of critical incidents by which people might establish true friendships (Tooby & Cosmides, 1996), the sense of powerlessness modern humans feel in large anonymous organizations compared with the small social hierarchies of the past (Wenegrat, 1990), and the increased opportunities for casual sex lacking in deep intimacy, that might lead people to feel emotionally empty (Buss, 1994). These discrepancies between modern and ancestral environments may interfere with the quest for a high quality of life.

Adaptations That Cause Subjective Distress

A second impediment to human happiness is that people have evolved an array of psychological mechanisms that are "designed" to cause subjective distress under some circumstances (e.g. Seligman, 1971). These include psychological pain (Thornhill & Thornhill, 1989), varieties of anxiety (Marks & Nesse, 1994), depression (Price & Sloman, 1987), specific fears and phobias (Marks, 1987), jealousy (Daly, Wilson, & Weghorst, 1982; Symons, 1979), and specific forms of anger and upset (Buss, 1989). These are all proposed to be evolved psychological mechanisms designed to solve specific adaptive problems, such as sexual coercion (psychological pain), inhabiting a subordinate position in the social hierarchy (depression), spousal infidelity (jealousy), and strategic interference (anger).[2] If these hypotheses are correct, they suggest that part of the operation of the normal psychological machinery *inevitably* entails experiencing psychological distress in certain contexts.

The emotion of jealousy provides an illustration. Much empirical evidence supports the hypothesis that sexual jealousy is an evolved psychological mechanism designed to combat the adaptive problem of threat to valued long-term mateships (Daly et al., 1982; Symons, 1979). Jealousy, according to this hypothesis, functions to alert a person to a mate's possible or actual infidelity and motivates action designed to prevent infidelity or deal with defection. Its design features include sex-linked activators, with men becoming more jealous in response to the threat of sexual infidelity and women becoming more jealous in response to emotional infidelity—hypotheses supported by psychological, physiological, and cross-cultural data (Buss et al., 1999; Buss, Larsen, Westen, & Semmelroth, 1992; Buunk, Angleitner, Oubaid, & Buss, 1996; Daly et al., 1982; Geary, Rumsey, Bow-Thomas, & Hoard, 1995; Wiederman & Allgeier, 1993).

Subjectively, jealousy is typically an extremely distressing emotion, a passion dangerous to the self and to others (Buss, 2000). It can create the torment of sleepless nights, cause a person to question his or her worth as a mate, create anxiety about losing a partner, and play havoc with social reputation. Jealousy can lead to an obsessive vigilance that crowds out all other thoughts and to terrifying violence that threatens the safety and well-being of the partner.

Despite the manifold unhappiness jealousy creates, jealousy has a crystalline functional logic, precise purposes, and supreme sensibility. It exists today in modern humans because those in the evolutionary past who were indifferent to the sexual contact that their mates had with others lost the evolutionary contest to those who became jealous. As the descendants of successful ancestors, modern humans carry with them the passions that led to their forebears' success. The legacy of this success is a dangerous passion that creates unhappiness, but the unhappiness motivated adaptive action over human evolutionary history (Buss, 2000).

Anger and upset, according to one evolutionary psychological hypothesis, are evolved psychological mechanisms designed to prevent *strategic interference* (Buss, 1989). These negative emotions function to draw attention to the interfering event, alert a person to the source of strategic interference, mark the interfering events for storage in and retrieval from memory, and motivate action designed to eliminate the interference or to avoid subsequent interfering events. Because men and women over evolutionary time have faced different sources of strategic interference, they are hypothesized to get angry and upset about different sorts of events. Empirical evidence supports these hypotheses, suggesting that women get more upset about sexual aggression (Buss, 1989), various forms of sexual harassment (Studd, 1996), and the horror of rape (Thornhill & Thornhill, 1989). Men, in contrast, tend to respond with more anger and upset than women when a potential mate leads them on or a current partner withholds sex (Buss, 1989). These and many other findings support the hypothesis that many apparently negative emotions may in fact be quite functional for humans, helping them to solve adaptive problems of social living (see Buss, 2000). Nonetheless, the subjective experience can be extremely painful and disturbing, reducing the quality of life a person experiences.

The negative emotions are not limited to sexual skirmishing. People experience distress when someone blocks their ascension in the social hierarchy, when they suffer a slide in status, when a friend betrays them, when their coalition is weakened, when their team loses, when their health is impaired, when they are threatened with violence, when a sibling is favored over them by a parent, when they are victimized by malicious gossip, when a partner rejects them, when tragedy befalls a loved one, and when a child dies. Human anguish in modern minds is tethered to the events that would have caused fitness failure in ancestral times.

Adaptations Designed for Competition

A third impediment to happiness stems from the competition inherent to evolution by selection. Reproductive *differentials* caused by design differences make up the engine of evolutionary change. Selection operates on differences, so one person's gain is often another person's loss. As Symons (1979) observed, "the most fundamental, most universal double standard is not male versus female but each individual human versus everyone else" (p. 229). The profound implication of this analysis is that humans have evolved psychological mechanisms designed to inflict costs on others, to gain advantage at the expense of others, to delight in the downfall of others, and to envy those who are more successful at achieving the goals toward which they aspire.

The evolutionary psychologist Steven Pinker provided an example using the German word *Schadenfreude,* a word that appears not to have a direct counterpart in the English language. Nonetheless,

> When English speakers hear the word *Schadenfreude* for the first time, their reaction is not "Let me see . . . Pleasure in another's misfortunes . . . What could that possibly be? I cannot grasp the concept; my language and culture have not provided me with such a category." Their reaction is, "You mean there's a *word* for it? Cool!!" (Pinker, 1997, p. 367; italics in original)

Ambrose Bierce even defined happiness as "an agreeable sensation arising from contemplating the misery of others" (quoted in Pinker, 1997, p. 390).

Empirical evidence supports the hypothesis that people do take pleasure in the "downfall of tall poppies" (Feather, 1994, p. 2). Across a series of studies, Feather (1994) discovered several important conditions under which people take pleasure in the fall of tall poppies. First, when the high status of a tall poppy was made salient, participants reported more happiness with the other's fall from grace. Second, when the success of a tall poppy was not perceived to be deserved, participants reported more pleasure with his or her fall than when the tall poppy was perceived to deserve the initial success. Third, *envy* was the most common emotional experience participants felt toward a tall poppy, especially if the other person's success was in a domain important to the participant, such as academic achievement among students.

Do people have adaptations to feel especially good about themselves when superseding or subordinating others (Gilbert, 1989)? Are envy and depression reliable consequences of being relatively low in the social hierarchy (Gilbert, 1989; Price & Sloman, 1987)? Given the apparent universality of status hierarchies in all groups and all cultures worldwide, escape from relative ranking may prove exceedingly difficult. If a person's happiness depends in part on another's misery or failure, then how can people design lives to improve the quality of all, not just those who happen to get ahead? These vexing questions become salient with the recognition that evolution has produced some psychological mechanisms that are inherently competitive.

Because *differential* reproductive success is the engine of the evolutionary process, one person's gain is often another person's loss. Consider two women competing to attract a particular desirable man as a husband. Research has shown that in addition to various self-enhancing attraction tactics, women also derogate their rivals (Buss & Dedden, 1990; Schmitt & Buss, 1996). Some women will call a rival promiscuous, spread rumors about how easy she is to get into bed, denigrate aspects of her face, body, and clothing style, and sometimes falsely tell others that she has contracted a sexually transmitted disease. Men are no less vicious in their derogation tactics. The content of gossip, in short, is adaptively targeted and undoubtedly affects success on the mating market. It can simultaneously create psychological anguish and ruin the reputations of victims. The outcome is inherently competitive—one person's success on the mating market is typically another person's loss. As Gore Vidal noted, "It is not enough to succeed. Others must fail" (quoted in Pinker, 1997, p. 390).

Some psychological mechanisms also produce predictable forms of conflict between the sexes. Men's evolved desire for sexual variety, for example, sometimes prompts sexual overtures that are sooner, more persistent, and more aggressive than women want (Buss, 1994). Simultaneously, women's strategies of imposing a longer courtship delay, requiring signs of emotional involvement, and delaying sex interfere with men's short-term sexual strategy (Buss, 1994). Both sexes deceive each other in ways well predicted by evolutionary theories (e.g., Tooke & Camire, 1991).

Jealousy provides another instructive example of competition and conflict (Buss, 2000). Jealousy is activated by perceived or real threats to romantic relationships—by a rival who is encroaching, a partner who is threatening defection, or both. Jealousy can undermine self-esteem, making a person feel "hurt, threatened, broken hearted, upset, insecure, betrayed, rejected, angry, possessive, envious, unhappy, confused, frustrated, lonely, depressed, resentful, scared, and paranoid" (Buss, 2000). Jealousy motivates conflict with partners, fights with rivals, and in some cases extreme violence. Despite the extensive suffering it creates, it served our ancestors well in the competitive currency of reproduction. Nonjealous men risked being cuckolded and spending a life devoted to nurturing a rival's children. Nonjealous women risked the diversion or loss of a partner's commitment to a female rival. Jealousy evolved to serve a variety of functions, including deterring a mate from straying, backing off interested rivals, and perhaps even communicating commitment to a partner (Buss, 2000). These competitive functions have come at the cost of conflict.

Three Additional Evolutionary Tragedies of Happiness

These various obstacles to improving human happiness obviously do not exhaust the evolved impediments to well-being. Evolutionary psychologist Steven Pinker (1997) described several other tragedies of happiness. One is the fact that humans seem designed to adapt quickly to their circumstances, putting us on a "hedonic treadmill" (Diener, Suh, Lucas, & Smith, 1999, p. 286). Americans today have more cars, color TVs, computers, and brand-name clothes than they did several decades ago, but Americans are no happier now than they were then (Myers & Diener, 1995). Reports of lottery winners suggest that individuals quickly adjust to their new riches and may be no happier than they were before (some even report increased conflicts with others). Happiness may track modern manifestations of ancestral signals of evolutionary fitness (Ketelaar, 1995), but people seem to adjust quickly to any gains they experience, creating the hedonic treadmill where apparent increments in rewards fail to produce sustained increments in personal happiness.

A second tragedy of human unhappiness stems from the fact that evolved mechanisms are designed to function well on average, although they will necessarily fail in some instances—what may be called *instance failure* (Cosmides & Tooby, 1999). For example, mechanisms of mate guarding are designed to ward off rivals and keep a partner from straying (Buss & Shackelford, 1997). Presumably, mate-guarding mechanisms evolved because, on average, they succeeded in successful mate retention. An individual woman or man, however, might fail to keep a partner, thus producing a cascade of psychological anguish and social humiliation, even though mate-guarding mechanisms have succeeded on average over the relevant sample space of evolutionary time. Instance failures may even be more frequent than successes over evolutionary time, as long as the net benefit of the strategy has exceeded its costs.

A third tragedy of human emotions is the asymmetry in affective experience following comparable gains and losses (Kahneman & Tversky, 1984). The pain people experience when they lose $100, for example, turns out to be affectively more disagreeable than the pleasure they experience when they win $100. Losses sting more keenly; the joy produced by comparable gains is more muted. As the former tennis star Jimmy Connors observed, "I hate to lose more than I like to win" (cited by Ketelaar, 1995). Evolved emotions, in short, may have been well designed to keep people's ancestors on track in the currency of fitness, but in some ways they seem designed to foil people's efforts to promote long-term happiness.

IMPROVING HUMAN HAPPINESS

Given the obstacles to well-being—discrepancies between modern and ancestral environments, evolved emotional mechanisms designed to cause subjective distress, and the existence of psychological mechanisms that are inherently competitive—it is clear that an evolutionary perspective does not offer easy or facile solutions to the problems of improving psychological well-being and the quality of life. In fact, they reveal how difficult such solutions will be to achieve. Nonetheless, evolutionary psychology does provide insights into how some of the more unpleasant and damaging features of the human condition might be ameliorated.

Closing the Gap between Modern and Ancestral Conditions

Modern humans cannot go back in time and live the lives of their Stone Age forebears, nor would an uninformed or uncritical move in that direction be inherently desirable, given that modern technology has eliminated many of the hostile forces of nature that formerly made life brutish, painful, and short. Nonetheless, the gap between former and modern conditions might be closed on some dimensions to good effect.

Increase Closeness of Extended Kin. If being deprived of extended close kin leads to depression in modern environments (L. Cosmides, personal communication, September 17, 1989), individuals can take steps to remain in closer proximity or to maintain greater emotional closeness to existing kin. Modern electronic communication, including E-mail, telephone, and video conferencing, might be exploited to this end when physical proximity is not possible. With people living longer, opportunities to interact with grandparents and grandchildren expand, offering the possibility of strengthening the network of extended kin.

Develop Deep Friendships. According to Tooby and Cosmides (1996), people may suffer a dearth of deep friendships in modern urban living. It's easy to be someone's friend when times are good. It's when you are really in trouble that you find out who your true friends are. Everyone has experienced fair-weather friends who are there only when times are good, but finding a true friend, someone that you know you can rely on when the going gets tough, is a real treasure.

The problem is that when times are good, fair-weather friends and true friends may act pretty much alike. It's difficult to know who your true friends are when the sailing is smooth. Because fair-weather friends can mimic true friends, the adaptive problem is how to differentiate those who are deeply engaged in your welfare from those who will disappear during your time of deep need (Tooby & Cosmides, 1996). Selection should fashion assessment mechanisms to make these differentiations. The strongest tests, the most reliable sources of evidence of friendship, come from the help you receive when you are desperately in need. Receiving help during these times is a far more reliable litmus test than help received at any other time. Intuitively, people do seem to have special recall for precisely these times. People take pains to express their appreciation, communicating that they will never forget the sacrifices made by those who helped them in their darkest hour.

Modern living, however, creates a paradox (Tooby & Cosmides, 1996). Humans generally act to avoid episodes of treacherous personal trouble, and in modern living, many of the hostile forces of nature that would have put people in jeopardy have been harnessed or controlled. Laws deter stealing, assault, and murder. A police force performs many of the functions previously performed by friends. Medical science has eliminated or reduced many sources of disease and illness. People live in an environment that in many ways is safer and more stable than the environment inhabited by their ancestors. Paradoxically, therefore, people suffer from a relative scarcity of *critical events* that would allow them to accurately assess who is deeply engaged in their welfare and to differentiate them from fair-weather friends. The loneliness and sense of alienation that many feel in modern living, a lack of a feeling of deep social connections despite the presence of many seemingly warm and friendly interactions, may stem from the lack of critical assessment events that tell them who is deeply engaged in their welfare (Tooby & Cosmides, 1996).

Several strategies may help to close this gap between modern and ancestral conditions to deepen social connectedness (Tooby & Cosmides, 1996). First, people should promote reputations that highlight their unique or exceptional attributes. Second, they should be motivated to recognize personal attributes that others value but have difficulty getting from other people. This involves cultivating a sensitivity to the values held by others. Third, they should acquire specialized skills that increase irreplaceability. If people develop expertise or proficiency in domains that most others lack, they become indispensable to those who value those competencies. Fourth, they should preferentially seek out groups that most strongly value what they have to offer and what others in the group tend to lack; in short, they should find groups in which their assets will be most highly cherished. Fifth, they should avoid social groups where their unique attributes are not valued or where these qualities are easily provided by others.

A sixth strategy involves the imposition of *critical tests* designed to deepen the friendship and test the strength of the bond (see also Zahavi, 1977; Zahavi & Zahavi, 1997). Although it would be foolish to subject oneself to a life-or-death situation merely to test the strength of a friendship, more modest tests are possible. Some friends may fail the tests, in which case they are deemed fair-weather friends. Those who pass the tests and provide help during these critical times make the transition to true friends marked by deep engagement.

Reducing Subjective Distress

If humans have evolved psychological mechanisms that function to produce subjective distress, one can design a social environment to reduce the likelihood of facing the adaptive problems that trigger psychological anguish. Although these problems are probably impossible to avoid completely, several strategies might lower the likelihood of their occurrence.

Selecting a Mate Who Is Similar—Reducing Jealousy and Infidelity. One strategy is to select a long-term mate or marriage partner who is similar to you on dimensions such as values, interests, politics, personality, and overall "mate value." A large body of empirical evidence supports the hypothesis that discrepancies between partners in these qualities lead to increased risk of infidelity, instability of the relationship, and a higher likelihood of eventual breakup (Buss, 2000; Hill, Rubin, & Peplau, 1976; Kenrick & Keefe, 1992; Thiessen & Gregg, 1980; Walster, Traupmann, & Walster, 1978; Whyte, 1990). Selecting a mate who is similar, conversely, should lower the likelihood of infidelity, and hence the agony experienced as a result of jealousy. Because jealousy appears to be an evolved emotion designed to combat threats to relationships, anything that reduces its activation should reduce the subjective pain people experience (Buss, 2000). Furthermore, assortative mating decreases the chance of divorce, and hence the sequelae caused by divorce—anguish experienced by the parties involved as well as by any children from the union.

Anything that leads to a higher divorce probability increases the odds of creating stepchildren. Evolutionary psychologists have demonstrated that stepchildren experience physical abuse and even homicide at rates 40 to 100 times greater than children residing with their genetic parents (Daly & Wilson, 1988). Selecting a mate who is similar lowers the odds of breaking up and hence decreases the odds of producing stepchildren who are at increased risk of abuse.

Extended Kin—Reducing Incest, Child Abuse, and Spousal Battering. Incest, child abuse, and wife battering may be greater now because modern humans live in isolated nuclear families, protected in a shroud of privacy. Having kin in close proximity has been discovered to offer a protective factor against some of these forms of abuse, notably wife battering (Figueredo, 1995). Although no studies have yet been conducted on the protective properties offered by extended kin for incest and child abuse, it is not unreasonable to expect that they will yield a similar effect.

Education about Evolved Psychological Sex Differences. Evolutionary psychology offers a precise metatheory about sex differences—the sexes are predicted to differ only in the domains in which they have faced different adaptive problems (Buss, 1995). Many such differences have been documented. Men more than women, for example, infer greater sexual interest when they observe a smile, which may lead to unwanted sexual advances that cause subjective distress in women (Abbey, 1982; Buss, 1994). This male bias in mind reading, however, can be shown to disappear under certain evolutionarily predicted conditions (Haselton & Buss, 2000). Education about the fact that men's and women's minds house somewhat different psychological mechanisms, and that the differences can be deactivated under certain conditions, may help to reduce the frequency of strategic interference.

Managing Competitive Mechanisms

Perhaps the most difficult challenge posed by our evolved psychological mechanisms is managing competition and hierarchy negotiation, given that selection has fashioned powerful mechanisms that drive rivalry and status striving. Status inequality produces a variety of negative consequences, such as the impairment of health (Wilkinson, 1996). One potential method of reducing such inequalities is to promote cooperation.

Evolutionists have identified one of the key conditions that promote cooperation—shared fate (Sober & Wilson, 1998). Shared fate occurs among genes within a body, for example—when the body dies, all the genes it houses die with it. Genes get selected, in part, for their ability to work cooperatively with other genes. A similar effect occurs with individuals living in some kinds of groups. When the fate of individuals within the group is shared—for example, when the success of a hunt depends on the coordination among all members of the hunting party, or when defense against attack is made successful by the cooperation of a group's members—then cooperation is enhanced. Knowledge of the evolutionary psychology of cooperation can lead to an improved quality of life for all cooperators.

Axelrod (1984), an evolutionary political scientist, suggested several ways in which this can be done. First, enlarge the shadow of the future. If two individuals believe that they will interact frequently in the extended future, they have a greater incentive to cooperate. If people know when the "last move" will occur and that the relationship will end soon, there is a greater incentive for people to defect and not cooperate. Enlarging the shadow of the future can be accomplished by making interactions more frequent and making a commitment to the relationship, which occurs, for example, with wedding vows. Perhaps one reason that divorces are so often ugly, marred by unkind acts of mutual defection, is that both parties perceive the last move and a sharply truncated shadow of the future.

A second strategy that Axelrod (1984) recommends is to teach reciprocity. Promoting reciprocity not only helps people by making others more cooperative, it also makes it more difficult for exploitative strategies to thrive. The larger the number of those who follow a tit-for-tat reciprocity strategy, the less successful it will be to attempt to exploit others by defecting. Essentially, the cooperators will thrive through their interactions with each other, whereas the exploiters will suffer because of a vanishing population of those on whom they can prey.

A third strategy for the promotion of cooperation is to insist on no more than equity. Greed is the downfall of many, exemplified by the myth of King Midas, whose lust for gold backfired when everything he touched, even the food he wanted to eat, turned to gold. The beauty of a tit-for-tat strategy is that it does not insist on getting more than it gives. By promoting equity, tit-for-tat succeeds by eliciting cooperation from others.

A final strategy for promoting cooperation is to cultivate a personal reputation as a reciprocator. People live in a social world where the beliefs others hold about them—their reputations—determine whether others will befriend or avoid them. Reputations are established through people's actions, and word about people's actions spreads. Cultivating a reputation as a reciprocator will make others seek them out for mutual gain. A reputation as an exploiter will foster social shunning. Exploiters risk vengeance and retribution from their victims. The combined effect of these strategies will create a social norm of cooperation, where those who were formerly exploiters are forced to rehabilitate their bad reputations by becoming cooperators themselves. In this way, cooperation will be promoted throughout the group.

By promoting cooperation, some evolved mechanisms designed to yield competitive advantage lie dormant.[3] Humans have within their menu of evolved strategies those that unleash treachery as well as those that produce harmony. By exploiting our knowledge of the conditions that promote cooperation, people might be able to mitigate some of the destruction inflicted by competition.

The Fulfillment of Desire

A fourth strategy for raising human happiness involves exploiting knowledge of evolved desires (Buss, 2000). Just as humans have evolved adaptations that create subjective distress, they have evolved desires whose fulfillment brings deep joy. Studies of private wishes reveal an evolutionary menu of motivations designed to achieve goals historically correlated with fitness. These include the desire for health, professional success, helping friends and relatives, achieving intimacy, feeling the confidence to succeed, satisfying the taste for high-quality food, securing personal safety, and having the resources to attain all these things (King & Broyles, 1997; Petrie, White, Cameron, & Collins, in press). Success at satisfying these desires brings episodes of deep happiness, even if people might habituate to their constant occurrence.

The fulfillment of mating desires provides another path. One of the most consistent findings in studies of well-being is the link to marriage (Diener et al., 1999). Married women and men are significantly happier than single women and men, even when other variables such as age and income are statistically controlled. Moreover, among married people, those who have succeeded in fulfilling their desire for a spouse who embodies the personality characteristics of agreeableness, conscientiousness, emotional stability, and openness to experience tend to be more emotionally and sexually satisfied with their marriages than those who fail to marry spouses with these qualities (Botwin, Buss, & Shackelford, 1997).

In addition to fulfilling major desires, evolution has equipped people with a host of mechanisms designed to allow people to bathe themselves in aesthetic pleasure. People can design environments to exploit evolved affective mechanisms that signal adaptive affordances. Landscape preferences provide a perfect illustration (Kaplan, 1992; Orians & Heerwagen, 1992). Research supports the hypothesis that humans have evolved specific habitat preferences that mimic certain aspects of the ancestral savanna terrain. People like natural over human-made environments, habitats with running water and terrain to house game. They like places where they can see without being seen (a "womb with a view"). They like environments that provide resources and safety, prospect and refuge, lush vegetation and fresh fruit. As noted by Orians and Heerwagen, "It may be difficult for many of us, with the year-round supplies of a wide array of fruits and vegetables in our supermarkets, to understand the importance of the first salad greens of the season to people throughout most of human history" (1992, p. 569). Appreciating the beauty of a blossom, the loveliness of a lilac, or the grace of a gazelle are all ways in which people can, in some small measure, fill their daily lives with evolutionarily inspired epiphanies of pleasure.

Having adequate resources to fulfill desires (Diener & Fujita, 1995), making progress toward fulfilling them (Cantor & Sanderson, 1999), achieving a state of "flow" in the process of achieving them (Csikszentmihalyi, 1990), and succeeding in fulfilling them in particular domains such as mating (Botwin et al., 1997) provide a few of the evolutionary keys to increasing human happiness.

CONCLUSIONS

Evolutionary psychology yields insight into some of the major obstacles to achieving a high quality of life—discrepancies between modern and ancestral conditions, the existence of evolved mechanisms designed to produce psychological pain, and the inherently competitive nature of some evolved mechanisms. Given these circumstances and constraints, improving the quality of life will not be easily or simply achieved. Knowledge of evolutionary obstacles, however, provides a heuristic for discovering places to intercede. The human menu of evolved strategies is large and varied, and modern humans have the power to create conditions to activate some strategies while leaving others dormant.

This article perforce has neglected or only obliquely touched on many of the complexities of human happiness, such as the finding that individual differences in dispositional happiness appear moderately heritable (Tellegan et al., 1988), that perpetual states of happiness would almost certainly have been maladaptive (Barkow, 1997), and that repeated short-term pleasures sometimes produce enduring long-term pain (Solomon, 1980). Comprehensive theories of human happiness will have to explain adaptively patterned phenomena such as why winners of competitions experience a hedonic and hormonal boost (Mazur & Booth, in press) and why women's feelings of well-being appear to peak during the late follicular phase of the ovulatory cycle, when fertility and chance of conception are maximal (Sanders, Warner, Backstrom, & Bancroft, 1983). A more complete theory must also explain why some sources of happiness and subjective distress differ profoundly for men and women, for parents and children, and for the same individuals at different stages of life as they confront predictably different adaptive problems (Buss, 1999). Future work could profitably include an account of the evolutionary psychology of hedonic trade-offs inherent in some activities, such as an extramarital affair that produces the immediate reward of sexual gratification, but a more distant and uncertain future risk of marital disruption and reputational damage.

As a species, humans have conquered many of the external hostile forces of nature that formerly threatened bodily survival. They have created environments that are relatively friction free; they have reduced infant mortality, polio, and malaria; conquered food shortages through agriculture; reduced the destructive impact of extremes of temperature and climate; and eliminated most predators. With a deeper understanding of the evolved mechanisms of mind that define who humans are and how they were designed to function, people may eventually acquire the ability to control some of the more destructive social conditions. Through this knowledge, people can take a few halting steps toward fulfilling the human desire for happiness.

ENDNOTES

1. The American legal system, of course, carries many blessings as well. It probably prevents or lowers the incidence of certain types of homicide, such as blood feuds, that are prevalent in many tribal societies and cultures lacking third-party legal systems (see Chagnon, 1992; Keeley, 1996).

2. Strategic interference occurs when a person's goals, or methods of achieving goals, are impeded or blocked (Buss, 1989).
3. An obvious exception is when people form cooperative groups to compete more effectively with other groups, as occurs in sports, warfare, and political coalitions (e.g., Alexander, 1979, 1987).

REFERENCES

Abbey, A. (1982). Sex differences in attributions for friendly behavior: Do males misperceive females' friendliness? *Journal of Personality and Social Psychology, 32,* 830–838.

Alexander, R. D. (1979). *Darwinism and human affairs.* Seattle: University of Washington Press.

Alexander, R. D. (1987). *The biology of moral systems.* Hawthorne, NY: Aldine de Gruyter.

Axelrod, R. (1984). *The evolution of cooperation.* New York: Basic Books.

Barkow, J. H. (1997). Happiness in evolutionary perspective. In N. L. Segal, G. E. Weisfeld, & C. C. Weisfeld (Eds.), *Uniting psychology and biology: Integrative perspectives on human development* (pp. 397–418). Washington, DC: American Psychological Association.

Botwin, M. D., Buss, D. M., & Shackelford, T. K. (1997). Personality and mate preferences: Five factors in mate selection and marital satisfaction. *Journal of Personality, 65,* 107–136.

Buss, D. M. (1989). Conflict between the sexes: Strategic interference and the evocation of anger and upset. *Journal of Personality and Social Psychology, 56,* 735–747.

Buss, D. M. (1994). *The evolution of desire: Strategies of human mating.* New York: Basic Books.

Buss, D. M. (1995). Psychological sex differences: Origins through sexual selection. *American Psychologist, 50,* 164–168.

Buss, D. M. (1999). *Evolutionary psychology: The new science of the mind.* Boston, MA: Allyn & Bacon.

Buss, D. M. (2000). *The dangerous passion: Why jealousy is as necessary as love and sex.* New York: Free Press.

Buss, D. M., & Dedden, L. A. (1990). Derogation of competitors. *Journal of Social and Competitive Relationships, 7,* 395–422.

Buss, D. M., Larsen, R., Westen, D., & Semmelroth, J. (1992). Sex differences in jealousy: Evolution, physiology, and psychology. *Psychological Science, 3,* 251–255.

Buss, D. M., & Shackelford, T. K. (1997). From vigilance to violence: Mate retention tactics in married couples. *Journal of Personality and Social Psychology, 72,* 346–361.

Buss, D. M., Shackelford, T. K., Kirkpatrick, L. A., Choe, J., Lim, H. K., Hasegawa, M., Hasegawa, T., & Bennett, K. (1999). Jealousy and the nature of beliefs about infidelity: Tests of competing hypotheses about sex differences in the United States, Korea, and Japan. *Personal Relationships, 6,* 125–150.

Buunk, A. P., Angleitner, A., Oubaid, V., & Buss, D. M. (1996). Sex differences in jealousy in evolutionary and cultural perspective: Tests from the Netherlands, Germany, and the United States. *Psychological Science, 7,* 359–363.

Cantor, N., & Sanderson, C. A. (1999). Life task participation and well-being: The importance of taking part in daily life. In D. Kahneman, E. Diener, & N. Schwarz (Eds.), *Well-being: The foundations of hedonic psychology* (pp. 230–243). New York: Russell Sage Foundation.

Chagnon, N. (1992). *Yanomamö: The last days of Eden.* San Diego, CA: Harcourt Brace Jovanovich.

Cosmides, L., & Tooby, J. (1999). Toward an evolutionary taxonomy of treatable conditions. *Journal of Abnormal Psychology, 108,* 453–464.

Csikszentmihalyi, M. (1990). *Flow: The psychology of optimal experience.* New York: Harper & Row.

Daly, M., & Wilson, M. (1988). *Homicide.* Hawthorne, NY: Aldine.

Daly, M., Wilson, M., & Weghorst, S. J. (1982). Male sexual jealousy. *Ethology and Sociobiology, 3,* 11–27.

Darwin, C. (1859). *The origin of the species.* London: Murray.

Diener, E., & Fujita, F. (1995). Resources, personal strivings, and subjective well-being: A nomothetic and idiographic approach. *Journal of Personality and Social Psychology, 68,* 926–935.

Diener, E., Suh, E. M., Lucas, R. E., & Smith, H. L. (1999). Subjective well-being: Three decades of progress. *Psychological Bulletin, 125,* 276–302.

Dunbar, R. I. M. (1993). Coevolution of neocortical size, group size, and language in humans. *Behavioral and Brain Sciences, 16,* 681–735.

Feather, N. T. (1994). Attitudes toward achievers and reactions to their fall: Theory and research concerning tall poppies. *Advances in Experimental Social Psychology, 26,* 1–73.

Figueredo, A. J. (1995). *Preliminary report: Family deterrence of domestic violence in Spain.* Unpublished manuscript, Department of Psychology, University of Arizona.

Geary, D. C., Rumsey, M., Bow-Thomas, C. C., & Hoard, M. K. (1995). Sexual jealousy as a facultative trait: Evidence from the pattern of sex differences in adults from China and the United States. *Ethology and Sociobiology, 16,* 355–383.

Gilbert, P. (1989). *Human nature and suffering.* Hillsdale, NJ: Erlbaum.

Gutierres, S. E., Kenrick, D. T., & Partch, J. J. (1999). Beauty, dominance, and the mating game: Contrast effects in self-assessment reflect gender differences in mate selection. *Personality and Social Psychology Bulletin, 25,* 1126–1134.

Haselton, M. G., & Buss, D. M. (2000). Error management theory: A new perspective on biases in cross-sex mindreading. *Journal of Personality and Social Psychology, 78,* 81–91.

Hill, C. T., Rubin, Z., & Peplau, L. A. (1976). Breakups before marriage: The end of 103 affairs. *Journal of Social Issues, 32,* 147–168.

Kahneman, D., & Tversky, A. (1984). Choices, values, and frames. *American Psychologist, 39,* 341–350.

Kaplan, S. (1992). Environmental preference in a knowledge-seeking, knowledge-using organism. In J. Barkow, L. Cosmides, & J. Tooby (Eds.), *The adapted mind* (pp. 581–598). New York: Oxford University Press.

Keeley, L. H. (1996). *War before civilization.* New York: Oxford University Press.

Kenrick, D. T., Gutierres, S. E., & Goldberg, L. (1989). Influence of erotica on ratings of strangers and mates. *Journal of Experimental Social Psychology, 25,* 159–167.

Kenrick, D. T., & Keefe, R. C. (1992). Age preferences in mates reflect sex differences in reproductive strategies. *Behavioral and Brain Sciences, 15,* 75–133.

Kenrick, D. T., Neuberg, S. L., Zierk, K. L., & Krones, J. M. (1994). Evolution and social cognition: Contrast effects as a function of sex, dominance, and physical attractiveness. *Personality and Social Psychology Bulletin, 20,* 210–217.

Ketelaar, T. (1995, June–July). *Emotions as mental representations of fitness affordances: I. Evidence supporting the claim that the negative and positive emotions map onto fitness costs and benefits.* Paper presented at the annual meeting of the Human Behavior and Evolution Society, Santa Barbara, CA.

King, L. A., & Broyles, S. J. (1997). Wishes, gender, personality, and well-being. *Journal of Personality, 65,* 49–76.

Marks, I. (1987). *Fears, phobias, and rituals: Panic, anxiety, and their disorders.* New York: Oxford University Press.

Marks, I. M., & Nesse, R. M. (1994). Fear and fitness: An evolutionary analysis of anxiety disorders. *Ethology and Sociobiology, 15,* 247–261.

Mazur, A., & Booth, A. (in press). Testosterone and dominance in men. *Behavioral and Brain Sciences.*

Myers, D. G., & Diener, E. (1995). Who is happy? *Psychological Science, 6,* 10–19.

Nesse, R. M., & Williams, G. C. (1994). *Why we get sick.* New York: New York Times Books.

Nolen-Hoeksema, S. (1987). Sex differences in unipolar depression: Evidence and theory. *Psychological Bulletin, 101,* 259.

Orians, G. H., & Heerwagen, J. H. (1992). Evolved responses to landscapes. In J. Barkow, L. Cosmides, & J. Tooby (Eds.), *The adapted mind: Evolutionary psychology and the generation of culture* (pp. 555–579). New York: Oxford University Press.

Petrie, K. J., White, G., Cameron, L. D., & Collins, J. P. (in press). Photographic memory, money, and liposuction: Wish lists of medical students. *British Medical Journal*

Pinker, S. (1997). *How the mind works.* New York: Norton.

Price, J. S., & Sloman, L. (1987). Depression as yielding behavior: An animal model based on Schjelderup-Ebb's pecking order. *Ethology and Sociobiology, 8,* 85–98.

Sanders, D., Warner, P., Backstrom, T., & Bancroft, J. (1983). Mood, sexuality, hormones and the menstrual cycle: 1. Changes in mood and physical state. *Psychosomatic Medicine, 45,* 487–501.

Schmitt, D. P., & Buss, D. M. (1996). Strategic self-promotion and competitor derogation: Sex and context effects on the perceived effectiveness of mate attraction tactics. *Journal of Personality and Social Psychology, 70,* 1185–1204.

Seligman, M. E. P. (1971). Phobias and preparedness. *Behavior Therapy, 2,* 307–320.

Sober, E., & Wilson, D. S. (1998). *Unto others.* Cambridge, MA: Harvard University Press.

Solomon, R. L. (1980). The opponent process theory of acquired motivation: The costs of pleasure and the benefits of pain. *American Psychologist, 35,* 691–712.

Studd, M. V. (1996). Sexual harassment. In D. M. Buss & N. M. Malamuth (Eds.), *Sex, power, conflict: Evolutionary and feminist perspectives* (pp. 54–89). New York: Oxford University Press.

Symons, D. (1979). *The evolution of human sexuality.* New York: Oxford.

Symons, D. (1987). If we're all Darwinians, what's the fuss about? In C. Crawford, D. Krebs, & M. Smith (Eds.), *Sociobiology and psychology* (pp. 121–145). Hillsdale, NJ: Erlbaum.

Tellegen, A., Lykken, D. T., Bouchard, T. J., Wilcox, K. J., Jr., Wilcox, K. J., Segal, N. L., & Rich, S. (1988). Personality similarity in twins reared apart and together. *Journal of Personality and Social Psychology, 54,* 1031–1039.

Thiessen, D. D., & Gregg, B. (1980). Human assortative mating and genetic equilibrium: An evolutionary perspective. *Ethology and Sociobiology, 1,* 111–140.

Thornhill, N., & Thornhill, N. W. (1989). The evolution of psychological pain. In R. W. Bell & N. B. Bell (Eds.), *Sociobiology and the social sciences* (pp. 73–103). Lubbock, TX: Texas Tech University Press.

Tooby, J., & Cosmides, L. (1996). Friendship and the banker's paradox: Other pathways to the evolution of adaptations for altruism. *Proceedings of the British Academy, 88,* 119–143.

Tooke, W., & Camire, L. (1991). Patterns of deception in intersexual and intrasexual mating strategies. *Ethology and Sociobiology, 12,* 345–364.

Walster, E., Traupmann, J., & Walster, E. (1978). Equity and extramarital sex. *Archives of Sexual Behavior, 7,* 127–141.

Wenegrat, B. (1990). *Illness and power: Women's mental disorders and the battle between the sexes.* New York: New York University Press.

Whyte, M. K. (1990). *Dating, mating, and marriage.* New York: Aldine de Gruyter.

Wiederman, M. W., & Allgeier, E. R. (1993). Gender differences in sexual jealousy: Adaptationist or social learning explanation? *Ethology and Sociobiology, 14,* 115–140.

Wilkinson, R. G. (1996). *Unhealthy societies: From inequality to well-being.* London: Routledge.

Zahavi, A. (1977). The testing of a bond. *Animal Behavior, 25,* 246–247.

Zahavi, A., & Zahavi, A. (1997). *The handicap principle.* New York: Oxford University Press.

Hunger, Eating, and Ill Health

JOHN P. J. PINEL, SUNAINA ASSANAND, AND DARRIN R. LEHMAN

Humans and other warm-blooded animals living with continuous access to a variety of good-tasting foods tend to eat too much and suffer ill health as a result—a finding that is incompatible with the widely held view that hunger and eating are compensatory processes that function to maintain the body's energy resources at a set point. The authors argue that because of the scarcity and unpredictability of food in nature, humans and other animals have evolved to eat to their physiological limits when food is readily available, so that excess energy can be stored in the body as a buffer against future food shortages. The discrepancy between the environment in which the hunger and eating system evolved and the food-replete environments in which many people now live has led to the current problem of overconsumption existing in many countries. This evolutionary perspective has implications for understanding the etiology of anorexia nervosa.

Thinking about hunger and eating has long been dominated by the set-point assumption: that declines in energy resources below their set points produce compensatory increases in hunger—and in eating, if food is available. Despite numerous failures to confirm the major predictions of this set-point theory (see, e.g., Brandes, 1977; Friedman, Emmerich, & Gil, 1980; Smith, Gibbs, Strohmayer, & Stokes, 1972; W. H. Wilson & Heller, 1975) and the proposal of more defensible theoretical alternatives (see, e.g., Toates, 1981; Weingarten, 1985; Wirtshafter & Davis, 1977; Woods, 1991), set-point theory continues to dominate the thinking about hunger and eating of most laypersons, psychologists, and other health professionals. Indeed, in a recent survey of dietitians, nurses, doctors, and senior-year psychology students, Assanand, Pinel, and Lehman (1998) found that almost all believed that deviations from energy set points were the primary source of their motivation to eat. The fact that many of the important developments in the study of the regulation of hunger and eating do not seem to have influenced the set-point thinking of many psychologists was the major impetus for this article.

Our purpose here is not to review the evidence against the set-point theory of hunger and eating—this evidence has already been reviewed several times (see, e.g., Epstein, Nicolaidis, & Miselis, 1975; Friedman & Stricker, 1976; Russek, 1981). Our primary focus is on the inability of set-point theory to account for the results of two

J. P. J. Pinel, S. Assanand, and D. R. Lehman, "Hunger, eating, and ill health," *American Psychologist, 55* (2000): 1105–1116. Copyright © 2000 by the American Psychological Association. Reprinted with permission.

important lines of recent research on eating and health. When considered together, the results of these two lines of research—one on humans and one on laboratory animals—lead to a startling conclusion of major significance: Individuals living with continuous ready access to a wide variety of good-tasting foods have a tendency to suffer ill health because they eat too much. The results also suggest that the negative health consequences of ad libitum consumption are not, as commonly presumed, restricted to the gluttonous and obese (i.e., those who can be viewed as pathological exceptions to the metabolic balance and optimal health maintained in the rest of the population by smoothly functioning set-point systems). Rather, the consequences of ad libitum consumption adversely affect most people and indeed, most other warm-blooded animals living in food-replete environments.

We begin this article by briefly describing the current problems of overconsumption and obesity in the United States and other wealthy nations. In the second section, we describe the two lines of research that together demonstrate that humans and other warm-blooded animals living in food-replete environments tend to eat more than is optimal for good health and long life. In the third section, we hypothesize why humans and other animals living with ad libitum access to a variety of foods tend to eat more than is optimal. Our hypothesis builds on the work of several theorists (e.g., Bolles, 1980; Brown, 1991, 1993; Collier, 1986; Neel, 1962); it is an amalgam of an evolutionary analysis of hunger and eating, of health psychology research on levels of consumption and health, and of biopsychological research and theory on the mechanisms of hunger and eating. Finally, in the fourth section, we discuss an implication of this hypothesis for understanding the etiology of anorexia nervosa.

THE TENDENCY OF HUMANS LIVING IN FOOD-REPLETE SOCIETIES TO OVEREAT

Overconsumption and obesity have reached epidemic proportions in many wealthy societies. These problems are best documented in the United States. Epidemiological studies estimate that between one third and one half of adult Americans are significantly overweight (see Brownell & Rodin, 1994; Gibbs, 1996; Manson et al., 1995; Millar & Stephens, 1987). These proportions have more than doubled in the past century, and they are still increasing (see Brownell & Rodin, 1994).

The adverse effects of excessive weight on health are well documented. Studies of obesity have linked it to cardiovascular disease, cerebrovascular disease, diabetes mellitus, gall bladder disease, gout, several types of cancer (e.g., breast, colorectal, ovary, prostate), endocrine abnormalities, kidney dysfunction, liver damage, pulmonary function impairment, and accelerated deterioration of the joints (see Foreyt, 1987; Polivy & Herman, 1985). As a result, obese people die sooner: The results of one study (Garrison & Castelli, 1985) found that, within a 30-year period, the mortality rate among people who were overweight was nearly four times higher than the mortality rate among people who were of so-called desirable weight. Indeed, it is estimated that the adverse health effects of obesity contribute to the premature deaths of approximately 300,000 Americans each year (Gibbs, 1996).

BENEFICIAL EFFECTS ON HEALTH OF
RESTRICTED LEVELS OF CONSUMPTION

Most research on levels of consumption and health has focused on the adverse effects of high levels of consumption. However, in this section, we describe studies that have focused on the beneficial effects of low levels of consumption—that is, on levels of consumption that are below the common ad libitum levels that occur when food is readily and continuously available. These studies are of two types: uncontrolled studies in humans and controlled experiments in other species. Together, the results of these lines of research demonstrate that humans and other warm-blooded animals living in food-replete environments tend to consume substantially more than is optimal for good health.

Uncontrolled Human Studies

Three studies of human subjects living in wealthy countries suggest that low levels of consumption can have beneficial effects on health. Two of the studies, the Okinawa study (Kagawa, 1978) and the Nurses' Health study (Manson et al., 1995), were correlational studies demonstrating that health and longevity are greatest in individuals whose levels of consumption and body weights, respectively, are below prescribed national norms. The third study, the Biosphere 2 study (Walford, Harris, & Gunion, 1992), was an uncontrolled experimental demonstration that an improvement in health can result from a substantial reduction of food intake in ostensibly normal-weight, healthy individuals.

In the Okinawa study (Kagawa, 1978), the caloric intake and health of inhabitants of the Japanese island of Okinawa were compared with those of inhabitants of other parts of Japan. Adult Okinawans were found to consume, on average, 20% fewer calories than other adult Japanese, and Okinawan school children were found to consume 38% fewer calories than recommended by Japanese health authorities. Remarkably, the rates of morbidity and mortality in Okinawa were found to be markedly lower than in other parts of Japan, a country in which overall levels of caloric intake and obesity are well below Western norms (see Kagawa, 1978). Most notably, the death rates from stroke, cancer, and heart disease in Okinawa were only 59%, 69%, and 59%, respectively, of those in the rest of Japan, and the death rate for Okinawans between 60 and 64 years of age was only 50% of the Japanese average. Indeed, the proportion of Okinawans living to be over 100 years of age was 5 to 40 times greater than that of inhabitants of various other areas of Japan.

In the Nurses' Health study (Manson et al., 1995), the association between body-mass index and mortality was assessed in a large cohort of U.S. female nurses—levels of consumption were not directly measured. In this study, over 100,000 female nurses were recruited and studied over a 16-year period. In contrast to previous studies of the relation between body-mass index and mortality (see, e.g., Stevens et al., 1992; Tuomilehto et al., 1987; Wilcosky, Hyde, Anderson, Bangdiwala, & Duncan, 1990), this study controlled the confounding effects of cigarette smoking, which is more prevalent among relatively lean people (Garrison, Feinleib, Castelli, & McNamara, 1983). In addition, it controlled the effects of several other potential confounds, including age, levels of alcohol consumption, levels of dietary fat intake, menopausal status, preexisting disease, illness-related weight loss, and levels of physical activity. Most notably, the results revealed a positive correlation between body-mass index and mortality, with the lowest mortality rate occurring among those nurses with body-mass indices below 19—that is, among those nurses weighing at least 15% below the average weight of U.S. women of a similar age and at least 10% below their recommended weights according to the widely used Metropolitan Life Insurance Company Table of 1983. Furthermore, negative correlations were observed between body-mass index and various measures of health: Diabetes, gall stones, hypertension, and nonfatal myocardial infarction were all less frequent in the leanest nurses than in the normal-weight or overweight nurses. Apparently, the various health advantages of a low body-mass index had not been detected in previous studies (e.g., Tuomilehto et al., 1987) because they had not controlled for cigarette smoking.

In the Biosphere 2 study (Walford et al., 1992), four normal-weight females, three normal-weight males, and one mildly overweight male lived continuously for two years in a self-contained ecosystem: the so-called Biosphere 2. During their first six months in Biosphere 2, the eight participants were limited to a diet of 1,780 calories per day, an intake nearly 600 calories less than the current North American average (Walford & Walford, 1994). Among the health benefits observed in participants following this six-month period were decreases of 15% in average body weight, 30%/27% in average blood pressure, 38% in average cholesterol level, 20% in average fasting blood glucose level, and 24% in average white blood cell count.

The results of the aforementioned studies have been the focus of attention (e.g., Weindruch, 1996) because of their provocative implication that consumption below levels prevalent in wealthy countries can improve health and longevity. However, because they were uncontrolled, these three studies, even when considered together, provide only equivocal support for this conclusion. For example, it is impossible to rule out the possibility that the effects on health in each of the three studies were mediated by differences in the constitution of the high-calorie and low-calorie diets, rather than by total caloric intake per se; because the constituents of the high-calorie and low-calorie diets were not equated in any of the three studies, the health gains may have resulted from the fact that the lower calorie diets were richer in health-promoting nutrients and lower in toxins and fats than the high-calorie diets. However, this and other methodological problems (e.g., self-selection) have been resolved by controlled experiments on dietary restriction in nonhuman species.

Controlled Experiments in Nonhuman Species

Over the past decade, experiments on more than a dozen different species (e.g., monkeys, dogs, rabbits, rats) representing at least five different orders of warm-blooded animals have addressed the same general question: What happens to an ostensibly healthy, normal-weight animal living with ad libitum access to a well-balanced commercial diet when its level of caloric intake is substantially reduced? The answer has been clear and consistent (for reviews, see Bucci, 1992; Masoro, 1988; Weindruch, 1996; Weindruch & Walford, 1988): In experiment after experiment, reductions from

30% to 70% in the caloric intake of ad libitum balanced diets have resulted in decreases in body weight, significant improvements in various indices of health, and substantial increases in longevity. The improvements in health that have been observed include lower levels of blood glucose and blood insulin; lower blood pressure; higher rates of DNA repair; enhanced immune functioning; greater physical endurance; the postponement of age-related declines in protein synthesis, bone and muscle mass, learning ability, and spontaneous locomotive activity; and a delay in the onset of numerous age-related diseases, including cancer, autoimmune disease, diabetes, hypertension, and kidney disease.

In one experiment on intake restriction (Weindruch, Walford, Fligiel, & Guthrie, 1986), groups of mice, once weaned, had their caloric intake of a well-balanced commercial diet reduced below typical ad libitum levels either by 25%, 55%, or 65%. In addition to lowering body weights, all three levels of dietary restriction substantially improved health and increased longevity. Moreover, the greatest degree of dietary restriction produced the greatest improvements. Those mice that had their intake reduced by 65% had the best immune responses, the lowest incidence of cancer, and the greatest average life span—a remarkable increase of 67% above the average life span of the ad libitum control subjects. In a similar experiment (see Maeda et al., 1985; Yu, Masoro, & McMahan, 1985), groups of rats had their caloric intake reduced to 40% below ad libitum levels starting at either six weeks or six months of age. In both groups, dietary restriction reduced body weight, slowed the progression of chronic nephropathy and cardiomyopathy, delayed tumor development and skeletal muscle degeneration, prevented age-related decreases in spontaneous locomotive activity, and increased median life span by over 40%.

Two experimental studies of intake restriction are currently ongoing in primate species. One of these experiments was initiated in Rhesus and squirrel monkeys by Roth in 1987; the other was initiated in Rhesus monkeys by Ershler, Kemnitz, and Roecker in 1989 (see Weindruch, 1996). In both of these studies, caloric intake for the experimental groups has been set at 70% of usual laboratory ad libitum levels. Because the dependent measures in both experiments include longevity, these experiments will not be completed until all of the monkeys have died. Still, at this point in both experiments, most indices of good health and predictors of long life clearly favor the restricted-intake groups. For example, on average, the calorie-restricted monkeys in Ershler et al.'s study weigh 10 pounds less, have 15% less body fat, have lower blood pressure, have lower levels of blood glucose and blood insulin, and are more responsive to insulin.

Although one must always display caution in generalizing to humans from laboratory experiments in nonhuman species, there are two reasons why it seems warranted in this case. First is the fact that the effects have been so great and so consistent in each of the species and situations in which they have been studied. Second is the similarity between the results of the aforementioned uncontrolled studies in humans and the experimental results in nonhuman species: The strength of the evidence lies in the convergence of the human and nonhuman research. Indeed, there is good reason to believe that the health benefits of intake restriction in humans might be underestimated by the experiments in nonhumans. This is because laboratory animals with ad libitum access to a single balanced diet of laboratory feed are likely to overeat to a lesser degree than are humans with ad libitum access to an almost unlimited variety of preferred tastes—the ability of so-called cafeteria diets to promote consumption is well established (see, e.g., Rothwell, 1980; Rothwell & Stock, 1979).

Set-Point Theories of Hunger and Eating and the Deleterious Effects of ad Libitum Eating

The discovery that humans and other animals living in food-replete environments tend to eat far more than is optimal for good health and longevity has clear implications for the prevailing set-point theories of hunger and eating. All set-point theories are based—often implicitly—on the presumption that set-point negative feedback mechanisms have evolved to maintain the internal environment of the body at levels that promote good health and survival in the face of environmental fluctuation. With respect to the hypothetical set-point regulation of food intake, hunger (i.e., the motivation to eat) is believed to be triggered by a decline in the body's energy resources below set-point levels (e.g., set points of blood glucose and body fat); satiety, on the other hand, is believed to be associated with levels of the body's energy resources that are either at or above set-point levels. Clearly, a set-point theory would account admirably for hunger and eating if eating and bodily energy resources were being regulated in most members of the population within a narrow range. However, the great variability of caloric intake and body-mass index both within and between people argues against a mechanism that is designed to maintain the body's energy resources at an optimal point. Rather than abandoning their set-point views in the face of this critical inconsistency, many proponents of set-point theory have reacted by assuming that people have vastly different energy set points, set points that change, or compensatory mechanisms that are sometimes ineffective. However, without an independent means of measuring energy set points—other than by inferring them from food intake and body-mass index—such post hoc assumptions are circular and, thus, impossible to refute.

The increasing rates of obesity in industrialized societies and the discovery of the deleterious effects of ad libitum consumption in food-replete environments create two more fundamental challenges to set-point theories of hunger and eating. First, theories whose primary objective is to explain the constancy of energy resources provide no insight whatsoever into the steadily increasing prevalence of obesity in many countries. Second, it is unlikely that evolution would or could have produced a strict regulatory mechanism that maintains energy resources at pathological levels in a substantial proportion of the population.

AN EVOLUTIONARY PERSPECTIVE ON THE REGULATION OF HUNGER AND EATING

If set-point theories cannot account for major realities of hunger and eating, how are hunger and eating regulated? Insights into the fundamental nature of the physiological system that regulates hunger and eating may be gleaned from a consideration of the environmental pressures that likely led to their evolution. In this section, we present an evolutionary perspective on hunger and eating and discuss some of its theoretical implications—see Bolles (1980) for an engaging presentation of a similar view.

Positive Incentives

One of the main challenges faced by any animal living in a natural environment is to consume enough food to survive and reproduce. This is a particular problem for humans and other warm-blooded animals because they need to continually consume energy at a relatively high rate to maintain their internal body temperature at homeostatic levels. However, in the natural environment, the supply of appropriate foods tends to be intermittent and unpredictable, and there is often life-or-death competition for food resources when they are available. What kind of hunger and eating mechanism would have been most likely to evolve in warm-blooded animals to deal with the discrepancy between their continual demand for energy and the intermittent and unpredictable food supply?

For a hunger and eating mechanism to be adaptive in a natural environment, it must anticipate and prevent energy deficits, not merely react to them. An animal that did not become hungry until it was experiencing an energy deficit would risk being caught short because of the unreliability of the food supply (see Bolles, 1980; Collier, 1986; Weingarten, 1985). Accordingly, the theory that hunger and eating are normally triggered when the energy resources of the body fall below their optimal level is incompatible with the harsh reality of the environment in which the hunger and eating system evolved—an environment in which competition for limited and unpredictable food resources was intense and starvation was a major cause of death. For a hunger and eating mechanism to be adaptive, it must promote levels of consumption that maintain the energy resources of the body well above the levels required to meet immediate needs, so that the excess energy can be stored in the body as a buffer against periods of food unavailability (see Brown, 1991, 1993). In short, a hunger and eating mechanism that is triggered by declines in energy resources below levels needed for current optimal functioning is unlikely to have evolved in warm-blooded animals because it would have been maladaptive in their natural environment.

If the decline in the body's energy resources below their homeostatic level is not the usual cause of hunger, what is? A number of theorists (e.g., Bolles, 1990; Hetherington & Rolls, 1996; Toates, 1981) have suggested that the primary stimulus for hunger and eating is the positive-incentive value of food. According to positive-incentive theory, people are not driven to eat by declines of their energy resources below set points. Rather, people are drawn to eat by the anticipated pleasure of eating (i.e., by food's positive-incentive value); under most natural conditions, people will consume highly palatable foods when such foods are available because they have evolved to find pleasure in this behavior.

Many factors interact to influence a food's positive-incentive value, but the most important of these is anticipated taste. According to the positive-incentive theory of hunger and eating, people eat because they normally develop—through the interactions of their genetic program and their experience—a relish for particular tastes that are in nature associated with foods that promote human survival. For example, humans normally develop a liking for sweet, fatty, and salty tastes—tastes that in nature are usually characteristic of foods that are rich in energy and essential vitamins and minerals. In contrast, the positive-incentive value of bitter-tasting substances is low—in nature, these are frequently associated with toxic chemicals. Superimposed on these species-characteristic taste preferences and aversions are individual preferences and aversions that each person develops through interactions with other members of the species (see, e.g., Galef, 1989) and through experiencing the health-promoting and health-disrupting effects of the foods he or she eats (see, e.g., Sclafani, 1990).

Positive-incentive theorists do not deny that major reductions in the body's energy resources below homeostatic levels increase hunger, as well as eating, if food is available. They do, however, view this relation differently than do set-point theorists. According to set-point theory, reduction of the body's energy resources below energy set points is the main motivating factor in food consumption; according to positive-incentive theory, humans and other animals living in food-replete environments rarely, if ever, experience an energy deficit. This is because they find the consumption of high positive-incentive value foods so rewarding that when such foods are readily available, they consume far more than they need to meet their energy requirements. However, in those rare instances in which starvation does occur, hunger and eating are triggered by a major increase in the positive-incentive value of all foods.

Rogers and Blundell (1980) increased the positive-incentive value of the diet available to a group of laboratory rats by adding two palatable food items to it: bread and chocolate. If eating were strictly regulated by an energy set-point mechanism, this manipulation of the diet's positive-incentive value should have had little or no effect on the level of ad libitum consumption—set points are mechanisms that are designed to defend the constancy of the internal environment against variation in the external environment. This is not what happened. The rats' caloric intake increased by an average of 84%, and within 120 days, their body weights had increased by an average of 49%. Conversely, Brandes (1977) decreased the positive-incentive value of the diet available to a group of rats by adulterating it with quinine, a bitter-tasting substance. The rats ate little of the quinine-adulterated chow and did not increase their food intake even when rendered severely hypoglycemic by insulin injections.

Warm-blooded animals survive in natural environments because they spend a large proportion of their waking hours foraging for food and consuming it when they find it, whether or not they have an immediate need for the energy that it contains. As a result, excess energy is stored in the body as a buffer against future food shortages. In fact, studies estimate that, in industrialized societies, lean humans store enough energy in fat reserves to sustain basal energy requirements for more than one month, average-sized individuals store enough energy in fat reserves to sustain basal energy requirements for more than two months, and obese individuals store enough energy in fat reserves to sustain basal energy requirements for more than a year (see Geiselman, 1987; Levine, Eberhardt, & Jensen, 1999).

Mechanisms of Satiety

Clearly, there is more to the regulation of eating behavior than the unrelenting drive to eat: Any reasonable theory of hunger and eating must be able to explain satiety (i.e., why bouts of eating are terminated in the midst of plenty). According to set-point theory, satiety occurs when eating returns the body's supply of readily utilizable energy—that is, the glucose circulating in the blood stream—to its homeostatic set point. Although appealing in its simplicity, this account is inconsistent with the empirical evidence. Eating in food-replete environments is usually initiated in the absence of deficits in blood glucose, and thus, a return of blood glucose levels to their set point could not possibly be the mechanism of satiety (see Ritter, Roelke, & Neville, 1978). Moreover, brief bouts of eating are typically terminated well before the food is digested and absorbed into the bloodstream (see Ramsay, Seeley, Bolles, & Woods, 1996).

According to the positive-incentive theory of hunger and eating, eating stops in the presence of palatable food when its positive-incentive value has declined to the point where it is no longer sufficient to motivate consumption. Studies in which humans have rated the positive-incentive value of different foods both before and after eating a meal indicate that there are two different kinds of satiety factors, one general and one specific (Booth, 1981). As a meal is consumed, there is a gradual, general decline in the positive-incentive value of all potential foods and a more precipitous, specific decline in the positive-incentive value of the foods that are being consumed—the latter effect has been termed *sensory-specific satiety* (see B. J. Rolls, 1986). Sensory-specific satiety provides an explanation for two related eating phenomena: It explains why individuals who are satiated on one food often recommence eating if offered a different food (see, e.g., B. J. Rolls, Rolls, Rowe, & Sweeney, 1981), and it explains why experimental animals with access to a varied diet (i.e., a cafeteria diet) consume substantially more than if they are offered only a single diet. For example, in one study, rats given simultaneous access to four different foods gained an average of 12% more in body weight and 22% more in body fat over the ensuing seven weeks than did rats given access to just one of the foods (see B. J. Rolls & Hetherington, 1989). These effects of sensory-specific satiety are inconsistent with the assumption that the amount that people eat is regulated by an energy set point.

Why would sensory-specific satiety have evolved? Not only is a human or other animal living in a natural environment faced with the problem of consuming enough energy, it must also consume a diet varied enough to supply it with all of the essential vitamins and minerals that it needs. This would not happen if the positive-incentive value of each available food were a fixed value for each animal. If this were the case, animals would tend to eat only the available food with the highest positive-incentive value. However, as a result of sensory-specific satiety, the positive-incentive value of a food being consumed declines more precipitously than does the positive-incentive value of other foods, thus encouraging the consumption of a varied diet (E. T. Rolls, 1981).

Body-Weight Regulation

Set-point theory attempts to account for the stability of adult body weight by assuming that eating is regulated over the long term by a body-fat set point. However, as previously mentioned, two major facts of body-weight regulation are inconsistent with any mechanism whose primary function is the defense of a fixed, healthy body weight: First is the increasingly high incidence of obesity in modern industrialized societies (see Thomas, 1995). Second, the body weights of many adults do undergo substantial and enduring changes during their lives (see Brownell & Rodin, 1994).

Many factors interact to determine an individual's body weight. These factors are of two types: those that influence energy intake (i.e., eating) and those that influence energy output. In contrast to the view that body weight is rigidly defended by changes in the level of consumption that occur in response to deviations from a body-fat set point, current evidence suggests that the relative stability of body weight is largely attributable to the fact that the body tends to use energy less efficiently as levels of body fat increase. A consequence of this fact is the declining effectiveness of a faithfully adhered-to weight-loss program: As the level of body fat declines, efficiency with which the body uses energy increases until an equilibrium is achieved, and body weight remains at this arbitrary level until the level of intake changes.

There are two known mechanisms by which increases in consumption increase energy expenditure. The first mechanism has been termed *diet-induced thermogenesis* (Rothwell & Stock, 1979). Higher levels of body fat trigger slight increases in body temperature, which tend to reduce the impact on body weight of continuing excessive consumption by, so to speak, wasting calories (Keesey & Powley, 1986). For example, in one study (Rothwell & Stock, 1982), the basal metabolic rate was found to be 45% greater in obese rats than in normal-weight rats. The second mechanism has been termed *nonexercise activity thermogenesis.* Levine et al. (1999) found that, in humans who overeat, there is a major increase in energy expenditure by fidgeting, which limits fat accumulation. Accordingly, both diet-induced thermogenesis and nonexercise activity thermogenesis contribute to the maintenance of reasonably stable body weights by damping the effects on body weight of changes in levels of consumption.

There are large individual differences in the degree to which excessive eating leads to weight gain. For example, Rose and Williams (1961) assessed the caloric intake of individuals of the same sex, age, height, weight, and activity level and found that it was not uncommon for one member of a matched pair to be consuming twice as many calories as the other member without gaining more weight. In addition, Sims and Horton (1968) attempted to increase the body weights of volunteer prisoners at the Vermont State Prison by 25% and found that, for some volunteers, this was very difficult: For example, one prisoner had to consume 7,000 calories a day—more than two times the number of calories that he normally consumed—to accomplish this weight gain. Levine et al. (1999) suggested that individual differences in the degree to which excessive eating leads to weight gain may be explained by individual differences in nonexercise activity thermogenesis: People who effectively activate nonexercise activity thermogenesis when overeating dissipate most of the excess energy and, thus, gain little weight, whereas people who do not effectively activate nonexercise activity thermogenesis when overeating retain most of the excess energy and, thus, gain weight.

One strength of set-point theory is that it constitutes an explanation of both hunger and weight regulation. In contrast, positive-incentive theory—although more consistent with evolutionary pressures and with the principle features of hunger—has little to say about weight regulation. However, the positive-incentive theory of hunger is compatible with various settling-point models of weight regulation that have been proposed. Settling-point models provide a loose kind of homeostatic regulation without a mechanism or mechanisms for returning body weight to a prescribed set point; as such, they are more consistent with the documented nature of body-weight regulation (Pinel, 2000).

According to the settling-point models (see Bolles, 1980; Wirtshafter & Davis, 1977), body weight tends to drift around the level at which the various factors that influence food consumption and energy expenditure achieve an equilibrium. Body weight stays stable as long as none of these factors change, but when one does change, body weight drifts to a new settling point. Although settling points are not actively defended, negative feedback mechanisms, such as satiety signals and diet-induced thermogenesis, play a role in limiting the amount of drift. The drift of body weight back to its original level after the termination of a diet is sometimes offered as evidence of set-point regulation (see Carterson et al., 1996); however, the settling-point model accounts for the drift more parsimoniously, without having to evoke a set-point mechanism for which there is no direct evidence. Indeed, no regulatory mechanism at all is needed to explain why body weight drifts back to its original level once the conditions that existed before the diet are reinstated. What appears to be evidence of a set-point mechanism is often only a constancy of relevant environmental factors (Bolles, 1980).

The distinction between the set-point model and the settling-point model is an important one because of the implications that it has for weight-control strategies (see Gibbs, 1996; Van Itallie, Yang, & Porikos, 1988). For example, set-point theory implies that efforts at permanent weight loss are futile and that people who are overweight should recognize that they have high body-fat set points and not fight nature (see, e.g., Seligman, 1993; Wooley & Garner, 1991). In contrast, the settling-point model implies that permanent weight loss can be affected by any permanent change in physiology or lifestyle that influences either energy intake or output; however, the change must be permanent because as soon as the person regresses to the original condition, body weight drifts back to its original settling point.

Mealtime Hunger

Perhaps the most compelling subjective support for the set-point theory of hunger and eating are the strong feelings of hunger experienced by people when they miss a regularly scheduled meal. Most people believe that these feelings are signals from the body that it is experiencing an energy deficit (Assanand et al., 1998). However, Woods (1991; see also Woods & Strubbe, 1994) has cast this premise in a very different light—one that is substantially more consistent with the evidence. The theory of Woods rests on two important, but seldom acknowledged, facts of energy regulation. First, as people approach mealtime, they are almost always in reasonable homeostatic balance: They have large stores of energy in the form of body fat from which withdrawals can be readily made and converted to glucose, and there are no substantial declines in blood glucose—indeed, levels of blood glucose rarely vary by more than one or two percent (Woods & Strubbe, 1994). Second, Woods emphasized that the consumption of a meal disrupts homeostasis, rather than reinstating it: Blood glucose level, body metabolic rate, and liver temperature all increase during a meal—sometimes to near pathological levels. This may be why virtually all mammalian species tested with ad libitum access to food choose to eat many small meals per day (i.e., snacks) rather than a few large meals (Collier, 1989)—whether or not humans would make a similar choice in the absence of social and cultural pressures remains a matter of conjecture.

Woods (1991) contended that because the consumption of meals is, in the short term, a homeostasis-disrupting event, meal-predictive cues elicit a number of physiological changes in the body that serve to reduce the impending meal's homeostasis-disturbing impact. For example, as scheduled mealtimes approach, insulin is released from the pancreas, which starts to extract glucose from the blood and reduces the subsequent increase in blood glucose resulting from the meal-if a meal does not ensue, blood glucose levels return to their homeostatic level. It is our view that these anticipatory meal-compensatory changes, rather than energy deficits, are the basis of the powerful feelings of hunger that many people—including extremely obese people, who clearly have no overall energy deficit—experience when they miss a regularly scheduled meal. Consistent with our view, Woods has noted that people who suffer from reactive hypoglycemia—that is, a tendency to oversecrete insulin in anticipation of, or in response to, a meal—often report extreme feelings of hunger at mealtime.

Why Do Humans Eat Too Much?

Discussion of the environmental pressures that likely led to the evolution of the human hunger and eating system and of several important empirical and theoretical advances in the study of hunger and eating brings us full circle to the two lines of research that began this article: (a) studies in humans demonstrating that ad libitum levels of consumption are associated with reduced health and (b) experiments in laboratory animals demonstrating that controlled reductions in food intake below ad libitum levels lead to improvements in health and increases in longevity. We have argued that these findings are incompatible with the widely held view that hunger and eating are regulated by set-point mechanisms that maintain the body's energy levels at optimal levels and have described an alternative theory of hunger and eating derived from an evolutionary analysis. Does this theory provide a more compelling perspective from which to understand the pathological tendency of humans to overeat when in the midst of plenty?

From the perspective of our evolutionary analysis, the reason humans living in modern industrialized societies tend to overeat is that the presence, the expectation, or even the thought of food with a high positive-incentive value promotes hunger. Because in nature high positive-incentive value foods are rich sources of vitamins, minerals, and energy, it is important that such foods be consumed each time the opportunity presents itself so that the nutrients they provide can be banked as protection against potential future food scarcity. The problem is that many humans, who are admirably suited to energy regulation in a natural environment characterized by a paucity and inconsistency of food supply, live in environments in which foods of the highest possible variety and positive-incentive value are almost always available.

The human hunger and eating system did not evolve to cope with the continuous attraction of salted french fries, chocolate mocha cheesecake, and southern fried chicken. Nor did the system evolve to deal with the variety of tastes that are readily available. In a natural environment, in which the number of tastes available at any one time is likely to be few, sensory-specific satiety is an important mechanism for promoting dietary diversity. However, when the number of available foods is great, sensory-specific satiety has the effect of promoting very high levels of intake—when one becomes satiated on one food or combinations of foods, one simply switches to another high positive-incentive value food and continues eating. Who has never been comfortably satiated after eating soup, salad, and a few too many dinner rolls only to find him- or herself half an hour later finishing a main course in some distress and wondering whether or not to have ice cream on the pecan pie? Indeed, in a recent study (Assanand, Pinel, & Lehman, 1996), 81% of respondents reported that in situations in which they have access to a large supply of preferred foods, they frequently eat until they feel ill.

Because set-point theories are expressly designed to explain how internal homeostasis is maintained in the face of environmental variation, the inability of the set-point theory of hunger and eating to explain the major variations in body weight and eating in the general population is one of its major weaknesses. The theory proposed herein does this job better because it is based on the premise that hunger, eating, and body-fat levels are not highly regulated. Instead, they are held to be part of a settling-point system that has evolved to encourage humans and other warm-blooded animals to eat enough to accumulate a store of energy as a buffer against future shortages. According to settling-point models, changes in any factors that increase the availability of high positive-incentive value foods would be expected to produce increases in hunger and eating. Indeed, the major thesis of this article is that the increases in the availability of high positive-incentive value foods that have occurred over the past few decades in industrialized nations—increases that have been much too rapid to produce adaptive evolutionary change—have promoted levels of ad libitum consumption that are far higher than those that are compatible with optimal health and long life.

Ironically, it is the individual who is most at risk in modern societies—the individual with an insatiable appetite who uses her or his energy efficiently and stores the excess—that would be most suited to life in a natural environment. Those with less than ravenous appetites or tendencies to use calories inefficiently so that substantial reserves of body fat do not accumulate would be unlikely to survive the first drought or serious incursion by competitors on their food supply (see Coleman, 1979).

Ad Libitum Consumption and Reproduction

From an evolutionary perspective, reproductive success is the overriding criterion of adaptiveness. Accordingly, the strongest evidence for our thesis that food-replete environments are maladaptive for many current species would come from demonstrations of the adverse effects of these environments on the number of viable offspring. Although no studies have been conducted to address this issue directly, a study by Merry, Holehan, and Phillips (1985) is germane.

Merry et al. (1985) found that the reproductive life spans of female rats who had continuous access to a commercial diet were more than one year shorter than the reproductive life spans of female rats who had been placed on a restricted diet that maintained their body weights at 50% of the weights of the ad libitum rats. Although the ad libitum rats reached puberty sooner, they were largely infertile by the end of their first year, whereas many of the rats that had been maintained on the restricted diet remained fertile well into their third year. Although reproductive senescence was accelerated in the ad libitum rats, the aging-related changes in vaginal cytology and associated hormonal profiles were similar to those observed in the restricted-diet rats. Consistent with findings that we have already discussed, the restricted-diet rats ($M = 3.9$ years) lived substantially longer than the ad libitum rats ($M = 2.9$ years).

Health Implications

There is one major factor that influences human eating and body-fat levels that does not have an equivalent in other species. Humans can understand that excessive consumption leads to obesity and ill health and have the potential to prevent these problems by cognitively overriding the powerful attraction of high positive-incentive value foods. In other words, they have the ability to engage in dietary restraint (Blundell, 1996; Polivy & Herman, 1975). Indeed, differences in the ability and propensity to engage in dietary restraint may be major factors responsible for differences in the eating behavior of individuals living in modern food-replete environments. Surveys conducted in North America (see, e.g., De Castro, 1995; Horm & Anderson, 1993; Serdula et al., 1993) suggest that virtually everybody displays some level of dietary restraint. Still, levels of obesity and health problems associated with overconsumption continue to increase (Thomas, 1995).

Set-point theory and the theory that we have proposed provide different perspectives on the impact of dietary restraint on health. From the perspective of set-point theory, the effects of dietary restraint are seen as negative for most people because they override a motivational system that is assumed to maintain most people's bodies in good health—although perhaps not in their most cosmetically pleasing form by current Western standards (see Fallon & Rozin, 1985). Although the set-point perspective does acknowledge that dietary restraint can benefit the frankly obese—people who are assumed to possess maladaptive set-point systems that maintain body weight at excessive levels—fighting against one's set point is seen as a losing proposition (see, e.g., Polivy & Herman, 1985; Seligman, 1993; Wooley & Garner, 1991).

In contrast to the perspective provided by set-point theory, the theory proposed here views dietary restraint as largely a positive influence on health in modern wealthy societies. Considerable restraint is needed to counteract the ill health promoted by the powerful attraction of the vast array of omnipresent, high positive-incentive value foods with which human hunger and eating systems have not evolved to deal. Given the recent evidence of the adverse effects on health and longevity of ad libitum diets (see Weindruch, 1996), the improvements in public health that could potentially result from promoting restrained eating are substantial.

The primary motive for dietary restraint in modern wealthy Western societies is the reduction of obesity, usually for cosmetic reasons but sometimes for health reasons (see Bray, 1992; Sjostrom, 1993). The improvement in health associated with the reduction of eating generally is assumed to result largely, if not entirely, from decreased obesity. However, the research on the beneficial effects of reduced intake suggest otherwise: Participants who were judged to be of normal weight were found to display improvements in health when they reduced their intake (see, e.g., Walford et al., 1992; Weindruch et al., 1986). Several theories have been proposed to explain this improvement (see Sohal & Weindruch, 1996). One such theory is that the rate of aging and the incidence of all age-related diseases (e.g., various cancers and cardiovascular diseases) are accelerated by the consumption of excessive energy whether or not the person becomes obese; this is presumed to be mediated by the accumulation in cells of deleterious reactive oxygen metabolites, a product of molecular oxygen. The main evidence supporting this theory is the finding that caloric restriction decreases the rate at which reactive oxygen metabolites are generated in cells and, in so doing, decreases the rate at which cellular damage responsible for aging occurs.

DEVELOPMENT OF ANOREXIA NERVOSA: A HYPOTHESIS

The amalgam of positive-incentive theory and settling-point theory proposed herein accounts well for the basic phenomena of hunger and weight regulation; however, the critical test of any theory is its ability to stimulate and guide future research. In this, the final section of the article, we consider the implications of our theory for understanding the etiology of anorexia nervosa.

Although some degree of dietary restraint appears to be essential for the maintenance of optimal health by most people in modern wealthy societies, the practice of restrained eating is associated with risks. Virtually all patients with eating disorders have a history of strict dieting prior to the onset of their disorder. For example, in one prospective study (Patton, 1988), 21% of teenage girls who were dieting at the time of their initial interview had developed an eating disorder one year later, compared with only 3% of nondieters. Of the eating disorders, anorexia nervosa is the most devastating, the most resistant to treatment, and the most difficult to understand in the face of the increasing prevalence of obesity. One study found that 17% of anorexics died after having completed an inpatient hospital treatment program (Theander, 1983).

Evidence suggests that people—primarily, adolescent females—under great pressure from a cultural emphasis on slenderness begin dieting, and those who are highly controlled, rigid, and obsessive overcome the attraction of food and develop the disorder (see G. T. Wilson, Heffernan, & Black, 1996). Virtually all of the research on the etiology of anorexia nervosa has focused on predisposing individual characteristics such as gender, age, culture, personality, and genetic factors (see Cooper, 1995; Garfinkel & Garner, 1983). We do not question the value of these approaches to the study of the etiology of anorexia nervosa; our point is that the theory proposed herein points to an important aspect of the etiology of anorexia nervosa that has been largely ignored.

The positive-incentive theory of hunger suggests that the decline in eating that defines anorexia nervosa is likely a consequence of a corresponding decline in the positive-incentive value of food; it also suggests that studying the positive-incentive value of food in anorexic patients would be productive. However, the positive-incentive value of food in anorexic patients has received little attention—in part because of the predominance of set-point thinking and in part because anorexic patients often display substantial interest in food. The fact that many anorexic patients are obsessed with food—they continually talk about it, think about it, and prepare it for others (Crisp, 1983)—seems to suggest that it holds a high positive-incentive value for them. The confusion lies in the fact that the positive-incentive value of interacting with food is not necessarily the same as the positive-incentive value of eating food—and it is the positive-incentive value of eating food that is critical when considering anorexia nervosa. Indeed, the behavior of rats that are housed with access to a single diet to which they have a conditioned taste aversion is reminiscent of the behavior of anorexic humans: They continually manipulate the food, sometimes putting it in their mouths and spitting it out, but they do not eat it.

A few studies have examined the positive-incentive value of various tastes in anorexic patients (see, e.g., Drewnowski, Halmi, Pierce, Gibbs, & Smith, 1987; Sunday & Halmi, 1990). In general, these studies found that the positive-incentive value of various tastes is lower in anorexic patients than in control participants. Be that as it may, these studies grossly underestimate the importance of reductions in the positive-incentive value of food in the etiology of anorexia nervosa because the anorexic participants and the control participants were not matched in weight. People who have had starvation imposed on them—although difficult to find—are the suitable equal-weight control subjects for anorexic participants. Starvation normally triggers a radical increase in the positive-incentive value of food. This has been best documented by the descriptions and behavior of volunteer participants undergoing experimental semistarvation. When asked how it felt to starve, one participant replied,

> I wait for mealtime. When it comes I eat slowly and make the food last as long as possible. The menu never gets monotonous even if it is the same each day or is of poor quality. It is food and all food tastes good. Even dirty crusts of bread in the street look appetizing. (Keys, Brozek, Henschel, Mickelsen, & Taylor, 1950, p. 852)

Although we agree that the value placed on slenderness by Western culture is the main precipitating factor in anorexia (Wilfley & Rodin, 1995), the extreme adaptive increases in the positive-incentive value of food seen in nonanorexic subjects facing starvation suggests that this is not the whole story. The positive-incentive value of food increases to such high levels under conditions of starvation that it is difficult to imagine how anybody—no matter how controlled, rigid, obsessive, and motivated—could refrain from eating in the presence of palatable food. Why this protective mechanism is not activated in severe anorexics is a key question about the etiology of anorexia nervosa that needs to be addressed. We believe that the answer lies in the study of positive incentives.

Our theory of hunger and eating suggests a means by which the positive-incentive value of food might be reduced to the point where particularly determined dieters could overcome food's attraction enough to reach the level of starvation characteristic of extreme anorexia. This hypothesis is based on the fact that eating meals can have a number of adverse physiological effects (e.g., increases in hepatic temperature; Woods, 1991; Woods & Strubbe, 1994), particularly if they are eaten after a period of deprivation (Brooks & Melnik, 1995). We suggest that meals, which produce adverse, but tolerable, effects in healthy individuals, may be extremely aversive for individuals who have undergone food deprivation and that these aversive effects might condition a wide array of taste aversions, making it easier for severe anorexics to starve themselves. Consistent with our view, Capaldi and Myers (1982) found that rats prefer flavors consumed under conditions of low food deprivation to flavors consumed under conditions of high food deprivation. Evidence for the extremely noxious effects that eating has on abstemious humans is found in the reactions of World War II concentration camp victims to refeeding—many were killed by the very food given to them by their liberators (Keys et al., 1950; see also Solomon & Kirby, 1990).

The purpose of this digression into the causal factors of anorexia nervosa is not to develop a new theory of anorexia nervosa; it is merely to demonstrate that our synthesis of current research on the nature of hunger and eating can serve as a basis for developing original hypotheses. We believe that the combination of the positive-incentive theory of hunger and eating with Woods's analysis of the aversive consequences of meals has important implications for the study of this eating disorder.

REFERENCES

Assanand, S., Pinel, J. P. J., & Lehman, D. R. (1996). *Common misconceptions about the regulation of feeding.* Unpublished manuscript, University of British Columbia, Vancouver, British Columbia, Canada.

Assanand, S., Pinel, J. P. J., & Lehman, D. R. (1998). Personal theories of hunger and eating. *Journal of Applied Social Psychology, 28,* 998–1015.

Blundell, J. E. (1996). Food intake and body weight regulation. In C. Bouchard & G. A. Bray (Eds.), *Regulation of body weight: Biological and behavioral mechanisms* (pp. 111–133). Chichester, England: Wiley.

Bolles, R. C. (1980). Some functionalistic thoughts about regulation. In F. M. Toates & T. R. Halliday (Eds.), *Analysis of motivational processes* (pp. 63–75). London: Academic Press.

Bolles, R. C. (1990). A functionalistic approach to feeding. In E. D. Capaldi & T. L. Powley (Eds.), *Taste, experience, and feeding* (pp. 3–13). Washington, DC: American Psychological Association.

Booth, D. A. (1981). The physiology of appetite. *British Medical Bulletin, 37,* 135–140.

Brandes, J. S. (1977). Insulin induced overeating in the rat. *Physiology and Behavior, 18,* 1095–1102.

Bray, G. A. (1992). Pathophysiology of obesity. *American Journal of Clinical Nutrition, 55,* 488S–494S.

Brooks, M. J., & Melnik, G. (1995). The refeeding syndrome: An approach to understanding its complications and preventing its occurrence. *Pharmacotherapy, 15,* 713–726.

Brown, P. (1991). Culture and the evolution of obesity. *Human Nature, 2,* 31–57.

Brown, P. (1993). Cultural perspectives on the etiology and treatment of obesity. In A. J. Stunkard & T. A. Wadden (Eds.), *Obesity: Theory and therapy* (pp. 179–193). New York: Raven Press.

Brownell, K. D., & Rodin, J. (1994). The dieting maelstrom: Is it possible and advisable to lose weight? *American Psychologist, 49,* 781–791.

Bucci, T. J. (1992). Dietary restriction: Why all the interest? An overview. *Lab Animal, 21,* 29–34.

Capaldi, E. D., & Myers, D. E. (1982). Taste preferences as a function of food deprivation during original taste exposure. *Animal Learning and Behavior, 10,* 211–219.

Carterson, I. D., Atkinson, R. L., Bray, G. A., Hansen, B. C., Reeds, P. J., Stock, M. J., Tremblay, A., & York, D. A. (1996). What are the animal and human models for the study of regulation of body weight and what are their respective strengths and limitations? In C. Bouchard & G. A. Bray (Eds.), *Regulation of body weight: Biological and behavioral mechanisms* (pp. 85–110). Chichester, England: Wiley.

Coleman, D. L. (1979, February 16). Obesity genes: Beneficial effects in heterozygous mice. *Science, 203,* 663–665.

Collier, G. H. (1986). The dialogue between the house economist and the resident physiologist. *Nutrition and Behavior, 3,* 9–26.

Collier, G. H. (1989). The economics of hunger, thirst, satiety, and regulation. *Annals of the New York Academy of Sciences, 575,* 136–154.

Cooper, Z. (1995). The development and maintenance of eating disorders. In K. D. Brownell & C. G. Fairburn (Eds.), *Eating disorders and obesity: A comprehensive handbook* (pp. 199–206). New York: Guilford Press.

Crisp, A. H. (1983). Some aspects of the psychopathology of anorexia nervosa. In P. L. Darby, P. E. Garfinkel, D. M. Garner, & D. V. Coscina (Eds.), *Anorexia nervosa: Recent developments in research* (pp. 15–28). New York: Alan R. Liss.

De Castro, J. M. (1995). The relationship of cognitive restraint to the spontaneous food and fluid intake of free-living humans. *Physiology and Behavior, 57,* 287–295.

Drewnowski, A., Halmi, K. A., Pierce, B., Gibbs, J., & Smith, G. P. (1987). Taste and eating disorders. *American Journal of Clinical Nutrition, 46,* 442–450.

Epstein, A. N., Nicolaidis, S., & Miselis, R. (1975). The glucoprivic control of food intake and the glucostatic theory of feeding behaviour. In G. J. Mogenson & R. R. Calaresu (Eds.), *Neural integration of physiological mechanisms and behaviour* (pp. 148–168). Toronto, Ontario, Canada: University of Toronto Press.

Fallon, A. E., & Rozin, P. (1985). Sex differences in perceptions of desirable body shape. *Journal of Abnormal Psychology, 94,* 102–105.

Foreyt, J. P. (1987). Issues in the assessment and treatment of obesity. *Journal of Consulting and Clinical Psychology, 55,* 677–684.

Friedman, M. I., Emmerich, A. L., & Gil, K. M. (1980). Effects of insulin on food intake and plasma glucose level in fat-fed diabetic rats. *Physiology and Behavior, 24,* 319–325.

Friedman, M. I., & Stricker, E. M. (1976). The physiological psychology of hunger: A physiological perspective. *Psychological Review, 83*, 409–431.

Galef, B. G. (1989). Laboratory studies of naturally-occurring feeding behaviors: Pitfalls, progress and problems in ethoexperimental analysis. In R. J. Blanchard, P. F. Brain, D. C. Blanchard, & S. Parmigiani (Eds.), *Ethoexperimental approaches to the study of behavior* (pp. 51–77). Dordrecht, The Netherlands: Kluwer Academic.

Garfinkel, P. E., & Garner, D. M. (1983). The multidetermined nature of anorexia nervosa. In P. L. Darby, P. E. Garfinkel, D. M. Garner, & D. V. Coscina (Eds.), *Anorexia nervosa: Recent developments in research* (pp. 3–14). New York: Alan R. Liss.

Garrison, R. J., & Castelli, W. P. (1985). Weight and thirty-year mortality of men in the Framingham study. *Annals of Internal Medicine, 103*, 1006–1009.

Garrison, R. J., Feinleib, M., Castelli, W. P., & McNamara, P. M. (1983). Cigarette smoking as a confounder of the relationship between relative weight and long-term mortality: The Framingham Heart Study. *JAMA, 249*, 2199–2203.

Geiselman, P. J. (1987). Carbohydrates do not always produce satiety: An explanation of the appetite- and hunger-stimulating effects of hexoses. *Progress in Psychobiology and Physiological Psychology, 12*, 1–46.

Gibbs, W. W. (1996, August). Gaining on fat. *Scientific American, 275*, 88–94.

Hetherington, M. M., & Rolls, B. J. (1996). Sensory-specific satiety: Theoretical frameworks and central characteristics. In E. D. Capaldi (Ed.), *Why we eat what we eat* (pp. 267–290). Washington, DC: American Psychological Association.

Horm, J., & Anderson, K. (1993). Who in America is trying to lose weight? *Annals of Internal Medicine, 119*, 672–676.

Kagawa, Y. (1978). Impact of westernization on the nutrition of Japanese: Changes in physique, cancer, longevity, and centenarians. *Preventive Medicine, 7*, 205–217.

Keesey, R. E., & Powley, T. L. (1986). The regulation of body weight. *Annual Review of Psychology, 37*, 109–133.

Keys, A., Brozek, J., Henschel, A., Mickelsen, O., & Taylor, H. L. (1950). *The biology of human starvation.* Minneapolis: University of Minnesota Press.

Levine, J. A., Eberhardt, N. L., & Jensen, M. D. (1999, January 8). Role of nonexercise activity thermogenesis in resistance to fat gain in humans. *Science, 283*, 212–214.

Maeda, H., Gleiser, C. A., Masoro, E. J., Murata, I., McMahan, C. A., & Yu, B. P. (1985). Nutritional influences on aging of Fischer 344 rats: II. Pathology. *Journal of Gerontology, 40*, 671–688.

Manson, J. E., Willett, W. C., Stampfer, M. J., Colditz, G. A., Hunter, D. J., Hankinson, S. E., Hennekens, C. H., & Speizer, F. E. (1995). Body weight and mortality among women. *New England Journal of Medicine, 333*, 677–685.

Masoro, E. J. (1988). Food restriction in rodents: An evaluation of its role in the study of aging. *Journal of Gerontology, 43*, B59–B64.

Merry, B. J., Holehan, A. M., & Phillips, J. G. (1985). Modification of reproductive decline and lifespan by dietary manipulation in CFY Sprague-Dawley rats. In B. Lofts & W. N. Holmes (Eds.), *Current trends in comparative endocrinology* (pp. 621–624). Hong Kong: Hong Kong University Press.

Millar, W. J., & Stephens, T. (1987). The prevalence of overweight and obesity in Britain, Canada, and United States. *American Journal of Public Health, 77*, 38–41.

Neel, J. V. (1962). Diabetes mellitus: A "thrifty" genotype rendered detrimental by "progress"? *American Journal of Human Genetics, 14*, 353–362.

Patton, G. C. (1988). The spectrum of eating disorders in adolescence. *Journal of Psychosomatic Research, 32*, 579–584.

Pinel, J. P. J. (2000). *Biopsychology* (4th ed.). Boston: Allyn & Bacon.

Polivy, J., & Herman, C. P. (1975). Dieting and binging: A causal analysis. *American Psychologist, 40*, 193–201.

Polivy, J., & Herman, C. P. (1985). Dieting as a problem in behavioral medicine. *Advances in Behavioral Medicine, 1*, 1–37.

Ramsay, D. S., Seeley, R. J., Bolles, R. C., & Woods, S. C. (1996). Ingestive homeostasis: The primacy of learning. In E. D. Capaldi (Ed.), *Why we eat what we eat* (pp. 11–27). Washington, DC: American Psychological Association.

Ritter, R. C., Roelke, M., & Neville, M. (1978). Glucoprivic feeding behavior in absence of other signs of glucoprivation. *American Journal of Physiology, 234*, E617–E621.

Rogers, P. J., & Blundell, J. E. (1980). Investigation of food selection and meal parameters during the development of dietary induced obesity [Abstract]. *Appetite, 1*, 85

Rolls, B. J. (1986). Sensory-specific satiety. *Nutrition Reviews, 44*, 93–101.

Rolls, B. J., & Hetherington, M. (1989). The role of variety in eating and body weight regulation. In R. Shepherd (Ed.), *Handbook of the psychophysiology of human eating* (pp. 57–84). Chichester, England: Wiley.

Rolls, B. J., Rolls, E. T., Rowe, E. A., & Sweeney, K. (1981). Sensory specific satiety in man. *Physiology and Behavior, 27*, 137–142.

Rolls, E. T. (1981). Central nervous mechanisms related to feeding and appetite. *British Medical Bulletin, 37*, 131–134.

Rose, G. A., & Williams, R. T. (1961). Metabolic studies of large and small eaters. *British Journal of Nutrition, 15*, 1–9.

Rothwell, N. J. (1980). Reversible obesity induced by "cafeteria" diets. *Appetite, 1*, 87

Rothwell, N. J., & Stock, M. J. (1979, September 6). A role for brown adipose tissue in diet-induced thermogenesis. *Nature, 281*, 31–35.

Rothwell, N. J., & Stock, M. J. (1982). Energy expenditure of "cafeteria"-fed rats determined from measurements of energy balance and indirect calorimetry. *Journal of Physiology, 328,* 371–377.

Russek, M. (1981). Current status of the hepatostatic theory of food intake control. *Appetite, 2,* 137–143.

Sclafani, A. (1990). Nutritionally based learned flavor preferences in rats. In E. D. Capaldi & T. L. Powley (Eds.), *Taste, experience, and feeding* (pp. 139–156). Washington, DC: American Psychological Association.

Seligman, M. E. P. (1993). *What you can change . . . and what you can't.* New York: Ballantine Books.

Serdula, M. K., Collins, M. E., Williamson, D. F., Anda, R. F., Pamuk, E. R., & Byers, T. E. (1993). Weight control practices of U.S. adolescents and adults. *Annals of Internal Medicine, 119,* 667–671.

Sims, E. A. H., & Horton, E. S. (1968). Endocrine and metabolic adaptation to obesity and starvation. *American Journal of Clinical Nutrition, 21,* 1455–1470.

Sjostrom, L. (1993). Impacts of body weight, body composition, and adipose tissue distribution on morbidity and mortality. In A. J. Stunkard & T. A. Wadden (Eds.), *Obesity: Theory and therapy* (pp. 13–41). New York: Raven Press.

Smith, G. P., Gibbs, J., Strohmayer, A., & Stokes, P. E. (1972). Threshold doses of 2-deoxy-D-glucose for hyperglycemia and feeding in rats and monkeys. *American Journal of Physiology, 222,* 77–81.

Sohal, R. S., & Weindruch, R. (1996, July 5). Oxidative stress, caloric restriction, and aging. *Science, 273,* 59–63.

Solomon, S. M., & Kirby, D. F. (1990). The refeeding syndrome: A review. *Journal of Parenteral and Enteral Nutrition, 14,* 90–97.

Stevens, J., Keil, J. E., Rust, P. F., Tyroler, H. A., Davis, C. E., & Gazes, P. C. (1992). Body-mass index and body girths as predictors of mortality in Black and White women. *Archives of Internal Medicine, 152,* 1257–1262.

Sunday, S. R., & Halmi, K. A. (1990). Taste perceptions and hedonics in eating disorders. *Physiology and Behavior, 48,* 587–594.

Theander, S. (1983). Long-term prognosis of anorexia nervosa: A preliminary report. In P. L. Darby, P. E. Garfinkel, D. M. Garner, & D. V. Coscina (Eds.), *Anorexia nervosa: Recent developments in research* (pp. 441–442). New York: Alan R. Liss.

Thomas, P. R., Ed. (1995). *Weighing the options: Criteria for evaluating weight-management programs.* Washington, DC: National Academy Press.

Toates, F. M. (1981). The control of ingestive behavior by internal and external stimuli: A theoretical review. *Appetite, 2,* 35–50.

Tuomilehto, J., Salonen, J. T., Marti, B., Jalkanen, L., Puska, P., Nissien, A., & Wolf, E. (1987). Body weight and risk of myocardial infarction and death in the adult population in eastern Finland. *British Medical Journal, 295,* 623–627.

Van Itallie, T. B., Yang, M., & Porikos, K. P. (1988). Use of aspartame to test the "body weight set point" hypothesis. *Appetite, 11,* 68–72.

Walford, R. L., Harris, S. B., & Gunion, M. W. (1992). The calorically restricted low-fat nutrient-dense diet in Biosphere 2 significantly lowers blood glucose, total leukocyte count, cholesterol, and blood pressure in humans. *Proceedings of the National Academy of Science, 89,* 11533–11537.

Walford, R. L., & Walford, L. (1994). *The anti-aging plan.* New York: Four Walls Eight Windows.

Weindruch, R. (1996, January). Caloric restriction and aging. *Scientific American, 274,* 46–52.

Weindruch, R., & Walford, R. L. (1988). *The retardation of aging and disease by dietary restriction.* Springfield, IL: Charles C Thomas.

Weindruch, R., Walford, R. L., Fligiel, S., & Guthrie, D. (1986). The retardation of aging in mice by dietary restriction: Longevity, cancer, immunity, and lifetime energy intake. *Journal of Nutrition, 116,* 641–654.

Weingarten, H. P. (1985). Stimulus control of eating: Implications for a two-factor theory of hunger. *Appetite, 6,* 387–401.

Wilcosky, T., Hyde, J., Anderson, J. J. B., Bangdiwala, S., & Duncan, B. (1990). Obesity and mortality in the Lipid Research Clinics Program Follow-up Study. *Journal of Clinical Epidemiology, 43,* 743–752.

Wilfley, D. E., & Rodin, J. (1995). Cultural influences on eating disorders. In K. D. Brownell & C. G. Fairburn (Eds.), *Eating disorders and obesity: A comprehensive handbook* (pp. 78–82). New York: Guilford Press.

Wilson, G. T., Heffernan, K., & Black, C. M. D. (1996). Eating disorders. In E. J. Mash & R. A. Barkley (Eds.), *Child psychopathology* (pp. 541–571). New York: Guilford Press.

Wilson, W. H., & Heller, H. C. (1975). Elevated blood glucose levels and satiety in the rat. *Physiology and Behavior, 15,* 137–143.

Wirtshafter, D., & Davis, J. D. (1977). Set points, settling points, and the control of body weight. *Physiology and Behavior, 19,* 75–78.

Woods, S. C. (1991). The eating paradox: How we tolerate food. *Psychological Review, 98,* 488–505.

Woods, S. C., & Strubbe, J. H. (1994). The psychobiology of meals. *Psychonomic Bulletin and Review, 1,* 141–155.

Wooley, S. C., & Garner, D. M. (1991). Obesity treatment: The high cost of false hope. *Journal of the American Dietetic Association, 91,* 1248–1251.

Yu, B. P., Masoro, E. J., & McMahan, C. A. (1985). Nutritional influences on aging of Fischer 344 rats: I. Physical, metabolic, and longevity characteristics. *Journal of Gerontology, 40,* 657–670.

Psychoactive Drug Use in Evolutionary Perspective

RANDOLPH M. NESSE AND KENT C. BERRIDGE

Pure psychoactive drugs and direct routes of administration are evolutionarily novel features of our environment. They are inherently pathogenic because they bypass adaptive information processing systems and act directly on ancient brain mechanisms that control emotion and behavior. Drugs that induce positive emotions give a false signal of a fitness benefit. This signal hijacks incentive mechanisms of "liking" and "wanting," and can result in continued use of drugs that no longer bring pleasure. Drugs that block negative emotions can impair useful defenses, although there are several reasons why their use is often safe nonetheless. A deeper understanding of the evolutionary origins and functions of the emotions and their neural mechanisms is needed as a basis for decisions about the use of psychoactive drugs.

The neural mechanisms that regulate emotion and behavior were shaped by natural selection to maximize Darwinian fitness, so psychoactive drugs that disrupt those mechanisms should impair adaptation. As the toll of substance abuse tragically demonstrates, they can. But psychoactive drugs can also improve adaptation in some circumstances (what would many scientists do without caffeine?), relieve the symptoms of mental disorders, and induce pleasures that can sometimes be safe. Here, we consider substance use and abuse from the perspective of Darwinian medicine, the enterprise of seeking evolutionary explanations for design characteristics that make organisms vulnerable to disorders (*1–3*). This perspective suggests that explanations of substance abuse based on brain mechanisms or on individual and social differences can be augmented by evolutionary explanations for the universal human vulnerability to the maladaptive effects of psychoactive drugs, and for the functions of emotions they influence.

Emotions are coordinated states, shaped by natural selection, that adjust physiological and behavioral responses to take advantage of opportunities and to cope with threats that have recurred over the course of evolution (*4, 5*). Thus, the characteristics and regulation of basic emotions match the requirements of specific situations that have often influenced fitness. Emotions influence motivation, learning, and decisions and, therefore, influence behavior and, ultimately, fitness (*6–10*). Subjective feelings

Reprinted with permission from R. M. Nesse and K. C. Berridge, "Psychoactive drug use in evolutionary perspective," *Science, 278* (October 3, 1997): 63–66. Copyright 1997 American Association for the Advancement of Science.

offer a window (often distorted) into motivation, but they are not the essence of emotion (*9, 11, 12*) and are not even always a necessary component (*13, 14*). For example, in a recent study of a forced-choice task, normal people start to avoid the poor choice and to show emotion-associated skin conductance changes even before they become aware of any preference (*15*). Nonetheless, subjective positive or negative valence is a prominent aspect of basic emotions, with distinct kinds of negative states outnumbering positive ones. These observations are consistent with the origins of emotions as specialized states shaped to cope with situations that involve opportunities or gains and a greater number of different kinds of situations that involve threats or losses. This offers a potential evolutionary explanation for the nonintuitive, but well-documented, relative independence of positive and negative affect (*16*), and suggests that the effects of psychoactive drugs on positive and negative emotions should be considered separately.

DRUGS THAT STIMULATE POSITIVE EMOTIONS

Substance abuse is explained, according to folk psychology, by human tendencies to repeat behaviors that bring pleasure or relieve suffering. This global explanation is correct but incomplete. Most drugs of abuse act on ancient and remarkably conserved neural mechanisms, associated with positive emotions, that evolved to mediate incentive behavior. Heroin, cocaine, alcohol, marijuana, amphetamine, and their synthetic analogs activate mesolimbic dopamine-containing neurons and associated opioid receptors in mammalian brains, a system that may be a "common neural currency" for reward and a substrate for regulating motivations (*17–21*). Some of the transmitter molecules used by these systems evolved as much as 1000 million years ago (*22*), and mammalian dopamine, serotonin, and norepinephrine neurotransmitters are also used by invertebrate phyla, such as mollusks and arthropods, that diverged from prevertebrate lines roughly 600 million years ago. Most vertebrate brains have μ opioid receptor-like DNA sequences (*23*), and even nonmammalian vertebrate brains have mesolimbic systems comprising dopamine-containing neurons that ascend from the midbrain to a dorsal and ventral striatal complex (*24*). Although these neurotransmitter systems may not all serve the same functions, some neurotransmitters play similar roles in very different organisms: Dopamine mediates feeding in organisms ranging from slugs to primates (*25*), and a similar molecule, octopamine, mediates the effects of sucrose rewards in bees (*26*). This conservation of function for reward-signaling chemicals contrasts with a diversity of receptors (*27, 28*), probably because a mutation that changes a transmitter is likely to disrupt a whole system, whereas gene duplication allows differentiation of receptors that can gradually take on new functions (*29*).

Drugs of abuse create a signal in the brain that indicates, falsely, the arrival of a huge fitness benefit. This changes behavioral propensities so that drug-seeking increases in frequency and displaces adaptive behaviors. Other novel aspects of the modern environment have similar effects. For instance, playing video games also displaces more adaptive behaviors but via psychological instead of direct neurochemical means. Snacks high in fat, salt, and sugar tend to displace more nutritious foods in the diet. We are vulnerable to such fitness-decreasing incentives because our brains are not designed to cope with ready access to pure drugs, video games, and snack foods (30). Hundreds of generations of exposure would likely shape resistance to their allure and their deleterious effects. Far less time might be sufficient, if the genetic deficit in alcohol dehydrogenase in many Asian populations is indeed a product of selection by a few thousand years of exposure to alcohol (31). In the meanwhile, the mismatch between our bodies and our modern environments is a major cause of behavioral and medical problems.

This simple perspective leaves many aspects of substance abuse unexplained. For instance, as addiction develops, drug-induced pleasure declines or remains constant, even as cravings increase and maladaptive consequences accumulate, thus making it clear that the pursuit of pleasure is an insufficient explanation. One likely reason is the separation of mammalian brain reward systems into components that correspond roughly to "liking" (hedonic pleasure on receiving a reward) and to "wanting" (incentive motivation and behavioral pursuit of a reward). Although the nature of these components is just beginning to be understood, they appear to have different neural substrates. "Liking" of sweet foods, for example, is mediated by certain opioid forebrain systems and by brain-stem systems, whereas "wanting" seems to be mediated by ascending mesolimbic dopamine neurons (12, 32). The separate neural mediation of "wanting" may have evolved so that disparate "likes" for food, sex, and other incommensurate incentives could be compared in a common currency of utility (33). The "liking" system is activated by receiving the reward, while the "wanting" system anticipates reward and motivates instrumental behaviors. When these two systems are exposed to drugs, the "wanting" system motivates persistent pursuit of drugs that no longer give pleasure, thus offering an explanation for a core paradox of addiction.

Another aspect of physiology that makes us susceptible to substance abuse is neural sensitization–hyperresponsivity in ascending dopamine projections induced by addictive drugs, through a mechanism gated by genetic and experiential factors (34, 35). Such sensitization of brain substrates that mediate "wanting" can result in compulsive seeking of a drug that causes neither pleasure nor withdrawal (32, 34). Any organism with a chemically mediated incentive system and technological capabilities is intrinsically vulnerable to addiction, but these special design features of vertebrate reward systems magnify the risks and may explain the otherwise bizarre phenomenon of addicts who sacrifice everything else in life to get drugs that do not reliably bring pleasure, and who return to drug use even after extended periods of abstinence.

Important implications follow from the origin of our vulnerability to drug abuse in the mismatch between ancient mechanisms and modern environments. From this evolutionary perspective, individual variations that increase susceptibility to drug abuse are better described as quirks than defects, because they probably had no deleterious effects in the ancestral environment. Genetic differences set parameters of basic neurobehavioral systems that are shared by all members of a species. Nongenetic differences in emotional experience can also influence susceptibility to drug use, as demonstrated by the substantial comorbidity of substance abuse and posttraumatic stress disorder. The strong association between emotional symptoms and susceptibility to addiction has been studied carefully for smoking, and the ability of nicotine to relieve these feelings has been interpreted in a sophisticated evolutionary perspective (*36*). Instead of only seeking explanations for substance abuse in individual differences in genes, temperament, early experiences, social conditions, cultural setting, or exposure to drug use, an evolutionary perspective suggests that we also consider how these factors interact with the emotional and behavioral mechanisms that make all humans vulnerable to substance abuse. This view encourages therapeutic attention to the diversity of factors that influence people's emotions, such as relationships, social support, social inequity, the experience of discrimination, and opportunities or blocked opportunities. There are reasons why people who are not succeeding in the social competition are likely to experience positive emotions less often and negative emotions more often, take drugs more often, and be less responsive to treatment. This view also suggests that the mismatch between novel pharmacological hyperincentives and ancient brain mechanisms is likely to worsen with the discovery of new drugs and new routes of administration. Finally, it suggests that we cannot reasonably expect to win the war on drug abuse, but we can use our knowledge to develop sensible strategies for prevention, treatment, and public policy to manage a problem that is likely to persist because it is rooted in the fundamental design of the human nervous system.

DRUGS THAT BLOCK NEGATIVE EMOTIONS

An evolutionary perspective also has implications for drugs that block anxiety, low mood, and other negative emotions. Psychiatrists may soon have drugs that control emotional suffering just as well as other drugs can control pain, cough, fever, diarrhea, and vomiting. Our understanding of when and how emotional reactions are useful remains superficial, but understanding the utility of many physical defenses has also proved elusive. While most physicians know that blocking a cough can lead to death in a patient with pneumonia, and many know that blocking *Shigella*-induced diarrhea leads to slower recovery and more complications (*37*), some do not appreciate the utility of defenses such as fever and low blood iron levels in infection (*38, 39*), and some do not readily differentiate between manifestations of disease that are aspects of defenses and those that arise from defects in the body's machinery (*3*). Such difficulties are magnified in psychiatry. The utility of anxiety is known but often ignored (*40–42*), the utility of jealousy remains controversial (*43*), and the utility of low mood and depression is just being considered (*44–47*). Quantitative studies that explicitly address the evolutionary functions of emotions have just begun. For example, new data support the function of embarrassment and guilt in regulating the individual's hierarchical role in a group (*48, 49*). Our understanding of the functional significance of negative emotions grows slowly, while new psychotropic drug development races far ahead at a furious pace. We lack the scientific knowledge about emotions that would support detailed advice on when these agents should or should not be used.

We do, however, have several reasons to think that psychotropic drugs can often be safe and useful, even if the capacities for negative emotions are adaptations. First, there are disease states, in which drugs can normalize or compensate for pathology, for example, lithium's ability to prevent mania. Second, many normal painful emotional responses may be no more useful in the modern environment than the pain caused by surgery. A panic attack may save the life of a hunter fleeing from a lion, but cost the life of a driver on an expressway. Third, the body has redundant defenses, so blocking one negative emotion may have few deleterious consequences, just as blocking fever does not necessarily slow the recovery from infection. Fourth, the biological systems that regulate defense expression must (according to signal detection principles) have been shaped to express the defensive response whenever, on average, it is worth it. Because many defenses are inexpensive but protect against potentially fatal threats whose presence is signaled by unreliable cues, even an optimal system will produce many false alarms (4). Like vomiting, which can eliminate a possibly fatal toxin at the cost of losing a few hundred calories, fear and low mood may decrease the tendency for behaviors that are dangerous or useless. Finally, the brain was not designed to benefit individuals, but their genes. As Wilson puts it, "Love joins hate, aggression, fear, expansiveness, withdrawal, and so on, in blends designed not to promote the happiness of the individual, but to favor the maximum transmission of the controlling genes." (50)

Such considerations make it possible to envision, or even to predict, a future in which drugs will eliminate much normal as well as pathological emotional suffering, just as they now relieve physical suffering. On the other hand, the same factors also undermine the simplistic view, advocated by some psychiatrists and pharmaceutical companies, that intense aversive emotions almost always result from a brain abnormality. Some anxiety and low mood has a primary cause in brain defects, but much also arises from normal brains and is caused by an imbalance of brain chemicals only in the same superficial sense that cough is caused by excessive neural activity in the brain locus that controls cough. Furthermore, just because a drug relieves a negative emotion does not mean that the emotion is abnormal, nor does it imply that the drug works by reversing a brain defect. Aspirin, after all, reduces body temperature only in people with fever, but fever is a defense against disease, not a disease itself.

CONCLUSION

Emotional capacities evolved to improve the Darwinian fitness of individuals as they seek resources and avoid dangers. The pursuit of emotion-associated goals tends to move organisms up a hedonic and adaptive gradient, but neurobehavioral systems are designed to maximize Darwinian fitness, not happiness, so our pleasures are often fleeting, and we experience much unnecessary suffering. The neurochemical mechanisms that mediate these states confer intrinsic vulnerability to substance abuse in environments where drugs are available. A better understanding of the mechanisms, origins, and functions of the emotions will enhance our ability to cope with substance abuse and our wisdom in making decisions about the therapeutic use of psychoactive drugs.

REFERENCES AND NOTES

1. G. W. Williams and R. M. Nesse, *Q. Rev. Biol.* **66**, 1 (1991).
2. R. M. Nesse, *Ethol. Sociobiol.* **15**, 339 (1994).
3. ——— and G. W. Williams, *Why We Get Sick: The New Science of Darwinian Medicine* (Vintage Books, New York, 1995).
4. R. M. Nesse, *Hum. Nat. 1,* 261 (1990).
5. J. Tooby and L. Cosmides, *Ethol. Sociobiol.* **11**, 375 (1990).
6. R. H. Frank, *Passions Within Reason: The Strategic Role of The Emotions* (Norton, New York, 1988).
7. N. H. Frijda, in *The Nature of Emotion,* P. Ekman and R. J. Davidson, Eds. (Oxford Univ. Press, New York, 1994), pp. 59–67.
8. K. Oatley and P. N. Johnson-Laird, in *Goals and Affect,* L. L. Martin and A. Tesser, Eds. (Erlbaum, Hillsdale, NJ, 1995).
9. J. LeDoux, *The Emotional Brain* (Simon & Schuster, New York, 1996).
10. T. Ketelaar and G. L. Clore, in *Personality, Emotion, and Cognitive Science,* G. Matthews, Ed. (Elsevier, Amsterdam, in press).
11. S. T. Murphy and R. B. Zajonc, *J. Pers. Soc. Psychol.* **64**, 723 (1993).
12. K. C. Berridge, in *Understanding Quality of Life: Scientific Understanding of Enjoyment and Suffering,* D. Kahneman, E. Diener, N. Schwarz, Eds. (Sage, New York, in press).
13. R. B. Zajonc, *Science* **228**, 15 (1985).
14. M. S. Gazzaniga, *The Integrated Mind* (Plenum, New York, 1987).
15. A. Bechara, H. Damasio, D. Tranel, A. R. Damasio, *Science* **275**, 1293 (1997).
16. G. G. Berntson, S. T. Boysen, J. T. Cacioppo, *Ann. N. Y. Acad. Sci.* **702**, 75 (1993).
17. B. G. Hoebel, in *Stevens' Handbook of Experimental Psychology,* R. C. Atkinson, R. J. Herrnstein, G. Lindzey, R. D. Luce, Eds. (Wiley, New York, 1988), vol. 1, pp. 547–626.
18. F. Bloom, in *The Cognitive Neurosciences,* M. Gazzaniga, Ed. (MIT Press, Cambridge, MA, 1995), pp. 1063–1070.
19. G. F. Koob, *Neuron* **16**, 893 (1996).
20. R. A. Wise, *Annu. Rev. Neurosci.* **19**, 319 (1996).
21. G. Tanda, F. E. Pontieri, G. Di Chiara, *Science* **276**, 2048 (1997).
22. R. J. Walker, H. L. Brooks, L. Holden-Dye, *Parasitol. Suppl.* **113**, S3 (1996).
23. X. Li, D. E. Keith Jr., C. J. Evans, *J. Mol. Evol.* **43**, 179 (1996).
24. A. B. Butler and W. Hodos, *Comparative Vertebrate Neuroanatomy* (Wiley, New York, 1996).
25. A. Gelperin, *Trends Neurosci.* **9**, 323 (1986).
26. B. Pribbenow and J. Erber, *Neurobiol. Learn. Mem.* **66**, 109 (1996).
27. S. Peroutka, *Neurochem. Int.* **25**, 533 (1994).
28. K. Fryxell, *J. Mol. Evol.* **41**, 85 (1995).
29. E. J. W. Barrington, *Br. Med. Bull.* **38**, 227 (1982).
30. S. B. Eaton and M. Konner, *N. Engl. J. Med.* **312**, 283 (1985).
31. M. Smith, *Adv. Hum. Genet.* **15**, 249 (1986).
32. K. C. Berridge, *Neurosci. Biobehav. Rev.* **20**, 1 (1996).
33. P. Shizgal, *Curr. Opin. Neurobiol.* **7**, 198 (1997).
34. T. E. Robinson and K. C. Berridge, *Brain Res. Rev.* **18**, 247 (1993).
35. P. W. Kalivas and J. Stewart, *ibid.* **16**, 223 (1991).
36. C. S. Pomerleau, *Addiction* **92**, 397 (1997).
37. H. L. DuPont and R. B. Hornick, *J. Am. Med. Assoc.* **226**, 1525 (1973).
38. M. J. Kluger, Ed., *Fever, Its Biology, Evolution, and Function* (Princeton, Princeton, NJ, 1979).
39. E. D. Weinberg, *Physiol. Rev.* **64**, 65 (1984).
40. J. A. Gray, *Fear and Stress* (Cambridge Univ. Press, Cambridge, UK, ed. 2, 1987).
41. D. H. Barlow, *Psychol. Inq.* **2**, 97 (1991).
42. I. M. Marks and R. M. Neese, *Ethol. Sociobiol.* **15**, 247 (1994).
43. D. M. Buss, R. J. Larsen, D. Westen, *Psychol. Sci.* **7**, 373 (1996).
44. R. M. Nesse, "What is mood for?" *Psycholoquy* [online] **2**, 9.2 (1991).
45. P. Gilbert, *Depression: The Evolution of Powerlessness* (Guilford, New York, 1992).
46. J. Price, L. Sloman, R. Gardner, P. Gilbert, P. Rodhe, *Br. J. Psychiatry* **164**, 309 (1994).
47. M. T. McGuire and A. Troisi, *Darwinian Psychiatry* (Harvard Univ. Press, Cambridge, MA, 1997).
48. D. Keltner and B. Busswell, *Cogn. Emotion* **10**, 155 (1996).
49. T. Ketelaar and W. T. Au, unpublished manuscript.
50. E. O. Wilson, *Sociobiology* (Harvard Univ. Press, Cambridge, MA, 1975).
51. We thank C. Brown, S. Cooper, D. Gribbin, K. Little, M. McGuire, C. Pomerleau, T. Robinson, E. Valenstein, and other colleagues for their helpful comments on an earlier version of this manuscript.

Evolutionary Social Psychology and Family Homicide

MARTIN DALY AND MARGO WILSON

Homicide is an extreme manifestation of interpersonal conflict with minimal report-ing bias and can thus be used as a conflict "assay." Evolutionary models of social motive predict that genetic relationship will be associated with mitigation of conflict, and various analyses of homicide data support this prediction. Most "family" homi-cides are spousal homicides, fueled by male sexual proprietariness. In the case of parent-offspring conflict, an evolutionary model predicts variations in the risk of violence as a function of the ages, sexes, and other characteristics of protagonists, and these predictions are upheld in tests with data on infanticides, parricides, and filicides.

Homicide within the family is a theme of great psychological significance. In many mythologies, the primordial murder was a fratricide or patricide. Freud's "Oedipal theory" made the urge to kill one's father a normal element of the male psyche (*1*); Bloch (*2*) maintains that the "central preoccupation of childhood" is the fear of parental filicide. Moreover, these murderous impulses are apparently man-ifest not just in imagination, but in action. Two prominent experts on domestic vio-lence in the United States have written (*3*, p. 88):

> With the exception of the police and the military, the family is perhaps the most vio-lent social group, and the home the most violent social setting, in our society. A per-son is more likely to be hit or killed in his or her home by another family member than anywhere else or by anyone else.

These allegations present a puzzle from the perspective of contemporary evolu-tionary theories of social motives and behavior (*4–7*). The species-typical appetites, aversions, motives, emotions and cognitive structures of all creatures, including *Homo sapiens,* have been shaped by selection to produce social action that is effec-tively "nepotistic": action that promotes the proliferation of the actor's genetic ele-ments in future generations, by contributing to the survival and reproductive success of the actor's genetic relatives. Apprehensions of self-interest—such as the absence of pain and hunger, or the positive satisfactions derived from social and sexual successes and from the well-being of one's children—evolve as tokens of expected posterity ("expected" in the statistical sense of that which would be anticipated from past evidence). It follows that individual self-interests conflict because of rivalry for representation in future gene pools (8). Genetic relatedness is a predictor of reduced conflict and enhanced cooperation because the genetic posterities of blood relatives co-vary (are promoted by common exigencies) in direct proportion to their degree of relatedness. The heuristic value and essential soundness of this theoretical framework have been abundantly confirmed by recent research on nonhuman animals (6, 7, 9), and there is a growing body of empirical studies indicating its applicability to human sociality, too (9–13).

What, then, of family violence? We propose (i) that genetic relationship is associated with the mitigation of conflict and violence in people, as in other creatures; and (ii) that evolutionary models predict and explain patterns of differential risk of family violence.

We shall focus on an extreme form of interpersonal violence: homicide. One may protest that homicides are too infrequent and extreme to illuminate conflict generally, but there is advantage in focusing on acts so dire. The issues over which people are prepared to kill are surely those about which they care most profoundly. Moreover, because homicide is viewed so seriously, there is less reporting bias in homicide archives than in the records of any lesser manifestation of conflict. Homicides thus provide an exceptionally valid "assay" of interpersonal conflict.

GENETIC RELATIONSHIP AND MITIGATION
OF HOMICIDE RISK WITHIN FAMILIES

Criminological studies of homicide in the United States (14) have generally used a limited categorization of victim-killer relationships. In a classic study of homicides in Philadelphia (15), for example, "relatives" constituted almost one-fourth of all victims, and most of these were spouses; blood relatives and in-laws were not distinguished, together constituting just 6.5% of solved cases. These results are apparently typical: "Relatives" have never been found to exceed one-third of any substantial sample of U.S. homicides, and, wherever spouses have been distinguished, they outnumber all other relatives combined. In two studies, genealogical and marital relatives were distinguished: 19% of Detroit homicide victims in 1972 were related to their killers by marriage compared to 6% by blood (16); 10% of Miami victims in 1980 were marital relatives of their killers compared to 1.8% blood relatives (17).

These data suggest that blood kin may be relatively immune from lethal violence in the United States (18), given the high frequency and intensity of interactions among relatives. However, in order to decide whether this is really so, one needs some sort of denominator representing "opportunity": the number and availability of potential victims in different categories of relationship to potential killers. One approach to this problem is to confine attention to cases involving members of the same household, so that the universe of accessible potential victims can be specified. Given the prevailing household compositions in Detroit in 1972, for example, coresidents unrelated to the killer by blood, whether spouses or not, were more than 11 times more likely to be slain than coresiding genetic relatives (11,16). Comparable analyses have not been conducted in other U.S. cities (nor can they be with information in typical data sets, since coresidence has not ordinarily been recorded); however, the fact that the distribution of victim-killer relationships in Detroit was unexceptional suggests that similar results would obtain.

Another approach to the issue of whether kinship mitigates conflict when opportunity is controlled entails comparing the distribution of relationships between killers and their victims with the distribution of relationships between collaborators in homicide. The logic is this: If conflict and cooperation were to arise merely in proportion to the frequency and intensity of interactions, relatively intimate types of relationships would provide more opportunities for both. Those intimate links that are prevalent among victim-killer relationships should thus prove to be similarly prevalent among cooffenders. But such is not the case. Among coaccused pairs of killers in Miami, for example, 29.6% were blood relatives as compared to just 1.8% of victims and killers (*17*). In fact, the average degree of relatedness between collaborative killers is far higher than the corresponding value for victim and killer in every society for which a relevant sample of cases is available, including tribal horticulturalists, medieval Englishmen, Mayan villagers, and urban Americans (*11*).

STEP-RELATIONSHIPS

A particularly apt comparison for assessing effects of (perceived) relationship on conflict is that between the parent-offspring relationship and surrogates thereof. Parental solicitude has evolved to expend animals' resources (and even their lives) in enhancing the reproductive prospects of their descendants (*19, 20*). It is therefore not surprising that parental solicitude evolves to be discriminative with respect to predictors of the offspring's probable contribution to the parent's genetic posterity (*21*). One implication is that substitute parents will often care less profoundly for "their" children than will genetic parents.

"Cruel stepparent" stories are cross-culturally ubiquitous (*22*) and reflect a recurring dilemma. Mothers and fathers have been widowed or abandoned with dependent children throughout human history, whereupon the fate of the children became problematic. A worldwide solution to the problem of single parents unable or unwilling to raise their children is fosterage to close relatives such as maternal grandparents (*23*). In some societies, widows are customarily married to their dead husbands' brothers (the levirate); in others, widows with dependent children may spurn remarriage and reside with siblings or other close relatives. In the absence of such arrangements, children come under the care of stepparents who may have no benevolent interest in their welfare. In a study of the foraging Ache Indians of Paraguay, for example, Hill and Kaplan (*24*) traced the careers of 67 children raised by mother and stepfather after the natural father's death: 43% had died, of various causes, before their 15th birthdays, as compared to just 19% of those raised by two surviving parents.

Children in stepparent families are disproportionately often injured in industrial nations, too. The specific kinds of injuries involved suggest that such children are not at risk merely by virtue of decreased parental vigilance and supervision, but are also more often assaulted (*25, 26*). When injuries are attributed to "child abuse," the difference between stepparent and genetic parent homes is large and is independent of risk attributable to low socioeconomic status, maternal youth, family size, or personality characteristics of the abusers (*27–29*). Abusive stepparents are discriminative, sparing their own children within the same household (*28, 30*). Presently available data do not reveal whether stepmother or stepfather households entail greater risks (*31*).

Overrepresentation of stepfamilies in child abuse samples might be dismissed as a product of reporting biases but for the fact that stepparents are even more strongly overrepresented in cases of child homicide, where biases of detection and reporting are presumably minimal. An English sample of "fatal battered baby cases" included 15 killed by stepfathers and 14 by genetic fathers (*32*), although fewer than 1% of same-age English babies dwelt with stepfathers (*25*). Similarly, an Australian sample of fatally battered babies included 18 slain by substitute fathers compared to 11 by genetic fathers (*33*). A child living with one or more substitute parents in the United States in 1976 was approximately 100 times more likely to be fatally abused than a same-age child living with genetic parents (*11*). Age-specific rates of being killed by step- or genetic parents in Canada are shown in Figure 1.

In view of the costs of prolonged "parental" investment in nonrelatives, it may seem remarkable that step-relationships are ever peaceful, let alone genuinely affectionate. However, violent hostility is rarer than friendly relations even among nonrelatives; people thrive by the maintenance of networks of social reciprocity and by establishing reputations for fairness and generosity that will make them attractive exchange partners (*34*). The kindly deportment of most stepparents may prove to be explicable mainly in the context of reciprocity with the genetic parent; moreover, insofar as indulgence toward unrelated children is a general attribute of men (or other male animals), it may be attributable to sexual selection as a result of female mate choice

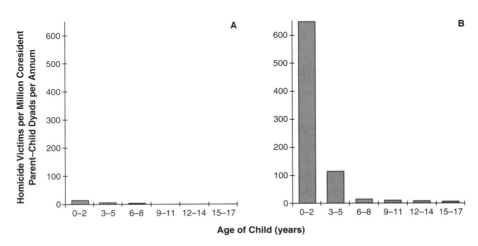

FIGURE 1   Age-specific rates of homicide victimization by (**A**) genetic parents (*n* = 341 victims) or (**B**) stepparents (*n* = 67), Canada, 1974 to 1983.

(*35*). The fact remains, however, that step-relationships lack the deep commonality of interest of the natural parent-offspring relationship, and feelings of affection and commitment are correspondingly shallower (*29, 36*). Differential rates of violence are one result.

SPOUSAL CONFLICTS

The customary extension of the category "relative" to encompass spouses and in-laws is metaphorical, but not arbitrary. By cooperative rearing of joint offspring, mates in a species with biparental care forge a powerful commonality of interest analogous to that existing between blood relatives (*37*). Indeed, the genetic interests of an exclusively monogamous pair coincide even more closely than those of blood relatives (*34*). However, two considerations act against the evolution of perfect harmony in mated pairs: (i) the possibility of extra-pair reproduction and (ii) the partners' nepotistic interests in the welfare of distinct sets of collateral kin.

Mutual progeny contribute to spousal harmony, whereas children of former unions contribute to spousal conflict (*38*). U.S. divorce statistics reflect these effects of children: For a given duration of marriage, children of former unions elevate divorce rates, whereas children of the present union reduce them (*39*). We predict parallel influences of children on spousal homicide rates. There is some evidence that the presence of stepchildren is associated with spousal homicide (*11, 40, 41*), but available data do not permit quantitative assessment of the risks in households of various compositions.

In many animals (including people in their environments of evolutionary adaptation), female reproduction is resource-limited whereas the reproductive capacities of females are themselves the limiting "resource" for males. Male reproductive output in such species has a higher ceiling and greater variance than that of females, with the result that reproductive competition is more intense and dangerous among males (*5, 19, 42*). One tactic in such competition is sequestering and guarding mates, which increases in utility (relative to alternative tactics like maximizing copulatory contacts) in species with biparental care, since parentally investing males can be fooled about paternity.

Human marriage is a cross-culturally general institutionalization of reproductive alliance, entailing mutual obligations between the spouses during child-rearing, rights of sexual access (often but not necessarily exclusive and usually controlled by the husband), and legitimization of the status of progeny. Men take a proprietary view of women and their reproductive capacity, as witness the widespread practices of bridewealth (*43*) and claustration and infibulation of reproductively valuable women (*44*), and the near universality of sexually asymmetrical adultery laws that treat poaching by rival males as a property violation (*45, 46*).

Male sexual proprietariness is the dominant issue in marital violence. In studies of "motives" of spousal homicide, the leading identified substantive issue is invariably "jealousy" (*11*). Interview studies of North American spouse killers indicate that the husband's proprietary concern with his wife's fidelity or her intention to quit the marriage led him to initiate the violence in an overwhelming majority of cases, regardless of whether it was the husband or wife who ended up dead (*11, 41*). Similarly, in other cultures, wherever motives in a sample of spousal homicides have been characterized in detail, male sexual proprietariness has proven relevant to more than half of those homicides (*11*). Sexual proprietariness evidently lies behind most non-lethal wife beating, too (*46, 47*), suggesting that spousal homicides are not primarily cold-blooded "disposals," but are the tip of the iceberg of coercive violence. Men strive to control women by various means and with variable success, while women strive to resist coercion and maintain their choices. There is brinkmanship in any such contest, and homicides by spouses of either sex may be considered the slips in this dangerous game (*48*).

This view of spousal violence as the coercive tactic of proprietary men suggests that women will be extremely at risk when perceived as likely to end the relationship. Indeed, there is a remarkable prevalence of recently estranged wives among homicide victims. In an Australian study (*33*), 98 of 217 women slain by their husbands (45%) were separated or in the process thereof, compared to just 3 of 79 men slain by their wives (4%). Estrangement has also been implicated in spousal homicides in Canada (*11*). A correct apprehension of the lethal risk in deserting a proprietary husband is surely one factor in the reluctance of many abused wives to leave.

The above considerations suggest, moreover, that young wives may be especially at risk, for two reasons: Youth per se makes the woman more attractive to rival men (*49*), and the short duration of the marriage means that deep commonalities of interest have yet to be forged, making the marriage potentially unstable (*50*). In Canada, young wives are indeed likeliest to be spousal homicide victims (Figure 2). One might

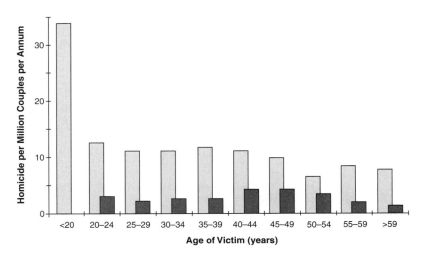

FIGURE 2 Age-specific rates of homicide victimization within legal marriages for (light-colored bar) women killed by their husbands (*n* = 528) and (dark-colored bar) men killed by their wives (*n* = 124), Canada, 1974 to 1983 (*11*). Age-related variations in spousal homicide victimization are significant for wives ($\chi^2(9) = 44.2$, $P < 0.001$), but not for husbands ($\chi^2(9) = 10.6$, $P > 0.3$).

attribute this differential risk to the fact that young women are married to young men, the most homicidal demographic category, but the woman's age is apparently more relevant to spousal homicide risk than the man's (*11*); the wife's declining risk as a function of age is apparent within each age class of husbands (although risk rises again for wives much older than their husbands). To date, no analysis has fully unconfounded the variables of the two parties' ages and marital and reproductive histories in order to assess their separate relevances to spousal homicide risk (*51*).

PARENT-OFFSPRING CONFLICT AND VIOLENCE

Parents and children engage in frequent battles of wills, major and minor. Traditional social scientific views of these conflicts attribute them to imperfect adaptation in one or the other party, for example, "immature" egoism in the child or poor parenting skills.

Trivers (*52*) proposed a radically different perspective on parenting and socialization: Even though offspring are the parents' means to genetic posterity, parent-offspring conflict is an endemic feature of sexually reproducing organisms, because the allocation of resources and efforts that would maximize a parent's genetic posterity seldom matches that which would maximize a particular offspring's. Selection favors inclinations in both parties to achieve one's own optimum against the wishes and efforts of the other. This theory accounts for the seemingly maladaptive phenomenon of weaning conflict, as well as for disparate parental and offspring attitudes to collateral kin, "regression" to earlier stages of development on the birth of a sibling, and adolescent identity crises (*7, 21, 52, 53*). In some circumstances, an offspring's reproductive prospects (according to cues that were predictive in the species' environment of evolutionary adaptation) may be insufficient to offset that offspring's detrimental effect on the parent's capacity to pursue other adaptive action, in which case parental solicitude may be expected to fail (*54*).

People everywhere recognize that parents may sometimes be disinclined to raise a child, and anthropologists have collected much information about the circumstances in which infanticide is alleged to be common, acceptable, or even obligatory. If parental inclinations have been shaped by selection, there are at least three classes of circumstances in which we might anticipate some reluctance to invest in a newborn: (i) doubt that the offspring is the putative parent's own, (ii) indications of poor offspring quality, and (iii) all those extrinsic circumstances, such as food scarcity, lack of social support, and overburdening from the demands of older offspring, that would have made a child unlikely to survive during human evolutionary history (*55*). The great majority of ethnographic accounts of infanticide in nonindustrial societies reflect one or another of these three categories of strategic allocation of lifetime parental effort (*56, 57*).

Moreover, we may expect maternal psychology to exhibit sensitivity to the mother's own residual reproductive value: A newborn's compromising effects on the mother's future diminish with maternal age, and hence maternal willingness to jettison an infant may also be expected to decrease. This prediction is upheld (Figure 3) (*58*). This maternal age effect is not an artifact of marital status; it is observed in both married and unmarried women (*11*).

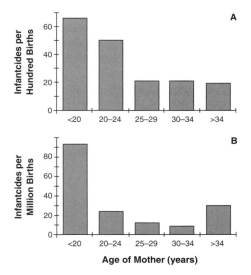

FIGURE 3 Rates of infanticides by mothers as a function of maternal age, among (**A**) Ayoreo Indians of South America (*58*) (*n* = 54 victims), and (**B**) in Canada, 1974 to 1983 (*11*) (*n* = 87).

Reprinted with permission from Martin Daly and Margo Wilson. *Homicide.* (New York: Aldine de Gruyter). Copyright © 1988 by Aldine de Gruyter.

Evolutionary considerations suggest several predictions about filicide in relation to the child's age, too. In ancestral environments, the child's probability of attaining adulthood and contributing to its own and its parents' genetic posterity increased with age, especially during infancy, as the child passed through a stage of high mortality risk. The predicted consequence is that parental psychology should have evolved to cherish the child increasingly over a prolonged period, as the child's reproductive value increased. Hence:

1. Parents are expected to be more willing to incur costs on behalf of offspring nearer to maturity (*59*) and to be more inhibited in the use of dangerous tactics when in conflict with such offspring. Filicide rates are thus predicted to decline with the child's age, whereas no such effect is predicted in the case of child homicides by non-relatives, whose valuation of the child is not expected to parallel that of the parents.

2. This decline is predicted to be negatively accelerated and concentrated in the first year postpartum, because (i) in the environments of human evolutionary adaptation, the lion's share of the prepubertal increase in reproductive value occurred within the first year, and (ii) insofar as parental disinclination reflects a "strategic" assessment of the reproductive episode, an evolved assessment mechanism should be such as to terminate hopeless ventures as early as possible.

3. Filicides perpetrated by the mother are predicted to be a more steeply declining function of the child's age than those perpetrated by the father, because (i) women's reproductive life spans end before those of men, so the utility of alternative reproductive efforts declines more steeply for women than for men; (ii) the extent to which children impose greater opportunity costs on mothers than on fathers is probably maximal in infancy; and (iii) phenotypic and other evidence of paternity may surface after infancy and is expected to be relevant to paternal but not maternal solicitude (*45, 60*).

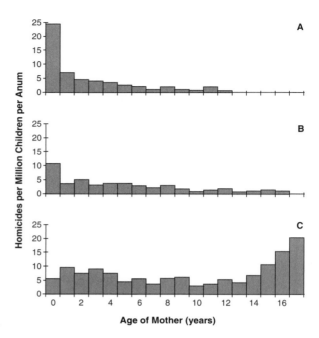

FIGURE 4 Age-specific rates of homicide victimization among Canadian children, 1974 to 1983. (**A**) Slain by mothers (n = 198 victims), (**B**) by fathers (n = 154), and (**C**) by persons other than genealogical relatives (n = 493).

All three predictions gain support from the Canadian data in Figure 4.

Offspring kill parents, too. Because violence toward parents, like violence toward children, is associated with economic and other stressors (*61*), and because parricides often follow a history of parental mistreatment of the eventual killer (*62*), one might expect factors related to the risk of filicide to affect the risk of parricide in a directionally similar fashion. An evolutionary theoretical perspective, however, suggests one likely exception to this generalization. Just as a parent's valuation of an offspring is predictably related to the ages (reproductive values) of both parties, so too is the offspring's valuation of the parent. An offspring of a given age may be expected to disvalue an elderly parent more than a younger one. These considerations suggest that parental age at the child's birth will have opposite effects on the rates of violence perpetrated by parent and offspring against each other, and the data in Figure 5 are supportive.

An alternative to Trivers's (*7, 52*) evolutionary analysis of parent-offspring conflict is Freud's "Oedipal theory": It is allegedly a normal phase of infant male psychosocial development to lust after mother and wish father dead (*1*). [Freud (*63*) later developed a less detailed theory of an analogous girlish love of father and antipathy toward mother.] An evolutionary perspective suggests that Freud apprehended two distinct parent-offspring conflicts and conflated them. There is indeed a conflict between father and infant son over the wife-mother, but it is not sexual rivalry. The optimal birth interval from the child's perspective exceeds that from the father's, and it is not implausible that toddlers have evolved specific adaptive strategies to delay the

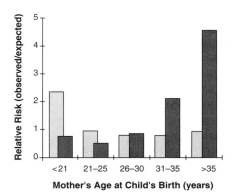

FIGURE 5   Parent-child homicides perpetrated (light-colored bar) by the mother (filicide, $n =$ 190 victims) or (dark-colored bar) upon her (matricide, $n = 61$), as a function of her age at the child's birth, Canada, 1974 to 1983. Relative risk is the ratio of the observed number of cases over the number expected if cases were distributed in proportion to the numbers of births to Canadian women in each age category in the calendar year of each filicide victim or matricide perpetrator's birth. Both distributions depart from number expected (filicides, $\chi^2(4) = 66.5$, $P < 0.001$; matricides, $\chi^2(4) = 56.9$, $P < 0.001$). No comparable analysis of paternal filicides and patricides is possible because of lack of information on age-specific fertility of men in the population-at-large.

conception of a sibling (*64*), including tactics to diminish mother's sexual interest and thwart father's access to her. In many societies, there is a later conflict between father and son over the timing of the son's accession to reproductive status, often subsidized by the father at a cost to his own continuing reproductive ambitions; this later conflict is "sexual," but it is not over the mother.

　　If Trivers's (*7, 52*) evolutionary model is correct, then conflict between parents and young children exists irrespective of the child's sex. According to Freud, children are in conflict primarily with the parent of the same sex, at least in the "Oedipal phase" (ages 2 to 5 years) (*65*) if not from birth; such a same-sex contingency in parent-offspring antagonisms is allegedly endemic to the human condition. Trivers's account predicts no such infantile same-sex contingency, although elements of sexual rivalry could arise later. Canadian data on parent-offspring homicide cases support Trivers's view (Table 1), as do British and U.S. data (*66*).

CONCLUDING REMARKS

Analyses of "family violence" have hitherto ignored crucial distinctions among relationships. Elucidation of the nature of relationship-specific confluences and conflicts of interest requires a conception of the fundamental nature of self-interests. Evolutionary theory provides such a conception by considering perceived self-interests to be evolved tokens of expected genetic posterity. From this perspective, the spousal relationship is unique in its potential for generating shared interests and betrayals

TABLE 1   Parent-offspring homicides in Canada, 1974 to 1983, cross-tabulated by sex of killer and victim and by offspring age. Table entries are numbers of victims; 13 cases in which both parents were charged are excluded. All cases in which the child was 10 years old or less are filicides; "circumpubertal" cases include 31 filicides and 24 parricides; "adult" off-spring cases include 26 filicides and 148 parricides. Only after puberty is there a same-sex contingency in parent-offspring violence; ns, not significant.

Offspring Stage (age, in years)	Victim's Sex	Killer's Sex		Test of Contingency
		Male	*Female*	
Infantile (0–1)	Male	24	53	
	Female	17	50	$\chi^2(1) = 0.6$
	Percentage male	58.5	51.5	ns
"Oedipal" (2–5)	Male	21	21	
	Female	27	27	$\chi^2(1) = 0.0$
	Percentage male	43.8	43.8	ns
"Latency" (6–10)	Male	21	19	
	Female	10	5	$\chi^2(1) = 0.9$
	Percentage male	67.7	79.2	ns
Circumpubertal (11–16)	Male	28	9	
	Female	14	4	$\chi^2(1) = 0.0$
	Percentage male	66.7	69.2	ns
Adult (≥ 17)	Male	104	8	
	Female	47	15	$\chi^2(1) = 10.1$
	Percentage male	68.9	34.5	$P < 0.01$

thereof, and the commonalities and conflicts of interest even among blood relatives are relationship-specific.

The application of such an evolutionary model to the study of violence (or other social behavior) is neither simple nor direct. In particular, an evolutionary model need not imply that the behavior in question effectively promotes the reproductive success of the actors or their relatives. Homicide is a rare, extreme product of motivational mechanisms whose outputs are only expected to be adaptive on average, and in environments not crucially different from those in which we evolved. Murder-suicides forcefully illustrate why adaptation is most usefully sought at a psychological level of abstraction rather than in each category of overt behavior. Men are far more likely than women to commit suicide after killing a spouse (*11, 33*) and are especially likely to do so when the couple are estranged. A frequently expressed rationale is "If I can't have her, no one can." In such a case, the killer has apparently fallen into futile spite, but the counterproductiveness of sexual proprietariness in these extreme cases hardly gainsays its candidate status as a masculine psychological adaptation. The more typical consequences of fierce proprietariness have surely been effective deterrence of rivals and coercive control of wives. Similarly, the proposition that discriminative parental affection has been favored by selection is not undermined by the consideration that fatal child abuse may land a stepfather in jail. Although specific acts may be maladaptive (especially in evolutionarily novel environments), selection has shaped the social motives, emotions, and cognitive processes underlying them. Evolutionary psychological constructs like "discriminative parental solicitude" or "male sexual proprietariness" are domain-specific, but they influence a range of actions both conflictual and cooperative. The evolutionary psychological hypotheses that we have tested against homicide data should be further assessed with less extreme behavioral measures of conflict and with positive measures of harmony and solicitude.

Evolutionary models have enabled us to predict and discover patterned variations in the risk of lethal violence, as a function of the parties' ages, circumstances, and specific relationships to one another. As predicted, genetic relationship is associated with a softening of conflict, and people's evident valuations of themselves and of others are systematically related to the parties' reproductive values. Evolutionary theory can provide a valuable conceptual framework for the analysis of social psychologies (*7, 11, 34, 49, 67*).

REFERENCES AND NOTES

1. S. Freud, *The Interpretation of Dreams* (Basic Books, New York, 1900); *Totem and Taboo* (Norton, New York, 1913).

2. D. Bloch, *So the Witch Won't Eat Me: Fantasy and the Child's Fear of Infanticide* (Grove, New York, 1978).

3. R. J. Gelles and M. A. Straus, in *Crime and the Family*, A. J. Lincoln and M A Straus, Eds. (Thomas, Springfield, IL, 1985), pp. 88–110.

4. W. D. Hamilton, *J. Theor. Biol.* **7**, 1 (1964).

5. G. C. Williams, *Adaptation and Natural Selection* (Princeton Univ. Press, Princeton, NJ, 1966).

6. E. O. Wilson, *Sociobiology* (Belknap, Cambridge, MA, 1975); J. F. Wittenberger, *Animal Social Behavior* (Duxbury, Boston, 1981); M. Daly and M Wilson, *Sex Evolution and Behavior* (Wadsworth, Belmont, CA, 1983); J. R. Krebs and N. B. Davies, Eds., *Behavioural Ecology* (Blackwell, Oxford, ed. 2 1984); D. I. Rubenstein and R. W. Wrangham, Eds., *Ecological Aspects of Social Evolution* (Princeton Univ. Press, Princeton, NJ, 1986).

7. R. L. Trivers, *Social Evolution* (Benjamin/Cummings, Menlo Park, CA 1985).

8. Notwithstanding the focus on individuals and their genetic nonidentity, theoretical work on social evolution and the research inspired thereby have been little concerned with genetically based phenotypic variation. Instead, researchers have been primarily concerned to identify adaptive, species-typical (or sex-typical), facultative social strategies.

9. R. D. Alexander and D. W. Tinkle, Eds., *Natural Selection and Social Behavior* (Chiron, New York, 1981).

10. N. A. Chagnon and W. Irons, Eds., *Evolutionary Biology and Human Social Behavior* (Duxbury, North Scituate, MA, 1979).

11. M. Daly and M. Wilson, *Homicide* (Aldine de Gruyter, Hawthorne, NY, 1988).

12. L. L. Betzig, M. Borgerhoff Mulder, P. W. Turke, Eds., *Human Reproductive Behaviour* (Cambridge Univ. Press, Cambridge, 1988).

13. C. Crawford, M. Smith, D. Krebs, Eds., *Sociobiology and Psychology* (Erlbaum, Hillsdale, NJ, 1987).

14. For example, see C. Loftin and R. N. Parker, *Criminology* **23**, 269 (1985); S. F. Messner and K. Tardiff, *ibid.*, p. 241; K. R. Williams and R. L. Flewelling, *ibid.* **25**, 543 (1987).

15. M. E. Wolfgang, *Patterns in Criminal Homicide* (Univ. of Pennsylvania Press Philadelphia, 1958).

16. M. Daly and M. Wilson, *Am. Anthropol.* **84**, 372 (1982).

17. W. Wilbanks, *Murder in Miami* (University Press of America, Lanham, MD, 1984).

18. Elsewhere, blood relatives often constitute a larger proportion of homicide victims than in the United States. Fratricides constitute a significant component of the homicide rate, for example, in certain agricultural societies in which the family farm is not practicably partitionable, so that one's brother is one's principal rival (*11*). In general, rates of family homicides seem to be less variable

between countries than rates of other killings *(11)*, so that family homicides are proportionately significant wherever the overall homicide rate is low. Further assessment of the influence of (perceived) relatedness on rates of violence will require the development of new models incorporating the effects of social access, competition, and other social structural variables.

19. R. L. Trivers, in *Sexual Selection and the Descent of Man 1871–1971*, B. Campbell, Ed. (Aldine, Chicago, 1972), pp. 136–179.
20. In most dyadic relationships, reciprocity is carefully monitored and imbalances are resented as exploitative [L. Betzig, in *(12)*, pp. 49–64; N. A. Berté, in *(12)*, pp. 83–96; S. M. Essock-Vitale and M. T. McGuire, *Ethol. Sociobiol.* **6**, 155 (1985); H. Kaplan and K. Hill, *Curr. Anthropol.* **26**, 223 (1985)]. Parental altruism is different in that the flow of benefits is prolongedly, cumulatively, and ungrudgingly unbalanced.
21. M. Daly and M. Wilson, *Nebr. Symp. Motiv.* **35**, 91 (1988).
22. M. R. Cox, *Cinderella: 345 Variants* (The Folklore Society, London, 1892); S. Thompson, *Motif-Index of Folk Literature* (Indiana Univ. Press, Bloomington, 1955).
23. J. B. Silk, *Am. Anthropol.* **82**, 799 (1980).
24. K. Hill and H. Kaplan, in *(12)*, pp. 291–305.
25. J. Wadsworth, I. Burnell, B. Taylor, N. Butler, *J. Epidemiol. Community Health* **37**, 100 (1983).
26. D. M. Fergusson, J. Fleming, D. P. O'Neill, *Child Abuse in New Zealand* (Government of New Zealand Printer, Wellington, 1972).
27. M. Wilson, M. Daly, S. Weghorst, *J. Biosoc. Sci.* **12**, 333 (1980).
28. M. Daly and M. Wilson, *Ethol. Socobiol.* **6**, 197 (1985).
29. M. Wilson and M. Daly, in *Child Abuse and Neglect*, R. J. Gelles and J. B. Lancaster, Eds. (Aldine de Gruyter, Hawthorne, NY, 1987), pp. 215–232.
30. J. L. Lightcap. J. A. Kurland, R. L. Burgess, *Ethol. Sociobiol.* **3**, 61 (1982).
31. Neither do presently available data permit the assessment of risks to adoptees. We predict that such risks will be less than to stepchildren for several reasons: (i) adoption "by stranger" is primarily the recourse of childless couples, strongly motivated to simulate a natural family experience, whereas step-relationships arise incidentally to the establishment of a desired mateship; (ii) adoptive parents are equally unrelated to their wards and thus avoid the conflict of one party's "parental" efforts benefiting the other's children; (iii) couples wishing to adopt are screened for suitability and may return children who do not work out; and (iv) adoptive couples are much more affluent on average than either stepparent or genetic parent families.
32. P. D. Scott, *Med. Sd. Law* **13**, 197 (1973).
33. A. Wallace, *Homicide: The Social Reality* (New South Wales Bureau of Crime Statistics and Research, Sydney, 1986).
34. R. D. Alexander, *The Biology of Moral Systems* (Aldine de Gruyter, Hawthorne, NY, 1987).
35. R. C. Connor, *Anim. Behav.* **34**, 1562 (1986); B. B. Smuts, *Sex and Friendship in Baboons* (Aldine de Gruyter, Hawthorne, NY, 1986); Y. Yanagisawa and H. Ochi, *Anim. Behav.* **34**, 1769 (1986).
36. L. Duberman, *The Reconstituted Family* (Nelson-Hall, Chicago, 1975); M. V. Flinn, *Ethol. Sociobiol.* **9**, 335 (1988).
37. Marital extension of the concept of "family" opens the door to a variety of manipulative metaphorical usages of kinship terminology [N. A. Chagnon, in *(12)*, pp. 23–48; N. W. Thornhill, thesis, University of New Mexico, Albuquerque (1987); G. R. Johnson, S. H. Ratwik, T. J. Sawyer, in *The Sociobiology of Ethnocentrism,* V. Reynolds, V. Falger, I. Vine, Eds. (Croom Helm, London, 1987), pp. 157–174.
38. L. Messinger, *J. Marriage Fam. Counseling* **2**, 193 (1976); A. M. Ambert, *J. Marriage Fam.* **48**, 795 (1986).
39. G. S. Becker, E. M. Landes, R. T. Michael, *J. Polit. Econ.* **85**, 1141 (1977); L. K. White and A. Booth, *Am. Social. Rev.* **50**, 689 (1985).
40. J. M. M. Binda, in *Crime and Punishment in the Caribbean*, R. Brana-Shute and G. Brana-Shute, Eds. (Center for Latin American Studies, Gainesville, FL, 1980); D. Kalmuss and J. A. Seltzer, *J. Marriage Fam.* **48**, 113 (1986); H. P. Lundsgaarde, *Murder in Space City* (Oxford Univ. Press, New York, 1977).
41. P. D. Chimbos, *Marital Violence* (R & E Research Associates, San Francisco, 1978).
42. A. T. Bateman, *Heredity* **2**, 349 (1948); R. Thornhill and N. W. Thornhill, *Ethol. Sociobio.* **4**, 137 (1983); M. Wilson and M. Daly. *ibid.* **6**, 59 (1985). Although the focus of this article is family homicides, the majority of lethal violence occurs between unrelated men and involves competition for material, social, and sexual resources that were directly related to reproductive success in the environments of human evolution [*(11)*; N. A. Chagnon, *Science* **239**, 985 (1988)].
43. J. L. Comaroff. Ed., *The Meaning of Marriage Payments* (Academic Press. London, 1980); M. Borgerhoff Mulder, in *(12)*, pp. 65–82.
44. M. Dickemann, in *(9)*, pp. 417–438; F. P. Hosken, *The Hosken Report: The Genital and Sexual Mutilation of Females* (Women's International Network News, Lexington, MA, 1979).
45. M. Wilson, *Univ. Toronto Fac. Law Rev.* **45**, 216 (1987).
46. M. Daly, M. Wilson, S. J. Weghorst, *Ethol. Sociobiol.* **3**, 11 (1982).

47. Anglo-American tort actions illustrate the proprietary rights of men over women's sexual and reproductive capacities [C. Backhouse, *Dalhousie Law J.* **10**, 45 (1986); M. B. W. Sinclair, *Law Inequality* **5**, 33 (1987); P. Brett. *Aust. Law J.* **29**, 321 (1955)].

48. Legal traditions all over the world acknowledge that violent rages on the part of cuckolds are to be expected and excuse them to varying degrees *(11, 45)*. The recognition that cuckolds are inclined to violence does not in itself explain why such violence should be deemed justified; the acknowledged temptations to theft, by contrast are usually considered an argument for stiffer (deterrent) penalties. Legitimation of the cuckold's use of violence is analogous to the legitimation of self-defense and protection of property and reflects a social contract among those men who "own" women.

49. D. Symons, *The Evolution of Human Sexuality* (Oxford Univ. Press. Oxford, 1979).

50. Age-specific divorce rates are maximal at shortest marital duration [A. J. Norton and J E. Moorman, *J. Marriage Fam.* **49**, 3 (1987)].

51. Homicide rates are 9 times higher in common-law unions than in legal marriages in Canada *(11)* and 13 times higher in Australia *(33)*. The large number of common-law couples in U.S. spousal homicide samples [J. Bourdouris, *J. Marriage Fam.* **33**, 667 (1971); *(11 15, 17)*] suggests that a similar situation prevails in the United States but the U.S. census does not distinguish common-law marriages. Common-law unions may be especially risky for several reasons, including short duration, lack of commitment, children of other unions, and relative poverty. Research into their exceptional risk is needed.

52. R. L. Trivers, *Am. Zool.* **14**, 249 (1974).

53. M. O. Slavin, *Psychoanal. Contemp. Thought* **8**, 407 (1985).

54. Evolutionary considerations suggest that human maternal attachment is likely to entail three distinct processes with different time courses: an assessment in the immediate postpartum of the prospects for a successful rearing, followed by a discriminative attachment to the child, and a gradual deepening of love and commitment proceeding over several years [M. Daly and M. Wilson, in *(13)*, pp. 293–309].

55. R. D. Alexander, *Darwinism and Human Affairs* (Univ. of Washington Press, Seattle, 1979).

56. M. Dickeman, *Annu. Rev. Ecol. Syst.* **6**, 107 (1975); L. Minturn and J. Stashak, *Behav. Sci. Res.* **17**, 70 (1982).

57. M. Daly and M. Wilson, in *Infantcide,* G. Hausfater and S. B. Hrdy. Eds. (Aldine de Gruyter, Hawthorne, NY, 1984), pp. 487–502.

58. P. Bugos and L. McCarthy, *ibid.,* pp. 503–520.

59. M. Andersson, C. G. Wiklund, H. Rundgren, *Anim. Behav.* **28**, 536 (1980); T. L. Patterson, L. Petrinovich, D. K. James, *Behav. Ecol. Sociobiol.* **7**, 227 (1980), P. H. Pressley, *Evolution* **35**, 282 (1981).

60 M. Daly and M. Wilson, *Ethol. Sociobiol.* **3**, 69 (1982).

61. K. A. Pillemer and R. S. Wolf, Eds., *Elder Abuse* (Auburn House, Dover, MA, 1986).

62. B. F. Corder, B. C. Ball, T. M. Haizlip, R. Rollins, R. Beaumont, *Am. J. Psychiatry* **133**, 957 (1976); D. H. Russell, *Int. J. Offender Ther. Comp. Criminol.* **28**, 177 (1984).

63. S. Freud, *Int. Z. Psychoanal.* **17**, 317 (1931).

64. N. G. Blurton Jones and E. da Costa, *Ethol. Sociobiol.* **8**, 135 (1987).

65. S. Freud, in *The Standard Edition of the Complete Psychological Works of Sigmund Freud,* J. Strachey, Transl. and Ed. (Hogarth, London, 1922). vol. 18.

66. M. Daly and M. Wilson. *J. Pers.,* in press.

67. D. Symons, in *(13),* pp. 121–146; J. H. Barkow, *J. Anthropol. Res.* **40**, 367 (1984); L. Cosmides, thesis, Harvard University, Cambridge, MA (1985); J. Tooby and I. DeVore, in *The Evolution of Human Behavior: Primate Models,* W. G. Kinzey, Ed. (State Univ. of New York Press, Albany, 1987), pp. 183–237.

68. Supported by grants from the Harry Frank Guggenheim Foundation, Health and Welfare Canada, the Natural Sciences and Engineering Research Council of Canada and the Social Sciences & Humanities Research Council of Canada. We thank M. W. Swanson, J. Bannon, and R. Hislop for access to Detroit homicide data, and J. Lacroix and C. McKie for access to Canadian homicide data. We also thank N. Chagnon, L. Cosmides, C. LaFramboise, P. Strahlendorf, D. Symons, N. Thornhill, R. Thornhill, and J. Tooby for critical comments on the manuscript.

Hawk-Eyed,
in *The Birder's Handbook*

PAUL R. EHRLICH, DAVID S. DOBKIN,
AND DARRYL WHEYE

B irds and people are "sight animals." For both, the eyes are the dominant sense organs, vastly more important than their inferior sense of smell. The reasons for our sensory similarity to birds can be found in human evolutionary history. At one point the ancestors of *Homo sapiens* were small, tree-dwelling primates. When leaping from limb to limb and snatching of insect prey with the hands, sharp, binocular vision was very handy; those of our forebears that tried instead to smell the location of a branch on which to land were unlikely to survive to reproduce. And since in the breezy treetops odors quickly dissipate, they do not provide good cues for detecting food, enemies, or mates. Birds, flying higher and faster than primates leap, naturally also evolved sight as their major device for orienting to the world.

Most birds have binocular vision. It is especially well developed in predators that must precisely estimate ever-changing distances to moving prey. Their eyes tend to be rotated toward the front of the head, so that the visual fields of each eye overlap to some degree. This trend is most pronounced in owls, whose eyes are almost as completely overlapping in field as ours. Small birds that are likely to be prey for raptors tend to have their eyes set on the sides of the head, permitting them to watch for danger in all directions. At the opposite extreme from the owls are the woodcocks, mud probers with eyes set high and back on the head, out of the way of vegetation and splattering mud and in a position to look out for predators. In fact, the woodcock has better binocular vision to the rear than to the front!

Shorebirds, waterfowl, pigeons, and other birds that have minimal binocular vision seem to depend on differences in apparent motion between close and distant objects for much of their depth perception. When a bird's eye is moving, closer objects appear to move at a faster rate than do distant objects—a phenomenon familiar from the way roadside, telephone poles seen from the window of a moving car appear to pass more rapidly than the distant landscape. Presumably to enhance this distance-measuring method, shorebirds and waterfowl often bob their heads up and down, and pigeons move theirs back and forth while walking. Even birds with relatively good binocular vision may use apparent motion to aid them in estimating distance; perched New Guinea kingfishers often "post" up and down on their legs before diving after prey. To see how this works, move your head with one eye closed and note the relative motion of close and distant objects.

From P. R. Ehrlich, D. S. Dobkin, and D. Wheye, "Hawk-eyed," in *The birder's handbook: A field guide to the natural history of North American birds* (New York: Fireside Press/Simon & Schuster, 1988), pp. 229, 231.

The term "hawk-eyed" accurately describes many birds. For example, both raptors that must see prey at great distances and seed eaters that must pick tiny objects off the ground have eyes designed for high "visual acuity"—the capacity to make fine discriminations. There is, in fact, evidence that hawks can distinguish their prey at something like two or three times the distance that a human being can detect the same creature. Interestingly, even with such visual acuity, Cooper's Hawks are known to hunt quail by their calls.

One way that birds have attained such a high degree of acuity is by having relatively large eyes. A human eye weighs less than 1 percent of the weight of the head, whereas a starling's eye accounts for some 15 percent of its head weight. But more than size alone appears to account for the astonishing performance of the eyes of hawks. Evolution has arranged the structure of their eyes so that each eye functions very much like a telescope. The eye has a somewhat flattened lens placed rather far from the retina, giving it a long "focal length," which produces a large image. A large pupil and highly curved cornea admit plenty of light to keep the image on the retina bright.

Visual acuity in birds is also enhanced by the structure of the retina itself, which has tightly packed receptors and possesses other adaptations for producing a fine-grained image. Most of those receptors are the type called "cones." "Rods," the receptors of the vertebrate retina that are specialized to function in dim light, are relatively rare. Thus daytime acuity is, in part, achieved at the expense of night vision—a small price to pay for birds that are inactive at night anyway. In those relatively few species that are nocturnal, such as owls, rods predominate.

Considering the frequent evolution of gaudy colored plumage, it is not surprising that birds active in the daytime have color vision (nocturnal birds are thought to be color blind), and that color perception is often obvious in bird behavior. One can watch a hummingbird moving from red flower to red flower; bowerbirds show color preferences when decorating their bowers. Just how refined that color vision may be has proven difficult to determine. However, the diversity of visual pigments found in birds' eyes, and the presence of an array of brightly colored oil droplets inside the cones, suggest that avian color perception may surpass our own. There is also evidence that some birds' eyes are sensitive to ultraviolet light. In hummingbirds the adaptive significance of this is clear, since some flowers from which they drink nectar have patterns visible in the ultraviolet end of the light spectrum. Why pigeons have the ability to see ultraviolet remains a mystery. Equally surprising is the recently discovered ability of pigeons to detect the plane of polarized light. This probably serves them well in homing.

Natural Categories

ELEANOR H. ROSCH

The hypothesis of the study was that the domains of color and form are structured into nonarbitrary, semantic categories which develop around perceptually salient "natural prototypes." Categories which reflected such an organization (where the presumed natural prototypes were central tendencies of the categories) and categories which violated the organization (natural prototypes peripheral) were taught to a total of 162 members of a Stone Age culture which did not initially have hue or geometric-form concepts. In both domains, the presumed "natural" categories were consistently easier to learn than the "distorted" categories. Even when not central, natural prototype stimuli tended to be more rapidly learned and more often chosen as the most typical example of the category than were other stimuli. Implications for general differences between natural categories and the artificial categories of concept formation research were discussed.

The concepts which an S learns in a typical concept formation experiment (cf. Bourne, 1968) are arbitrary. That is, the stimuli generally consist of discrete attributes (such as red vs green, square vs circle, one vs two borders); the categories to which those attributes themselves belong are generally already well known to the S (e.g., American college sophomores have long since learned the concepts "red" and "square"); and the subset of attribute combinations which comprise the to-be-learned concepts can be formed, at the will of the $E,$ out of any logically possible combinations of the attributes (e.g., the E can call "red and square" the positive subset or "two borders or circle" the positive subset). For such concepts, once the S has learned the rule(s) defining the positive subset, any one stimulus which fits the rule is as good an exemplar of the concept as any other—it makes no sense to ask S whether the red square on one of E's cards is a better example of the concept "red square" than one on another card. Concept formation tasks were designed to test questions about problem-solving which could only be approached with limited and controlled stimuli like these; such tasks do not, however, represent the full range of actual human concepts.

In contrast, many "real" categories (concepts designable by words in "natural languages") partition domains whose stimuli are not discrete but composed of continuous physical variations; natural language categories are not necessarily composed of combinations of simpler, already learned attributes; and, in most, if not all, natural

Reprinted from *Cognitive Psychology,* vol. 4, E. H. Rosch, "Natural categories," pp. 328–350, Copyright 1973, with permission from Elsevier.

language concepts, some stimuli are clearly better exemplars of the concept than others. The domain of color serves as an example of all three points: physical properties of light, such as wavelength, intensity, or reflectance, are continuous variables; perceived colors are not "analyzable" into combinations of discrete dimensions (Shepard, 1964); and, as is apparent from natural language terminology, there are colors which are considered "better" members of particular color categories than other colors (a "good" red vs an "off" red).

Concepts somewhat more like those in natural languages have been employed in a series of studies of the "process of abstraction," reviewed by Posner (1969). In this work, categories were typically composed of distributions of attributes, and some instances of categories were designed to be more "typical" members of the category than others. However, the categories themselves were invariably artificial; for example, Posner and Keele's (1968) categories were sets of distortions of random dot patterns; Reed's (1970) were combinations of Brunswik schematic faces. With such stimuli, subjects appear to operate inductively by abstracting a "prototype" (a central tendency) of the distribution (e.g., of dot patterns, schematic face features), a "prototype" which then appears to "operate" in classification and recognition of instances.

It is the contention of the research to be reported that there are categories in perceptual domains such as color and form which are not arbitrary. Neither a "concept-formation model" of category formation in terms of learning the "correct" (defined either by an experimenter or a culture) combination of discrete attributes nor an "abstraction-process model" of category formation in terms of abstraction of the central tendency of an (experimentally or culturally determined) arbitrary grouping of distributions of attributes is adequate to account for the nature and development of categories in these perceptual domains. The following alternative account of the development of color and form categories is proposed: there are colors and forms which are more perceptually salient than other stimuli in their domains. A working hypothesis is that salient colors are those areas of the color space previously found to be most exemplary of basic color names in many different languages (Berlin & Kay, 1969) and that salient forms are the "good forms" of Gestalt psychology (circle, square, etc.). Such colors and forms more readily attract attention than other stimuli (Heider, 1971) and are more easily remembered than less salient stimuli (Heider, 1972). When category names are learned, they tend to become attached first to the salient stimuli (only later generalizing to other instances), and by this means "natural prototypes" become foci of organization for categories.

From this account it can be predicted that learning natural perceptual categories differs from the abstraction process found in previous studies of artificial category learning in the following specific ways: (a) It is easier to learn categories in which the natural prototype is central to a set of variations than it is to learn categories in which a distortion of a prototype is central and the natural prototype occurs as a peripheral member. (b) The natural prototype will tend to be learned first whether or not it is central to the category. (c) Ss will tend to "define" the category as a set of variations on the natural prototype (operationally, they will identify the natural prototype as the "most typical" example of the category) even when the natural prototype is not central to the category.

EXPERIMENT I: COLORS

The color space was long considered a domain of uniform, physical variation which languages could partition arbitrarily into color name categories (cf. Lenneberg, 1967). Thus, colors were considered an ideal domain in which "language-cognition" research could demonstrate the effects of linguistic categories on nonverbal cognitive processes such as memory (Brown & Lenneberg, 1954; Lantz & Stefflre, 1964; Stefflre, Castillo Vales, & Morley, 1966). Such a view of the nature of the color space has been challenged recently from several sources.

Berlin and Kay (1969) argued that there were a limited number of "basic" color terms (defined by linguistic criteria) in any language—three achromatic and eight chromatic terms. When informants from diverse languages were asked to choose the best examples of their language's basic color terms from an array of Munsell chips, they tended to choose the same areas of the color space. Berlin and Kay called these clusters of best examples of color terms "focal points," and argued that the previous anthropological emphasis on cross-cultural differences in color names was derived from looking only at the boundaries of color names—a more variable aspect of categorization than the focal points. Although Berlin and Kay's data do not constitute unequivocal support for their claims (cf. Hickerson, 1971), the claims are arresting and clearly warrant further research.

Previous work of the present author (Heider, 1971, 1972) provided evidence that the focal points of basic color terms represented areas of the color space which possessed a particular perceptual-cognitive salience "prior" to color naming. "Prior to naming" can be taken in two senses: developmentally, Heider (1971) showed that 3-yr-old American children oriented toward focal colors in preference to nonfocal colors. Cross culturally, Heider (1972) demonstrated that the Dani of New Guinea, speakers of a language which lacks all of the basic chromatic color terms (K. G. Heider, 1970), remembered focal colors more accurately than nonfocal colors—both in a short-term recognition task similar to that used by Brown and Lenneberg (1954) and in a long-term memory task.

The research to be reported here was designed to explore the manner in which color categories are learned. The basic research design involved comparison of the learning of color categories structured according to the supposed natural organization of the color space (focal colors the physically central members of categories) with the learning of color categories structured in other "unnatural" ways. Such a study obviously could not be adequately performed with Ss who already knew a set of basic chromatic color terms provided by their language. Even young children of a culture whose language contained basic color terms were not appropriate Ss since, among other problems, their prior history of exposure to the color terms of their language could not be controlled.

Ideally, Ss were required whose language did not contain basic color terms; for such Ss, the input stimuli for learning color categories could be precisely specified and controlled within the context of the experiment. Such a language is spoken by the Dani of Indonesian New Guinea, a Stone Age people previously described by K. G. Heider (1970) as possessing only two color terms, which divide the color space on the basis of brightness rather than hue. Color systems of that character have been reported for other cultures as well; they are classified by Berlin and Kay (1969) as Stage I, the first and simplest stage of a proposed evolutionary ordering of color systems. A description of a study verifying the nature of Dani color terminology and tables showing the distribution of the two basic color terms over arrays of Munsell chips are available in Heider and Olivier (1972).

If the color space were undifferentiated or if the saliency of focal color areas were irrelevant to the learning of color categories, then any set of color categories should be as easy for *S*s to learn as any other set of equal discriminability. In contrast, the basic hypothesis of the present study is that colors are "natural categories" and conform to the hypotheses for the learning of natural categories stated in the introduction; that is, it is predicted that focal colors themselves and sets in which focal colors are central will be learned faster than nonfocal colors and than unnaturally structured sets.

A secondary interest of the study concerned a different aspect of the structure of color categories—the relative "learnability" of the different basic colors within the domain of colors as a whole. Berlin and Kay (1969) argued, from a review of the anthropological literature, that color terms enter languages in a fixed evolutionary order which is: (a) black, white (b) red (c) yellow, green (d) blue (e) brown (f) pink, purple, orange, gray. If the salience of focal colors is found to play a role in the learning of basic color names, then it is not unreasonable to suppose that salience differences among focal colors might lead to an evolutionary order in the development of color names within languages. In the present research, it was possible to see whether the speed with which color categories were learned (in the naturally constructed sets) corresponded to the evolutionary order proposed by Berlin and Kay.

Methods

Subjects. A total of 68 male Dani, prescreened for color blindness, served as *S*s. Only Dani whose color term usage was restricted to the two basic Dani color terms "mili" (roughly "dark") and "mola" (roughly "light") were used. Because the learning task required a number of days of consecutive attendance, it was necessary to use *S*s who were physically present at a local school; however, care was taken to use only *S*s who were still monolingual in their own language (that is, *S*s who, essentially, had not yet learned anything verbal in the school which was conducted in Indonesian). Dani do not measure age, but, from their size and general physical maturity, *S*s were judged to be 12–15 yr of age or older. Because the number of volunteers was limited, *S*s who learned the three different types of color category sets were matched in threes according to height (as a rough estimate of age), and according to their ability to interpret the logic of their own kinship structure (as a rough estimate of "intelligence"—see K. G. Heider, 1971). Subjects were volunteers and were paid after they had learned the set assigned them to criterion.

Stimuli. Munsell color chips of glossy finish were used, and are referred to in Munsell notation. The C. I. E. tristimulus values and chromaticity coordinates are obtainable from Nickerson, Tomaszewski, and Boyd (1953).

Six different category sets were used: two sets in which focal colors were central; two sets in which internominal colors were central; and two sets in which focal colors were peripheral. In three of the six sets (one set of each type), categories were composed of chips of the same brightness varying only in hue; in the other three sets (one of each type), categories were composed of chips of the same hue, varying only in brightness. The three brightness-varying sets were considered a replication with different stimuli, of the design of the three hue-varying sets.

Each set consisted of eight categories (consistent with the eight basic chromatic color terms claimed by Berlin & Kay, 1969). Categories were composed of three chips because a pilot study showed this the optimum number for Dani learning in this task. Each S learned one, and only one, of the sets.

The stimuli used in all categories for all sets are shown in Munsell notation in Table 1. Sets 1, 2, and 3 were composed of hue-varying categories. The presumed "natural prototypes" of color categories were represented by eight focal color chips, that is, by one chip from the center of each of the areas where best examples of the eight basic chromatic color names clustered in Berlin and Kay's (1969) study. (A more complete description of the method of selection of these chips is available in Heider 1972.) In Set 1, each category was composed of one central natural prototype (a "focal" chip) and chips of the same brightness two Munsell steps to either "side" (roughly longer and shorter wavelength) in hue. For example, for an English speaker, the "blue" category might be described as a "pure" blue chip, a blue chip (two Munsell steps) toward green and a blue chip (two Munsell steps) toward purple. Step 1 was, thus, constructed to coincide with the proposed natural structure of the color space.

In contrast, Set 2 was constructed to violate that proposed natural structure. Artificial (nonnatural) prototypes for categories were represented by eight chips from the "internominal" areas of the color space; that is from the centers of those areas in which no chips had been designated as the best example of a basic color name by any language in the Berlin and Kay (1969) study. For the present study, eight internominal chips were chosen which, in addition to being central to internominal areas fell "between" two basic color name areas. Set 2 categories were composed in a manner analogous to those of Set 1; each category consisted of the central internominal chip and the chip of same brightness two Munsell step to the longer and two Munsell steps to the shorter wavelength of the central chips. However, because internominal chips had been chosen that fell between two different basic name areas, Set 2 categories tended to "violate natural hue concepts." That is, the two peripheral chips in each Set 2 category consisted of chips from areas that speakers of languages containing basic hue terms would label with two *different* basic color names—e.g., an English speaker might label Set 2 categories "red *and* brown," "yellow *and* green."

Set 3 differed from Set 1 only in that the focal color was a peripheral rather than the central member of each three-chip category. Each category of Set 3 contained a focal chip and the two chips of the same Munsell brightness but two and four Munsell steps of longer wavelength than the focal chips (for purposes of defining the "red" category in this set, the color space was considered circular with red adjacent to purple).

Sets 4–6 were constructed in a manner analogous to Sets 1–3 with the exception that categories were composed of chips of the same Munsell hue, varying in brightness. In Set 4, the same focal colors were central to categories as in Set 1; however, the other two chips in each category were the chips one Munsell step lighter in brightness and one Munsell step darker in brightness than the focal chip. For example, the "blue" category in this set contained the same central chip as in Set 1 but with it were now a lighter blue and a darker blue. In Set 5, categories were composed of the same central

TABLE 1   Sets of Stimuli Used in Color Learning Experiment

	STIMULI					
	Hue-Varying Sets					
	Set 1[a]		*Set 2*		*Set 3*	
Category	*Central Color*	*Peripheral Colors*	*Central Color*	*Peripheral Colors*	*Central Color*	*Peripheral Colors*
1	5R 8/6	10RP 8/6 10R 8/6	7.5YR 8/8	2.5YR 8/6 2.5Y 8/10	10RP 8/6	5R 8/6 5RP 8/6
2	5R 4/14	10RP 4/14 10R 4/12	10R 4/10	5R 4/14 5YR 4/10	10RP 4/14	5R 4/14 5RP 4/12
3	2.5Y 8/16	10YR 8/14 5Y 8/12	2.5GY 8/12	10Y 8.5/12 5GY 8/10	10YR 8/14	2.5Y 8/16 5YR 8/16
4	2.5YR 6/16	10 R 6/14 5YR 6/12	5YR 6/12	2.5YR 6/16 7.5YR 6/14	10R 6/14	2.5YR 6/16 5R 6/12
5	5YR 3/6	2.5YR 3/8 10YR 3/4	5Y 3/4	2.5 Y3/2 7.5Y 3/6	2.5YR 3/8	5YR 3/6 10R 3/10
6	2.5G 5/12	7.5GY 5/10 7.5G 5/10	5BG 5/8	10G 5/10 10BG 5/8	7.5B G5/10	2.5G 5/12 2.5GY 5/10
7	2.5PB 4/10	10B 4/10 5PB 4/12	7.5PB 4/12	2.5PB 4/10 2.5P 4/10	10B 4/10	2.5PB 4/10 2.5B 4/Max
8	5P 3/10	10PB 3/8 10P 3/10	5RP 3/10	10P 3/8 10RP 3/10	10PB 3/8	5P 3/10 5PB 3/10

	Brightness-Varying Sets					
	Set 4[a]		*Set 5*		*Set 6*	
Category	*Central Color*	*Peripheral Colors*	*Central Color*	*Peripheral Colors*	*Central Color*	*Peripheral Colors*
1	5R 8/6	5R 9/2 5R 7/6	7.5YR 8/8	7.5YR 9/2 7.5YR 7/10	5R 7/6	5R 8/6 5R 6/12
2	5R 4/14	5R 5/14 5R 3/12	10R 4/10	10R 5/16 10R 3/10	5R 3/12	5R 4/14 5R 2/8
3	2.5Y 8/16	2.5Y 9/4 2.5Y 7/12	2.5GY 8/12	2.5GY 9/6 2.5GY 7/10	2.5Y 7/12	2.5Y 8/16 2.5Y 6/10
4	2.5YR 6/16	2.5YR 7/10 2.5YR 5/12	5YR 6/12	5YR 7/Max 5YR 5/12	2.5YR 5/12	2.5YR 6/16 2.5YR 4/8
5	5YR 3/6	5YR 4/10 5YR 2/4	5Y 3/4	5Y 4/6 5Y 2/2	5YR 2/4	5YR 3/6 5YR 1/2
6	2.5G 5/12	2.5G 7/10 2.5G 3/10	5BG 5/8	5BG 7/8 5BG 3/6	2.5G 3/10	2 5G 5/12 2.5G 1/6
7	2.5PB 4/10	2.5PB 6/10 2.5PB 2/8	7.5PB 4/12	7.5PB 6/10 7.5PB 2/10	2.5PB 3/10	2.5PB 4/10 2.5PB 2/8
8	5P 3/10	5P 4/Max 5P 2/8	5RP 3/10	5RP 4/12 5RP 2/8	5P 2/8	5P 3/10 5P 1/6

Note—Munsell steps between stimuli sometimes uneven to balance discriminability (measured by technique described in Brown & Lenneberg, 1954) between categories.

[a] Categories of these sets correspond to "basic" color terms: 1 = pink, 2 = red, 3 = yellow, 4 = orange, 5 = brown, 6 = green, 7 = blue, 8 = purple.

internominal chips as in Set 2, however, combined with the Munsell chips one step lighter and one step darker in brightness. Because of this change in construction, the chips of a Set 5 category, instead of cross-cutting basic name areas as those of the Set 2 categories had done, tended to fall into the same internominal area. That is, whereas a Set 3 category might be labeled "yellow *and* green," by an English speaker, the equivalent Set 5 category would probably be considered three brightnesses of "yellow-green." The categories of Set 6 (analogous to Set 3) consisted of the focal color and the two chips of the same hue but one and two steps darker in brightness (special chips of 1/brightness were obtained for the brown, green, and purple categories).

For purposes of the present study, the comparison between hue-varying and brightness-varying sets was not of particular concern; the comparison of primary interest was between sets composed of categories in which focal colors were central, internominal colors central, or focal colors peripheral (i.e., the comparison between Sets 1 vs 2 vs 3, and between Sets 4 vs 5 vs 6). Before sets were completed, discriminability between chips within and between categories for each set were computed by the formulas (omitting the correction for "edges") in Brown and Lenneberg (1954). Neither the mean discriminability within nor between categories differed between Sets 1–3 nor Sets 4–6. However, all three of the latter (the sets composed of brightness-varying categories) had lower mean discriminability within categories and greater mean discriminability between categories than the former (the sets composed of hue-varying categories). Triads of Ss matched in height and understanding of the logic of their own kinship system were taught Sets 1–3; other matched triads were taught 4–6.

Procedure. Twelve Ss learned Set 1; 12 Ss learned Set 2, and 11 Ss learned each of the other sets. An S learned one set only.

The Ss learned a set as a paired associate task; colors as stimuli, the same Dani word as correct response for the three colors in a category. Finding suitable response words at first seemed a serious obstacle to the study; however, it proved possible to use as responses names of Dani *sibs* (a *sib* is a nonterritorial, unilineal descent group, somewhat like a clan). *Sib* names were all well known to Dani and, as nearly as could be determined in pretesting, all approximately equally frequent, familiar, and meaningful. Furthermore, measures of association between *sib* names were easily obtained (Dani readily listed *sib* names), and it was possible to use names with approximately equal interassociation value. In order to randomize effects of any uncontrolled memorability differences in *sib* names, each S received a different set of pairings of colors and names. An S's own *sib* name was never used as one of his responses.

The task was described to each S as learning a new language which the E would teach him and for which he would be paid when learning was completed. He was warned that the learning could take several days. At the start of the first testing session, the colors (mounted on 3 × 5-in. white cards) were laid in random order in front of the S; and he was told the "name" of each which he repeated after the E. Thereafter, the cards were gathered into a pack, shuffled, and presented one at a time to the S who was required to say the name of the color. The S received feedback after each response; he was praised if correct and told the correct response if incorrect. After each test, the cards were reshuffled. Ss received five tests a day on successive days until the criterion of one perfect test had been achieved. A record was kept of the stimulus color and the S's response on each trial.

Immediately after reaching criterion, Ss performed two additional tasks: the first intended to ascertain whether the three-chip category had been learned as a transferable concept, the second designed to measure the S's ideas of the central (most typical) member of each of the categories in the set he had learned. As a transfer task, Ss were asked to "name" eight colors which had not been in the training categories. For the hue-varying sets, each transfer color was the chip one Munsell step darker than the central chip of each category; for the brightness-varying sets, each transfer color was the chip two Munsell steps of shorter wavelength than the central chip. To measure the second variable, the S was shown, successively, all three chips of each category of his learning set and asked to point to the best (most typical) example. There is a Dani verb form used specifically for usual or typical activities which served to make such questions readily understood, at least in regard to some stimuli.

Results

Of the 68 Dani who undertook the learning task, 63 completed learning to criterion. That categories within a set were learned as transferable concepts was shown by the results of the transfer task. By chance, Ss would have been correct in the transfer task one-eighth of the time; the obtained overall ratio of correct transfers was 7.2/8.

The first basic hypothesis of the study concerned differences in the relative ease with which the different sets were learned. Figure 1 shows the learning curves for all six sets. Each point in Figure 1 represents an average over subjects and over the five tests for that day. The mean number of errors per stimulus chip per S learning each of the sets to criterion was—for hue-varying sets: Set 1, 8.54; Set 2, 18.96; Set 3, 12.91; for brightness-varying sets: Set 4, 6.67; Set 5, 8.77; Set 6, 9.58. A two-way analysis of variance, Treatments × Levels (Lindquist, 1953) was performed on number of errors to criterion. Classification of sets by the type of color categories in the set (focal colors central, internominal colors central, focal colors peripheral) constituted the Treatment variable; whether the sets were hue-varying or brightness-varying constituted the Levels variable.

Both main effects were significant ($p < .05$): Treatments, $F(2,61) = 7.02$; Levels, $F(2,61) = 1.63$. The significant effect of Treatment is directly relevant to the main hypothesis of the study. Individual comparisons between all pairs of sets confirmed that

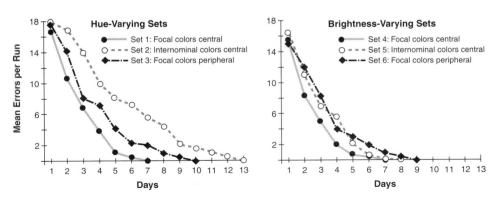

FIGURE 1   Mean errors per test per day for the six color category learning sets.

the following differences between sets were statistically significant ($p < .05$ or better): within hue-varying sets—Set 1 < Set 3 < Set 2; within brightness-varying sets—Set 4 < Set 5, Set 6. These results show that, in both the hue- and brightness-varying sets, sets in which the presumed natural prototype were central (Sets 1 and 4) were learned with significantly fewer errors than either of the other sets. Set 2, composed of "hue-violating" categories, was more difficult to learn than any of the other sets. (There is additional anecdotal evidence for the difficulty of Set 2; not only were three of the five Ss who failed to reach criterion assigned to Set 2, but an additional four Set 2 Ss could only be persuaded to continue to criterion with great effort on the part of the E, a difficulty not encountered with the Ss who had been assigned to other sets.) The significant main effect of Level was of less interest to the purpose of the study. It was not surprising that the brightness-varying sets (4–6) should be learned with fewer errors than the hue-varying sets (1–3); such an effect was predictable on the basis of discriminability differences between the hue- and brightness-varying categories.

The second basic hypothesis of the study concerned the relative ease with which names were learned for colors as individual stimuli within categories; the prediction was that focal colors would be learned faster than nonfocal even when the focal colors were peripheral members of categories. In light of the abstraction research findings concerning the central tendencies of artificial categories (Posner, 1969), it was also reasonable to expect that central members of categories would be learned more rapidly than peripheral members. The data from Sets 1, 3, 4, and 6 could be grouped into an R × C table: Focal versus Nonfocal, and Central versus Peripheral. A two-way analysis of variance for the variable number-of-errors-per-stimulus was performed on this data. The main effect for the focal dimension was significant, $F(1,26) = 8.72$, $p < .01$; however, neither the main effect for centrality, $F(1,26) = 1.94$, nor the interaction, $F(1,26) = 1.13$, reached significance. Such results indicated that focal colors were learned with fewer errors than nonfocal, an effect which was independent of the centrality of the colors. That names for focal colors were learned faster than for nonfocal colors is consistent with Heider's (1972) finding that focal chips were better remembered than nonfocal in memory tasks which did not involve category learning. It was, however, surprising that central members of categories were not learned faster than peripheral. The ease of learning central and peripheral colors could also be compared for Sets 2 and 5 (which did not contain focal colors). Errors per stimulus for central and peripheral chips were compared by t test for each of these two sets. The difference was not significant in Set 2, but the hypothesis that central would be learned more rapidly than peripheral was weakly supported in Set 5, $t(10) = 2.01$, $p < .10$.

The final basic hypothesis concerned Ss' judgments of the "most typical" examples of categories—this hypothesis could not be tested for Dani color learning. Dani Ss, although they readily transferred color category names to new instances, were unwilling to designate one of the color chips as the most typical member of the three-chip category. Since Dani easily made such a judgment for form categories, discussion of the color task will be deferred until the form data have been presented.

In addition to the main interest of the experiment, the study provided an opportunity to look at the relative "salience" (learnability) of different basic color areas compared to each other. The simplest hypothesis about the relation of colors was that the relative ease of learning color categories within the naturally structured sets (1 and 4) would correspond to the linguistic order in which Berlin and Kay (1969) proposed that color terms evolve. The order of difficulty for learning color categories in the present study (Sets 1 and 4 combined—least difficult shown first) was: red, green, pink, blue, purple, yellow, brown, orange. The rank order correlation of this order with the specific order proposed by Berlin and Kay did not reach significance. However, Berlin and Kay's first four color term categories (red, yellow, green, blue) were, as a group, learned with significantly fewer errors than brown, pink, orange, and purple as a group, $t(19) = 2.41$, $p < .05$. These results are similar to Heider's (1972) finding that neither length of color names, latency of naming, nor short- or long-term memory for focal colors correlated with the exact Berlin and Kay evolutionary order but that there was a consistent tendency for the four "primary" focal colors to prove different from the four "secondary" colors.

A second, and perhaps more interesting, hypothesis about relations among colors was the possibility that the structure of the color space derived from the confusion errors in learning (calling chips from one category by the name of another category) might mirror the "name structure" of the color space which Berlin and Kay propose for different stages of color name evolution. For example, Ss might go through an early "stage" in which they applied the word for the red category to the pink, orange, and purple, as well as to the red, chips. However, absolutely no such tendency was observable in the confusion data for either Sets 1, 3, 4, or 6, even at the very beginning of learning. The Ss were more likely to confuse categories which were physically more similar; however, they were as likely to call the "evolutionarily earlier" color name categories by the name assigned to the "later" colors as vice versa; e.g., in the above example, they were as likely to call the red chips "orange" as they were to call the orange chips "red."

Of course, the above is not evidence against Berlin and Kay's proposed evolutionary order; there need be no simple relation between order of individual acquisition of terms and linguistic evolution. The present study only represents a case in which a possible evolutionary order could have been, but was not, reflected on the level of individual learning.

In summary, the first two basic hypotheses of the research were supported: Dani Ss could learn the presumed natural prototypes of color categories and sets in which those stimuli were central faster than they learned other color stimuli or sets organized around other areas of the color space.

EXPERIMENT II: FORMS

Learning of form categories was studied for two reasons: (a) to demonstrate the role of natural prototypes in category formation in more than one perceptual domain, and (b) to replicate the logic of the color research with stimuli in which "natural" and "unnatural" category sets could be constructed in a more controlled manner than had been possible with colors. That is, because of the nature of the color space, it had not been possible for focal colors to occur as peripheral members of sets in which internominal colors were central, nor, using both focal and internominal colors had it been possible to construct a group of sets in which all stimuli occurred both as central and as peripheral members. Such manipulations were possible with forms.

The Dani language does not possess readily accessible monolexemic codes for geometric forms (K. G. Heider, 1970), not surprising in light of the fact that Dani live in an "uncarpentered world" (Segall, Campbell, & Herskovitz, 1966) in which three-dimensional shapes are irregular and in which two-dimensional geometric line drawings do not occur. Even so, it was possible that Dani had nonverbal concepts which would lead them to group the experimental forms in a particular way prior to the category learning of the experiment itself and/or that Dani had readily available verbal circumlocutions which could designate the experimental form categories. Three pilot studies were, therefore, performed designed to determine whether Dani showed evidence of pre-experimental biases in categorizing the experimental stimuli.

Pilot Studies

The stimuli used in the pilot studies were 21, two-dimensional line drawings, three "basic" forms (circle, square, triangle), and six transformations of each of the basic forms. These were the forms of Set 1 described in detail below. The object of the pilot research was to determine whether Dani showed tendencies to group these stimuli into circle, square, and triangle categories prior to the experimental name learning.

The possibility of nonverbal grouping of the stimuli was tested in two tasks: free sorting of the 20 figures, and a series of oddity problems in which the S was required to point to the two figures most alike when his choice was two variants of one basic form and one variant of one of the other forms. Seven Ss performed the sorting task; nine performed the oddity problems. The results were uniform and unequivocal. Both in the sorting and in the oddity problems, grouping of variants of the same form was at chance.

The possibility of verbal circumlocutions to designate the form categories was tested in a two-person communication task. Two Ss were seated on either side of a screen; each had before him (arranged in different orders), the 21 figures of Set 1. One S, designated as speaker was required to describe each form so that the listener could pick the correct form from among the others. When the listener thought he had found the form, he held up the card so the speaker could see his choice. If incorrect, the speaker was required to give a new description and the listener to choose a second time. Twenty pairs of Ss performed the task. This communication task is one in which American Ss tend to verbalize both the basic form category and the variation (e.g., "It's the square with a hole in it."); Dani codings, however, were almost all the names of specific objects ("It's a pig," "It's a broken fence."). If the form class of the figure had affected Dani verbalizations, listener errors should have been greater within the form class of the encoded stimulus; for example if the intended stimulus were a variant of the circle, and the listener's choice were incorrect, he should be more likely to choose a different variant of the circle than some other form. The actual result was that errors were randomly distributed over the three form classes—even on the second guess where the speaker had been given a chance to correct an initially erroneous choice.

It appeared safe to conclude, from the pilot research, that the two-dimensional figures used in the form learning study were not already classified into form classes by Dani Ss. The main form learning study is, thus, reported in detail below.

Method

Subjects. A total of 94 Dani were *S*s in the form learning experiment. None had participated either in the color research or in the pilot studies. Because form learning required fewer days to reach criterion than color learning, it was possible to use *S*s from the surrounding villages who had no contact with the local school. As in the previous experiment, *S*s were paid after they reached criterion on the learning task. Approximately 14 *S*s learned each form set.

Stimuli. The "good forms" of Gestalt psychology were presumed the natural prototypes of form categories. Two-dimensional line drawings of a "perfect" square, circle, and equilateral triangle, approximately 1 sq. in. in area, served as prototype (focal) forms.

Seven sets of stimuli were constructed. In Set 1, the presumed natural set, a "perfect" basic circle, square, and equilateral triangle were "central" to a group of transformations. By "central" it is meant that the transformations were performed on the "perfect" basic forms. As an aid to visualization, Figure 2 shows the square and its transformations. There were six transformations: (a) Gap—a ¼ in. gap was placed in one side of the figure. (b) Line-to-curve—for square and triangle, one line was changed to a curve the midpoint of which was ¼ in. to the inner side of the figure; for the circle, an arc was changed to a line which cut off an equivalent amount of the area of the circle. (c) One-line-extended—for the square and triangle, one line was extended ¼ in. with the adjoining line extended to meet it; for the circle, an equivalent extension of the arc was produced. (d) Two-lines-extended—two opposite lines (or, for circle, arcs) were extended as in c; thus, the square became a rhombus, the triangle a scalene triangle, and the circle a regular ellipse. (e) Irregular figure—all four sides of the square and the three sides of the triangle were of different length; the circle was changed to an ameboid form. (f) Freehand—all three forms were changed to freehand drawings of the prototype forms, modeled after actual copies made by Dani of the original forms.

Each of the other sets of stimuli were derived by using the three figures produced by one of the transformations as prototype and performing the listed transformations upon the new prototypes. The perfect figures occurred peripherally in those sets (Sets 2–7) in the place which the prototype of the new set had occupied in Set 1. For example, in Set 2, gapped figures were the prototypes; the line-to-curve, one-line-extended, etc., transformations were all performed upon the gapped figures. The perfect (nongapped) figures were produced by a "gap closing" transformation which took the place of the gap producing transformation which had yielded the gapped figures as peripheral members of Set 1. In Set 3, the line-to-curve (arc-to-line) figures were the prototypes; in Set 4, the one-line-(arc)-extended figures; in Set 6, the irregular figures; and in Set 7, the freehand figures.

Figures were printed on 2 × 3-in. white cards. During learning and testing, they could appear randomly in any orientation.

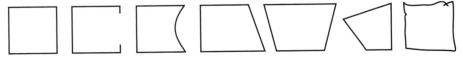

FIGURE 2   Basic square and six transformations.

Procedures. Each learning set consisted of 21 figures, 7 in each of the categories. Each *S* learned one, and only one, set. As in the color learning task, *S*s learned a set as a paired associate task: figures as stimuli, a Dani word (*sib* name) as correct response for the seven figures in a category. Figures were shown in a different random order each test, five tests a day, with feedback after each response. When the criterion of one perfect test was achieved, *S*s performed two additional tasks: a transfer task and a task designed to elicit the *S*s conception of the most typical member of each of the categories in the set he had learned. As a transfer task, each *S* was asked to name three irregular figures (4 sided, 3 sided, ameboid) constructed as variants of the central form (actual prototype) of the set he had learned but differing from the irregular figures of his own set. To measure the second variable, the seven figures in a category were placed before the *S* and he was asked to pick the "most typical" example of the category name. The figure which he chose was then removed and he was asked to pick the most typical of those that remained. This technique was applied successively until the *S* had rank ordered each member of each category.

Results and Discussion

Of the 94 *S*s who participated in the form learning, only two failed to complete learning to criterion. Scores on the transfer task were almost perfect—of 92 *S*s, each making three transfer choices (one per category), there were only six errors. Dani *S*s clearly could learn two-dimensional form categories as transferable concepts.

The logic of the form learning experiment was essentially the same as that of color learning. Tables 2 and 3 show the means and significance test results for the variables: (a) errors to criterion per set, (b) errors to criterion per stimulus type, and (c) mean rank of best example per stimulus type. From these two tables, it may be seen that all three basic hypotheses of the form learning study were supported. From line 1 of Tables 2 and 3, it is apparent that Set 1, in which the presumed natural prototypes were central to a set of distortions was learned with fewer errors than any of the other sets, in all of which the distorted forms were central and the presumed natural prototypes peripheral. In regard to the second hypothesis, the form stimuli could provide a more controlled test than had the colors. In the seven form sets, each stimulus type (basic, gap, line-to-curve, etc.) occurred once as the prototype of a set and six times as peripheral members of other sets. It was, thus, possible to compare the mean number of errors made in learning each stimulus type across all sets. The means for the three categories (square, circle, triangle) combined are shown in the second row of Table 2 and the significance test results for differences between those means in the second row of Table 3. It is clear that the natural prototypes were learned faster than other stimuli, even when they were peripheral members of categories.

Although Dani *S*s had been unable to pick a most typical example of the color categories, they easily made this judgment in the case of the forms.[1] Thus, it became possible to test the third basic hypothesis. Table 2, line 6, shows the means of the rankings of best example for each stimulus type combined across categories, and Table 3, line 3, shows significant differences between those rankings. For forms, it was confirmed that Dani *S*s were more likely to choose presumed natural prototypes than distortions as the most typical member of a category, a difference which cuts across sets in which the natural prototypes were and were not actually central.

TABLE 2   Errors and Best-Example Rank for Each Form Type

Category	Basic	Gap	Line-to-Curve	One-Line-Extended	Two-Lines-Extended	Irregular	Freehand
				Form Type			
Mean Errors per Stimulus per Person for Each Set[a]							
Form types and categories combined within sets	2.62	4.07	4.32	3.91	3.78	5.88	7.47
Mean Errors per Stimulus per Person for Each Form Type (all sets combined)							
All categories combined	1.97	3.87	3.86	3.11	2.92	6.07	7.29
Circle	.57	1.71	1.40	1.79	1.67	6.02	6.24
Square	2.06	6.29	4.30	4.47	4.24	8.57	9.21
Triangle	3.27	3.58	5.86	3.09	2.84	3.62	6.43
Mean Rank[b] **as Best Example for Each Form Type (all sets combined)**							
All categories combined	1.81	3.82	4.37	3.77	3.32	4.99	5.94
Circle	1.18	4.00	3.63	4.09	3.22	5.54	6.72
Square	1.54	3.91	4.28	4.11	3.56	6.27	4.90
Triangle	2.69	3.54	5.17	3.07	3.18	3.16	6.19

[a] For these means, "form type" designates the set in which that form type was the set prototype.

[b] Rank of 1 meant first choice as best example.

The results presented so far have rested on data combined across the three form categories. Was the same direction of results characteristic of all three of the forms? Table 2, lines 3–5 and 7–9 shows, separated into form category, mean errors and mean rank as best example for each figure. The same methods of statistical analysis, one-way analysis of variance and *t* tests between all pairs of figures, that had been applied to the combined data were applied to the data of each separate form category. For circle and square, the results were essentially identical to those already reported for the combined data; the one difference was that, for both circle and square, errors for the irregular variant did not differ from errors for the freehand variant. However, the triangle category showed a somewhat different pattern. Neither in errors nor in mean rank as best example was there a significant difference between the basic (equilateral) triangle, gap, one-line-extended, two-lines-extended or the irregular figure. All five of those figures were learned with fewer errors than the line-to-curve and the freehand figure. Thus, for the triangle, it appeared that any three-sided, straight-line figure was an equally good "triangle prototype," and that all such figures were superior to the curved and freehand figures.

TABLE 3   Summary of Form Learning Results

Dependent variable	F test of overall variation[a]	Significant differences between sets and stimuli on dependent variable[b]
Errors to criterion per set	$F = 4.19$ $p < .05$	Set 1 < Set 2, Set 3, Set 4, Set 5 < Set 6 < Set 7
Errors to criterion per stimulus[c]	$F = 3.82$ $p < .05$	basic < gap, line-to-curve, one-line-extended, two-lines-extended < irregular, freehand
Rank most typical example	$F = 5.73$ $p < .01$	basic < gap, line-to-curve, one-line-extended, two-lines-extended < irregular < freehand

[a] One-way analysis of variance, $df = 6,12$.
[b] T tests performed between all pairs of stimuli: "<" represents differences significant at least $p < .05$.
[c] Combined over all sets.

Statistics combined across sets fail to represent with full force the effects obtained for basic circle and square in the sets in which they were peripheral. It was not simply that, on the average, the basic figures were more easily learned and ranked higher as best example than the other figures. In five of the sets (1, 2, 4, 5, 7), the basic circle actually received a higher mean best-example rank than any of the other figures in those sets, although the basic circle was not the actual prototype in four of the sets. Basic square received the highest mean best-example rank in the four sets (1, 2, 5, 7). Basic circle was actually learned with fewest errors of any figure in the set in four sets (1, 4, 5, 7) although it was the actual prototype only in Set 1; basic square was learned with fewest errors in two sets (1, 5).

The fact that there was a strong and consistent effect in errors to criterion and rank as best example associated with whether stimuli were natural prototypes or not and that this effect cut across whether they were the central or peripheral members of sets, does not rule out the possibility that there was also an effect of centrality. That is, for all stimuli combined, the central figure (actual prototype) of a set might tend to be learned more rapidly and ranked higher as best example than peripheral members. The mean errors per S for the actual (central) prototype figures for all stimuli and sets combined was 3.36; the mean errors for peripheral figures was 4.95, a difference which was statistically significant, $t(12) = 3.61$, $p < .01$. Similarly the mean best-example rank of the actual prototypes for all stimuli and sets combined was 3.12; the mean rank for those same figures when they occurred as peripheral members of categories was 4.90, a difference which was also statistically significant, $t(12) = 2.83$, $p < .02$. Such a finding is consistent with the effects of centrality in the learning of artificial categories (Reed, 1970). However, the effects of the natural prototype on learning and definition of best example of categories is one which could not have been discovered except with the use of natural categories.

One final finding, which should now be quite apparent from the data, is that the three basic measures—ease of learning sets of form categories when a particular type of figure was the prototype, ease of learning individual types of figures within sets, and rank order of judgment of types as best example of categories—were highly correlated. Almost identical orders have emerged from analysis of each of the three variables (see Table 3), a correlation which invites the speculation that it is generally true that categories whose central members are, in their own right, easy to learn stimuli will be easier to learn than categories whose central members are more difficult to learn.

GENERAL DISCUSSION

Evidence has been presented that there are nonarbitrary color and form categories which form around perceptually salient "natural prototypes." The evidence was of three basic types: (a) Ss from a culture which did not initially possess hue or form concepts could learn names for the presumed natural prototypes faster than for other stimuli even when the natural prototypes were not the central members of categories, (b) members of that culture could more easily learn hue and form concepts when the presumed natural prototypes were the central members of categories than when the categories were organized in other ways, and (c) at least for the forms, Ss tended to "distort" their definition of the category toward the natural prototype; that is, they tended to choose the natural prototype as the most typical member of the category even when it was actually peripheral. These findings have several more general implications.

In the first place, the results bear directly on the claim of "language and cognition" research (cf. Lenneberg, 1967) that color categories affect certain cognitive processes, such as memory for colors. That claim was partially refuted earlier by Heider's (1972) demonstration that the same areas of the color space were the most codable across many different languages and the best remembered even by speakers of a language which lacked basic hue terms. The present study went further in demonstrating the way in which perceptual-cognitive factors (the salience and memorability of certain areas of the color space) can influence the formation of linguistic categories.

For the specific case of colors, a fairly strong connection may be drawn between color language categories and what is already known of the physiology of color perception. The dominant wavelengths (as provided by Munsell Color Company, 1970) of the focal chips for the four primary basic color terms (see Table 1) correspond roughly to the "unique hue points" proposed by Hering (1964)—a theory now supported by physiological evidence of opponent color cells in the primate lateral geniculate (De Valois & Jacobs, 1968)—and evidence for a more direct match of focal yellow, green, and blue to unique hue points is provided in McDaniel (1972).

In the present study, form categories were shown to be influenced by natural prototypes in much the same way as color categories. More generally, similar perceptual influence on the structure of categories may well exist for many other domains. In fact, such a hypothesis is as tenable for the nonverbal categories developed by animals as for human semantic categories, a recent case in point being Wright and Cumming's (1971) demonstration of color categorizing "preferences" in the pigeon.

Color and form were cases in which the structure of "real" categories made the learning of those categories unlike the learning of the type of artificial categories traditional in concept formation research. Other natural semantic categories (e.g., categories such as "fruit," "bird"), although unlikely to possess a perceptually determined natural prototype, may well have artificial prototypes; and, in fact, there is evidence that semantic categories are learned and processed in a manner more similar to that of color and form than to that of artificial categories (Rosch, in press).

In short, the evidence which has been presented regarding the structure and learning of color and form categories may have implications beyond the domains of color and form: (a) there may be other domains which are organized into natural categories, and (b) even in nonperceptual domains, artificial prototypes (the best examples of nonperceptual categories) once developed, may affect the learning and processing of categories in that domain in a manner similar to the effects of natural prototypes.

ENDNOTE

1. This was not the only difference between the color and form learning; however, before speculating, it should be recalled that the present research was designed to measure the effect of category structure on learning *within* the modalities of color and form and was not designed to compare color-category with form-category learning.

REFERENCES

Berlin, B., & Kay, P. *Basic color terms: Their universality and evolution.* Berkeley: University of California Press, 1969.

Bourne, L. E. *Human conceptual behavior.* Boston: Allyn and Bacon, 1968.

Brown, R., & Lennebebg, E. A study in language and cognition. *Journal of Abnormal and Social Psychology,* 1954, **49**, 454–462.

De Valois, R. L., & Jacobs, G. H. Primate color vision. *Science,* 1968, **162**, 533–540.

Heider, E. R. "Focal" color areas and the development of color names. *Developmental Psychology,* 1971, **4**, 447–455.

Heider, E. R. Universals in color naming and memory. *Journal of Experimental Psychology,* 1972, **93**, 10–20.

Heider, E. R., & Olivier, D. C. The structure of the color space in naming and memory for two languages. *Cognitive Psychology,* 1972, **3**, 337–345.

Heider, K. G. *The Dugum Dani: a Papuan culture in the Highlands of West New Guinea.* Chicago: Aldine, 1970.

Heider, K. G. Development of kinship competency: the New Guinea Dani. Paper presented at a meeting of the American Anthropological Association, New York, November, 1971.

Hickerson, N. P. Review of "Basic color terms: their universality and evolution." *International Journal of American Linguistics,* 1971, **37**, 257–270.

Hering, E. *Outlines of a theory of the light sense* (translated by L. M. Hurvich and D. Jameson). Cambridge: Harvard University Press, 1964.

Lantz, D., & Stefflre, V. Language and cognition revisited. *Journal of Abnormal and Social Psychology,* 1964, **69**, 472–481. .

Lenneberg, E. *Biological foundations of language.* New York: Wiley 1967.

Lindquist, E. F. *Design and analysis of experiments in psychology and education.* Boston: Houghton Mifflin, 1953.

McDaniels, C. K. Hue perception and hue naming. Unpublished B.A. thesis. Harvard College, 1972.

Munsell Color Company. *Dominant wavelength and excitation purity for designated Munsell color notation.* Baltimore: Munsell Color Company, 1970.

Nickerson, D., Tomaszewski, J. J., & Boyd, T. F. Colorimetric specifications of Munsell repaints. *Journal of the Optical Society of America,* 1953, **43**, 163–171.

Posner, M. I. Abstraction and the process of recognition. In G. H. Bower & J. T. Spence (Eds.), *The psychology of learning and motivation.* Vol. 3. New York: Academic Press, 1969.

Posner, M. I., & Keele, S. On the genesis of abstract ideas. *Journal of Experimental Psychology,* 1968, **77**, 353–363.

Reed, S. K. Decision processes in pattern classification. Technical Report 32, Perceptual Systems Laboratory, University of California at Los Angeles, 1970.

Rosch, E. H. On the internal structure of perceptual and semantic categories. In T. M. Moore (Ed.), *Cognitive development and the acquisition of language.* New York: Academic Press, in press.

Segall, M. H., Campbell, D. T., & Herskovitz, M. J. *The influence of culture on visual perception.* Indianapolis: The Bobbs-Merrill Company, 1966.

Stefflre, V., Casttllo Vales, V., & Morley, L. Language and cognition in Yucatan: a cross cultural replication. *Journal of Personality and Social Psychology,* 1966, **4**, 112–115.

Wright, A. A., & Gumming, W. W. Color-naming functions for the pigeon. *Journal of the Experimental Analysis of Behavior,* 1971, **15**, 7–17.

Biological Boundaries of Learning
The Sauce-Béarnaise Syndrome

MARTIN E. P. SELIGMAN AND JOANNE L. HAGER

Some years ago one of us (Seligman) went out to dinner. He had an excellent *filet mignon* with *sauce Béarnaise,* his favorite, and then he went off with his wife Kerry to see the opera *Tristan und Isolde.* Some hours later he became violently ill with stomach flu and spent most of the night in utter misery. Later, when he attempted to eat *sauce Béarnaise* again, he couldn't bear the taste of it. Just thinking about it nauseated him.

At first glance, his reaction seemed to be a simple case of Pavlovian conditioning: a conditioned stimulus (the sauce) had been paired with an unconditioned stimulus (the illness), which elicited an unconditioned response (throwing up). So future encounters with the sauce caused a conditioned response (nausea). At second glance, however, he realized that the *sauce Béarnaise* phenomenon had violated all sorts of well-established laws:

1. The interval between tasting the sauce and throwing up was about six hours. The longest interval between two events that produce learning in the laboratory is about 30 seconds.
2. It took only one such experience for him to associate the sauce with sickness; learning rarely occurs in only one trial in the laboratory.
3. Neither the *filet mignon,* nor the white plate on which it was served, nor his wife, became distasteful to him; he associated none of them with the illness, only the *sauce Béarnaise.* But, according to laws of Pavlovian conditioning, all events or objects that occur along with the illness (the unconditioned stimulus) should have become unpleasant.
4. His reaction had no cognitive or "expectational" components, unlike most conditioning phenomena. When he found out that another close colleague got sick the same night, he knew that the sauce hadn't caused the malaise at all—stomach flu had caused it. But knowing that the sauce was not the culprit did not inhibit his aversion to it one bit.
5. Finally, his loathing of *sauce Béarnaise* stayed with him about five years, whereas associations formed by Pavlovian conditioning generally die out in about a dozen trials.

Laws. This experience led us to reconsider the phenomena that pass for conditioning in the laboratory.

Psychologists have long assumed that in the simple, controlled world of the laboratory they would find general laws of behavior. Learning theorists in particular have relied on the deliberately unnatural quality of the experiment: they argued that the arbitrary pairing of any stimuli with any response, or of any response with any reinforcer, would guarantee the generality of the results.

For example, Ivan Pavlov, in his textbook example of classical conditioning, taught dogs to salivate to a clicking sound by giving them meat along with the clicks. When he stopped handing out the meat, the dog eventually stopped salivating to the sound. Pavlov assumed that this illustrated a behavioral law—extinction—that would apply beyond the specific stimulus (the clicks) and response (salivation) of his experiment. Similarly, psychologists have assumed that if they trained a rat to press a lever in order to get pellets of flour—an example of instrumental conditioning—the rules describing the rat's behavior would transcend the particular instance of bar-pressing and flour pellets.

Smile. Learning theorists, whether they study classical conditioning or instrumental conditioning, thus tend to believe that what an animal learns about is relatively unimportant. They believe that virtually all stimuli, responses and reinforcers can be paired equally well, if they but use correct techniques. Moreover, we have general laws that describe the acquisition, inhibition, or extinction of such pairings. We can teach a pigeon to peck for grain as easily as we teach a rat to run for water and as easily as we teach a child to smile for approval. The underlying psychological laws are the same for all three behaviors.

This belief—the *equipotentiality premise*—is the foundation of mainstream learning theory today. Our most eminent learning theorists have shared the premise: Ivan Pavlov, B. F. Skinner, Clark Hull, and William K. Estes. But it is wrong. There are limits to learning, limits that evolution and natural selection have set for each species.

Advantage. Learning theorists may argue that 60 years of research have indeed found certain general laws that hold for a wide range of arbitrarily chosen events. For instance, we know that intermittent reinforcement will keep an animal working longer for a reward than continuous reinforcement will. This is true whether the subjects are rats, pigeons, or human beings, whether the response is running, pecking, or bar-pressing, and whether the reinforcer is food, water, or sex.

Perhaps, we reply, but the activities that we teach animals in the laboratory do not generally occur in the real world. When do rats normally have to press levers in order to get flour pellets? When do dogs come across little metronomes that signal meat? Learning theorists say that such random associations are intentionally artificial; that way the results are not contaminated by the animal's biology or previous experience.

But biology and experience do make a difference, and the emphasis that psychologists place on arbitrary events does not ensure laws that are general; it produces laws that are specific to arbitrary events, arbitrarily paired. Evolution has not prepared dogs and rats to learn about clicks that predict food or levers that turn off shock when they are pressed. Not so for the *sauce Béarnaise* phenomenon. In nature, stomach illness frequently follows unusual-tasting food, often with a delay of a few hours. An animal that has been poisoned by a new taste—and lived to tell the tale—would have a selective advantage: if he could learn to stay away from that taste in the future; if he could learn that lesson quickly, preferably with only one experience; if he could avoid being misled by other stimuli surrounding the new taste; and if that knowledge did not disappear (extinguish) rapidly.

From this evolutionary standpoint, mankind has long been prepared for the *sauce-Béarnaise* phenomenon. By contrast, natural selection has not prepared most animals for such typical laboratory experiences as buzzers paired with electric shock.

Readiness. Thus we have come to disagree with the assumption that conditioning has no limits. We propose a *preparedness dimension* to describe and delineate the limits of learning. We suggest that an animal brings to any experiment certain physiological equipment and predispositions, some of which are appropriate to the situation and others that are less so. The animal has a specialized sensory and motor system, we know; but more important, it has an associative apparatus that also has a long evolutionary history. This history will make some lessons easier to learn than others, some lessons more difficult to forget than others, and some more generalizable to other experiences than others.

We think it likely that *the very laws of learning vary from one situation to another, depending on the preparedness of the animal* to learn the contingency at hand. We see this preparedness concept as a continuum. In a given situation, an animal may be *prepared, unprepared,* or *contraprepared* to learn its lesson.

- By *prepared* we mean that the biology and genetics of the animal contribute greatly to its ability and readiness to make the association at hand. We can make the parameters of the task difficult, and it will still learn its lesson, and frequently the very first time.
- By *unprepared* we mean that nothing in the animal's natural history contributes to its learning the association; it learns after many trials.
- By *contraprepared* we mean that the animal is not at all biologically and genetically suited to make the association—dogs, for instance, are contraprepared for learning to yawn to get fed. No matter how easy we make the task, the animal will never learn.

Rock. This approach puts instinct and learning on the same continuum. Instinct, in our formulation, is simply an extreme case of preparedness. Further, we can measure the animal's extent of preparedness by the number of trials it requires to learn the association; it is this simple measure that makes the dimension continuous.

Thus, if we confront an animal with a stimulus, and it makes the response we are looking for the first time, we may say that its behavior is a clear illustration of instinct or a reflex. (A falling rock, for example, will elicit a startle reflex that is instinctive in human beings.) If the animal makes the conditioned response after only a few trials, we may say that it is somewhat prepared. If the animal responds correctly after many trials, it is unprepared. And if it never learns to make the association, or if it does so only after very many trials, we say that the animal is contraprepared.

Rats. Typically ethologists, who in studying wild animals in their natural habitats, have explored events on the prepared end of the scale, such as imprinting; learning theorists have restricted themselves to the unprepared region, teaching rats to associate colors, say, with food. Few researchers have studied the contraprepared end of the continuum. We use this continuum to integrate the evidence that learning is not equipotential.

The same week that Seligman was undergoing the agonies of the stomach flu, John Garcia of the State University of New York at Stony Brook published the first of a series of articles in what were then relatively obscure journals. Though the series had been rejected by the blue-ribbon journals of psychology, they are now recognized as perhaps the most important studies of animal learning of the decade. Among their consequences was that they explained the *sauce-Béarnaise* phenomenon.

Garcia and Robert A. Koelling confronted their rats with a sweet-tasting liquid and a light-sound stimulus, both paired with radiation sickness—a malaise characterized by stomach upset. But only the taste, not the bright light or loud sound, became unpleasant to the rats. In the complementary experiment, they paired the sweet taste and the light-sound stimuli with electric shock. This time, the rats associated the light-sound combination, not the taste, with the shock.

Cuckoo. This one experiment illustrates both ends of the preparedness spectrum. The rats were *prepared* to associate taste with illness, and this association occurred in spite of the hour-long delay between the taste and the illness. But the rats were *unprepared*—perhaps contraprepared—to associate taste with electric shock, to link external events (light and noise) with nausea. The evolutionary advantage is obvious: animals that are poisoned by a distinctively flavored food and survive, do well not to eat that food again.

Garcia's research was not well received in traditional quarters. One psychologist, who had worked for years on delay of reinforcement, remarked publicly, "Those findings are no more likely than bird shit in a cuckoo clock." Nevertheless, researchers have replicated the findings many times since.

Wisdom. Garcia's research helped solve a long-standing problem in physiological psychology: that of specific hungers. We had known that animals deficient in a given nutrient, such as thiamine or riboflavin, seek out substances that contain the missing nutrient. How do they manage this? The wisdom-of-the-body hypothesis proposed that foods containing the needed vitamin somehow taste better; or that the animal's ability to detect foods with the needed nutrient is increased. But such a hypothesis is unparsimonious and inelegant; it requires that there be a separate mechanism to handle each of the dozen or more nutrients for which specific hungers have been identified. When an animal lacks calcium, for example, why should foods with calcium come to taste better, rather than foods with riboflavin?

At the time Garcia was working on stomach poisoning, Paul Rozin and his colleagues Willard Rodgers and James Kalat at the University of Pennsylvania made a breakthrough. Rozin showed that specific hungers and specific aversions are symmetrical: when an animal becomes thiamine-deficient on one diet, he is sick to his stomach, and this in turn makes the animal dislike its deficient diet. Thiamine-deficiency, in short, is a form of food poisoning; and Rozin's rats were biologically prepared to associate the illness with the taste of the deficient diet. This association held over long intervals between the conditioned stimulus (the diet) and the unconditioned stimulus (the illness); and the animals always connected the illness with the food, never with such irrelevant external stimuli as the food container or the location of the food.

In addition, Steven Maier and Donna Zahorik of the University of Illinois found that animals will prefer new tastes that accompany the recovery from their illness.

In sum, one mechanism—biological preparedness to associate tastes with gastrointestinal consequences—replaces the dozen-odd mechanisms that were previously needed to account for specific hungers.

Snake. Garcia's insights are also relevant to psychopathology in man. We can interpret human phobias as prepared classical conditioning. Phobias too are selective: we have phobias about heights, the dark, crowds, animals and insects, but we do not have phobias about pajamas, electric outlets, or trees, even though the latter may accompany trauma as often as the former. Isaacs Marks of London's Maudsley Hospital related a typical case. A seven-year-old girl, playing one day in the park, saw a snake, but she was not particularly alarmed. Several hours later she accidentally smashed her hand in a car door, and soon thereafter developed a fear of snakes that lasted into adulthood. Notice that she did not develop a car-door phobia, which would have been more logical. Moreover, considerable time elapsed between her seeing the snake and having the accident.

Phobias are highly resistant to extinction—they last a long time; and, like taste aversions, they are unaffected by cognitive understanding. It does not help a person with a cat phobia to know that cats are harmless, just as it didn't help Seligman to know that the flu, and not *sauce Béarnaise,* caused his sickness.

Cats. The preparedness dimension applies to instrumental learning as well as Pavlovian (classical) learning. (In instrumental learning the animal finds that its behavior will produce a reward or a punishment—the reward will maintain its response and punishment will diminish it.) We actually had evidence for this 70 years ago, when E. L. Thorndike began his pioneer studies of animal learning.

Thorndike put cats into large puzzle boxes and studied the ways that they learned to escape: in one the cat would have to pull a string to get out, in another it had to find the crucial lever, and so on. The last one, box Z, had only a door, which Thorndike would open for the cat whenever it licked or scratched itself. Each of these actions has an instrumental function: the cat scratches itself when it itches, and licks itself when it is dirty.

Thorndike found that freedom—getting out of the puzzle boxes—was sufficient reward for his cats; their freedom reinforced the behaviors of pulling strings, pushing buttons, or pressing levers. But his cats had a great deal of trouble learning to get out of box Z. They found it exceedingly difficult to associate scratching and licking with the opening of the door. Thorndike himself suggested that there may be some instrumental associations that the nervous system just cannot make; his box-Z cats were demonstrating their contrapreparedness to learn that lesson. But Thorndike's suggestion has been lost on modern-learning theorists.

Key. Similarly, psychologists have long taught pigeons to peck at keys for grain. Key-pecking, they assumed, was an arbitrary behavior that they could reward. But we must note one important difference between a pigeon's pecking and, say, a rat's pressing levers. In nature, lever-pressing has nothing to do with getting food; but pecking has everything to do with the bird's eating. Thus we would infer that birds are more prepared to peck keys than rats are to press levers. Indeed, Paul Brown and Herbert Jenkins of McMaster University in Hamilton, Ontario found that the pigeon will learn to peck keys even when this behavior does not produce grain. They confronted the birds with a lit-up key, then gave them some grain, and this was enough to get them to start pecking. The pigeons even continued to peck when the probability of getting food did not increase—in fact, even when the probability decreased.

Robert Bolles of the University of Washington found that similar considerations hold in avoidance learning—what animals will and will not learn to do to avoid certain painful things. Rats learn to press bars for food pellets, and also readily learn to jump or run from a dangerous place to a safe one to avoid electric shock. From this, equipotentiality theorists would deduce that rats should be able to learn to press bars to avoid shock. But it isn't so. It is a long and tedious procedure to train a rat to press a bar to avoid shock. Similarly, pigeons will peck keys for grain, but not to avoid shock. They can certainly avoid danger in other ways, however: if we ask pigeons to fly or run from shock, they learn quickly. Bolles concluded that to train an animal to avoid a painful stimulus, we must choose from among its species-specific repertoire of *defensive* actions, not from its appetitive repertoire. Natural selection must have prepared the animal before human beings can train it.

Gulls. As learning theorists encounter more and more experimental anomalies of the kind we have described, they are becoming more open to the importance of ethological findings on prepared behaviors—an area with which comparative psychologists such as Daniel Lehrman, T. C. Schneirla, M. E. Bitterman, and Gilbert Gottlieb have long been familiar.

Beginning with its modern founders, Konrad Lorenz and Nikolaas Tinbergen, ethology has been concerned with the behavior of animals in the wild, scrupulously noting the behaviors specific to each species rather than searching for common laws of learning. Ethologists had therefore known for years that learning is not equipotential.

For instance, Tinbergen found that herring gulls (in their natural environment) learn to recognize their own chicks within hours, but they will not learn to recognize their own eggs even after weeks—though both eggs and chicks are easily distinguishable to the human observer. Lorenz studied imprinting: the fact that ducklings, at a critical period of development, begin to follow whatever object (mother, locomotives, Lorenz himself) is moving in their environment. This following apparently relieves the ducklings' distress, and is highly resistant to change.

Songs. Stephen T. Emlen, a Cornell University ethologist, thinks that genetically prepared learning is relevant in bird migration as well ["Birds," PT, April]. His indigo buntings apparently are prepared to learn about the circumpolar constellations, and to use these cues in migration, for they will learn to migrate to and from Orion when they are raised in a planetarium with this constellation at the pole rather than the Little Dipper (the real polar constellation).

Birds also are prepared to learn the songs appropriate for their species and studies of the critical periods in song-learning may illuminate human language learning. Peter Marler of Rockefeller University studied the white-crowned sparrow. In nature, this bird learns its song by listening to adults of the species. If the young bird does not hear the song between 10 and 50 days of age, however, its song is deficient when it is adult. Moreover, its ability to learn during this period is selective: it will not pick up the song of another species, even if this is the only song it hears.

Children. Marler's research meshes with that of Noam Chomsky at M.I.T. and Eric Lenneberg at Cornell, both of whom have studied language learning in children. Their data show that children do not learn to speak and understand language the way rats learn to press levers—contrary to B. F. Skinner's argument that reinforcement shapes both kinds of behavior. In all but the most impoverished linguistic environments, children will speak and understand the language that they hear. We do not need to arrange our words carefully for them to do so, nor need we reward or punish their verbal attempts.

It appears that both young sparrows and young human beings are prepared to focus on the sounds of their own species, and that species only.

Evidence. One might ask what difference it makes if there are strong biological and genetic constraints on what can and cannot be learned. We now have tentative evidence that different laws of learning, different physiological bases, and even different cognitive mechanisms may underlie prepared and unprepared learning.

1. *Different Laws of Learning.* Unprepared associations disappear readily if they are not continually reinforced. Prepared learning is much more robust. Imprinting, phobias, and taste aversions persist in the absence of reinforcement. They last even when they have lost their purpose; they seem to take on autonomous lives of their own that remain impervious to extinction.
2. *Different Physiological Bases.* Prepared associations are neither fragile nor plastic. Taste aversions can be learned under anesthesia, and they are not to be broken down by electroconvulsive shock or by inactivation of the cerebral cortex. Unprepared associations are much more fragile and plastic. We can mold them and shape them and destroy them with reasonable ease.

3. *Different Cognitive Mechanisms.* Finally, unprepared learning is largely cognitive—it involves expectations, selective attention, and intention. Prepared learning, by comparison, seems blind and noncognitive. When unprepared learning occurs, information-seeking is important: stimuli that are redundant do not become conditioned. In contrast, even redundant tastes become aversive when they are paired with nausea.

Evolution has not left the learning of prepared associations to cognitive processes alone. Perhaps this is why love and sexual attachments—to say nothing of phobias—are irrational: they are all survival related. An animal that must act instantaneously cannot take time out to ruminate.

Order. So we must recognize that the learning apparatus of men and animals may be just as evolutionarily specialized as perceptual and motor apparatus. The environmentalist model, which tries so hard to be an uncontaminated situation for the study of behavioral laws, inadvertently may have injected a bias of its own: that because the animals would learn to do most of the odd things the experimenters wanted them to do, there were no biological limits on what animals could learn. We now know that this is not true. Learning theorists played a major part in showing us that biology is not destiny, that the environment can shape and focus behavior. But they went to an unwarranted extreme. A truly general learning theory must take into account the entire spectrum of preparedness. And we hold out some hope that laws of a higher level of generality may emerge.

If, for example, future work supports the existing evidence that ease of extinction varies with preparedness, we would have a truly general law of extinction. We cannot say what will develop in the future as the largely unexplored areas of prepared and contraprepared learning are studied; it may be that any search for general laws will prove to be a will-o'-the-wisp. But we think otherwise; scientists seem to be prepared to create order out of chaos.

The preparedness dimension should generate some important questions and new directions for research. We may learn how prepared man is to learn about aggressive and sexual behaviors in various situations. We can examine the things we do—the things we learn, perceive, remember, understand, fail to understand, believe, disbelieve—and find out whether we do them as we do because we are *Homo sapiens,* animals evolved and still evolving. By finding and probing these biological boundaries, we may open vast dimensions of experience for man.

Illness-Induced Aversions in Rat and Quail

Relative Salience of Visual and Gustatory Cues

HARDY C. WILCOXON, WILLIAM B. DRAGOIN,
AND PAUL A. KRAL

Bobwhite quail, like the rat, learn in one trial to avoid flavored water when illness is induced by a drug ½ hour after drinking. In contrast to the rat, quail also learn to avoid water that is merely darkened by vegetable dye. The visual cue is even more salient than the taste cue in quail.

E arlier work on illness-induced aversions to eating and drinking shows rather clearly that the rat, at least, must have either a gustatory or an olfactory cue in order to learn to avoid ingesting a substance if the illness that follows ingestion is delayed by ½ hour or more. Visual, auditory, and tactual cues, even though conspicuously present at the time of ingestion, do not become danger signals for the rat in such circumstances (1, 2). On the other hand, blue jays (*Cyanocitta cristata bromia* Oberholser, Corvidae) easily learn to reject toxic monarch butterflies (*Danaus plexippus* L., subfamily Danainae) on sight, although the model suggested for this learning gives emetic reinstatement of taste during illness a prominent, mediating role (3).

Impetus for our experiments came from the general view that the behavior of an organism, including what it can and cannot readily learn, is largely a product of its evolutionary history. In view of the rat's highly developed chemical senses, nocturnal feeding habits, and relatively poor vision, its ability to learn to avoid toxic substances on the basis of their taste or smell, rather than their appearance, is not surprising. But how general is this phenomenon across species? Might we not expect a diurnal bird, with its superior visual equipment and greater reliance upon vision in foraging for food and drink, to show a different pattern? Perhaps such birds, even in situations involving long delay between the time of ingestion of some food and the onset of illness, can learn to avoid ingesting substances that are distinctive in appearance only.

We report here two experiments which show that bobwbite quail (*Colinus virginianus*) can associate a purely visual cue with a long-delayed, illness consequence. In the first experiment we investigated the relative salience of a visual cue and a gustatory cue in both rats and quail. In the second experiment, in which we used quail only, we controlled for two variables which, unless accounted for, would not have allowed clear-cut interpretation of the first experiment.

Forty 90-day-old male Sprague-Dawley rats and 40 adult male bobwhite quail were subjects (4) in the first experiment. All were caged individually and had free access to food throughout the experiment. At the start, both species were trained over a period of several days to drink all of their daily water from 30-ml glass Richter tubes. Water was presented at the same time each day, and the time allowed for drinking was gradually reduced to a 10-minute period. Baseline drinking was then measured for 1 week, after which experimental treatments were imposed.

On treatment day, subgroups of each species received an initial 10-minute exposure to water that was either dark blue ($N = 8$), sour ($N = 8$), or both blue and sour ($N = 24$). Water was made blue by the addition of three drops of vegetable food coloring to 100 ml of hydrochloric acid solution (0.5 ml per liter). One-half hour after removal of the distinctive fluid all subjects were injected intraperitoneally with the illness-inducing drug, cyclophosphamide. The dosage for the rats was 66 mg/kg, a dosage known to be effective for establishing one-trial aversions to distinctive tastes in the rat. We used a larger dose (132 mg/kg) for the quail, however, because exploratory use of the drug with the birds showed that this larger dose was necessary in order to produce the primary symptom of illness that rats exhibit, namely, extensive diarrhea.

TABLE 1   Means and standard deviations (S.D.) of drinking scores in all groups of both experiments from the last baseline day through the first extinction test (E_1). Probabilities (P) of differences between means of the treatment day (TD) and E_1 were calculated by the t-test for repeated measures.

Group	N	Last Baseline Day Mean (ml)	S.D.	TD Mean (ml)	S.D.	First Recovery Day Mean (ml)	S.D.	Second Recovery Day Mean (ml)	S.D.	E_1 Mean (ml)	S.D.	P
						Experiment 1						
S : S quail	8	12.9	3.16	9.1	3.24	9.8	4.49	12.6	3.75	6.0	3.77	< .05
S : S rat	8	17.8	4.60	10.6	2.31	17.6	2.04	19.0	3.16	6.2	3.99	< .02
B : B quail	8	12.4	2.52	14.1	2.83	9.5	4.50	11.4	1.90	5.1	3.66	< .01
B : B rat	8	17.4	2.71	19.6	3.70	13.1	2.60	17.6	2.27	18.1	3.71	
BS : BS quail	8	13.0	1.80	6.8	2.49	12.2	3.03	13.0	2.35	2.2	2.68	< .001
BS : BS rat	8	20.4	2.30	13.1	2.29	15.9	3.38	19.4	3.09	5.0	2.92	< .001
BS : S quail	8	13.2	3.07	6.6	3.03	13.2	4.81	12.2	2.59	7.1	3.61	
BS : S rat	8	17.9	2.90	12.0	2.24	17.6	2.53	17.8	2.17	4.5	2.96	< .001
BS : B quail	8	11.5	2.55	8.8	3.19	11.8	3.70	11.9	2.06	2.2	3.19	< .001
BS : B rat	8	18.5	3.08	12.2	3.73	15.9	1.93	17.5	2.96	12.2	4.35	
					Experiment 2, Quail Only (tinted tube)							
Drug-treated	20	14.1	2.61	13.2	3.58	9.5	3.24	11.4	3.44	7.0	3.63	< .001
Saline-treated	20	13.3	2.86	13.5	3.98	13.0	3.87	13.5	3.30	12.5	3.10	

For 2 days after treatment all subjects drank plain water at the regular 10-minute daily drinking period. This allowed them time to recover from the illness, as evidenced by remission of diarrhea and a return to baseline amounts of water consumption. Extinction tests were then begun to determine whether aversive conditioning had been established to the cues present in the water on treatment day. Five 10-minute tests were conducted, one every third day, with 2 days intervening between tests during which subjects were allowed to drink plain water to reestablish the baseline.

Animals that drank sour water on treatment day were tested with sour water (S : S); those that drank blue water on treatment day received blue water in the extinction tests (B : B). However, the 24 animals of each species that had drunk blue-sour water on treatment day were divided into three subgroups for testing. One group of each species was tested on blue-sour water (BS : BS), another on sour water (BS : S), and the third on blue water (BS : B).

Figure 1 shows a comparison of the amount of water drunk by rats and quail over five extinction trials for each of the five treatment : test conditions. Differences between mean drinking scores on treatment day and the first extinction trial (E_1) were assessed for statistical significance by the *t*-test. Results in the S : S condition show that the sour taste by itself was an effective cue for avoidance in both rat ($P < .02$) and

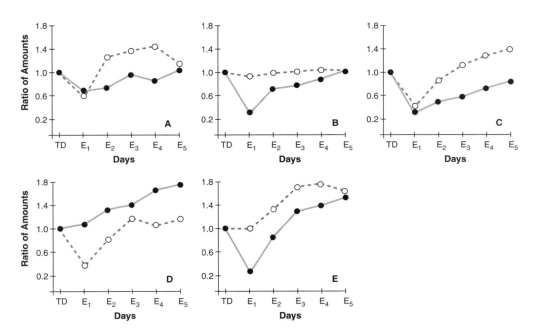

FIGURE 1 Comparison of the amount of water consumed by quail (solid lines) and rats (dashed lines) expressed as a ratio of the amount consumed on a given day to the amount consumed on treatment day (TD); E_1 through E_5 are the five extinction trials given at 3-day intervals after the single conditioning trial on TD. **(A)** Group S : S; **(B)** group B : B; **(C)** group BS : BS; **(D)** group BS : S; **(E)** group BS : B.

quail ($P < .05$). Only the quail, however, showed reduced drinking ($P < .01$) of water that was colored blue on treatment and test days (B : B). In the BS : BS condition, both species again showed significantly reduced drinking in the tests ($P < .001$).

Perhaps the most striking results were shown by the last two subgroups for which the compound cue (BS) of the treatment day conditioning trial was split for separate testing of each component. In the latter two conditions (BS : S and BS : B) rats and quail showed a remarkable difference with respect to the salience of gustatory and visual cues. When the sour element of the compound conditioning stimulus was the test cue (BS : S), rats avoided it ($P < .001$) but quail did not. On the other hand, when the blue color was the element tested (BS : B), quail avoided it ($P < .01$) but rats did not. The behavior of the quail in these split-cue tests is especially informative. Although the quail learned the aversion to taste alone (S : S condition), removal of the visual element from the compound conditioning stimulus (BS : S condition) apparently constituted such a radical change in stimulus for them that it rendered the remaining taste element ineffective. The results demonstrate, therefore, not only that quail can associate a visual cue with long-delayed illness, but also that a visual cue can be so salient as to overshadow taste when the two cues are compounded.

The most important result of this experiment is that quail were somehow able to associate blue water with a subsequent illness which we induced arbitrarily ½ hour after removal of the drinking tube. Failure of the rats used in our experiments to do so does not, of course, constitute a powerful argument that this species cannot associate a visual cue over a long delay. It is conceivable, although we think it unlikely, that rats see no difference between plain and dark blue water. In any event, Garcia and his co-workers (1) have reported much more convincing evidence than ours that rats do not utilize a visual cue in delayed-illness avoidance learning. Thus, our main concern after the first experiment was whether the results for quail were unequivocal, rather than whether rats could actually see our visual cue.

In the second experiment we attempted to answer two questions: (i) Could the quail have been relying on some subtle taste of the dyed water rather than solely upon its appearance?; and (ii) Was the effective consequence that produced aversion to blue water really the drug-induced illness, or was it the considerable trauma of being caught, handled, and injected?

Birds from each of the five earlier subgroups were assigned to one of two groups, assignment being random except for the restriction that the groups be balanced with respect to prior treatment and test conditions. Procedural details were the same as in the first experiment. On treatment day, however, both groups drank from tinted blue tubes filled with the same plain water to which they were accustomed. One group ($N = 20$) was then injected with cyclophosphamide ½ hour after drinking, whereas the other group ($N = 20$) was injected with normal saline.

Figure 2 shows the result. Birds that received the illness-inducing drug drank less from the tinted tube when they next encountered it ($P < .001$), whereas those injected with saline did not.

Although Figures 1 and 2 give a clear picture of the relative changes in drinking occasioned by treatment-day and test conditions, they give no information on the absolute amounts ingested or the degree of variability. Accordingly, means and standard

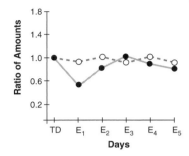

FIGURE 2   A comparison of the amount of plain water drunk from tinted tubes by drug-treated quail (solid line) and saline-treated quail (dashed line). The amount drunk is expressed as a ratio of the amount ingested on a given day to the amount consumed on treatment day (TD).

deviations are shown in Table 1 for all groups each day from the last baseline day through the first extinction test. Comparison of baseline scores with those of treatment day shows that sour water, whether blue or not, was somewhat aversive to both species at first encounter, that is, before induction of illness; blue water alone was not. The amount of plain water drunk on the two recovery days after treatment shows a return to baseline levels. Effects of the delayed-illness conditioning trial are seen best by comparing scores of treatment day with those of the first extinction test.

Despite the controls introduced in the second experiment, it could be argued that the results represent not true associative learning but only the birds' increased wariness of strange-looking fluids as a result of recent illness. However, studies now completed in our laboratory (5) show that, although such sensitization or heightened neophobia contributes to the effect, there is a significant associative learning component as well. We are confident, therefore, that at least one avian species can associate a purely visual cue with a delayed illness without mediation by means of peripheral mechanisms such as reinstated taste.

It seems reasonable to expect that this capacity will be widespread among animals whose visual systems are highly developed and whose niches demand great reliance upon vision in foraging. If so, the implications for ecology, behavior theory, and evolutionary theory are of considerable importance.

REFERENCES AND NOTES

1. J. Garcia and R. A. Koelling, *Psychonom. Sci.* **4**, 123 (1966); J. Garcia, B. K. McGowan, F. R. Ervin, R. A. Koelling, *Science* **160**, 794 (1968).
2. P. Rozin, J. Camp. *Physiol. Psychol.* **67**, 421 (1969).
3. L. P. Brower, W. N. Ryerson, L. L. Coppinger, S. C. Glazier, *Science* **161**, 1349 (1968); L. P. Brower, *Sci. Amer.* **220**, 22 (Feb. 1969).
4. We thank Dr. G. McDaniel of Auburn University for supplying the quail and Dr. P. Tavormina of Mead Johnson Research Center for experimental samples of cyclophosphamide.
5. H. C. Wilcoxon, W. B. Dragoin, P. A. Kral, in preparation.
6. This research is part of the program of the John F. Kennedy Center for Research on Education and Human Development, George Peabody College for Teachers, Nashville, Tennessee, under a Biomedical Sciences Support grant from the National Institutes of Health.

The Hunter-Gatherer Theory of Spatial Sex Differences
Proximate Factors Mediating the Female Advantage in Recall of Object Arrays

MARION EALS and IRWIN SILVERMAN

Based on their theory that sex differences in spatial abilities originated in human evolution as a function of division of labor, Silverman and Eals (1992) demonstrated in a series of studies that females consistently surpassed males in recall of locations of objects in a spatial array. The present studies were replications of the above, but with the inclusion of uncommon objects, for which subjects would not possess verbal labels. Female superiority for recall of locations of common objects as observed in Silverman and Eals was replicated across incidental and directed learning conditions. The female advantage occurred as well for uncommon objects, but only under incidental learning conditions. Conjectures are offered regarding sex differences in attentional and imagery processes that could account for this pattern of results.

The paradigm of evolutionary psychology (Tooby and Cosmides 1992) appears well suited to the topic of human spatial sex differences for several reasons. For one, male biases in spatial task performance are near universal across regions, classes, ethnic groups, ages, and virtually every other conceivable demographic variable (Gaulin and Hoffman 1988; Harris 1978; Jahoda 1980; Linn and Peterson 1985; Maccoby and Jacklin 1974; McGee 1979; Samuel 1983; Vandenberg and Kuse 1978.) Further, hormonal bases for these differences have been amply demonstrated (Kimura and Hampson 1993; Nyborg 1984; Reinish et al. 1991; Silverman and Phillips 1993). Finally, selection pressures for sex-specific spatial behaviors can be readily attributed to division of labor during the "environment of evolutionary adaptedness" (Tooby and DeVore 1987), whereby males were primarily hunters and females primarily foraged.

As described by Silverman and Eals (1992):

> Tracking and killing animals entail different kinds of spatial problems than does foraging for edible plants; thus, adaptation would have favored diverse spatial skills between sexes throughout much of their evolutionary history. The cognitive mechanisms of contemporary homo sapiens appear to reflect these differences, insofar as the various spatial measures showing male bias (e.g. mental rotations, map reading,

maze learning) correspond to attributes that would enable successful hunting. Essentially, these attributes comprise the abilities to orient oneself in relation to objects or places, in view or conceptualized across distances, and to perform the mental transformations necessary to maintain accurate orientations during movement. This would enable the pursuit of prey animals across unfamiliar territory and, also, accurate placement of projectiles to kill or stun the quarry (pp. 514–15).

Previous writers have demonstrated a correlation between scores on male-biased spatial tests and skills related to hunting (Jardine and Martin 1983; Kolakowski and Molina 1974). Silverman and Eals extended this analysis, however, contending that if the disposition for the development of specific spatial attributes evolved in the male in conjunction with hunting, females may have developed parallel spatial specializations associated with foraging.

Successful foraging, Silverman and Eals surmised, would require locating food sources within complex arrays of vegetation and finding them again in ensuing growing seasons. This would involve:

> the recognition and recall of spatial configurations of objects; that is, the capacity to rapidly learn and remember the contents of object arrays and the spatial relationships of the objects to one another. Foraging success would also be increased by peripheral perception and incidental memory for objects and their locations, inasmuch as this would allow one to assimilate such information non-purposively, while walking about or carrying out other tasks (p. 489).

Based on these notions, Silverman and Eals compared sexes on the ability to learn contents and spatial configurations of object arrays, using various techniques. In one, developed for group administration, subjects were presented with drawings of common objects in an array and asked to examine them for one minute. Other studies used actual objects. In these studies subjects were left alone for two minutes in a small, cubicle-type room, outfitted as a graduate student office, containing a variety of work-related and personal items. In some conditions they were instructed to try to learn the objects in the room and their locations (directed learning); in others they were unaware that their time in the room was related to the study (incidental learning). Dependent variables in these studies comprised memory for items (object memory) and their locations (location memory), assessed independently, using both recall and recognition as performance criteria. Results were that females' scores consistently, significantly exceeded those of males across all studies.

One question raised by Silverman and Eals about their findings was whether females' advantages in recall of object arrays was based on their superior verbal skills; specifically, their greater capacity to recall object names (Maccoby and Jacklin 1974). It was suggested that if this were the case, it may be speculated that female verbal superiority; at least in its rudimentary form, emerged also in human evolution as a function of its adaptive value for division of labor. Similar to spatial differences, verbal sex differences are near universal and show hormonal correlates (Burstien, Bank, and Jarvick 1980). Nevertheless, there has been no prior attempt to explore their ultimate causation.

The present research was designed to assess whether verbal processes could account for the female spatial specializations revealed by Silverman and Eals. Their original studies were repeated with the inclusion of uncommon objects; that is, items for which subjects would not possess verbal labels. The primary question of these studies was whether the female advantages in object and location recall would be maintained under this condition.

STUDY ONE

The first study used the group testing procedure of Silverman and Eals, but with drawings of uncommon rather than common objects. Subjects for this study were volunteers, solicited from undergraduate courses and administered the test in groups of various sizes.

As in Silverman and Eals' study, subjects were first shown the stimulus array (Figure 1) for one minute and were asked to "examine the objects." Then they were presented with the array depicted in Figure 2, which contained the same objects in the same locations as the stimulus array, but with a number of objects added. They were instructed to put a cross through all of the objects that were not in the original array and were told they would be allowed one minute and would be penalized for items incorrectly crossed. (One point was given for each item correctly crossed and, to correct for guessing, a deduction of .31 was made for each item incorrectly crossed, based on the proportion of items added.) This score served as the measure of object memory.

Finally, subjects received the array shown in Figure 3, comprising the same items as the stimulus array but with some moved to new locations. Subjects were asked to put a cross through the objects that had been moved and circle the objects that had not, and were informed that they would have a minute for this task as well. A point was scored for each correct response and, in the few cases of items left blank, a half point was given to compensate for guessing. This was the measure of location memory.

Hypotheses were that females would show significantly higher scores for both object and location memory, as found by Silverman and Eals with familiar objects.

Results are shown in Table 1. There was a nonsignificant trend favoring females for object memory and a significant difference in the same direction for location memory.

TABLE 1   Mean Object Memory and Location Memory Scores, by Sex, for Study One

	N	Mean	SD	*t* Value	Significance (2-Tail)
Object Recall					
Females	42	4.17	2.79	1.40	.167
Males	41	3.94	2.16		
Location Recall					
Females	42	26.38	3.00	2.99	.004
Males	41	24.32	3.29		

FIGURE 1 The stimulus array for study one.

FIGURE 2 The stimulus array with items added.

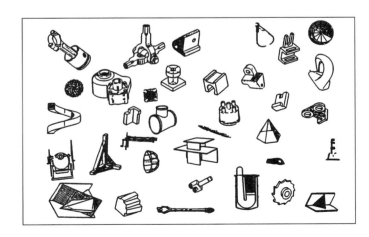

FIGURE 3 The stimulus array with items moved.

STUDY TWO

Study two was designed to replicate the studies of Silverman and Eals with actual objects, but with the inclusion of unfamiliar items. Subjects were 40 male and 40 female paid volunteer undergraduates from York University, solicited for an ambiguously labeled experiment. Subjects were administered the procedures individually.

The study used both directed and incidental learning conditions. For both conditions, subjects were met at the laboratory where they were encouraged to leave their coats and any books and other materials they were carrying. Then they were taken to a six by eight foot, cubicle-type office nearby (the stimulus room).

The stimulus room was outfitted as a typical graduate student office, containing a variety of common work related and personal items and located in an aisle of such offices. Interspersed among the common items, however, were the same number of unusual items, either found or specially constructed for the study. Figure 4 shows two views from the stimulus room, illustrating the manner in which common and uncommon items were dispersed.

For the incidental learning condition, the experimenter asked subjects to wait in the room for several minutes while he completed preparations in the laboratory for the study in which they were to participate. If the subject asked about the unusual items, the experimenter said that they were being used for a different study. Exit interviews following the research session indicated that no subjects were suspicious that they would be tested for recall of the room contents.

The experimenter returned for the subject in precisely two minutes and, when they re-entered the laboratory, explained that the actual purpose of the study was to assess, "how people naturally process their environments." Subjects were then administered the measures of object and location memory, described below.

The directed learning condition was similar in procedure, except that when subjects were taken to the stimulus room they were told that they would have two minutes to "try to memorize as many objects in the room as possible and their approximate locations."

A

B

FIGURE 4   Two views of the stimulus room for study two, showing arrangements of common and uncommon objects.

DEPENDENT VARIABLE MEASURES

Measures of object and location memory were identical for incidental and directed learning conditions.

For object memory, tested first, subjects were shown a series of cards containing either the names of common objects or drawings of uncommon objects. Half the items in each category had been present in the stimulus room, and subjects were required to indicate which items were and which items were not. Subjects were scored in terms of percentages of objects correctly designated as being either in or out of the room, separately for common and uncommon items.

For the measures of location memory, subjects were given a schematic drawing of the stimulus room divided into seven numbered areas. They were shown another series of cards depicting either common or uncommon objects in the same manner as above, but this series contained only items that had been in the room. Subjects were instructed to mark the number of the area that contained each item. Scores were again recorded in terms of percentages correct, separately for common and uncommon items.

DATA ANALYSES AND HYPOTHESES

The data for common and uncommon objects were analyzed in separate 2×2 MANOVAs for sex and condition, with object and location memory as dependent variables. The analyses for common objects was intended to replicate the original findings. Hypotheses were that females' scores for object and location memory would significantly exceed males' across directed and incidental learning conditions. The same hypotheses applied to data for uncommon objects.

RESULTS

Tables 2 and 3 present the findings, respectively, for common and uncommon objects.

Table 2 reveals a nonsignificant trend for higher female object memory scores across incidental and directed learning conditions, and a significant difference in the same direction for location memory. There were no interaction effects.

Table 3 reveals a more complex pattern of results. There were no main effects of sex for either object or location memory, but there were interactions between sex and learning condition approaching significance at $p = .07$ for object memory and reaching significance at $p < .05$ for location memory. In both cases, females surpassed males in the incidental learning condition and the reverse occurred for directed learning. In terms of simple effects, significance was achieved for male superiority in object memory in the directed learning condition ($t = 2.06; p < .05$) and for female superiority in location memory in the incidental learning condition ($t = 2.05; p < .05$).

CONCLUSIONS AND DISCUSSION

Hypotheses for study one were substantially, though not wholly, supported. The group test based on drawings of uncommon objects showed the same significant sex difference in location memory favoring females as did the same test with common ob-

TABLE 2   Mean Percentage Object and Location Memory Scores for Common Objects in Study Two by Sex and Incidental vs. Directed Learning Conditions

Condition		Males			Females	
		Mean	SD		Mean	SD
Object Memory						
Incidental		77.50	(13.18)		82.77	(19.15)
Directed		91.94	(10.27)		94.72	(8.91)
	F tests:	Sex	1.79	NS		
		Condition	19.20	$p < .001$		
		Interaction	.17	NS		
Location Memory						
Incidental		45.50	(21.36)		62.31	(27.33)
Directed		65.00	(20.19)		85.00	(13.31)
	F tests:	Sex	15.70	$p < .001$		
		Condition	20.38	$p < .001$		
		Interaction	.11	NS		

Ns = 20 for each sex, in each condition: Total = 80

jects used by Silverman and Eals. Sex differences for object memory, however, also favored females but did not achieve significance.

The same pattern was obtained for common objects in study two; the stimulus room study. Female scores for location memory across learning conditions were significantly higher, replicating Silverman and Eals. Sex differences were in the same direction for object memory, but at a nonsignificant level. Again, hypotheses received qualified support.

A diverse trend was observed for uncommon objects in study two. For object memory scores, the only significant difference was contrary to the hypotheses; male scores were higher in the directed learning condition. Results for location memory, on the other hand, provided partial support for the hypotheses; females were significantly higher in the incidental learning condition only.

In considering the entire pattern of results, it is important to note that location memory scores in the group test were considered to represent incidental learning. As Silverman and Eals (1992, p. 541) indicated, subjects were instructed solely to "examine the objects." Hence, they probably surmised they would be tested for how many items they recalled, but not for item locations. Thus, the most parsimonious interpretation incorporating all of the data is that for unfamiliar objects, the female advantage occurs solely for location memory in incidental learning conditions.

This interpretation supports the notion that the sex factor in location memory is more accurately conceived as a difference in perceptual style rather than learning ability (Silverman and Eals 1992, p. 545). Based on their ancestral roles as food gatherers, keepers of the habitat, and caretakers of the young, the attentional styles of females may have evolved as more inclusive of the environment than males. Further, the capacity of females to recall locations of objects without verbal references may sug-

TABLE 3   Mean Percentage Object and Location Memory Scores for Uncommon Objects in Study Two by Sex and Incidental vs. Directed Learning Conditions

		Males			Females	
Condition		*Mean*	*SD*		*Mean*	*SD*
Object Memory						
Incidental		48.97	(8.60)		51.03	(13.06)
Directed		69.56	(11.18)		62.79	(9.51)
	F tests:	Sex	.96	NS		
		Condition	45.52	$p < .001$		
		Interaction	3.39	$p < .07$		
Location Memory						
Incidental		20.39	(8.19)		27.50	(11.72)
Directed		33.08	(10.40)		30.58	(12.07)
	F tests:	Sex	.93	NS		
		Condition	10.85	$p < .001$		
		Interaction	4.04	$p < .05$		

Ns = 20 for each sex, in each condition: Total = 80

gest that they continuously record details of their environments through some imaging process akin to eidetic imagery. Thus, they are able to retrieve a comprehensive image of a previous physical surrounding without having attempted to remember it or even given it particular conscious attention.

Both of these proposed sex differences may explain recent findings that females show greater memory for and use of physical landmarks in spatial mapping and route learning tasks; that is, tasks requiring the plotting or recall of directions between two points in space (Bever 1992; Galea and Kimura 1993; Miller and Santoni 1986).

It seems feasible, however, that these attributes would also contribute to the female advantage for location memory in directed learning conditions, as demonstrated for common objects in Silverman and Eals and in the present study two. Thus, it remains problematic as to why the female bias did not occur as well for directed learning of uncommon objects. Perhaps subjects were inclined to adopt a particular strategy when consciously attempting to learn uncommon objects; for example, assigning verbal labels to them, which interfered with females' spontaneous attentional and imaging processes. This may also account for the unexpected lower female object memory scores for uncommon objects under the directed learning condition.

An alternative explanation of greater female recall of uncommon objects in incidental learning conditions is that they are more naturally curious about novel things and tended to examine them more closely. If this occurred, however, females would have had less opportunity in the stimulus room study to examine common objects, whereas their scores were superior to males' for these as well.

In sum, Silverman and Eals' findings were generally replicated in the present studies, providing additional support for their hunter-gatherer model of spatial sex differences. The present studies demonstrated as well that in the case of incidental location learning, which may be regarded as the most salient measure of foraging related spatial behaviors, the female advantage occurs independently of verbal skills. The various proposed interpretations of these data can lead to novel investigations of sex differences in attentional styles and imaging processes, and may provide an evolutionarily based explanation for differences between sexes in route learning and spatial mapping strategies.

REFERENCES

Bever, T. The logical and extrinsic sources of modularity. In *Modularity and Constraints in Language and Cognition,* M. Gunnar and M. Maratsos (Eds.). Vol. 25 of Minnesota Symposia on Child Psychology. Hillsdale: Lawrence Erlbaum, 1992, pp. 179–212.

Burstien, B., Bank, L., and Jarvick, L.F. Sex differences in cognitive functioning: Evidence, determinants, implications. *Human Development* 23: 299–313, 1980.

Galea, L.A.M., and Kimura, D. Sex differences in route learning. *Personality and Individual Differences* 14:53–65, 1993.

Gaulin, S.J.C., and Hoffman, H.A. Evolution and development of sex differences in spatial ability. In *Human Reproductive Behavior: A Darwinian Perspective,* L. Betzig, M.B. Mulder and P. Turke (Eds.). Cambridge: Cambridge University Press, 1988, pp. 129–152.

Harris, L.J. Sex differences in spatial ability: possible environmental, genetic and neurological factors. In *Asymmetric Function of the Brain,* Kinsbourn, M. (Ed.). Cambridge: Cambridge University Press, 1978, pp. 465–522.

Jahoda, G. Sex and ethnic differences on a spatial-perceptual task: Some hypotheses tested. *British Journal of Psychology* 71:425–431, 1980.

Jardine, R., and Martin, N.G. Spatial ability and throwing accuracy. *Behavior Genetics,* 13:331–340, 1983.

Kimura, D., and Hampson, E. Neural and hormonal mechanisms mediating sex differences in cognition. In *Biological Approaches to the Study of Human Intelligence,* P.A. Vernon (Ed.). New Jersey: ABLEX Publishers, 1993, pp. 375–397.

Kolakowski, D., and Molina, R.M. Spatial ability, throwing accuracy and man's hunting heritage. *Nature* 251:410–412, 1974.

Linn, M.C., and Peterson, A.C. Emergence and characterization of sex differences in spatial ability a meta-analysis. *Child Development* 56:1479–1498, 1985.

Maccoby, E.E., and Jacklin, C.N. *Psychology of Sex Differences.* Stanford: Stanford University Press, 1974.

McGee, M.G. Human spatial abilities: psychometric studies and environmental, genetic, hormonal and neurological influences. *Psychological Bulletin* 80:889–918, 1979.

Miller, L.K., and Santoni, V. Sex differences in spatial abilities: strategic and experiential correlates. *Acta Psychologica* 62:225–235, 1986.

Nyborg H. Performance and intelligence in hormonally different groups. *In Sex Differences in the Brain: Progress in Brain Research, vol. 61,* G.D. De Vries, J.P.C. DeBruin, H.B.M. Uylings, M.A. Corner (Eds.). Amsterdam: Elsevier, 1984, pp. 491–508.

Reinish, J., Ziemba-Davis, M., and Saunders, S. Hormonal contributions to sexually dimorphic behavioral development in humans. *Psychoneuroendocrinology* 16:213–278, 1991.

Samuel, W. Sex differences in spatial ability reflected in performance on I.Q. sub-tests by black or white examinees. *Personality and Individual Differences* 4:219–221, 1983.

Silverman, I., and Eals, M. Sex differences in spatial abilities: evolutionary theory and data. In *The Adapted Mind: Evolutionary Psychology and the Generation of Culture,* J. Barkow, L. Cosmides, and J. Tooby (Eds.). New York: Oxford University Press, 1992, pp. 487–503.

Silverman, I., and Phillips, K. Effects of estrogen changes during the menstrual cycle on spatial performance. *Ethology and Sociobiology* 14: 257–270, 1993.

Tooby J., and Cosmides, L. The psychological foundations of culture. In *The Adapted Mind: Evolutionary Psychology and the Generation of Culture,* J. Barkow, L. Cosmides, and J. Tooby (Eds.). New York: Oxford University Press, 1992, pp. 19–136.

Tooby J., and DeVore, I. The reconstruction of hominid behavioral evolution through strategic modeling. In *The Evolution of Human Behavior: Primate Models,* W.G. Kinzey (Ed.). SUNY Press, New York: 1987.

Vandenberg, S.G., and Kuse, A.R. Mental rotations: a group test of three-dimensional spatial visualization. *Perceptual and Motor Skills* 47:599–604, 1978.

Cross-Cultural Evidence of Cognitive Adaptations for Social Exchange among the Shiwiar of Ecuadorian Amazonia

LAWRENCE S. SUGIYAMA, JOHN TOOBY,
AND LEDA COSMIDES

On the basis of evolutionary game theory, it was hypothesized that humans have an evolved cognitive specialization for reasoning about social exchange, including a subroutine for detecting cheaters. This hypothesis led to a specific prediction: Although humans are known to be poor at detecting potential violations of conditional rules in general, they should nevertheless detect them easily when the rule involves social exchange and looking for violations corresponds to looking for cheaters. This prediction was subsequently confirmed by numerous tests. Evolutionary analyses further predict that: (i) in humans, complex adaptations will be distributed in a species-typical fashion; and (ii) aspects of cognitive organization relevant to performing the evolved function of an adaptation should be more buffered against environmental and cultural variation than function-irrelevant aspects. Here we report experiments testing whether social exchange reasoning exhibits these properties of adaptations. Existing tests of conditional reasoning were adapted for nonliterate experimental subjects and were administered to Shiwiar hunter–horticulturalists of the Ecuadorian Amazon. As predicted, Shiwiar subjects were as highly proficient at cheater detection as subjects from developed nations. Indeed, the frequency of cheater-relevant choices among Shiwiar hunter–horticulturalists was indistinguishable from that of Harvard undergraduates. Also as predicted, cultural variation was confined to those aspects of reasoning that are irrelevant to social exchange algorithms functioning as an evolutionarily stable strategy. Finally, Shiwiar subjects displayed the same low performance on descriptive conditionals as subjects from developed nations. Taken together, these findings support the hypotheses that social exchange algorithms are species-typical and that their evolutionarily stable strategy (ESS)-relevant subroutines are developmentally buffered against cultural variation.

reciprocation	cooperation	economics
game theory	evolutionary psychology	

From L. S. Sugiyama, J. Tooby, and L. Cosmides, "Cross-cultural evidence of cognitive adaptations for social exchange among the Shiwiar of Ecuadorian Amazonia," *Proceedings of the National Academy of Sciences, 99* (2002): 11537–11542. Reprinted with permission of the authors.

Although zoologically rare, social exchange has evolved in a variety of species, from vampire bats to baboons, indicating that some species have evolved the adaptations necessary for engaging in this behavior whereas others have not (1, 2). Evidence that social exchange behavior has been an ancient and enduring characteristic of our own species can be found throughout the ethnographic record, and both paleoanthropological research and its presence in chimpanzees suggest that this particular form of social interaction may be older than the genus *Homo* (3–8). Selection pressures favoring social exchange exist whenever one organism (the provisioner) can change the behavior of a target organism to the provisioner's advantage by making the target's receipt of a provisioned benefit *conditional* on the target acting in a required manner. This mutual provisioning of benefits, each conditional on the other's compliance, is what is meant by social exchange or reciprocation (9, 10).

Evolutionary biologists have shown through game-theoretic techniques that adaptations for social exchange can be favored and stably maintained by natural selection, provided they include design features that (*i*) enable them to detect cheaters (i.e., those who do not comply or reciprocate), and (*ii*) cause them to channel future benefits to reciprocators, not cheaters[1] (11–14). These analyses prompted the hypothesis that the human neurocognitive architecture includes *social contract algorithms:* a set of circuits that were specialized by selection for solving the intricate computational problems inherent in adaptively engaging in social exchange behavior. Among these is a subroutine for cheater detection (9, 15, 16).

A *social contract* specifies a situation in which an individual must satisfy a requirement of some kind (often at some cost to him- or herself), in order to be eligible to receive a benefit from another individual or group. Cheating is a violation of a social contract in which the benefit is illicitly taken (i.e., without satisfying the requirement upon which provision of that benefit was made conditional) (9, 15, 16).

Conditional Reasoning

Because conditionally delivered behavior requires conditional reasoning for its regulation, methods drawn from the study of conditional reasoning have been used to conduct a series of experiments testing for the presence of social contract algorithms and their predicted properties. The hypothesis that the brain contains social contract algorithms (the *adaptive specialization hypothesis*) predicts a sharply enhanced ability to reason adaptively about conditional rules when those rules specify a social exchange. The null hypothesis is that there is nothing specialized in the brain for social exchange: This hypothesis predicts no enhanced conditional reasoning performance specifically triggered by social exchanges as compared with other contents.

The Wason selection task (17–19) is a test of conditional reasoning in which subjects are asked to identify possible violations of a conditional rule of the form *If P then Q* (see Figure 1a). As predicted by the adaptive specialization hypothesis, when the conditional expresses a social contract and detecting a violation corresponds to detecting a cheater, subjects perform very well—65–80% of subjects answer correctly (15, 16, 20–24). In contrast, the hypothesis that high performance on social exchange conditionals is a byproduct of a general cognitive ability to reason well about all conditionals has been repeatedly falsified: A large literature shows that people are

a General Structure of a Descriptive Problem

The following rule holds: If **P** then **Q**.

The cards below have information about four situations. Each card represents one situation. One side of a card tells whether *P* happened, and the other side of the card tells whether *Q* happened. Indicate only those card(s) you definitely need to turn over to see if any of these situations violate the rule.

b General Structure of a Social Contract Problem

The following rule holds:

standard form:
  If you take the **benefit,** then you satisfy the **requirement.**

switched form:
  If you satisfy the **requirement,** then you take the **benefit.**

  If   **P**   then   **Q**

The cards below have information about four people. Each card represents one person. One side of a card tells whether a person accepted the benefit, and the other side of the card tells whether that person satisfied the requirement. Indicate only those card(s) you definitely need to turn over to see if any of these people are violating the rule.

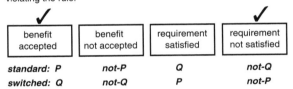

FIGURE 1   The Wason selection task. The conditional rule (If *P* then *Q*) always has specific content (see *Methods* for examples). **(a)** The general structure of the task in logical terms. Check marks indicate the logically correct card choices. **(b)** The general structure of the task when the content of the conditional rule expresses a social contract. It can be translated into either logical terms (*P*s and *Q*s) or social contract terms (benefits and requirements). Here, check marks indicate the correct card choices if one is looking for cheaters. The benefit term appears in the antecedent (*P*) in the standard form, and in the consequent (*Q*) in the switched form.

very poor at detecting violations of conditional rules when the conditional describes almost any other state of the world. A correct response (*P and not-Q*) on such rules is typically elicited from only 5–30% of subjects tested (15–19). People reason poorly even about conditionals that are almost identical to social contracts, but that lack even one of their key defining features (15, 16, 20–24).

Variants of the null hypothesis—that people's facility at cheater detection is a byproduct of some more general cognitive ability—have been empirically tested in many ways (15, 16, 20–26). For example, the accompanying article (25) reports that focal brain damage can selectively impair social exchange reasoning while leaving intact other cognitive abilities (including conditional reasoning about closely parallel rules). This discovery provides support for the hypothesis that social exchange reasoning is an adaptive specialization, rather than the expression of some more general cognitive ability.[2] Similarly, it has been shown that cheater detection is not a byproduct or special case of the activation of logical reasoning (15, 16, 20–23). As in the experiments reported here, a generic social contract can be expressed in a number of ways: e.g., "If you take the benefit, then you (must) satisfy the requirement" (standard form) or "If you satisfy the requirement, then you (may) take the benefit" (switched form). Subjects routinely check for cheating by choosing the cards that represent a person who has accepted the benefit and a person who has not satisfied the requirement, regardless of the logical category these choices fall into. Specifically, by detecting cheaters, subjects produce an adaptively correct response that incidentally corresponds to the logically correct answer (*P and not-Q*) on standard social contracts, but that corresponds to a logically incorrect answer (*Q and not-P*) on switched social contracts (15, 16, 20–23). (See Figure 1*b*).

Ontogeny and the Logic of Cross-Cultural Tests

If the algorithms that produce social exchange reasoning are an evolved adaptation, their development should be buffered against disruption by cultural or environmental variability, with acquisition caused by mechanisms selected for that function (as in the case of language[3]) (27–30). In contrast, the null hypothesis is that all apparent cognitive specializations are the product of a few general-purpose, content-independent acquisition processes acted on during ontogenesis by differentiated local cultural and physical environments (31, 32)[4]. Contrary to the predictions of this general-purpose acquisition hypothesis, performance on conditional reasoning problems that do not involve social contracts (or other evolutionarily significant domains) remains at low levels even when the rules tested are culturally familiar[5] (15–19), or when subjects are trained, taught logic, or given incentives to perform well (17–19, 33). Even more striking, however, is that, contrary to the general-purpose acquisition hypothesis, subjects perform just as well on their very first exposure to culturally unfamiliar social contracts as they do on culturally familiar ones, so that there is no evidence for improvement even with a lifetime of exposure (15, 16, 20–24).

Still, the key divergence between the two explanations involves the predicted distribution of specialized reasoning skills or abilities across the human species (20, 21). Social contract algorithms are predicted to be cross-culturally universal, because complex adaptations in long-lived species with open population structures, such as humans, will almost always be distributed in a species-typical fashion (34).[6] Similarly, selection favors buffering the functional aspects of adaptations against environmental disruption—a selection pressure that is absent from functionally irrelevant aspects of adaptations, which are therefore more free to vary (34). In contrast, skills acquired through more general-purpose inductive processes are distributed across cultures in a more variable fashion: this is true even when adaptations play some part in building them [e.g., counting; lexically distinguishing yellow from black, white, and red; (35–39)[7]]. If social exchange reasoning is acquired by means of more general-purpose processes, then it might be absent from many cultures, its features might vary in widely divergent settings, and, in particular, they need not exhibit the narrow properties necessary for it to constitute an evolutionarily stable strategy (ESS). Indeed, under the null hypothesis there is no reason to expect ESS-relevant aspects of social exchange reasoning to be less variable than ESS-irrelevant ones, because general-purpose acquisition machinery has not been designed to distinguish between them.

Although cognitive experiments supporting the hypothesis that there is a reasoning specialization for cheater detection have been conducted in a number of different societies, these sites were all in developed nations (e.g., U.S., Hong Kong, U.K., Germany), and all involved literate subjects (20–24, 31). Although each instance is informative, the evidence for species-typicality gains strength in proportion to the diversity of subject populations tested, and cannot be considered strong if the only populations tested are from modern market economies. For this reason, we chose as our study population the Shiwiar of Ecuadorian Amazonia, a group of hunter–horticulturalists whose way of life is as different from life in industrialized societies as any that presently exists, and one that in several key respects more closely reflects the kind of social environment in which humans evolved. The focus of research was to test whether the Shiwiar would exhibit the same subtle patterns of reasoning as all other tested populations do, despite major differences in cultural, social, and physical environments.

METHODS

Shiwiar Participants

Shiwiar in the study area have no everyday direct contact with outsiders (see *Appendix*). The rivers the Shiwiar live along become unnavigable long before they reach the frontiers of colonization, and there are no roads. They depend on hunting (often with blowguns), fishing, gardening, and foraging for their livelihood. Relatively few Shiwiar speak Spanish, and Shiwiar, a non-Indo-European language, is the language of daily life. Traditional ties of kinship and affinity dominate social relationships mediated by gossip, witchcraft, and the threat or use of violence, and the Shiwiar continue to interpret the world through a culturally distinctive worldview. Although it is impossible now to find a group of people who are not subject to some influence from the industrialized world, Shiwiar in the study villages are at the far end of this spectrum. To the extent that they have been influenced by the outside world, it has been largely a material influence, such as the gradual adoption of some nonindigenous crops, and the acquisition of various tools and artifacts.

Stimuli and Procedures

Figure 2 depicts how we modified the Wason task for use with nonliterate subjects (see *Appendix*). Each subject was presented with a descriptive problem, a standard social exchange problem, and a switched social exchange problem. The rules were embedded in a story context. All of the problems had unfamiliar content and study participants had no direct or prior experience with the rules. The order of the problems was reversed for half of the subjects.

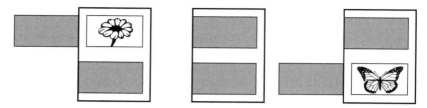

FIGURE 2 Wason selection task modified for nonliterate subjects: Schematic representation of the "cards." Both doors are closed on the middle card. Opening the top door reveals a photo representing either a true or false antecedent (e.g., the presence of a particular flower). Opening the bottom door reveals a photo representing either a true or false consequent (e.g., the presence of a butterfly).

PREDICTIONS

For well-established reasons (40, 41), experimentation under field conditions injects higher levels of error variance into results than are obtainable under well-controlled laboratory conditions.[8] Nevertheless, if social contract algorithms are an evolved adaptation, and hence a reliably developing species-typical feature of the human neurocognitive architecture, then:

(*i*) Shiwiar subjects should show the same strong propensity to select the cards that correspond to detecting cheaters as subjects do in developed nations.

(*ii*) To the extent that cultural variation is exhibited, it should be differentially found in card selections that are irrelevant to performing the function of the adaptation—that is, to detecting cheaters. Only cheater-detecting choices reflect the operation of evolved algorithms necessary to make social exchange an evolutionarily stable strategy, and so only those are predicted to be developmentally buffered against cultural variation and other sources of perturbation.

(*iii*) For social contracts, social exchange categories (benefit accepted/requirement met) are hypothesized to be a deeper representational format than logical categories (antecedent = P/consequent = Q). For these problems, Shiwiar card choices should parallel each other when the cards are analyzed in terms of their role in social exchanges, but not when analyzed in terms of their logical role in the propositional calculus (which differs for the standard and switched forms).

RESULTS

If mechanisms specialized for cheater detection are universal features of the human cognitive architecture, then one would expect Shiwiar to say "yes" to the *benefit accepted* and *requirement not satisfied* cards. Errors of omission—failing to choose either of these cards—would suggest a failure to understand what events are relevant to detecting cheaters, and would therefore be very damaging to the hypothesis. Such errors were rare. The *benefit accepted* card was chosen by 86% of subjects on both social contracts (chance = 50%; $p = 0.00013$). The *requirement not satisfied* card was chosen by 86% of subjects for the standard social contract ($p = 0.00013$), and by 81%

for the switched social contract ($p = 0.0011$). These figures are almost identical to those from a comparable study done at Harvard (15, 16): 75–92% of the Harvard undergraduates tested chose the cheater-relevant cards in response to parallel problems (see Figure 3[9]). Shiwiar made more correct cheater detection selections in two cases, Harvard students in the other two, and the average difference between these populations in cheater detection card choices was just 1 percentage point, favoring the Shiwiar.

In other words, like Harvard undergraduates, Shiwiar subjects almost always chose the cards necessary for detecting cheaters. This result was not because of a nonspecific tendency to choose all cards. Although the surface content of the three problems differs, all express conditional rules of the form *If P then Q*. Therefore, card choices can be classified by *logical* category, and compared across problems (e.g., *P* is cheater relevant for a standard social contract, but not for a switched one; see Figure 1, Table 1). Holding logical category constant, each card in a social contract was chosen significantly more often when it was relevant to cheater detection than when it was not

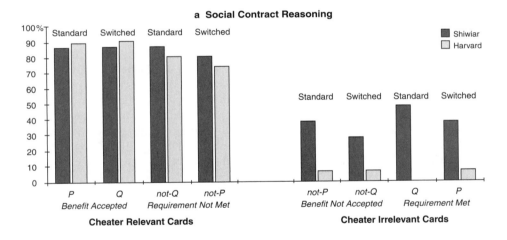

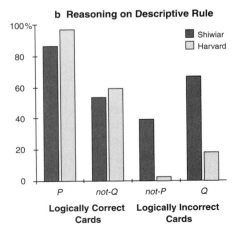

FIGURE 3   Individual card selections: Comparison of the performance of Shiwiar subjects with that of Harvard undergraduates. (**a**) Performance on social contracts. (**b**) Performance on descriptive rules.

TABLE 1   For social contracts (SC), frequency of card choices follows social contract category, not logical category; Shiwiar subjects ($n = 21$)

Card Category	Standard SC	Switched SC	Descriptive
Social contract category			
Benefit accepted	18	18	
Benefit not accepted	8	6	
Requirement met	10	8	
Requirement not met	18	17	
Logical category			
P	18	8	18
Not-P	8	17	8
Q	10	18	14
Not-Q	18	6	11

Cheater-relevant cards: *Benefit accepted* corresponds to *P* for standard version, *Q* for switched. *Requirement not met* corresponds to *not-Q* for standard version, *not-P* for switched.

(P: 86% vs. 38%; *not-P*: 81% vs. 38%; Q: 86% vs. 48%; *not-Q*: 86% vs. 29%; range of values: $0.0045 > p > 0.00018$; $0.69 > r > 0.54$[10]). Additionally, for both social contracts, the number of subjects choosing cheater irrelevant cards (*benefit not accepted*; *requirement satisfied*) was below chance, although not always significantly so (see Table 1[11]). In every case, however, selection frequencies were in the predicted direction (above 50% for cheater-relevant cards and below 50% for cheater-irrelevant cards). The probability of obtaining this pattern by chance alone is only 1 in 256 ($2^{-8} = 0.004$).

Thus cheater-relevant cards were overwhelmingly and selectively chosen by Shiwiar subjects. When they made errors, these were disproportionately on cards irrelevant to cheater detection, through sometimes exhibiting an interest in additional cards—errors of curiosity. As predicted by the hypothesis that functionally important aspects of an adaptive specialization should be more buffered against disruption, the Harvard and Shiwiar subjects did not differ in their propensity to choose ESS-relevant, cheater-detection cards. Also as predicted, these populations differed more in their propensity to choose ESS-irrelevant cards than ESS-relevant ones: the magnitude of this difference was more than 6 times greater for ESS-irrelevant cards.

We also scored responses by using the most stringent scoring criterion: an answer was counted as correct only if the subject chose the two necessary cards *and no others*. Although this very strict scoring criterion penalizes errors of curiosity [and, given task pragmatics, non-Western subjects (40)[k]], it is nevertheless relevant: Finding that this exact pattern is the modal response, despite error variance due to task pragmatics, would further militate against the hypothesis that Shiwiar are choosing the correct cheater-detection cards merely because of an indiscriminate interest in all cards. In contrast, if Shiwiar construe the world in a way that is incommensurate with Western conceptions, or have reasoning mechanisms that embody very different principles, or even answer randomly, then there is no reason to expect the stringent pattern to occur more often than chance.[12]

Sixty-two percent of Shiwiar subjects produced this pattern in response to at least one of the two social contracts (chance = 12%; $p = 2.0 \times 10^{-7}$, $h' = 1.106$). It was also the modal response if one considers each social contract problem individually: this pattern was elicited from 47.6% of Shiwiar subjects for the switched social contract and from 33.3% for the standard one (chance = 6.25%[13]). Each of these proportions is much higher than chance, and the effect sizes are large by conventional standards ($p = 1.54 \times 10^{-6}$, $h' = 1.018$; $p = 0.00044$, $h' = 0.726$, respectively).

Another way of assaying for the presence of domain-specific social contract algorithms is to see whether the social contracts elicited a different pattern of responses than the descriptive problem. Table 1 shows that the response profile for the descriptive problem does not match that for either social contract: Like American subjects, Shiwiar treat descriptive rules differently from social contracts. The same is true if one compares responses by using the stringent scoring criteria. No Shiwiar answered *Q and not-P* to the descriptive problem, but 47.6% produced this otherwise unusual pattern in response to the switched social contract ($t^* = 4.26$, $p < 0.00025$, $r = 0.69$). *P and not-Q*, the logically correct response for a descriptive problem, is also the correct cheater-detection response for a standard social contract. Yet more Shiwiar subjects gave this response to the standard social contract than to the descriptive problem (33.3% vs. 14.3%, $t^* = 1.71$, $p = 0.052$, $r = 0.38$[14]). By conventional standards, the first effect size (0.69) is large and the second (0.38) is medium; these Shiwiar effect sizes are not significantly different from those for the Harvard students.[15] [The descriptive problem did not elicit the logically correct answer (*P and not-Q*) more often than chance (14.3%, $p = 0.14$), and it elicited *Q and not-P* less often than chance (0%; $p < 0.05$)[16].]

Most importantly, the response profiles in Table 1 reveal which problems the Shiwiar were construing as similar, and what dimensions they were using to do so. When sorted by social contract category (i.e., benefits and requirements), the two social contracts elicited response profiles that are almost identical. But when sorted by logical category, the selection frequencies for standard and switched social contracts are notably at variance with one another (and neither profile matches the descriptive rule). This means (*i*) Shiwiar minds construed the two social contract problems as similar to each other and different from the descriptive problem, and (*ii*) for social contract problems, a social contract categorization scheme captures dimensions that are psychologically real for Shiwiar subjects, whereas a logical categorization scheme does not. The same result obtains for the Harvard undergraduates (15, 16).

CONCLUSIONS

The function of a cheater-detection subroutine is to draw attention to potential cheaters, regardless of whatever else in the situation might be of interest. If this subroutine is a reliably developing, species-typical feature of the human mind, then Shiwiar should overwhelmingly choose the cards necessary for detecting cheaters on social contracts. They did. Indeed, Shiwiar hunter–horticulturalists and Harvard undergraduates had identical response profiles for these ESS-relevant cards.

This finding is consistent with the prediction that responses necessary for social exchange to function as an ESS will be developmentally buffered against cultural variation. It is difficult to imagine two populations that differ more than Shiwiar villagers and Harvard students in their exposure to Western-style schooling, word problems, the institution of science, or the concept of an experimental situation—factors that are known to affect performance in cross-cultural studies of cognition. The extreme cultural unfamiliarity of the test situation should introduce error into the Shiwiar data, thereby lowering their performance ceiling. Yet this effect appears only when one looks at the propensity to choose cards with information that, while interesting, is irrelevant to detecting cheaters (errors of curiosity). ESS-relevant choices were culturally uniform; ESS-irrelevant choices were free to vary with the cultural situation.

In short, Shiwiar performance on reasoning problems involving social exchange is what was predicted on the hypothesis that social contract algorithms are a reliably developing, universal feature of the human cognitive architecture, functioning as an evolutionarily stable strategy. Such a universal competence, if it exists, would serve as one of the cognitive foundations for human economic activity, as well as certain other cooperative dimensions of human sociality.

APPENDIX

Subjects

Twenty-one male and female Shiwiar individuals ranging from 16 to approximately 60 years of age participated in the experiment. Verbal consent was obtained to carry out this study from all individuals who participated, as well as from village leaders and other appropriate authorities.

Shiwiar live in a remote area, and have little direct contact with outsiders. What contact they have is possible primarily by means of missionary emergency medical airlift on small dirt airstrips cut in the forest with machetes and axes. These flights typically do not enter a given village for months on end and in smaller villages may not be made for periods as long as a year. Missionaries are not resident in study villages and Shiwiar leaders prohibit the presence of most outsiders.

Task and Stimuli

The Wason task was modified for use with nonliterate subjects (see Figure 2). First, we used actual cards to present the experimental stimuli and presented content information visually in photographs instead of in writing. Second, instead of having information presented on two sides of the card we presented the information about the antecedent and consequent in two photos on one side of the card. These photos were covered by "doors," which could be opened to reveal a photo. In every experiment, the photo depicting the antecedent appeared on top, while the photo depicting the consequent appeared on the bottom. Third, we presented subjects with one card at a time. That is, they were presented with one photo and asked whether they needed to see the covered photo on the same card to know if that card broke the rule being tested. When the subject gave his/her response, the experimenter presented the next card until all four alternatives were presented. All of this was done to reduce memory load, given that this is a verbally administered version of what is usually a written task.

Translation of Instructions

Because no Shiwiar speak English, protocols were first translated into Spanish. The method, along with the Spanish versions of the switched social contract and descriptive rule, were then pretested on 33 13- and 14-year-olds at a Quito junior high school with results similar to those found among U.S. college populations (social contract: 61% correct; descriptive: 12% correct). The protocols were then translated from Spanish to Shiwiar by a bilingual assistant, and recorded onto a cassette tape, with independent translation back into Spanish serving as a check on the accuracy of the Shiwiar version.

Procedures

Subjects were presented instructions and experimental content in Shiwiar from a cassette tape. Before testing, subjects were familiarized with the task as follows. Each subject was presented with a Wason selection task employing a descriptive rule: *"Chinki keakau nakumkamau yakinini, turasha yurank naranja nukamkamau nunkanini"* ("If there is a red bird in the drawing on top, then there is an orange on the drawing below"). All photos on six cards were shown to the subject. The experimenter emphasized that on top there was always one class of item, in this case different colored birds, and on the bottom there was always a different class of item, in this case different kinds of fruit. The cards were then covered and shuffled, and the test was run to familiarize the subject with the test and to test subjects' understanding of the procedures. No feedback about correct versus incorrect responses was given.

After this instruction set, each subject was presented with another descriptive problem, a standard social exchange problem, and a switched social exchange problem. The rules were embedded in a story context. All of the problems had unfamiliar content and study participants had no direct or prior experience with the rules. The standard social contract was a social contract law "If you eat mongongo nut [described as an aphrodisiac], then you must have a tattoo on your chest" [described as a mark denoting married status]. The switched social contract was a personal exchange "If you give me a basket of fish when you return from fishing, then you may use my motorboat." (Residents of the study villages have seen boats with outboard motors, and consider them desirable, but no one there owns one.) The descriptive problem was "If there is a green butterfly in the picture on the top part of the card, then there is a red flower in the picture on the bottom part of the card." The order of the problems was reversed for half of the subjects.

ENDNOTES

1. These features are necessary for the adaptations causing the behavior to be an evolutionarily stable strategy or ESS (14). For the application of the game-theoretic constraints to cognition, see ref. 9.

2. For an opposite dissociation, where social exchange reasoning is preserved but more general cognitive abilities are impaired (in schizophrenia), see ref. 26.

3. Functionally specialized acquisition mechanisms buffer development by solving problems of combinatorial explosion in environments that do not uniquely determine an outcome when analyzed by more general inductive procedures (27, 28).

4. For discussion of acquisition views, see refs. 29 and 30.

5. That familiarity *per se* does not facilitate logical reasoning on this task is uncontroversial at this point (15–19).

6. This condition holds if the adaptation is complex—that is, its genetic basis depends on the simultaneous presence of specific alleles at several different independent loci. The more loci involved, the more likely the adaptation in question is ancient and species-typical. Almost all cognitive adaptations will require, for their specification, more than a few loci, and so will be complex in this sense. (Also, adaptations for cheater detection are not predicted to be expressed facultatively.)

7. Although counting systems vary widely, there are adaptations that make them possible and place certain constraints on them (35, 36). The same is true for color terms (37–39).

8. Experimentation under field conditions injects higher levels of error variance into results than are obtainable under well-controlled laboratory conditions. More significant than factors such as added distractions, interruptions, and language difficulties is the extreme cultural strangeness of experimental testing itself, with its unfamiliar necessity of adhering to formal, abstract, and seemingly arbitrary behavioral and communicative constraints. Shiwiar subjects had no prior experience with experimental test-taking situations. This situation introduces confusion into the communicative pragmatics inherent in the task situation, and error variance into results. Restricting one's responses to the question *explicitly* asked, and ignoring information (such as who may be exhibiting generosity to whom) that is relevant to real life but not to a test problem, is a skill one learns in classrooms and courtrooms. Presumably, this is why schooling affects how people reason about problems involving hypotheticals (40) (such as those posed by Wason tasks). In virtually every other social context, when a question is asked, the pragmatic implication is that the asker does not already know the answer, and would like to be told whatever information might be relevant to solving his problem (41). Thus we predicted that Shiwiar performance would reflect two factors: (*i*) their lack of familiarity with the culturally specific pragmatics of Western testing situations (such as the task demand to ignore interesting information), which would cause cheater-irrelevant cards to sometimes be selected, and (*ii*) the presence of a species-typical cheater

detection mechanism, which would cause a strong propensity to select cheater-relevant cards.

9. The Harvard data (15, 16) were chosen for purposes of comparison because (*i*) these problems most closely paralleled the ones given to the Shiwiar, (*ii*) it was the most complete parallel data set, and (*iii*) this comparison placed the hypothesis in greatest jeopardy. Shiwiar look even more similar to subjects from developed nations when other data sets are used.

10. Paired t tests: For P: $t* = 4.16$, $r = 0.68$, $p = 0.00024$; for *not-P*: $t* = 3.21$, $r = 0.58$, $p = 0.0022$; for Q: $t* = 2.89$, $r = 0.54$, $p = 0.0045$; for *not-Q*: $t* = 4.28$, $r = 0.69$, $p = 0.00018$.

11. The frequency of choosing the *benefit not accepted* card was significantly below chance ($p = 0.02$) for the switched social contract, and for all other irrelevant card choices in the predicted direction, but not significantly so (i.e., $p > 0.05$). For the descriptive problem, only the P card was chosen more often than chance.

12. A yes/no judgment for each of four cards results in $2^4 = 16$ combinatorial possibilities; hence the probability of choosing all and only the correct cards by chance is $1/16 = 6.25\%$. The probability of getting at least one of two social contracts right by chance is $[1 - (15/16)^2] = 12\%$.

13. This result is very robust to changes in assumptions about what counts as chance. Suppose, for example, that people everywhere think that one particular card needs to be chosen for any conditional rule, regardless of content. If it happened to be one of the cards that a person looking for cheaters would choose, then 8 of the 16 combinatorial possibilities would be eliminated, and 12.5% of subjects would answer correctly by chance. Nevertheless, such an arbitrary doubling of the value of chance does not affect the conclusions: cheater detection among Shiwiar would still be higher than chance at the $p < 0.01$ level.

14. Given $n = 21$ and a medium effect size of 0.38, the probability of finding a difference that is significant at the 0.05 level is only 34% (42). Increasing sample size to increase the power of the test was not an option: we tested everyone in the village who was willing (to get 80% power, $n = 80$).

15. Significance test for differences in effect size uses Fisher's z transformation of r (43).

16. Q and *not-P* is the correct response if one is looking for cheaters on a switched social contract, but for a descriptive conditional, it is both logically incorrect and almost never produced by subjects from developed nations.

REFERENCES

1. Wilkinson, G. (1988) *Ethol. Sociobiol.* **9**, 85–100.
2. Packer, C. (1977) *Nature (London)* **265**, 441–443.
3. Cashdan, E. (1989) in *Economic Anthropology*, ed. Plattner, S. (Stanford Univ. Press, Stanford, CA), pp. 21–48.
4. Fiske, A. (1991) *Structures of Social Life* (Free Press, New York).
5. Isaac, G. (1978) *Sci. Am.* **238** (4), 90–108.
6. Lee, R. & DeVore, I., eds. (1968) *Man the Hunter* (Aldine, Chicago).
7. de Waal, F. (1989) *J. Human Evol.* **18**, 433–459.
8. de Waal, F. & Luttrell, L. (1988) *Ethol. Sociobiol.* **9**, 101–118.
9. Cosmides, L. & Tooby, J. (1989) *Ethol. Sociobiol.* **10**, 51–97.
10. Tooby, J. & Cosmides, L. (1996) *Proc. Br. Acad.* **88**, 119–143.
11. Axelrod, R. (1984) *Evolution of Cooperation* (Basic, New York).
12. Axelrod, R. & Hamilton, W. D. (1981) *Science* **211**, 1390–1396.
13. Trivers, R. (1971) *Q. Rev. Biol.* **46**, 35–57.
14. Maynard Smith, J. (1982) *Evolution and the Theory of Games* (Cambridge Univ. Press, Cambridge, U.K.).
15. Cosmides, L. (1989) *Cognition* **31**, 187–276.
16. Cosmides, L. (1985) *Ph. D. dissertation* (Harvard Univ., Cambridge, MA).
17. Wason, P. (1966) in *New Horizons in Psychology*, ed. Foss, B. (Penguin, Harmondsworth, U.K.), pp. 135–151.
18. Wason, P. & Johnson-Laird, P. (1972) *Psychology of Reasoning: Structure and Content* (Harvard Univ. Press, Cambridge, MA).
19. Wason, P. (1983) in *Thinking and Reasoning: Psychological Approaches*, ed. Evans, J. S. B. T. (Routledge & Kegan Paul, London), pp. 44–75.
20. Cosmides, L. & Tooby, J. (1992) in *The Adapted Mind*, eds. Barkow, J., Cosmides, L. & Tooby, J. (Oxford Univ. Press, New York), pp. 163–228.
21. Cosmides, L. & Tooby, J. (1997) in *Characterizing Human Psychological Adaptations, CIBA Foundation Symposium*, eds. Bock, G. R. & Cardew, G. (Wiley, Chichester, U.K.), Vol. 208, pp. 132–156.
22. Fiddick, L., Cosmides, L. & Tooby, J. (2000) *Cognition* **77**, 1–79.
23. Gigerenzer, G. & Hug, K. (1992) *Cognition* **43**, 127–171.
24. Platt, R. & Griggs, R. (1993) *Cognition* **48**, 163–192.
25. Stone, V. E., Cosmides, L., Tooby, J., Kroll, N. & Knight, R. T. (2002) *Proc. Natl. Acad. Sci. USA* **99**, 11531–11536.
26. Maljkovic, V. (1987) *A.B. thesis* (Harvard Univ., Cambridge, MA).
27. Pinker, S. (1984) *Language Learnability and Language Development* (Harvard Univ. Press, Cambridge, MA).
28. Cosmides, L. & Tooby, J. (1987) in *The Latest on the Best: Essays on Evolution and Optimality*, ed. Dupre, J. (MIT Press, Cambridge, MA), pp. 277–306.
29. Cheng, P. & Holyoak, K. (1985) *Cognit. Psychol.* **17**, 391–416.
30. Holland, J., Holyoak, K., Nisbett, R. & Thagard, P. (1986) *Induction* (MIT Press, Cambridge, MA).
31. Tooby, J. & Cosmides, L. (1992) in *The Adapted Mind*, eds. Barkow, J., Cosmides, L. & Tooby, J. (Oxford Univ. Press, New York), pp. 19–136.
32. Hirschfeld, L. & Gelman, S. (1994) *Mapping the Mind* (Cambridge Univ. Press, New York), pp. 3–35.
33. Cheng, P., Holyoak, K., Nisbett, R. & Oliver, L. (1986) *Cognit. Psychol.* **18**, 293–328.
34. Tooby, J. & Cosmides, L. (1990) *J. Pers.* **58**, 17–67.
35. Gallistel, C. R. (1990) *The Organization of Learning* (MIT Press, Cambridge, MA).
36. Wynn, K. (1992) *Nature (London)* **358**, 749–750.
37. Shepard, R. (1992) in *The Adapted Mind*, eds. Barkow, J., Cosmides, L. & Tooby, J. (Oxford Univ. Press, New York), pp. 495–532.
38. Berlin, B. & Kay, P. (1969) *Basic Color Terms: Their Universality and Evolution* (Univ. of California Press, Berkeley, CA).
39. Rosch, E. (1975) *J. Exp. Psychol. Hum. Percept. Perform.* **1**, 303–322.
40. Sharp, D., Cole, M. & Lave, C. (1978) *Education and Cognitive Development: The Evidence from Experimental Research, Monographs of the Society for Research in Child Development* (Univ. of Chicago Press, Chicago), Vol. 44 (n1-sup-2), pp. 1–112.
41. Sperber, D. & Wilson, D. (1995) *Relevance: Communication and Cognition* (Blackwell, Oxford)
42. Cohen, J. (1988) *Statistical Power Analysis for the Behavioral Sciences* (Erlbaum, Mahwah, NJ), pp. 179–212.
43. Rosenthal, R. & Rosnow, R. (1991) *Essentials of Behavioral Research* (McGraw-Hill, Boston), 2nd Ed., pp. 448–455.

Error Management Theory
A New Perspective on Biases in Cross-Sex Mind Reading

MARTIE G. HASELTON AND DAVID M. BUSS

A new theory of cognitive biases, called error management theory (EMT), proposes that psychological mechanisms are designed to be predictably biased when the costs of false-positive and false-negative errors were asymmetrical over evolutionary history. This theory explains known phenomena such as men's overperception of women's sexual intent, and it predicts new biases in social inference such as women's underestimation of men's commitment. In Study 1 (N = 217), the authors documented the commitment underperception effect predicted by EMT. In Study 2 (N = 289), the authors replicated the commitment bias and documented a condition in which men's sexual overperception bias is corrected. Discussion contrasts EMT with the heuristics and biases approach and suggests additional testable hypotheses based on EMT.

S everal independent traditions of research have documented systematic errors in human judgment and decision making. The most famous of these was established by Tversky and Kahneman (1974) and is influential in cognitive and social psychology as well as in business and economics (Lopes, 1991). Social cognition researchers in this tradition have documented cognitive errors such as base-rate neglect, confirmation bias, and illusory correlation (Nisbett & Ross, 1980). Typically the goal in these studies was to identify biased heuristics—"rules of thumb" or "shortcuts"— that are the hypothesized source of errors (Tversky & Kahneman, 1974). A second line of research concerns a particular domain of judgment: inferences about the thoughts and intentions of members of the opposite sex. A potentially harmful error is that men appear to over-infer sexual intent in women in response to cues such as a smile or friendliness (see, e.g., Abbey, 1982, 1991). These errors have typically been attributed to sex-role socialization rather than to the operation of simplifying heuristics.

These two lines of research are related in that they concern judgment under uncertainty. Judging the likelihood of probabilistic events, such as in tasks used in heuristics and biases research, requires judgment under uncertainty. Similarly, inferences about the sexual intentions of others, which are not directly observable, are based on probabilistic cues and hence also uncertain.

This article describes two hypotheses about cross-sex mind-reading biases, one that explains men's overperception of women's sexual intent and one that predicts a

M. G. Haselton and D. M. Buss, "Error management theory: A new perspective on biases in cross-sex mind reading," *Journal of Personality and Social Psychology,* 78 (2000): 81–91. Copyright © 2000 by the American Psychological Association. Reprinted with permission.

new error. These hypotheses are derived from a theory of errors that challenges the position that errors reflect shortcomings or limitations of psychological design (see, e.g., Kahneman, Slovic, & Tversky, 1982; Nisbett & Ross, 1980) or susceptibility to erroneous social messages caused by socialization. This new theory proposes that cognitive errors result from *adaptive biases* that exist in the present because they led to survival and reproductive advantages for humans in the past.

ERROR MANAGEMENT THEORY

When judgments are made under uncertainty, two general types of errors are possible—false positives (Type I errors) and false negatives (Type II errors). A decision maker cannot simultaneously minimize both errors because decreasing the likelihood of one error necessarily increases the likelihood of the other (Green & Swets, 1966).

The costs of these two types of errors are rarely symmetrical. In scientific hypothesis testing, Type I errors are usually considered more costly than Type II errors. Scientists, therefore, typically bias their decision-making systems (e.g., inferential statistics) toward making Type II errors. Errors are also asymmetrical in warning devices like fire alarms, which are biased in the opposite direction. Missed detections (Type II errors) are more costly; therefore, the bias is toward making false alarms (Type I errors). Whenever the costs of errors are asymmetrical, humanly engineered systems should be built to be biased toward making less costly errors (Green & Swets, 1966). This bias might increase overall error rates, but it minimizes overall cost.

According to error management theory (EMT; Haselton, Buss, & DeKay, 1998), decision-making adaptations have evolved through natural or sexual selection to commit predictable errors. Whenever there exists a recurrent cost asymmetry between two types of errors over the period of time in which selection fashions adaptations, they should be biased toward committing errors that are less costly. Because it is exceedingly unlikely that the two types of errors are ever identical in the recurrent costs associated with them, EMT predicts that human psychology will contain decision rules biased toward committing one type of error over another (also see Cosmides & Tooby, 1996; Nesse & Williams, 1998; Schlager, 1995; Searcy & Brenowitz, 1988; Tomarken, Mineka, & Cook, 1989).

The logic of EMT extends to benefit asymmetries as well as to cost asymmetries. Consider two types of correct inferences, hits and correct rejections. If the benefits associated with these two different correct inferences differ recurrently over evolutionary time, other things being equal, then selection will favor the reasoning strategy that is biased toward the more beneficial inference, even if it results in more errors overall. In cases where the costs of the two different errors are the same, but the benefits are asymmetrical, the benefit asymmetry will be the driving selective force. In cases where the benefits of correct inferences are the same but the costs of errors are asymmetrical, the cost asymmetry will be the driving selective force. The key point of EMT is that selection will favor biased decision rules that produce more beneficial or less costly outcomes (relative to alternative decision rules), even if those biased rules produce more frequent errors. In this article we apply the logic of EMT to two social adaptive problems: inferences about sexual interest and commitment intent.

SEX DIFFERENCES IN READING SEXUAL INTENT

In the early 1980s, Abbey launched a tradition of research into sex differences in sexual perceptions. In Abbey's (1982) pioneering study, unacquainted male–female dyads participated in a short discussion while a hidden man and woman observed the interaction through one-way glass. The observers rated the degree to which the target individuals' behaviors indicated their sexual intentions and estimated the target individuals' sexual attraction to one another. The targets provided parallel self-ratings and ratings of their conversation partner. The men in the study perceived greater sexual intent in women than did the women.

Men's greater inference of women's sexual intent has been replicated in laboratory studies similar to the original study (e.g., Saal, Johnson, & Weber, 1989), studies using photographs (e.g., Abbey & Melby, 1986), videos (e.g., Johnson, Stockdale, & Saal, 1991), and short vignettes (e.g., Abbey & Harnish, 1995). In these studies male and female targets were depicted in sexually ambiguous circumstances and third-party perceivers rated the sexual intent of the depicted men and women.

ARE MEN MISREADING WOMEN'S ACTUAL INTENT?

There is no direct gauge of intentions analogous to a thermometer for measuring temperature. Researchers must rely on indirect measures of mental states. Two commonly used indirect measures are (a) reports from the target whose intentions are read (see, e.g., Ickes, 1997) and (b) reports from other knowledgeable sources, such as same-sex third-party perceivers (see, e.g., Abbey, 1982).

Both of these types of ratings may be biased. Self-ratings are susceptible to self-enhancement biases (e.g., Sedikides, 1993). Women's self-ratings, for example, may underestimate their true sexual intent (Einon, 1994) because signals of sexual promiscuity may cause reputational damage (Buss, 1994; Einon, 1994). Third-party women's ratings may be biased in the opposite direction, as in derogation of same-sex competitors (Buss & Dedden, 1990; Schmitt & Buss, 1996). The same enhancement and derogation counterbiases may also exist in men's self-ratings and their ratings of other men. Men may under-rate their true sexual intent in order to highlight other intentions, such as intentions of commitment and love (Schmitt & Buss, 1996), which are desired by women (Buss, 1994). Men, like women, derogate their same-sex competitors' sexual fidelity and long-term romantic intentions (Buss & Dedden, 1990; Schmitt & Buss, 1996), resulting in potentially inflated third-party sexual intent ratings provided by men.

If this reasoning is correct, the true state of women's sexual intent should be bracketed by women's self-ratings and the ratings provided by third-party women. One standard for evaluating whether men err is therefore to evaluate cross-sex perceptions relative to self-perceptions and third-party women's ratings. When men's perceptions exceed or underestimate both women's self-perceptions and third-party women's perceptions, men may be in error. Similarly, evidence of a possible error in women's cross-sex perceptions would occur if their perceptions simultaneously exceed (or underestimate) both men's self-perceptions and third-party men's perceptions. Past studies have failed to compare these three ratings separately (e.g., Abbey, 1982).

WHY DO MEN AND WOMEN PERCEIVE
WOMEN'S SEXUAL INTENT DIFFERENTLY?

Researchers have developed several hypotheses about men's apparent overperception of women's sexual intent. The first is the *general oversexualization hypothesis:* Because men tend to rate women's and men's sexual intent more highly than do women, men appear to "oversexualize the world" (see, e.g., Abbey, 1982, 1991). According to this hypothesis, men do this because they are socialized to be sexual, whereas women are socialized to be coy (Abbey, 1982, 1991). The second is the *media hypothesis* (Abbey, 1991): Men are exposed to leading media images depicting women as initially coy but then overcome with sexual desire. The third is the *default-model hypothesis,* which is closely related to the false consensus model in social–cognitive research (see Marks & Miller, 1987, for a review). This hypothesis suggests that men exceed women in sexual desire and use their own desires as an erroneous gauge of women's desires (Shotland & Craig, 1988). A weakness shared by these hypotheses is that they have been offered post hoc and have not yet been supported with independent tests or novel predictions based on their premises.

HYPOTHESES ABOUT CROSS-SEX MIND-READING BIASES

We applied EMT to the domain of cross-sex mind reading. EMT offers a new explanation for men's sexual overperception and predicts a new bias in mind reading.

> *Hypothesis 1: Sexual overperception bias.* Men possess intention-reading adaptations designed to minimize the cost of missed sexual opportunities by over-inferring women's sexual intent.

One primary factor limiting men's reproductive success over evolutionary history was their ability to gain sexual access to fertile women (Symons, 1979). Ancestral men who tended to falsely infer a prospective mate's sexual intent (a false-positive error) paid the fairly low costs of failed sexual pursuit: perhaps some lost time and wasted courtship effort. In contrast, men who tended to falsely infer that a woman lacked sexual intent (a false-negative error) paid the costs of losing a sexual opportunity and hence a reproductive opportunity. In the currency of natural selection—the replicative success of one design relative to other designs (Dawkins, 1989)—the latter error was more costly.

> *Hypothesis 2: Commitment-skepticism bias.* Women possess intention-reading adaptations designed to minimize the cost of feigned commitment by men by underinferring men's commitment intent.

Using EMT logic, we hypothesized that women's inferences of men's commitment intent would show a reverse bias. For women, the costs of falsely inferring a prospective mate's commitment when little or none exists (a false-positive error), according to this hypothesis, were greater than the costs of failing to infer commitment that does exist (a false-negative error). An ancestral woman who consented to sex with a man who abandoned her shortly thereafter because of his low level of commitment could have suffered the costs of an unwanted or untimely pregnancy, raising a child without an investing mate, a reduction in her mate value, and reputational damage (Buss, 1994). These were substantial costs given the lowered survival of the child and impairment of future reproductive potential (Hurtado & Hill, 1992). An ancestral woman who erred by underestimating a man's commitment, in contrast, may have merely evoked more numerous and more frequent displays of commitment by the man who truly was committed (Buss, 1994). Given the tremendous importance to women of securing a committed mate, according to this hypothesis, modern women are descendants of ancestral mothers who erred in the direction of being cautious—a commitment-skepticism bias.

These hypotheses require the assumption that men and women, over the course of human evolutionary history, were able to exercise some degree of individual choice in entering or leaving mateships. All available cross-cultural and anthropological evidence supports this assumption (Buss, 1994). Most cultures permit individuals to exercise choice, either directly or indirectly. Even in cultures where marriages are arranged by elders, individuals manage to influence their parents' choices, sometimes refuse to marry a designated partner, sometimes elope with a loved one against parents' wishes, and sometimes marry one person while having sex with a lover of choice (Buss, 1994; Jankowiak, 1995). Similarly, choice can be exercised through divorce or abandonment, patterns observed in every known culture (Betzig, 1989; Buss, 1994).

Hypothesis 3: The sister correction.   Men possess intention-reading adaptations designed to correctly read their sisters' sexual intentions.

EMT proposes that cost asymmetries lead to the evolution of biased inferential mechanisms. When the specific targets of cross-sex mind reading vary, however, cost asymmetries vary, and the bias when mind reading one target should shift accordingly. Hypothesis 1 proposed that the costs to men of missing a sexual opportunity were greater than the costs of failed pursuit, causing misperceptions of sexual intent. But what happens when the target represents a class of individuals who are not reproductively appropriate sex partners, such as sisters?

From an evolutionary perspective, ancestral men and their sisters had a large degree of shared fate. Differential gene replication could occur either directly through individual reproduction or indirectly if individuals aided the reproduction of their close genetic relatives who were likely to possess the gene (Hamilton, 1964). Men who recognized their sisters' upset when their intentions were misread (perhaps if she were the victim of unwanted sexual advances or attempted rape) may have been better able to protect their sisters' ability to exercise choice in mating and preserve their sisters' reputations. In contrast, men who extended their overinference of sexual intent to all targets, including sisters, would have failed to protect the interests of their kin. If men's overperception of women's sexual intent is indeed an error designed to minimize the likelihood of missed sexual opportunities, sisters would have been inappropriate targets of these inferences. We hypothesized that men "correct" their biased inferences about women's sexual intent when the target is a sister.

STUDY 1: DO WOMEN UNDERPERCEIVE MEN'S COMMITMENT INTENT?

To test the commitment-skepticism hypothesis we compared cross-sex perceptions of commitment intent with same-sex perceptions of commitment intent. Because the commitment-intent items were worded in the direction of noncommitment (e.g., "he will avoid getting committed . . . "), the prediction derived from the hypothesis was that women's ratings would exceed the criterion measure: men's perceptions of other men. We also examined perceptions of sexual intent. We predicted that men's ratings of women's sexual intent would exceed women's ratings.

Method

Participants. The participants were 217 undergraduates, 113 men and 104 women. Participation partially fulfilled a course requirement. The average age was 18.56 for men and 18.64 for women.

Materials. The instructions were "Please rate the following statements on whether or not you agree with them or disagree with them. Use the following 7-point scale." The scale ranged from 1 (*strongly disagree*) to 4 (*neutral*) to 7 (*strongly agree*). Items pertaining to men's commitment and women's commitment appeared on the same page but were interspersed between items assessing other aspects of relationships (such as the frequency with which men and women discuss their relationships). The items appeared in the same order for all participants. The items about men appeared before the items about women. Three items assessed perceptions of commitment: (a) "Men [women] tend to be afraid of long-term commitments such as marriage"; (b) "Men [women] tend to keep their emotions to themselves in order to avoid making a commitment to a woman [man]"; (c) "As long as a man [woman] can have lots of sex without commitment, he [she] will avoid getting committed to one woman [man]."

Items pertaining to sexual intent appeared in the same order (perceptions of men first) but on different pages. The instructions were "To what extent do the following behaviors indicate 'sexual interest' on the part of a man [woman]?" Each behavior was rated on a 7-point rating scale ranging from 1 (*no sexual interest*) to 4 (*moderate sexual interest*) to 7 (*a lot of sexual interest*). Eight behaviors were presented: ". . . on the first day of work, approaching a male [female] co-worker, smiling brightly, and striking up a friendly conversation"; ". . . smiling at a man [woman] at a party"; ". . . being friendly to a man [woman] she [he] just met at the party"; ". . . touching a man [woman] on the arm at the party"; ". . . reducing the distance between her [him] and a man [woman] to a few inches at the party"; ". . . prolonged eye contact with the woman [man] he [she] just met at the party"; ". . . going to a bar alone"; and ". . . dancing provocatively with a woman [man] he [she] just met at the party."

Procedure. Participants completed the questionnaire in small same-sex groups. A same-sex researcher was present to answer questions.

Results

A commitment composite was created by computing the arithmetic mean of the ratings provided for the three commitment items ($\alpha = .74$ and $\alpha = .62$ for perceptions of men and women, respectively). A mixed-model 2×2 analysis of variance (ANOVA), with sex of rater and sex of target as between- and within-group factors, revealed a significant interaction, $F(1, 213) = 14.87$, $p < .001$, suggesting that the pattern of ratings of the target (same sex vs. opposite sex) differed for men and women raters.

Two Bonferroni-corrected planned contrasts ($\alpha = .025$ for each pair of contrasts) compared men's and women's ratings of each target. As predicted by the commitment-skepticism hypothesis, women's ratings of men's commitment avoidance ($M = 4.52$, $SD = 1.19$) were significantly greater than men's ratings of men's commitment avoidance ($M = 3.96$, $SD = 1.31$), $F(1, 213) = 10.63$, $p < .01$. We did not predict a difference between men's ratings of women's commitment and women's self-perceived commitment, and none were found (for men, $M = 2.90$, $SD = 1.11$; for women, $M = 2.69$, $SD = 0.97$), $F(1, 213) = 2.22$, $p = .14$.

A sexual-intent composite was created by computing the arithmetic mean of the ratings provided for the eight sexual-intent items ($\alpha = .84$ and $\alpha = .82$ for perceptions of men and women, respectively). A mixed-model 2×2 ANOVA was conducted with sex of rater and sex of target as between- and within-group factors. There was neither a significant interaction of the factors nor a main effect of sex of target ($ps > .90$). There was a significant main effect of rater, with men's ratings ($M = 3.70$, $SD = 0.85$) exceeding women's ratings ($M = 3.39$, $SD = 0.88$), $F(1, 211) = 6.73$, $p = .01$.

Discussion

Using error management theory, we hypothesized that women underperceive men's commitment. Our prediction derived from this hypothesis that women would overperceive men's commitment avoidance was confirmed. In contrast to the sex difference in perceptions of men's commitment, there were no significant sex differences in perceptions of women's commitment. This suggests that commitment underperception is specific to women's cross-sex perceptions and does not occur in men's cross-sex perceptions.

We predicted and found that men perceive greater sexual intent in women; however, as in past studies, men's perceptions of men's sexual intent were also greater than women's perceptions of men's intent. This may indicate that women underperceive men's sexual intent or that men's overperception extends to targets of both sexes. In Study 2, we attempted to resolve this ambiguity by examining an additional criterion measure of men's sexual intent.

Study 1 had several important limitations. First, the questions about men's sexual intent and commitment appeared before the questions about women. It is therefore possible that the results were affected by item order. Second, the commitment items were all "commitment avoidance" items, which may have been somewhat leading.

STUDY 2

Study 2 consisted of two parts. In Part 1, we assessed cross-sex perceptions relative to self-report criterion measures. In Part 2, we assessed cross-sex perceptions relative to same-sex and self-report criterion measures. Our first goal in Study 2 was to replicate the new finding in Study 1. Our second goal was to eliminate the two potential threats to validity in Study 1 by counterbalancing the order in which participants were asked about men and women targets and by asking participants nonleading questions about commitment. Our third goal was to assess cross-sex perceptions relative to an additional criterion measure: self-perceptions. This criterion measure allowed further investigation of women's perceptions of men's sexual intent. Collecting same-sex, cross-sex, and self-perceptions in Study 2 also allowed us to test the *default model hypothesis,* which proposes that men's overperception of women's sexual intent is a result of an erroneous extension of self-perceptions to others. Our fourth goal was to test Hypothesis 3: the sister correction.

Specific Predictions

Predicted Mind Reading Biases.   In Part 1 of this study, men's and women's self-perceptions were the criterion measures. We predicted that men's ratings of women's sexual intent would exceed women's self-perceived sexual intent and that women's ratings of men's commitment intent would be lower than men's self-perceived commitment intent.

In Part 2 of this study, there were two criterion measures: same-sex perceptions and self-perceptions. We predicted that men's ratings of women's sexual intent would exceed the criterion measures, whereas women's ratings of men's commitment would be lower than the criterion measures.

The Predicted Correction for Sisters.   Hypothesis 3 proposed that men's overperception of women's sexual intent will not occur when the mind-reading target is a sister. This hypothesis predicts that men's perceptions of a sister's sexual intent will be lower than men's perceptions of unrelated women's sexual intent.

Method

Participants.   The participants were 289 undergraduate students, 168 women and 121 men. The average age of the women was 19.14, and the average age of the men was 19.25. Their participation partially fulfilled a research requirement for a psychology course.

Materials
Sex and Commitment Contrast Instrument.   Participants completed two forms of the sex and commitment contrast instrument. The order was counterbalanced. On one they reported their own likely intentions given that they engaged in each of 15 different behaviors. On the other form, they reported analogous perceptions of the intentions of members of the opposite sex. The instructions for women's cross-sex perception form were

> Imagine a man you might date. Imagine that you had been out on a few casual dates with him and you had *not* had sex with him. Imagine that he engaged in each of the acts listed below. For each act, make two ratings: (1) Rate the *man's interest in having sex* with you, given that he engaged in that act. (2) Rate the *man's interest in developing a committed relationship* with you, given that he engaged in that act.

The instructions for the women's self-report form were

Imagine a man you might date. Imagine that you had been out on a few casual dates with him and you had *not* had sex with him. Imagine engaging in each act listed below. For each act, make two ratings: (1) Rate how likely it would be that you would *want to have sex* with the man, given that you engaged in that act. (2) Rate how likely it would be that you would be *interested in developing a committed relationship* with the man, given that you engaged in that act.

The rating scale had seven anchored points (−3 = *extremely unlikely,* −2 = *moderately unlikely,* −1 = *somewhat unlikely,* 0 = *neutral,* +1 = *somewhat likely,* +2 = *moderately likely,* and +3 = *extremely likely*). The scale was followed by 15 cues in the form, "If he did X he [she] would want . . ." (cross-sex form) or "If I did X, I would want . . ." (self-report form), where X represents each of 15 different cues. Representative examples of the cues are "held hands with me [him/her]"; "complimented me [him/her] on my [his/her] appearance"; "passionately kissed me [him/her]"; "told me [him/her] that he [she/I] loved me [him/her]"; "bought me [him/her] expensive jewelry." To the right of each cue were spaces in which to rate how much the cue indicated (a) sexual intent and (b) commitment intent.

Cross-Sex Perception Instrument. Participants completed three forms: a same-sex, an opposite-sex, and a self-perception form. The order of the forms was randomized across participants. Each of the six possible orders of forms was administered to approximately equal numbers of men and women participants.

The rating scale had seven anchored points (−3 = *strongly disagree,* −2 = *moderately disagree,* −1 = *somewhat disagree,* 0 = *neutral,* +1 = *somewhat agree,* +2 = *moderately agree,* and +3 = *strongly agree*). It was followed by 24 items, 5 of which were designed to test the commitment-skepticism hypothesis (the remaining items assessed perceptions not related to our hypotheses, such as perceptions of concern with social status and physical appearance). These items were (a) "If a man [woman] could have lots of sex without commitment, he [she] would avoid getting committed to one woman [man]"; (b) "Most men [women] prefer many different sex partners over one committed sex partner"; (c) "A typical man [woman] needs to know that a woman [man] loves him [her] before he [she] is willing to have sex with her [him]"; (d) "In order for a typical man [woman] to feel comfortable having sex with a woman [man], he [she] needs to know that she [he] feels committed to him [her]"; and (e) "Men [women] tend to avoid long-term commitments like marriage."

Following these items was a depiction of the 7-point *extremely unlikely–extremely likely* scale used in the sex and commitment contrast questionnaire (see above). This scale was followed by four items designed to test the sexual overperception hypothesis (Hypothesis 1): (a) "At a party, if a man [woman] smiles at a woman [man] repeatedly over the course of the evening, what is the likelihood that he [she] wants to have sex with her [him]?"; (b) "When a man [woman] touches a woman's [man's] arm when he [she] is out on a date with her [him], how likely is it that he [she] is interested in having sex with her [him]?"; (c) "When a man [woman] goes out to a bar, how likely is it that he [she] is interested in finding someone to have sex with that night?"; and (d) "In class, if a man [woman] smiles at a female [male] student repeatedly over the course of the lecture, what is the likelihood that he [she] wants to have sex with her [him]?" Self-perception items contained appropriate pronoun substitutions; for example: "If I could have lots of sex without commitment, I would avoid getting committed to one woman [man]."

Cross-Sex Sibling Perception Instrument. The instructions for the cross-sex sibling perception instrument were

> The following questions are about a member of your family. Please think about your sister [brother]. If you have more than one, think of the one who is *closest to you in age*. Answer the following questions about this person.

These instructions were followed by a short biographical information section requesting the sibling's initials, age, degree of relationship (full biological sibling, adopted, etc.), and the number of years the participant and the sibling lived in the same household. The siblings' initials were requested in an effort to "commit" the participant to answering the questions about only one specific sibling and to help the participant think more vividly about this person.

Following the 7-point *extremely unlikely–extremely likely* scale was a subset of the items from the cross-sex perception questionnaire. These items were (a) "At a party, if your sister [brother] smiles at a man [woman] repeatedly over the course of the evening, what is the likelihood that she [he] wants to have sex with him [her]?"; (b) "If your sister [brother] touches a man's [woman's] arm when they are out on a date, how likely is it that she [he] is interested in having sex with him [her]?"; and (c) "If your sister [brother] goes out to a bar, how likely is it that she [he] is interested in finding someone to have sex with that night?"

Procedure. Participants were tested in same-sex groups of 20 individuals or fewer. The same-sex researcher conducting the sessions was available to answer questions. Participants with cross-sex siblings completed the sibling instrument after completing the other questionnaires.

Data Analysis. We created composite ratings by calculating the arithmetic mean of the sexual intent items within each instrument and by calculating the arithmetic mean of the commitment intent items within each instrument. To confirm that the pattern of target ratings differed systematically for each sex, we first conducted a mixed-model factorial ANOVA for each dependent variable. Sex of rater and target type (e.g., cross-sex vs. self-report) were within- and between-groups factors, respectively. We followed this analysis with Bonferroni-corrected planned contrasts ($\alpha = .025$ for each pair of contrasts) designed to assess differences between men's and women's cross-sex ratings and the criterion measures.[1]

Results: Sex and Commitment Contrast

Commitment Intent. Reliabilities (αs) for composites were .88 for ratings of men and .86 for ratings of women. As in Study 1, a significant rater by target interaction, $F(1, 273) = 30.10$, $p < .001$, suggested that the pattern of target ratings differed for male and female raters.

As predicted by the commitment-skepticism hypothesis, women's perceptions of men's commitment intent as indicated by the men's display of the 15 dating cues ($M = 1.21$, $SD = 0.74$) were significantly lower than men's perception of their own commitment intent given their display of the cues ($M = 1.65$, $SD = 0.50$), $F(1, 279) = 31.58$, $p < .001$. Men's perception of women's commitment intent as indicated by the women's display of the 15 dating cues ($M = 1.65$, $SD = 0.48$) was not significantly different from women's perception of their own commitment intent given their display of the cues ($M = 1.60$, $SD = 0.76$), $F(1, 276) = .44$, $p = .51$).

Sexual Intent. Reliabilities for the composites were .95 for ratings of men and .96 for ratings of women. There was a significant rater by target interaction, $F(1, 265) = 80.33$, $p < .001$, indicating that the pattern of target ratings differed for men and women raters.

As predicted by Hypothesis 1 and as documented in past studies, men's ratings of women's sexual intent as indicated by women's display of dating cues were greater ($M = 1.02$, $SD = 0.90$) than women's self-perceived sexual intent given the cues ($M = 0.13$, $SD = 1.60$), $F(1, 270) = 28.84$, $p < .001$. Women's ratings of men's sexual intent as indicated by the men's display of dating cues ($M = 1.42$, $SD = 1.00$) were greater than men's self-perceived sexual intent given the cues ($M = 1.10$, $SD = 1.23$), $F(1, 273) = 2.40$, $p = .02$, though to a lesser degree. This result contradicts the hypothesis that men's perceptions are generally oversexualized, because women's ratings exceeded men's ratings.

Results: Cross-Sex Perception

Commitment Intent. Reliabilities of the composites were .74, .70, and .83 for perceptions of men, women, and self, respectively. A significant rater by target interaction, $F(2, 566) = 104.70$, $p < .001$, indicated that the rating pattern differed for men and women raters.

As predicted, women's ratings of men's commitment intent ($M = -1.27$, $SD = 1.10$) were significantly lower than men's perceptions of other men's commitment intent ($M = -0.99$, $SD = 1.02$), $F(1, 281) = 4.80$, $p < .02$, and men's self-perceived commitment intent ($M = 0.55$, $SD = 1.35$), $F(1, 281) = 156.25$, $p < .001$. These results confirm the predictions derived from Hypothesis 2.

We did not have a priori predictions about differences between men's perceptions of women's commitment intent and the criterion measures. Men's and women's perceptions of women's commitment intent ($M = 1.29$, $SD = 0.87$, and $M = 1.17$, $SD = 1.00$, respectively) did not differ significantly, $F(1, 281) = 1.17$, $p = .28$, but men's perceptions were significantly lower than women's self-perceived commitment intent ($M = 2.04$, $SD = 1.03$), $F(1, 281) = 41.86$, $p < .01$.

Figure 1 summarizes these findings. The data presented in the left panel test Hypothesis 2—women's perceptions of men's commitment. The right panel depicts data for men's perceptions of women's commitment. For ratings of men and women separately, composite cross-sex ratings are contrasted with each of the criterion measures. Evidence of a possible cross-sex mind-reading error exists when cross-sex perceptions exceed or underestimate both criterion measures. This occurred for women's

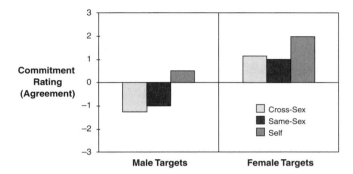

FIGURE 1   Women's perception of men's commitment appears in the left panel. Cross-sex perceptions represent women's perceptions of men and men's perceptions of women. Same-sex and self-perception ratings are the criterion measures. Evidence of a possible cross-sex mind-reading error is obtained if the cross-sex perception significantly exceeds or underestimates both criterion measures, as is the case for women's perception of men's commitment (left panel). This effect suggests that women underperceive men's commitment intent, as predicted by Hypothesis 2. Men's perception of women's commitment fell between the two criterion measures (right panel), suggesting the possibility that men accurately perceive women's commitment.

perceptions of men's commitment intent, which were significantly lower than each criterion measure (the predicted effects), but not for men's perceptions of women's commitment. Men's perceptions fell between the two criterion measures, suggesting that men may correctly infer women's commitment.

Sexual Intent.   Composite reliabilities were .83, .83, and .91 for perceptions of men, women, and self, respectively. A significant rater by target interaction, $F(2, 566) = 104.70$, $p < .001$, confirmed that the pattern of target ratings differed for men and women raters.

As predicted, men's ratings of women's sexual intent ($M = 0.12, SD = 1.01$) were significantly greater than women's ratings of women ($M = -0.34$, $SD = 1.19$), $F(1, 283) = 11.70$, $p < .01$, and significantly greater than women's self-perceived sexual intent ($M = -1.69, SD = 1.38$), $F(1, 283) = 136.89$, $p < .001$. These results confirm the predictions derived from Hypothesis 1.

Women's perceptions of men's sexual intent were between the two criterion measures. Women's perceptions of men's sexual intent ($M = 1.01, SD = 1.02$) were significantly lower than men's perceptions of other men's sexual intent ($M = 1.29, SD = 1.04$), $F(1, 283) = 4.97$; $p < .05$, but significantly greater than men's self-perceived sexual intent ($M = 0.54, SD = 1.34$), $F(1, 283) = 11.63$, $p < .01$.

Figure 2 summarizes these findings. The left panel depicts results testing Hypothesis 1—men's perceptions of women's sexual intent. The right panel depicts women's perceptions of men's sexual intent. Men's perceptions of women significantly exceeded each of the criterion measures (left panel), providing evidence of a potential cross-sex mindreading error. Women's perceptions of men were between the criterion measures (right panel), suggesting potentially accurate perceptions.

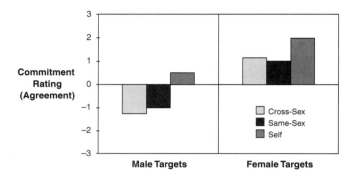

FIGURE 2   Men's perception of women's sexual intent appears in the left panel. Cross-sex perceptions represent men's perceptions of women and women's perceptions of men. Same-sex and self-perception ratings are criterion measures. Evidence of a possible cross-sex mind-reading error is obtained if the cross-sex perception significantly exceeds or underestimates both criterion measures. This is the case for men's perception of women's sexual intent (left panel). Women's perception of men's sexual intent fell between the two criterion measures (right panel), suggesting the possibility that women accurately perceive men's sexual intent.

Results: Cross-Sex Sibling Inferences

One hundred sixty-eight participants completed cross-sex sibling instruments (69 men and 99 women). Average sibling age was 20.57 (ranging from 6 to 36 years). Most siblings were full biological siblings (85%). The analysis was limited to full siblings and to siblings who were at least 15 years old.[2] There were 131 eligible participants (72 women and 59 men) using these criteria. The average age of the women's brothers was 20.42 (ranging from 15 to 31) and the average age of men's sisters was 21.49 (ranging from 15 to 31).

Reliability of the sibling composite was .87. A significant rater by target (cross-sex other vs. cross-sex sibling) interaction, $F(1, 127) = 8.89$, $p < .01$, indicated that the pattern of differences across target ratings differed for men and women raters.

As predicted, men's perceptions of their sisters' sexual intent ($M = -1.03$, $SD = 1.44$) were significantly lower than their perceptions of other women's sexual intent ($M = .02$, $SD = 1.09$), $F(1, 57) = 23.62$, $p < .001$. This confirms the prediction that men would perceive less sexual intent in sisters than in unrelated women.[3] Men's perceptions of their sisters fell between the two criterion measures (composite ratings of women's perceptions of women and women's self-perceptions for the three items appearing on the sibling form). Men's perceptions of sisters were lower than women's perceptions of women's sexual intent ($M = -0.21$, $SD = 1.19$), $F(1, 223) = 18.15$, $p < .001$, and greater than women's self-perceived sexual intent ($M = -1.69$, $SD = 1.39$), $F(1, 222) = 10.00$, $p < .01$.

We did not have an a priori prediction about women's perception of their brother's sexual intent. We found that women's perceptions of their brothers' sexual intent ($M = -0.50$, $SD = 1.69$) were also significantly lower than women's perceptions of other men's sexual intent ($M = 1.37$, $SD = 0.87$), $F(1, 70) = 111.94$, $p < .001$. Women's perceptions of their brothers' sexual intent fell below each criterion measure. Women's ratings of brothers were lower than men's ratings of men ($M =$ 1.37, $SD = 1.00$), $F(1, 189) = 92.74$, $p < .001$, and lower than men's self-ratings ($M =$ 0.47, $SD = 1.37$), $F(1, 189) = 18.92$, $p < .001$.

Discussion

Each part of Study 2 built on Study 1 by eliminating two potential threats to validity in Study 1: order effects and leading questions. Because Study 2 replicated the effects observed in Study 1, the findings in Study 1 cannot be attributed to these threats to validity.

Predicted Mind-Reading Biases. The predictions derived from Hypotheses 1 and 2 were confirmed in each part of Study 2. In Part 1, women's ratings of men's commitment were lower than men's self-perceived commitment, and men's ratings of women's sexual intent exceeded women's self-perceived sexual intent. In Part 2, women's ratings of men's commitment underestimated each criterion measure of men's commitment,[4] and men's ratings of women's sexual intent exceeded each criterion measure of women's sexual intent. In sum, as assessed relative to each type of criterion measure, men appear to overinfer women's sexual intent and women appear to underinfer men's commitment.

Other Potential Mind-Reading Biases. In contrast to these replicable effects, there was little evidence that men's inferences about women's commitment were erroneous. In Part 1, men's ratings did not differ significantly from the criterion measure. In Part 2, men's cross-sex perceptions fell between the two criterion measures, suggesting the possibility of reasonable accuracy.

There was little evidence that women's inferences about men's sexual intent were erroneous. In Part 1 of Study 2, women's perceptions exceeded men's self-perceived sexual intent. In Part 2 of Study 2, women's perceptions fell between the two criterion measures. The finding in Part 1 of Study 2 superficially seems at odds with the results of Study 1 and the results of past studies, which tend to document greater sexual perceptions of men relative to women. However, past studies have assessed women's perceptions of men's sexual intent relative to men's perceptions of men—not relative to men's self-perceived sexual intent as we have done in this study.[5] The final results were the sibling effects, which are considered in the General Discussion.

GENERAL DISCUSSION

Women's Commitment Skepticism

These studies document a new effect predicted by EMT. We hypothesized that women have commitment-reading adaptations biased toward underperceiving men's commitment. We hypothesized this psychological adaptation on the basis of the proposition that ancestral women suffered greater costs when they erred by falsely inferring a prospective mate's commitment. We confirmed this hypothesis. Women underperceived men's commitment as assessed relative to two criterion measures in two independent studies. In contrast, we found no consistent evidence that men misperceive women's commitment.

Men's Sexual Overperception

Using a minimal method with brief descriptions of cues, these studies replicated the sex differences in perceptions of sexual intent documented in previous studies (e.g., Abbey, 1982; Abbey & Melby, 1986). We extended the past research by showing that men overestimate women's sexual intent as assessed relative to two criterion measures: women's perceptions of women and women's self-perceived sexual intent. Whereas past research focused specifically on whether men err in perceiving sexual intent, we also examined the accuracy of women's perceptions of sexual intent. In contrast to evidence of men's erroneous cross-sex perception, women's cross-sex perception of sexual intent falls between the two criterion measures of accuracy, suggesting that women may perceive men's sexual intent with reasonable accuracy.

In summary, the results of these studies suggest that men and women are biased mind readers. As predicted by EMT, men's and women's errors occur in different domains and in different directions. In the language of inferential statistics, men tend to make Type I errors in inferring women's sexual intent, and women tend to make Type II errors in inferring men's commitment.

The Sister Effect

Based on the adaptive-bias hypothesis, we predicted that men's sexual overperception would not occur when the target was their sister. This prediction was confirmed. Men's perceptions of their sisters' sexual intent were lower than their perceptions of other women's sexual intent. Moreover, men's perceptions of their sisters fell between the two criterion measures (women's perceptions of women and women's self-perceptions), suggesting that men may perceive their sisters' sexual intent fairly accurately.

In sharp contrast to men's correction for sisters, we found an opposite adjustment in women's perceptions of their brothers. Whereas women's perceptions of other men were between the two criterion measures, their perceptions of their brothers underestimated each criterion measure. We did not have an a priori hypothesis about women's perceptions of their brothers.

Our initial prediction of the sister effect was based on the hypothesis that men have evolved an adaptive bias to overinfer sexual interest only when forming inferences about a delimited group of women: those of reproductive age who are potential sexual partners. An alternative explanation, compatible with the current pattern of results, is that the sibling adjustments are driven by the well-known phenomenon whereby individuals tend not to think of their siblings sexually, perhaps as a product of incest-avoidance mechanisms (e.g., Westermarck, 1921), and as a consequence see them as less sexually interested in others when observing cues such as a smile. Thus, more definitive tests of the adaptive-bias explanation will rest with studies that examine inferences about the sexual intent of other targets. According to the adaptive-bias explanation, for example, the overinference of sexual intent should not occur when men evaluate smiles and other cues from postmenopausal women or prepubescent girls—a prediction not made by the incest-avoidance hypothesis or other explanations unique to siblings.

Limitations

There are several important limitations of these studies. The first is the uncertainty of our criterion measures. We have argued that self-perceptions and same-sex perceptions may be biased in opposite directions, bracketing the true state of reality. We therefore view cross-sex perceptions that exceed or underestimate both of these criterion measures as possible errors. The specific pattern of the results we obtained—men's and women's errors in opposite directions in the hypothesized domains, but possible accuracy in other domains—is difficult to attribute to a systematic bias in our criterion measures alone. An alternative explanation for our findings based on criterion-measure bias would face the substantial burden of explaining why women's and men's criterion measures are biased in different directions only for the hypothesized effects.

A second important limitation is that the tests of our hypotheses involved hypothetical scenarios rather than real-life encounters. Men's sexual overperception has been reported by women in surveys of naturally occurring events (Abbey, 1987) and has been documented using a wide variety of methodologies, including laboratory studies of interactions between newly acquainted men and women, studies using photos and films as stimuli, and studies (such as the present studies) using hypothetical scenarios. Men's apparent error transcends the method used to study it. This cross-method consistency corroborates the validity of using the hypothetical scenarios to study biases in interpersonal perception.

Ideally, the new effects we have documented—women's commitment underperception, the sibling effects, and the finding that men's self-perceived sexual intent is lower than women's perception of men's sexual intent—should be verified with the use of other methods, such as laboratory studies or other studies of live interactions. Pending explorations using other methods, it is worth noting that hypothetical scenarios are likely to reveal the default impressions that women and men have of the intentions of members of the opposite sex. Methods involving live interactions may reveal impressions that are affected by the somewhat idiosyncratic cues associated with particular interaction partners or particular settings. Default impressions of the opposite sex are important because they may be the starting points that anchor subsequently updated perceptions.

Future studies should also use the innovative methods of other accuracy researchers, such as the empathic accuracy method (Ickes, 1997), behavioral prediction methods (e.g., Levesque & Kenny, 1993), and other methods (e.g., Aron, Aron, Tudor, & Nelson, 1991; Sanitioso, Kunda, & Fong, 1990). Replication with these methods would also be useful because they offer alternative criterion measures.

Alternative Sexual Overperception Hypotheses

The hypothesis proposed to account for men's overperception of women's sexual intent contrasts with three previous hypotheses: the general oversexualization hypothesis, the media hypothesis, and the default-model hypothesis. The default model hypothesis, which proposed that men extend their self-perceptions to others, predicted that men should provide similar ratings for themselves, other men, and women. In Study 2, however, women's perception of men's sexual intent was significantly greater than men's self-perceived sexual intent and significantly lower than men's perceptions of other men's sexual intent, suggesting that men's self- and other perceptions are different. The oversexualization hypothesis and media hypothesis are challenged by the sister effect, which showed that men do not overperceive the sexual intent of all women. Men appear to correct their perceptions for their sisters.

One reviewer noted another possible explanation involving a socialized double-standard in American culture. According to this explanation, American society socializes men (and promotes stereotypes of men) to be interested in casual sex, whereas it socializes women (and promotes stereotypes of women) to be interested in commitment. Although it is undoubtedly true that men and women experience different socialization practices in the sexual domain (see, e.g., Low, 1989), we feel that this hypothesis and others like it are imprecise and lack the explanatory power to cogently account for the particular patterns of results, both from the current studies and the cumulative body of research findings. Nothing in the tenets of these alternative hypotheses predicts that men's and women's inferences will be biased in any direction. Why would men overinfer sexual interest in women just because they are socialized to be freer than women to pursue casual sex? In fact, using this same double-standard of socialization explanation, one might predict the opposite inferential bias on the part of men—that women tend not to be sexually interested—because they can plainly observe that women have been socialized to be sexually restricted. The key point is that nothing in the socialization and stereotype explanations or their variants appears to predict specific inferential biases, let alone particular patterns of inferential biases based on sex of actor and sex of target. These hypotheses tend to be sufficiently vague in their premises that they can be molded post hoc to explain any pattern of findings— bias in one direction, bias in the other direction, or no bias at all.

Future Directions

According to error management logic, varying the balance of false-positive and false-negative errors should cause shifts in the errors we have hypothesized. For ancestral men, for example, the costs of a missed sexual opportunity (false-negative error) would have been far lower, relative to the costs of failed pursuit (false-positive error), if a target woman was pre- or postreproductive, as indicated by cues to youth, health, or attractiveness. EMT predicts that such women will not trigger sexual overperceptions.

EMT should also be tested in other domains of inference, such as inferences about sexual infidelity and inferences about aggressive intent. For men, the costs in compromised paternity of failing to detect cues to sexual infidelity may have been sufficiently large to create biased mind reading, causing men to err by inferring infidelity even where none exists (Buss, in press). Similarly, the ancestral costs of failing to correctly detect aggressive intentions, relative to the costs of being overcautious, may have created biased mind-reading adaptations, which lead men and women to overestimate the aggressive intentions of others.

Error Management Theory and the Heuristics and Biases Approach

In most imaginable circumstances, the best possible reasoning system is one that is always 100% accurate. This is impossible, however, when decisions are made under uncertain conditions. A cue used once to successfully predict an event may later fail. According to EMT, the criterion of good reasoning under such conditions is not overall or on-average correctness (also see Funder, 1987). Instead, optimal designs are sometimes those that result in errors that historically minimized overall costs or maximized overall benefits. This rule of good design contrasts with the nearly ubiquitous assumption in psychology that optimal reasoning systems are those that best correspond to normative rules or that best produce veridical inferences.

In the heuristics and biases approach, the optimal accuracy assumption has been made explicit. In introducing the approach, Kahneman et al. (1982) lauded the influence of Bayes's theorem in psychology because it offered "a fully articulated model of optimal performance" (p. xi). Later, in summarizing the empirical harvest generated by the approach, Shafir and Tversky (1995) explained the difference between the "normative approach," which describes the "rational decision maker," and the "descriptive approach," which describes how "decisions are actually made" (p. 77). The assumed optimality of accuracy is also evident in the labels heuristics-and-biases researchers apply to reasoning effects that deviate from normative standards. Such deviations are called "illusions," "sins" (Piatelli-Palmarini, 1994), and "fallacies" (Tversky & Kahneman, 1974), and are described as "ludicrous" and "indefensible" (Tversky & Kahneman, 1971).

The view that evolved psychological mechanisms may be designed to be biased has an important implication for the interpretation of errors. Heuristics and biases researches have assumed that because cognitive capacity and information processing time are limited, systematic errors reveal information-processing shortcuts (Kahneman et al., 1982; Kahneman & Tversky, 1996; Tversky & Kahneman, 1974). This interpretation of errors appears to be the most common interpretation of errors in judgment and decision making (e.g., Lopes, 1991; Osherson, 1995). EMT, in contrast, proposes that some errors reveal the cost and benefit asymmetries present over evolutionary history. Errors may be evidence of evolved adaptive biases, not simplifying heuristics.

CONCLUSIONS

Errors have intrigued psychologists because they help to reveal the underlying design of the mind. They also point out human fallibility—something many psychologists endeavor to correct. The explanations for reasoning errors, however, remain in dispute (Cosmides & Tooby, 1996; Gigerenzer, 1996; Kahneman & Tversky, 1996). We offer an interpretation of errors that contrasts with the dominant interpretation of cognitive errors in psychology. Error management theory explains men's sexual overperception, predicts a new mind-reading error made by women, and predicts a case in which men's sexual overperception is corrected. We know of no alternative theory that would have predicted this specific pattern of results.

An important implication of error management theory is that many reasoning mechanisms are not designed to be maximally correct. This insight may alter the interpretation of known cognitive errors and may lead to the discovery of new cognitive errors. We have suggested several avenues for testing error management theory in domains such as inferences about infidelity and aggressive intent. Ultimately, these tests will determine the usefulness of error management theory as a broader model of error and bias in reasoning.

ENDNOTES

1. The three commitment-avoidance items in the cross-sex perception instrument were reverse-scored before creating the composite. All contrasts were conducted using local error terms. Contrasts designed to test a priori predictions were one-tailed tests; contrasts assessing differences for which there were no a priori predictions were two-tailed.
2. The analysis was limited to full biological siblings because the hypotheses pertained most directly to full biological siblings. The analysis was limited to siblings 15 years old or older because at this age most individuals have reached puberty and questions about sexual and commitment intent become relevant to them. Analysis using all siblings did not significantly alter the results.
3. An alternative explanation for men's more accurate reading of sisters' minds is familiarity—perhaps cross-sex siblings' minds are read more accurately because of the increased familiarity associated with living in the same household. To examine this hypothesis, we correlated the number of years that participants lived in the same household with their sibling (range: 4 to 21 years; $M = 15.66$, $SD = 3.09$) with the difference between participants' cross-sex and sibling perceptions. The difference between men's perceptions of women's sexual intent and their perceptions of their sisters' sexual intent was not significantly correlated with the number of years they lived in the same household (range of correlations with individual sexual-intent items was $-.08$ to $.05$, $p >$

.05), nor was the difference between women's perceptions of their brothers and their perceptions of men significantly correlated with the number of years they lived with their brothers (range of correlations was $-.01$ to $.15$, $ps > .05$). On the basis of this particular measure of familiarity, there is little support for the familiarity hypothesis. This is an imperfect measure of familiarity, given that it is confounded with variables such as the time at which siblings move away from home, and other tests of this alternative explanation may be warranted.
4. One reviewer suggested that the commitment avoidance items included in Study 2 may have primed an "uncommitted man" stereotype, which may have contaminated the results of each part of the study. In an independent sample the effects documented in Study 2 have been replicated using an instrument containing none of the potential priming items. Interested readers may contact the authors to obtain the replication results.
5. The two exceptions are Abbey's original lab study (Abbey, 1982) and an independent replication (Saal et al., 1989). In these studies, self-perceptions and same-sex perceptions were collected; however, the cross-sex perceptions not compared with each of these potential criterion measures. The statistical analyses did not differentiate between these measures, and these studies therefore could not address the question of whether men's self-perception differed from women's perception of the men.

REFERENCES

Abbey, A. (1982). Sex differences in attributions for friendly behavior: Do males misperceive females' friendliness? *Journal of Personality and Social Psychology, 42*, 830–838.

Abbey, A. (1987). Misperceptions of friendly behavior as sexual interest: A survey of naturally occurring instances. *Psychology of Women Quarterly, 11*, 173–194.

Abbey, A. (1991). Misperception as an antecedent of acquaintance rape: A consequence of ambiguity in communication between men and women. In A.

Parrot & L. Bechhofer (Eds.), *Acquaintance rape: The hidden crime* (pp. 96–111). New York: Wiley.

Abbey, A., & Harnish, R. J. (1995). Perception of sexual intent: The role of gender, alcohol consumption, and rape supportive attitudes. *Sex Roles, 32*, 297–313.

Abbey, A., & Melby, C. (1986). The effects of nonverbal cues on gender differences in perceptions of sexual intent. *Sex Roles, 15*, 283–289.

Aron, A., Aron, E. N., Tudor, M., & Nelson, G. (1991). Close relationships as including other in the self.

Journal of Personality and Social Psychology, 60, 241–253.

Betzig, L. (1989). Causes of conjugal dissolution. *Current Anthropology, 30,* 654–676.

Buss, D. M. (1994). *The evolution of desire: Strategies of human mating.* New York: Basic Books.

Buss, D. M. (in press). *The dangerous passion: Why jealousy is as necessary as love and sex.* New York: Free Press.

Buss, D. M., & Dedden, L. A. (1990). Derogation of competitors. *Journal of Social and Personal Relationships, 7,* 395–422.

Cosmides, L., & Tooby, J. (1996). Are humans good intuitive statisticians after all? Rethinking some conclusions from the literature on judgment under uncertainty. *Cognition, 58,* 1–73.

Dawkins, R. (1989). *The selfish gene* (2nd ed.). Oxford, England: Oxford University Press.

Einon, D. (1994). Are men more promiscuous than women? *Ethology and Sociobiology, 15,* 131–143.

Funder, D. C. (1987). Errors and mistakes: Evaluating the accuracy of social judgment. *Psychological Bulletin, 101,* 75–90.

Gigerenzer, G. (1996). On narrow norms and vague heuristics: A reply to Kahneman and Tversky (1996). *Psychological Review, 103,* 592–596.

Green, D. M., & Swets, J. A. (1966). *Signal detection and psychophysics.* New York: Wiley.

Hamilton, W. D. (1964). The genetical evolution of social behavior. *Journal of Theoretical Biology, 7,* 1–52.

Haselton, M. G., Buss, D. M., & DeKay, W. T. (1998, July). *A theory of errors in cross-sex mindreading.* Paper presented at the Human Behavior and Evolution Society Meeting, Davis, CA.

Hurtado, A. M., & Hill, K. R. (1992). Paternal effect on offspring survivorship among Ache and Hiwi hunter-gatherers. In B. S. Hewlett et al. (Eds.), *Father–child relations: Cultural and biosocial contexts* (pp. 31–55). New York: Aldine de Gruyter.

Ickes, W. (1997). *Empathic accuracy.* New York: Guilford Press.

Jankowiak, W. (Ed.). (1995). *Romantic passion: A universal experience?* New York: Columbia University Press.

Johnson, C. B., Stockdale, M. S., & Saal, F. E. (1991). Persistence of men's misperceptions of friendly cues across a variety of interpersonal encounters. *Psychology of Women Quarterly, 15,* 463–475.

Kahneman, D., Slovic, P., & Tversky, A. (1982). *Judgment under uncertainty: Heuristics and biases.* New York: Cambridge University Press.

Kahneman, D., & Tversky, A. (1996). On the reality of cognitive illusions. *Psychological Review, 103,* 582–591.

Levesque, M. L., & Kenny, D. A. (1993). Accuracy of behavioral predictions at zero acquaintance: A social relations analysis. *Journal of Personality and Social Psychology, 65,* 1178–1187.

Lopes, L. (1991). The rhetoric of irrationality. *Theory and Psychology, 1,* 65–82.

Low, B. S. (1989). Cross-cultural patterns in the training of children: An evolutionary perspective. *Journal of Comparative Psychology, 103,* 313–319.

Marks, G., & Miller, N. (1987). Ten years of research on the false-consensus effect: An empirical and theoretical review. *Psychological Bulletin, 102,* 72–90.

Nesse, R. M., & Williams, G. C. (1998). Evolution and the origins of disease. *Scientific American, 11,* 86–93.

Nisbett, R. E., & Ross, L. (1980). *Human inference: Strategies and shortcomings of social judgment.* Englewood Cliffs, NJ: Prentice Hall.

Osherson, D. N. (1995). Probability judgment. In E. E. Smith & D. N. Osherson (Eds.), *Thinking: An invitation to cognitive science* (2nd ed., Vol. 3, pp. 35–75). Cambridge, MA: MIT Press.

Piatelli-Palmarini, M. (1994). *Inevitable illusions.* New York: Wiley.

Saal, F. E., Johnson, C. B., & Weber, N. (1989). Friendly or sexy? It may depend on whom you ask. *Psychology of Women Quarterly, 13,* 263–276.

Sanitioso, R., Kunda, Z., & Fong, G. T. (1990). Motivated recruitment of autobiographical memories. *Journal of Personality and Social Psychology, 59,* 229–241.

Schlager, D. (1995). Evolutionary perspectives on paranoid disorder. *Delusional Disorders, 18,* 263–279.

Schmitt, D. P., & Buss, D. M. (1996). Strategic self-promotion and competitor derogation: Sex and context effects on the perceived effectiveness of mate attraction tactics. *Journal of Personality and Social Psychology, 70,* 1185–1204.

Searcy, W. A., & Brenowitz, E. A. (1988, March 10). Sex differences in species recognition of avian song. *Nature, 332,* 152–154.

Sedikides, C. (1993). Assessment, enhancement, and verification determinants of the self-evaluation process. *Journal of Personality and Social Psychology, 65,* 317–338.

Shafir, E., & Tversky, A. (1995). Decision making. In E. E. Smith & D. N. Osherson (Eds.), *Thinking: An invitation to cognitive science* (2nd ed., Vol. 3, pp. 77–100). Cambridge, MA: MIT Press.

Shotland, R. L., & Craig, J. M. (1988). Can men and women differentiate between friendly and sexually interested behavior? *Social Psychology Quarterly, 51,* 66–73.

Symons, D. (1979). *The evolution of human sexuality.* New York: Oxford University Press.

Tomarken, A. J., Mineka, S., & Cook, M. (1989). Fear-relevant selective associations and covariation bias. *Journal of Abnormal Psychology, 98,* 381–394.

Tversky, A., & Kahneman, D. (1971). Belief in the law of small numbers. *Psychological Bulletin, 76,* 105–110.

Tversky, A., & Kahneman, D. (1974, September 27). Judgment under uncertainty: Heuristics and biases. *Science, 185,* 1124–1131.

Westermarck, E. (1921). *The history of human marriage.* London: Macmillan.

Constants across Cultures in the Face and Emotion

PAUL EKMAN AND WALLACE V. FRIESEN

This study addresses the question of whether any facial expressions of emotion are universal. Recent studies showing that members of literate cultures associated the same emotion concepts with the same facial behaviors could not demonstrate that at least some facial expressions of emotion are universal; the cultures compared had all been exposed to some of the same mass media presentations of facial expression, and these may have taught the people in each culture to recognize the unique facial expressions of other cultures. To show that members of a preliterate culture who had minimal exposure to literate cultures would associate the same emotion concepts with the same facial behaviors as do members of Western and Eastern literate cultures, data were gathered in New Guinea by telling subjects a story, showing them a set of three faces, and asking them to select the face which showed the emotion appropriate to the story. The results provide evidence in support of the hypothesis that the association between particular facial muscular patterns and discrete emotions is universal.

Prolonged and at times heated controversy has failed to demonstrate whether facial behaviors associated with emotion are universal for man or specific to each culture. Darwin (1872) postulated universals in facial behavior on the basis of his evolutionary theory. Allport (1924), Asch (1952), and Tomkins (1962, 1963) have also postulated universals in emotional facial behavior, although each writer offered a different theoretical basis for his expectation. The culture-specific view, that facial behaviors become associated with emotion through culturally variable learning, received support from Klineberg's (1938) descriptions of how the facial behaviors described in Chinese literature differed from the facial behaviors associated with emotions in the Western world. More recently, Birdwhistell (1963) and LaBarre (1947) have argued against the possibility of any universals in emotional facial behavior supplying numerous anecdotal examples of variations between cultures.

Ekman (1968) and Ekman and Friesen (1969) considered these contradictory viewpoints within a framework which distinguished between those elements of facial behavior that are universal and those that are culture specific. They hypothesized that the universals are to be found in the relationship between distinctive patterns of the facial muscles and particular emotions (happiness, sadness, anger, fear, surprise, disgust, interest). They suggested that cultural differences would be seen in some of the stimuli, which through learning become established as elicitors of particular

P. Ekman and W. V. Friesen, "Constants across cultures in the face and emotion," *Journal of Personality and Social Psychology, 17* (1971): 124–129. Copyright © 1971 by the American Psychological Association. Reprinted with permission.

emotions, in the rules for controlling facial behavior in particular social settings, and in many of the consequences of emotional arousal.

To demonstrate the hypothesized universal element, Ekman and Friesen (1969) conducted experiments in which they showed still photographs of faces to people from different cultures in order to determine whether the same facial behavior would be judged as the same emotion, regardless of the observers' culture. The faces were selected on the basis of their conformity to Ekman, Friesen, and Tomkins's (in press) a priori descriptions of facial muscles involved in each emotion. College-educated subjects in Brazil, the United States, Argentina, Chile, and Japan were found to identify the same faces with the same emotion words, as were members of two preliterate cultures who had extensive contact with Western cultures (the Sadong of Borneo and the Fore of New Guinea), although the latter results were not as strong (Ekman, Sorenson, & Friesen, 1969). Izard (1968, 1969), working independently with his own set of faces, obtained comparable results across seven other culture-language groups.

While these investigators interpreted their results as evidence of universals in facial behavior, their interpretation was open to argument; because all the cultures they compared had exposure to some of the same mass media portrayals of facial behavior, members of these cultures might have learned to recognize the same set of conventions, or become familiar with each other's different facial behavior.

To overcome this difficulty in the interpretation of previous results, it is necessary to demonstrate that cultures which have had minimal visual contact with literate cultures show similarity to these cultures in their interpretation of facial behavior. The purpose of this paper was to test the hypothesis that members of a preliterate culture who had been selected to insure maximum visual isolation from literate cultures will identity the same emotion concepts with the same faces as do members of literate Western and Eastern cultures.

METHOD

Subjects

Members of the Fore linguistic-cultural group of the South East Highlands of New Guinea were studied. Until 12 years ago, this was an isolated, Neolithic, material culture (Gajdusek, 1963; Sorenson & Gajdusek, 1966). While many of these people now have had extensive contact with missionaries, government workers, traders, and United States scientists, some have had little such contact. Only subjects who met criteria established to screen out all but those who had minimal opportunity to learn to imitate or recognize uniquely Western facial behaviors were recruited for this experiment. These criteria made it quite unlikely that subjects could have so completely learned some foreign set of facial expressions of emotion that their judgments would be no different from those of members of literate cultures. Those selected had seen no movies, neither spoke nor understood English or Pidgin, had not lived in any of the Western settlement or government towns, and had never worked for a Caucasian (according to their own report). One-hundred and eighty-nine adults and 130 children, male and female, met these criteria. This sample comprises about 3% of the members of this culture.

In addition to data gathered from these more visually isolated members of the South Fore, data were also collected on members of this culture who had had the most contact with Westerners. These subjects all spoke English, had seen movies, lived in a Western settlement or government town, and had attended a missionary or government school for more than 1 year. Twenty-three male adults, but no females, met these criteria.

Judgment Task

In a pilot study conducted 1 year earlier with members of this same culture, a number of different judgment tasks were tried. The least Westernized subjects could not be asked to select from a printed list of emotion terms the one that was appropriate for a photograph, since they could not read. When the list was repeated to them with each photograph, they seemed to have difficulty remembering the list. Further, doubts remained about whether the meaning of a particular emotion concept was adequately conveyed by translating a single English word into a single South Fore word. Asking the subject to make up his own story about the emotions shown in a picture was not much more successful, although the problems were different. Subjects regarded this as a very difficult task, repeated probes were necessary, and as the procedure became lengthy, subjects became reluctant.

To solve these problems, it was decided to employ a task similar to that developed by Dashiell (1927) for use with young children.[1] Dashiell showed the child a group of three pictures simultaneously, read a story, and told the child to point to the picture in which the person's face showed the emotion described in the story. The advantages of this judgment task in a preliterate culture are that (a) the translator recounts well-rehearsed stories which can be recorded and checked for accurate translation; (b) the task involves no reading; (c) the subject does not have to remember a list of emotion terms; (d) the subject need not speak, but can point to give his answer; and (e) perfect translation of emotion words is not required since the story can help provide connotations.

Emotion Stories

With the exception of the stories for fear and surprise, those used in the present study were selected from those which had been most frequently given in the pilot study. Considerable care was taken to insure that each story selected was relevant to only one emotion within the Fore culture, and that members of the culture were agreed on what that emotion was. Since the stories told by the pilot subjects for fear and surprise did not meet these criteria, the authors composed stories for these emotions based on their experience within the culture. The stories used are given below:

Happiness: His (her) friends have come, and he (she) is happy.

Sadness: His (her) child (mother) has died, and he (she) feels very sad.

Anger: He (she) is angry; or he (she) is angry, about to fight.

Surprise: He (she) is just now looking at something new and unexpected.

Disgust: He (she) is looking at something he (she) dislikes; or He (she) is looking at something which smells bad.

Fear: He (she) is sitting in his (her) house all alone, and there is no one else in the village. There is no knife, axe, or bow and arrow in the house. A wild pig is standing in the door of the house, and the man (woman) is looking at the pig and is very afraid of it. The pig has been standing in the doorway for a few minutes, and the person is looking at it very afraid, and the pig won't move away from the door and he (she) is afraid the pig will bite him (her).[2]

Pictures and Emotions

The six emotions studied were those which had been found by more than one investigator to be discriminable within any one literate culture (cf. Ekman, Friesen, & Ellsworth, in press, for a review of findings). The photographs used to show the facial behavior for each of the six emotions had been judged by more than 70% of the observers in studies of more than one literate culture as showing that emotion. The sample included pictures of both posed and spontaneous behavior used by Ekman and Friesen (1968), Frijda (1968), Frois-Wittmann (1930), Izard (1968), Engen, Levy, and Schlosberg (1957), and Tomkins and McCarter (1964). A total of 40 pictures were used of 24 different stimulus persons, male and female, adult and child. The photographs were prepared as 3 × 5 inch prints, cropped to show only the face and neck.

Story-Photographs Trial

A single item consisted of an emotion story, a correct photograph, in which the facial behavior shown in the photograph was the same as that described in the story, and either one or two incorrect photograph(s). Adult subjects were given two incorrect pictures with each correct picture; children were given only one because of a shortage of copies of the stimuli.

Because of a limitation on the number of available photographs, and upon the subjects' time, not all of the possible pairings of correct and incorrect photographs were tested. Instead, the subjects were presented with some of the presumably more difficult discriminations among emotions. The emotion shown in at least one of the incorrect photographs was an emotion which past studies in literate cultures had found to be most often mistaken for the correct emotion. For example, when *anger* was the emotion described in the story, the incorrect choices included *disgust, fear,* or *sadness,* emotions which have been found to be often mistaken for anger. The age and sex of the stimulus persons shown in the correct and incorrect photographs were held constant within any trial.

No one subject was given all the emotion discriminations, because again the stimuli would have been too few and the task too long. Instead, subjects from different villages were required to make some of the same and some different discriminations. Subjects were shown from 6 to 12 sets of photographs, but no picture appeared in more than 1 of the sets shown to any one particular subject.[3] A subject's task included making at least three different emotion discriminations; the same story was told more than once, with differing correct and incorrect photographs, and often requiring discrimination among differing sets of emotions. For example, the anger story might have been read once with Anger Picture A, Sadness Picture B, and Fear Picture C; the same anger story might have been read again to the same subject, but now with Anger Picture D, Disgust Picture E, and Surprise Picture F.

Procedure

Two-person teams conducted the experiment. A member of the South Fore tribe recruited subjects, explained the task, and read the translated stories; a Caucasian recorded the subjects' responses. Three such teams operated at once within a village; one team with a male Caucasian worked with male adult subjects; the two others with female Caucasians worked with the female adult subjects and the children. In most instances, almost all members of a village participated in the experiment within less than 3 hours.

Considerable practice and explanation was given to the translators. They were told that there was no correct response and were discouraged from prompting. Repeated practice was given to insure that the translators always repeated the stories in the same way and resisted the temptation to embellish. Spot checks with tape recordings and back translations verified that this was successful. The Caucasians, who did know the correct responses, averted their faces from the view of the subject, looking down at their recording booklet, to reduce the probability of an unwitting experimenter bias effect. Data analysis did not reveal any systematic differences in the responses obtained with different translators.

RESULTS

No differences between male and female subjects were expected, and no such differences had been found in the literate culture data. In this New Guinea group, however, the women were more reluctant to participate in the experiment, and were considered by most outsiders to have had less contact with Caucasians than the men. The number of correct responses for each subject was calculated separately for males and females and for adults and children. The t tests were not significant; the trend was in the direction of better performance by women and girls. The data revealed no systematic differences between male and female subjects in the discrimination of particular emotions, or in relation to the sex of the stimulus person shown on the photographs. In the subsequent analyses, data from males and females were combined.

Table 1 shows the results for the least Westernized adults for each emotion discrimination. Within each row, the percentage of subjects who gave the correct response for a particular discrimination between three emotions was calculated across all subjects shown that particular discrimination, regardless of whether the photographs used to represent the three emotions differed for individual subjects. Within each row, each subject contributed only one response, and thus the sum of responses was derived from independent subjects. However the rows are not independent of each other. Data from a given subject appear in different rows, depending upon the particular discriminations he was asked to make. If a group of subjects was requested to discriminate the same emotion from the same two other emotions more than once, only one randomly chosen response was included in the table.

TABLE 1 Adult Results

Emotion Described in the Story	Emotions Shown in the Two Incorrect Photographs	No. *Ss*	% Choosing Correct Face
Happiness	Surprise, disgust	62	90**
	Surprise, sadness	57	93**
	Fear, anger	65	86**
	Disgust, anger	36	100**
Anger	Sadness, surprise	66	82**
	Disgust, surprise	31	87**
	Fear, sadness	31	87**
Sadness	Anger, fear	64	81**
	Anger, surprise	26	81**
	Anger, happiness	31	87**
	Anger, disgust	35	69*
	Disgust, surprise	35	77**
Disgust (smell story)	Sadness, surprise	65	77**
Disgust (dislike story)	Sadness, surprise	36	89**
Surprise	Fear, disgust	31	71*
	Happiness, anger	31	65*
Fear	Anger, disgust	92	64**
	Sadness, disgust	31	87**
	Anger, happiness	35	86**
	Disgust, happiness	26	85**
	Surprise, happiness	65	48
	Surprise, disgust	31	52
	Surprise, sadness	57	28[a]

*$p < .05$.
**$p < .01$.
[a] Subjects selected the surprise face (67%) at a significant level ($p < .01$, two-tailed test).

A binomial test of significance assuming chance performance to be one in three showed that the correct face was chosen at a significant level for all of the discriminations (rows) except that of fear from surprise. Twice, fear was not discriminated from surprise, and once surprise was chosen more often than fear, even though the story had been intended to describe fear. A binomial test assuming chance to be one in two (a more conservative test, justified if it was thought that within a set of three pictures, there may have been one which was obviously wrong) still yielded significant correct choices for all but the fear-from-surprise discriminations.

The results for the most Westernized male adults were almost exactly the same as those reported in Table 1 for the least Westernized male and female adults. The number of correct responses for each subject was calculated; the *t* test showed no significant difference between the most and least Westernized subjects. Again, the only failure to select the correct picture occurred when fear was to be distinguished from surprise.

Table 2 shows the results for the children, tabulated and tested in similar fashion. The children selected the correct face for all of their discriminations. Through an oversight, the one discrimination which the adults could not make, fear from surprise, was not tried with the children. The percentages reported in Table 2 are generally higher than those in Table 1, but this is probably due to the fact that the children were

TABLE 2   Results for Children

Emotion Described in the Story	Emotion Shown in the *One* Incorrect Photograph	No. S*s*	% Choosing the Correct Face
Happiness	Surprise	116	87*
	Sadness	25	96*
	Anger	25	100*
	Disgust	25	88*
Anger	Sadness	69	90*
Sadness	Anger	60	85*
	Surprise	33	76*
	Disgust	27	89*
	Fear	25	76*
Disgust (smell story)	Sadness	19	95*
Disgust (dislike story)	Sadness	27	78*
Surprise	Happiness	14	100*
	Disgust	14	100*
	Fear	19	95*
Fear	Sadness	25	92*
	Anger	25	88*
	Disgust	14	100*

*$p \geq .01$.

given two photographs rather than three, and chance performance would be 50% rather than about 33%. Six-and 7-year-old children were compared with 14- and 15-year-olds, by the same procedures as described for comparing males and females. No significant differences or trends were noted.

DISCUSSION

The results for both adults and children clearly support our hypothesis that particular facial behaviors are universally associated with particular emotions. With but one exception, the faces judged in literate cultures as showing particular emotions were comparably judged by people from a preliterate culture who had minimal opportunity to have learned to recognize uniquely Western facial expressions. Further evidence was obtained in another experiment, in which the facial behavior of these New Guineans was accurately recognized by members of a literate culture. In that study, visually isolated members of the South Fore posed emotions, and college students in the United States accurately judged the emotion intended from their videotaped facial behavior. The evidence from both studies contradicts the view that all facial behavior associated with emotion is culture specific, and that posed facial behavior is a unique set of culture-bound conventions not understandable to members of another culture.[4]

The only way to dismiss the evidence from both the judgment and posing studies would be to claim that even these New Guineans who had not seen movies, who did not speak or understand English or Pidgin, who had never worked for a Caucasian, still had *some* contact with Westerners, sufficient contact for them to learn to recognize and simulate culture-specific, uniquely Western facial behaviors associated with each emotion. While these subjects had some contact with Westerners, this argument seems implausible for three reasons. First, the criteria for selecting these subjects makes it highly improbable that they had learned a "foreign" set of facial behaviors to such a degree that they could not only recognize them, but also display them as well as those to whom the behaviors were native. Second, contact with Caucasians did not seem to have much influence on the judgment of emotion, since the most Westernized subjects did no better than the least Westernized and, like the latter, failed to distinguish fear from surprise. Third, the women, who commonly have even less contact with Westerners than the men, did as well in recognizing emotions.

The hypothesis that there are constants across cultures in emotional facial behavior is further supported by Eibl-Eibesfeldt's (1970) films of facial behavior occurring within its natural context in a number of preliterate cultures. Evidence of constants in facial behavior and emotion across cultures is also consistent with early studies which showed many similarities between the facial behavior of blind and sighted children (Fulcher, 1942; Goodenough, 1932; Thompson, 1941). Universals in facial behavior associated with emotion can be explained from a number of nonexclusive viewpoints as being due to evolution, innate neural programs, or learning experiences common to human development regardless of culture (e.g., those of Allport, 1924; Asch, 1952; Darwin, 1872; Huber, 1931; Izard, 1969; Peiper, 1963; Tomkins, 1962, 1963). To evaluate the different viewpoints will require further research, particularly on early development.

The failure of the New Guinean adults to discriminate fear from surprise, while succeeding in discriminating surprise from fear, and fear from other emotions, suggests that cultures may not make *all* of the same distinctions among emotions, but does not detract from the main finding that most of the distinctions were made across cultures. Experience within a culture, the kinds of events which typically elicit particular emotions, may act to influence the ability to discriminate particular pairs of emotions. Fear faces may not have been distinguished from surprise faces, because in this culture fearful events are almost always also surprising; that is, the sudden appearance of a hostile member of another village, the unexpected meeting of a ghost or sorcerer, etc.

The growing body of evidence of a pan-cultural element in emotional facial behavior does not imply the absence of cultural differences in the face and emotion. Ekman (1968) and Ekman and Friesen (1969) have suggested that cultural differences will be manifest in the circumstances which elicit an emotion, in the action consequences of an emotion, and in the display rules which govern the management of facial behavior in particular social settings. Izard (1969) agrees with the view that there are cultural differences in the antecedent and consequent events, and has also found evidence suggesting differences in attitudes about particular emotions.

ENDNOTES

1. Carrol E. Izard brought Dashiell's procedure to our attention. This method has also been used in recent studies of referential communications (e.g., Rosenberg & Gordon, 1968).
2. The fear story had to be long in order to eliminate possibilities for anger or surprise being associated with the story.
3. The number of sets of photographs shown varied among villages, because a limited number of photographs were available in this field setting; the need to assure that the three pictures in any one set were comparable (in terms of the configuration of the mouth, the tilt of the head, and the age of the stimulus persons) restricted the number of sets

which could be composed for some of the combinations.

4. If posed behavior were simply a set of arbitrary conventions, it would be unlikely that the same conventions would be utilized in the cultures discussed here. That does not, however, imply that posed facial behavior is identical with spontaneous behavior. Ekman, Friesen, and Ellsworth (in press) have suggested that most posed behavior is similar in appearance to that spontaneous facial behavior which is of extreme intensity and unmodulated, although it may still differ in onset, duration, and decay time.

REFERENCES

Allport, F. H. *Social psychology.* Boston: Houghton Mifflin, 1924.

Asch, S. E. *Social psychology.* Englewood Cliffs, N.J.: Prentice-Hall, 1952.

Birdwhistell, R. L. The kinesic level in the investigation of the emotions. In P. H. Knapp (Ed.), *Expression of the emotions in man.* New York: International Universities Press, 1963.

Darwin, C. *The expression of the emotions in man and animals.* London: Murray, 1872.

Dashiell, J. F. A new method of measuring reactions to facial expression of emotion. *Psychological Bulletin,* 1927, **24**, 174–175.

Eibl-Eibesfeldt, I. *Ethology, the biology of behavior.* New York: Holt, Rinehart & Winston, 1970.

Ekman, P. Research findings on recognition and display of facial behavior in literate and nonliterate cultures. *Proceedings of the 76th Annual Convention of the American Psychological Association,* 1968, **3**, 727. (Summary)

Ekman, P., & Friesen, W. V. Nonverbal behavior in psychotherapy research. In J. Shlien (Ed.), *Research in psychotherapy.* Vol. 3. Washington, D.C.: American Psychological Association, 1968.

Ekman, P., & Friesen, W. V. The repertoire of nonverbal behavior—Categories, origins, usage and coding. *Semiolica,* 1969, **1**, 49–98.

Ekman, P., Friesen, W. V., & Ellsworth, P. *Emotion in the human face: Guidelines for research and integration of findings.* New York: Pergamon Press, in press.

Ekman, P., Friesen, W. V., & Tomkins, S. S. Facial affect scoring technique: A first validity study. *Semiolica,* in press.

Ekman, P., Sorenson, E. R., & Friesen, W.V. Pan-cultural elements in facial displays of emotions. *Science,* 1969, **164**, 86–88.

Engen, T., Levy, N., & Schlosberg, H. A new series of facial expressions. *American Psychologist,* 1957, **12**, 264–266.

Frijda, N. H. Recognition of emotion. In L. Berkowilz (Ed.), *Advances in experimental social psychology.* New York: Academic Press, 1968.

Frois-Wittmann, J. The judgment of facial expression. *Journal of Experimental Psychology,* 1930, **13**, 113–151.

Fulcher, J. S. "Voluntary" facial expression in blind and seeing children. *Archives of Psychology,* 1942, **38**, 272.

Gajdusek, D. C. Kuru. *Transactions of the Royal Society of Tropical Medicine and Hygiene,* 1965, **57**, 151–169.

Goodenough, F. L. Expression of the emotions in a blind-deaf child. *Journal of Abnormal and Social Psychology,* 1932, **27**, 328–333.

Huber, E. *Evolution of facial musculature and facial expression.* Baltimore: Johns Hopkins Press, 1931.

Izard, C. E. Cross-cultural research findings on recognition in recognition of facial behavior. *Proceedings of the 76th Annual Convention of the American Psychological Association,* 1968, **3**, 727. (Summary)

Izard, C. E. The emotions and emotion constructs in personality and culture research. In R. B. Cattell (Ed.), *Handbook of modern personality theory.* Chicago: Aldine Press, 1969.

Klineberg, O. Emotional expression in Chinese literature. *Journal of Abnormal and Social Psychology,* 1938, **33**, 517–520.

Labarre, W. The cultural basis of emotions and gestures. *Journal of Personality,* 1947, **16**, 49–68.

Peiper, A. *Cerebral function in infancy and childhood.* New York: Consultants Bureau, 1963.

Rosenberg, S., & Gordon, A. Identification of facial expressions from affective descriptions: A probabilistic choice analysis of referential ambiguity. *Journal of Personality and Social Psychology,* 1968, **10**, 157–166.

Sorenson, E. R., & Gajdusek, D. C. The study of child behavior and development in primitive cultures. A research archive for ethnopediatric film investigations of styles in the patterning of the nervous system. *Pediatrics,* 1966, **37** (1, Pt. 2).

Thompson, J. Development of facial expression of emotion in blind and seeing children. *Archives of Psychology,* 1941, **37**, 264.

Tomkins, S. S. *Affect, imagery, consciousness.* Vol. 1. *The positive affects.* New York: Springer, 1962.

Tomkins, S. S. *Affect, imagery, consciousness.* Vol. 2. *The negative affects.* New York: Springer, 1963.

Tomkins, S. S., & McCarter, R. What and where are the primary affects? Some evidence for a theory. *Perceptual and Motor Skills,* 1964, **18**, 119–158.

Language as an Adaptation
to the Cognitive Niche

STEVEN PINKER

This chapter defends the theory that the human language faculty is a biological adaptation. It reviews the design of language and its distribution across the species, which suggest that complex language is an innate specialization of humans, and, like other examples of complex adaptive design in the natural world, a product of natural selection. Language is designed to code propositional information for the purpose of sharing it with others, and thus fits with other features of our zoologically distinctive "cognitive niche." The theory has recently been supported by two new areas of research: evolutionary game theory, and tests for selection in molecular evolution.

Keywords: Language evolution, Human evolution, Adaptation, Natural selection, Evolutionary psychology, Evolutionary game theory, Molecular evolution

INTRODUCTION

This chapter outlines the theory (first explicitly defended by Pinker & Bloom, 1990), that the human language faculty is a complex biological adaptation that evolved by natural selection for communication in a knowledge-using, socially interdependent lifestyle. This claim might seem to be anyone's first guess about the evolutionary status of language, and the default prediction from a Darwinian perspective on human psychological abilities. But the theory has proved to be controversial, as shown by the commentaries in Pinker & Bloom (1990) and the numerous debates on language evolution since then (Fitch, 2002; Hurford, Studdert-Kennedy, & Knight, 1998).

In the chapter I will discuss the design of the language faculty, the theory that language is an adaptation, alternatives to the theory, an examination of what language might be an adaptation for, and how the theory is being tested by new kinds of analyses and evidence.

THE DESIGN OF HUMAN LANGUAGE

The starting point in an analysis of the evolution of language must be an analysis of language itself (for other overviews, see Bickerton, 1990; Jackendoff, 2002; Miller, 1991). The most remarkable aspect of language is its *expressive power*: its ability to

From S. Pinker, "Language as an adaptation to the cognitive niche," in *Language evolution: Reports from the research frontier*, edited by M. Christiansen & S. Kirby (New York: Oxford University Press, 2000), Chapter 2. Reprinted by permission of Oxford University Press.

convey an unlimited number of ideas from one person to another via a structured stream of sound. Language can communicate anything from soap opera plots to theories of the origin of the universe, from lectures to threats to promises to questions. Accordingly, the most significant aspects of the language faculty are those that make such information transfer possible (Pinker, 1994; Pinker, 1999). The first cut in dissecting the language faculty is to separate the two principles behind this remarkable talent.

Words

The first principle underlies the mental lexicon, a finite memorized list of words. As Ferdinand de Saussure pointed out, a word is an arbitrary sign: a connection between a signal and a concept shared by the members of the community. The word *duck* doesn't look like a duck, walk like a duck or quack like a duck, but I can use it to convey the idea of a duck because we all have learned the same connection between the sound and the meaning. I can therefore bring the idea to mind in a listener simply by making that noise. If instead I had to shape the signal to evoke the thought using some perceptible connection between its form and its content, every word would require the inefficient contortions of the game of Charades.

The symbols underlying words are bidirectional. Generally if I can use a word I can understand it when someone else uses it, and vice-versa. When children learn words, their tongues are not molded into the right shape by parents, and they do not need to be rewarded for successive approximations to the target sound for every word they hear. Instead, children have an ability upon hearing somebody else use a word to know that they in turn can use it to that person or to a third party and expect to be understood.

Grammar

Of course we do not just learn individual words; we combine them into larger words, phrases, and sentences. This involves the second trick behind language, grammar. The principle behind grammar was articulated by Wilhelm von Humboldt as "the infinite use of finite media." Inside every language-user's head is a finite algorithm with the ability to generate an infinite number of potential sentences, each of which corresponds to a distinct thought. For example, our knowledge of English incorporates rules that say "a sentence may be composed of a noun phrase (subject) and a verb phrase (object)" and "a verb phrase may be composed of a verb, a noun phrase (object), and a sentence (complement)." That pair of rules is *recursive:* a phrase is defined as a sequence of phrases, and one or more of those daughter phrases can be of the same kind as the mother phrase. This creates a loop that can generate sentences of any size, such as "I wonder whether she knows that I know that she knows that he thinks she is interested in him." By means of generating an infinite number of sentences, we can convey an infinite number of distinct thoughts (see also Studdert-Kennedy, this volume), since every sentence has a different meaning (most linguists believe that true synonymy is rare or nonexistent).

Grammar can express an astonishing range of thoughts because our knowledge of grammar is couched in abstract categories such as "noun" and "verb" rather than concrete concepts such as "man" and "dog" or "eater" and "eaten" (Pinker, 1994; Pinker, 1999). This gives us an ability to talk about new kinds of ideas. We can talk about a dog biting a man, or, as in the journalist's definition of "news," a man biting a dog. We can talk about aliens landing in Roswell, or the universe beginning with a big bang, or Michael Jackson marrying Elvis's daughter. The abstractness of grammatical categories puts no restriction on the content of sentences; the recursive, combinatorial nature of grammar puts no limits on their complexity or number.

A grammar comprises many rules, which fall into subsystems. The most prominent is *syntax,* the component that combines words into phrases and sentences. One of the tools of syntax is linear order, which allows us to distinguish, say, *Man bites dog* from *Dog bites man.* Linear order is the most conspicuous property of syntax, but it is a relatively superficial one. Far more important is *constituency.* A sentence has a hierarchical structure, which allows us to convey complex propositions consisting of ideas embedded inside ideas. A simple demonstration comes from an ambiguous sentence such as *On tonight's program Dr. Ruth will discuss sex with Dick Cavett.* It is composed of a single string of words in a particular order but with two different meanings, which depend on their constituent bracketings: [*discuss*] [*sex*] [*with Dick Cavett*] versus [*discuss*] [*sex with Dick Cavett*]. Of course, most sentences in context are not blatantly ambiguous, but ambiguity illustrates the essential place of constituency in interpreting meaning from sentences. As with other symbolic systems that encode logical information, such as arithmetic, logic, and computer programming, it is essential to get the parentheses right, and that's what phrase structure in grammar does.

Syntax also involves *predicate-argument* structure, the component of language that encodes the relationship among a set of participants (Pinker, 1989). To understand a sentence one cannot merely pay attention to the order of words, or even the way they are grouped; one has to look up information associated with the predicate (usually the verb) which specifies how its arguments are placed in the sentence. For example, in the sentences *Man fears dog* and *Man frightens dog*, the word *man* is the subject in both cases, but its semantic role differs: in the first sentence the man causes the fear; in the second he experiences it. In understanding a sentence, one has to look up information stored with the mental dictionary entry of the verb and see whether it says (for instance) "my subject is the one experiencing the fear" or "my subject is the one causing the fear."

A fourth trick of syntax is known as transformations, movement, or binding traces. Once one has specified a hierarchical tree structure into which the words of a sentence are plugged, a further set of operations can alter it in precise ways. For example, the sentence *Dog is bitten by man* contains the verb *bite*, which ordinarily requires a direct object. But here the object is missing from its customary location; it has been "moved" to the front of the sentence. This gives us a way of shifting the emphasis and quantification of a given set of participants in an event or state. The sentences *Man bites dog* and *Dog is bitten by man* both express the same information about who did what to whom, but one of them is a comment about the man and the other is a comment about the dog. Similarly, sentences in which a phrase is replaced by a *wh*-word and moved to the front of a sentence, such as *Who did the dog bite?*, allow the speaker to seek the identity of one of the participants in a specified event or relationship. Transformations thus provide a layer of meaning beyond who did what to whom; that layer emphasizes or seeks information about one of the participants, while keeping the actual event being talked about constant.

Syntax, for all that complexity, is only one component of grammar. All languages have a second combinatorial system, morphology, in which simple words or parts of words (such as prefixes and suffixes) are assembled to produce complex words. The noun *duck*, for example, comes in two forms—*duck* and *ducks*—and the verb *quack* in four—*quack, quacks, quacked,* and *quacking.* In languages other than English morphology can play a much greater role. In Latin, for example, case suffixes on nouns convey information about who did what to whom, allowing one to scramble the left-to-right order of the words for emphasis or style. For example, *Canis hominem mordet* and *Hominum canis mordet* (different orders, same cases) have the same non-newsworthy meaning, and *Homo canem mordet* and *Canem homo mordet* have the same newsworthy meaning.

Language also embraces a third combinatorial system called phonology, which governs the sound pattern of a language. In no language do people form words by associating them directly with articulatory gestures like a movement of the tongue or lips. Instead, an inventory of gestures is combined into sequences, each defining a word. The combinations are governed by phonological rules and constraints that work in similar ways in all languages but whose specific content people have to acquire. English speakers, for example, sense that *bluck* is not a word but could be one, whereas *nguck* is not a word and could not be one (though it could be a word in other languages). All languages define templates for how words may be built out of hierarchically nested units such as feet, syllables, vowels and consonants, and features (articulatory gestures). Interestingly, whereas syntax and morphology are semantically compositional—one can predict the meaning of the whole by the meanings of the elements and the way they are combined—this is not true of phonology. One cannot predict the meaning of *duck* from the meaning of *d*, the meaning of *c*, and the meaning of *k*. Phonology is a combinatorial system that allows us to have large vocabularies (for example, 100,000 words is not atypical for an English speaker) without having to pair each one of them with a distinct noise. The presence of these two kinds of discrete combinatorial systems in language is sometimes called duality of patterning.

Phonology also contains a set of adjustment rules which, after the words are defined and combined into phrases, smooth out the sequence of articulatory gestures to make them easier to pronounce and comprehend. For instance, one set of rules in English causes us to pronounce the past-tense morpheme *-ed* in three different ways, depending on whether it is attached to *jogged, walked,* or *patted.* The adjustment for *walked* keeps the consonants at the end of a word either all voiced or all unvoiced, and the adjustment for *patted* inserts a vowel to separate two *d*-like sounds. These adjustments often function to make articulation easier or speech clearer in a way that is consistent across the language, but they are not merely products of a desire to be lazy or clear. These two goals are at cross-purposes, and the rules of phonology impose shared conventions among the speakers of a language as to exactly when one is allowed to be lazy in which way.

Interfaces of Language with Other Parts of the Mind

Grammar is only one component of language, and it has to interface with at least four other systems of the mind: perception, articulation, conceptual knowledge (which provides the meanings of words and their relationships), and social knowledge (how language can be used and interpreted in a social context). While these systems also serve nonlinguistic functions, and may have been carried over from earlier primate designs, at least some aspects of them may have evolved specifically to mesh with language. A likely example is the vocal tract: Darwin pointed to the fact that in humans every mouthful of food has to pass over the trachea, with some chance of getting lodged in it and causing death by choking. The human vocal tract has a low larynx compared to those of most other mammals, an arrangement that compromises a number of physiological functions but allows us to articulate a large range of vowel sounds. Lieberman has plausibly argued that physiological costs such as the risk of death by choking were outweighed in human evolution by the benefit of rapid, expressive communication (Lieberman, 1984).

IS LANGUAGE AN ADAPTATION?

In the biologist's sense of the word, an "adaptation" is a trait whose genetic basis was shaped by natural selection (as opposed to the everyday sense of a trait that is useful to the individual). What are the alternatives to the theory that language is an adaptation? And what are the reasons for believing it might be one?

Is Language a Distinct Part of the Human Phenotype?

One alternative is that language is not an adaptation itself, but a manifestation of more general cognitive abilities, such as "general intelligence," "a symbolic capacity," "cultural learning," "mimesis," or "hierarchically organized behavior" (see, e.g., Bates, Thal, & Marchman, 1991; Deacon, 1997; Tomasello, 1999). If so, these more general cognitive capacities would be the adaptation.

These alternatives are difficult to evaluate, because no one has spelled out a mechanistic theory of "general intelligence" or "cultural learning" that is capable of acquiring human language. Intelligence, learning, symbol comprehension, and so on don't happen by magic but need particular mechanisms, and it is likely that different mechanisms are needed in different domains such as vision, motor control, understanding the physical and social worlds, and so on (Pinker, 1997b). The ability to acquire and use the cultural symbols called "language" may require learning mechanisms adapted to that job. Attempts to model the acquisition of language using general-purpose algorithms such as those in traditional artificial intelligence or connectionist neural networks have failed to duplicate the complexity of human language (Pinker, 1979; Pinker, 1999; Pinker & Prince, 1988).

Though it is hard to know exactly what is meant by terms like "cultural learning" or "general intelligence," one can see whether mastery of language in the human species resembles abilities that are unambiguously culturally acquired, like agricultural techniques, chess skill, knowledge of government, and mathematical expertise, or whether it looks more like a part of the standard human phenotype, like fear, humor, or sexual desire. Some very general properties of the natural history of language suggests that the latter is more accurate (see Jackendoff, 2002; Lightfoot & Anderson, 2002; Pinker, 1994).

First, language is universal across societies and across neurological normal people within a society, unlike far simpler skills like farming techniques or chess. There may be technologically primitive peoples, but there are no primitive languages: the anthropologists who first documented the languages of nonstate societies a century ago were repeatedly astonished by their complexity and abstractness (Voegelin & Voegelin, 1977). And despite stereotypes to the contrary, the language of uneducated, working class, and rural speakers has been found to be systematic and rule-governed, though the rules may belong to dialects that differ from the standard one (Labov, 1969; McWhorter, 2002).

Second, languages conform to a universal design. A language is not just any conceivable code that maps efficiently from sound to meaning. The design specs listed in the preceding section—and indeed, far more subtle and complex properties of grammar—can be found in all human languages (Baker, 2001; Comrie, 1981; Greenberg, Ferguson, & Moravcsik, 1978; Hockett, 1960).

A third kind of evidence is the ontogenetic development of language. Children the world over pass through a universal series of stages in acquiring a language (Brown, 1973; Ingram, 1989; Pinker, 1994). That sequence culminates in mastery of the local tongue, despite the fact that learning a language requires solving the daunting problem of taking in a finite sample of sentences (speech from parents) and inducing a grammar capable of generating the infinite language from which they were drawn (Pinker, 1979; Pinker, 1984). Moreover, children's speech patterns, including their errors, are highly systematic, and often can be shown to conform to linguistic universals for which there was no direct evidence in parents' speech (Crain, 1998; Gordon, 1985; Kim et al., 1994).

A fourth kind of evidence also comes from the study of language acquisition. If children are thrown together without a pre-existing language that can be "culturally transmitted" to them, they will develop one of their own. One example, studied by Bickerton, comes from the polyglot slave and servant plantations in which the only lingua franca among adults was a pidgin, a makeshift communicative system with little in the way of grammar. The children in those plantations did not passively have the pidgin culturally transmitted to them, but quickly developed creole languages, which differ substantially from the pidgins and which have all the basic features of established human languages (Bickerton, 1981). Another example comes from deaf communities, where complex sign languages emerge quickly and spontaneously. A recent study in Nicaragua has tracked the emergence of a complex sign language in little more than a decade, and has shown that the most fluent and creative users of the language were the children (Senghas & Coppola, 2001).

A fifth kind of evidence is that language and general intelligence, to the extent we can make sense of that term, seem to be doubly dissociable in neurological and genetic disorders. In aphasias and in the genetically caused developmental syndrome called Specific Language Impairment, intelligent people can have extreme difficulties speaking and understanding (Leonard, 1998; Siegal, Varley, & Want, 2001; van der Lely,

Rosen, & McClelland, 1998). Conversely, in a number of retardation syndromes, such as Williams syndrome and the sequelae of hydrocephalus, substantially retarded children may speak fluently and grammatically and do well on tests of grammatical comprehension and judgment (Clahsen & Almazen, 1998; Curtiss, 1989; Rossen, Klima, Bellugi, Bihrle, & Jones, 1996). Few of these dissociations are absolute, with language or nonlinguistic cognition completely spared or completely impaired. But the fact that the two kinds of abilities can dissociate quantitatively and along multiple dimensions shows that they are not manifestations of a single underlying ability.

Did Language Evolve by Means Other Than Natural Selection?

A different alternative to the hypothesis that language is an adaptation is the possibility that it evolved by mechanisms other than natural selection, a hypothesis associated with Stephen Jay Gould and Noam Chomsky (Chomsky, 1988; Gould, 1997; see Piatelli-Palmarini, 1989 and Pinker & Bloom, 1990 for discussion). On this view, language may have evolved all at once as the product of a macromutation. Or the genes promoting language may have become fixed by random genetic drift or by genetic hitchhiking (i.e., genes that were near other genes that were the real target of selection). Or it may have arisen as a by-product of some other evolutionary development such as a large brain, perhaps because of physical constraints on how neurons can be packed into the skull.

This theory is hard to evaluate (though as we shall see, not impossible), because there have been no specific proposals fleshing out the theory (for example, specifying the physical constraint that makes language a neurobiological necessity). So what is the appeal of the nonselectionist theories?

One is a general misconception, spread by Gould, that natural selection has become an obsolete or minor concept in evolutionary biology, and that explanations in terms of by-products (what he called "spandrels") or physical constraints are to be preferred in principle (e.g., Piatelli-Palmarini, 1989). This is a misconception because natural selection remains the only evolutionary force capable of generating complex adaptive design, in which a feature of an organism (such as the eye or heart) has a nonrandom organization that enables it to attain an improbable goal that fosters survival and reproduction (Dawkins, 1986; Williams, 1966). Moreover, natural selection is a rigorous concept which can be modeled mathematically or in computer simulations, measured in natural environments, and detected by statistical analyses of organisms' genomes (Kreitman, 2000a; Maynard Smith, 1988; Przeworski, Hudson, & Di Rienzo, 2000; Weiner, 1994).

A second appeal of nonselectionist theories comes from a skepticism that language could have provided enough reproductive benefits to have been selected for. According to one objection, popular among linguists, language has arbitrary features that do not obviously contribute to communication. However, *all* communication systems have arbitrary features (such as the particular sequences of dots and dashes making up Morse code), because arbitrary ways of linking messages to signals are useful as long as they are shared by sender and recipient. Moreover, since a feature that eases the task of the speaker (by omitting information or reducing the complexity of the signal) will complicate the task of the listener (by making the message more ambiguous or vulnerable to noise), a shared code must legislate arbitrary conventions that don't consistently favor any single desideratum (Pinker & Bloom, 1990).

Another argument for nonselectionist theories is that grammar is more complicated than it needs to be to fulfill the communicative needs of a hunter-gatherer lifestyle. As one skeptic put it, "How does recursion help in the hunt for mastodons?" But as Bloom and I pointed out, complex grammar is anything but a useless luxury: "It makes a big difference whether a far-off region is reached by taking the trail that is in front of the large tree or the trail that the large tree is in front of. It makes a difference whether that region has animals that you can eat or animals that can eat you." Since selection can proceed even with small reproductive advantages (say, one percent), the evolution of complex grammar presents no paradox.

A third misconception is that if language is absent from chimpanzees, it must have evolved by a single macromutation. This is seen as an argument for a macromutational theory by those who believe that human language is qualitatively distinct from the communicative abilities of chimpanzees, and as an argument that human language cannot be qualitatively distinct from the communicative abilities of chimpanzees by those who believe that macromutations are improbable. But both arguments are based on a misunderstanding of how evolution works. Chimpanzees and bonobos are our closest living relatives, but that does not mean that we evolved from them. Rather, humans evolved from an extinct common ancestor that lived six to eight million years ago. There were many other (now-extinct) species in the lineage from the common ancestor to modern humans (australopithecines, *habilis, ergaster,* archaic *sapiens*, etc.), and more important, many individuals making up the lineages that we group into species for convenience. Language could well have evolved gradually *after* the chimp-human split, in the 200,000–300,000 generations that make up the lineage leading to modern humans. Language, that is, could be an autapomorphy: a trait that evolved in one lineage but not its sister lineages.

The final appeal of the nonselectionist hypothesis is that language could only have been useful once it was completely in place: a language is useless if you are the only one to have evolved the ability to speak it. But this objection could be raised about the evolution of *any* communicative system, and we know that communication has evolved many times in the animal kingdom. The solution is that comprehension does not have to be in perfect synchrony with production. In the case of language, it is often possible to decode parts of an utterance in a language one has not completely mastered. When some individuals are making important distinctions that can be decoded by listeners only with cognitive effort, it could set up a pressure for the evolution of neural mechanisms that would make this decoding process become increasingly automatic and effortlessly learned (Pinker & Bloom, 1990). The process whereby environmentally-induced responses set up selection pressures for such responses to become innate, triggering conventional Darwinian evolution that superficially mimics a Lamarckian sequence, is known as the Baldwin Effect (Hinton & Nowlan, 1987).

Opposing these spurious arguments for the nonselectionist hypothesis is a strong prima facie reason to favor the selectionist one: the standard argument in evolutionary biology that only natural selection can explain the evolution of complex adaptive design (Dawkins, 1986; Williams, 1966). The information processing circuitry necessary to produce, comprehend, and learn language requires considerable organization.

Randomly organized neural networks, or randomly selected subroutines from an artificial intelligence library, do not give rise to a system that can learn and use a human language. As we saw, language is not just a set of symbolic labels for concepts, not just the use of linear order, not just the use of hierarchical structure, and not just a blurting out of a sequence of sounds. It is an integrated system containing a lexicon, several components of grammar, and interfaces to input-output systems, possibly with language-specific modifications of their own. And this complexity is not just there for show, but makes possible a remarkable ability: language's vast expressive power, rapid acquisition by children, and efficient use by adults.

As with other complex organs that accomplish improbable feats, the necessary circuitry for language is unlikely to have evolved by a process that is insensitive to the functionality of the end product, such as a single mutation, genetic drift, or arbitrary physical constraints. Natural selection is the most plausible explanation of the evolution of language, because it is the only physical process in which how well something works can explain how it came into existence.

WHAT DID LANGUAGE EVOLVE FOR?

If language is an adaptation, what is it an adaptation for? Note that this is different from the question of what language is typically *used* for, especially what it is used for at present. It is a question about the "engineering design" of language and the extent to which it informs us about the selective pressures that shaped it.

What is the machinery of language trying to accomplish? The system appears as if it was put together to encode propositional information—who did what to whom, what is true of what, when, where and why—into a signal that can be conveyed from one person to another. It is not hard to see why it might have been adaptive for a species with the rest of our characteristics to evolve such an ability. The structures of grammar are well suited to conveying information about technology, such as which two things can be put together to produce a third thing; about the local environment, such as where things are; about the social environment, such as who did what to whom, when where and why; and about one's own intentions, such as "If you do this, I will do that," which accurately convey the promises and threats that undergird relations of exchange and dominance.

The Cognitive Niche

Gathering and exchanging information is, in turn, integral to the larger niche that modern *Homo sapiens* has filled, which John Tooby and Irven DeVore (Tooby & DeVore, 1987) have called "the cognitive niche" (it may also be called the "informavore" niche, following a coinage by George Miller). Tooby and DeVore developed a unified explanation of the many human traits that are unusual in the rest of the living world. They include our extensive manufacture of and dependence on complex tools, our wide range of habitats and diets, our extended childhoods and long lives, our hypersociality, our complex patterns of mating and sexuality, and our division into groups or cultures with distinctive patterns of behavior. Tooby and DeVore proposed that the human lifestyle is a consequence of a specialization for overcoming the evolutionary fixed defenses of plants and animals (poisons, coverings, stealth, speed, and so on) by cause-and-effect reasoning. Such reasoning enables humans to invent and use new technologies (such as weapons, traps, coordinated driving of game, and ways of detoxifying plants) that exploit other living things before they can develop defensive countermeasures in evolutionary time. This cause-and-effect reasoning depends on intuitive theories about various domains of the world, such as objects, forces, paths, places, manners, states, substances, hidden biochemical essences, and other people's beliefs and desires.

The information captured in these intuitive theories is reminiscent of the information that the machinery of grammar is designed to convert into strings of sounds. It cannot be a coincidence that humans are special in their ability to outsmart other animals and plants by cause-and-effect reasoning, and that language is a way of converting information about cause-and-effect and action into perceptible signals.

A distinctive and important feature of information is that it can be duplicated without loss. If I give you a fish, I don't have the fish, as we know from sayings like "you can't eat your cake and have it." But if I tell you how to fish, it is not the case that I now lack the knowledge of how to fish. Information is what economists call a nonrival good, a concept recently made famous by debates about intellectual property (such as musical recordings that can be shared without cost on the Internet).

Tooby and DeVore have pointed out that a species that has evolved to rely on information should thus also evolve a means to *exchange* that information. Language multiplies the benefit of knowledge, because a bit of know-how is useful not only for its practical benefits to oneself but as a trade good with others. Using language, I can exchange knowledge with somebody else at a low cost to myself and hope to get something in return. It can also lower the original acquisition cost—I can learn about how to catch a rabbit from someone else's trial and error, without having to go through it myself.

A possible objection to this theory is that organisms are competitors, so sharing information is costly because of the advantages it gives to one's competitors. If I teach someone to fish, I may still know how to fish, but they may now overfish the local lake, leaving no fish for me. But this is just the standard problem of the evolution of any form of cooperation or altruism, and the solution in the case of language is the same. By sharing information with our kin, we help copies of our genes inside those kin, including genes that make language come naturally. As for non-kin, if we inform only those people who are likely to return the favor, both of us can gain the benefits of trade. It seems clear that we do use our faculties of social cognition to ration our conversation to those with whom we have established a nonexploitative relationship; hence the expression "to be on speaking terms."

Language, therefore, meshes neatly with the other features of the cognitive niche. The zoologically unusual features of *Homo sapiens* can be explained parsimoniously by the idea that humans have evolved an ability to encode information about the causal structure of the world and to share it among themselves. Our hypersociality comes about because information is a particularly good commodity of exchange that makes it worth people's while to hang out together. Our long childhood and extensive biparental investment are the ingredients of an apprenticeship: before we go out in the world, we spend a lot of time learning what the people around us have figured out.

And because of the greater payoff for investment in children, fathers, and not just mothers, have an incentive to invest in their children. This leads to changes in sexuality and to social arrangements (such as marriage and families) that connect men to their children and to the mothers of those children.

Humans depend on culture, and culture can be seen in part as a pool of local expertise. Many traditions are endemic to a people in an area because know-how and social conventions have spread via a local network of information sharing. Humans have evolved to have a long lifespan (one end of the evolutionary ubiquitous tradeoff between longevity and fecundity) because once you've had an expensive education you might as well make the most out of it by having a long period in which the expertise can be put to use. Finally, the reason that humans can inhabit such a wide range of habitats is that our minds are not adapted to a narrow, specialized domain of knowledge, such as how to catch a rabbit. Our knowledge is more abstract, such as how living things work and how objects collide with and stick to each other. That mindset for construing the world can be applied to many kinds of environments rather than confining us to a single ecosystem.

On this view, then, three key features of the distinctively human lifestyle—know-how, sociality, and language—coevolved, each constituting a selection pressure for the others.

Alternatives to the Cognitive Niche Theory

Several alternative hypotheses acknowledge that language is an adaptation but disagree on what it is an adaptation for. One possibility, inspired by an influential theory of the evolution of communication by Dawkins and Krebs (Dawkins, 1982), is that language evolved not to inform others but to manipulate and deceive them. The problem with this theory is that unlike signals with the physiological power to manipulate another organism directly, such as loud noises or chemicals, the signals of language are impotent unless the recipient actively applies complicated computations to decode them. It is impossible to use language to manipulate someone who doesn't understand the language, so hominids in the presence of the first linguistic manipulators would have done best by refusing to allow their nascent language systems to evolve further, and language evolution would have been over before it began.

Another possibility is that language evolved to allow us to think rather than to communicate. According to one argument, it is impossible to think at human levels of complexity without a representational medium for propositions, and language is that medium (Bickerton, 1990). According to another argument, we spend more time talking to ourselves that talking to other people, so if language has any function at all, it must be thought rather than communication (Chomsky, 2002). These theories have two problems. One is that they assume the strongest possible form of the Whorfian hypothesis—that thought depends entirely on language—which is unliklely for a number of reasons (see Pinker, 1994; Pinker, 2002; Siegal et al., 2001; Weiskrantz, 1988). The other is that if language evolved to represent information internally, much of the apparatus of grammar, which converts logical relationships into perceptible signals, would be superfluous. Language would not need rules for defining word orders, case markers, phonological strings, adjustment rules, and so on, because the brain could more efficiently code the information to itself silently using tangled networks of variables and pointers.

Considerations of language design rule out other putative selectional pressures. Language is unlikely to have evolved as a direct substitute for grooming (Dunbar, 1998), or as a courtship device to advertise the fitness of our brains (Miller, 2000), because such pressures would not have led to an ability to code complex abstract propositions into signals. A fixed set of greetings would suffice for the former; meaningless displays of virtuosity, as in scat singing, would suffice for the latter.

NEW TESTS OF THE THEORY THAT
LANGUAGE IS AN ADAPTATION

Contrary to the common accusation that evolutionary hypotheses, especially ones about language, are post hoc "just-so" stories, the hypothesis that language is an evolutionary adaptation can be made rigorous and put to empirical test. I will conclude by reviewing two new areas of research on the evolution of language that have blossomed since my 1990 paper with Bloom and which are beginning to support its major predictions.

Language and Evolutionary Game Theory

Good theories of adaptation can be distinguished from bad ones (Williams, 1966). The bad ones try to explain one bit of our psychology (say, humor or music) by appealing to some other, equally mysterious bit (laughing makes you feel better; people like to make music with other people). The good ones use some *independently established* finding of engineering or mathematics to show that some mechanism can efficiently attain some goal in some environment. These engineering benchmarks can serve as predictions for how Darwinian organisms ought to work: the more uncannily the engineering specs match the facts of the organism, the more confidently one infers that the organism was selected to carry out that function.

Evolutionary game theory has allowed biologists to predict how organisms ought to interact with other organisms coevolving their own strategies (Maynard Smith, 1982). Language, like sex, aggression, and cooperation, is a game it takes two to play, and game theory can provide the external criteria for utility enjoyed by the rest of evolutionary biology. Modelers assume only that the transmission of information between partners provides them with an advantage (say, by exchanging information or coordinating their behavior), and that the advantage translates into more offspring, with similar communicative skills. The question then is how a stable communication system might evolve from repeated pairwise interactions, and crucially, whether such systems have the major design features of human language.

The first such attempt was a set of simulations by Hurford showing that one of the defining properties of human language, the arbitrary, bi-directional sign, will drive out other schemes over evolutionary time (Hurford, 1989). More recently, Nowak and his collaborators have now done the same for two of the other central design features of language (Nowak & Krakauer, 1999; Nowak, Krakauer, & Dress, 1999a; Nowak, Plotkin, & Jansen, 2000).

Nowak and his colleagues pointed out that in all communication systems, errors in signaling or perception are inevitable, especially when signals are physically similar. Imagine organisms that use a different sound (say, a vowel) for every concept they wish to communicate. As they communicate more concepts, they will need additional sounds, which will be physically closer and hence harder to discriminate. At some point adding new signals just makes the whole repertoire more confusable and fails to increase its net communicative power. Nowak and colleagues showed that this limitation can be overcome by capping the number of signals and stringing them together into sequences, one *sequence* per concept. The sequences are what we call words, and as I mentioned earlier, the combination of meaningless vowels and consonants into meaningful words by rules of phonology is a universal property of language, half of the trait called "duality of patterning." Nowak and his colleagues have shown how its evolution is likely among communicators with a large number of messages to convey, a precondition that plausibly characterizes occupants of the cognitive niche.

Nowak and his colleagues have recently motivated another hallmark of language. Imagine a language in which each message was conveyed by a single word. For any word to survive in a community, it must be used frequently enough to be heard and remembered by all the learners. As new words are added to the vocabularies of speakers, old words must be used less often, and they are liable to fade, leaving the language no more expressive than before. Nowak et al. point out that this limitation can be overcome by communicators who use compositional syntax: rather than pairing each word with an entire event, they pair each word with a *component* of an event (a participant, an action, a relationship), and string the words together in an order that reflects their roles (e.g., *Dog bites man*). Such communicators need not memorize a word for every event, reducing the word-learning burden and allowing them to talk about events that lack words. Syntax and semantics, the other half of the duality of patterning, will evolve.

Nowak et al. note that syntax has a cost: the requirement to attend to the order of words. Its benefits exceed the costs only when the number of events worth communicating exceeds a threshold. This "syntax threshold" is most likely to be crossed when the environment, as conceptualized by the communicators, has a combinatorial structure: for example, when any of a number of actors (dogs, cats, men, women, children) can engage in any of a number of actions (walking, running, sleeping, biting). In such a world, the number of words that have to be learned by a syntactic communicator equals the sum of the number of actors, actions, places, and so on, whereas the number that must be learned by a nonsyntactic communicator equals their *product,* a potentially unlearnable number. Nowak et al. thus proved the theoretical soundness of the conjecture of Pinker and Bloom (1990) that syntax is invaluable to an analytical mind in a combinatorial world.

Language and Molecular Evolution

Mathematical models and computer simulations can show that the advantages claimed for some feature of language really can evolve by known mechanisms of natural selection. These models cannot, of course, show that language *in fact* evolved according to the proposed scenario. But recent advances in molecular and population genetics may provide ways of testing whether selection in fact occurred.

Evolution is a change in gene frequencies, and the first prediction of the theory that language is an evolutionary adaptation is that there should be genes that have as one of their distinctive effects the development of normal human language abilities. Such a gene would be identifiable as an allelic alternative to a gene that leads to an impairment in language. Since pleiotropy is ubiquitous, one need not expect that such a gene would affect *only* language, but its effects on language should not be consequences of some more general deficit such as a hearing disorder, dysarthria, or retardation.

Clinical psycholinguists have long known of the collection of syndromes called Specific Language Impairment (SLI), in which a child fails to develop language on schedule and struggles with it throughout life (Bishop, North, & Donlan, 1995; Leonard, 1998; van der Lely et al., 1998). By definition SLI is not a consequence of autism, deafness, retardation, or other nonlinguistic problems, though it may co-occur with them. In one form of the syndrome, sometimes called "Grammatical SLI," the children are normal in intelligence, auditory perception, and the use of language in a social context, but their speech is filled with grammatical errors and they are selectively deficient in detecting ungrammaticality and in discriminating meaning based on a sentence's grammar (van der Lely et al., 1998; van der Lely & Stollwerck, 1996). Though it was once thought that SLI comes from a deficit in processing rapidly changing sounds, that theory has been disproven (Bishop, Carlyon, Deeks, & Bishop, 1999; Bishop, Bishop, & Norbury, 2001; van der Lely et al., 1998).

SLI runs in families and is more concordant in monozygotic than in dizygotic twins, suggesting it has a heritable component (Bishop et al., 1995; Stromswold, 2001; van der Lely & Stollwerck, 1996). But the inheritance patterns are usually complex, and until recently little could be said about its genetic basis. In 1990 investigators described a large multi-generational family, the KEs, in which half the members suffered from a disorder of speech and language, distributed within the family in the manner of an autosomal dominant gene (Hurst et al., 1990). Extensive testing by psycholinguists showed a complex phenotype (Bishop, 2002). The affected family members on average have lower intelligence test scores (perhaps because verbal coding helps performance in a variety of tasks), but their language impairment cannot be a simple consequence of low intelligence, because some of the affected members score in the normal range, and some score higher than their unaffected relatives (Bishop, 2002; Lai et al., 2001). And though the affected members have problems in speech articulation (especially as children) and in fine movements of the mouth and tongue (such as sticking out their tongue or blowing on command), their language disorder cannot be reduced to a motor problem, because they also have trouble identifying phonemes, understanding sentences, judging grammaticality, and other language skills (Bishop, 2002).

In 2001, geneticists identified a gene on Chromosome 7, FOXP2, that is perfectly associated with the syndrome within the KE family and in an unrelated individual (Lai et al., 2001). They also argued on a number of grounds that the normal allele plays a causal role in the development of the brain circuitry underlying language and speech, rather than merely disrupting that circuitry when mutated.

A second crucial prediction of the language-as-adaptation theory is that there should be *many* genes for language. If human language can be installed by a single gene, there would be no need to invoke natural selection, because it is not staggeringly improbable that a single gene could have reached fixation by genetic drift or hitchhiking. But if a large set of coevolved genes is necessary, probability considerations would militate against such explanations. The more genes are required for normal language, the lower the odds that our species could have accumulated them all by chance.

It seems increasingly likely that in fact many genes are required. In no known case of SLI is language wiped out completely, as would happen if language was controlled by a single gene which occasionally is found in mutated form. Moreover, SLI is an umbrella term for many distinct syndromes (Leonard, 1998; Stromswold, 2001; The SLI Consortium, 2002). Grammatical SLI, for example, is distinct from the syndrome affecting the KE family, which in turn is distinct from other cases of SLI known to clinicians (van der Lely & Christian, 1998). In yet another syndrome, language delay, children are late in developing language but soon catch up and can grow up without problems (Sowell, 1997). Language delay is highly heritable (Stromswold, 2001) and its statistical distribution in the population suggests that it is a distinct genetic syndrome rather than one end of a continuum of developmental timetables (Dale et al., 1998). There are yet other heritable disorders involving language (Stromswold, 2001), such as stuttering and dyslexia (a problem in learning to read which may often be a consequence of more general problems with language). Both have been associated with specific sets of chromosomal regions (Stromswold, 2001).

With recent advances in genomics, the polygenic nature of language is likely to become more firmly established. In 2002, an "SLI Consortium" discovered two novel loci (distinct from FOXP2) that are highly associated with SLI but not associated with low nonlinguistic intelligence (The SLI Consortium, 2002). Moreover, the two loci were associated with different aspects of language impairment, one with the ability to repeat nonwords, the other with expressive language, further underscoring the genetic complexity of language.

The most important prediction of the adaptation theory is that language should show evidence of a history of selection. The general complaint that evolutionary hypotheses are untestable has been decisively refuted by the recent explosion of quantitative techniques that can detect a history of selection in patterns of statistical variation among genes (Kreitman, 2000b; Przeworski et al., 2000). The tests depend on the existence of neutral evolution: random substitutions of nucleotides in noncoding regions of the genome, or substitutions in coding regions that lead to synonymous codons. These changes have no effect on the organism's phenotype, and hence are invisible to natural selection. The genetic noise caused by neutral evolution can thus serve as a baseline or null hypothesis against which the effects of selection (which by definition reduces variability in the phenotype) can be measured.

For example, if a gene has undergone more nucleotide replacements that alter its protein product than replacements that do not, the gene must have been subject to selection based on the function of the protein, rather than having accumulated mutations at random, which should have left equal numbers of synonymous and amino-acid-replacing changes. Alternatively, one can compare the variability of a gene among the members of a given species with the variability of that gene across species; a gene that has been subjected to selection should vary more between species than within species.

Still other techniques compare the variability of a given gene to estimates of the variability expected by chance, or check whether a marker for an allele is found in a region of the chromosome that shows reduced variation in the population because of a selective sweep. About a dozen such techniques have been devised so far. The calculations are complicated by the fact that recombination rate differences, migrations, population expansions, and population subdivisions can also cause deviations from the expectations of neutral evolution, and therefore can be confused with signs of selection. But techniques to deal with these problems have been developed as well.

It is now obvious how one can test the language-as-adaptation hypothesis (or indeed, any hypothesis about a psychological adaptation). If a gene associated with a trait has been identified, one can measure its variation in the population and apply the tests for selection. The day that I wrote this paragraph, the first of such tests has been reported in *Nature* (Enard et al., 2002). A team of geneticists examined the FOXP2 protein (the cause of the KE family's speech and language disorder) in the mouse, several primate species, and several human populations. They found that the protein is highly conserved among mammals: the chimpanzee, gorilla, and monkey versions of the protein are identical to each other and differ in only one amino acid from the mouse version and two from the human version. But two of the three differences between humans and mice occurred in the human lineage after its separation from the common ancestor with the chimpanzee. And though the variations in the gene sequence among all the nonhuman animals produce few if any functional differences, at least one of the changes in the human lineage significantly altered the function of the protein. Moreover, the changes that occurred in the human lineage have become fixed in the species: the team found essentially no variation among 44 chromosomes originating in all the major continents, or in an additional 182 chromosomes of European descent. The statistical tests showed that these distributions are extremely unlikely to have occurred under a scenario of neutral evolution, and therefore that the FOXP2 genes has been a target of selection in human evolution. The authors further showed that the selection probably occurred during the last 200,000 years, the period in which anatomically modern humans evolved, and that the gene was selected for directly, rather than hitchhiking on an adjacent selected gene. Alternative explanations that rely on demographic factors were tested and at least tentatively rejected.

This stunning discovery does not *prove* that language is an adaptation, because it is possible that FOXP2 was selected only for its effects on orofacial movements, and that its effects on speech and language came along for the ride. But this is implausible given the obvious social and communicative advantages that language brings, and the fact that the deficient language in SLI is known to saddle the sufferers with educational and social problems (Beitchman et al., 1994; Snowling, Adams, Bishop, & Sothard, 2001).

The studies I reviewed in this section are, I believe, just a beginning. I predict that evolutionary game theory will assess the selective rational for an increasing number of universal properties of human language, and that new genes for language disorders and individual variation in language will be discovered and submitted to tests for a history of selection in the human lineage. In this way, the theory that language is an adaptation, motivated originally by the design features and natural history of language, will become increasingly rigorous and testable.

REFERENCES

Baker, M. (2001). *The atoms of language.* New York: Basic Books.

Bates, E., Thal, D., & Marchman, V. (1991). Symbols and syntax: A Darwinian approach to language development. In E. A. Krasnegor (Ed.).

Beitchman, J. H., et al. (1994). Seven-year follow-up of speech/language-impaired and control children: Speech/language stability and outcome. *Journal of the American Academy of Child and Adolescent Psychiatry, 31,* 1322–1330.

Bickerton, D. (1981). *Roots of language.* Ann Arbor: Karoma.

Bickerton, D. (1990). *Language and species.* Chicago: University of Chicago Press.

Bishop, D. V. M. (2002). Putting language genes in perspective. *Trends in Genetics.*

Bishop, D. V. M., et al. (1999). Auditory temporal processing impairment: Neither necessary nor sufficient for causing language impairment in children. *Journal of Speech, Language, and Hearing Research, 42,* 1295–1310.

Bishop, D. V. M., North, T., & Donlan, C. (1995). Genetic basis of Specific Language Impairment. *Developmental Medicine and Child Neurology, 37,* 56–71.

Bishop, J., Bishop, D. V. M., & Norbury, C. F. (2001). Phonological processing, language, and literacy: A comparison of children with mild to moderate sensorineural hearing loss and those with specific language impairment. *Journal of Child Psychology and Psychiatry, 42,* 329–340.

Brown, R. (1973). *A first language: The early stages.* Cambridge, MA: Harvard University Press.

Chomsky, N. (1966). *Cartesian linguistics: A chapter in the history of rationalist thought.* New York: Harper & Row.

Chomsky, N. (1988). *Language and problems of knowledge: The Managua lectures.* Cambridge, MA: MIT Press.

Chomsky, N. (2002). *The evolution of language.* Paper presented at the 4th International Conference on the Evolution of Language, Harvard University.

Clahsen, H., & Almazen, M. (1998). Syntax and morphology in Williams syndrome. *Cognition, 68,* 167–198.

Comrie, B. (1981). *Language universals and linguistic typology.* Chicago: University of Chicago Press.

Crain, S. (1998). *Behavioral and Brain Sciences.*

Curtiss, S. (1989). The independence and task-specificity of language. In A. Bornstein & J. Bruner (Eds.), *Interaction in human development.* Hillsdale, NJ: Erlbaum.

Dale, P. S., et al. (1998). Genetic influence on language delay in two-year-old children. *Nature Neuroscience, 1,* 324–328.

Dawkins, R. (1982). *The extended phenotype.* New York: Oxford University Press.

Dawkins, R. (1986). *The blind watchmaker: Why the evidence of evolution reveals a universe without design.* New York: Norton.

Deacon, T. (1997). *The symbolic species: The coevolution of language and the brain.* New York: Norton.

Dunbar, R. (1998). *Grooming, gossip, and the evolution of language.* Cambridge, MA: Harvard University Press.

Enard, W., et al. (2002). Molecular evolution of *FOXP2,* a gene involved in speech and language. *Nature.*

Fitch, T. (Ed.). (2002). *Proceedings of the Fourth International Conference on the Evolution of Language.* Cambridge, MA: Department of Psychology, Harvard University.

Gordon, P. (1985). Level-ordering in lexical development. *Cognition, 21,* 73–93.

Gould, S. J. (1997). Darwinian fundamentalism. *New York Review of Books* (June 12), 34–52.

Greenberg, J. H., Ferguson, C. A., & Moravcsik, E. A. (1978). *Universals of human language* (Vol. 4). Stanford, CA: Stanford University Press.

Hinton, G. E., & Nowlan, S. J. (1987). How learning can guide evolution. *Complex Systems, 1,* 495–502.

Hockett, C. F. (1960,). The origin of speech. *Scientific American, 203,* 88–111.

Hurford, J. R. (1989). Biological evolution of the Saussurean sign as a component of the language acquisition device. *Lingua, 77,* 187–222.

Hurford, J. R., Studdert-Kennedy, M., & Knight, C. (Eds.). (1998). *Approaches to the evolution of language: Social and cognitive bases.* New York: Cambridge University Press.

Hurst, J. A., et al. (1990). An extended family with a dominantly inherited speech disorder. *Developmental Medicine and Child Neurology, 32,* 347–355.

Ingram, D. (1989). *First language acquisition: Method, description, and explanation.* New York: Cambridge University Press.

Jackendoff, R. (2002). *Foundations of language: Brain, meaning, grammar, evolution.* New York: Oxford University Press.

Kim, J. J., et al. (1994). Sensitivity of children's inflection to morphological structure. *Journal of Child Language, 21,* 173–209.

Kreitman, M. (2000). Methods to detect selection in populations with applications to the human, *Annual Review of Genomics and Human Genetics* (pp. 539–559).

Labov, W. (1969). The logic of nonstandard English. *Georgetown Monographs on Language and Linguistics, 22,* 1–31.

Lai, C. S. L., et al. (2001). A novel forkhead-domain gene is mutated in a severe speech and language disorder. *Nature, 413,* 519–523.

Leonard, L. B. (1998). *Children with Specific Language Impairment.* Cambridge, MA: MIT Press.

Lieberman, P. (1984). *The biology and evolution of language.* Cambridge, MA: Harvard University Press.

Lightfoot, D., & Anderson, S. (2002). *The language organ.* New York: Cambridge University Press.

Maynard Smith, J. (1982). *Evolution and the theory of games.* New York: Cambridge University Press.

Maynard Smith, J. (1988). *An introduction to the mathematical theory of evolution.* New York.

McWhorter, J. (2002). *Power of Babel.* New York.

Miller, G. A. (1991). *The science of words.* New York: W. H. Freeman.

Miller, G. F. (2000). *The mating mind: How sexual choice shaped the evolution of human nature.* New York: Doubleday.

Nowak, M. A., & Krakauer, D. C. (1999). The evolution of language. *Proceedings of the National Academy of Science USA, 96,* 8028–8033.

Nowak, M. A., Krakauer, D. C., & Dress, A. (1999a). An error limit for the evolution of language. *Proceedings of the Royal Society of London B, 266,* 2131–2136.

Nowak, M. A., Plotkin, J. B., & Jansen, V. A. (2000). The evolution of syntactic communication. *Nature, 404,* 495–498.

Piatelli-Palmarini, M. (1989). Evolution, selection, and cognition: From "learning" to parameter setting in biology and the study of language. *Cognition, 31,* 1–44.

Pinker, S. (1979). Formal models of language learning. *Cognition, 7,* 217–283.

Pinker, S. (1984). *Language learnability and language development.* Cambridge, MA: Harvard University Press.

Pinker, S. (1989). *Learnability and cognition: The acquisition of argument structure.* Cambridge, MA: MIT Press.

Pinker, S. (1994). *The language instinct.* New York: HarperCollins.

Pinker, S. (1997b). *How the mind works.* New York: Norton.

Pinker, S. (1999). *Words and rules: The ingredients of language.* New York: HarperCollins.

Pinker, S. (2002). *The blank slate: The modern denial of human nature.* New York: Viking.

Pinker, S., & Bloom, P. (1990). Natural language and natural selection. *Behavioral and Brain Sciences, 13,* 707–784.

Pinker, S., & Prince, A. (1988). On language and connectionism: Analysis of a Parallel Distributed Processing model of language acquisition. *Cognition, 28,* 73–193.

Przeworski, M., Hudson, R. R., & Di Rienzo, A. (2000). Adjusting the focus on human variation. *Trends in Genetics, 16,* 296–302.

Rossen, M., et al. (1996). Interaction between language and cognition: Evidence from Williams syndrome. In J. H. Beitchman, N. J. Cohen, M. M. Konstantareas, & R. Tannock (Eds.), *Language, learning, and behavior disorders.* New York: Cambridge University Press.

Senghas, A., & Coppola, M. (2001). Children creating language: How Nicaraguan sign language acquired a spatial grammar. *Psychological Science, 12,* 323–328.

Siegal, M., Varley, R., & Want, S. C. (2001). Mind over grammar: Reasoning in aphasia and development. *Trends in Cognitive Sciences, 5,* 296–301.

Snowling, M., et al. (2001). Educational attainments of school leavers with a preschool history of speech-language impairments. *International Journal of Language and Communication Disorders, 36,* 173–183.

Sowell, T. (1997). *Late-talking children.* New York: Basic Books.

Stromswold, K. (2001). The Heritability of Language: A Review and Metaanalysis of Twin and Adoption Studies. *Language,* in press.

The SLI Consortium. (2002). A genomewide scan identifies two novel loci involved in Specific Language Impairmen. *American Journal of Human Genetics, 70,* 384–398.

Tomasello, M. (1999). *The cultural origins of human cognition.* Cambridge, MA: Harvard University Press.

Tooby, J., & DeVore, I. (1987). The reconstruction of hominid evolution through strategic modeling. In W. G. Kinzey (Ed.), *The evolution of human behavior: Primate models.* Albany, NY: SUNY Press.

van der Lely, H. K. J., & Christian, V. (1998). *Lexical word formation in specifically language impaired children* (Unpublished manuscript). London: Department of Psychology, Birkbeck College, University of London.

van der Lely, H. K. J., Rosen, S., & McClelland, A. (1998). Evidence for a grammar-specific deficit in children. *Current Biology, 8,* 1253–1258.

van der Lely, H. K. J., & Stollwerck, L. (1996). A grammatical specific language impairment in children: An autosomal dominant inheritance? *Brain and Language, 52,* 484–504.

Voegelin, C. F., & Voegelin, F. M. (1977). *Classification and index of the world's languages.* New York: Elsevier.

Weiner, J. (1994). *The beak of the finch.* New York: Vintage.

Weiskrantz, L. (Ed.). (1988). *Thought without language.* New York: Oxford University Press.

Williams, G. C. (1966). *Adaptation and natural selection: A critique of some current evolutionary thought.* Princeton, NJ: Princeton University Press.

Nonverbal Courtship Patterns in Women
Context and Consequences

MONICA M. MOORE

There is a class of nonverbal facial expressions and gestures, exhibited by human females, that are commonly labeled "flirting behaviors." I observed more than 200 randomly selected adult female subjects in order to construct a catalog of these nonverbal solicitation behaviors. Pertinent behaviors were operationally defined through the use of consequential data; these behaviors elicited male attention. Fifty-two behaviors were described using this method. Validation of the catalog was provided through the use of contextual data. Observations were conducted on 40 randomly selected female subjects in one of four contexts: a singles' bar, a university snack bar, a university library, and at university Women's Center meetings. The results indicated that women in "mate relevant" contexts exhibited higher average frequencies of nonverbal displays directed at males. Additionally, women who signaled often were also those who were most often approached by a man; and this relationship was not context specific.

I suggest that the observation of women in field situations may provide clues to criteria used by females in the initial selection of male partners. As much of the work surrounding human attraction has involved laboratory studies or data collected from couples in established relationships, the observation of nonverbal behavior in field settings may provide a fruitful avenue for the exploration of human female choice in the preliminary stages of male–female interaction.

Key Words: Nonverbal behavior; Courtship; Female solicitation; Female choice.

INTRODUCTION

Biologically, one of the most important choices made by an organism is the selection of a mate. The evolution of traits that would assist in the identification of "superior mates" prior to the onset of mating is clearly advantageous. One legacy of anisogamy is that errors in mate selection are generally more expensive to females than to males (Trivers 1972). Hence, the females of a wide variety of species may be expected to exhibit traits that would facilitate the assessment of the quality of potential suitors in respect to their inherited attributes and acquired resources. There are many examples of female selectivity in a variety of species, including elephant seals (LeBoeuf and Peterson 1969; Bertram 1975), mice (McClearn and Defries 1973), fish (Weber and

Reprinted from *Ethology and Sociobiology,* vol. 6, M. M. Moore, "Nonverbal courtship patterns in women," pp. 237–247, Copyright 1985, with permission from Elsevier.

Weber 1975), rats (Doty 1974), gorillas (Nadler 1975), monkeys (Beach 1976), birds (Selander 1972; Wiley 1973; Williams 1975), and a few ungulates (Beuchner and Schloeth 1965; Leuthold 1966).

Very few studies in the area of human mate selection and attraction have focused on the issue of female choice. Fowler (1978) interviewed women to identify the parameters of male sexual attractiveness. The results showed that the male's value as a sexual partner correlated with the magnitude of emotional and material security he provided. Baber (1939) found that women emphasize qualities such as economic status, disposition, family religion, morals, health, and education in a prospective marriage partner, whereas men most frequently chose good looks, morals, and health as important qualities. More recent studies (Coombs and Kenkel 1966; Tavris 1977) also found women rating attributes such as physical attractiveness as less important than did men. Reiss (1960) believes than many more women than men choose "someone to look up to" and Hatkoff and Luswell (1977) presented data that indicated that women want the men with whom they fall in love to be persons whom they can respect and depend on. Daly and Wilson (1978) conclude from cross-cultural data that a male's financial status is an important determinant of his mating success.

Although these reports are valuable, it is clear that the mechanisms and expression of male assessment and female choice in humans have received little attention. In addition, much of the information available regarding human female choice is derived from interviews or questionnaires. Few studies have focused on initial choice situations in field observations. There are several difficulties with a field approach. A major problem surrounds the determination that a choice situation is being observed when verbal information is unavailable. I suggest that this problem may be solved through observations of nonverbal behavior. Indeed, there appears to be a repertoire of gestures and facial expressions that are used by humans as courtship signals (Birdwhistell 1970), much as there is signaling between members of the opposite sex in other species. Even in humans courtship and the choice of a mate have been characterized as largely nonverbal, with the cues being so persuasive that they can, as one observer put it, "turn a comment about the weather into a seductive invitation" (Davis 1971, p. 97).

The focus of much study in the area of nonverbal communication has been description (Scheflen 1965; Birdwhistell 1970; Mehrabian 1972). The primary aim of this research has been the categorization and analysis of nonverbal behaviors. By employing frame-by-frame analysis of films, Birdwhistell and his associates have been able to provide detailed descriptions of the facial expressions and movements or gestures of subjects in a variety of contexts. Observations conducted in this fashion as well as field studies have resulted in the labeling of many nonverbal behaviors as courtship signals. For example, Givens (1978) has described five phases of courtship between unacquainted adults. Scheflen (1965) investigated flirting gestures in the context of psychotherapy, noting that both courtship behaviors and qualifiers of the courtship message were exhibited by therapists and clients. Eibl-Eibesfeldt (1971) used two approaches to describe flirting behavior in people from diverse cultural backgrounds. Employing a camera fitted with right angle lenses to film people without their knowledge, he found that an eyebrow flash combined with a smile was a common courtship behavior. Through comments made to women, Eibl-Eibesfeldt has been able to elicit the "coy glance," an expression combining a half-smile and lowered eyes. Kendon

(1975) filmed a couple seated on a park bench in order to document the role of facial expression during a kissing round. He discovered that it was the female's behavior, particularly her facial expressions that functioned as a regulator in modulating the behavior of the male. Cary (1976) has shown that the female's behavior is important in initiating conversation between strangers. Both in laboratory settings and singles' bars conversation was initiated only after the female glanced at the male. These results are valuable in documenting the importance of nonverbal behavior in human courtship. But what is lacking is an ethogram of female solicitation behavior.

The purpose of this study was to describe an ensemble of visual and tactile displays emitted by women during initial meetings with men. I shall argue here that these nonverbal displays are courtship signals; they serve as attractants and elicit the approach of males or ensure the continued attention of males. In order to establish the immediate function of the described behaviors as courtship displays, I employed two classes of evidence described by Hinde (1975) for use in the establishment of the immediate function of a behavior: contextual evidence and consequential evidence. The rationale behind the use of consequential data was that behavior has certain consequences and that if the consequence appears to be a "good thing" it should have relevance for the immediate function of the behavior in question. It should be noted, however, that Eibl-Eibesfeldt (1970) has pointed out the danger in this approach because of interpretations of value on the part of the observer. Therefore, contextual information was provided as further documentation that the nonverbal behaviors in question were courtship signals. Hinde has noted that if certain behaviors are seen in some contexts but are absent in others their function must relate to those contexts in which they were observed. Together these two classes of information provide an indication of the immediate function of the behavior, in this case nonverbal behavior in women interacting with men. Thus, this study consisted of two parts: catalog compilation based on consequential information and validation of the catalog obtained through contextual data.

DEVELOPMENT OF THE CATALOG

Method

Subjects. For the initial study, more than 200 subjects were observed in order to obtain data to be used in the development of the catalog of nonverbal solicitation signals. Subjects were judged to be between the ages of 18 and 35 years. No systematic examination was made of background variables due to restrictions imposed by anonymity. All subjects were white and most were probably college students.

Procedure. Subjects were covertly observed in one social context where opportunities for male–female interaction were available, a singles' bar. Subjects were observed for 30 minutes by two trained observers. Focal subjects were randomly selected from the pool of possible subjects at the start of the observation period. We observed a woman only if she was surrounded by at least 25 other people (generally there were more than 50 others present) and if she was not accompanied by a male. In order to record all instances of the relevant behaviors, observers kept a continuous narrative account of all behaviors exhibited by a single subject and the observable consequences of those actions (Altmann 1974). The following criteria were used for identifying behaviors: a nonverbal solicitation behavior was defined as a movement of body part(s) or whole body that resulted in male attention, operationally defined, within 15 seconds following the behavior. Male attention consisted of the male performing one of the following behaviors: approaching the subject, talking to her, leaning toward her or moving closer to her, asking the subject to dance, touching her, or kissing her. Field notes were transcribed from concealed audio tape recorders. Estimates of interobserver reliability were calculated for 35 hours of observation using the formula:

$$\frac{\text{No. of agreements (A + B)}}{\text{No. of agreements (A + B) + No. seen by B only + No. seen by A only}}$$

(McGrew 1972). The range of interobserver reliability scores was 0.72–0.98, with the average score equaling .88. Low reliability scores were obtained only for behaviors difficult for an observer to catch in a darkened room, such as glancing behaviors.

Subsequently, five randomly selected subjects were observed for a period of at least 1 hour. Again observers kept a continuous narrative account of all nonverbal behavior exhibited by the woman.

The behaviors observed in courting women can be conceptualized in various ways: distance categories (Crook 1972), directional versus nondirectional, or on the basis of body part and movement employed in the exhibition of the nonverbal pattern (McGrew 1972). The third framework was chosen because the displays were most discretely partitioned along these dimensions.

Results

Fifty-two different behaviors were exhibited by the subjects in the present study. Nonverbal solicitation behaviors and their frequencies are summarized in Table 1 according to category. These behaviors were highly visible and most appeared very similar in form in each subject. In other words, each behavior was discrete, or distinct from all other solicitation behaviors.

Descriptions of Nonverbal Solicitation Behaviors
Facial and Head Patterns. A number of different facial and head patterns were seen in the women we observed. All women performed glancing behaviors, although the particular pattern varied among the individual subjects in the duration or length of time involved in eye to eye contact.

Type I glance (the room encompassing glance) was not restricted to an identifiable recipient. It was usually exhibited early in the evening and often was not seen later in the evening, particularly if the woman made contact with a man. The woman moved her head rapidly, orienting her face around the room. This movement was followed by another head movement that reoriented the woman's face to its original position. The total duration of the glance was brief, 5–10 seconds, with the woman not making eye contact with any specific individual. In some women this pattern of behavior was exaggerated: the woman stood up as her glance swept about the room.

The glancing behavior called the *type II glance (the short darting glance)* was a solicitation behavior that appeared directed at a particular man. The woman directed her gaze at the man, then quickly away (within 3 seconds). The target axis of the

TABLE 1 Catalog of Nonverbal Solicitation Behaviours

Facial and Head Patterns	Frequency	Gestures	Frequency	Posture Patterns	Frequency
Type I glance (room-encompassing glance)	253	Arm flexion	10	Lean	121
		Tap	8	Brush	28
		Palm	18	Breast touch	6
Type II glance (short darting glance)	222				
Type III glance (gaze fixate)	117				
Eyebrow flash	4	Gesticulation	62	Knee touch	25
Head toss	102	Hand hold	20	Thigh touch	23
Neck presentation	58	Primp	46	Foot to foot	14
Hair flip	139	Hike skirt	4	Placement	19
Head nod	66	Object caress	56	Shoulder hug	25
Lip lick	48	Caress (face/hair)	5	Hug	11
Lipstick application	1	Caress (leg)	32	Lateral body contact	1
Pout	27	Caress (arm)	23	Frontal body contact	7
Smile	511	Caress (torso)	8	Hang	2
Coy smile	20	Caress (back)	17	Parade	41
Laugh	249	Buttock pat	8	Approach	18
Giggle	61			Request dance	12
Kiss	6			Dance (acceptance)	59
Whisper	60			Solitary dance	253
Face to face	9			Point/permission grant	62
				Aid solicitation	34
				Play	31

horizontal rotation of the head was approximately 25–45 degrees. This behavior was usually repeated in bouts, with three glances the average number per bout.

In contrast, the *type III glance (gaze fixate)* consisted of prolonged (more than 3 seconds) eye contact. The subject looked directly at the man; sometimes her glance was returned. Again, this behavior was seen several times in a period of minutes in some subjects.

Another movement involving the eye area was an *eyebrow flash*, which consisted of an exaggerated raising of the eyebrows of both eyes, followed by a rapid lowering to the normal position. The duration of the raised eyebrow portion of the movement was approximately 2 seconds. This behavior was often combined with a smile and eye contact.

Several behaviors involved the head and neck region. In *head tossing*, the head was flipped backwards so that the face was tilted upwards briefly (less than 5 seconds). The head was then lowered to its original position. The head toss was often combined with or seen before the *hair flip*. The hair flip consisted of the woman raising one hand and pushing her fingers through her hair or running her palm along the surface of her hair. Some women made only one hand movement, while in others there were bouts of hair stroking; the woman put her hand to her hair several times within a 30-second interval. The *head nod* was seen when the woman was only a short distance from the man. Usually exhibited during conversation, the head was moved forward and backward on the neck, which resulted in the face of the subject moving up and down. Another head pattern was called *face to face*. In this behavior pattern the head and face of the woman were brought directly opposite another person's face so that the noses almost touched, a distance of approximately 5 cm. A final behavior involving the head and neck was the *neck presentation*. The woman tilted her head sideways to an angle of approximately 45 degrees. This resulted in the ear almost touching the ipsilateral shoulder, thereby exposing the opposite side of the neck. Occasionally the woman stroked the exposed neck area with her fingers.

There were a number of signals that involved the lips and mouth of the observed subjects. *Lipstick application* was a rare behavior. The woman directed her gaze so that she made eye contact with a particular man. She then slowly applied lipstick to her lips. She engaged in this behavior for some time (15 seconds), repeatedly circling her lips. In contrast, the *lip lick* was seen quite often, particularly in certain subjects. The woman opened her mouth slightly and drew her tongue over her lips. Some women used a single lip lick, wetting only the upper or the lower lip, while others ran the tongue around the entire lip area. The *lip pout* was another behavior involving the mouth. The lips were placed together and protruded. Generally, the lower lip was extended somewhat farther than the upper lip, so that it was fuller in appearance.

Smiling was among the most prevalent behaviors observed in the sampled women. The smile consisted of the corners of the mouth being turned upward. This resulted in partial or sometimes full exposure of the teeth. In some women the smile appeared fixed and was maintained for long periods of time. The *coy smile* differed from the smile in that the woman displaying a coy smile combined a half-smile (the teeth were often not displayed or only partially shown) with a downward gaze or eye contact which was very brief (less than 3 seconds). In the latter case the woman's glance slid quickly away from an onlooker who had become aware that he was being looked at.

Laughing and giggling were generally responses to another person's comments or behavior and were very common. In some women the *laugh* was preceded by a head toss. *Giggling* was less intense laughter. The mouth of the woman was often closed and generally the sounds were softer.

Kissing was rather unusual in the bar context. The slightly protruded lips were brought into contact with another person's body by a forward head movement. Variations consisted of the area touched by the woman's lips. The most common targets were the lips, face, and neck of the man. The woman, however, sometimes puckered her lips and waited, as if "offering" them to the male.

Finally, the *whisper* was used by most of the subjects in the sample. The woman moved her mouth near another person's ear and soft vocalizations presumably were produced. Sometimes body contact was made.

Gestures. There were several nonverbal patterns that involved movement of the hands and arms. Most were directed at a particular person. Some involved touching another individual. Others functioned at a distance.

Arm flexion occurred when the arm was flexed at wrist and elbow and was moved toward the body. It was often repeated two or three times in a bout. This behavior was often followed by the approach of another individual toward whom the subject gazed. If the male was in close physical proximity, the female sometimes used *tapping* instead to get his attention. The elbow or wrist was flexed repeatedly so that the woman's finger was moved vertically on an object (usually another person's arm).

Women occasionally *palmed*. Palming occurred when the hand was extended or turned so that the palm faced another person for a brief period of time, less than 5 seconds. In this study, palming was also recorded when the woman coughed or touched herself with the palm up.

In several women rapid movements of the hands and arms were seen accompanying speech. This behavior was labeled *gesticulation*. Arms and hands, while held in front of the woman's torso, were waved or extended upwards in an exaggerated, conspicuous manner. This behavior was often followed by a lean forward on the part of the man.

A hand gesture sometimes initiated by a woman was the *hand hold*. The woman grasped the man's hand so that her palm was next to the man's palm. This occurred on the dance floor as well as when the man was seated at the table with the woman. Generally, this behavior had a long duration, more than 1 minute

There were several behaviors that appeared related to each other because they involved inanimate objects. The first of these was the *primp*. In this gesture the clothing was patted or smoothed, although to the observer it appeared in no need of adjustment. A shirt was tucked in or a skirt was pulled down. On the other hand, the *skirt hike* was performed by raising the hem of the skirt with a movement of the hand or arm so that more leg was exposed. This behavior was only performed by two women and was directed at a particular man. When another man looked the skirt was pushed rapidly into place. Instead of patting or smoothing clothing, subjects sometimes "played with" an object, called *object caress*. For example, keys or rings were often fondled. Glasses were caressed with the woman sliding her palm up and down the surface of the glass. A cigarette pack was another item frequently toyed with in an object caress.

Finally, many women touched other people in a caressing fashion. Each incidence of caressing was considered separately in terms of the part of the body that was touched, because the message, in each case, may have been quite different. In *caress (face/hair)* the woman moved her hand slowly up and down the man's face and neck area or tangled her hands in his hair. While the couple was seated, women have been observed stroking the man's thigh and inner leg, *caress (leg)*. The *buttock pat*, however, occurred while the couple was standing, often while dancing. In this gesture the woman moved her hand, palm side down, up and down the man's buttocks. Other items in this group included *caress (arm), caress (torso),* and *caress (back).*

Posture Patterns. Compared to the two categories just presented, there were some behaviors which involved more of the body in movement. These I called posture patterns. Many of these behaviors could only be accomplished while the woman was standing or moving about the room.

Lean was a common solicitation pattern. Generally while seated, the woman moved her torso and upper body forward, which resulted in closer proximity to the man. This movement was sometimes followed by a *brush* or a *breast touch*. The brush occurred when brief body contact (less than 5 seconds) was initiated by the woman against another individual. This occurred when a woman was walking across the room; she bumped into a man. The result was often conversation between the man and the woman. The breast touch also appeared accidental; and it was difficult to tell, except by length of time of contact, whether or not the movement was purposeful. The upper torso was moved so the breast made contact with the man's body (usually his arm). Most often the contact was brief (less than 5 seconds), but sometimes women maintained this position for several minutes.

There were four other actions that were similar to the brush and breast touch in that the woman made bodily contact with the man. In the *knee touch* the legs were brought into contact with the man's legs so that the knees touched. Interactants were always facing one another while seated. If the man and woman were sitting side by side, the woman may have initiated a *thigh touch*. The leg was brought into contact with the man's upper leg. *Foot to foot* resulted in the woman moving her foot so that it rested on top of the man's foot. Finally, rather than make contact with some part of her own body, an observed woman sometimes took the man's hand and placed it on her body. I called this behavior *placement*. For example, on two occasions, a woman put a man's hand in her lap. Other targets were the thigh or arm.

There was another constellation of behaviors that appeared related to each other. All of these behaviors were variations of some contact made between the woman's upper body and her partner's upper body. These were generally behaviors of long duration, more than 1 minute. The most common of these behaviors was the *shoulder hug*. In this signal, the partially flexed arm was draped on and around another person's shoulder. In contrast, the *hug* occurred when both arms were moved forward from a widespread position and around the man, thereby encircling him. The duration of this behavior, however, was brief (less than 10 seconds). *Lateral body contact* was similar to shoulder hug except that the woman moved under the man's arm so that his arm was draped around her shoulders rather than vice versa. Similarly, *frontal body contact* occurred when the chest and thighs of the woman rested against the chest and thighs of the man. This behavior was like the hug except that there was no squeeze pressure and the arms did not necessarily encircle the other person. This posture pattern was often seen on the dance floor or when a couple was standing at the bar. *Hanging* was similar to frontal body contact except that the man was supporting the woman's weight. This behavior was initiated by the woman who placed her arms around the man's neck. She was then lifted off her feet while her torso and hips rested against the man's chest and hip. This was a behavior low in frequency and brief in duration, less than 5 seconds.

There were two behaviors that involved whole body movement. These were called *parade* and *approach*. Parade consisted of the woman walking across the room, perhaps on her way to the bar or the restroom. Yet rather than maintaining a relaxed attitude, the woman exaggerated the swaying motion of her hips. Her stomach was held in and her back was arched so that her breasts were pushed out; her head was held high. In general she was able to make herself "look good." The other behavior that involved walking was approach. The woman went up to the man and stood very close to him, within 2 feet. Usually verbal interaction ensued.

Some women followed an approach with a *request dance*. This was demonstrated nonverbally by the woman pointing and/or nodding in the direction of the dance door. Two other categories involving dancing behavior were included in the catalog. *Dance (female acceptance)* was included because by accepting a dance with the man the woman maintained his attention. Another dancing behavior was one of the most frequently seen signals. It was called the *solitary dance* because, while seated or standing, the woman moved her body in time to the music. A typical male response was to request a dance.

Just as a woman, in agreeing to dance with a man, was telling him, nonverbally, that he was acceptable for the moment she also told him so when she allowed him to sit at her table with her. Thus, *point/permission grant* was given a place in the catalog. The woman pulled out the chair for the man or pointed or nodded in the direction of the chair. There was generally a verbal component to the signal which could not be overheard.

Aid solicitation consisted of several behaviors that involved the request of help by the subject. For example, the woman handed her jacket to the man and allowed him to help her put it on. Other patterns in this category included indicating that a drink be refilled, waiting to be seated, or holding a cigarette for lighting.

The final category of solicitation behavior was also a variety of posture patterns. Called *play*, these behaviors consisted of the woman pinching the man, tickling him, sticking out her tongue at him, of approaching him from behind covering his eyes. Some women sat on the man's lap, and several women in the sample came up behind men and stole their hats. All of these behaviors were simply recorded as play behavior.

VALIDATION OF THE CATALOG

Method

Subjects. Forty women were covertly observed for the second portion of the study, validation of the catalog. Subjects were judged between the ages of 18 and 35. All subjects were white. Again no systematic examination of background variables was possible.

Procedure. To justify the claim that the nonverbal behaviors described above were courtship signals, that is, carried a message of interest to the observing man, women were covertly observed in different social contexts. The four contexts selected for study were a singles' bar, a university snack bar, a university library, and university Women's Center meetings. These contexts were chosen in order to sample a variety of situations in which nonverbal solicitation might be expected to occur as well as situations in which it was unlikely to be exhibited. The selection of contexts was based on information collected through interviews and pilot observations. If nonverbal solicitation was found in situations where male–female interaction was likely but either was not found or occurred in lower frequencies where male–female interactions were impossible, then the immediate function of nonverbal solicitation can be said to be the enhancement of male–female relationships.

The methodology employed in this section was similar to that used in the development of the catalog. Focal individual sampling was the method of choice for the 40 subjects, 10 in each of the 4 contexts. Each subject was randomly selected from those individuals present at the beginning of the observation period. Sessions were scheduled to begin at 9:00 P.M. and end at 11:00 P.M. in the bar context. This time was optimal because crowd density was at its peak. Sessions in the Women's Center context always began at noon or at 7:00 P.M. because that was the time at which programs were scheduled. Observations were randomly made in both the library and the snack bar contexts; for each context, four sessions were conducted at 11:00 A.M., three at 2:00 P.M., and three at 7:00 P.M. Subjects were observed for a period of 1 hour. (Any subject who did not remain for 1 hour of observation was excluded from the analyses.) Observations were conducted using either a concealed audio recorder or, when appropriate, paper and pen. No subject evidenced awareness of being observed. Again, we observed a woman only if she was surrounded by at least 25 other people and if she was not accompanied by a male.

Data for each woman consisted of a frequency measure, the number of nonverbal solicitation behaviors, described above, that she exhibited during the hour of observation. Observers counted not only the total number of nonverbal solicitation behaviors, but also kept a tally of the specific behaviors that were used by each woman.

Results

Frequency and Categorization of Nonverbal Solicitation Behaviors. Data collected on 40 subjects and the respective frequencies of their solicitation displays are given in Table 2. The results show that the emission of the catalogued behaviors was context specific in respect to both the frequency of displays and the number of different categories of the repertoire. The subjects observed in the singles' bar emitted an average of 70.6 displays in the sampled interval, encompassing a mean number of 12.8 different categories of the catalog. In contrast, the corresponding data from the snack bar, library, and women's meetings were 18.6 and 7.5, 9.6 and 4.00, and 4.7 and 2.1, respectively. The asymmetry in display frequency was highly significant ($\chi^2 = 25.079$, df = 3, $p < 0.001$). In addition, the asymmetry in the number of categories utilized was also significant ($\chi^2 = 23.099$, df = 3, $p < 0.001$).

Rate of Display. The quartile display frequencies for the four contexts are given in Figure 1. As can be seen, the display frequency accelerated over time in the singles' bar context but was relatively invariant in the other three contexts.

Frequency of Approach. If subjects are pooled across contexts in which males are present and partitioned into high- and low-display categories, where the high display category is defined as more than 35 displays per hour, the data show that the high-

TABLE 2   Social Context: Display Frequency and Number of Approaches[a]

	Singles' Bar	Snack Bar	Library	Women's Meetings
Number of subjects	10	10	10	10
Total number of displays	706	186	96	47
Mean number of displays	70.6	18.6	9.6	4.7
Mean number of categories utilized	12.8	7.5	4.0	2.1
Number of approaches to the subject by a male	38	4	4	0
Number of approaches to a male by the subject	11	4	1	0

[a]The tabulated data are for a 60-minute observation interval. Assymetry in display frequency: $\chi^2 = 25.079$, df = 3, $p < 0.001$; asymmetry in number of categories utilized: $\chi^2 = 23.099$, df = 3, $p < 0.001$.

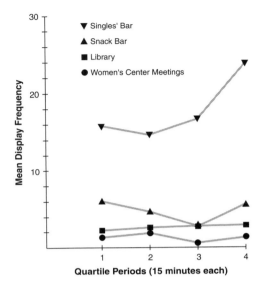

FIGURE 1   Frequency of occurrence for all solicitation behaviors for each quartile of the observational interval for each of the four social contexts.

display subjects elicited greater than 4 approaches per hour, whereas low display subjects elicited less than 0.48 approaches per hour. The number of approaches to subjects by a male in each context is presented in Table 2. Approaches were most frequent in the singles' bar where displays were also most frequent.

For the three contexts in which males were present (the singles' bar, the snack bar, and the library), the number of approaches to the subject was compared to the number of categories employed in solicitation displays. Subjects were pooled across these contexts and divided into two groups—those who utilized less than ten categories and those who employed ten or more categories. The results were highly significant ($\chi^2 = 12.881$, df = 1, $p < 0.025$): regardless of when the woman utilized a high number of categories she was more likely to be approached by a male.

Also given in Table 2 are the figures for female-to-male approaches. In both cases (female to male, and male to female), approaches were much higher in the bar context. To show that the number of male approaches correlated with frequency of female solicitation, Spearman rank correlations were determined for these measures. The correlation between number of male approaches and total number of solicitations, across all three contexts, equaled 0.89 ($p < 0.05$). Clearly, those women who signaled often were also those who were most often approached by a man; and this relationship was not context specific.

DISCUSSION

The results of this study are in no way discoveries of "new" behaviors. The behaviors catalogued here have been described as courtship behaviors by others. But there has been little firm evidence to support this claim of their function, aside from references to context. This study was the first attempt to bring all the behaviors together in catalog form and provide documentation of their function.

When we compare those behaviors contained in the catalog compiled in this study to other descriptions of courtship in humans, we find many areas of congruence. Scheflen (1965) has outlined four categories of heterosexual courtship behavior: courtship readiness, preening behavior, positional cues, and actions of appeal or invitation. Many of the behaviors observed in courting women are similar to those seen by Scheflen during psychotherapy sessions. For example, Scheflen's category of courtship readiness bears resemblance to parade behavior. Preening behaviors, as described by Scheflen, are similar to the hair flip, primp, skirt hike, and object caress catalogued here. Positional cues are found in the catalog under leaning, brushing, and caressing or touching signals. Finally, Scheflen's actions of appeal or invitation are included as aid solicitation, point/permission grant, request dance, palm and solitary dance. What appears to be absent in courting women are the qualifiers of the courtship message observed by Scheflen during psychotherapy.

There is a significant continuity between the expressions and gestures described in this study and those Givens (1978) believed to be important during the first four phases of courtship. According to Givens, the essence of the first stage, the attention phase, is ambivalence. Behaviors seen by Givens during this stage and observed in this study include primping, object caressing, and glancing at and then away from the male. During the recognition phase Givens has observed head cocking, pouting, primping, eyebrow flashing and smiling, all of which were seen by me. During the interaction stage, conversation is initiated and the participants appear highly animated. Indeed, women in this study, while talking to men, appeared excited, laughing, smiling, and gesticulating frequently. Givens has indicated that in the fourth stage, the sexual arousal phase, touching gestures are exchanged. Similarly, it was not unusual to see couples hold hands, caress, hug, or kiss after some period of interaction.

Given's work has indicated that it is often the female who controls interaction in these early phases. The observations of Cary (1976) seem to bear this out and glancing behavior appears to be a significant part of the female role. In this study glancing often took place over a period of time prior to a male approach. As Crook (1972) has stated, males are generally hesitant to approach without some indication of interest from the partner, and repeated eye contact seems to demonstrate that interest. Rejection behaviors were not catalogued here, but it is entirely possible that one way women reject suitors is by failing to recognize their presence through eye contact.

Eibl-Eibesfeldt has also stressed importance of the eye area in two flirting gestures he has observed in several cultures. The first, a rapid raising and lowering of the eyebrows, accompanied by a smile and a nod, was seen rarely in this study. Raised eyebrows were sometimes seen in the bar context and when directed a man with a quick glance to the dance floor were often followed by a request to dance. Raised eyebrows also sometimes followed comments by a man when he had joined a woman at their table. Eibl-Eibesfeldt (1970) has also presented pictures of women exhibiting what he calls the coy glance. Although the coy glance was sometimes seen in this study (here called the coy smile), it was more usual for a young American woman to use direct eye contact and a full smile. Yet the fact that these behaviors were observed is significant, and later cross-cultural studies may demonstrate that there are more behaviors that share the courtship message.

It appears then that although glancing behaviors were important in signaling interest, initially, other behaviors seemed to reaffirm the woman's interest later in the observation period. Behaviors such as nodding, leaning close to the man, smiling and laughing were seen in higher frequencies after the man had made contact with the woman and was dancing with her or was seated at her table. This accounts for the rise in frequency of solicitation near the end of the observation period in the bar context. Yet it is difficult to make any firm statements about a sequential pattern in the exhibition of solicitation behavior. Although these behaviors are distinct in form, variability among subjects with regard to timing was great. Neither was it possible to determine the potency of particular behaviors. Indeed, it often appeared as though behaviors had a cumulative effect; that is, the man waited to respond to the woman until after he had observed several solicitations.

However, it is clear that there is a constellation of nonverbal behaviors associated with female solicitation that has been recognized by many investigators in several contexts and with similar results (Morris 1971; Kerdon and Ferber 1973; Nieremberg and Calero 1973; Clore et al. 1975; Key 1975; Knapp 1978; Lockard and Adams 1980). This is strong circumstantial evidence supporting the current results that these are "real" contextually valid movements, not random behaviors. Furthermore, these expressions and gestures appear to function as attractants and advertisers of female interest.

Traditionally, women have had more control in choosing men for relationships, being able to pace the course of sexual advances and having the prerogative to accept or decline proposals (Hatkoff and Luswell 1977). Nonverbal solicitation is only one of the first steps in the sequence of behaviors beginning with mate attraction and culminating with mate selection. However, these courtship gestures and expressions appear to aid the woman in her role as discriminating chooser. Females are able to determine when and where they wish to survey mate potential by exhibiting or withholding displays. They can elicit a high number of male approaches, allowing them to choose from a number of available men. Or they may direct solicitations at a particular male.

What happens after the approach of a man then becomes increasingly important. Much of the basis of actual choice must rest on what the man says to the woman in addition to his behavior toward her and others. It seems reasonable that females would enhance their fitness by making the most informed judgment possible. Yet before interaction is initiated some initial choice is made. These initial impressions and the selection of those men deemed interesting enough to warrant further attention by a woman have been virtually ignored. If, indeed, the woman is exercising her right to choose, what sort of filter system is she using? Which men are chosen for further interaction and which are rejected? Literature cited earlier indicates that the behaviors that indicate status, wealth, and dependability are attributes that women may assess in initial encounters. At present data are not available to address these issues. But I believe that hypotheses regarding the particulars of human female choice can be tested through covert observation of female invitational behavior. Information obtained through observation in field settings can be added to verbal reports. The results of such a venture may present us with a more complete picture of the levels of selection involved in human female choice.

REFERENCES

Altmann, J. Observational study of behavior: sampling methods. *Behavior* 49: 227–267 (1974).

Baber, R.E. *Marriage and Family.* New York: McGraw-Hill, 1939.

Beach, R.A. Sexual attractivity, proceptivity and receptivity in female mammals. *Hormones and Behavior* 7: 105–138 (1976).

Bertram, B.C. Social factors influencing reproduction in wild lions. *Journal of Zoology* 177: 463–482 (1975).

Beuchner, H.K., Schloeth, R. Ceremonial mating system in Uganda kob (*Adenota kob thomase* Neuman). *Zeitschrift fur Tierpsychologie* 22: 209–225 (1965).

Birdwhistell, R. L. *Kinesics and Context.* Philadelphia: University of Pennsylvania Press, 1970.

Cary, M.S. Talk? Do you want to talk? Negotiation for the initiation of conversation between the inacquainted. Ph.D. dissertation. University of Pennsylvania, 1976.

Clore, G.L., Wiggins, N.H., Itkin, I. Judging attraction from nonverbal behavior: the gain phenomenon. *Journal of Consulting and Clinical Psychology* 433: 491–497 (1975).

Coombs, R.H., Kenkel, W.F. Sex differences in dating aspirations and satisfaction with computer selected partners. *Journal of Marriage and the Family* 28: 62–66 (1966).

Crook, J.H. Sexual selection, dimorphism, and social organization in primates. In *Sexual Selection and the Descent of Man 1871–1971,* B. Campbell (Ed.), Chicago: Aldine, 1972.

———— The socio-ecology of primates. In *Social Behavior in Birds and Mammals: Essays on the Social Ethology of Animals and Man,* J.H. Crook (Ed.). London: Academic, 1972.

Daly, M., Wilson, M. *Sex, Evolution, and Behavior.* North Scituate, MA: Duxbury, 1978.

Davis, F. *Inside Intuition.* New York: McGraw-Hill, 1971.

Doty, R.L. A cry for the liberation of the female rodent: Courtship and copulation in Rodentia. *Psychological Bulletin* 81: 159–172 (1974).

Eibl-Eibesfeldt, I. *Ethology: The Biology of Behavior.* New York: Holt, Rinehart, and Windston, 1970.

———— *Love and Hate.* New York: Holt, Rinehart and Winston, 1971.

Fowler H.F. Female choice: An investigation into human breeding system strategy. Paper presented to Animal Behavior Society. Seattle, June 1978.

Givens, D. The nonverbal basis of attraction: Flirtation, courtship, and seduction. *Psychiatry* 41: 346–359 (1978).

Hatkoff, T.S., Luswell, T.E. Male-female similarities and differences in conceptualizing love. In *Love and Attraction,* M.Cook. G. Wilson (Eds.). Oxford: Pergamon, 1977.

Hinde, R.A. The concept of function. In *Function and Evolution in Behavior,* S. Bariends, C. Beer, and A. Manning (Eds.). Oxford: Clarendon, 1975.

Kendon, A. Some functions of the face in a kissing round. *Semiotica* 15: 299–334 (1975).

————, Ferber, A. A description of some human greetings. In *Comparative Ecology and Behavior of Primates,* R. P. Michael and J.H. Crook (Eds.). London: Academic, 1973.

Key, M.R. *Male/Female Language.* Metuchen NJ: Scarecrow, 1975.

Knapp, M.L. *Nonverbal Communication in Human Interaction.* New York: Holt, Rinehart, and Winston, 1978.

LeBoeuf, B.J., Peterson, R.S. Social status and mating activity in elephant seals. *Science* 163: 91–93 (1969).

Leuthold, W. Variations in territorial behavior of Uganda kob *Adenota kob thomasi* (Neumann 1896). *Behaviour* 27: 215–258 (1966).

Lockard, J.S., Adams R.M. Courtship behaviors in public: Different age/sex roles. *Ethology and Sociobiology* 1(3): 245–253 (1980).

McClearn, G.E., Defries, J.C. *Introduction to Behavioral Genetics.* San Francisco: Freeman, 1973.

McGrew, W.C. *An Ethological Study of Children's Behavior.* New York: Academic, 1972.

Mehrabian, A. *Nonverbal Communcation.* Chicago: Aldine, 1972.

Morris, D. *Intimate Behavior.* New York: Random House, 1971.

Nadler, R.D. Sexual cyclicity in captive lowland gorillas. *Science* 189: 813–814 (1975).

Nieremberg, G. I., Calero, H.H. *How to Read a Person Like a Book.* New York: Hawthorne, 1973.

Reiss, I.L. Toward a sociology of the heterosexual love relationship. *Marriage and Family Living* 22: 139–145 (1960).

Scheflen, A.E. Quasi-courtship behavior in psychotherapy. *Psychiatry* 28: 245–257 (1965).

Selander, R.K. Sexual selection and dimorphism in birds. In *Sexual Selection and the Descent of Man 1871–1971,* B. Campbell (Ed.). Chicago: Aldine, 1972.

Tavris, C. Men and women report their views on masculinity. *Psychology Today* 10: 34–42 (1977).

Trivers, R.L. Parental investment and sexual selection. In *Sexual Selection and the Descent of Man 1871–1971,* B. Campbell (Ed.). Chicago: Aldine, 1972.

Weber, P.G., Weber, S.P. The effect of female color, size, dominance and early experience upon mate selection in male convict cichlids, *cichlosoma nigrofasciatum Gunther* (pisces, cichlidae). *Behavior* 56: 116–135 (1975).

Wiley, R.H. Territoriality and nonrandom mating in sage grouse. *Centrocerus urophasiamis. Animal Behavior Monographs* 6: 85–169 (1973).

Williams, G.C. *Sex and Evolution.* Princeton NJ: Princeton University Press, 1975.

Competitiveness, Risk Taking, and Violence
The Young Male Syndrome

MARGO WILSON AND MARTIN DALY

Sexual selection theory suggests that willingness to participate in risky or violent competitive interactions should be observed primarily in those age–sex classes that have experienced the most intense reproductive competition (fitness variance) during the species' evolutionary history, and in those individuals whose present circumstances are predictive of reproductive failure.

Homicidal conflicts in the city of Detroit in 1972 are reviewed in the light of the above perspective. Homicide in Detroit, as elsewhere, is overwhelmingly a male affair. Victim and offender populations are almost identical, with unemployed, unmarried, young men greatly overrepresented. The most common conflict typologies are described, and it is suggested that many, perhaps most, homicides concern status competition.

Other manifestations of "taste for risk," such as daredevilry and gambling, are briefly reviewed. The evidence suggests that such a taste is primarily a masculine attribute, and is socially facilitated by the presence of peers in pursuit of the same goals.

Such dangerous, competitive acts as the classic "trivial altercation" homicide often appear foolhardy to observers. However, it remains unknown whether the typical consequences of such acts are ultimately beneficial or detrimental to the perpetrators' interests.

Key Words: Homicide, Risk-taking, Young male syndrome

Homicidal conflicts, in America and elsewhere, usually involve men who already know each other. Most cases are not robbery related, and the issues of contention often seem ludicrously small to police, and to criminologists.

The classic study of American homicide is Wolfgang's (1958) analysis of 588 criminal homicides in Philadelphia. Wolfgang classified 560 of the killings into 12 motive categories. "Altercation of relatively trivial origin; insult, curse, jostling, etc." accounted for 37% of cases, and was far and away the leading motive type. Eighty-

Reprinted from *Ethology and Sociobiology,* vol. 6, M. Wilson and M. Daly, "Competitiveness, risk taking, and violence: The young male syndrome," pp. 59–73, Copyright 1985, with permission from Elsevier.

seven percent of offenders in these altercations were men. Wolfgang's findings have been corroborated in many subsequent studies. According to an authoritative staff report on criminal homicide in 17 American cities, presented to the National Commission on the Causes and Prevention of Violence, "Altercations appeared to be the primary motivating forces both here and in previous studies. Ostensible reasons for disagreements are usually trivial, indicating that many homicides are spontaneous acts of passion, not products of a single determination to kill" (Mulvihill, Tumin, and Curtis 1969, p. 230). The report then quotes a Dallas homicide detective: "Murders result from little ol' arguments over nothing at all. Tempers flare. A fight starts, and somebody gets stabbed or shot. I've worked on cases where the principals had been arguing over a 10 cent record on a juke box, or over a one dollar gambling debt from a dice game" (Mulvihill, Tumin, and Curtis 1969, p. 230). The authors of the report go on to describe a series of astonishingly petty but fatal disputes.

These altercations have intrigued many commentators, but to call them "trivial" is surely to misunderstand them. The participants behave as if a great deal more is at stake than small change or access to a pool table. Our own study of similar cases in Detroit has convinced us that something important *is* at stake: Violent male–male disputes are really concerned with "face," dominance status, and what Goffman (1959) calls "presentation of self" in a highly competitive social milieu. This interpretation of altercations is not original with us; it has been developed especially by Toch (1969), Luckenbill (1977) and Felson (1978), each of whom describes the typical, almost tragic, progression of events, in which neither victim nor offender finds it possible to back down and a violent resolution seems almost agreed upon. But just *why* men should value intangible social resources like "face" enough to risk deadly conflict over them is a profound question that we think can best be addressed from the broad comparative perspective of evolutionary biology.

SOCIOBIOLOGICAL THEORY OF MALE COMPETITIVENESS

Dangerous, confrontational competition among males is not unique to our species. Violent conflict with attendant mortality risk is widespread in the animal kingdom, and it is usually a male affair. To the evolutionist, such ubiquitous behavioral inclinations demand explanation in terms of their adaptive functions for the actors: How can competitiveness and a taste for risky confrontation contribute to male fitness?

The principal body of relevant sociobiological theory has been developed and discussed by various authors, especially Bateman (1948), Williams (1966) and Trivers (1972). This theory attributes male competitiveness and related phenomena to different selective pressures producing distinct female and male behavioral strategies. In most animal species, including *Homo sapiens,* male fitness is limited by access to fecund females, whereas female fitness is limited by physiological and energetic constraints. It follows that very successful males can enhance their fitness by monopolizing the reproductive performance of several females, whereas the fitness of females cannot profit from multiple mates to the same extent. Females are therefore a "resource" for which males compete. This competition need not take the form of a direct contest for females. Instead males are in competition for those resources, including feeding territories, nest sites, and more intangible "resources" like political influence and social status, that can be converted into reproductive opportunity, whether because they are directly attractive to females or because they help quell rival males.

Recently, several writers have protested that this orthodox view of intrasexual competition is unsound because it implies that females do not compete or because it ignores nonagonistic avenues of competition (see, e.g., Wasser 1983). These complaints are directed against an alleged bias in the literature. Perhaps male–male competition *has* been overemphasized, but such complaints, whether justified or not, do not seriously challenge the theory. Of course females compete, but there is a straightforward logic according to which males compete *more intensely.*

The intensity of reproductive competition can be conceptualized in terms of the within-sex variance in fitness. Competition is generally more intense among males than among females in that male fitness variance exceeds female fitness variance. And although competition need not be confrontational and dangerous (or indeed direct at all), the likelihood of risky competitive tactics increases as the payoff variance increases: in any competition, the more disparate the outcomes for winners versus losers, the greater the expected expenditure of effort and tolerable risk.

Where within-sex fitness variance is large, some individuals are monopolizing reproduction while others are losing out. The degree of such monopolization of females by males is the degree of "effective polygyny" of the breeding system, and the more polygynous, the more intense the male–male competition. The more intense this competition, the more we can expect males to be inclined to risky tactics, and hence the more excess mortality they should be expected to suffer in comparison to females. These theoretical expectations are amply verified by studies comparing groups of related species within an order or family: The degree of polygyny characteristic of the various species tends to be correlated with the extent to which males are larger and better armed than females, and with the extent to which male mortality exceeds female mortality (e.g., Leutenegger and Kelley 1977; Wittenberger 1978; Alexander et al. 1979; Clutton-Brock, Albon, and Harvey 1980). In those rare cases, primarily certain birds, in which the breeding system is polyandrous and females compete to monopolize the parental effort of several males, the females tend to be larger and more combative (Jenni 1974; Maxson and Oring 1980).

THE CASE OF HOMO SAPIENS

Placed in comparative perspective within the primates, *Homo sapiens* exhibits sex differences in body size, armament, pugnacity, age at puberty, rate of senescence and life expectancy, all of which suggest a natural selective history of effective polygyny. This is also the implication of the ethnographic record: In most extant human societies, women are a contested resource. Successful men routinely convert high status and power into monopolization of multiple women (e.g., Betzig 1982). It follows that males at the other end of the scale are likelier than females to suffer complete reproductive failure (e.g., Howell 1979).

Men in all cultures find themselves involved in networks of significant relationships with other men within which face and relative status are at issue (e.g., Jayawardena 1963; Safilios-Rothschild 1969; Tiger 1969; Fox 1972; Horowitz and Schwartz 1974; Paige and Paige 1981). Typically, these networks are arenas of alliance, rivalry, marital exchange politics, obligation reputation, and resource distribution. We would expect a man's performance within the local competitive–cooperative male milieu to have important fitness consequences. It follows that both appetite for and aptitude in this milieu should be basic evolved attributes of masculine psychology.

If variations in the intensity of sexual selection have indeed been relevant to the evolution of competitive inclinations and dangerous risk taking, certain predictions about violent conflict would seem to follow. The participants should be mostly males; in the case of homicide, that means a preponderance of men among both victims and offenders. In an effectively polygynous breeding system, competition for access to reproductive status is most intense among young adult males, and so we might expect that age class to be most conflictual and prone to risk. Furthermore, insofar as status and face disputes constitute a significant proportion of homicides, we expect that victims and offenders will often be peers and will exhibit similar demographic and socioeconomic profiles, except that victims may tend to be wealthier than offenders where robbery is involved. Both victim and offender populations should include disproportionate representation of the segment of society that is relatively "disenfranchised" (reproductively and otherwise), and therefore has the least to lose in escalated conflict over status:—unemployed, single, young men. With respect to these demographic characteristics, we may furthermore expect participants in *other* dangerous activities to resemble the principals in homicides.

HOMICIDAL CONFLICT IN DETROIT

The homicide bureau of the Detroit police department investigated 690 nonaccidental homicides committed in 1972. By October, 1980, 512 of these cases were closed, which means that the police had identified a perpetrator to their own satisfaction regardless of whether a conviction or prosecution had been attained. Police files on all 690 homicides were examined in detail during 1973–74 by Marie Wilt, a sociologist who coded cases with respect to 70 variables, including ages, sexes, victim–offender relationship, and a set of conflict typologies of her own devising (Wilt 1974). We have examined the police files to make additional codings, and have updated the data from files completed since Wilt's study.

Wilt categorized homicides as "crime specific" (incidental to the commission of another crime, usually robbery) or "social conflict." In 508 closed cases, the relationship between victim and offender was known. These two categorizations of cases are cross tabulated in Table 1. It is clear from Table 1 that homicides involving strangers usually occur incidentally to the commission of another crime. (Of closed cases, 32.8% are "crime-specific," but circumstantial evidence suggests that a much larger proportion of the 178 cases remaining open are also of this type.) Cases involving relatives have been analyzed elsewhere (Daly and Wilson 1982; Daly, Wilson, and Weghorst 1982).

TABLE 1 Five Hundred Twelve Closed Homicide Cases in the City of Detroit, 1972, Classified by Type of Case and by Victim–Offender Relationship

Victim–Offender Relationship	Crime Specific	Social Conflict	Unknown
Relatives			
Genealogical kin	1	31	0
Spouse	1	79	0
Affinal or step	0	15	0
Nonrelatives			
Friends and acquaintances	47	193	3
Strangers	119 (34 by police; 6 police victims)	19 (2 by police)	0 / 2
Unknown	0	2	
TOTAL	168	339	5

PARTICIPANTS IN HOMICIDE

Table 2 breaks down the 512 closed homicides according to the sex of offender and victim. Figure 1 presents age-specific homicide rates for men and women relative to the population of the city of Detroit (U.S. Bureau of the Census 1971, Table 24). As expected, participants in homicidal conflict are predominantly young men. Victim rates are based on 682 cases; excluded are six cases where the victim was a police officer, plus two cases where the body was not identified. Offender rates necessarily exclude the 178 open cases, and also exclude 36 police-action homicides.[1] The figure is based on 467 cases where offenders' age and sex were known. In 53 multiple offender

TABLE 2 Five Hundred Twelve Detroit Homicides by Type of Case and Sex of the Principals

Type of Case	Offender–Victim[a] M–M	M–F	F–M	F–F
Social conflict	195[b]	61	67	16
Crime specific	148[c]	13[d]	7	0
Type unknown	5	0	0	0
All closed cases	348	74	74	16

[a] M, male; F, female.

[b] Includes 2 by police.

[c] Includes 33 by police, 6 police victims.

[d] Includes 1 by police.

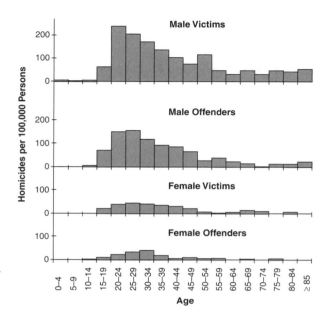

FIGURE 1 Homicide rates per 100,000 persons for the city of Detroit in 1972, by age and sex.

cases, we have included only the first offender in the police records. Ten offenders killed two victims each, and four killed three; for the sake of consistency in treating each victim as a "case," we have included these offenders multiply.

The huge sex difference in homicidal violence is not peculiar to Detroit. Figure 2 presents homicide victimization rates for the United States as a whole. (Offenders cannot be similarly portrayed, since national data are based only on major convictions and exclude self-defense and justified homicides, among others.) The sex difference is furthermore not peculiar to America—indeed it appears to be a cross-cultural universal (Daly and Wilson, in press).

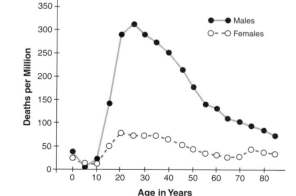

FIGURE 2 Homicide victimization rates by age and sex for the United States in 1975.

Data from U.S. Department of Health, Education, and Welfare (1979) and U.S. Bureau of the Census (1977).

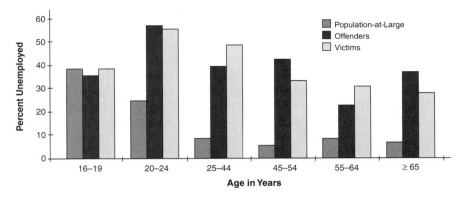

FIGURE 3   Unemployment rates among male homicide offenders, male victims, and the male population-at-large in the city of Detroit in 1972.

Population-at-large data from U.S. Department of Labor (n.d., Table II).

Victim and offender populations are remarkably alike—and not just in age and sex. Forty-three percent of adult male victims and 41% of adult male offenders were unemployed, compared to 11.2% of adult men in the city of Detroit (Figure 3). Sixty-nine percent of male victims and 73% of male offenders over 14 years of age were unmarried, compared to 43% of same-age men in Detroit (Figure 4). Among both male victims and male offenders, 36% had previous criminal records (excluding convictions for motor vehicle violation, drunkenness, and narcotics offenses). Our expectations about the participants in homicidal conflicts are confirmed: They indeed tend to be unemployed, single, young men. Further insight will require further categorization of conflict typologies.

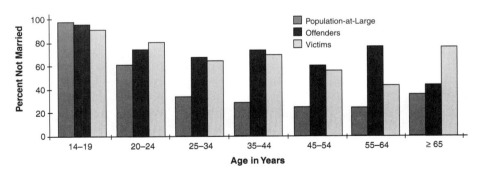

FIGURE 4   Proportions unmarried among male homicide offenders, male victims, and the male population-at-large in the city of Detroit in 1972.

Population-at-large data courtesy of the Planning Department of the City of Detroit.

SOCIAL CONFLICT HOMICIDES

Three hundred thirty-nine cases out of our sample of solved homicides were "social conflicts," not incidental to the commission of another crime. In 125 of these cases, victim and offender were "relatives" (Table 1); these familial homicides have been discussed elsewhere (Daly and Wilson 1982). Here we wish to focus upon the 214 cases in which victim and offender were unrelated. (Spouses, whether legally married or common-law, are considered "relatives" and excluded from present analysis, as are in-laws.)

Wilt originally classified Detroit social conflict homicides into four categories, atheoretically derived from her preliminary reading of a hundred cases. These she called "jealousy conflicts," "business conflicts," "family conflicts," and "arguments between friends, acquaintances, or neighbors." Each of these major categories was subdivided into a number of narrower substantive types. We have retained the "jealousy" and "business" categories, and reorganized the other classifications into similarly broad classes of motives. The resulting classification is outlined in Table 3.

A total of 58 homicides in this study were attributed to sexual jealousy: the 34 cases in Table 3, plus 24 cases in which victim and offender were related (23 spousal homicides and 1 involving intervention by an in-law). Among the sexual jealousy cases in Table 3, the predominant variety involved two men contesting a particular woman. We have reviewed the 58 sexual jealousy cases, and the prevalence of this motive in homicide generally, in another paper (Daly, Wilson, and Weghorst 1982). In addition to the 13 business conflict cases in Table 3, an additional two intrafamilial homicides could be so classified.

More than half of the 214 cases summarized in Table 3 are of the sort that criminologists have called "trivial altercations." These include what we have called "escalated showing-off disputes" (29 cases; 16.1% of the 180 classifiable, non-

TABLE 3   Two Hundred Twelve Detroit "Social Conflict" Homicides Where Victim and Offender Were Unrelated, by Conflict Typology and Sex of the Principals

Conflict Typology	Offender–Victim[a]			
	M–M	M–F	F–M	F–F
Jealousy conflicts	20	5	6	3
Business conflicts	10	1	2	0
Escalated showing-off disputes	26	0	2	1
Retaliation for previous verbal or physical abuse	75	9	6	5
Intervention in family quarrels	5	0	0	0
Miscellaneous unique disputes	2	0	1	1
Insufficient information to categorize	26	4	1	1
Total social conflicts among nonrelatives	164	19	18	11

[a] M, male; F, female.

relative, social conflict homicides) and "disputes arising from retaliation for previous verbal or physical abuse" (95 cases; 52.8%).

The escalated showing-off dispute involves two or more individuals trying to best one another in front of witnesses. There were no such cases in which the disputants were relatives. We offer two illustrative synopses based on Wilt's summaries of the police documentation:

Case 121: Victim (male, age 19), offender (male, age 23) and others had been drinking together. Victim was a boxer and was talking about his fights. Offender showed off with his night stick by placing it between the victim's legs and lifting him in the air. Victim was embarrassed and asked offender to let him down. Victim accused offender of tearing his pants and told offender to pay for them. Offender and others were laughing at victim. Victim hit offender and both were told to leave. Victim left first, then stood on the porch. Offender says victim hit him again when he came out, so he shot him.

Case 185: Victim (male, age 22) and offender (male, age 41) were in a bar when a mutual acquaintance walked in. Offender bragged to victim of "this guy's" fighting ability and that they had fought together. Victim replied "you are pretty tough" and an argument ensued over whether victim or offender was the better man. Victim then told offender "I got mine" (gun) and the offender replied "I got mine too," both indicating their pockets. The victim then said "I don't want to die and know you don't want to die. Let's forget about it." But the offender produced a small automatic, shot the victim dead, and left the bar.

Such escalated showing-off disputes as these are overwhelmingly a male affair. The two cases in which a woman killed a man both involved the woman's intervening in a dispute between two men, killing one in defense of the other. Only one of 29 cases involved an escalated showing-off dispute between women.

The category of "disputes arising from retaliation for previous verbal or physical abuse," accounting for the largest number of cases, is a little more heterogeneous. It includes retaliation for insults, for accusations of cheating or theft, and for physical attacks at some time past. The unifying characteristic of these cases is the affront and loss of face that seem to demand redress. Here are two brief illustrative synopses of disputes arising from verbal or physical abuse:

Case 79: Victim (male, age 23) accused an acquaintance, the offender (male, age 17), of having broken into his home, and proceeded to beat up offender. The latter left, got a gun from a friend, returned and killed his assailant before several witnesses.

Case 324: Victim (male, age 25), walking down street with his brother, directed an insulting remark at two brothers (ages 20, 22), who responded aggressively, whereupon victim and victim's brother walked home. When they reemerged, the brothers whom they had insulted were waiting with guns and killed victim and wounded his brother.

CRIME-SPECIFIC HOMICIDES

Alexander (1979) has argued, from the same perspective adopted here, that young men are expected to be the principal participants in law breaking and in dangerous attempts to accrue material resources as well as status:

> Sexual competition is demonstrably more intense among males than among females; and one can easily show from the accumulated differences between modern males and females powerful evidence that this has consistently been the case during human history, and that as a general consequence the entire life history strategy of males is a higher-risk, higher-stakes adventure than that of females . . . This finding leads to the prediction that lawbreaking will occur more frequently among males, which of course is already well known . . . It also seems to predict that laws are chiefly made by men (as opposed to women) to control men (as opposed to women) (Alexander 1979, p. 241).

In this regard, it is interesting to note that Bacon, Child, and Barry (1963) found that crime rates tend to be higher in more polygynous societies, males being everywhere the criminals.

Our "crime-specific" homicide sample may also be viewed as supporting Alexander's analysis. The offenders in such homicides are even more often male (95% of 134 cases) than are "social conflict" offenders (75% of 337 cases). The seven crime-specific homicides committed by women include four in self-defense against male burglars or attempted rapists, leaving only three cases where the woman was the party engaged in criminal activity. A predominance of male offenders is of course characteristic not just of homicide, but of all types of crime except prostitution. Ninety-three percent of robberies, 94% of burglaries, and 91% of motor vehicle thefts in America in 1980, for example, were committed by males (U.S. Department of Justice, 1981, Table 34). Men are not poorer than women, but they help themselves to other people's property more often, and they are evidently readier to use violence to do so. It may be suggested that the chronic competitive situation among males is ultimately responsible for a greater felt need for surplus—as opposed to subsistence—resources.

Not only are crime-specific offenders in Detroit more often male than social conflict offenders, but they also match our predicted demographic profile better. The crime-specific male offenders are younger (27.8 ± 12 years) than their social conflict counterparts (34.2 ± 13 years), are more often unemployed (43.6% vs. 38.9%) and are more often unmarried (73.8% vs. 57.8%). The age and marital status differences are significant ($p < 0.01$).

It is also noteworthy how few of the *victims* of crime-specific homicide are female (Table 2). If these cases were simply to be understood as violent appropriation of other's resources, then we might expect male offenders to pick on females fairly often. Women are not infrequently robbed (50% of victims of theft in Detroit according to U.S. Department of Justice, 1976), but they are relatively infrequently killed (14% of 49 murdered robbery victims in the present study). There are several possible reasons for this, but at least part of the explanation seems to lie in the fact that crime-specific homicides contain some of the same elements of face and male competitiveness that characterize so many social conflict homicides. This point has been especially well developed by Toch (1969), who has analyzed violent escalation in police–suspect interactions in terms of the stubborn aggressiveness of both parties when concerned to maintain face in front of witnesses.

RISK TAKING MORE GENERALLY

We expect a taste for competitive risk taking to be an evolved aspect of masculine psychology as a result of sexual selection. If male fitness derives from success in risky competition, then males are expected to join such competition willingly, given reasonable prospects of success. Thus, for example, the addition of an element of competition, especially face to face, makes males but not females more willing to persevere in a rather dull, laboratory, skill-testing task (Weinberg and Ragan 1980). A taste for risk, with or without competition, may also be manifested in many other spheres than the violent conflicts that we have thus far considered (see also Rubin and Paul 1979).

In a sociable species such as our own, in which there are long-term consequences of success and failure in competition, mediated by rank and reputation, we furthermore expect an evolved inclination toward the social display of one's competitive risk-taking skills, and again this should be especially a masculine trait. Just why the maintenance of reputation should require incurring risk can be answered in terms of pressures favoring "honest advertising." A signal or display that is supposed to be indicative of high resources or estimable personal qualities is only convincing when it cannot be counterfeited by individuals with fewer resources or lesser qualities (Zahavi 1977; see also Popp and DeVore 1979). A boast is only impressive if it implies a challenge and if those who might take up the challenge hear it (Borgia 1979).

Successful risk taking certainly evokes admiration. An entertaining case study is Wolfe's (1979) *The Right Stuff,* an account of machismo and prestige in test pilots and astronauts. Wolfe's title refers to a coveted, intangible substance that successful daredevils possess. Some men have it and are revered for it; others don't have it and never will. The fact that people accord prestige to successful risk takers in this way only makes sense on the assumption that there is something predictive about past success—that competence, judgment, physical prowess, and good "luck" are enduring qualities of individuals. Acceptance of defeat or subordinate status also requires the same assumption—that there is some enduring quality that makes past victors likely to win again if challenged again. For this reason, the acceptance of risk seems to have acquired a generalized prestige value that may transfer, irrationally, to pure chance situations where past success is *not* predictive of future success. People are not always good intuitive statisticians and they use many imperfect rules of thumb in making behavioral decisions (see, e.g., Nisbett and Ross 1980). One such rule of thumb is to follow the successful, so that being followed and admired can augment the rewards of the initial success.

One laboratory operationalization of risk taking is to confront subjects with hypothetical dilemmas (whether to recommend major surgery, for example, or how to invest a pension fund). With the hazards and expectations of benefit specified probabilistically, the subjects are called upon to choose from the various options. A riskier decision is then one that incurs relatively large or probable hazards in exchange for relatively large or probable benefits. In this sort of situation, groups generally tend to arrive at riskier decisions than do individuals (e.g., Kogan and Wallach 1964; Zaleska 1976). As we would expect, this effect appears to be stronger in men than in women (e.g., Johnson, Stemler, and Hunter 1977) and most studies have used male subjects only. A leading candidate as an explanation for the group effect is that social desirability or prestige accompanies the advocacy of risky choices in group situations (Brown 1965), perhaps because advocates of risk are perceived as especially capable (Jellison and Riskind 1970). These interpretations are of course quite compatible with the arguments we have presented.

A similar operationalization of risk taking in the real world is gambling. If the odds are equal, then the larger bet is the riskier bet. Gambling is predominantly a male activity (e.g., Downes et al. 1976; Kallick et al. 1979) and the larger the stakes, the more male dominated it becomes (e.g., Newman 1972; Cornish 1978). There is some evidence that the presence of other players leads blackjack players to elevate their bets against the house (Blascovich, Ginsburg, and Howe, 1976; Ginsburg, Blascovich, and Howe 1976), a result similar to the group shift-to-risk effect described above. Furthermore, "high rollers" sometimes enjoy considerable prestige.

A rather different sort of risk is incurred by drug users. In American surveys, adolescents and young adults are the major users of illegal drugs, and males use all such substances more than do females. Married persons show the lowest rates of use. In predicting drug usage, parental influence is minor and peer influence preeminent (Kandel 1980). We predict that high-risk behaviors, such as experiments with high dosages of drugs and novel or unknown substances, can be shown to be socially facilitated and admired by peers, especially among males.

ON THE SEX DIFFERENCE IN MORTALITY

We have already remarked that it is characteristic of a polygynous species that the males tend to suffer higher mortality than the females. This sex difference is ultimately attributable to the greater degree of reproductive competition among males. Its more proximate causes are various, including a variety of consequences of the males' risk-taking behavior. Demographers draw a distinction between "external" and "internal" sources of mortality. The former category consists primarily of deaths by accident (approximately 80% of "external" deaths in America), as well as deaths by suicide, homicide, poisoning, and medical misadventure. Internal sources of mortality include disease and senescence. Males exceed females, in the Western world, in both sorts of mortality, but the pattern of sex differences is distinct (Figure 5). The sex differential is considerably larger in external than in internal mortality and it is maximal in young adulthood, whereas the sex difference in internal mortality is maximal in later years. The substantial sex difference in external mortality risk in young adulthood may be interpreted as another manifestation of the dangerous-young-male syndrome.

Some efforts have been made to construct life tables for ancient men and women from archaeological materials, and it is generally concluded that female mortality

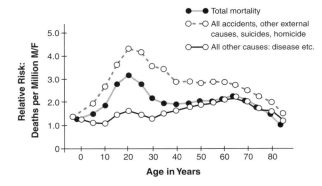

FIGURE 5 The ratio of male mortality over female mortality for the United States in 1975, according to type of mortality.

Data from U.S. Department of Health, Education, and Welfare (1979) and U.S. Bureau of the Census (1977).

exceeded male mortality at most ages in most prehistoric skeletal series (Acsádi and Nemeskéri 1970). This result appears to contradict modern evidence and our expectation that excess male mortality is characteristic of our species. In this regard, it should be noted that virtually all the archaeological materials are postagricultural and are therefore no more representative of our hunting-and-gathering prehistory than are modern samples; that sexing of prepubertal skeletons is acknowledged to be guess-work; and that data are based on burial groups and may therefore exclude adventurous, emigrant young men. The fact that males surpass females in "internal" mortality (Figure 5), and in particular that males senesce more rapidly than females, supports our hypothesis that the female life-span has exceeded male life-span for a significant period of our evolutionary history.

MORTALITY IN MOTOR VEHICLE ACCIDENTS

Men, particularly young men, incur many more accidents and fatalities in motor vehicles than do women (Peck, Coppin, and Marsh 1965; Shaw and Sichel 1971). It would appear likely that this is not a matter of lesser skill, but rather of more risky behavior, such as speeding (Organisation for Economic Cooperation and Development 1975), tailgating (Ebbesen and Haney 1973), refusing to yield right of way (Jamieson 1977), and running amber lights (Konečni, Ebbesen, and Konečni 1976). Men also react more aggressively than women to inconsiderate behavior by other drivers (Turner, Layton, and Simons 1975).

It has been suggested, however, that the sex difference in motor vehicle fatalities may be an artifact of sex differences in exposure to risk: males drive more than females (Organisation for Economic Cooperation and Development 1975). We have therefore combined three sorts of data—motor vehicle fatalities (U.S. Department of Health, Education, Welfare 1974, Table 4-1); estimates of the numbers of miles driven by licensed drivers in different age-sex classes according to a U.S. National Probability Sample (U.S. Bureau of the Census 1979); and numbers of licensed drivers by age and sex (U.S. Department of Transportation, n.d., Table DL-P1)—to arrive at estimates of driver mortality per mile driven (Figure 6). Although men indeed drive more

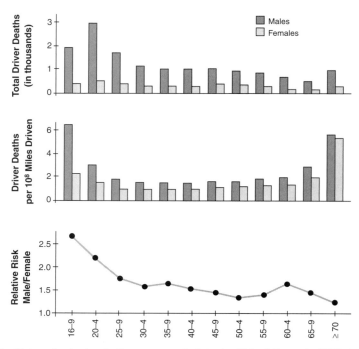

FIGURE 6   Driver deaths (excluding motorcycles) in the United States in 1970, by age and sex; death rates on a per driving distance basis; and the ratio of male mortality over female mortality.

See text for data sources.

than women, a dramatic sex difference in driver mortality remains when the data are corrected for miles driven, and the sex difference is strongly age dependent. Dangerous driving by young men moreover appears to be a social display. For example, male drivers are much quicker to hazard a turn into traffic when they have male passengers than when they have female passengers or are alone, whereas female drivers are not evidently influenced by passengers (Jackson and Gray 1976).

THE FIELD OF HONOR

The risky competitive inclinations of young men are variously manifested, then, but we should like to return, in conclusion, to the sort of confrontational disputes with which we began. The typical "trivial altercation" homicide in America is an affair of honor with strong resemblances to the affairs of honor that have been described in other cultures (e.g., Eckert and Newmark 1980; Caro Barajo 1966; Safilios-Rothschild 1969). The precipitating insult may appear petty, but it is usually a deliberate provocation (or is perceived to be), and hence constitutes a public challenge that cannot be shrugged off. It often takes the form of disparagement of the challenged party's "manhood": his nerve, strength or savvy, or the virtue of his wife, girlfriend, or female relatives. Where there is a disparity in social rank, the individual of higher status may be able to refuse a challenge without loss of face, but not when the two parties are approximate equals. The challenge is itself often issued in response to a perception of status-inappropriate behavior—offense is taken because the other party appears to be elevating himself either by putting on superior "airs" or by failing to show adequate deference to those of slightly higher rank. There seems to be almost an "agreement" that the conflict will be resolved violently (Luckenbill 1977) and it is often the eventual victim who presses the conflict to its violent end (Wolfgang 1958). The eventual killer may announce and justify his deadly intentions both to his victim and to their audience. In all of these features, the homicidal altercation seems more like a formal duel (Thimm 1896; Baldick 1965; Williams 1980) than a senseless eruption of violence.

One interesting question is why these cases must be carried to their deadly conclusion. They may be contrasted, for example, with the ritualized "hold-me-back-or-I'll-kill-him" Irish barroom disputes described by Fox (1977), in which satisfaction is routinely achieved without bloodshed. The difference is of course largely attributable to reporting bias—our starting point is a sample of homicide cases and we have no knowledge of the incidence of defused conflicts. But homicide *is* more frequent in America than in Europe (see, e.g., United Nations 1975, Table 27). One possible explanation is that low-status men in American ghettos may often be immigrants from out of state, perhaps cut off from extended family ties, and are therefore playing a higher-stakes, higher-risk game (cf. Alexander's formulation quoted above) than the young contestants Fox observed "at home" in more enduring social networks. Of the male–male, nonrelative homicides in our Detroit sample, 53% of victims and 47% of offenders were born outside Michigan; however, 41% of *all* Detroiters were born out of state (U.S. Bureau of the Census 1973), and so it is not clear that immigrant men are at higher risk of involvement in homicide than men in Detroit generally. We would still expect that the participants in homicidal conflicts are relatively isolated from family and the opportunities for enhancement of inclusive fitness that family affords, and hence have relatively little to lose. We would expect further that the demographic characteristics of participants in homicidal conflicts are associated with high risks of non-marriageability and total reproductive failure. These are issues for future research.

It is evident that the principal protagonists in homicide are young adults (Figures 1, 2), but we are not satisfied that the sociobiological theories reviewed earlier in this article explain why. Several authors have suggested that a young adult peak in risk-prone competitiveness is a prediction from sexual selection theory. We know of no formal derivation of this "prediction," which seems to be more of a generalization from comparative knowledge. One might instead predict that where two men find themselves similarly disenfranchised—their circumstances similarly predictive of failure—that it is the *older,* not the younger, who has less to lose and should therefore be readier to employ dangerous competitive tactics. Development of theory about competitive strategies in relation to life histories seems called for.

A final area in which research should prove illuminating is the question of the social significance and sequelae of competition and confrontation. Who are the actors most concerned to impress—women, their opponents, or other men? Is success in dangerous confrontation in fact predictive of later status, resource accrual, social accomplishments, perhaps even fitness? What are the social consequences of refusing to accept risks—is cowardice an enduring and consequential stigma? The motives in fatal altercations between young men are often portrayed as "trivial," implying that homicide is an irrational overreaction. But this conclusion is too hasty. For all we know, the principals may be acting as shrewd calculators of the probable costs and benefits of alternative courses of action. Once a conflict becomes dangerous, the *most* negative outcome befalls the man who is shot. Men in such situations may have quite realistic knowledge of the lesser costs (not to mention possible benefits) of shooting first. In our Detroit sample, we know the eventual dispositions in 121 solved, male–male, social conflict, nonrelative homicide cases. Fifty-seven offenders (47.1%) were not convicted of any crime in connection with the homicide (56 cases dismissed, primarily as "justifiable," "excusable," or "self-defense," and a single acquittal after trial). Of 64 convicted offenders, only 2 were first-degree murders, 12 second-degree murders, 34 manslaughters, and 16 lesser charges. Thus fewer than 12% of apprehended offenders in this sample were convicted of an offense more serious than manslaughter (although the rate of murder convictions may well be higher in the 43 cases for which we lacked final dispositions). A typical sentence for manslaughter was 3 to 5 years in state prison, with parole available after 18 months.

We cannot then conclude that the offenders in "trivial altercation" homicides, swept up by irrational passions, act without concern for the consequences to themselves. We should need a great deal more information to decide whether pulling the trigger is ultimately beneficial or detrimental to the perpetrator's welfare. But, of course, most people are able to avoid situations in which they will be obliged or provoked to kill. What is clear is that it is young adult males, with few resources and poor prospects, who most often become involved in such dangerous, competitive situations.

ENDNOTE

1. Police are excluded from subsequent analyses of both victims and offenders, since their involvement in dangerous conflict is peculiar to their profession rather than being indicative of the demographic categories to which they belong. The city of Detroit employed 6148 police officers in 1972 (U.S. Department of Justice 1973, Table 71), six of whom were homicide victims in the line of duty. Thirty-six homicides were committed by police in the line of duty.

REFERENCES

Acsádi, Gy., Nemeskéri, J. *History of Human Life Span and Mortality*. Budapest: Akadémiai Kiadó, 1970.

Alexander, R.D. *Darwinism and Human Affairs*. Seattle: University of Washington. 1979.

———, Hoogland, J.L., Howard, R.D., Noonan, K.M., Sherman, P.W. Sexual dimorphisms and breeding systems in pinnipeds, ungulates, primates, and humans. In *Evolutionary Biology and Human Social Behavior: An Anthropological Perspective*, N.A. Chagnon and W. Irons, (Eds.). North Scituate, MA: Duxbury. 1979, pp.402–435.

Bacon, M.K., Child, I.L., Barry, H. A cross-cultural study of correlates of crime. *Journal of Abnormal and Social Psychology* 66: 291–300 (1963).

Baldick, R. *The Duel*. New York: Clarkson N. Potter, 1965.

Bateman, A.J. Intra-sexual selection in Drosophila. *Heredity* 2: 349–368 (1948).

Betzig, L.L. Despotism and differential reproduction: A cross-cultural correlation of conflict asymmetry, hierarchy, and degree of polygyny. *Ethology and Sociobiology* 3: 209–221 (1982).

Blascovich, J., Ginsburg, G., Howe, R. Blackjack, choice shifts in the field. *Sociometry* 39: 274–276 (1976).

Borgia, G. Sexual selection and the evolution of mating systems. In *Sexual Selection and Reproductive Competition in Insects,* M.S. Blum and N.A. Blum (Eds.). New York: Academic, 1979, pp. 19–80.

Brown, R. *Social Psychology.* New York: Free Press, 1965.

Caro Barajo, J. Honour and shame: A historical account of several conflicts. In *Honour and Shame,* J.G. Peristiany (Ed.). London: Weidenfeld and Nicolson, 1966, pp. 81–137.

Clutton-Brock, T.H., Albon, S.D., Harvey, P.H. Antlers, body size and breeding group size in the Cervidae. *Nature* 285: 565–567 (1980).

Cornish, D.B. *Gambling: A Review of the Literature and its Implications for Policy and Research.* London: Home Office, 1978.

Daly, M., Wilson, M.I. Homicide and kinship. *American Anthropologist* 84: 372–378 (1982).

———, ———. On the adaptive significance of motives in homicide. In *Evolution, Adaptation and Behavioral Science,* I. DeVore and J. Tooby (Eds.). New York: Aldine, in press.

———, ———, Weghorst, S.J. Male sexual jealousy. *Ethology and Sociobiology* 3: 11–27 (1982).

Downes, D.M., Davies, D.P., David, M.E., Stone, P. *Gambling, Work and Leisure: A Study Across Three Areas.* London: Routledge and Kegan Paul, 1976.

Ebbesen, E.B., Haney, M. Flirting with death: Variables affecting risk-taking at intersections. *Journal of Applied Psychology* 3: 303–324 (1973).

Eckert, P., Newmark, R. Central Eskimo song duels: A contextual analysis of ritual ambiguity. *Ethnology* 19: 191–211 (1980).

Felson, R.B. Aggression as impression management. *Social Psychology* 41: 205–213 (1978).

Fox, R. Alliance and constraint: Sexual selection in the evolution of human kinship systems. In *Sexual Selection and the Descent of Man, 1871–1971,* B. Campbell (Ed.). Chicago: Aldine, 1972.

———. The inherent rules of violence. In *Social Rules and Social Behaviour,* P. Collett (Ed.). Oxford: Basil Blackwell, 1977.

Ginsburg, G.P., Blascovich, J.J., Howe, R.C. Risk-taking in the presence of others: blackjack in the laboratory and in the field. In *Gambling and Society,* W.R. Eadington (Ed.). Springfield, IL: Thomas, 1976.

Goffman, E. *The Presentation of Self in Everyday Life.* Garden City, NY: Doubleday Anchor Books, 1959.

Horowitz, R., Schwartz, G. Honor, normative ambiguity and gang violence. *American Sociological Review* 39: 238–251 (1974).

Howell, N. *Demography of the Dobe !Kung.* New York: Academic, 1979.

Jackson, T.T., Gray, M. Field study of risk-taking behavior of automobile drivers. *Perceptual and Motor Skills* 43: 471–474 (1976).

Jamieson, B.D. Sex differences among drivers in yielding right-of-way. *Psychological Reports* 41: 1243–1248 (1977).

Jayawardena, C. Conflict and solidarity in a Guianese plantation. *London School of Economics Monographs in Social Anthropology, no. 25.* London: Athlone, 1963.

Jellison, J.M., Riskind, J. A social comparison of abilities interpretation of risk-taking behavior. *Journal of Personality and Social Psychology* 15: 375–390 (1970).

Jenni, D.A. Evolution of polyandry in birds. *American Zoologist* 14: 129–144 (1974).

Johnson, N.R., Stemler, J.G., Hunter, D. Crowd behavior as "risky shift": A laboratory experiment. *Sociometry* 40: 183–187 (1977).

Kallick, M., Suits, D., Dielman, T., Hybels, J. *A Survey of American Gambling Attitudes and Behavior.* Ann Arbor, MI: Institute for Social Research, 1979.

Kandel, D.B. Drug and drinking behavior among youth. *Annual Review of Sociology* 6: 235–285 (1980).

Kogan, N., Wallach, M. *Risk-taking: A Study in Cognition and Personality.* New York: Holt, Rinehart, and Winston, 1964.

Konečni, V.J., Ebbesen, E.B., Konečni, D.K. Decision processes and risk-taking in traffic: Driver response to the onset of yellow light. *Journal of Applied Psychology* 61: 359–367 (1976).

Leuttenegger, W., Kelley, J.T. Relationship of sexual dimorphism in canine size and body size to social, behavioral, and ecological correlates in anthropoid primates. *Primates* 18: 117–136 (1977).

Luckenbill, D.F. Criminal homicide as a situated transaction. *Social Problems* 25: 176–186 (1977).

Maxson, S.J., Oring, L.W. Breeding season time and energy budget of the polyandrous spotted sandpiper. *Behaviour* 74: 200–263 (1980).

Mulvihill, D.J., Tumin, M.M., Curtis, L.A. *Crimes of Violence. Vol. 11. A Staff Report Submitted to the National Commission on the Causes & Prevention of Violence.* Washington, D.C.: U.S. Government Printing Office, 1969.

Newman, O. *Gambling: Hazard and Reward.* University of London: Athlone, 1972.

Nisbett, R., Ross, L. *Human Inference: Strategies and Shortcomings of Social Judgment.* Englewood Cliffs, NJ: Prentice-Hall, 1980.

Organisation for Economic Cooperation and Development. *Young Driver Accidents.* Paris: OECD, 1975.

Paige, K.E., Paige. J.M. *The Politics of Reproductive Ritual.* Berkeley, CA: University of California Press, 1981.

Peck, R.C., Coppin, R.S., Marsh, W.C. *Driver Record by Age, Sex and Marital Status. The 1964 Driver Record Study. Part 5.* Department of Motor Vehicles, State of California, 1965.

Popp, J.L., DeVore. I. Aggressive competition and social dominance theory: synopsis. In *The Great Apes,* D.A. Hamburg and E.R. McCown (Eds.). Memo Park, CA: Benjamin/Cummings, 1979.

Rubin, P.H., Paul, C.W. An evolutionary model of taste for risk. *Economic Inquiry* 17: 585–596 (1979).

Safilios-Rothschild, C. "Honour" crimes in contemporary Greece. *British Journal of Sociology* 20: 205–218 (1969).

Shaw, L., Sichel, H.S. *Accident Proneness. Research in the Occurrence, Causation, and Prevention of Road Accidents.* Oxford: Pergamon, 1971.

Thimm, C.A. *A Complete Bibliography of Fencing and Duelling.* New York: Benjamin Blom, 1896 (Reissued 1968).

Tiger, L. *Men in Groups.* New York: Vintage Books, 1969.

Toch, H. *Violent Men. An Inquiry into the Psychology of Violence.* Chicago: Aldine, 1969.

Trivers, R.L. Parental investment and sexual selection. In *Sexual Selection and the Descent of Man 1871–1971,* B. Campbell (Ed.). Chicago: Aldine, 1972.

Turner, C.W., Layton, J.F.. Simons, L.S. Naturalistic studies of aggressive behavior: Aggressive stimuli, victim visability, and horn honking. *Journal of Personality and Social Psychology* 31: 1098–1107 (1975).

United Nations. *Demographic Yearbook 1974. Special Topic: Mortality Statistics.* New York: United Nations, 1975.

U.S. Bureau of the Census. *Census of Population: 1970. General Population Characteristics. Final report PC(1)-B24 Michigan.* Washington, D.C.: U.S. Government Printing Office, 1971.

———. *Census of Population: 1970 Subject Reports. Final Report PC(2)-2A. State of Birth.* Washington, D.C.: U.S. Government Printing Office, 1973.

———. *Current Population Reports, Series P-25, No. 643, Estimates of the Population of the United States, by Age, Sex, and Race: July 1, 1974 to 1976.* Washington, D.C.: U.S. Government Printing Office, 1977.

———, Federal Highway Administration. *National Personal Transportation Survey 1969–70.* Cited in "Study of California Driving Performance (Phase II)," a research report of the Rate Regulation Division, California Department of Insurance, 1979.

U.S. Department of Health, Education, Welfare. *Vital Statistics of the United States 1970. Vol. II—Mortality, Part A.* Washington, D.C.: U.S. Government Printing Office, 1974.

———. *Vital Statistics of the United States 1975. Vol. II—Mortality, Part A.* Washington, D.C.: U.S. Government Printing Office, 1979.

U.S. Department of Justice, Federal Bureau of Investigation. *Uniform Crime Reports of the United States 1972.* Washington, D.C.: U.S. Government Printing Office, 1973.

———. *Uniform Crime Reports for the United States 1980.* Washington, D.C.: U.S. Government Printing Office, 1981.

U.S. Department of Justice, Law Enforcement Assistance Administration. *Criminal Victimization Surveys in Chicago, Detroit, Los Angeles, New York and Philadelphia: A Comparison of 1972 and 1974 Findings.* Washington, D.C.: U.S. Government Printing Office, 1976.

U.S. Department of Labor, Bureau of Labor Statistics. *Current Population Survey 1972 Annual Average Area Supplement.* Washington, D.C., no date.

U.S. Department of Transportation. *Drivers Licenses, by Sex and Age Groups, for 40 States—1970.* Washington, D.C., no date.

Wasser, S.K. (Ed.). *Social behavior of female vertebrates.* New York: Academic, 1983.

Weinberg, S., Ragan, J. Effects of competition, success-failure and sex or intrinsic motivation. In *Psychological and Sociological Factors in Sport,* P. Klavora and K.A.W. Wipper (Eds.). Toronto: University of Toronto Press, 1980.

Williams, G.C. *Adaptation and Natural Selection.* Princeton, NJ: Princeton University Press, 1966.

Williams, J.H. *Dueling in the Old South. Vignettes of Social History.* College Station, TX: Texas A & M University Press, 1980.

Wilt, G.M. *Toward an Understanding of the Social Realities of Participating in Homicides.* Doctoral dissertation, Wayne State University, 1974, unpublished.

Wittenberger, J.F. The evolution of mating systems in grouse. *Condor* 80: 126–137 (1978).

Wolfe, T. *The Right Stuff.* New York: Farrar, Straus, and Giroux, 1979.

Wolfgang, M.E. *Patterns in Criminal Homicide.* Philadelphia: University of Pennsylvania Press, 1958.

Zahavi, A. The cost of honesty (further remarks on the handicap principle). *Journal of Theoretical Biology* 67: 603–605 (1977).

Zaieska, M. Majority influence in group choices among bets. *Journal of Personality and Social Psychology* 33: 8–17 (1976).

A Few Good Men
Evolutionary Psychology and Female Adolescent Aggression

ANNE CAMPBELL

Criminologists have drawn attention to the fact that crime peaks in the teens and early 20s and that this pattern shows invariance over culture, history, offense, and sex. Wilson and Daly (1985) have proposed that among young, disadvantaged males, the age-crime curve reflects risky tactics aimed at averting "reproductive death." Though young women's rate of involvement in violent crime is much lower than men's, they also show a similar age-violence curve for assault. This paper proposes that this may be the result of aggressive mate selection among young women and that, under certain specified circumstances, women may engage in low-key intra-sexual strategies in addition to epigamic strategies. This paper reviews material on sex differences in violent crime and in mate selection strategies, and offers predictions about the likely circumstances under which females will use intrasexual strate-gies. The scant available data on female adolescent fighting suggest that female-female assaults are more common than official statistical estimates and that they are frequently triggered by three key issues related to reproductive fitness: management of sexual reputation, competition over access to resource-rich young men, and pro-tecting heterosexual relationships from takeover by rival women.

Key Words: Aggression; Female; Mate selection

H irschi and Gottfredson (1983) make a compelling argument for the invari-ance of the age-crime curve. The association between youth and height-ened crime rate, they argue, holds constant regardless of historical period, country, race, type of crime, and (most relevant for the present discussion) sex. While males far exceed females in the volume and rate of crime they commit, females show a similar (although muted) rise in involvement during the teen years. I shall begin by examining data on sex and age distributions for crimes of violence, with particular reference to assault.

Official statistics typically measure arrest or findings of guilt. With regard to the United States, Kruttschnitt (1994) presents 1989 arrest rates for various forms of violent crime for males and females as a function of age (see Figure 1). The correla-tion over age between male and female rates for assault is 0.89 ($p < .01$) with males

Reprinted from *Ethology and Sociobiology,* vol. 16, A. Campbell, "A few good men: Evolutionary psychology and female adolescent aggression," pp. 99–123, Copyright 1995, with permission from Elsevier.

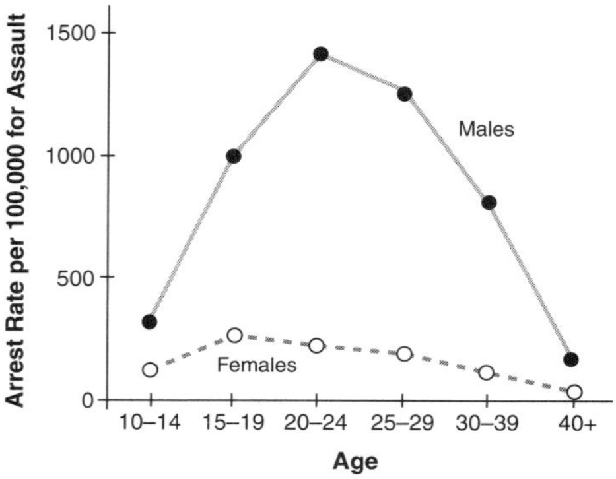

FIGURE 1   Arrest rates for assault by sex and age.

Data from the United States Department of Justice 1989 (reported in Kruttschnitt 1994).

peaking at ages 20–24 and females at 15–19. For aggravated assault the correlation is 0.99 ($p < .0001$) with both sexes peaking at 20–24. The same pattern is evident in British arrest rate data. The correlation between the sexes for convictions for violent offences is 0.98 ($p < .01$). This effect does not seem to be a function of differential willingness to prosecute or find guilty, for the same pattern is evident with cautioning rate ($r = 0.98, p < .01$). Piper (1983) used official data to examine a cohort of Philadelphia youths, focusing explicitly on age of initiation into violent offending. The proportion of violent offenders who committed their first violent offense at a particular age was computed as a function of all those originally at risk for such offenses. The age range was 10 to 18. The data again reveal a remarkable similarity in the age distribution for the two sexes. As with national rate figures for assault, we see a tendency for girls' initiation to peak somewhat earlier (age 12–15) than boys' (age 15–16).

The use of official data is vulnerable to the criticism that it reflects police and prosecutorial bias rather than true rates of offending. To obviate such criticisms, self-report delinquency studies can be used, where youth are asked to indicate their involvement in various crimes under condition of anonymity. The National Youth Survey has been collecting such data from a national United States sample for several years. Elliott, Huizinga, and Morse (1983) report data on involvement in serious violence as a function of sex and age. As with official data, prevalence rates (the proportion of individuals classified as serious offenders in a given year) are similar for the two sexes ($r = 0.77, p < .005$), as are survival rates, which reflect the proportion of individuals at each age who have never been classed as serious violent offenders ($r = 0.92, p < .0001$). Like Piper, the authors present hazard rates reflecting age of initiation but this time based upon self-report. While females peak between 13 and 15, the male peak occurs at 16–18.

This parallel between the development of aggression in males and females is not confined to measures of reported or official criminal violence nor to the teenage years. In a cross-sectional Finnish study, Bjorkvist, Lagerspetz, and Kaukiainen (1992) report age trends (at ages 8, 11, and 15) for a variety of forms of aggression measured by peer nomination. For kicking/striking and pushing/shoving, the sexes show remarkable similarity, with both sexes peaking at age 11. Gender differences in absolute frequency are significant (for kicking/striking at all three ages and for pushing/shoving at ages 11 and 15) in the expected direction. These authors and many others, however, overlook the remarkable similarity between boys and girls in developmental trends. Eron et al. (1983) report longitudinal data on aggression, again measured by peer report. As they note, "The shape of the curve is the same for boys and girls." Both sexes show an identical trend, with aggression rising consistently from age 7 to peak at their last data point, age 11.

Gottfredson and Hirshi (1990) have argued that the age-crime curve is not explicable by any social correlates of age that have so far been advanced (e.g., dropout from school, unemployment/employment, marriage, and parenthood), although some have pointed for the need to examine such correlates more rigorously. (Daly and Wilson 1990 see such variables as potentially relevant and interpretable within an evolutionary psychological account of violence in terms of mate selection and differential fitness.) In their paper on homicide, Daly and Wilson argue that males' higher rates of involvement reflect their greater fitness variance—the Bateman effect—and their consequent willingness to engage in risky tactics. They rightly note that the female homicide rate is only a fraction of that of males, pointing out that "women compete too and may even kill one another in the process but their lesser fitness variance has generally meant that they have little to gain and at least something to lose by dangerous tactics." Females consequently receive little further attention, despite the authors' comment that "the shapes of age distributions are remarkably similar" across the sexes.

In this paper I will argue that the peaking of aggression in the teenage and early adult years can be explained by recourse to the same theoretical framework for boys and girls: the evolutionary psychology of mate selection. In doing so, I make the assumption that the evolved psychology responsible for intrasexual aggression in mate selection results from selection pressures that were at work in Pleistocene society, but that to the extent that the same social and life course circumstances are present today, we see evidence of the activation of these same psychological mechanisms.

In arguing for the presence of intrasexual aggression among young women, I concur with Daly and Wilson (1990) that females have more to risk than do males by acts of aggression and, because of this, I predict smaller sex ratios for minor acts of violence than for the serious offense of homicide on which their argument was based. They select homicide as an assay for aggression based on its greater frequency of reporting and consequent higher reliability. It is, however, only an assay of relatively severe attack, and among younger females we would expect this to be the exception rather than the rule (for reasons to be discussed shortly). This turns out to be the case. While female percentages of all arrests (FP/A) for assault and aggravated assault decrease with age, FP/A for homicide increases with age (Kruttschnitt 1994; Steffensmeier and Alien 1988). Wilbanks (1982) found that female homicide offenders peaked at 25 to 44 years while males peaked at 15–24. Weisheit (1984) found female killers' mean age to be 27; Bunch, Foley, and Urbina (1983), age 29; Hewitt and Rivers (1986), age 40; and Mann (1988), age 33. We know that homicide is usually an intersexual crime for women and is principally directed at sexual intimates. The increasing rate with age reflects women's partnered status, and data suggest that killing usually occurs as an act of defense against abusive partners who threaten the woman or her offspring (Browne 1987).

THE EVOLUTIONARY PSYCHOLOGY
OF FEMALE ADOLESCENT AGGRESSION

Daly and Wilson's (1988) evolutionary explanation of young males' high level of violence is founded upon competitive access to females. For a male, reproductive success is a function of number of sexual partners, while for a female, success depends upon material resources and her ability to convert them to offspring, rather than number of mates (Bateman 1948). The woman makes a greater parental investment in offspring both in terms of the relative cost of gamete production (egg vs. sperm) and in gestation, lactation, and other nurturance. It is this greater parental investment that makes the female the resource for which males compete (Trivers 1972). (In species where males make the greater parental investment, it is females who actively compete for mates.) Human sexual selection has operated on an effectively polygynous system in which males' fitness variance is greater than females' because men are more likely than women to leave more descendants than any single woman could bear or none at all. Thus males compete for females while females are characterized by "discriminating passivity" (Bateman 1948).

Sexual selection involves the twin processes of intrasexual competition (within-sex contests aimed at subduing rivals) and epigamic selection (within-sex competition to display a particular attribute that is preferentially valued in a mate by the opposite sex). While Daly and Wilson (1988) have examined risk and violence as aspects of male intrasexual competition, recent work by Buss and Schmitt (1993) has examined epigamic selection as a factor in both male and female mate preferences. They are concerned with the way in which the sexes compete with one another to attract the most desirable partners. To date, the belief has been that while men may engage in intrasexual contest (especially where other avenues of reproductive success are cut off), to the extent that women compete it is in terms of epigamic display—they attempt to secure the best males by excelling in demonstrating those characteristics that are most valued by males. "Human females compete with one another in the currency of physical attractiveness because that is primarily what males value" (Symons 1979). In short, a woman's sexual strategy is passive; she exercises choice by allowing sexual access to the most desirable mate who presents himself, and she seeks to attract him by exhibiting those qualities that the opposite sex finds desirable. Man's sexual strategy is active; he pursues a variety of females, attempting both to advertise those qualities that will make him more desirable than his rivals and to deter (either directly or through the development of a fierce, risk-taking reputation) other suitors.

Though the male rate of violence exceeds that of women by a factor of about 9:1, I have demonstrated that the age distribution of female aggression and violence follows that of males very closely indeed. Yet the evolutionary argument as it stands provides no means of accounting for this because young women, it is argued, do not engage in the intrasexual strategies that typify males as they enter their most reproductively valuable years. In the following sections I shall consider the risks and the advantages attached to a female intrasexual strategy and then consider the circumstances that may tilt the balance toward such a (conservatively) risky strategy.

Risks

The most straightforward explanation of women's avoidance of intrasexual strategies is that the threat to their reproductive fitness is too great. Women's lesser fitness variance means that there is a greater probability that a woman will produce offspring during her lifetime. In addition, while men can never be certain of their own paternity, women know that any progeny of theirs contains half of their genes. So, it is argued, there is little evolutionary incentive to risk their life (and that of their future offspring) to ensure the quality of the remaining half (Daly and Wilson 1994; Symons 1979). This fact may account for why the rate of female homicide is so much lower than that of men and why female-female homicide is a particularly rare event. Though I shall argue that females may fight where the stakes are high enough, mate preference may not be worth risking one's life for and this may explain why the sex differential is less for assault than for homicide. O'Brien (1988), in an analysis of within- and between-sex patterns of violence, notes that despite females' underrepresentation in crimes of violence, there is a clear relationship among women between degree of violence and sex of opponent: "Females offend against other females *more often* than expected for simple assault and, albeit to a lesser extent, for aggravated assault. For homicides, females murder females *less often* than expected." In a cross-cultural analysis of female aggression, Burbank (1987) finds that although attacks are more often directed against other females than against males, the damage women do is often slight, and women are much less likely to use weapons in a female-female context. A similar trend has been noted among primates for whom "the central organizing principle of primate social life is competition between females and especially female lineages" (Hrdy 1981). Hrdy is puzzled by the fact that female gelada rarely inflict serious injury on one another: "Even though the female-female quarrels are more frequent than fights between males in most species, encounters between adult males are much more likely to result in one or both animals being wounded." Yet this paradox of frequent but low-key antagonisms between females in primates and humans can be explained parsimoniously in terms of women's lesser fitness variance, certainty of maternity and consequent high investment in conceiving and rearing a child to adulthood. Fight tactics would be expected to be nonlethal to the extent that the risk of serious injury or death carries with it the certain knowledge that the woman's genes will not be carried forward (see Dawkins 1989; Maynard-Smith 1974). Indeed, fights may be avoided unless there is a severe paucity of resource-provisioning males. Bjorkvist et al. (1992) report that while males exceed females on measures of direct physical and verbal aggression, females score significantly higher on indirect forms, such as gossiping, excluding, and spreading false rumors. Such tactics may have served females well in discrediting rivals' sexual reputations (and consequent chances of mating) as well as inducing stress (with its attendant consequences in terms of ovulation suppression, see Hrdy 1981). Though lower-key in terms of visibility and immediate effect, such tactics can be pursued with minimum risk.

Another argument against female intrasexual strategies has been made by Symons (1979), who suggests that men may discriminate against aggressive females: "There is no reason to believe that men find woman's ability to compete successfully with other women a particularly desirable characteristic in a wife." However, this has the status of a hypothesis rather than a fact. Male fascination with female-female aggression seems evident in its popularity in films and the wrestling ring, and is usually associated with a frisson of sexuality. In addition physical competence may well be a good indicator of health (and hence reproductive value); willingness to risk injury in pursuit of her mate may augur well for her future fidelity and signal equal bellicosity in defending future offspring.

An effectively polygynous system, in which males actively seek as many partners as is economically and legally possible, suggests also that females may have little incentive to fight over men because, like the proverbial bus, "there's bound to be another one along soon." This position, however, assumes that all males who present themselves will be equally desirable as partners or that male intrasexual competition itself will select the fittest mate. I shall discuss these possibilities in the next section.

Advantages

Those who have concerned themselves with human reproductive strategies are in accord that choice of mate carries far greater future implications and significance among women than among men (Buss and Schmitt 1993; Daly and Wilson 1983; Symons 1979). In an effectively polygynous system, men may find other or additional women to bear them children if the current choice of mate proves infertile, and they can do this at relatively little cost because their parental investment is so much lower than that of the female. As Symons (1979) sums it up, "Selection can be expected to favour humans who prefer to copulate with and to marry the fittest members of the opposite sex, and since human female parental investment may typically exceed male investment, females might be expected to be choosier than males." It is in a woman's best interests to attract and retain a man who can provide good genetic material and who is able and willing to make a considerable parental investment in their offspring. Yet while genes and resources are the fundamental recipe for fitness, the literature on female selection has consistently overemphasised the latter at the expense of the former (Buss and Schmitt 1993; Feingold 1990; Symons 1979).

This stress upon women's interest in men as resource providers rather than as phenotypically desirable mates is emphatically underscored by Symons (1979): "I trust no one believes that women compete for opportunities to copulate. In the West, as in all human societies, copulation is a female service or favor: women compete for husbands and for other relationships with men, not for copulation." He speculates that "the human female 'evaluative mechanism' has been designed by selection more for detecting the most reproductively valuable husbands than for detecting the most reproductively valuable sex partners." In other accounts of human mating strategy (Buss and Schmitt 1993, pp. 219, 226; Hrdy 1981, p. 150; Small 1992, p. 143), the possibility that male genetic quality affects female choice is mentioned but not elaborated upon, despite Trivers' (1972) original contention that females enhance the fitness of their offspring by selecting males with superior genotypes. Buss and Schmitt (1993) mention male gene quality only in consideration of short-term sexual strategies, noting that "this benefit remains currently controversial." Yet because male resources are of little benefit to a woman if there are no offspring or only poor quality offspring on which to use them, good genetic choice is logically prior to assessment of resources.

For example, Buss and Schmitt (1993) argue that "the reproductive success of women, in contrast to men, is not as closely linked with obtaining reproductively valuable mates." According to them, men look for attractive, healthy physical appearance and energetic behavior as guides to the likely fertility of women, while women concern themselves with cues to the material resources that a potential mate has and is willing to share. But fertility cuts both ways. Given the disproportionate investment that a woman makes in selecting a mate, it should be in a woman's best interests to select a man who is neither impotent nor sterile. Physical characteristics that provide reliable cues to sexual potency should be selected for by females. Though both Symons (1979, p. 201) and Buss and Schmitt (p. 209) suggest that male reproductive value cannot be judged by physical appearance, it seems unlikely that females would disregard available information on youth, strength, and libido in screening out undesirable mates. Women should also prefer men who display signs of sexual maturity and full sexual differentiation. Apart from providing cues to maturity and potency, male appearance is important on terms of providing an estimate of the likely quality of children that the couple may produce. A female choosing to mate with a strong, athletic, and dominant male increases the likelihood of producing sons with similar traits and thus augmenting her inclusive fitness.

Buss (1988) presents data on male and female tactics of mate selection that demonstrate, despite his original prediction of no sex difference, that males significantly more than females attempt to attract the opposite sex by displaying strength, showing off, and athleticism. The latter is related to body build and to ideal male form (shoulder-to-hip ratio), which can be readily discerned from appearance. Weisfeld et al. (1987) found that athleticism is related to dominance. Girls are more attracted to dominant, athletic boys (Weisfeld et al. 1987), and women also show a preference for more dominant males as husbands (Buss 1987; Howard, Blumstein, and Schwartz 1987; Weisfeld, Bloch, and Ivers 1983; Weisfeld et al. 1992). Dominance may have direct implications for sexual success. In primates, reproductive success is related to dominance (Barkow 1989) and in humans, Masters and Johnson (1970) found that sexual difficulties were more frequent among couples where the man was subordinate. Dominance may be decodable from facial features—Keating (1985) found that males with "dominant" facial features (such as prominent jaws and brows) were rated as more attractive by women. These latter features are also signs of full sexual maturity. Dominant boys tend to reach sexual maturity earlier than their peers (Weisfeld and Billings 1988).

Female mate choice is likely to be strongly driven by judgments about attractiveness that may, in the long evolutionary haul, derive from concerns with potency, sexual maturity, dominance, and a preference for "sexy" sons who will increase her inclusive fitness. There is a considerable social psychological literature that points to the importance of physical attractiveness in mate choice, and preference for attractive phenotypes may have taken on a social and cultural life of its own. By the age of three, children prefer pretty children to less attractive peers (Dion 1977), and attractiveness is perceived to be related to a host of desirable characteristics (Feingold 1990). Conversely, individuals who excel at athletics or academia are judged more attractive than

their less gifted peers (Felson and Bohrnstedt 1979). This may go beyond a mere attri-
bution effect; attractive individuals do indeed report more pleasurable interactions
with others and higher satisfaction with relationships (Reis, Neziek, and Wheeler
1980).

That women evaluate men in terms of more than just their likely resource investment in offspring is also indicated by the prevalence of women's short-term liaisons
and extramarital affairs. Ethological data suggest that females of many species mate
with males other than their main partners even under risky conditions, and physiological evidence suggests that sperm from such matings have preference over that from
their long-term mates (Mock and Fujioka 1990). The phenomenon of female "promiscuity" has been discussed in both primate and human females (see Hrdy 1986). There
is evidence that the father of the child is not the woman's current partner in 20% to
30% of human births (Bellis and Baker 1990), and Russell and Wells (1987) found
that people behave as if they were seven-eighths certain that the husband of their
mother is their father. A possible account is that the wife attempts to improve upon the
genetic quality of the husband by consorting with more dominant males (Benshoof
and Thornhill 1979).

The distinction between genetic quality and resources that has been drawn in
prior work may be overstated, for it is likely that the two variables are correlated. Buss
and Schmitt (1993) hypothesize that for women, short-term liaisons (dating and extramarital affairs) function as a testing ground for long-term choices rather than as a distinct mating strategy. In support of this, they note that there is a higher correlation for
females than for males between the qualities considered desirable in a short-term and
long-term mate. Symons (1979) suggests that, in general, males with the most resources are likely to be those whose genes are the fittest: "A high-status male is both
the best choice for a husband and for a sex partner." Yet he goes on to argue that resource differences are unlikely to be attributable to genetics (and therefore that
women's mating preference is not driven by genetic concerns). Buss and Schmitt,
however, suggest that variables in the qualities that lead to resource acquisition may
be heritable and that this will confer reproductive advantage on her offspring. Intelligence, for example, has a substantial genetic component and is correlated with earn-
ings and social class. It would be to a woman's advantage to mate with a man who
may pass on such a desirable genotype and thus enhance the fitness of her offspring as
well as benefitting her and her children by means of the material resources that he can
provide. The same point has been made with respect to the traits of dominance and
athleticism (Weisfeld and Billings 1988). If women can passively rely on intramale
competition to present them with the best and the brightest as a mate, then there is little incentive for them to risk injury in intrafemale competition. Symons (1979) believes that intramale competition will do the job: "Females may be expected to exercise minimum choice both because they will not normally have much opportunity to
do so and because the best choice almost invariably is a male who is successful in
intrasexual competition." Yet there are a number of reasons to doubt this. First, most
females broadly value the same characteristics in a man (e.g., genes, resources, and,
arguably, the ability to offer protection). Notwithstanding male preference for sexual
variety and the fact that 80% of societies allow polygyny, monogamy, or serial
monogamy is the rule rather than the exception for most individuals. These two facts

alone suggest that many women, given the passive scenario, are likely to find themselves with mates who fall short of their preference. Indeed Symons (1979) suggests that the impact may be even more severe: "Possibly the effect of status on male attractiveness is not linear, but instead, only a few males of the highest status benefit substantially from intense female interest." There are likely to be considerable reproductive benefits for women who succeed in securing and holding these highly valued males. Under certain circumstances, to be discussed in the next section, it may well be to her advantage to actively compete with other females for them.

What are the advantages that accrue to a female who is able to use aggression successfully against other females? Primate research has suggested a far more active and assertive view of female reproductive strategies and has indicated some of the ensuing benefits (Hrdy 1981). High-ranking females mate with higher-status males, are freer from harassment by other females, get pregnant more quickly, breed more successfully, have infants with a higher rate of survival, and have daughters who breed at significantly earlier ages. Many of these benefits derive from the fact that high-ranking females' harassment of subordinates is a stressor that can result in maturational delay, inhibition of ovulation, lengthening of the menstrual cycle, and even spontaneous abortion, as well as preventing rivals from being inseminated by desirable males. Furthermore, dominance is related to age; assertive females reach the top at about the time of their first or second offspring and subsequently lose rank with age, suggesting that intrafemale aggression may well be tied to reproductive concerns.

When Is It Worth the Risk?

In this section I will draw out some of the factors that may have an effect on the likelihood of female intrasexual strategies. It is likely that many of the population-level forces I discuss (youth, sex ratios, unemployment, social mobility, absent fatherhood, female choice, and sexual freedom among women) themselves are interrelated in ways too complex to be considered here.

Age. Wilson and Daly (1985) have described the particular significance of youth for violence among men. Early adulthood is the time at which reproductive issues are most salient, and, among humans, status acquired by this time may endure for many years as a function of reputation. Because Wilson and Daly are at pains to stress the polygynous nature of humans, they omit serious consideration of the fact that marriage partners are decided in this period of life and, extramarital opportunities notwithstanding, the quality of a long-term mate is of considerable significance in terms of fitness of offspring and social prestige associated with securing a highly valued partner.

If, among women, short- and long-term mate selection strategies are correlated and short-term liaisons function as a testing ground for evaluating their own ability to attract desirable partners and for vetting prospective long-term mates, then the teenage years are of particular significance for girls. Girls reach puberty earlier than boys (Savin-Williams and Weisfeld 1989) and menarche occurs relatively late in the sequence of pubertal changes—approximately 18 months after their growth spurt has reached its peak. Menstrual periods occur without ovulation for about 12 to 18 months (Boxer, Tobin-Richards, and Peterson 1983). Thus, from the time that a girl begins to show signs of sexual development, she has as long as 3 years during which time she is unlikely to conceive. This provides a period of safe sexual experimentation in preparation for the establishment of a more permanent long-term commitment. Her reproductive value (and that of her age cohort) is at its peak, and she has a competitive advantage over younger and older women. This is likely to be the time at which similarly aged girls will compete with one another for access to the most desirable males. In primates, as I have noted, female aggression and dominance are closely tied to the early reproductive years. Recall also that self-report studies and criminal statistics suggest that girls' involvement in aggressive acts peaks about two years earlier than that of boys. Could it be that this reflects their earlier development and the consequently earlier combative struggle for the fittest mates?

Choice. Symons (1979) notes that arranged marriages negate effective female choice and thereby female competition. (Presumably they have a similar effect on men.) In societies where such practices continue and where parental choice of partner is uninfluenced by the daughter's preferences, we should expect to see little female intrasexual contest. Epigamic strategies of enhancing her physical appearance may be present and encouraged by parents to the extent that they increase her desirability and price as a wife and so can be used by her parents to attract a higher-status male. The remainder of the discussion is confined to those societies where women exercise choice in mating.

Sex Ratio. Intensity of competition will vary as a function of sex ratio (Daly and Wilson 1990). In societies where the number of women exceeds that of men, the competition among women for long-term mates presumably will be more intense. Though women currently exceed men in Western populations, such broad demographic considerations may not impinge upon individual choice and action. For a given woman living in a particular ecological niche, such statistics are of little interest. The thesis of assortative mating and empirical data affirms that a woman is likely to find a mate within the geographical area in which she resides who approximately matches her in social class, ethnicity, education, and IQ (Hill, Rubin, and Peplau 1976; Tharp 1963). It is the availability of possible mates within this pool that forms the effective sex ratio for her age cohort in which she must compete. For example, the high rate of youthful male mortality in the black community suggests that female-female competition for mates here should be more intense, as it should be in societies after a war.

Proportion of Resource-Rich Mates. In societies with an effectively equal sex ratio, there may still be variations in the proportion of desirable males. Though a relatively high proportion of middle-class and upper-class males are likely to be economically successful and therefore good providers for future offspring, the same is not likely to be true in poverty-level neighborhoods (see Draper and Harpending 1988). In recent years, rising levels of unemployment and the (arguable) development of an economic underclass has increased the pool of resource-poor males who not only cannot contribute to childrearing but may actually be a drain upon economic resources destined for the woman's children. Wilson (1987) has argued that within the black community affirmative action and increased access to higher education have benefited the best and the brightest while consigning the majority to underclass status. Here, high rates of unemployment, homicide, incarceration, mental illness, and substance abuse mean that a smaller proportion of available males will be good mate potential, with the result that competition should be more intense.

Men Who Commit. Men seek to increase the number of their offspring by pursuing a greater number of premarital and extramarital partners. This is reflected in men's greater sexual desire (Symons and Ellis 1989), their tendency to fall in love more readily (Dion and Dion 1985; Peplau and Gordon 1985), and their preference for a "fast-track" approach to intimacy (Fisher 1992). Symons (1979) suggests that women's sexual "liberation" may also have the effect of increasing female competition for long-term mates because the easy availability of female sexual partners may dissuade men from making a long-term commitment to one woman. Realization of male preference for such short-term liaisons may be assisted by women's willingness to engage in them. Draper and Harpending (1988) note that in societies where male parental investment is low, it goes hand in hand with a female strategy of intense maternal nurturance followed by loss of interest in the child, who is then fostered out to relatives upon the arrival of the next boyfriend. Thus, a male preference for low paternal investment may lead to female accommodation, which allows this pattern of behaviour to repeat itself. Dunbar and Waynforth (1994), however, suggest that women are increasingly seeking the capacity for responsible fatherhood in their partners and that resource provision now takes second place to reliability and nurturance.

Male ability to offer protection to their mates has been considered as a factor in female mate selection and may be reflected in women's preference for athletic males, discussed earlier. Criminal victimization is highest in those demographic groups and urban locations where the crime rate is highest (Fagan, Piper, and Cheng 1987). If underclass women are at higher risk of victimization than more-affluent women, protection may well be an issue in mate selection. However, women are more likely to be killed by a husband or lover than by a stranger (Kruttschnitt 1994). Wife abuse is commonly prompted by concerns with infidelity and, among women who accommodate males by practicing serial monogamy, such doubts on the part of her partner may be more prevalent. Though wife abuse occurs throughout the social strata, there is a significant negative correlation with social class (Straus, Gelles, and Steinmetz 1981), and Draper and Harpending (1988) note that in subcultures where male-female pairings are of short duration, there are higher rates of violence against women: As Hrdy (1981) has pointed out, a male may also pose a threat to the female's offspring rather than being a source of protection, and in humans, as well as primates, such aggression occurs more frequently where the child is not the father's own (Daly and Wilson 1988). For these reasons, whether females would compete to secure a male as a form of protection remains an open question.

Absent Fathers. To the extent that women can now depend upon other (though less generous) sources of support such as the state, they may be willing to assume motherhood without demanding the father's long-term investment. In "pure" cases where the mother has no interest in a continued relationship with the father, his genetic contribution (estimated by possession of phenotypically attractive characteristics) will take precedence over consideration of his resources (Weisfeld and Billings 1988). It is likely, however, that this would engender much competition among females because desirable males would be willing to impregnate women quite promiscuously in circumstances where no further contribution would be demanded or expected, and a purely sexual involvement would not represent a resource loss to other women.

Such "pure" cases of a man providing a woman with sperm are rare (possibly confined to sperm-bank donation) and sexual involvement often carries with it the potential for further involvement and for paternal commitment to the woman and their child. It is when paternity offers the woman the possibility of support that competition is most likely for those males who are best able to provide it. Even in cultures characterized by father-absence, resource provision may not be entirely absent: Draper and Harpending (1988) conclude that in such societies the male parental role is devalued and economic resources are extracted early in the relationship in full knowledge that the man's stay will be brief. Even in short-term dating relationships where parental investment is not an issue, women still evaluate men in terms of their available resources and their likely willingness to share them (Buss and Schmitt 1993). Thus even short-term relationships may carry the possibility of investment of male resources, and consequent female-female competition is likely to be greatest in severely economically deprived areas (see Taylor 1993).

Individual Differences. Gardner's (1993) analysis of youthful risk-taking proposes that aggression (and other risky behaviors) are rational if one assumes that youthful impulsiveness is the result of a greater positive time preference. This preference for immediate rather than delayed rewards is a function of (realistic) uncertainty about the future. Since males' fitness variance is greater than females', we should expect them to display more risky behavior. However, Hrdy (1986) notes that aggregate statistical data indicating lower female fitness variance may obscure important individual differences between women in fecundity. Any given teenage girl cannot be certain that she will secure a mate, and individual differences in subjective assessments of this likelihood may affect the risks she is willing to take. Girls who believe that they are less attractive to boys may be more willing to engage in risky tactics. It is unlikely that unusually attractive women would engage in intrasexual combat for men because (1) their probability assessment of successfully attracting a mate would be realistically higher and the attractions of risky strategies consequently lower, and (2) their larger number of suitors would offer ample choice within which to secure the best mate. However, attractive women may find themselves the target of other women's aggression if they attract a disproportionate fraction of available men's attention and resources. Girls who mature early may also be the target of jealousy among other girls. Unlike early maturing boys who are popular with their peers, girls who reach menarche ahead of their age-mates seem to be rejected by other girls, though they are popular with boys (Faust 1960). Explanations of this effect have included asynchronicity as a source of awkwardness among adolescents who strive for conformity (Jones and Mussen 1958), early curvaceousness being too threatening in our sexually repressive society (Tobin-Richards, Boxer, and Peterson 1983), and the association of early menarche with shortness and chubbiness, which are not valued as ideal body types (Tobin-Richards et al. 1983). I suggest that among girls early menarche and bodily maturity confer considerable advantage in terms of mate selection. Such girls have the long-term advantage of a greater "fertile life expectancy" as well as the immediate advantages of attracting disproportionate male interest and resources and of having a wider selection of available males from which to choose than those entering the mate selection arena later. Early maturing girls may then be the target of attack by their later-maturing peers. Finally, because intrasexual strategies are only an adaptive choice if the negative consequences are small, we would expect that women (as well as men) who are particularly skilled in fighting would be most likely to engage in such tactics.

To fully evaluate all the above proposals, we would require a considerable body of data that to date has not been collected. The dearth of both theory and research in this area has been discussed by Hrdy (1986) in a review of the androcentric bias of traditional ethological studies. She notes, "Studies in the social sciences say almost nothing about competition among women; certainly no firm data have been collected," (Hrdy 1981), and Buss (1988) concurs: "Female-female competition appears to be an unnecessarily neglected area of research in social psychology and evolutionary biology." Nevertheless, we can make a preliminary examination of the thesis that the age-violence curve for women reflects intrasexual combat over reproductive success by examining available research on girls' adolescent fights with special reference to the sex of the combatants and the reasons for the fight. In the next section I will review the rather scant data that is available.

ADOLESCENT GIRLS' FIGHTING

Campbell (1986) used questionnaires to obtain data on the frequency and form of involvement in fighting from British schoolgirls, from inmates of a juvenile prison for young offenders, and from adult prisoners. The institutionalized samples were considerably more aggressive, representing as they did a selected criminal population; their data will not be discussed here. The schoolgirls ($N = 251$) were 16 years old and were drawn from comprehensive schools in working-class areas of London, Glasgow, Liverpool, and Oxfordshire. All of the girls had witnessed a fight, 89% had been involved in one (25% had been involved in more than six fights) and 43% had fought within the preceding year. The majority of fights were against another girl (73%) and predominantly occurred in the street (47%) or at school (29%). The fight itself rarely involved weapons (10%) and was most often restricted to punching (80%), kicking (79%), and slapping (57%). While 25% reported no injuries from the fight, 41% reported bruises, 22% scratches, and 11% cuts. Seventy-eight percent had seen their opponent since the fight, suggesting that they were either friends or acquaintances.

Of those responding to the question asking for a brief description of the reason for the fight, 46% were coded as attacks on personal integrity. This category included accusations of promiscuity, false accusations, and gossiping behind her back. The majority of responses fell in the first category. The second-most-frequent reason for fighting (endorsed by 13%) was loyalty, which included a personal integrity attack directed at a third person, such as a girl's friend, sister, or mother. The third-most-frequently endorsed response was jealousy over romantic partners (12%). (It is interesting to note that this figure rose with age. Among the Borstal sample whose ages ranged from 16 to 20, jealousy accounted for 25% of fights, and among adult inmates, the figure was 42%.) The emphasis upon sexual reputation was clear from responses to a question asking about the last remark that was made before the fight began; the two most-frequent responses were accusations of promiscuity ("slut," "slag"), endorsed by 31%, and dispute-related remarks ("Takes one to know one"), endorsed by a similar percentage.

A second study involved analysis of fights ($N = 64$) reported by female gang members in New York City (Campbell 1984). These girls had left school, and the majority were cohabiting with men. Because of this, domestic assaults (usually over issues of male infidelity) were the most-frequently reported form of fighting (36%) and half of all the reported fights were against males. The second-largest category (24%) included responses to perceived slights against an individual's reputation, including cuckoldry, promiscuity, cowardice, or stupidity; these fights were almost exclusively against other girls.

These data suggest that female adolescent aggression is more common than might be supposed from examination of official statistics—among the British schoolgirls, only 10% occasioned police involvement. They also suggest that issues connected with sexual relations figure prominently in the reasons for fighting. This is reflected in ethnographic and interview material in which girls are asked about the reasons for female fighting. Marsh and Paton (1986) conducted extensive interviews with British girls, concluding that "highest on their list, however was 'rumour spreading' or sexual insult." It was agreed that it was wholly justifiable to use physical violence in the defence of one's sexual reputation; "If someone slags you off—calls you a tart or something you've got to be able to do something about it." Their transcripts (Marsh and Paton 1984) clearly substantiate this conclusion:

> If a girl is going out with a boy and he's two-timing her, they tend to take it out on the other girl. Well, it takes two doesn't it?
> (I) Are most fights generally over boyfriends?
> Mainly.
> The thing you said earlier about girls being accused of being sluts, they fight for their reputation. [Marsh and Paton 1984, 1:10]

> (I) What do you reckon is the reason girls fight?
> Jealousy.
> Yeah.
> (I) What over?
> Boys usually.
> Like a lot of girls say they fight to protect their reputation.
> Yeah. [Marsh and Paton 1984, 1:65]

> (I) Why do girls fight?
> Over boys—yeah, there ain't really any other main reason is there? [Marsh and Paton 1984, 1:74]

A similar theme was evident in Campbell's open-ended interviews with schoolgirls (Contemporary Violence Research Centre 1979):

> (I) What do girls fight about?
> Boys.
> Ripping up one another's clothes and calling each other names.
> Jealousy.

(I) So do girls and boys fight about the same things or not?
Boils down to the same thing really 'cos girls fight over boys, boys fight over girls. Fight for their pride, things like that and boys fight about the same things.

Sexuality as a sensitive and explosive issue for teenage girls can be more finely differentiated. Evolutionary theory alerts us to three principal areas of challenge: sexual reputation, competition over access to a desirable partner, and jealousy about proprietary ownership of an established partner and his resources. While at a theoretical level this distinction is valuable, ethnographic work indicates that they are far from distinct in the real world. An accusation of promiscuity rarely occurs out of the blue and in isolation from other causes. Rather, it can be seen as the immediate trigger that propels the accused into fighting as a means of reclaiming a threatened social identity (Athens 1980; Felson 1978; Luckenbill 1977). Such an accusation often flows from the other two issues, which themselves are not always clearly separated. A girl who is attracted to a boy and flirting with him may in her mind have already established an implicit ownership of him, and any other female's interest in him will be understood and expressed in the language of jealousy rather than competition for access. Nevertheless, I shall attempt to understand these different forms of competition in turn.

The significance of a *sexual reputation* (for promiscuity) has been articulated in terms of evolutionary theory by Buss (1988). A woman's chance of securing a desirable long-term mate depends in large part upon his evaluation of her likely fidelity, which in turn is related to his future parental investment and the problem of (uncertainty of) paternity. Though willingness to engage in sexual relations without elaborate courtship is considered desirable in a short-term mate, it is undesirable in a long-term partner (Buss and Schmitt 1993). Male preference for sexually discriminative women is a theme that has been echoed in sociological writing, though here the emphasis is upon the resulting "double standard" of morality enforced by men and the inhibiting impact upon women's sexual psychology. Wilson (1978), in a study of working-class teenage girls, noted the repressive triangle of love, sex, and marriage: Girls take love to be a prerequisite for sex, and this, in turn, is a precursor to marriage: Sex without at least lip service to love places the girl in danger of developing a reputation. Problematic from a feminist perspective was the fact that the girls themselves were forceful in maintaining this code: "The girls regulated their contact with other girls who were known as 'lays' in order to preserve their own reputations. In fact they openly ridiculed the girls, referring to them as 'whores'" (Wilson 1978). One teenage girl (Campbell 1982) remarked that "a girl that's been called a slag is the same as a boy that's been called a chicken," and indeed from the viewpoint of future reproductive success their impact is similar. A male can demonstrate that he is not a chicken by fighting anyone who so impugns him. A girl, however, is unable to demonstrate in any convincing and public way that the accusation is false. Her best hope is to forcefully repel anyone who so accuses her and thus minimize the chance of anyone else repeating such a reputational attack, as in the following example:

She started spreading rumours about me saying that I used to sneak out in the middle of the night in my night-dress and meet ten boys or something, really stupid. . . . Well we were arguing with each other about the rumour mainly and she was saying she didn't say it . . . and then she starting calling me names like that and then she started to walk off across the road and she said "I'll get you some time, you fucking bitch." And that made me mad because if she was going to get me she was going to get me there and then, I mean there was no point in getting me later and so I kicked her in the back and she fell flat on her face and I said "If you are going to get me, get me now" and we started fighting. [Marsh and Paton 1984; 1:8]

I was walking round to your house and you know one of the girls that we used to go to school with said "Oh, my God. You look a right slut. Look at all that makeup you've got on." Now I never batted an eyelid. I just told her to shut her mouth—there was three of them. I said "Oh, shut your mouth." Yet that was on my mind all night and we got up to Scamps (nightclub), didn't we? And she was sat there and, I just went over to her and hit her round the face. "Now say it," I said, and she poked me in the eye. [Marsh and Paton 1984, 1:33]

Competition for desirable partners can also engender female aggression. Schuster (1983; 1985), using data from China and Zambia, concludes that adult female aggression is principally driven by competition over scarce resources and often this includes men. The degree of female economic and social dependence on men is related to the intensity with which women are prepared to fight to secure high-status males. This same theme, less evident in more-affluent Western societies, is seen in ethnographies of the American "underclass" where the high levels of homicide reduce the pool of male candidates, where males are in plentiful supply as sexual partners but conspicuously absent as long-term parents, and where poverty, drug addiction, and prison sentences make many of them more of a liability than an asset. A study of young women involved in drugs and gangs in Detroit clearly indicates that it is male resources that are the commodity in shortest supply. The women clearly differentiate drug users from high-level drug dealers, the former being rejected as the "living dead" and the latter being in a position to furnish abundant resources to their partners. As Taylor (1993) vividly describes it, "They can see the power of the gang, the celebrity status. This is real, it can happen to people just like them. These women can remember seeing 'that girl' at school, in the shopping malls, driving a new Mercedes, BMW, Corvette, sporting Gucci, Louis Vuitton, Fendi and smelling of expensive perfume, going to Auburn Palace to see the Pistons, meeting John Salley at parties." The desirability of access to such material resources meant that even among college girls drug dealers were considered desirable partners worth fighting for.

It's hard to get a good man and girls grab any fella that treat you special. . . . It's just tight out here, the campus is fucked up 'cause we ain't got nothing but girls, girls, girls, girls and the guys got their pick. We just start fighting each other over the same guys. Dope guys is straight if they think you ain't dissing them. They got coin and they will spend on you, and that's better than getting messed up over nothing. At least dope guys will buy you dinner at some place besides Mickey Dees. . . . Word, my girlfriend is at another university and her man is this big time roller. My boy got big paper and will spend it on her with a quickness. I tell her take all his paper, all of it, 'cause it's just a matter of time and he's gonna do some rotten dog shit to her, take all his money while you can. Got to get it when you can. You never know when it's gonna stop and you better get much as you can while you can. [Taylor 1993]

Male preference for novelty in sexual relations is not lost on young women. Girls involved in mixed sex groups are acutely sensitive to incursions by other females who by virtue of their novelty have an inbuilt advantage over the home group of women. Fights can occur when new females seek to enter the group or to establish relations with males whom the home team of girls regard as their pool of resources. As a British girl described it:

> If you get some girls what come in the Oranges [pub], they have been in there once and they come in. They really start slagging themselves around. They ain't been in there for about two years kind of thing and they just start hanging around all the boys showing off.
>   I cannot stand that.
>   And that attracts the blokes more than anything. [Marsh and Paton 1984, 1:51]

> Well most of the fights are in the Oranges and Lemons [pub] between the girls. Get a bird in the bog and beat her up. You've done it. Rosie has done it. We are really possessive. If there is a bloke, we like think "Oh he's eyeing her up" so I follow her into the toilet. [Marsh and Paton 1984, 1:156]

> There was a fair and there was all these girls up there and there is this girl called Della she is supposed to be a right old scrubber and she went up to Jackie and she said "You are nicking our boys" and she kept walking up to her, in front of her and that . . . and then she pushed her so Jackie had a fight with her. [Marsh and Paton 1984. 2:231]

A virtually identical scenario was described by a female member of a New York City mixed-sex gang (Campbell 1991):

> So she was new on the block. She just came to the block, right, and you know how the guys are. I used to be going out with Chico? And the guys they see a new girl? This guy—our guys when they see a new girl, they be checking her out you know. We don't like that. So she came to the block but she didn't come to make friends with us, she just came to make friends with the guys, you know? . . . So then one day she was in the corner and Big L was in the corner with her and she was over there you know real flashy and everything. . . . And I see her laughing and I tell Booby "I bet you I'll go over there and slap her in the face" I tell Booby and she tell me, "Go ahead, Weeza."

Within groups of girls, physical attractiveness confers a marked advantage on some individuals. Male preference for good looks in a partner (Buss and Schmitt 1993) may release them from the need to fight for boys, but it simultaneously can make them the target for other females who resent their "head start" in the competition for mates.

> They were jealous of Beverley because she could get quite a few boyfriends and half of them [the other girls] were too fat or too skinny. They were following us and we got up and started walking off and they was calling out names and I turned around and said "Just because you are too fucking fat Smith." They come from the pub and I was walking ahead of Bev and next minute I heard them slap Bev round the face. There was a whole gang of them onto her. [Marsh and Paton 1984, 1:36]

As I have noted already, the distinction between competition and jealousy is, in practice, a fine one. *Jealousy* in the form of proprietary ownership of a boy carries with it the right to fight off potential interlopers. But the time horizon of "ownership" spills over in both directions. For some girls mere association with a desirable male is taken to confer ownership, while at the other end of the time spectrum a girl may continue to "own" a boy even when the relationship is over. With regard to the former, two British boys described their typical experience of a female fight:

> Supposing that two girls fancy him, then there is a fight between the two girls to get in first.
>
> Yeah.
>
> If he went to a disco and she went with him and the next disco this other girl went with him, the two girls would fight about it. That's what happens.
>
> "He's mine." "No he isn't, you bitch." [Marsh and Paton 1984, 1:104]

The dispute arises when an association becomes a steady relationship that the girl has a right to protect. From the female partner's point of view, this point may be reached long before the boy (or any other girls) are aware that this line has been crossed. At the other end of the time spectrum, some girls feel that it is justifiable to repel female rivals even when they themselves have abandoned any exclusive claim to the boy:

> Me and my boyfriend finished for a while. I went to London. Then I came back and if I see him with any bird I just went mad and then seeing him with her as well. . . . I walked up to her and I says, "You fucking leave him alone or else you've had it." I really went mad at her. (Marsh and Paton 1984, 1:134)

> This girl [Susie] has been going out with this boy for a year and she packed him up and her friend [Linda] goes out with him so Susie keeps calling the girl a slut all the time but the girl don't say nothing. She just takes it. She just sort of sits there and don't say nothing.
>
> Well it's only because Linda can't have her [beat her] though isn't it?
>
> Because she knows that she would probably get beaten up. [Marsh and Paton 1984, 2:215]

A more straightforward scenario involves a steady relationship in which another female knowingly attempts to use her sexuality as a way of luring the boy away.

> This mate of mine, her boyfriend was sat talking to this other girl. And my mate she was really drunk and she's the type of person—she's really possessive over her boyfriend. I mean I can put up with it to a certain extent but anybody will lash out. And she followed this girl into the toilets and I was sat in there and she threatened her with a bottle and this girl started pulling her hair and Karen was slapping her and it just amazed me. The bouncer come in and tried to split it up. [Marsh and Paton 1984, 1:28]

> (I) What sorts of things do you argue with your friends about?
>
> Boyfriends and that. Other things.
>
> Say she was leading him on, I would tell her to shut her mouth or something like that. She would either lay off or if she carries on she gets the worst doesn't she?

It just goes into an argument and then it could end up in a fight. . . . Well I was going out with this boy called Steven. This was on holiday, because I met him on holiday, and this girl I was going about with—her name was Mary—she was flirting round with him and that and I didn't like it and one night I saw her just about to kiss him so I went up and hit her. . . I called her the biggest slag walking. [Marsh and Paton 1984, 4:2–3]

Burbank's (1987) cross-cultural review of adult female aggression finds that 52% of aggression between women is precipitated by a husband's adultery (with his adultery accounting for 23% of attacks on the husband). In matters of sexual jealousy, it is unclear why the aggression is directed at the same-sex rival rather than at the partner. It seems probable that the length and social legitimacy of the relationship may play a role. In a long-term partnership, the partner has undertaken an explicit or implicit commitment to fidelity, and so aggression may be directed at the partner for his failure to honor this obligation and the ensuing betrayal that it carries with it. However, where the partnership has been of short duration, occasional rather than continuous or carries with it no explicit understanding of sexual exclusivity, a direct attack on the partner may be inappropriate in two senses. First, the partner can justifiably argue that he never agreed to an exclusive relationship and, secondly, aggression toward the partner may be more likely to drive him away rather than to save the relationship. (Among males, issues of sexual unfaithfulness may be so critical as to eliminate this second consideration—knowledge of a woman's infidelity may be so devastating to the relationship that the aim of the aggression is to injure or even kill her rather than to secure her future faithfulness.) Among women, however, evidence suggests that jealousy is principally experienced as a threat to her partner's continued provision of emotional and material resources (Buss and Schmitt 1993). If this is indeed the case, her aim may be to secure the relationship without risking a direct attack on him. This is especially common in situations where her legitimate hold over him is tenuous. This is likely to be the case among young women who are dating rather than married and particularly where the relationship is just beginning (and may not yet be acknowledged by the young man or their social group) or has even ended. Among female Puerto Rican young gang members, a rhetorical justification for attacking the female rival rather than the male partner was often employed: Men are considered to be driven by an insatiable need for sex that they cannot resist. Because this is beyond their control, it is the rival female who is to blame for their infidelity (Campbell 1991).

CONCLUSION

Criminologists' traditional emphasis upon crime as a male phenomenon has often resulted in inattention to the female experience. Yet despite differences in absolute rates of commission, girls show a similar age-assault curve to boys. While rates of homicide climb with age among women, assault and aggravated assault are most frequent in the teenage years. An evolutionary account that stresses both the importance of mate selection for young women, together with the restraining influence of women's smaller fitness variance and their certainty of maternity, offers a potential explanation. Elaboration of the argument allows us to make specific predictions about the effects of age, freedom of choice, sex ratio, social class, father absence, male commitment, and individual differences such as attractiveness, sexual maturity, and physical prowess. Available data suggest that female assaults are more numerous than official statistics would suggest, that same-sex fights are more common than between-sex fights in the teenage years, and that issues of sexual reputation, competition, and ownership of men figure large in girls' own accounts of their fighting. Further data are required to investigate the specific hypotheses suggested by an evolutionary account.

When such data are available, it will be necessary to consider the evolutionary circumstances that may have given rise to the potential for intrafemale as well as intramale aggression at adolescence. A critical question is whether the two sexes have each evolved distinctive modes of adaptation or, more likely, whether there has been a single adaptation with sex-specific threshold settings (see Cloninger et al. 1978). Behavioral genetic research has investigated the heritability of a number of personality traits. If the genetic determinants of a given trait differ between the sexes, then male-female siblings should show a lower level of correlation for that trait than do same-sex siblings. The fact that they do not suggests that the same influences are at work in both sexes (Eaves, Eysenck, and Martin 1989). Rowe (1994) concludes that "the same set of genes receive a somewhat different level of expression in men and women." He suggests that phenotypic differences between the sexes may result from sex-linked hormonal modulation of gene expression. But external rather than internal factors may also play a role. Male and female intrasexual aggression may be a response to similar social cues (e.g., perceived local sex ratio, proprietary emotions about mates) but with females having a higher threshold for response and thus requiring a more extreme environmental or emotional trigger. Cultural approval (at a societal and peer-group level) of males' aggression and disapproval of females' may play an important role in this parameter setting (Campbell 1993). No direct examination has yet been made of same-sex/cross-sex siblings in concordance for aggression. Rowe (1994) notes that where sex differences are very large, such as in criminality, some genes may also be sex-linked. Clearly, further data are required to elaborate the evolutionary pressures toward intrasexual aggression and the extent to which these have resulted in two sex-linked adaptations or in a single facultative adaptation with threshold differences in readiness to employ aggressive tactics.

REFERENCES

Athens, L. *Violent Criminal Acts and Actors,* London: Routledge and Kegan Paul, 1980.

Barkow, J. Darwin. *Sex and Status: Biological Approaches to Mind and Culture,* Toronto: University of Toronto Press, 1989.

Bateman, A. Intra-sexual selection in drosophila. *Heredity* 2:349–368, 1948.

Bellis, M., and Baker, R. Do females promote sperm competition? Data from humans. *Animal Behaviour* 40:997–999, 1990.

Benshoof, L., and Thornhill, R. The evolution of monogamy and concealed ovulation in humans. *Journal of Biological Structures* 2:95–106, 1979.

Bjorkvist, K., Lagerspetz, K., and Kaukiainen, A. Do girls manipulate and boys fight? Developmental trends regarding direct and indirect aggression. *Aggressive Behavior* 18:117–127, 1992.

Boxer, A., Tobin-Richards, M., and Peterson, A. Puberty: Physical change and its significance in early adolescence. *Theory into Practice* 22:85–90, 1983.

Browne, A. *When Battered Women Kill,* New York: Free Press, 1987.

Bunch, B., Foley, L., and Urbina, S. The psychology of violent female offenders: A sex-role perspective. *The Prison Journal* 63:66–79, 1983.

Burbank, V. Female aggression in cross-cultural perspective. *Behavioural Science Research* 21:70–100, 1987.

Buss, D. Sex differences in human mate selection criteria: An evolutionary perspective. In *Sociobiology* and Psychology: Ideas. Issues and Applications, C. Crawford. M. Smith, and D. Krebs (Eds.). Hillsdale, NJ: Erlbaum, 1987.

Buss, D. The evolution of human intrasexual competition. *Journal of Personality and Social Psychology* 54:616–628, 1988.

Buss, D., and Schmitt, D. Sexual strategies theory: An evolutionary perspective on human mating. *Psychological Review* 100:204–232, 1993.

Campbell, A. Female aggression. In *Aggression and Violence,* P. Marsh and A. Campbell (Eds.). Oxford: Blackwell, 1982.

Campbell, A. Girls-talk: The social representation of aggression by female gang members. *Criminal Justice and Behavior* 11:217–222, 1984.

Campbell, A. Self-report of fighting by females. *British Journal of Criminology* 26:28–46, 1986.

Campbell, A. *The Girls in the Gang,* 2nd ed. Oxford: Basil Blackwell, 1991.

Campbell, A. *Men Women and Aggression,* New York: Basic Books, 1993.

Cloninger, C., Christiansen, K., Reich, T., and Gottesman, I. Implications of sex differences in the prevalences of antisocial personality, alcoholism, and criminality for familiar transmission. *Archives of General Psychiatry* 35:941–951. 1978.

Contemporary Violence Research Centre. *Final Report to Whitbread Ltd,* Oxford University: Contemporary Violence Research Centre, 1979.

Daley, M., and Wilson, M. *Sex; Evolution and Behavior,* Belmont. CA: Wadsworth, 1983.

Daly, M., and Wilson, M. *Homicide,* New York: Aldine de Gruyter, 1988.

Daly, M., and Wilson, M. Killing the competition: Female/female and male/male homicide. *Human Nature* 1:81–107, 1990.

Daly, M., and Wilson, M. Evolutionary psychology of male violence. In *Male Violence,* J. Archer (Ed.). London: Routledge, 1994.

Dawkins, R., *The Selfish Gene,* 2nd ed. Oxford: Oxford University Press, 1989.

Dion, K.K. The incentive value of physical attractiveness for young children. *Personality and Social Psychology Bulletin* 3:67–70, 1977

Dion, K.K., and Dion, K.L. Personality, gender and the phenomenology of romantic love. In *Review of Personality and Social Psychology,* Vol. 6. P. Shaver (Ed.). Beverly Hills, CA: Sage, 1985.

Draper, P., and Harpending, H. A sociobiological perspective on the development of human reproductive strategies. In *Sociobiological Perspectives on Human Development,* K. McDonald (Ed.). New York: Springer Verlag, 1988.

Dunbar, R., and Waynforth, D. *Conditional Mate Choice Strategies in Humans.* Paper presented to the British Psychological Society Annual Conference, Brighton, England, 1994.

Eaves, L. Eysenck, H., and Martin, N. *Genes, Culture and Personality: An Empirical Approach,* London: Academic Press, 1989.

Elliott, D., Huizinga, D., and Morse, B. Self-reported violent offending: A descriptive analysis of juvenile violent offenders and their offending careers. *Journal of Interpersonal Violence* 1:472–514, 1983.

Eron, L., Huesmann, R., Brice, P., Fisher, P., and Mermelstein. R. Age trends in the development of aggression, sex typing and related television habits. *Developmental Psychology* 19:71–77, 1983.

Fagan, J., Piper, E., and Cheng, Y. Contributions of victimization to delinquency in inner cities. *The Journal of Criminal Law and Criminology* 78:586–613, 1987.

Faust, M. Developmental maturity as a determinant of prestige in adolescent girls. *Child Development* 31:173–184, 1960.

Feingold, A. Gender defferences in effects of physical attractiveness on romantic attraction: A comparison across five research paradigms. *Journal of Personality and Social Psychology* 59:981–993, 1990.

Felson, R. Aggression as impression management. *Social Psychology* 41:205–213, 1978.

Felson, R., and Bohrnstedt, G. Are the good beautiful or the beautiful good? The relationship between children's perceptions of ability and perceptions of physical attractiveness. *Social Psychology Quarterly* 42:386–392, 1979.

Fisher, H. *Anatomy of Love,* New York: Simon and Schuster, 1992.

Gardner, W. A life-span rational-choice theory of risk taking. In *Adolescent Risk Taking,* N. Bell and R Bell (Eds.). London: Sage, 1993.

Gottfredson, M., and Hirschi, T. *A General Theory of Crime,* Stanford, CA: Stanford University Press, 1990.

Hewitt, J., and Rivers, G. *The Victim-Offender Relationship in Convicted Homicide Cases 1960–1984.* Paper presented at annual meeting. Academy of Criminal Justice Sciences, 1986.

Hill, C., Rubin, Z., and Peplau, L. Breakups before marriage: The end of 103 affairs. *Journal of Social Issues* 32:147–168, 1976.

Hirschi, T., and Gottfredson, M. Age and the explanation of crime. *American Journal of Sociology* 89:552–584, 1983.

Howard, J., Blumstein, P., and Schwartz, P. Social or evolutionary theories? Some observations on preferences in human mate selection. *Journal of Personality and Social Psychology* 53:194–200, 1987.

Hrdy, S. *The Woman That Never Evolved,* Cambridge, MA: Harvard University Press, 1981.

Hrdy, S: Empathy, polyandry and the myth of the coy female. In *Feminist Approaches to Science,* R. Bleier (Ed.). New York: Pergamon Press, 1986.

Jones, M. and Mussen, P. Self-conceptions, motivations and interpersonal attitudes of early and late-maturing girls. *Child Development* 29:492–501, 1958.

Keating, C. Gender and physiognomy of dominance and attractiveness. *Social Psychology Quarterly* 48: 61–70, 1985.

Kruttschnitt, C. Gender and interpersonal violence. In *Understanding and Preventing Violence,* Vol. 3. A. Reiss and J. Roth (Eds.). Washington, DC: National Academy Press, 1994.

Luckenbill, D. Criminal homicide as a situated transaction. *Social Problems* 25: 76–186, 1977.

Mann, C. Getting even? Women who kill in domestic encounters. *Justice Quarterly* 5:33–51, 1988.

Marsh, P., and Paton, R. Unpublished interview transcripts, Volumes 1–5. Research supported by Social Science Research Council (HR 8379) and the Economic and Social Research Council (GOO230113). Oxford: Oxford Brookes University, 1984.

Marsh, P., and Paton, R. Gender, social class and conceptual schemas of aggression. In *Violent Transactions: The Limits of Personality,* A. Campbell and J. Gibbs (Eds.). Oxford: Basil Blackwell, 1986.

Masters, W., and Johnson, V. *Human Sexual Inadequacy,* Boston: Little Brown, 1970.

Maynard-Smith, J. The theory of games and the evolution of animal conflict. *Journal of Theoretical Biology* 47:209–221, 1974.

Mock, D., and Fujioka, M. Monogamy and long-term pair bonding in vertebrates. *Trends in Ecology and Evolution* 5:39–43, 1990.

O'Brien, R. Exploring the intersexual nature of violent crimes. *Criminology* 26:151–170, 1988.

Peplau, L., and Gordon. S. Women and men in love: Gender differences in close heterosexual relationships. In *Women, Gender and Social Psychology,* V. O'Leary, R. Unger, and B. Wallston (Eds.). Hillsdale, NJ: Erlbaum, 1985.

Piper, E. *Patterns of Violent Juvenile Recidivism.* Unpublished doctoral dissertation. University of Pennsylvania, 1983.

Reis, H., Nezlek, J., and Wheeler, L. Physical attractiveness in social interaction. *Journal of Personality and Social Psychology* 38:604–617, 1980.

Rowe, D. *The Limits of Family Influence: Genes, Experience and Behavior,* New York: Guildford Press, 1994.

Russell, R., and Wells, P. Estimating paternity confidence. *Ethology and Sociobiology* 8:215–220, 1987.

Savin-Williams, R., and Weisfeld, G. An ethological perspective on adolescence. In *Biology of Adolescent Behaviour and Development,* G. Adams, R. Montemayor, and T. Gullotta (Eds.). Newbury Park: Sage, 1989.

Schuster, I. Women's aggression: An African case study. *Aggressive Behaviour* 9:319–331, 1983.

Schuster, I. Female aggression and resource scarcity: A cross-cultural perspective. In *The Aggressive Female,* M. Haug, D. Benton, P. Brain, B. Oliver, and J. Mos (Eds.). Netherlands: CIP-Gegevens Koninklijke Bibliotheek, 1985.

Small, M. The evolution of female sexuality and mate selection in humans. *Human Nature* 3:133–156, 1992.

Steffensmeier, D., and Alien, E. Sex disparities in arrests by residence, race and age: An assessment of the gender convergence/crime hypothesis. *Justice Quarterly* 5:53–80, 1988.

Straus, M., Gelles, R., and Steinmetz, S. *Behind Closed Doors: Violence in the American Family,* New York: Anchor, 1981.

Symons, D. *The Evolution of Human Sexuality,* Oxford: Oxford University Press, 1979.

Symons; D., and Ellis, B. Human male-female differences in sexual desire. In *The Sociobiology of Sexual and Reproductive Strategies,* A. Rasa, C. Vogel, and E. Voland (Eds.). London: Chapman and Hall, 1989.

Taylor, C. *Girls, Gangs, Women and Drugs,* East Lansing: Michigan State University Press, 1993.

Tharp, R. Psychological patterning in marriage. *Psychological Bulletin* 60:97–117, 1963.

Tobin-Richards, M., Boxer, A., and Peterson, A. The psychological significance of pubertal change: Sex differences in perception of self during early adolescence. In *Girls at Puberty: Biological and Psychosocial Perspectives,* J. Brooks-Gunn and A. Peterson (Eds.). New York: Plenum, 1983.

Trivers, R. Parental investment and sexual selection. In *Sexual Selection and the Descent of Man,* B. Campbell (Ed.). Chicago: Aldine-Atherton, 1972.

Weisfeld, G., and Billings, R. Observations on adolescence. In *Sociobiological Perspectives on Human Development,* K. McDonald (Ed.). New York: Springer Verlag, 1988.

Weisfeld, G., Bloch, S., and Ivers, J. A factor analytic study of peer-perceived dominance in adolescent boys. *Adolescence* 18:229–243, 1983.

Weisfeld. G., Muczenski, D., Weisfeld. C., and Omark, D. Stability of boys' social success among peers over an eleven year period. In *Interpersonal Relations: Family, Peers, Friends,* J. Meacham (Ed.). Basel: Karger, 1987.

Weisfeld, G., Russell, R., Weisfeld, C., and Wells, P. Correlates of satisfaction in British marriages. *Ethology and Sociobiology* 13:125–145, 1992.

Weisheit, R. Female homicide offenders: Trends over time in an institutionalized population. *Justice Quarterly* 1:471–489, 1984.

Wilbanks W. Murdered women and women who murder: A critique of the literature. In *Judge, Lawyer, Victim, Thief: Women, Gender Roles and Criminal Justice,* N. Rafter and E. Stanko (Eds.). Boston: Northeastern University Press, 1982, pp. 151–180.

Wilson, D. Sexual codes and conduct: A study of teenage girls. In *Women, Sexuality and Social Control,* C. Smart and B. Smart (Eds.). London: Routledge and Kegan Paul, 1978.

Wilson, M., and Daly, M. Competitiveness, risk taking, and violence: The young male syndrome. *Ethology and Sociobiology* 6:59–73, 1985.

Wilson, W. *The Truly Disadvantaged,* Chicago: University of Chicago Press, 1987.

Nepotism and the Evolution of Alarm Calls

Alarm calls of Belding's ground squirrels warn relatives, and thus are expressions of nepotism

PAUL W. SHERMAN

A larm calls, vocalizations that alert other animals to impending danger, give the appearance of altruism. Identifying the function of the alarm calls of any species has proved difficult, both because predation is rarely seen in the field (*1*) and because individual identity of and kinship among members of prey species are usually unknown. Moreover, members of many species give several different, predator-specific alarm calls.

During a 3-year field study, I investigated the function of the alarm call that Belding's ground squirrels (*Spermophilus beldingi,* Rodentia: Sciuridae) give when a terrestrial predator approaches. Because the ground squirrel population that I studied contains individually marked animals of known age, among which familial relationships through common female ancestors are also known, discriminating among several hypothesized advantages of giving alarm calls is for the first time possible. A disadvantage of calling is also demonstrated. My investigation indicates that assisting relatives, nepotism, is the most likely function of the ground squirrels' alarm call; this result implicates kin selection (*2*) in the evolution of a behavior that, because it may involve risks to the alarm caller's phenotype, appears to be altruistic.

FUNCTIONS OF ALARM CALLS

Individuals may benefit from giving alarm calls in any of several contexts, because alarm calls may result in one or more of the following six effects.

1. *Diversion of predators' attention to other prey.* This hypothesis would be implicated if, in the absence of cover, alarm calls or screams from captured individuals stimulate aggregation (*3*), group mobbing (*4, 5*), or pandemonium (*5–7*); or, if the prey are already hidden, alarm calls cause them to behave in a manner that would enhance their crypticity (*6, 7*). Observations suggesting that "ventriloquial" alarm calls occur that increase the jeopardy of others (*8*) or that callers mislead or manipulate conspecifics so as to increase their own safety (*6*) would also support this hypothesis for the species and call at issue.

2. *Discouragement of predator pursuit.* By calling, potential prey may reduce the likelihood and costs of attacks on themselves, if calls cause predators to terminate pursuits. For example, fleet and elusive prey might discourage predators by indicating

to the predators that they have been seen and that the advantage of surprise has thus been removed (9). Sudden or erratic changes in prey behavior as well as alarm calls may startle or momentarily confuse predators, and may indicate to them that an attack is unlikely to succeed (10). In addition, poisonous prey might signal their distasteful-ness by giving an alarm call (4). Under this hypothesis, callers gain by indicating to a predator that it has been detected or that the probability of a successful or profitable attack is low. This second hypothesis would thus be implicated if predators consis-tently turn away from or suddenly release callers, regardless of the presence, proxim-ity, or behavior of other suitable prey.

3. *Alerting relatives.* Callers may gain by having placed themselves in some jeopardy if kin are thereby consistently warned (2, 11, 12). Captured individuals might also give distress (alarm) calls in this context, thereby soliciting assistance from relatives (4) or else warning them to flee or to hide. Under this, the third hypothesis, year-round alarm calls must be associated with the continuous presence of relatives [compare Williams (12, p. 206)]. If alarm calls are given during only part of the year, they must coincide with proximity of kin. For a given species, this hypothesis would be strongly supported if individuals with relatives living within earshot call more fre-quently than do conspecifics without them.

4. *Helping the group.* Alarm calling might spread by a process of between-group selection, either if (i) prey populations are composed of small, genetically iso-lated demes (13) or if (ii) between periods of dispersal and panmixia, prey populations are sedentary and composed of isolated aggregations of individuals that are similar to each other in their propensity to call (14, 15). Then either (i) the persistence of groups must be proportional to the percentage of callers within them and groups containing more callers must recolonize areas left vacant by the extinction of groups containing fewer callers (13) or else (ii) temporary aggregations of sedentary individuals must produce dispersing young in proportion to the percentage of callers within each aggre-gation (14). In both cases (i) and (ii), unlike the case where the nepotism hypothesis (that is, the third hypothesis) is applicable, fully or partially isolated groups of con-specifics must be identifiable (13–16), and these groups must differ in the proportion of alarm callers versus noncallers. If identifiable groups exist and if between-group differences in percentage of callers are demonstrable, the familial relationships among group members must then be considered (16, 17) because between-group differences in the percentage of callers could be brought about by the association of either family members or of nondescendants. If the former, the differential reproduction of such groups is most appropriately analyzed in terms of kin selection [(16, 17); but see (18)]. If the latter, hypothesis 4 can be distinguished from hypothesis 3.

5. *Reduction of the likelihood of later attacks by the same predator.* If predators become better at hunting similar prey with experience or if they return to hunt near sites of previous successful kills [for examples, see (19)], alarm callers may benefit by warning conspecifics if by so doing they deny predators sustenance and a search image (20). Hypothesis 5 implies that the phenotypic risk of calling is at least lower than the danger of being surprised during a later hunt by the same predator. The hy-pothesis requires that predators are more often successful in populations without alarm callers than in populations containing them. Hypothesis 5 does not require a particular population structure or familial relationship among callers and those

warned. If predators return to sites of previous successful kills, hypothesis 5 predicts that the most sedentary individuals should call most frequently, because they will be in jeopardy from returning predators more often than less sedentary conspecifics.

6. *Warning of others likely to reciprocate.* If individual callers and listeners associate long and consistently enough for them to exchange risks associated with alerting each other and benefits accompanying being alerted, alarm calling may spread on the basis of reciprocity (*20*). As proposed by Trivers, this hypothesis assumes that callers and warned individuals are either distantly related or unrelated (*20*); however, reciprocity may also occur among related conspecifics [(*21*); see also (*15*)], complicating efforts to contrast hypotheses 6 and 3. Hypothesis 6 would be supported if the likelihood of calling increases directly with the probability of warning reciprocators or if this likelihood decreases with the probability of warning nonreciprocators [for a possible example of reciprocity among primates, see (*22*)].

Under hypotheses 1 and 2, alarm calling is favored because of benefits to the caller's phenotype. Under hypotheses 3 to 6, alarm calls are phenotypically but not genotypically altruistic (*21,* p. 336).

STUDY AREA AND STUDY ANIMAL

During the summers of 1974 through 1976, ten different field assistants (three in 1974, five in 1975, and five in 1976) and I studied the responses of Belding's ground squirrels (Figure 1) to terrestrial predators at Tioga Pass Meadow, in the Sierra Nevada mountains of California (*23*). Ground squirrels in the study population have been permanently marked yearly since 1969: between 1969 and 1973, M. L. Mortori and his students individually toe-clipped 731 of them; from 1974 to 1976 my assistants and I double-ear-tagged another 1135, including the 451 young from 101 complete litters. Therefore, exact ages (up to 8 years) of and familial relationships through

FIGURE 1   Belding's ground squirrel at Tioga Pass, Mono County, California.

common female ancestors among groups of ground squirrels are known. Most animals were marked with human hair dye for visual identification at a distance, and their burrows were marked with stakes and painted rocks.

During 3082 hours of observation, members of five species of terrestrial predators and marked ground squirrels of known age were seen simultaneously 102 times: long-tailed weasels (*Mustela frenata*) 67 times, badgers (*Taxidea taxus*) 11 times, dogs (*Canis familiaris*) unaccompanied by humans 11 times, coyotes (*Canis latrans*) 10 times, and pine martens (*Martes americana*) 3 times. On these occasions nine ground squirrels (six adults and three juveniles) were killed (that is, one was killed every 342 observation hours): two by pine martens, three by coyotes, and four by long-tailed weasels. I use these observations to discriminate among hypotheses 1 to 6 for this species' alarm call.

Belding's ground squirrels are diurnal rodents that inhabit alpine and subalpine meadows in the Far West (*24, 25*). At the study area, elevation 3040 meters, they are active from May through September, and they hibernate the rest of the year (*23*). Although conspecific ground squirrels interact daily, they do not group their burrows into circumscribed aggregations nor do they produce young synchronously as do colonial species such as black-tailed prairie dogs (*Cynomys ludovicianus*) (*26–28*).

Like many other terrestrial sciurids (*29, 30*), Belding's ground squirrels give a segmented alarm call in the 4- to 6-kilohertz range when a predatory mammal approaches them (Figure 2); by contrast they give a single-note, high-pitched whistle to aerial predators [(*31*); see also (*32*)]. Their alarm call to terrestrial predators is easily localized by humans, perhaps because of certain acoustical properties of the sound (*33*) (Figure 2) and because individuals usually call repeatedly [$\bar{X}$ ± standard error (S.E.) = 27.8 ± 3.8 calls per individual per predator appearance, with N = 13; $\bar{X}$ = 6.1 ± 1.3 minutes of calling per individual per predator appearance, N = 16], even after a predator has apparently disappeared ($\bar{X}$ = 3.7 ± 0.9 minutes of calling per individual, after the predator disappeared from an observer's view; N = 19). Vigorous vibrations of chest cavities of calling ground squirrels and their open mouths enhanced our ability to determine callers' identities, even when several animals were close together. Eighty-two times ground squirrels gave calls that sounded like alarm calls (that is, Figure 2) when no predator was seen. Because these calls might not have been predator-related, I report here only behavior taking place on the 102 occasions when predators and ground squirrels were simultaneously seen, regardless of whether or not alarm calls

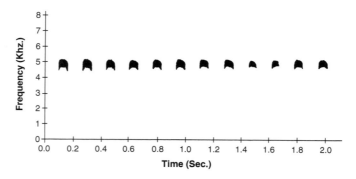

FIGURE 2 Sound spectrogram of the alarm call that Belding's ground squirrels give when predatory mammals appear. No frequency harmonics between 6 and 16 khz were found. Frequency is given in kilohertz and time in seconds.

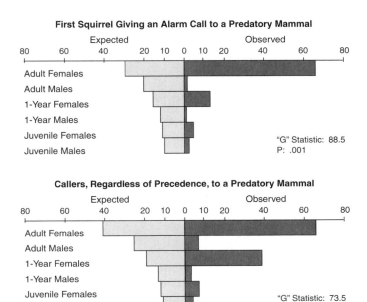

FIGURE 3 Expected and observed frequencies of alarm calling by various sex and age classes of Belding's ground squirrels. "Expected" values were computed by assuming that animals call randomly, in direct proportion to the number of times they are present when a predatory mammal appears. The overall significance of both comparisons is largely due to females calling more often than "expected" and males calling infrequently. Data are from 102 interactions between ground squirrels and predators (1974–76).

were heard. For Tables 2 and 3 and Figure 3, I combined data from appearances of all five species of predatory mammals after determining that neither the proportions of sex and age categories of ground squirrels present when a predator appeared (Figure 3) nor the percentage of animals that called differed among predator species (all $P \geq .1$, two-tailed G statistics).

POPULATION STRUCTURE AND MATING SYSTEM

At Tioga Pass Meadow, the average genetic relatedness among female ground squirrels inhabiting any small area is high as a result of common ancestry. As in several other terrestrial sciurids (*34, 35*), females successfully rearing young are sedentary between years, and daughters mature and breed near their birthplaces until they die or disappear from the study area. In contrast to their sisters (Table 1), males permanently emigrate from the area where they were born, usually before their first winter hibernation (*36*). Males do not return to their natal area to copulate, and brothers do not aggregate elsewhere. Seven males born in 1974 were sexually active for the first time in 1976 (that is, as 2-year-olds), and the mated 422.0 ± 89.8 m ($\bar{X} \pm$ S.E.; $N = 11$ copulations) from their natal burrows; the brothers' matings took place 341.3 ± 107.6 m from each other ($N = 6$ pairs of copulations by brothers). By contrast, 12 females born in

1974, each a sister of one of the 2-year-old males, mated 43.2 ± 11.7 m from their natal burrows [*N* = 19 copulations; some females mate more than once (*36*)]; the sisters' matings took place 39.2 ± 9.2 m from each other (*N* = 7 pairs of copulations by sisters).

Some male Belding's ground squirrels are apparently highly polygynous. In 1975, for example, the three most successful males in one area of Tioga Pass Meadow that was under nearly continuous observation (21 percent of the sexually active males present) accounted for 21 of 37 completed copulations (57 percent); the most successful male mated with eight different females and he accounted for 22 percent of all completed copulations. Similarly, in 1976, of ten males the top two (20 percent) accounted for 19 of 32 completed copulations (59 percent); the most successful male mated with nine different females and he accounted for 31 percent of all completed copulations (*36*). Unlike males in harem-polygynous sciurid species (*27, 37, 38*), male Belding's ground squirrels do not defend mating areas or territories after mating, identifiable physical resources valuable to females or to young, or sexually receptive females. Nor do males appear to behave parentally toward their mates' offspring.

TABLE 1   Within-family sexual asymmetries in emigration distances among Belding's ground squirrels at Tioga Pass Meadow, California. For females, the home burrow is either the one from which their offspring emerged or, if their young died or disappeared before emergence, the burrow to which they carried nesting material and in which they spent the nights at about the time the young were emerging. For males, the home burrow is the one to which they carried nesting material and in which they spent the nights at about the time the young were emerging. All distances were measured in the field.

Home Burrow Distance Category	Sample Size	Distance (m)	
		Mean ± S.E.	*Range*
2-to 8-year females, interyear	24	17.4 ± 3.2	0.0– 60.0
2-to 5-year males, interyear	10	175.0 ± 25.4*	56.0– 288.0
Females' mating site(s)—her burrow that year (13 different females)	19	36.4 ± 18.1	13.6– 148.9
Males' mating site(s)—his burrow that year (5 different males)	10	176.3 ± 37.1*	106.7– 380.0
1-year females' burrow—their natal burrow	27	38.4 ± 6.3	5.5– 140.8
1-year males' burrow—their natal burrow	13	223.7 ± 39.9*	58.3– 510.0
2-year females' burrow—their natal burrow	9	47.1 ± 13.7	7.6– 132.4
2-year males' burrow—their natal burrow	7	449.7 ± 161.3*	113.0–1385.0
1-year sisters' burrows	17	38.5 ± 7.2	2.9– 115.0
1-year brothers' burrows	6	273.2 ± 49.0*	108.9– 437.8
2-year sisters' burrows	7	71.8 ± 21.2	14.0– 171.5
2-year brothers' burrows	4	325.0 ± 94.8†	87.9– 393.0
Mother—1-year daughter	21	49.7 ± 5.9	2.7– 158.0
Mother—1-year son	10	239.4 ± 37.8*	61.5– 537.6

*Differences significant, $P < .005$.

†Difference significant, $P < .01$, Mann-Whitney U test.

During their 4- to 6-hour period of sexual receptivity, females mate with a mean of 2.1 ± 0.2 different males (± S.E., $N = 34$ females, 69 copulations). Females rear their young alone, and they protect their offspring from conspecifics that find neonatal ground squirrels acceptable prey by excluding nondescendants from the area surrounding their nest burrows (*36*). About the time that their mates' young are born, the males that copulated most frequently abandon areas where their mates will rear young and inhabit burrows elsewhere (Table 1); unsuccessful males do not move. The successful males usually remain near their new burrows until after they have attempted to mate there the following spring. During the lactation period, a male that had mated to completion with more than one female returned to and entered the area defended by one of his mates only once every 19.3 ± 3.2 hours (data from 7 males, 17 females); similarly, nonmates entered a female's defended area during the same period only once every 16.9 ± 4.1 hours (data from 11 females, 13 adult males). A returning mate was chased away by the resident female 42 of 53 times (79 percent). Similarly, during the lactation period, males who had either not mated at all or else had not copulated with particular females were chased, if they trespassed, from the defended areas of those nonmates 32 of 38 times (84 percent).

KINSHIP AND ASYMMETRIES IN TENDENCIES TO GIVE ALARM CALLS

When a predatory mammal appears, adult and 1-year-old female Belding's ground squirrels give alarm calls more frequently than would be expected if the animals called in direct proportion to the number of times they were present when a predator arrived (that is, expected if calls were "random"); by contrast, males call considerably less often than would be expected under randomness (Figure 3). Twenty-two times only males were present (that is, no females were there) when a predatory mammal appeared, and four times (18 percent) alarm calls were given by one of them. Conversely, only females were present 47 times when a predator appeared, and alarm calls were given in 40 (85 percent) of these cases. (For this comparison, the number of males present in alarm-call-evoking situations when no females were there and the number of females present when no males were there did not differ significantly; $P > .09$, Mann-Whitney U test.) Because of the matrilineal kin group structure of Belding's ground squirrel populations (Table 1) and because females are the more parental sex in this species, the sexual dimorphism in calling frequency (Figure 3) suggests that the alarm call under consideration might function to warn kin (that is, hypothesis 3).

In apparent support of the nepotism hypothesis (*2, 11*) are data (Table 2) suggesting that when a predatory mammal appears (i) reproductive females without living mothers, sisters, or descendants call more frequently than do nonreproductive females similarly lacking close female relatives, (ii) reproductive females without living mothers or sisters but with at least one living female descendant (that is, a daughter or a granddaughter) call more frequently than do reproductive females without living mothers, sisters, or descendants, (iii) reproductive females without living female descendants but whose mothers or at least one sister are alive call more frequently than do reproductive females lacking all three classes of close female relatives, and (iv) temporary "invaders," reproductive but nonresident females, known not to have lived on a study plot within Tioga Pass Meadow in the previous year or years and present less than 1 hour, call less frequently than do reproductive residents (*39*) (for this latter comparison, all reproductive females were considered whether or not their family members were alive).

Although the data are sparse, it appears that females with living female relatives call whether or not those family members are actually present when a predatory mammal appears (Table 2). Destruction of the current year's litter also does not seem to affect calling tendencies (Table 2).

Analysis of variance of 1974–75 data from 87 encounters between ground squirrels and predators (involving 174 different reproductive females of known age) indicates that time of year (*40*) has no effect on calling frequency ($F = 2.03$, d.f. = 2, $P =$ .17), but that the age of the female does have a significant effect ($F = 19.8$, d.f. = 1, $P =$ .005); the likelihood that alarm calls will be given by females increases with increasing

TABLE 2   Kinship and asymmetries in tendencies to give alarm calls among female Belding's ground squirrels. Expected calling frequencies were computed as in Figure 3; N is the number of times ground squirrels in each category were present when a predatory mammal appeared.

Category of Females	N	Number Observed to Call	Number Expected to Call If Calls Are "Random"	Significance $G*$	P
Reproductive,[†] with no known living relatives	19	14	9	5.80	< .025
Nonreproductive, with no known living relatives	14	2	7		
Reproductive, with a living daughter or granddaughter, but no other living relatives	27	18	12	5.58	< .025
Reproductive, with no known living relatives	24	5	11		
Reproductive, with their mother or at least one sister alive, but no living descendants	18	13	8	5.37	< .025
Reproductive, with no known living relatives	17	3	8		
Reproductive residents: known to have lived in the same area the previous year or years	168	64	56	4.90	< .05
Reproductive nonresidents: temporary invaders to an area (see text)	49	9	17		
Reproductive, with either their mother, a sister, or a descendant alive and present when a predatory animal appears	21	9	9	—	N.S.[‡]
Reproductive, with at least one relative alive but not present when a predatory mammal appears	11	6	6		
Reproductive, without their mother or any sisters, but with nursing young known to be alive	46	21	22	0.38	N.S.
Reproductive, without their mother or any sisters, and whose young were destroyed	16	4	3		

*G statistic is correct for continuity, and levels of significance are given.

[†]"Reproductive" means pregnant, lactating, or living with postweaning young of the year.

[‡]Not significant.

age (*41*). Among males, alarm calling and copulatory success seem to be unrelated. When predatory mammals appeared in 1975, seven males that had copulated at least once called no more frequently (that is, in no greater percentage of the times when a predator appeared) than did eight males that had not copulated in 1975 (*P* > .2, Mann-Whitney U test). Among the seven 1975 males that copulated at least once, there was no correlation between the number of matings with different females and the percentage of alarm-call-evoking situations in which each male called (*P* > .3, Kendall's rank correlation test).

Neither the first ground squirrel that behaved as if it saw a predator (Table 3), the animal closest to the danger, nor the one closest to its own burrow always sounded the first alarm. On 54 occasions, the animal first reacting to a predator was identified and its sex was ascertained. In 6 of the 31 times that an adult male reacted first (19 percent), the first-reacting male also called first, and in 9 of the 23 times that a reproductive female reacted first (39 percent), the first-reacting female also called first. In 68 instances, the ground squirrel closest to a predator when the predator was first seen by a human observer was identified and its sex was ascertained. In 5 of the 36 times that an adult male was the closest (14 percent), the closest male also called first, and in 9 of the 32 times that a reproductive female was the closest (28 percent), the closest female also called first. Among reproductive residents, 21 females giving alarm calls were no closer to their home burrows than were 19 simultaneously present noncallers (*P* > .1, Mann-Whitney U test). Thus, when a predatory mammal appears, old (that is, 4 to 7+ years), reproductive, resident females with living kin are most likely to call, while males are the most consistent noncallers. Again the implication is that warning family members, hypothesis 3, is a likely function of this alarm call.

DISCRIMINATING AMONG THE ALTERNATIVE HYPOTHESES

Could these data be better explained by any of the five hypotheses alternative to nepotism? Contrary to hypothesis 1, alarm calls did not divert predators' attention to other prey by causing pandemonium among the ground squirrels, and the animals did not aggregate to mob or to flee from predators (Table 3). Four times an adult female chased a long-tailed weasel from the neighborhood of her burrow, and in none of these cases did any conspecifics aid her (*42*). Whether or not they were near their burrows, most ground squirrels either sat up or ran to a rock upon sighting a predatory mammal or upon hearing an alarm call (Table 3). Occasionally juveniles squeaked when hand-held, and these screams from captured individuals sometimes attracted their mothers or other reproductive females. Such squeaks were clearly different from the alarm calls under discussion (that is, Figure 2), and they ceased 3 to 4 weeks after juveniles appeared above the ground for the first time. First callers and other alarmers did not seek cover in the center of an aggregation of conspecifics. Neither did alarm callers appear to sequester information on the whereabouts of approaching predators, and the calls did not seem ventriloquial to us or, apparently, to predators (below). Alarm callers usually sat upright, often on prominent rocks, and looked directly toward the advancing predator, thereby seemingly directing the attention of conspecifics toward it (*43*). Indeed, I could often locate the predator by following the gaze of several alerted animals, whether or not they were calling. I do not know whether ground

TABLE 3 Behavior of Belding's ground squirrels toward predatory mammals or toward alarm calls from conspecifics. Data are from 102 ground squirrel–predator interactions (1974 to 1976).

| | | | | OBSERVED RESPONSES | | | | |
| | | | | Runs Toward | | | | |
Class of Animal	None	Sits Up but Does Not Change Location	Conspecific	Rock	Bush	Mouth of Any Burrow Other Than Home	Mouth of the Home Burrow	Defended Area
Ground Squirrels within the Defended Area Surrounding the Burrow								
Adult females (2 to 8 years)	6 (8%)	29 (37%)	3 (4%)	33 (43%)	1 (1%)	2 (3%)	3 (4%)	—
1-year females	2 (5%)	14 (37%)	2 (5%)	15 (40%)	0 (0%)	2 (5%)	3 (8%)	—
Juveniles of both sexes	2 (5%)	13 (33%)	3 (8%)	6 (15%)	1 (3%)	6 (15%)	8 (21%)	—
Total	10 (7%)	56 (36%)	8 (5%)	54 (35%)	2 (1%)	10 (7%)	14 (9%)	—
Ground Squirrels Not within the Defended Area Surrounding the Burrow								
Adult females	2 (3%)	12 (23%)	3 (5%)	15 (29%)	1 (2%)	1 (2%)	3 (5%)	16 (31%)
1-year females	1 (4%)	5 (22%)	0 (0%)	8 (35%)	0 (0%)	1 (4%)	2 (8%)	6 (26%)
Juveniles of both sexes	0 (0%)	2 (11%)	1 (6%)	6 (33%)	0 (0%)	4 (22%)	1 (6%)	4 (22%)
Total	3 (3%)	19 (20%)	4 (4%)	29 (31%)	1 (1%)	6 (6%)	6 (6%)	26 (29%)
Adult males (2 to 5 years)	5 (11%)	16 (35%)	4 (9%)	17 (37%)	1 (2%)	1 (2%)	2 (4%)	*
1-year males	3 (11%)	9 (32%)	2 (7%)	13 (46%)	0 (0%)	0 (0%)	1 (4%)	*
Total	8 (11%)	25 (34%)	6 (8%)	30 (41%)	1 (1%)	1 (1%)	3 (4%)	*

*Males do not defend areas surrounding burrows as do females.

squirrels also use this cue. However, in 11 instances a ground squirrel probably could not see an advancing predator because of the ground squirrel's position in a swale; on eight of these occasions (73 percent), the ground squirrel sat up and oriented itself in the same direction as a conspicuous, calling conspecific, thus toward the apparently unseen predator. Only one of nine times (11 percent) did a ground squirrel in the same swale orient toward an apparently unseen predator when no conspecific was calling. Thus, no evidence supports the hypothesis that the alarm call results in the diversion of predators' attention to other prey (that is, hypothesis 1).

Members of all five mammalian predator species appeared undeterred by ground squirrel alarm calls, suggesting that the call does not function to discourage predator pursuit (that is, hypothesis 2). Indeed, members of all five species stalked or chased alarm callers, suggesting that calling may in fact make alarmers more conspicuous. Three of six adult ground squirrels preyed upon during this study had called just prior to being attacked. Also, calling ground squirrels were stalked or chased by predators significantly more often than were noncallers. A marked ground squirrel was stalked or chased 22 times; 14 of 107 calling animals (13 percent) were so attacked, but only 8 of 168 noncallers (5 percent) were similarly attacked ($P < .025$, two-tailed G statistic, corrected for continuity). To test hypothesis 2 further, I considered the responses of coyotes to callers separately. Because coyotes sometimes hunted by remaining motionless or hidden near bushes for long periods as if the element of surprise were important to their success, and provided that the alarm call under consideration discourages predator pursuit by indicating that the advantage of surprise has been removed, coyotes in particular might be deterred by "it." A coyote caught a mountain vole (*Microtus montanus*) and behaved as if it were continuing to hunt this species or other prey on ten occasions; in these cases, 39 ground squirrels gave alarm calls and 41 were silent. Five of the 39 callers (13 percent) were apparently stalked or were chased by the predator, while only 3 of the 41 noncallers (7 percent) were similarly pursued (this difference is not significant at the $P < .05$ level, G statistic). Thus, coyotes do not turn away from calling ground squirrels; if anything they, like other predators, are attracted to callers. None of the predators seemed to be startled or confused by alarm calls. On the four occasions when we observed the behavior of a predatory mammal toward the ground squirrel that it had just killed, the predator consumed its victim, suggesting that Belding's ground squirrels are not distasteful (nor poisonous) and that, therefore, alarm calling is not an aposematic display. The abundance of noncallers and the male-bias among them (Figure 3) do not support the second hypothesis, the lack of correspondence between the nearest ground squirrel to the predator (that is, the one likely to be in greatest proximate danger) and the first alarm caller, or the first one behaving as if it saw the predator (Table 3) and the first alarm caller also do not support the hypothesis that the alarm call functions to discourage predator pursuit (hypothesis 2).

Although this population of ground squirrels was not divided up into identifiable, physically isolated demes (*13*), females successfully raising young were relatively sedentary during 1974–76 (Table 1). Behaviors observed among these stable aggregations might have spread by a process of between-group selection [that is, hypothesis 4; see (*14, 15*)]. Because these aggregations are composed mainly of close relatives—mothers, daughters, sisters, cousins, and nieces—the "groups" are appropriately characterized as matrilineal kinship associations. The likelihood that female family members are consistently alerted by alarm calls and the apparent interdependence of kinship and calling (Table 2) make it impossible in this species to support between-group selection over kin selection (that is, hypothesis 3) [(*16, 17*); but see (*18*)]. With a dog, I visited six Sierra Nevada populations of Belding's ground squirrels other than the primary population under study; all visited populations were greater than 0.5 km but less than 23 km from Tioga Pass Meadow. At least one alarm call, usually many, was heard at each soon after the dog was released. Thus I have no evidence that noncalling groups or populations of ground squirrels occur in the vicinity of Tioga Pass Meadow. These data are obviously inadequate to determine whether there are between-group or between-population differences in the percentages of alarm callers. Because I found no noncalling populations of Belding's ground squirrels and because aggregations of related females do not predictably break up, emigrate from their natal area, and reassemble with alarm callers not sharing common ancestry, however, the most important prerequisites (*13–15*) for the operation of between-group selection (that is, hypothesis 4) are seemingly absent.

Because female ground squirrels are more sedentary than are males (Table 1), females might be more frequently in jeopardy than males if predators return to hunt near sites of previous successful kills. Females also give alarm calls more frequently than do males (Figure 3). Taken together, these observations suggest that the alarm call might function to reduce the likelihood of later attacks by the same predator (that is, hypothesis 5). However, mammalian predators at Tioga Pass Meadow do not preferentially return to sites of previous successes. For seven diurnal predations by coyotes and long-tailed weasels, the time between visits by a member of the successful species to a ground squirrel's defended area contiguous to one on which a kill had been made, 20.9 ± 6.2 days, was not different from ($P \geq .10$, Mann-Whitney U tests) the time between visits to seven randomly chosen defended areas, 18.9 ± 8.4 days, on which ground squirrels had never been captured [this comparison was made five times with seven different, randomly chosen defended areas each time; in no case were any significant differences found]. If predators did return to hunt near sites of previous successes, under hypothesis 5 young females should give alarm calls more frequently than older females; because the probability of dying increases with increasing female age in this species (*36*), young females would be in jeopardy from returning predators more often in their lifetimes than would older females [but see (*41*)]. Contrary to the prediction of decreases in calling with increases in female age, tendencies to give alarm calls increase with increasing female age. Discrimination among alarm-call-evoking situations, apparently on the basis of kinship with individuals likely to be alerted (Table 2), is also not predicted by hypothesis 5, but this observed discrimination does support the hypothesis that one function of the alarm call is to warn relatives (that is, hypothesis 3).

Because aggregations of (closely related) female Belding's ground squirrels are more stable through time than are male-male or male-female associations (Table 1), reciprocity (*20*) might be more likely to occur among females than among males. Therefore, the sexual dimorphism in probability of giving an alarm call (Figure 3) could indicate that the call functions to warn conspecifics likely to reciprocate (that is, hypothesis 6). If so, the "reciprocators" are also family members, and reciprocation might therefore benefit callers genotypically as well as phenotypically (*21*). Because reciprocity, as Trivers (*20*) formulated the hypothesis, refers only to an exchange of phenotypic benefits, circumstances (*20*, p. 35) ". . . when the recipient is so distantly related to the organism performing the altruistic act that kin selection can be ruled out," the alarm call under discussion does not function only in the context described by hypothesis 6. The degree to which alarm callers discriminate against distantly related or unrelated individuals known not to call might indicate the degree to which the alarm call functions to warn phenotypic reciprocators (*20, 22*). Limited evidence suggests that the presence of certain kinds of noncallers at least does not deter females with living relatives from calling. Using data from 28 encounters between predatory mammals and reproductive females whose mothers or at least one sister or daughter were alive, I compared the time between the moment a human observer first saw a predator and the first alarm call and the percentage of callers versus noncallers under two circumstances: when no noncallers were present, and when at least one unrelated male, temporary female "invader," or one nonreproductive female not known to be related to any of the residents in a study plot was present. In neither of these comparisons did callers' responses differ significantly on the basis of the presence of noncallers ($P \geq .2$ for each comparison, Mann-Whitney U tests). In assessing the importance of this apparent lack of a difference, note that discrimination on the basis of whether certain relatives are alive does occur (Table 2). In other words, females call more frequently when relatives might be alerted; they refrain from calling when no kin are alive despite being surrounded by (unrelated) females, members of the sex that calls. Although reciprocation might occur between related ground squirrels with reciprocators benefiting genotypically as well as phenotypically (*15*)—because nonreciprocators are not obviously discriminated against when rather subtle discrimination on the basis of relatedness apparently occurs—it is not possible to support the phenotypic reciprocity hypothesis [that is, hypothesis 6 (*20*)] apart from the nepotism hypothesis (that is, hypothesis 3).

CONCLUSIONS

My observations suggest that it is possible to begin discriminating among theoretical alternative functions of alarm calls and other behaviors that, because they may be phenotypically hazardous, appear altruistic. Data and arguments deriving from them imply that, of the six hypothesized alternative benefits of giving alarm calls, warning relatives, hypothesis 3 (*2, 11*) is a likely function of the alarm call that Belding's ground squirrels give when terrestrial predators approach. Regarding the other possible functions of this alarm call, no evidence supports hypotheses 1 (diverting predators' attention), 2 (discouraging predator pursuit), or 5 (reducing the likelihood of later attacks by the same predator). That the alarm call may function to help the group (hypothesis 4) or to warn reciprocators (hypothesis 6) is possible; but when assumptions of the fourth and sixth hypotheses and predictions derived from them and from the hypothesis 3 that the call alerts relatives are contrasted and are compared with field observations of the ground squirrels' behavior, both appear to be at most less important functions than warning kin.

Among the sciurids in which males give little or no parental care and in which matrilineal kin groups are known or are appropriately suspected to be a basic population unit (*34*), there exist similarities in the form (*29–31*) and female sex- and age-specificity of alarm calls to terrestrial predators (*11, 29, 34, 44*). Further, in at least one sciurid in which males have harems and live with and probably protect their mates and their mates' offspring year-round, harem-males call most frequently (*45*). These observations suggest that warning kin might be a common function of sciurid alarm calls to predatory mammals and they imply that asymmetries in tendencies to call may be expressions of discriminative nepotism (*21*).

REFERENCES AND NOTES

1. For example, D. P. Barash [*Am. Midl. Nat.* **94**, 468 (1975)] reported that "During 7 years of study of free-living marmots (Rodentia: Sciuridae), I observed eight instances of predation and numerous cases of alarm-calling in 3017 hr. of direct field observations on five marmot species. . . ."

2. W. D. Hamilton, *J. Theor. Biol.* **7**, 1 (1964); M. J. West Eberhard, *Q. Rev. Biol.* **50**, 1 (1975).

3. W. D. Hamilton, *J. Theor. Biol.* **31**, 295 (1971); I. Vine, *ibid.* **30**, 405(1971); M. Treisman, *Anim. Behav.* **23**, 779 (1975).

4. As suggested by S. Rohwer, S. D. Fretwell, and R. C. Tuckfield [*Am. Midl. Nat.* **96**, 418 (1976)].

5. For example, J. L. Hoogland and P. W. Sherman, *Ecol. Monogr.* **46**, 33 (1976); D. Windsor and S. T. Emlen, *Condor* **77**, 359 (1975).

6. E. L. Charnov and J. R. Krebs, *Am. Nat.* **109**, 107 (1975).

7. N. W. Owens and J. D. Goss-Custard, *Evolution* **30**, 397 (1976).

8. C. Perrins, *Ibis* **110**, 200 (1968).

9. N. Smythe, *Am. Nat.* **104**, 491 (1970); A. Zahavi, in *Evolutionary Aspects of Ecology,* B. Stonehouse and C. M. Perrins, Eds. (Macmillan, London, in press).

10. P. M. Driver and D. A. Humphries, *Ibis* **111**, 243 (1969); D. A. Humphries and P. M. Driver, *Science* **156**, 1767 (1967).

11. J. Maynard Smith, *Am. Nat.* **99**, 59 (1965); C. Dunford, *Am. Nat.* **111**, 782(1977).

12. G. C. Williams, *Adaptation and Natural Selection* (Princeton Univ. Press, Princeton, N.J 1966). See also H. W. Power, *Science* **189**, 142 (1975); D. H. Hirth and D. R. McCullough, *Am. Nat.* **111**, 31 (1977).

13. R. Levins, *Am. Math. Soc. Publ.* **1**, 77 (1970); B. R. Levin and W. L. Kilmer, *Evolution* **28**, 527 (1974); I. Eshel, *Theor. Popul. Biol.* **3**, 258 (1972).

14. D. S. Wilson, *Proc. Natl. Acad. Sci. U.S.A.* **72**, 143 (1975); *Am. Nat.* **111**, 157 (1977).

15. A similar suggestion was made by W. D. Hamilton [in *Biosocial Anthropology,* R. Fox, Ed. (Wiley, New York, 1975), p. 133].

16. J. Maynard Smith, *Q. Rev. Biol.* **51**, 277 (1976).

17. M. J. West Eberhard, *ibid.*, p. 89; J. Maynard Smith, *Nature (London)* **201**, 1145 (1964); R. D. Alexander and G. Borgia, in preparation; J. L.

Brown, *Nature (London)* **211**, 870 (1966). See also M. Gadgil, *Proc. Natl. Acad. Sci. U.S.A.* **72**, 1199 (1975).

18. E. O. Wilson, *BioScience* **23**, 631 (1973).

19. E. Curio, *The Ethology of Predation,* vol. 7 of the series *Zoophysiology and Ecology,* D. S. Farner, Ed. (Springer-Verlag, Berlin, 1976), p. 58.

20. R. L. Trivers, *Q. Rev. Biol.* **46**, 35 (1971).

21. R. D. Alexander, *Annu. Rev. Ecol. Syst.* **5**, 325.

22. Olive baboons, *Papio anubis:* see C. Packer, *Nature (London)* **265**, 441 (1977).

23. The study area, an alpine meadow about 1000 m long by 450 m wide, adjoins and lies just east of California State Highway 120, between Lake Tioga and the Yosemite National Park boundary at Tioga Pass, Mono County. For a description of the area and the annual cycle of ground squirrels there, see M. L. Morton, *Bull. South. Calif. Acad. Sci.* **74**, 128 (1975); _____, C. S. Maxwell, C. E. Wade, *Great Basin Nat.* **34**, 121 (1974); M. L. Morton and J. S. Gallup, *ibid.* **35**, 427 (1975).

24. E. R. Hall and K. R. Kelson, *The Mammals of North America* (Ronald, New York, 1959) vol. 1, p. 340; S. D. Durrant and R. M. Hanson, *Syst. Zool.* **3**, 82 (1954).

25. L. W. Turner, thesis, University of Arizona, Tucson (1972).

26. J. L. Hoogland, thesis, University of Michigan, Ann Arbor (1977); in preparation.

27. J. A. King, *Contrib. Lab. Vertebr. Biol. Univ. Mich.* **67**, 1 (1955).

28. C. B. Koford, *Wildl. Monogr.* **3**, 1 (1958).

29. For a discussion of the genus *Spermophilus,* see R. H. Manville, *J. Mammal,* **40**, 26 (1959); D M. Balph and D. F. Balph, *ibid.* **47**, 440 (1966); J. P. W. Harris, thesis, University of Michigan, Ann Arbor (1967); B. J. Betts, *Anim. Behav.* **24**, 652 (1976); D. H. Owings, M. Borchert, R. Virginia, *ibid.* **25**, 221 (1977). For a discussion of the genus *Eutamias,* see L. R. Brand, *ibid.* **24**, 319 (1976). For a discussion of the genus *Tamias,* see C. Dunford, *Behavior* **36**, 215 (1970). Species in the genus *Cynomys* give mono or bisyllable alarm barks in the 1- to 7-khz range, several in succession. In this regard see G. H. Waring, *Am. Midl. Nat.* **83**, 167 (1970); J. J. Pizzimenti and L. R. McClenaghan, Jr., *ibid.* **92**, 130 (1974).

30. For example, for Arctic ground squirrels, *Spermophilus undulatus*, see H. R. Melchior, *Oecologia (Berlin)* **7**, 184 (1971).

31. L. W. Turner, *J. Mammal.* **54**, 990 (1973).

32. For descriptions of audibly distinct alarm calls to aerial and terrestrial predators in California ground squirrels, *Spermophilus beecheyi*, see J. M. Linsdale, *The California Ground Squirrel* (Univ. of California Press, Berkeley, 1946); H S. Fitch, *Am. Midl. Nat.* **39**, 513 (1948); D. H. Owings and R. A. Virginia, *Z. Tierpsychol.*, in press.

33. P. Marler, *Nature (London)* **176**, 6 (1955); *Ibis* **98**, 231 (1956); *Behavior* **11**, 13 (1957); E. A. Armstrong, *A Study of Bird Song* (Oxford Univ. Press, London, 1963).

34. For a discussion of *Spermophilus armatus*, see R. E. Walker, thesis, Utah State University, Logan (1968); N. A. Slade and D. F. Balph, *Ecology* **55**, 989 (1974). For a discussion of *S. richardsoni*, see R. I. Yeaton, *J. Mammal.* **53**, 139 (1972); D. R. Michener, thesis, University of Saskatchewan, Regina (1972); _____ and G. R Michener, *J. Mammal*, **52**, 853 (1971); *Ecology* **54**, 1138 (1973). For a discussion of suggestive data on *S. tridecemlineatus*, see O. J. Rongstad, *J. Mammal.* **46**, 76 (1965); H. McCarley, *ibid.* **47**, 294 (1966).

35. For a discussion of *Marmota flavivetrins*, see K. B. Armitage and J. F. Downhower, *Ecology,* **55**, 1233 (1974).

36. P. W. Sherman, thesis, University of Michigan, Ann Arbor (1976).

37. For a discussion of *Marmota flaviventris*, see J. F. Downhower and K. B. Armitage, *Am. Nat.* **105**, 355 (1971); K. B. Armitage, *J. Zool.* **172**, 233 (1974). For a discussion of *M. caligata*, see D. P. Barash, *J. Mammal.* **56**, 613 (1975); of *M. olympus*, see _____, *Anim. Behav. Monogr.* **6**, 171 (1973); of *Spermophilus columbianus*, see A. L. Steiner, *Rev. Comp. Anim.* **4**, 23 (1970).

38. For reports of the defense of sexually receptive females by males among sciurids that are probably not harem-polygynous, see: for *Spermophilus undulatus*, E. A. Carl, *Ecology* **52**, 395 (1971); for *Sciurus aberti*, R. C. Farentinos, *Anim. Behav.* **20**, 316 (1972).

39. Similarly, E. A. Carl (see (*38*)] noted that for a nonreproducuvc, transient or "refugee" population of *Spermophilus undulatus*, that included members of both sexes, "The population was singularly silent; only occasionally did I hear a squirrel vocalization, in sharp contrast to the barrage of alarm calls that greeted me whenever I walked across the study area" (*38*, p. 410).

40. The 1974 and 1975 breeding seasons were divided into three segments for each reproductive female considered in the analysis: (i) spring emergence-parturition, (ii) parturition-first appearance of young above ground, and (iii) first appearance of young–fall disappearance of the female (hibernation). The arc sine square root transformation was used to produce normality in the data analyzed. The data consist of the percentage of times that calls were given by females of each age class, 1 to 7+ years, when a predatory mammal appeared.

41. D. P. Barash (*1*) observed an apparently similar effect of age on tendency to give alarm calls among marmots. The effect that he and I observed might result if older, more experienced females either (i) are more familiar with routes of escape near their burrows, thus more able than less experienced females to evade predators once they have rendered themselves conspicuous by giving an alarm call, or (ii) are redirecting nepotism from current or future (expected) young to offspring or grandchildren that have reached reproductive age, or both (i) and (ii). Advantages of assisting descendants whose likelihood of future reproduction is higher than a female's own reproductive potential may favor increasing nepotism with advancing age among female mammals generally [a similar suggestion was made by S. B. Hrdy and D. B. Hrdy, *Science* **193**, 913 (1976)]. Menopause-like termination of reproduction coupled with extensive maternal care in, for example, elephants [R. M. Laws, I. S. C. Parker, R. C. B. Johnstone, *Elephants and Their Habits* (Clarendon, Oxford, 1975)] may suggest that nepotism is sometimes completely redirected toward relatives that have survived to reproductive age [see also (*21*)].

42. L. W. Turner (*25, 31*) made similar observations on *Spermophilus beldingi*. E. R. Warren [*J. Mammal.* **5**, 265 (1924)] also reported single *S. armatus* chasing long-tailed weasels while conspecific ground squirrels looked on. Once K. Loehr [thesis, University of Nevada, Reno (1974), p. 22] observed ". . . several adult Belding Ground Squirrels . . ." chasing a weasel.

43. H. R. Melchior (*30*) and E. A. Carl (*38*) reported that *Spermophilus undulatus* behave similarly. R. C. Farentinos [*Z. Tierpsychol.* **34**, 441 (1974)] reports parallel observations for *Sciurus aberti*.

44. See also J. P. Fitzgerald and R. R. Lechleitner, *Am. Midl. Nat.* **92**, 146 (1974); R. A. Grizzell, Jr., *ibid.* **53**, 257 (1955).

45. For a discussion of *Marmoia marmota*, see D. P. Barash, *Anim. Behav.* **24**, 27 (1976).

46. I thank my field assistants L. Blumer, K. Dunny, S. Flinn, M. Flinn, C. Kagarise, D. Kuchapsky, B. Mulder, J. Odenheimer, M. Roth, and B. Schultz. The support of M. L. Morton was invaluable. For other assistance, I thank R. Alexander, J. Blick, J. Hoogland, R. Huey, C. Kagarise, R. Koford, R. Payne, F. Pitelka, S. Steams, and D. Tinkle. The Southern California Edison Company provided housing, and the Clairol Company donated hair dye. Supported by NSF grant GB-43851, the Theodore Roosevelt Memorial Fund, the Museum of Zoology and the Rackham School of Graduate Studies at the University of Michigan, and the Museum of Vertebrate Zoology and the Miller Institute at the University of California, Berkeley.

Primates—A Natural Heritage of Conflict Resolution

FRANS B. M. DE WAAL

The traditional notion of aggression as an antisocial instinct is being replaced by a framework that considers it a tool of competition and negotiation. When survival depends on mutual assistance, the expression of aggression is constrained by the need to maintain beneficial relationships. Moreover, evolution has produced ways of countering its disruptive consequences. For example, chimpanzees kiss and embrace after fights, and other nonhuman primates engage in similar "reconciliations." Theoretical developments in this field carry implications for human aggression research. From families to high schools, aggressive conflict is subject to the same constraints known of cooperative animal societies. It is only when social relationships are valued that one can expect the full complement of natural checks and balances.

With the early provocative description of *Australopithecus* as a lustful killer and the appearance of Konrad Lorenz's *On Aggression* in 1967, the origins of violence became a central theme in debates about human social evolution (*1, 2*). Popular authors spun the now familiar scenario according to which inborn aggressiveness, combined with male bonding in hunting and warfare, explains the human success story. The extraordinary appeal of this "killer ape" myth (*3*) has been attributed to the horrors of World War II. Confidence in human nature was at a low after the war, and the view that we are murderous psychopaths—or "a mentally unbalanced predator, threatening an otherwise harmonious natural realm" [(*4*), p. 14]—went down remarkably easily with scientists and the general public alike.

If we disregard this larger evolutionary debate and focus on the original research, it is obvious that aggressive behavior was studied as an individual rather than a social phenomenon. For example, Lorenz proposed his controversial drive concept according to which aggressive energy builds up endogenously, after which it seeks an outlet, whether in sports or warfare. He also emphasized genetic determinants, postulating an aggressive instinct (*1*). Psychologists, in contrast, developed their frustration-aggression hypothesis and studied the effects of role models and authorities (*5*). However different these outlooks, authors on both sides of the nature-nurture divide agreed on the antisocial character of aggressive behavior. According to ethologists, its main function was to cause dispersal, a view derived from territorial fish and birds in which threat displays do indeed serve to keep intruders at a distance. Psychologists, too, only saw negative consequences when a mouse was placed in a rat's cage to provoke an attack, when pain-induced aggression was incited among rats on an electric grid, or when human subjects were instructed to deliver high-voltage shocks to strangers (*6*). Focusing on aggression among individuals that did not know each other, students of both human and animal behavior thus laid the groundwork for what may be called the individual model [(*7*) and Figure 1].

Inasmuch as the individual model is oblivious to social context, it fails to address how families or societies deal with the disruptive consequences of conflict. The model tells us how aggression starts, but not how it ends or is kept under control. In the real world, however, the vast majority of aggression involves familiar individuals, which means that aggressors and victims share a past and can be expected to share a future. A different model was needed, therefore, one that regards individuals as socially embedded. Inspired by gregarious study objects, primatologists were the first to move toward this more integrated paradigm.

Primate societies are characterized by cooperation. Some species, such as chimpanzees [*Pan troglodytes* (*8*)] and humans, show collective intercommunity violence. More often, however, alliances are formed within the group with two or more individuals banding together to defeat a third (*9*). As a result, high-ranking individuals are not necessarily the strongest, but the ones that can mobilize most support (*10*). The ubiquitous primate activity of grooming serves an important role in this political arena by fostering valuable partnerships (*11*). All members of a group are actively establishing and maintaining histories of interaction, known as social relationships. Studying monkeys and apes in cohesive groups, in both captivity and the field, primatologists increasingly made relationships, rather than individuals, the unit of analysis (*12*).

At the same time that these ideas arose, a simple observation changed the way we look at the social impact of conflict. Earlier research on nonhuman primates had emphasized appeasement and reassurance gestures (*13, 14*) and had hinted at relationship repair after fights (*15–17*). The latter phenomenon was named and empirically defined as the result of an incident in the world's largest chimpanzee colony at the Arnhem Zoo, in the Netherlands. When the alpha male fiercely attacked a female, other apes came to her defense, causing prolonged screaming and chasing in the group. After the chimpanzees had calmed down, a tense silence followed, broken when the entire colony burst out hooting. In the midst of this pandemonium, two chimpanzees kissed with their arms wrapped around each other (Figure 2). These two chimpanzees turned out to be the same male and female central in the previous fight.

After reconciliation was defined as a friendly reunion between former opponents not long after an aggressive confrontation, data on hundreds of instances showed the

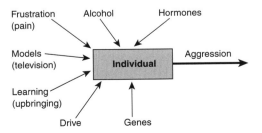

FIGURE 1   The individual model of aggression. Many different influences, both external (e.g., role models) and internal (e.g., hormones), determine an individual's propensity to become aggressive. Because social consequences and feedback are not part of the model, it makes no predictions about conflict resolution.

FIGURE 2   Chimpanzees typically seal a postconflict reunion, or reconciliation, with a mouth-to-mouth kiss, as here by a female (right) to the dominant male.

Photograph by the author.

pattern to be a regular, conspicuous part of social life in the Arnhem chimpanzee colony (*18*). Combined with other developments in the 1970s, this meant that a solid framework for the study of conflict resolution had come into place revolving around the following three elements: (i) indications of a calming function of grooming and other body contacts, (ii) recognition of long-term social relationships and their survival value, and (iii) demonstration of a connection between aggressive conflict and subsequent interopponent reunions, called "reconciliations."

PRIMATE RESEARCH

The reconciliation concept applies to animals a familiar human interpretation, which comes with connotations of rapprochement, conflict settlement, and even forgiveness (*19*). Reconciliation is best regarded as a heuristic concept capable of generating testable predictions regarding the problem of relationship maintenance (*20*). One central assumption is that a motivational state can be replaced relatively rapidly by its opposite: hostility and fear make way for a positive inclination. Another assumption is that this motivational shift serves the restoration of relationships. Since its introduction, more than 100 reports on 27 different primate species have been published, mostly in support of predictions derived from the reconciliation concept (*21*).

The first aim of research in this area has been to compare different expectations regarding the social consequences of aggression. The traditional notion that aggression serves a spacing function would predict decreased contact between individuals after open conflict. The reconciliation hypothesis, in contrast, predicts that individuals try to "undo" the social damage inflicted by aggression, hence, that they will actively seek contact, specifically with former opponents.

Testing these predictions requires a comparison with baseline data. The standard procedure is a controlled design known as the PC-MC method (*22*). One of the participants in a spontaneous fight is followed for a given time window (e.g., 10 min) to collect postconflict (PC) data, which is then compared with baseline information on the contact tendencies of the same individual in the absence of previous aggression (matched control or MC). These two sets of data allow for a division of opponent pairs into "attracted" pairs (i.e., contacting each other earlier in the PC than the MC) and "dispersed" pairs (i.e., contacting each other earlier in the MC than the PC). The conciliatory tendency (CT) after all observed fights can then be expressed as (*23*): CT = (attracted pairs – dispersed pairs)/(all pairs).

This measure has a built-in correction for normal contact rates, such that a CT of 0% means that the rate of friendly interaction between any two individuals is unaffected by previous aggression. Studies adopting this paradigm for primates have almost universally demonstrated positive CT values (for some species exceeding 50%), meaning that former opponents systematically contact each other more often than expected [(*23*) and Figure 3]. Thus far, most studies have concerned captive primates. One comparative study found no difference in conciliatory tendency between a captive and wild population of the same species (*24*). That former opponents frequently engage in friendly interaction flies in the face of earlier assumptions about the dispersive impact of aggression, which should have resulted in negative CT values. Moreover, some species show behavioral specificity, that is, their PC reunions stand out by special gestures, vocalizations, or body contacts. Dependent on the species, postconflict reunions may include mouth-to-mouth kissing, embracing, sexual intercourse, clasping the other's hips, grooming, grunting, and holding hands.

With regard to the pacifying function implied by the reconciliation label, several studies have confirmed that the chance of renewed aggression is reduced and tolerance restored after PC reunion. For example, the probability of revival of a conflict is lower for reconciled than unreconciled conflicts (*25, 26*). When conflict was experimentally induced in pairs of monkeys, individuals permitted to reconcile were more tolerant of each other around a juice dispenser than individuals that had been prevented from reconciling, suggesting that reconciliation reduces aggression in the dominant and fear in the subordinate (*27*).

Displacement activities, such as self-scratching, may provide clues about arousal due to anxiety and social tension (*28*). Thus, self-directed behavior increases after anxiogenic drug treatment but decreases after anxiolytic drug treatment (*29*). Using self-scratching as a behavioral index, anxiety has been found to rise when an individual has just received aggression and to drop back to baseline more rapidly after reconciliation than without it (*30*). Reconciliation thus seems to have a calming effect. This is not to say that anxiety is restricted to the victims of aggression: the

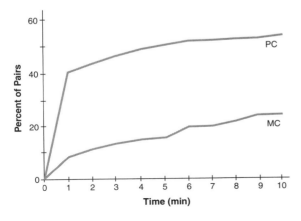

FIGURE 3 Most primates show a dramatic increase in body contact between former opponents during postconflict (PC) as compared with matched-control (MC) observations. Earlier notions about aggression would have predicted the exact opposite, i.e., distancing between previous antagonists. The graph provides the cumulative percentage of opponent-pairs seeking friendly contact during a 10-min time window after 670 spontaneous aggressive incidents in a zoo group of stumptail macaques (*79*).

reconciliation concept, which revolves around social relationships, implies that not only losers but also winners have something to "worry" about. Behavioral signs of anxiety have indeed been measured in aggressors, especially after conflict in high-quality relationships. These findings fit the prediction that aggression-induced anxiety concerns the social tie and suggest an interesting emotional mechanism: Conflict in valuable relationships induces greater anxiety, which in turn creates a greater need for calming PC contact with the opponent (*31*).

Whereas all of these findings support the specific function suggested by the reconciliation label, which is to repair damaged relationships, it is hard to measure lasting effects. Could it be that the effects concern merely the immediate future (*32*)? This has been a point of debate, and careful data collection on long-term effects is needed. It has been argued, however, that because long-term social relationships are an emergent property of short-term interactions, a distinction between the two is artificial (*33*). Moreover, in virtually all primates studied, reconciliation is typical of partners with close ties even after controlling for their high level of interaction. Thus, in macaques, which form matrilineal societies with kin-based alliances, fights among kin are more often reconciled than those among nonkin [(*23*) and Figure 4]. There are also the unifying group-hugs after rare aggression among male muriquis (*Brachyteles arachnoides*), a species in which males collectively defend a territory (*34*). Chimpanzee males, too, band together against neighbors and counter the disruptive effects of status competition within the group with a conciliatory tendency that far exceeds that of females (*35*). All of these cases support the prediction that long-term cooperative arrangements are associated with frequent relationship repair.

As a testimony to the effectiveness of these mechanisms, aggression can become quite common in close relationships without endangering them. Thus, not only do macaque mothers, daughters, and sisters show high levels of grooming and mutual support, they also frequently fight; in fact, they do so more often than unrelated females (*36, 37*). This paradoxical finding can be explained by assuming that the more compatible or secure a relationship (*38*), the more the threshold for conflict can be lowered without posing a threat to that relationship. The same may apply to entire

FIGURE 4   Reconciliations allow rhesus monkeys to maintain tight kinship bonds despite frequent intrafamilial squabbles. Shortly after two adult sisters bit each other, they reunite sitting on the left and right of their mother, the alpha female of the troop, each female holding her own infant. The sisters smack their lips while the matriarch loudly grunts.

Photograph by the author.

species, such as some conciliatory and tolerant macaques, which also exhibit high rates of mild aggression (*39, 40*). These high rates may reflect the reduced cost associated with aggression in a society in which reconciliation is easy.

One of the generalizations to come out of reconciliation research on nonhuman primates is the valuable relationship hypothesis (*41*), according to which reconciliation will occur especially after conflict between parties that represent a high social or reproductive value to each other. In other words, social relationships are commodities the deterioration of which needs to be prevented (*42, 43*). Apart from the above-mentioned observational data, experimental evidence comes from a study that manipulated the degree of cooperation among monkeys. Pairs of longtail macaques (*Macaca fascicularis*) were trained to obtain rewards by acting in a coordinated fashion: The only way to obtain popcorn would be for two monkeys to sit side by side at a dispenser, a procedure that attached significant benefits to their relationship. After this training, subjects showed a three times greater tendency to reconcile after an induced fight than subjects that had not been trained to cooperate (*44*).

With these mechanisms in place, it is obvious that from a relationship perspective the central problem is not aggressive conflict per se, but the perceived value of the relationship and the way conflict is dealt with. In nonhuman primates, aggression is a well-integrated part of social life: it occurs in the best relationships, and its potentially negative impact is countered by a flurry of friendly social interaction. The individual model has therefore been replaced by a relational model, which places conflict in a social context (*7*). Instead of treating aggression as an instinct or an automatic response triggered by frustration, this model sees it as one of several options for the resolution of conflicts of interest. Other options are avoidance of the adversary (common in hierarchical and territorial species) and the sharing of resources (common in tolerant species). After having weighed the costs and benefits of each option, conflict may escalate to the point of aggression, after which there still is the option of undoing its damage by means of reconciliation, which option will be favored by parties with shared interests (Figure 5).

The relational model thus allows for a cycling through conflict and reconciliation over time, representing negotiations that define or redefine the terms of the relationship. The prototypical example is the relationship between mother and offspring during weaning. A very intense, valuable relationship, which neither party can afford to break, is disturbed by rejections of nipple access mandated by the mother's future reproduction. The offspring's interests are quite different and would be served by continued nursing (*45*). A prolonged series of conflicts plays out between the two, sometimes involving aggression and often leading to temper tantrums, in which the offspring squirms and screams. After having cycled for months through daily confrontations and reconciliations, the new terms of the relationship may be reflected in a compromise: The offspring substitute-nurses by sucking on the mother's lower lip or by taking a skin fold close to her nipple into its mouth (Figure 6). These outcomes show how conflict can shape relationships without permanently disturbing them.

The development of reconciliation in young primates has been little studied, but there is increasing evidence that we are dealing with a "skill" (i.e., a learned behavioral strategy) rather than hard-wired behavior (*38, 46*). This was demonstrated by an experiment that exploited interspecific variation in conciliatory tendency. Rhesus

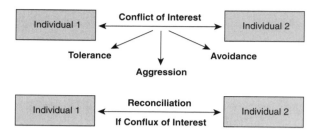

FIGURE 5 According to the relational model, aggressive behavior is one of several ways in which conflicts of interest can be settled. Other possible ways are tolerance (e.g., sharing of resources), or avoidance of confrontation (e.g., by subordinates to dominants). If aggression does occur, it depends on the nature of the social relationship whether repair attempts will be made, or not. If there is a strong mutual interest in maintenance of the relationship, reconciliation is most likely. Parties negotiate the terms of their relationship by going through cycles of conflict and reconciliation.

monkeys (*Macaca mulatta*)—a relatively aggressive, intolerant macaque with low levels of reconciliation—were exposed to a highly conciliatory close relative, the stumptail monkey (*M. arctoides*). Juveniles of both species were housed in mixed groups for 5 months. Following this, they were observed for 6 weeks with conspecifics only. This manipulation created a different social culture by producing rhesus monkeys with a three to four times higher conciliatory tendency than age mates that had never met the other species. Peacemaking tendencies rose gradually during cohousing with the gentle "tutor" species and remained high after its removal. This experiment demonstrated that reconciliation behavior of monkeys can be modified by social experience (*47*).

   Cognitive prerequisites for reconciliation are minimal. It is essential that members of the species recognize each other individually and that participants in a fight remember their opponent's identity (*22*). In addition, as seen above, reconciliation probably involves evaluation of the benefits derived from relationships: Appreciation

FIGURE 6 A weaning compromise has been arrived at between a mother chimpanzee and her 4-year-old son. After repeated nursing conflicts, the son is permitted to suck on a part of the mother's body other than the nipple.

Photograph by the author.

of relationship value will prevent risky overtures (any rapprochement carries the possibility of renewed conflict) for little gain. For most nonhuman primates, the above prerequisites are easily met. They are capable of much more, as reflected in the following examples of conflict resolution involving third parties.

Policing and Pacification. High-ranking individuals sometimes adopt a control role, breaking up fights or systematically protecting the weak against the strong (*48*). At other times they intervene peacefully or try to calm down one of the participants (*49, 50*). In species in which large males defend units of several females, such as Chinese golden monkeys (*Rhinopithecus roxellanae*), the leading male may maintain harmony by interposing himself between female contestants while holding their hands, and stroking or grooming both of them (*51*).

Triadic Reconciliation. In macaques and vervets (*Cercopithecus aethiops*), relatives of the victim may seek contact with the opponent. For example, a mother may approach and groom the attacker of her daughter in what appears a reconciliation "on behalf" of her offspring. Such third-party contacts seem to serve the relations between entire matrilines (*52, 53*). Similarly, there exist field reports of intergroup reconciliations spearheaded by the alpha females of different monkey groups (*54*).

Third-Party Mediation. In perhaps the most complex pattern, thus far known of chimpanzees only, a female acts as catalyst by bringing male rivals together. After a fight between them, males may remain oriented toward each other, staying close, but without either one initiating an actual reunion. Females have been observed to break the deadlock by grooming one male, then the other, until she has brought the two of them together, after which she withdraws (*18*).

All of these tactics are elaborations on a basic behavioral mechanism that protects cooperative bonds. Many animals other than primates would stand to gain from such a mechanism and have the cognitive capacities to permit it. From the beginning, therefore, there have been calls to look beyond the primate order. Only very recently, however, has PC behavior become a topic of systematic research in such disparate mammals as spotted hyenas [*Crocuta crocuta* (*55*)], domestic goats [*Capra hircus* (*56*)], and bottlenose dolphins [*Tursiops* spp. (*57*)]. The results have been positive, suggesting that conflict resolution may be widespread indeed.

The evolutionary advantages of reconciliation are obvious for animals that survive through mutual aid: Reconciliation ensures the continuation of cooperation among parties with partially conflicting interests. At the same time, it should be realized that reconciliation was never predicted or even remotely considered by evolutionary theorists. Traditionally, cost-benefit analyses have started from the assumption that animals neither know nor need each other. Thus, the rarity of lethal aggression was attributed entirely to the physical deterrent posed by the opponent's fighting abilities (*58*). In many social animals, however, both parties stand to lose if escalated fighting damages relationships. The widespread occurrence of reconciliation, therefore, questions assumptions underlying earlier modeling and leads theorists to look at individuals as part of the larger benefit-benefit arrangements that we call societies.

IMPLICATIONS FOR HUMAN BEHAVIOR

Ironically, research on how animals spontaneously make up after fights was for a long time ahead of how humans accomplish the same goals (59). This situation is rapidly changing, though, now that basic human research in this area is gathering steam, with some research shifting focus from aggression to conflict, negotiation, and compromise. For example, projects are under way in several countries to measure the development of conciliatory behavior in children.

The same ethological observation techniques developed for animals are applicable to children in the schoolyard or other settings of unstructured activity. Among preschoolers, two forms of conflict resolution have been noticed: peaceful associative outcomes, in which both opponents stay together and work things out on the spot (60), and friendly reunions between former opponents after temporary distancing (61). These two complementary forms of child reconciliation, expressed in play invitations, body contacts, verbal apologies, object offers, self-ridicule, and the like, have been found to reduce aggression, decrease stress-related agitation (such as jumping up and down), and increase tolerance (62). The striking similarity of these findings to those on nonhuman primates suggests causal, as well as functional, parallels. One of the single best predictors of peacemaking is positive contact between children before eruption of the conflict, suggesting a concern with the continuity and integrity of interactions with peers (61, 63).

Preference for integrative versus confrontational solutions to conflict is different for children from different cultural backgrounds (64, 65). For example, Kalmyk and Russian children hold hands after fights while reciting *mirilka,* or peacemaking rhymes such as, "Make peace, make peace, don't fight; if you fight, I'll bite, and we can't bite since we're friends" (66). Recent reviews of the literature on child conflict resolution stress the same themes as the primate literature, such as how friendship increases conciliatory tendency and how peacemaking skills are acquired through interaction with peers and siblings (67, 68). An impoverished social environment (as in the homeless) deprives children of this essential aspect of socialization (68), causing deficits in conflict management and moral development (69, 70). With the recent interest in conflict resolution at schools (71), there is a great need for basic information about how children behave among peers. Conflict resolution programs will need to be evaluated against behavioral change. This will require observational techniques not unlike those applied in the above primate studies complemented with attention to the unique role of language (72, 73).

In human adults, the topic of peacemaking is less well studied. The little systematic research that exists confirms that, rather than the rate and intensity of open conflict, it is the way conflict is being handled and resolved that matters most, for example, for marriage stability (74). There also exist cross-cultural comparisons that indicate how in human society reconciliation has been institutionalized, elaborated on, ritualized, and surrounded with a great many societal influences, such as the role of elders, conciliatory feasts, and compensatory payments (75). Peacemaking is a universal human preoccupation: some societies, such as the Malayan Semai, say that they fear a dispute more than they fear a tiger. No wonder that the Semai's *becharaa'*—an assembly of the disputants, their relatives, and the rest of the community—is opened by lengthy monologues in which the elders emphasize the mutual dependency within the community and the need to maintain harmony (*76*).

People everywhere seem to follow the relational model by taking overlapping interests into account when facing conflict, even at the international level. The European Community was founded on the premise that the best way to bring the parties together after World War II, and to ensure a peaceful future, was to promote economic ties, hence to raise the cost of damage to these relationships.

The conclusion from this growing area of research is that human aggressive conflict is best understood as an integral part of the social network. It operates within a set of constraints as old as the evolution of cooperation in the animal kingdom. Certain forms of aggression, such as warfare and random shootings, fall outside this framework, but the majority of aggression arises within the face-to-face group or family. It is this context that shaped human social psychology for millions of years, including both discordant and integrative social tendencies. And so, in a time when Lorenz's message about the dark side of human nature still finds an echo in popular writings about nonhuman primates (*77, 78*), other research is increasingly taking a perspective that includes the social impact of conflict, and how that impact is being buffered. Without denying the human heritage of aggression and violence, this research demonstrates an equally old heritage of countermeasures that protect cooperative arrangements against the undermining effects of competition.

REFERENCES AND NOTES

1. K. Lorenz, *On Aggression* (Methuen, London, 1967).
2. R. A. Dart, *Nature* **115**, 195 (1925).
3. R. Ardrey, *African Genesis* (Atheneum, New York, 1961).
4. M. Cartmill, *A View to a Death in the Morning: Hunting and Nature Through History* (Harvard Univ. Press, Cambridge, MA, 1993).
5. L. Berkowitz, *Aggression: Its Causes, Consequences, and Control* (McGraw-Hill, New York, 1993).
6. R. N. Johnson, *Aggression in Man and Animals* (Saunders, Philadelphia, 1972).
7. F. B. M. de Waal, in *Great Ape Societies*, W. C. McGrew, L. F. Marchant, T. Nishida, Eds. (Cambridge Univ. Press, Cambridge, 1996), pp. 159–172.
8. J. Goodall, *The Chimpanzees of Gombe: Patterns of Behavior* (Harvard Univ. Press, Cambridge, MA, 1986).
9. H. Harcourt and F. B. M. de Waal, *Coalitions and Alliances in Humans and Other Animals* (Oxford Univ. Press, Oxford, 1992).
10. F. B. M. de Waal, *Chimpanzee Politics: Power and Sex Among Apes* (Johns Hopkins Univ. Press, Baltimore, MD, ed. 2, 1998/1982).
11. H. Kummer, *Soc. Sci. Inf.* **17**, 687 (1978).
12. R. A. Hinde, *Man (London)* **11**, 1 (1976).
13. W. A. Mason, in *Advances in Experimental Psychology*, L. Berkowitz, Ed. (Academic Press, New York, 1964), pp. 277–305.
14. J. van Lawick-Goodall, *Anim. Behav. Monogr.* **1**, 161 (1968).
15. D. Lindburg, in *Behavioral Regulators of Behavior in Primates*, C. Carpenter, Ed. (Bucknell Univ. Press, Lewisburg, PA, 1973), pp. 85–105.
16. R. M. Seyfarth, *Anim. Behav.* **24**, 917 (1976).
17. J. McKenna, *Am. J. Phys. Anthropol.* **48**, 503 (1978).
18. F. B. M. de Waal and A. van Roosmalen, *Behav. Ecol. Sociobiol.* **5**, 55 (1979).
19. P. J. Asquith, in *The Meaning of Primate Signals*, R. Harré and V. Reynolds, Eds. (Cambridge Univ. Press, Cambridge, 1984), pp.138–176.
20. F. B. M. de Waal, *Behaviour* **118**, 297 (1991).
21. F. Aureli and F. B. M. de Waal, *Natural Conflict Resolution* (Univ. of California Press, Berkeley, 2000).
22. F. B. M. de Waal and D. Yoshihara, *Behaviour* **85**, 224 (1983).
23. H. C. Veenema, M. Das, F. Aureli, *Behav. Processes* **31**, 29 (1994).
24. F. Aureli, *Behav. Ecol. Sociobiol.* **31**, 329 (1992).
25. _____ and C. P. van Schaik, *Ethology* **89**, 89 (1991).
26. F. B. M. de Waal, in *Primate Social Conflict*, W. A. Mason and S. P. Mendoza, Eds. (SUNY Press, Albany, NY, 1993), pp. 111–144.
27. M. Cords, *Anim. Behav.* **44**, 57 (1992).
28. D. Maestripieri, G. Schino, F. Aureli, A. Troisi, *Anim. Behav.* **44**, 967 (1992).

29. G. Schino, G. Perretta, A. M. Taglioni, V. Monaco, A. Troisi, *Anxiety* **2**, 186 (1996).
30. F. Aureli, F. C. P. van Schaik, J. A. R. A. M. van Hooff, *Am. J. Primatol.* **19**, 39 (1989).
31. F. Aureli, *Aggr. Behav.* **23**, 315 (1997).
32. J. B. Silk, *Evol. Anthropol.* **5**, 39 (1996).
33. M. Cords and F. Aureli, *Evol. Anthropol.* **5**, 42 (1996).
34. K. B. Strier, D. S. Carvalho, N. O. Bejar, in *Natural Conflict Resolution,* F. Aureli and F. B. M. de Waal, Eds. (Univ. of California Press, Berkeley, 2000), pp. 315–317.
35. F. B. M. de Waal, *Q. Rev. Biol.* **61**, 459 (1986).
36. J. A. Kurland, *Kin Selection in the Japanese Monkey,* vol. 12 of *Contributions to Primatology* (Karger, Basel, Switzerland, 1977).
37. I. S. Bernstein, P. G. Judge, T. E. Ruehlmann, *Am. J. Primatol.* **31**, 41 (1993).
38. M. Cords and F. Aureli, in *Juvenile Primates: Life History, Development and Behavior,* M. E. Pereira and L. A. Fairbanks, Eds. (Oxford Univ. Press, New York, 1993), pp. 271–284.
39. F. B. M. de Waal and L. M. Luttrell, *Am. J. Primatol.* **19**, 83 (1989).
40. B. Thierry, in *Natural Conflict Resolution,* F. Aureli and F. B. M. de Waal, Eds. (Univ. of California Press, Berkeley, 2000), pp. 106–128.
41. F. B. M. de Waal and F. Aureli, *Ann. N.Y. Acad. Sci.* **807**, 317 (1997).
42. F. B. M. de Waal, in *Comparative Socioecology: The Behavioural Ecology of Humans and Other Mammals,* V. Standen and R. A. Foley, Eds. (Blackwell, London, 1989), pp. 243–263.
43. P. M. Kappeler and C. P. van Schaik, *Ethology* **92**, 51 (1992).
44. M. Cords and S. Thurnheer, *Ethology* **93**, 315 (1993).
45. R. L. Trivers, *Am. Zool.* **14**, 249 (1974).
46. A. C. F. Weaver and F. B. M. de Waal, in *Natural Conflict Resolution,* F. Aureli and F. B. M. de Waal, Eds. (Univ. of California Press, Berkeley, 2000), pp. 216–218.
47. F. B. M. de Waal and D. L. Johanowicz, *Child Dev.* **64**, 897 (1993).
48. F. B. M. de Waal, *Ethol. Sociobiol.* **5**, 239 (1984).
49. C. Boehm, in *Chimpanzee Cultures,* R. W. Wrangham, W. C. McGrew, F. B. M. de Waal, P. G. Heltne, Eds. (Harvard Univ. Press, Cambridge, MA, 1994), pp. 211–226.
50. O. Petit and B. Thierry, *Anim. Behav.* **48**, 1427 (1994).
51. R. Ren et al., *Primates* **32**, 321 (1991).
52. P. G. Judge, *Am. J. Primatol.* **23**, 225 (1991).
53. D. L. Cheney and R. M. Seyfarth, *Behaviour* **110**, 258 (1989).
54. P. G. Judge and F. B. M. de Waal, *Folia primatol.* **63**, 63 (1994).
55. H. Hofer and M. L. East, in *Natural Conflict Resolution,* F. Aureli and F. B. M. de Waal, Eds. (Univ. of California Press, Berkeley, 2000), pp. 232–234.
56. G. Schino, *Behaviour* **135**, 343 (1998).
57. A. Samuels and C. Flaherty, in *Natural Conflict Resolution,* F. Aureli and F. B. M. de Waal, Eds. (Univ. of California Press, Berkeley, 2000), pp. 229–231.
58. J. Maynard-Smith and G. R. Price, *Nature* **246**, 15 (1973).
59. F. B. M. de Waal, *Peacemaking Among Primates* (Harvard Univ. Press, Cambridge, MA, 1989).
60. S. Sackin and E. Thelen, *Child Dev.* **55**, 1098 (1984).
61. P. Verbeek and F. B. M. de Waal, *Peace Conflict: J. Peace Psychol.,* in press.
62. T. Ljungberg, K. Westlund, A. J. Lindqvist-Forsberg, *Anim. Behav.* **58**, 1007 (1999).
63. B. Laursen and W. W. Hartup, *Merrill-Palmer Q.* **35**, 281 (1989).
64. D. P. Fry, *Child Dev.* **59**, 1008 (1988).
65. S. Kagan and M. Madsen, *Dev. Psychol.* **5**, 32 (1971).
66. M. Butovskaya, P. Verbeek, T. Ljungberg, A. Lunardini, in *Natural Conflict Resolution,* F. Aureli and F. B. M. de Waal, Eds. (Univ. of California Press, Berkeley, 2000), pp. 243–258.
67. M. Cords and M. Killen, in *Piaget, Evolution, and Development,* J. Langer and M. Killen, Eds. (LEA, Mahwah, NJ, 1998), pp. 193–218.
68. P. Verbeek, W. W. Hartup, W. A. Collins, in *Natural Conflict Resolution,* F. Aureli and F. B. M. de Waal, Eds. (Univ. of California Press, Berkeley, 2000), pp. 34–53.
69. J. D. Coie and A. H. N. Cillessen, *Curr. Dir. Psychol. Sci.* **2**, 89 (1993).
70. M. Killen and L. P. Nucci, in *Morality in Everyday Life: Developmental Perspectives,* M. Killen and D. Hart, Eds. (Cambridge Univ. Press, Cambridge, 1995), pp. 52–86.
71. D. W. Johnson and R. T. Johnson, *Rev. Educ. Res.* **66**, 459 (1996).
72. J. Dunn and C. Slomkowski, in *Conflict in Child and Adolescent Development,* C. U. Shantz and W. W. Hartup, Eds. (Cambridge Univ. Press, Cambridge, 1992), pp. 70–92.
73. M. Killen and L. Naigles, *Discourse Processes* **19**, 329 (1995).
74. J. Gottman, *Why Marriages Succeed or Fail* (Simon & Schuster, New York, 1994).
75. D. P. Frye, in *Natural Conflict Resolution,* F. Aureli and F. B. M. de Waal, Eds. (Univ. of California Press, Berkeley, 2000), pp. 334–351.
76. C. A. Robarchek, *Ethos (Washington)* **7**, 104 (1979).
77. R. W. Wrangham and D. Peterson, *Demonic Males: Apes and the Evolution of Human Aggression* (Houghton Mifflin, New York, 1996).
78. M. P. Ghiglieri, *The Dark Side of Man: Tracing the Origins of Violence* (Perseus, New York, 1999).
79. F. B. M. de Waal and R. Ren, *Ethology* **78**, 129 (1988).
80. The author thanks M. Killen, F. Aureli, P. Verbeek, and *Science*'s anonymous referees for constructive comments on a previous version of this manuscript.

Mate Selection among Second Generation Kibbutz Adolescents and Adults
Incest Avoidance and Negative Imprinting

JOSEPH SHEPHER

Premarital sexual behavior and marriage patterns were investigated in Israeli kib-butzim. All adolescents and adults of the second generation (N = 65) in one kibbutz were studied. There were no cases of heterosexual activity between any two native adolescents of the same peer group and no cases of marriage between any two mem-bers of the same peer group. The avoidance was completely voluntary. Among 2769 marriages contracted by second generation adults in all kibbutzim, there were no cases of intra–peer group marriage. These findings could represent a case of nega-tive imprinting whereby collective peer group education which includes an incessant exposure to peers from the first days of life and an unimpeded tactile relationship among the peers between ages 0–6 results in sexual avoidance and exogamy.

INTRODUCTION

Imprinting is probably the most primitive learning process. It has been studied mainly in animal behavior, but some authors agree that there is some imprinting in humans (Sluckin, 1965; Taketomo, 1968; Money, 1960). In a recent publication, Money writes:

> Falling in love resembles imprinting, in that a releaser mechanism from within must encounter a stimulus from without before the event happens. Then that event has re-markable longevity, sometimes for a lifetime. The kind of stimulus that, whether it be acceptable or pathological, will be the effective one for a given individual will have been written in his psychosexual program, so to speak, in the years prior to puberty and dating back to infancy. (Money, 1971)

Money is very careful in formulating his hypothesis-like statement: "falling in love resembles imprinting"; "human beings stay remarkably stable in their erotic preferences." The question is, What is being imprinted? A vague ideal type of the op-posite sex (or the same sex)? In that case, the releaser would be the appearance of any representative of the opposite sex (or the same sex in case of homosexuality) who fits the imprinted ideal type. To what extent is this ideal type specific in its traits? Is it of the wide type of "some prefer blondes"? Or is it narrowly defined so that only a few representatives would fit it?

From J. Shepher, "Mate selection among second generation kibbutz adolescents and adults: Incest avoidance and negative imprinting," *Archives of Sexual Behavior, 1* (1971): 293–307. Reprinted with permission of Kluwer Academic/Plenum Publishers.

It is not only hard to answer these questions, it is even hard to imagine how to investigate them. We need a theoretically sound and operative definition of love or the state of falling in love, and this still seems to elude us (Rubin, 1970). The commonsense fact is that some people fall in love many times whereas others do so once in a lifetime. Is this the result of idiosyncratic imprinting or variance in availability of releasers fitting the imprinted ideal type?

I have no answers to these questions; yet I think that the research to be described herein may elucidate some of the basic questions about the genesis of erotic preference, as against love, which may be only a specific case of erotic attraction.

COLLECTIVE SOCIALIZATION AND SEXUAL PERMISSIVENESS

Kibbutz socialization has been described by various authors (Spiro, 1958; Neubauer, 1965; Rabin, 1965; Bettelheim, 1969; Shepher, 1969a). The most important characteristic traits of the system are the following:

1. Children are socialized from the earliest days of their lives by trained nurses in educational, heterosexual, one-age peer groups (Hebrew *kitah,* literally "class").
2. Children live separately from their parents during most of the day and in most of the kibbutzim during the night as well.[1]
3. Children meet their parents and siblings during afternoon hours (1–4 hr, according to age) when they visit their parents' house. These hours are devoted to the children exclusively and suffice to create very warm and affective relationships between children and parents.
4. From ages 0–4, children remain in small one-age peer groups with a maximum age range of 2 years. In kindergarten, two age groups are usually together, and from the age of 6 or 7 until 18 again a one-age peer group forms the educational framework.
5. Group solidarity is emphasized very much in the educational ideology of the kibbutz. Individualistic, competitive attitudes are discouraged; cooperation and affective friendly peer relations are encouraged. Until the sixth grade, there is no use of marks in school.
6. The children are exposed to each other constantly. Sexual play is not interfered with by the educators. This sexual play begins in infancy, is very intensive during early childhood, and is somewhat less intensive in the first school years.
7. At the age of 9–10, sexual shame appears and the relations between the sexes become tense. This tension disappears at the age of 13–14 and its place is taken by a warm and friendly relationship among the peers which, however, is completely de-eroticized.

The authorities have repeatedly stated that between peers of the same peer group there seems to be no heterosexual relationship, no erotic attraction, and consequently no marriage (Spiro, 1958; Rabin, 1965; Bettelheim, 1969; Talmon, 1964). These statements, however, were based on observations which were focused on the children's general development and dealt with the problem of adolescent sexual behavior only marginally. Talmon's article is an exception. However, she analyzed the data of three kibbutzim only and focused mainly on marriage.

THE STUDY: ITS SCOPE AND METHODS

In this study, anthropological as well as sociological methods were used. Since I had to investigate both premarital sexual activity and marriage, I faced the problem of uneven access to the data. Marriage is easily detected—being a formal act—by such convenient methods as a census, whereas premarital sexual activity must be revealed by years of observation. Present attitudes render it unavailable through the use of sociological methods such as questionnaires or interviews. Therefore, I decided to investigate premarital data and marriage data in one kibbutz intensively and only marriage data in all the kibbutzim. Since during the long years of observation I have learned that marriage patterns closely follow premarital affairs, I assumed the following:

1. If premarital sexual relations are similar to mate selection patterns in marriage in one kibbutz, and,
2. If mate selection patterns in marriage are similar to those in all the kibbutzim, then
3. I can infer that premarital sexual relations in all the kibbutzim are similar to those investigated in one kibbutz, and
4. This would be the best possible inference under the existing conditions.

I have observed all adolescents and adults of the second generation ($N = 65$) in one kibbutz where I was engaged for years in various educational tasks. Observations included all the phases of preadolescent and adolescent socialization and were focused on courtship behavior. The observations were checked through interviews with all the educators who ever worked with adolescents, including ones who were graduates of the system. All the heterosexual affairs of whatever intensity have been recorded and analyzed according to composition of the partners (i.e., whether or not they were natives of the kibbutz). All the marriages have been analyzed and compared with the premarital partnerships.

Using the data of a complete census of the adult second generation in the three big kibbutz federations,[2] I analyzed the marriage patterns according to their marriage partners. The data from the census were computer-processed, and all the marriages between second generation members were checked with the respective kibbutzim. Those couples in which the partners were ever members of the same peer group were personally contacted through a mailed questionnaire. A complete response has been obtained.

FINDINGS

In Yaara (the fictitious name of the kibbutz investigated), I found the following:

1. There is not a single case of heterosexual activity between any two native adolescents of the same peer group (Table 1).
2. There is no case of marriage between any two members of the same peer group (Table 2).
3. There is one single case of heterosexual activity within a peer group, but the boy is not a native and joined the kibbutz at the age of 10.
4. The avoidance is completely voluntary. There is absolutely no sign of formal or informal pressure or sanction against heterosexual activity within the peer group

TABLE 1   Partners in Premarital Sexual Affairs[a]

Subject/Partner	Males	Females
Same peer group	0	0
Other peer groups	1	1
Educated in the kibbutz	3	3
Adults of the kibbutz	2	7
Adults of other kibbutzim	4	4
From outside the kibbutz	12	4
Total	22	19

[a]Twenty-two premarital sexual affairs of 30 native males and 19 affairs of 20 native females have been recorded.

TABLE 2   Partners in Marriages[a]

Subject/Partner	Males	Females
Same peer group	0	0
Other peer group	0	0
Educated in the kibbutz	0	1
Adults of the kibbutz	2	2
Adults of other kibbutzim	1	3
From outside the kibbutz	4	1
Total	7	7

[a]Seven marriages of 30 native males and seven marriages of 20 native females.

either from the educators or parents or from the members of the peer group itself. Contrarily, the only affair, mentioned under (3), was benevolently accepted by the peer group, the educators, and the parents, and when it was discontinued, everybody regretted it.

5. The adolescents and later the full-grown adults are aware of the lack of mutual sexual attraction between them, and they actually regret it. The following observation is illustrative of their attitude:

D.14 male, 22 years old, comes home from the army on leave. He wears a uniform; tall, beautiful youngster. He meets his classmate D.1, also 22. The girl is dressed beautifully for the festive dinner of the eve of the Shabbat. The two youngsters shake hands, giving signs of greatly enjoying the meeting.

D.14 stares at D.1 and says, "What a pity that we are classmates! We would make a beautiful couple!"

D.1 answers, "Why, that would be a blaze!"

Both laugh heartily and go on their way.

6. Classmates are tied together by a very warm, friendly relationship. They accept each other ascriptively. They are always prepared to help each other, to share joys and sorrows. In one single case of a native of Yaara who fell in the second year of the Six Day War, the reaction of the peer group was a terrible emotional shock which lasted for weeks.

The analysis of the marriage statistics of the kibbutz movement revealed that among 2769 marriages[3] contracted by second generation adults there is not a single case of true intra–peer group marriage to be found. Fourteen couples were reported as intra–peer group couples. These couples were directly contacted, and their respective cosocialization periods are summarized in Table 3. In one case, the married partners were never in the same peer group. In eight cases, they joined the same peer group after the age of 6. Only in five cases were they together in the same peer group before the age of 6 but never for more than 2 years of the period 0–6.

DISCUSSION

Here we have a curiously pure case of a scientific statement of the pattern "if *A* then *B*" invariably, always, without exception. If children are socialized in a system like that in our Yaara, in Spiro's Quiryat Yedidim, and in Bettelheim's Atid, they do not

TABLE 3 Summary of Borderline Cases: Quasi Intra–Peer Group Couples[a]

Identification No.	I		T		K		ES						HS						
	0	1	2	3	4	5	6	7	8	9	10	11	12	13	14	15	16	17	18
01-09-103-104									―	―	―	―	―						
01-09-411-412									―	―	―	―	―	―					
01-10-118-121	Were in separate peer groups																		
01-55-79-81										―	―	―	―	―					
02-01-321-322															―	―	―	―	―
02-02-427-28										―	―	―	―	―	―	―	―	―	―
02-10-051-052												―	―	―	―	―	―	―	―
02-15-041-042														―	―	―	―	―	―
03-06-131-132									―	―	―	―	―	―	―	―	―	―	―
03-08-077-078									―	―	―	―	―	―	―	―	―	―	―
03-08-146-145				⌐	▨	▨	▨	▨	▨	▨	▨	▨	▨	▨	▨	▨	▨	▨	▨
03-10-013-014									―	―	―	―	―	―	―	―	―	―	―
03-18-063-064									―	―	―	―	―	―	―	―	―	―	―
03-026-013-014	▨	▨	▨				▨	▨	▨	▨	▨	▨	▨	▨	▨	▨	▨	▨	▨

[a] Abbreviations: I, infancy; T, toddler; K, kindergarten; ES, elementary school; HS, high school. Solid line: uninterrupted cosocialization. Cross-hatched line: interrupted cosocialization. Identification numbers: the first two digits are numbers of the federation, the second two of the kibbutz, and the remaining numbers of the married.

have sexual relationships with their peers and do not intermarry. In fact, I could have stopped here and been content with what I have established and let psychologists, psychiatrists, or biologists solve the problem of explanation. But the facts were so challenging that I—risking arrogant intrusion into neighboring disciplines—tried to find at least the direction to explanation.

In the first place, we have to turn to the explanation offered by Fox (1962). Dealing with the Westermarck–Freud controversy and trying to specify Westermarck's concepts of closeness and propinquity, Fox uses, among others, the example of the kibbutz as reported by Spiro. The explanation of the "positive aversion" between brother and sister reads as follows:

> Mutual stimulation during play (tickling, wrestling, exploring, soothing, stroking— all tactile interaction) between brother and sister leads to heightened sexual excitement, which while nearing climax cannot be (or rather is not) consummated by a successful act of coitus. The frustration engendered by the lack of tumescence will lead to anger and aggression and the episode will end in pain and tears. This if repeated enough, should act as an effective negative reinforcement. Thus, when sexual maturity is reached, each will try to avoid sexual approaches to or from the object of painful sexual experience. (Fox, 1962)

There is a serious problem in Fox's explanation: If the sexual play is so frustrating and painful that it ends in pain and tears, why is this sexual play not discontinued? Why do children engage again and again from early childhood until latency in sexual play? Why should they wait until puberty in order to avoid the painful partner? What is the independent evidence that the intensive sexual play is indeed painful and frustrating? It seems that the tension of the sexual arousal simply dies off and the overall balance of the sensations remains positive; otherwise, children would avoid it

Fox himself suggested that there is another possibility, namely, that the children stop at a pregenital level of soothing–stroking–petting type which does not overexcite the participants. This would happen *when* genital sexuality was traumatic. This means that genital sexuality is not always traumatic. One has to infer from the actual behavior of the children that it is not, because children engage again and again in sexual play.

In 1962, the data about sexual avoidance and exogamy between second generation kibbutz peers were scanty. Now there are the data from the entire kibbutz movement. The avoidance and the exogamy are so complete that their origin cannot be rooted in negative conditioning since such conditioning does not seem to be well established.

There are characteristics of the phenomenon which lead me to think that we are confronted here with a case of *imprinting:*

1. In a large population of 2769 marriages, there was not a single case of intra–peer group marriage, and, if the inference is correct, neither are there any premarital sexual relationships between adolescents of the same peer group in all the kibbutzim.
2. If cosocialization does not occur within a definite period, no avoidance and exogamy result.

Although almost 100 years old, imprinting theory has not yet reached a final crystallization, and authorities do not agree completely on its definitions. Thus Taketomo cites the original definition of Spalding, who was the creator of the concept 98 years ago:

> Imprinting (*Prägung*) is the name we have given to the process by which the releaser of an innate reaction to a fellow member of the species is acquired. (Taketomo, 1968)

Sluckin quotes Konrad Lorenz's definition of 1937:

> 1. The process is confined to a very definite period of individual life, a period which in many cases is of extremely short duration: the period during which the young partridge gets its reactions of following the parent birds condition to their object lasts literally but a few hours.
> 2. The process, once accomplished, is totally irreversible, so that from then on the reaction behaves exactly like an "unconditioned" or purely instinctive response. This absolute rigidity is something we never find in behavior acquired by associative learning, which can be unlearned or changed, at least to a certain extent. (Sluckin, 1965)

Thorpe (1956) adds two very important characteristics to Lorenz's definition, namely, that imprinting "is often completed long before the various specific reactions to which the imprinted pattern will ultimately become linked are established" and that imprinting is "supraindividual learning" and "a learning of the broad characteristics of the species."

In order to establish the presence of imprinting, Sluckin requires two tests: the recognition test and the discrimination test, through which animals can reveal that they have recognized the other animal to which they have been imprinted and that they do not recognize and follow others to which they have not been imprinted.

In the 1950s, imprinting was distinguished from other forms of learning (Taketomo, 1968). This distinction is not so clear at present. Especially difficult is the distinction between imprinting and conditioning (Sluckin, 1965). Nevertheless, certain characteristics of imprinting are clear:

> In conditioning, the reinforcing stimulus is necessary for the building up of the bond between the conditioned stimulus and the conditioned response; but reinforcing stimulus itself is separate from, or external to, the pair which are becoming associated. Primary reinforcing agents in conventional conditioning are conditions that meet the basic physiological needs of the organism and restore its psychological homeostasis. In imprinting there is no external reinforcement. The development of an attachment to the stimulus figure does not depend on a psychological reward, such as food, water, warmth, etc. The releasing stimulus itself is attractive from the start, and becomes more attractive as the organism continues to be exposed to it. In this sense such a stimulus could be regarded as reward. Therefore although it does not depend on external reinforcement, imprinting may be said to be a self reinforcing process. . . . However, in so far as the term, reinforcement, implies or suggests external reinforcement, imprinting may equally, if not preferably, be described as a form of *nonreinforced learning*. (Sluckin, 1965)

One of the most important characteristics of imprinting is the critical period during which imprinting must happen in order to have its results later. Neither before nor after the critical period can imprinting be successful. Sensitive periods characterize all learnings of early childhood, but they are not critical (Sluckin, 1965; Scott, 1962).

The application of the concept of imprinting to human behavioral development is still in its beginnings. Taketomo (1968) in his survey of these applications seems to accept completely only Salk's famous experiments on the imprinting of the mother's heartbeat rhythm on the human and nonhuman primate infant. Taketomo rejects the argument of Money *et al.* (1957) and Money (1960) that gender role and orientation, sexual aberrations, and falling in love are imprinted.

The data will now be examined in light of this short and far from exhaustive summary of imprinting theory.

Using Thorpe's (1956) definition, which seems to be most widely accepted by the authorities, the following may be argued:

1. The process is confined to a very definite and very brief period of the individual's life and possibly also to a particular set of environmental circumstances.

The particular set of environmental circumstances in our case is collective peer group education which includes an incessant exposure to peers from the very first days of life and an unimpeded tactile relationship among the peers.

The very definite and very brief period in the present case seems to be the period of the child's life between ages 0–6. The borderline cases (see Table 3) demonstrate that if during the critical period of 0–6 the collective education is interrupted or nonexistent, marriage and/or premarital sexual relationship may occur.

2. Once accomplished; it is often very stable, in some cases perhaps totally irreversible.

The data show the complete stability of the avoidance; there is no exception, either among those who married late in their lives or those who married several times.

3. It is often completed long before the various specific reactions to which the imprinted pattern will ultimately become linked are established.

The specific reactions in our case are the avoidance of sexual relations with peers and peer group exogamy, and these come at least 8 years after the imprinting process is completed.

4. It is supraindividual learning—a learning of the broad characteristics of the species. . . .

Unfortunately, there are not many examples of this particular set of environmental circumstances in human societies, at least not with the controllably uniform features of the kibbutz. But we have some comparative data, and more can be added. Fox (1962) gives the example of Tallensi, the Pondo, the Mountain Arapesh, although there are no conclusive data of actual occurrence of brother–sister incest.

Wolf (1966, 1968,1970) describes the effect of *sim-pua* marriages in one region of Taiwan on the sexual life of the spouses. In the *sim-pua* marriages, "the bride enters her future husband's home as a child. She is seldom more than three years of age and often less than a year."

> From the time the girl enters the family she and the boy are in contact almost every hour of every day. Until seven or eight years of age they sleep on the same tatami platform with his parents; they eat together and play together, they bathe with the other children of the family in the same tub. (Wolf, 1966)

Wolf (1970) found (first in one village, later in a sample of household registration records of two districts, in Sanshia Chen) that people married in the *sim-pua* form of marriage as compared with the other forms of marriage tend to (1) be reluctant to consummate their marriage, (2) have more extramarital sexual relationships (both sexes), (3) have a higher divorce rate, and (4) have fewer children. His conclusion is that the *sim-pua* marriage case is a further proof of the Westermarckian thesis. While we tend to assume that the disposition–imprinting–avoidance between coeducated children having unimpeded tactile relations is characteristic of the species, we need to be careful in accepting Wolf's data as additional decisive proof.

First, Wolf does not describe the socialization process. We do not know whether the spouses-to-be have or do not have tactile relationships, whether there are taboos or punishments. Second, we have no data about age and age differences of the children involved. In his second article, Wolf (1968) quotes the case of an 8-year-old boy of Foochow who carried his baby-wife. Wolf's method of accepting information from "gossip-sessions" (Wolf, 1970), while amusing, leaves doubts as to the reliability and exhaustiveness of the data.

Assuming that the future will bring more exact and more exhaustive data, may we dare conclude that this case fits the four requirements of Thorpe's definition of imprinting? Yet a formal fit of the requirements of the definition is certainly not sufficient.[4] We have to examine further tests.

It is very difficult to submit the case of the kibbutzim to Sluckin's experimental tests, as such things are difficult with any human behavior. But *ex post facto* I can conclude that kibbutz natives avoid sexual relationships and marriage *only* with their peers. They do not avoid other kibbutz youngsters, although they usually do not tend to prefer them as alternative partners. They have a normal sex life, and eventually almost all of them get married even earlier than the first generation in the kibbutz or the total Jewish population in Israel. Thus the case passes Sluckin's "test of discrimination."

It is possible, however, that the case is not one of imprinting but another form of learning, namely, conditioning, as Fox (1962) indicated or as Wolf suggested, proposing the following line of argument:

> The socialization process inevitably involves a good deal of punishment and pain, and children who are socialized together must come to one another with this experience. (Wolf, 1968)

Wolf asserts that in socialization punishment and pain are the unconditioned stimuli, whereas the conditioned stimulus would be sexual attraction during adolescence. Whereas I readily accept that kibbutz socialization necessarily includes punishment, I think that to compare that with Beach's experimental shock effect on mating dogs (Wolf, 1968) is hardly plausible. Just as I could not see the shocking effect of the sexual frustration of the kibbutz children in sexual play, so I cannot accept that punishment in socialization would have this conditioning result.

Having thus eliminated alternative explanations, I will venture the following explanation:

1. Sexual avoidance and exogamy between peers in the kibbutz are imprinted.
2. This imprinting takes place between ages 0–6.
3. Once imprinting has taken place, the peers as adolescents or adults will avoid each other sexually, will not intermarry, and cannot help but act accordingly even if they cognitively want to.

As to what actually happens during the imprinting process, I tentatively suggest Salzen's (1968) hypothesis based on a model suggested by Sokolov.

According to this hypothesis, early patterns of sensory stimulation set up neuronal assemblies which form a model. Familiar social and physical environments are thus modeled in these neuronal assemblies. Peers are the most important part of the kibbutz child's social environment from the very first days of life. Frequent bodily contact as well as utmost familiarity with the peers establishes a model of warm solidarity in the perception of these children. This basic model is confirmed and corroborated by education. Adolescent and adult sexuality bring new and different perceptive and sensory experiences which do not fit the basic model of warm solidarity. Thus whereas Salzen is right in stating that "appropriate stimulus objects may release sexual behavior only when they are also familiar enough not to evoke avoidance and fear," I have to add that appropriate stimulus objects may release sexual behavior if they are *not too familiar* and not modeled as part of a basic solidarity group, the members of which are liked or even cherished but not desired and loved and certainly "are not fallen in love with."

What is innate here is the capability or disposition of creating neuronal models which absorb and perceive such complicated objects as maternal figures (Bowlby, 1958), fetish objects and systems of sexual symbols (Money *et al.,* 1957, Money, 1960), and basic familiarity figures such as peers.

These models are created during definite, limited periods and once established they are stubbornly resistant to pattern change. Thus the model created by gender imprinting would be resistant to change even if genetic or gonadal or even anatomical sex assignment is opposite.

This tentative explanation does not stand alone, and it seems that a whole set of behavior patterns connected with sex may be similarly imprinted. Thus Money (1960) claims that gender role and orientation are imprinted: "The critical period for the imprinting of gender role and orientation seemed to be between the ages of 18 months and three or four years depending among other things on the child's I.Q. and ability to comprehend what was going on."

Thus this research seems to contribute to these findings by indicating that childhood exposure and experience do not only define with whom one will fall in love but under certain circumstances *they define with whom one will not fall in love.* This means that one is confronted here with a case of negative imprinting. The established imprinted model prevents the sexual attraction toward subjects who were imprinted in early childhood and forms a part of a neuronal model with which the erotic attraction is incompatible.

INCEST REGULATIONS: PREVENTIONS, INHIBITIONS, PROHIBITIONS

If this reasoning is correct that the sexual avoidance of peers in the kibbutz is imprinted and reveals a supraindividual learning process of the species (Thorpe, 1956), maybe one can understand better the controversy about Westermarck's insistence that "there is an innate aversion to sexual intercourse between persons living closely together from early youth. . . ."

Westermarck was severely criticized by Frazer:

> It is not easy to see why any deep human instinct should need to be reinforced by law. There is no law commanding men to eat and drink or forbidding them to put their hands in the fire. Men eat and drink and keep their hands out of the fire instinctively for fear of natural, not legal penalties, which would be entailed by violence done to these instincts. The law only forbids men to do what their instincts incline them to do; what nature itself prohibits and punishes, it would be superfluous for the law to prohibit or punish. Accordingly we may always safely assume that crimes forbidden by law are crimes which many men have a natural propensity to commit. If there was no such propensity there would be no such crimes, and if no such crimes were committed what need to forbid them? Instead of assuming, therefore, from the legal prohibition of incest that there is a natural instinct in favor of it, and that if the law represses it, as it represses other natural instincts, it does so because civilized men have come to the conclusion that the satisfaction of these natural instincts is detrimental to the general interests of Society. (Frazer, 1910, Vol. 4)

This is a very convincing argument, but it is based on two erroneous premises: (1) that incest aversion has the effectiveness and immediacy of such instincts as hunger and (2) that incest is universally forbidden by law. Frazer is caught in the nature–culture, heredity–environment dichotomy of his time; incest is prevented by a biologically programmed instinct, or it must be prohibited by law. *Tertium non datur.* Westermarck's use of the word "innate" (German *angeborene*) does not necessarily mean instinct in the sense of an inexorably universal pattern of behavior dictated by genetic heredity. True, Westermarck's use of the words "instinct," "instinctual," and "innate" is somewhat loose.

Freud does not speak of the presence of incestuous desire in *adults,* whereas Westermarck does. Freud speaks of the earliest sexual excitations of youth which are invariably incestuous (Freud, 1950). The whole Westermarck–Freud controversy may be reduced to Westermarck's unfortunate use of the word "innate":

> There is an *innate* aversion to sexual intercourse between persons living very closely together from early youth and that, as such persons are in most cases related, this feeling displays itself chiefly as a horror of intercourse between near kin. (Westermarck, 1889)

In the German original, Westermarck uses the word *angeborene,* and according to the German structure of the sentence it sounds as if there were a contradiction: *"das zwischen Personen, die von Kindheit an beisammen leben, eine angeborene Abneigung gegen den Geselhechtsvorkehr herrscht. . . ."* If the aversion is innate, how can it account for a behavior pattern which is dependent on certain residence and/or socialization patterns? We have to infer that Westermarck meant an innate *disposition* to develop aversion under certain conditions, which is quite different, and probably neither Freud nor Frazer would dispute it.

Freud himself was not very far from assuming the same. After telling the fascinating story of the primeval parricide, he remarks:

> No one can have failed to observe, in the first place, that I have taken as the basis of my whole position the existence of a *collective mind,* in which mental processes occur just as they do in the mind of the individual. In particular, I have supposed that the sense of guilt for an action has persisted for many thousands of years and has remained operative which can have had no knowledge of that action. (Freud, 1950) [Italics added.]

Freud himself was very unhappy about the invoking of "collective mind" and found a partial solution in the term "disposition":

> A part of the problem seems to be met by the inheritance of psychical *dispositions* which, however, need to be given some sort of impetus in the life of the individual before they can be roused into actual operation. (Freud, 1950) [Italics added.]

Freud not less than Westermarck presupposes a (biologically) inherited, i.e., innate, disposition to react specifically to certain particular stimuli which is not "roused into actual operation" if the stimuli are absent. That is, by the way, the core of Malinowski's (1927) criticism of Freud: ". . . . it appears necessary to draw in more systematically the correlation, between biological and social influences; not to assume the universal existence of the Oedipus complex, but in studying every type of civilization, to establish the special complex which pertains to it."

"The correlation between biological and social influences" would be, then, that the species has the innate disposition to be imprinted under certain conditions, namely, an intensive tactile relationship of peers in any socialization process. The case of the kibbutz is peculiar because of its institutionally controllable uniformity. But the same avoidance will be present in any family where siblings are reared under the same conditions. The variability among cultures from the point of view of the presence and absence of avoidance-creating conditions has been indicated by Fox (1962). But it is logical to assume that there may be variation among individual families within cultures, especially in modern societies. Some indication of such variability can be found in the study of Weinberg:

> Sibling incest frequently was transitory, hence the sibling participants did not behave like marriage partners. But six pairs of siblings, who were separated from early childhood and who became mutually attached, did contemplate marriage. (Weinberg, 1955)

It must be pointed out that Westermarck saw the real factor behind the genesis of the avoidance: close relationship from early childhood, not belonging to the same family. For him, the avoidance of sibling incest in the family is a matter of statistics; since in most families siblings live very closely together from early childhood, sexual attraction in adolescence is absent between most of the siblings. But not between all of them, and that is why incest is also prohibited sometimes by law. Since most people have been imprinted, they consider sexual relationship between members of the close family, in Levy-Bruhl's words,

> *L'étude des témoignages établira, qu'en effet l'inceste, à leurs yeux, est avant tout quelque chose d'anormal, d'insolite, de contre nature, qui porte malheur, en un mot, une "transgression."*
>
> *Non pas, . . . un acte moralement condamnable, mats un acte inhabituel et contra nature, qui revêle une mauvaise influence, en train de s'exercer, comme celui de la chèvre qui mange ses excrêments. . . .* (Levy-Bruhl, 1931)

Following Westermarck's reasoning, one has to ask two questions:

1. If the disposition to be imprinted during early childhood against sexual attraction to peers is independent of the family, could we not assume that it is earlier than the family?
2. Incest is not a unitary concept. There are at least[5] four basic forms of incest: mother–son, uterine siblings, agnatic siblings, and father–daughter. Is the corrected Westermarckian theory applicable to all of them? Fox (1967, 1968) expresses his doubt about the necessary connection between incest and the nuclear family:

> All this reasoning fits in with the doubts I had expressed about incest theories based on the "nuclear family hypothesis." The basic fact of the hierarchy was allowed for and indeed became central, and much about human incestuous behavior made more sense when viewed in this evolutionary framework, than when it was linked to the "preservation of the nuclear family." (Fox, 1968)

If one accepts the thesis that to understand early human behavior it is sufficient to assume two dyads, mother–child and uterine siblings, and a band of dominant and subdominant males, one can assume that the uterine sibling inhibition was very early, as was the mother–son inhibition.

Sade (1968) found in one group of rhesus macaques in the colony of Cayo Santiago that although adolescents are not expelled by dominant males, 75% left their group and joined another group. Some, but not all of them, returned later to the original group. According to Sade, only three males mounted their mothers in "single mountings," and only one copulated with his mother. Sade considers single mounting as a compromise, "a displacement activity," and explains the rarity of copulation between sons and mothers by the fact that young males "are inhibited from mating with their mothers by the reverberance of the role of infant in their adult relationships with their mothers." Moreover, "if the son can successfully challenge his mother's dominance, the inhibition is broken and he will mate with her."

Even mother–son avoidance is not general in the nonhuman primates, and there are no indications of avoidance between uterine siblings. We can assume that mother–son avoidance was earlier and that only uterine sibling avoidance is peculiarly human. The avoidance of sexual relationships within the two basic dyads is probably earlier than agnatic sibling and father–daughter relations, which were probably not inhibited. First, they were recognized later.[6] Second, if Sade's analysis of the role conflict in the young male monkey is right, then it is not applicable to the father–daughter relation: the father was dominant before the maturation of his daughter and remains dominant in the sexual relationship.

Slater (1959), Fox (1968), and Livingstone (1969) argue that besides inhibitions certain other mechanisms *prevented* incest. Thus Slater asserts that in the early hominids incest was highly improbable because of demographic factors such as short life expectation, high infant mortality, and wide spacing of children due to long lactation. Fox, quoting Chance, points to expulsion of maturing males from primate bands. Cohen (1964) found in societies where children are socialized by the parents and the members of the child's descent group that extrusion of prepubescent male children is widely accepted.

Thus there are three ways in which incest can be regulated: inhibitions, preventive mechanisms, and prohibitions. They are different in the various incestuous relationships, and they probably were different in various stages of the evolutionary scale. Instead of being caught in an impasse arrived at by an impressive group of scientists,

> There are no criteria, save aesthetics and logical consistency for choosing among theories, since there is no possibility of demonstrating that A varies with B if both A and B are universally and invariably present. (Aberle et al., 1963)

would it not be better to deal with the problem of incest according to a set of three variables: (1) types of regulations (inhibition, prevention, prohibition); (2) types of dyads involved (mother–son, uterine siblings, agnatic siblings, father–daughter); and (3) evolutionary stages and/or cross-cultural types ?

ENDNOTES

1. For some variations in this, see Shepher (1969b).
2. The religious kibbutzim as well as two unaffiliated kibbutzim are not included. However, these kibbutzim include less than 3% of the second generation and probably even less of the married second generation population.
3. To be sure, these are the marriages contracted by those who were members of their respective kibbutzim at the time of the census (1969). As to those who left the kibbutz, we have demographic data from one federation which includes about 35% of the second generation. In this federation, 16% of the children ever born into these kibbutzim have left them during 45 years of the existence of these kibbutzim (Survey of Deserters in the Second Generation Giva't Haviva, 1969, Hebrew). If we suppose that the rate of desertion is not different in the other federations and we ac-

cept Talmon's (1964) hypothesis that the probability of desertion is the lowest when the mates both have been reared in the kibbutz, we can argue that the probability that an intra–peer group couple have been among those who left the kibbutz is extremely small. Then too, such a marriage is so exceptional that people would remember it and it would have been brought to my attention.

4. The best case in point would probably be Spiro's (1956) proposal that, based on Murdock's (1949) definitions, marriage and family in the kibbutz are nonexistent. Spiro eventually corrected his assumptions (Bell and Vogel, 1960).
5. One can add adopted children and step-parents.
6. I am aware of the fact that it is very difficult to prove this thesis—as it is to prove most hypotheses of evolutionary theory.

REFERENCES

Aberle, D. F., Bronfenbrenner, U., Hess, E. H., Miller, D. L., Schneider, D. M., Spuhler, J. N. (1963). The incest taboo and the mating pattern of animals. *Amer. Anthropologist* **65:** 253–266.

Bell, N. W., and Vogel, E. F. (1960). *A Modern Introduction to the Family,* Free Press, New York.

Bettelheim, B. (1969). *The Children of the Dream,* Macmillan, New York.

Bowlby, J. (1958). The nature of the child's tie to his mother. *Int. J. Psychoanal.* **39:** 360–373.

Cohen, Y. A. (1964). *The Transition from Childhood to Adolescence,* Aldine, Chicago.

Fox, R. (1962). Sibling incest. *Brit. J. Social.* **13:** 128–150.

Fox, R. (1967). In the beginning: Aspects of hominid behavioural evolution. *Man* **2:** 415–433.

Fox, R. (1968). Incest, inhibition and hominid evolution. Paper presented to Wenner-Gren Symposium, Burg Wartenstein, August.

Frazer, J. (1910). *Totemism and Exogamy,* 4 vols., Macmillan, London.

Freud, S. (1940) (orig. 1913). *Totem und Tabu,* Gesammelte Werke DC, Imago, London.

Freud, S. (1950). *Totem and Taboo* (James Strachey, trans.), Routledge & Kegan Paul, Ltd., London.

Levy-Bruhl, L. (1931). *Le surnatwel et la nature dans la mentalite primitive,* Paris.

Livingstone, F. B. (1969). Genetics, ecology and the origins of incest and exogamy. *Curr. Anthropol.* **10:** 45–61.

Malinowski, B. (1927). *Sex and Repression in Savage Society,* Routledge & Kegan Paul, Ltd., London.

Money, J. (1960). Components of eroticism in man: Cognitive rehearsals. *Rec. Advan. Biol. Psychiat.* **2:** 210–225.

Money, J. (1962). Factors in the genesis of homosexuality. In Winakur, G. (ed.). *Determinants of Human Sexual Behavior,* Charles C Thomas, Springfield, Ill.

Money, J. (1971). Determinants of human sexual behavior. In Freedman, A. M., Kaplan, H. I., and Kaplan, H. S. (eds.). *Comprehensive Textbook of Psychiatry,* Williams and Wilkins, Baltimore.

Money, J., Hampson, J. G., and Hampson, J. L. (1957). Imprinting and the establishment of gender role. *Arch. Neurol. Psychiat.* **77:** 333–336.

Murdock, G. P. (1949). *Social Structure,* Macmillan, New York.

Neubauer, P. B. (ed.) (1965). *Children in Collectives,* Charles C Thomas, Springfield, Ill.

Rabin, I. A. (1965). *Growing Up in a Kibbutz,* Springer, New York.

Rubin, Z. (1970). Measurement of romantic love. *J. Personal. Soc. Psychol.* **16:** 265–273.

Sade, D. S. (1968). Inhibition of son-mother mating among free-ranging rhesus monkeys. *Sci. Psychoanal.* **7:** 18–35.

Salzen, E. A. (1968). Discussion of Taketomo. *Sci. Psychoanal.* **12:** 184–189.

Scott, J. P. (1962). Critical periods in behavioral development. *Science* **138:** 949–957.

Shepher, J. (1969a). The child and the parent-child relationship in kibbutz communities in Israel. *Assignment Children,* Vol. 10, UNESCO, Paris.

Shepher, J. (1969b). Familism and social structure: The case of the kibbutz. *J. Marriage and Family* **31:** 568–573.

Slater, M. K. (1959). Ecological factors in the origin of incest. *Amer. Anthropologist* **61:**1042–1059.

Sluckin, W. (1965). *Imprinting and Early Learning,* Methuen & Co., London.

Spiro, M. E. (1956). Is the family universal? *Amer. Anthropologist* **56:** 839–846.

Spiro, M. E. (1958). *Children of the Kibbutz,* Harvard University Press, Cambridge.

Taketomo, Y. (1968). The application of imprinting to psychodynamics. *Sci. Psychoanal.* **12:** 166–183.

Talmon, Y. (1964). Mate selection in collective settlements. *Amer. Social. Rev.* **29:** 491–508.

Thorpe, W. H. (1956). *Learning and Instinct in Animals,* Methuen & Co., London.

Weinberg, S. K. (1955). *Incest Behavior,* Citadel Press, New York.

Westermarck, E. A. (1889). *The History of Human Marriage I–III,* Allerton Press, New York.

Wolf, A. P. (1966). Childhood association, sexual attraction, and the incest taboo: A Chinese case. *Amer. Anthropologist* **68:** 883–898.

Wolf, A. P. (1968). Adopt a daughter-in-law, marry a sister: A Chinese solution to the problem of the incest taboo. *Amer. Anthropologist* **70:** 864–874.

Wolf, A. P. (1970). Childhood association and sexual attraction: A further test of the Westermarck hypothesis. *Amer. Anthropologist* **72:** 503–515.

Evolution, Traits, and the Stages of Human Courtship

Qualifying the Parental Investment Model

DOUGLAS T. KENRICK, EDWARD K. SADALLA,
GARY GROTH, AND MELANIE R. TROST

Individual differences are explicitly connected to social interaction in Darwin's notion of sexual selection: Traits that increase the probability of successful reproduction will tend to increase in frequency. This process operates partly through differential choice, by one sex, of certain traits in the other. According to the parental investment model, females frequently have more stringent criteria for the traits they will accept in a mate because they have a relatively larger investment in each offspring. Because human mating arrangements often involve a substantial commitment of resources by the male, it is necessary to invoke a distinction between the selectivity involved during casual mating opportunities and the selectivity exercised when choosing a long-term partner. Ninety-three undergraduate men and women rated their minimum criteria on 24 partner characteristics at four levels of commitment. In line with an unqualified parental investment model, females were more selective overall, particularly on status-linked variables. In line with a qualified parental investment model, males' trait preferences depended upon the anticipated investment in the relationship. Males had lower requirements for a sexual partner than did females, but were nearly as selective as females when considering requirements for a long-term partner.

One hears much talk these days about the need for a rapprochement between personality and social psychology (e.g., Blass, 1984; Kenrick, 1986). The December 1987 issue of the *Journal of Personality and Social Psychology* was dedicated to articles integrating the two areas. When the two subdisciplines were emerging at the turn of the century, both were influenced by the same intellectual tradition—Darwinian evolutionary theory. Sigmund Freud, whom many regard as the originator of the modern field of personality, took his ideas about life instincts and the primal horde directly from Darwin. The first psychology text with the title *Social Psychology,* written in 1908 by William McDougall, took an even more explicitly Darwinian approach.

This common birthplace may be the ideal ground for a reunion between personality and social psychology. We have argued elsewhere that a biosocial model can

From D. T. Kenrick, E. K. Sadalla, G. Groth, and M. R. Trost, "Evolution, traits, and the stages of human courtship: Qualifying the parental investment model," *Journal of Personality, 58* (1990): 97–117. Reprinted with permission of Blackwell Publishing.

connect the proximate processes of social cognition and social learning with the ultimate framework of sociobiology (Kenrick, 1987; Kenrick, Montello, & MacFarlane, 1985). We have also argued that there are two areas where this framework is particularly relevant: (*a*) in explaining gender differences in personality and social behavior (Kenrick, 1987); and (*b*) in explaining how those gender differences are intimately connected to different mating strategies (Kenrick & Trost, 1987, 1989; Sadalla, Kenrick, & Vershure, 1987). In this article, we discuss research that uses an evolutionary perspective to connect gender differences in personality to the social-psychological process of mate selection.

SEXUAL SELECTION

From its inception, Darwinian theory assumed an intimate association between social processes and gender differences in traits. Darwin connected the two via the process of *sexual selection,* first discussed in *The Origin of Species:*

> ... I believe, that when the males and females of any animal have the same general habits of life, but differ in structure, colour, or ornament, such differences have been mainly caused by sexual selection: that is, by individual males having had, in successive generations, some slight advantage over other males, in their weapons, means of defence, or charms, which they have transmitted to their male offspring alone. (Darwin, 1859/1958, p. 95)

In humans, individual differences in "charms" are more likely to be expressed in social behavior than in physical ornaments like antlers. Given that humans interact with familiar others over long time periods, human traits related to social dominance may be at least as important as physical weapons of defense are to other animals. Darwin further divided sexual selection into *intrasexual selection,* which results from competition between members of the same sex, and *epigamic selection,* which results from the fact that the members of one sex make choices about which members of the opposite sex they prefer to mate with:

> The rock-thrush of Guiana, birds of paradise, and some others, congregate; and successive males display with the most elaborate care, and show off in the best manner, their gorgeous plumage: they likewise perform strange antics before the females, which standing by as spectators, at last choose the most attractive partner. (Darwin, 1859/1958, p. 94)

The fact that males and females across the spectrum of human cultures differ reliably in certain personality traits (Williams & Best, 1982) may be due, in part, to sexual selection. It is assumed that our male and female ancestors fancied slightly different traits in one another. Presumably males were chosen for traits related to dominance and social status which signaled their capacity to contribute external resources to offspring. Because of their special mammalian abilities to contribute direct biological resources to potential offspring, females were chosen for traits signaling reproductive value and potential nurturance toward offspring (Buss & Barnes, 1986). Traits such as male dominance and female nurturance may have their evolutionary roots in natural selection (tangible advantages are conferred on individuals who manifest such behavior), intrasexual selection (males who compete effectively with other males have more access to both resources and mates), and epigamic selection (individuals engaging in such behavior are more desirable as mating partners).

DIFFERENTIAL PARENTAL INVESTMENT BY MALES AND FEMALES

Darwin saw sexual selection as more relevant to males' than to females' characteristics. He believed that males are more likely to compete amongst themselves for access to females, and that females are more likely to exercise selectivity in their choice of mates. Modern evolutionary theorists follow Darwin in assuming that females are choosier about a mate's traits than are males. This difference is generally explained in terms of *differential parental investment* (Trivers, 1972; Williams, 1966). Parental investment is typically defined (e.g., Trivers, 1985) as the contributions a parent makes to one offspring's reproductive success at a cost to its own ability to invest in other offspring. In mammals, females typically make a greater investment in each offspring because the female carries the fetus, nurses the infant, and is, compared with the male, limited in the number of offspring she can produce. Because of their different levels of investment in each offspring, females and males should engage in different mating strategies. Females should attempt to maximize the viability and reproductive potential of each offspring, while males should attempt to maximize the number of offspring. In terms of the criteria for a sexual partner, females should be more selective. Males, conversely, are presumed to have less to lose from an ill-chosen mating.

The human sexuality literature provides ample evidence to suggest that humans fit the typical mammalian pattern of differential parental investment, with greater consequent female selectivity (Daly & Wilson, 1983). Men are generally more eager and less discriminating with regard to sexuality (Hinde, 1984; Kenrick & Trost, 1987, 1989; Symons 1979). For instance, Kenrick, Stringfield, Wagenhals, Dahl, and Ransdell (1980) found men more likely to volunteer for experiments on erotica than were women, and there is abundant evidence that men seek more experience with erotica outside the laboratory (Kinsey, Pomeroy, & Martin, 1948; Kinsey, Pomeroy, Martin, & Gebhard, 1953; Shepher & Reisman, 1985). Likewise, men are overrepresented in virtually every category of sexual deviation (Davison & Neale, 1982).

We applied the differential parental investment model to humans in a series of studies on dominance and heterosexual attraction (Sadalla et al., 1987). In line with the above discussion, the model predicts that females will be attracted to males who show characteristics associated with social dominance. Males, who have less to lose from an ill-chosen mating, should be less discriminating about those characteristics in potential female partners. In support of the model, we found that males who expressed nonverbal dominance were, compared with less dominant males, rated as more sexually attractive by female subjects. Male subjects did not discriminate between dominant and nondominant female targets, but rated both as equally attractive. The effect was robust, appearing in four studies with three distinct manipulations of dominance. Sadalla and Fausal (1980) replicated the pattern across several different age samples of employees at a local manufacturing plant, and Buss (1989) found that characteristics related to dominance and social status were associated with male attractiveness across a wide range of different cultures.

PAIR BONDING INCREASES MALE PARENTAL INVESTMENT

The parental investment model implies that the sex investing more (most commonly the female) will be most choosy; whereas the sex investing least (most commonly the male) should be most competitive. Compared to most mammalian species, however, human males make a substantial parental investment in their progeny. In our own society there is a well-established pattern of parental bonding. Approximately 95% of all Americans get married at least once, and Daly and Wilson (1983) note that there is some form of marriage in every known society. While the specific details of courtship vary within and across cultures, mate bonding is a universal feature of human society. It is important to keep in mind that high male parental investment in humans contrasts with most other mammalian species.

For the above reasons, one must take care in applying ideas about differential parental investment from other mammals (in which low-investing males are often indiscriminate in mate choice) to humans (in which males may be quite discriminating). Consider a study by Buss and Barnes (1986). These authors asked students to rank the characteristics they preferred in a mate and found some sex differences. Females ranked "earning potential" and "college graduate" higher than did males, whereas males ranked physical attractiveness higher than did females. Those gender differences are consistent with an evolutionary model: Males have historically contributed indirect resources (like food and protection) to the offspring, which increase with education and socioeconomic status, whereas females have contributed direct physical resources via gestation and nurturing. Since physical attractiveness judgments are partially dependent on a female's youthfulness, those judgments correlate with her remaining reproductive potential (Buss & Barnes, 1986; Kenrick & Keefe, 1989; Symons, 1979). The most relevant feature of Buss and Barnes's data, however, is the striking similarity between male and female preferences. Of the top 10 preferences, 7 were the same for the two sexes. Consistent with our discussion above, Buss and Barnes note that gender differences in mate criteria are diminished in monogamous species.

What accounts for the fact that Sadalla et al. (1987) found strong sex differences supporting an unqualified parental investment model, whereas Buss and Barnes found fewer sex differences? Symons (1979) suggests that it is necessary to distinguish between sex differences in *typical* parental investment, and sex differences in *minimum possible* parental investment. Humans are like other mammals in that a male's minimum possible parental investment is very small, but different from other mammals in that a male's typical parental investment is very large.

QUALIFYING THE PARENTAL INVESTMENT MODEL

The distinction between typical and minimum possible parental investment may allow us to specify the circumstances under which humans will show the strong gender differences found in most other mammals, and distinguish those from the circumstances under which humans will show the lack of gender differences found in many monogamous species. Note that Sadalla et al. (1987) focused on the sexual attractiveness of a stranger. Sexual liaisons between strangers have the potential for very low investment by males, and these authors found sex differences similar to those found in other mammalian species. Buss and Barnes, on the other hand, examined the characteristics desired in a long-term mate (associated with high parental investment by both sexes), and they found many gender similarities. The difference between these studies suggests a central qualification on the parental investment model in its application to human courtship. In line with a *relationship-qualified parental investment model,* we hypothesize that anticipated investment in the relationship is a crucial moderator of the variations in gender differences found in earlier studies.

In the present study, we examine the degree to which preferences in a partner are associated with the level of anticipated investment in the relationship. At the level of casual dating, there is relatively little investment by either sex, so few male/female differences in selectivity should be observed. As the relationship moves to the level of sexual involvement, potential female investment increases greatly, so a corresponding increase in female selectivity would be predicted. Since sexual involvement does not involve a similar increase in investment for males, no concomitant increase in male selectivity would be expected at that level. At the level of exclusive dating, investment increases substantially for males and should be accompanied by parallel increases in selectivity. At the marriage level, both males and females make sizable investments, so both sexes should be highly selective.

A second difference between the Sadalla et al. (1987) and the Buss and Barnes (1986) studies also suggests a limiting condition on when gender differences do and do not occur. Sadalla et al. examined only dominance-related characteristics, whereas Buss and Barnes examined a wide range of characteristics. In line with the earlier findings, and with the classical Darwinian view that females preferentially mate with males who show signals that indicate their relative dominance over other males, we expect that characteristics related to dominance will be differentially valued by the two sexes.

METHOD

Subjects

Ninety-three undergraduate students (29 males, 64 females) participated in the study during class time. Participation was voluntary and students were given extra course credit.

Procedure

Students were asked to consider the criteria that they would use in choosing a partner for involvement in (*a*) a single date, (*b*) sexual relations (*c*) steady dating, and (*d*) marriage. For each level of involvement, they were asked to rate the importance of 24 criteria. Thirteen of these criteria were from Buss and Barnes (1986, Study 2): kind and understanding, religious, exciting personality, creative and artistic, good housekeeper, intelligent, good earning capacity, wants children, easygoing, good heredity, college graduate, physically attractive, and healthy. Eleven additional descriptors were also added: aggressive, emotionally stable, friendly, popular, powerful, sexy, wealthy, ambitious, good sense of humor, high social status, and dominant. Participants were asked to give the minimum and maximum percentiles of each characteristic that they would find acceptable in a partner at each level of involvement. Several examples were given to clarify any questions about the percentile concept, e.g., "A person at the 50th percentile would be above 50% of other people on kind and understanding, and below 49% of the people on this dimension." For ease of description, subjects were simply told to use 100 to indicate someone who was above the rest of the population, and 0 to indicate someone below the rest of the population.

RESULTS

The minimum acceptable criteria are of most relevance to our present hypotheses.[1] Using gender as a between-subjects factor, and level of involvement as a within-subjects factor, we conducted a repeated measures analysis of variance using the MANOVA approach (O'Brien & Kaiser, 1985) on an aggregate composed of the mean minimum values (averaged across all dependent variables). In line with the general parental investment hypothesis, this analysis indicated that females were generally more selective, $F(1, 86) = 10.99, p < .001$. Consistent with the qualified parental investment hypothesis, there was also a significant interaction of Gender × Level of Involvement, $F(3, 84) = 5.57, p < .002$. As shown in Table 1, the data supported the expectation that gender differences would be most pronounced at the level of sexual relations. Females showed a steady increase in criteria, whereas males' criteria did not increase between the level of date and sexual relations, but paralleled the female pattern after that. There was also a main effect of level of involvement, $F(3, 84) = 80.0, p < .001$. As shown in Table 1, the main effect is accounted for by the general increase in criteria with increasing level of involvement (qualified by the interaction discussed above).

Fine-Grained Analyses

Given that earlier findings have indicated that males and females select one another based on different criteria, it was of interest to examine the individual variables. Univariate analyses indicated significant Gender × Level of Involvement interactions on 11 of the variables: intelligent, friendly, kind, exciting, healthy, easygoing, creative, emotionally stable, sense of humor, college graduate, and social status. In line with the overall analysis, the general tendency on these variables was for gender differences to be strongest at the level of sexual relations. Figure 1 presents the results for intelligence.

As shown in Figure 1, males were actually willing to accept a slightly lower standard for intelligence in a sexual partner than in a date. The analysis of variance for the intelligence variable was $F(3, 90) = 44.2, p < .001$, for level of involvement; $F < 1$ for gender; and $F(3, 90) = 7.3, p < .01$, for the interaction. (F values for simple gender comparisons at each level of involvement will be presented in more detail below.)

TABLE 1   Aggregate Minimum Value for Each Sex at Each Level of Involvement

Sex of Subject	Involvement Level			
	Date	*Sexual Relations*	*Date Exclusively*	*Marry*
Female	39.1	45.6	52.7	56.9
Male	35.0	35.1	45.1	48.9

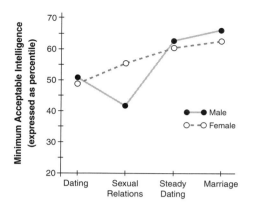

FIGURE 1 Minimum Acceptable Values of Intelligence at Each Level of Involvement

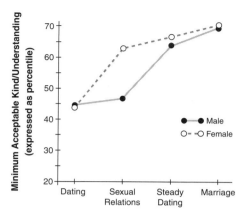

FIGURE 2 Minimum Acceptable Values of "Kind and Understanding" at Each Level of Involvement

For several of the other variables showing an interaction, males failed to increase their demands from the dating level to the sexual relations level. Figure 2 shows the results for the variable "kind and understanding." The analysis of variance for this variable yielded $F(3, 90) = 73.4$, $p < .001$, for level of involvement, $F(1, 92) = 2.4$, *ns* for gender, and $F(3, 90) = 9.6$, $p < .01$, for the interaction. Once again, the figure (and detailed analyses we present below) indicates that the largest sex differences are found at the level of sexual relations.

For 13 of the variables, females were more selective at all levels of involvement. Figure 3 shows the results for "earning capacity." Note again that males and females differ most at the level of sexual relations. However, these data show a main effect of subject sex, $F(1, 90) = 44.52$, $p < .001$, that is somewhat larger than the interaction, $F(3, 88) = 2.4$, *ns*. Once again there was a main effect of level of involvement, $F(3, 88) = 31.22$, $p < .001$. Variations in denominator degrees of freedom for univariate analyses are due to some subjects' failure to complete all items.

In addition to earning capacity, females also were generally more selective for the following variables: powerful, wealthy, high social status, dominant, ambitious, popular, wants children, good heredity, good housekeeper, religious, and emotionally stable. The only reversal of this tendency occurred for physical attractiveness. In fact, males were more selective about physical attractiveness at every level of involvement, but only significantly so at the level of marriage, $F(1, 92) = 3.99$, $p < .05$. Figure 4 plots the results for this variable.

Factor Analysis

In order to empirically organize any further examination of the 24 separate variables, we performed a principal components analysis using the average score for each variable across all levels of involvement (with varimax rotation to orthogonal factors). The factor structure is displayed in Table 2.

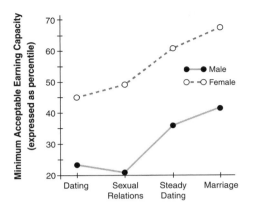

FIGURE 3 Minimum Acceptable Earning Capacity at Each Level of Involvement

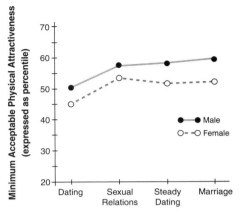

FIGURE 4 Minimum Acceptable Physical Attractiveness at Each Level of Involvement

Analyses of variance were performed on composite scores (derived by averaging scores across all variables within each of the five factors). Table 3 plots the means for each of those composite scores (bold face) along with results for each of the constituent variables (listed below each composite). As indicated, the different factors resulted in different patterns of results. For the aggregate status (I) variable (Table 3, Row 1), for instance, the analysis for main effect of gender, $F(1, 86) = 18.5, p < .001$, indicated a larger effect than did the analysis for a Gender × Level of Involvement interaction, $F(3, 84) = 3.8, p < .05$. (The F value for involvement level was $F[3, 84] = 45.7, p < .001$.) An examination of the mean values for variables listed under the status (I) factor in Table 3 indicates that females generally have higher status requirements than do males at each level of involvement. For variables related to attractiveness (II) and friendliness (III), on the other hand, significant gender effects occurred mainly at the level of sexual relations. Variables related to health (IV) and family orientation (V) also showed relatively greater gender differences at the level of sexual relations.

As indicated in Table 3, minimum standards for a mate tended to increase for both sexes as the level of involvement increased. From these analyses, it appears that two things account for most of the sex differences. First, the gender difference tends to occur at the level of sexual relations regardless of the factor being considered. Second, the variables related to status show a sex difference regardless of the level of involvement being considered. The importance of these two distinctions was shown in a final analysis. We repeated the initial aggregate analysis of variance, removing the level of sexual relations, and including all variables *except* those related to status. Although this analysis left a significant effect of level of involvement, $F(2, 88) = 125.04, p < .001$, it indicated neither a main effect of gender, $F(1, 89 = 1.78, ns,$ nor a Gender × Level of Involvement interaction, $F(2, 88) = 1.31, ns.$ Thus, by removing the effects of status variables and the sexual relations level, gender differences in selectivity were erased.

TABLE 2   Orthogonal Factor Structure from Factor Analysis of All Dependent Variables

Factor I: Status		*Factor III: Friendliness*	
Powerful	.88	Sense of humor	.83
Status	.86	Friendliness	.72
Popular	.82	Easygoing	.55
Wealthy	.78		
Good heredity	.72	*Factor IV: Health*	
Earning capacity	.63	Emotionally stable	.69
Dominance	.62	Healthy	.63
Good housekeeper	.57		
College degree	.56	*Factor V: Family Orientation*	
		Wants children	.75
Factor II: Attractiveness		Religious	.64
Attractiveness	.80	Kind and understanding	.54
Intelligence	.69		
Sexy	.64		
Exciting	.60		
Creative	.53		

Note. Only variables having loadings > .50 are shown.

DISCUSSION

In general, the results of the present study supported the modified parental investment model. We found larger gender differences in trait requirements for a sexual partner than for a partner at other levels of courtship. At the level of a single date, neither sex is highly invested, whereas at the level of serious commitment, both sexes are highly invested. When considering sexual relations, however, females risk a much larger investment than males do, and are consequently more demanding about a partner's characteristics at this level of involvement.

Studies of nonhuman species support the value of a distinction between low and high levels of relationship commitment. Monogamous species typically have lengthy courtship periods, during which both members of the pair appraise one another (Barash, 1977). Polygynous species, on the other hand, have very brief courtships in which multiple females mate with males who are demonstrably superior to their competitors (as indicated by dominance rankings and/or physical characteristics).

Regarding particular traits, we found support for the hypothesis that the sexes would differ most on criteria related to status and dominance. This follows the typical mammalian pattern, in which a female selects a dominant male who, even if he contributes few direct resources, will contribute desirable genes. Our findings on the particular variables replicated the findings of both Buss and Barnes (1986) and Sadalla et al. (1987). In line with Buss and Barnes's results, males were generally more selective regarding physical attractiveness, whereas females were more selective regarding traits related to resource allocation. In line with Sadalla et al., dominance was also found to be more important to women as a minimum criterion for mate selection. At the same time, these results extend those earlier findings and put them in a larger interactional context.

TABLE 3   Gender Comparison by Level: Means and Significance Levels for Factors and Individual Variables

	Sex	Date	Sexual Relations	Date Exclusively	Marry
I. Status	F	**33.84**	**38.25**	**47.89**	**52.27**
	M	**24.09**	**23.35**	**33.27**	**36.24**
		***	***	***	***
1. Powerful	F	33.38	34.63	42.12	44.80
	M	21.15	20.07	26.67	28.15
		**	**	***	***
2. High social status	F	32.23	35.98	43.80	47.57
	M	26.50	24.58	32.85	34.00
		ns	**	*	**
3. Popular	F	37.45	38.85	42.65	44.49
	M	28.11	26.67	34.78	34.22
		*	**	*ns*	**
4. Wealthy	F	34.38	36.08	44.95	48.94
	M	22.48	19.04	30.33	33.67
		**	***	***	**
5. Good heredity	F	30.82	41.46	52.80	58.63
	M	22.29	26.37	38.48	44.04
		ns	**	**	**
6. Good earning capacity	F	44.58	49.01	61.08	67.17
	M	23.79	19.93	36.86	42.21
		***	***	***	***
7. Dominant	F	30.80	38.02	41.75	43.03
	M	28.20	30.04	35.80	36.00
		ns	*ns*	*ns*	*ns*
8. Good housekeeper	F	24.77	31.58	46.11	53.35
	M	21.93	21.07	38.25	45.43
		ns	*	*ns*	*ns*
9. College graduate	F	37.31	40.34	59.12	66.82
	M	24.79	21.29	31.89	37.71
		*	***	***	***
II. Attractiveness	F	**43.97**	**53.55**	**56.32**	**60.61**
	M	**46.05**	**47.65**	**57.83**	**60.99**
		ns	*ns*	*ns*	*ns*
1. Physically attractive	F	45.45	54.98	51.59	52.73
	M	50.18	57.14	57.57	59.96
		ns	*ns*	*ns*	*
2. Intelligent	F	49.39	55.23	62.88	66.36
	M	50.93	43.21	63.21	67.32
		ns	**	*ns*	*ns*
3. Sexy	F	43.17	57.25	56.46	58.69
	M	44.07	53.52	54.44	56.69
		ns	*ns*	*ns*	*ns*

(continued)

TABLE 3 Continued

	Sex	Date	Sexual Relations	Date Exclusively	Marry
4. Exciting personality	F	42.03	54.52	59.06	70.26
	M	46.25	46.61	62.68	67.14
		ns	*ns*	*ns*	*ns*
5. Creative	F	38.94	45.45	51.36	54.77
	M	39.32	37.43	52.68	57.68
		ns	*ns*	*ns*	*ns*
III. Friendliness	F	**49.14**	**52.13**	**59.73**	**62.42**
	M	**46.07**	**43.23**	**54.95**	**59.08**
		ns	**	*ns*	*ns*
1. Good sense of humor	F	52.37	53.83	62.49	64.37
	M	52.59	46.29	59.07	61.67
		ns	*	*ns*	*ns*
2. Friendly	F	55.23	58.85	63.08	64.92
	M	47.32	48.86	58.57	66.43
		*	**	*ns*	*ns*
3. Easygoing	F	44.09	48.56	54.47	57.12
	M	44.46	38.79	53.21	55.04
		ns	**	*ns*	*ns*
4. Ambitious	F	43.95	47.05	58.64	63.26
	M	39.26	38.52	49.63	54.26
		ns	*	**	**
IV. Health	F	**50.52**	**60.81**	**64.96**	**67.85**
	M	**46.71**	**48.93**	**57.50**	**62.36**
		ns	***	**	*ns*
1. Emotionally stable	F	52.57	60.00	67.23	70.62
	M	43.07	43.39	56.61	62.32
		**	***	***	*
2. Healthy	F	47.88	61.44	62.50	64.85
	M	50.36	54.46	58.39	62.39
		ns	*ns*	*ns*	*ns*
V. Family orientation	F	**31.32**	**41.29**	**50.94**	**57.75**
	M	**28.11**	**28.24**	**42.07**	**49.68**
		ns	***	**	*
1. Wants children	F	21.12	27.15	45.03	55.48
	M	16.43	17.14	31.04	43.82
		ns	*ns*	*	*ns*
2. Religious	F	27.31	32.94	40.03	45.71
	M	22.54	19.71	30.14	34.00
		ns	*	*ns*	*ns*
3. Kind and understanding	F	45.29	63.32	67.41	71.71
	M	45.36	47.86	65.04	71.21
		ns	***	*ns*	*ns*

	Sex	Date	Sexual Relations	Date Exclusively	Marry
VI. Aggressiveness	F	**26.12**	**31.40**	**33.63**	**35.77**
	M	**28.50**	**30.61**	**34.86**	**36.82**
		ns	*ns*	*ns*	*ns*
Average of all variables	F	**39.09**	**45.60**	**52.71**	**56.89**
	M	**35.00**	**35.06**	**45.09**	**48.87**
		ns	***	***	**

Note. The means for each main factor (indicated by Roman numerals) are presented in bold face. Below each main factor, we present the means for each variable that constituted a given factor (numbered with Arabic numerals within a given factor). Significance levels refer to comparisons of male and female means within a given level of involvement.
*$p < .05$
**$p < .01$
***$p < .001$.

CONNECTING PERSONALITY WITH SOCIAL PSYCHOLOGY

Our decision to examine sex differences in mate criteria at the different stages of relationships was instigated by our involvement with social-psychological models of relationship formation (Kenrick & Trost, 1987, 1989). Social-psychological models commonly distinguish between different levels of involvement in a relationship, and this distinction is crucial to understanding how the parental investment model should be qualified when applied to humans. Social-psychological approaches to relationships, however, have two important limitations. First they have almost completely ignored the crucial importance of reproduction in heterosexual relationships. Social psychologists have instead focused on immediate cognitive variables and explained relationships in terms of unexamined assumptions about cultural norms. We have argued elsewhere (Kenrick, 1987; Kenrick & Trost, 1987, 1989) that such a focus has led to difficulties in explaining a number of findings, including: (*a*) gender differences in courtship that are inconsistent with a cultural model; (*b*) cross-cultural universalities in human mating patterns (e.g., Buss, 1989); and (*c*) hormonal influences on human courtship. An evolutionary perspective can address these findings and can also incorporate the proximate findings from social-psychological studies into the most powerful explanatory theory in the life sciences.

An evolutionary perspective can also connect the social-psychological enterprise with research on personality assessment. A central postulate of Darwinian theory is that there is an inherent connection between individual differences and reproduction. Other theorists have pointed out that by attending to the central dimensions of personality, our ancestors may have improved their chances of survival (Goldberg, 1981; Hogan, 1982). To survive in a hominid group, it may well have been essential for our progenitors to recognize dominance, agreeableness, conscientiousness, emotional stability, and intellect in other group members (Goldberg, 1981). However, survival is only the first half of evolutionary success. Reproduction, the primary payoff for survival, is the other half. From the biosocial view, we are sensitive to personality traits partly because those traits reflect adaptive characteristics of potential mates. To mate carelessly after successful survival would be like squandering a hard-earned life savings.

ENDNOTE

1. Since the criteria were generally positive characteristics, analyses of maximum acceptable levels resulted in ceiling effects. From an evolutionary perspective, the interesting differences will show up in the minimum criteria people are willing to settle for (Symons. 1979), not in the maximum benefits they are willing to accept.

REFERENCES

Barash, D. P. (1977). *Sociobiology and behavior.* New York: Elsevier.

Blass, T. (1984). Social psychology and personality: Toward a convergence. *Journal of Personality and Social Psychology, 47*, 1304–1309.

Buss, D. M. (1989). Sex differences in human mate preferences: Evolutionary hypothesis tested in 37 cultures. *Behavioral and Brain Sciences, 12*, 1–49.

Buss, D. M., & Barnes, M. (1986). Preferences in human mate selection. *Journal of Personality and Social Psychology, 50*, 559–570.

Daly, M. & Wilson, M. (1983). *Sex, evolution, and behavior* (2nd ed.). Boston: Willard Grant Press.

Darwin, C. (1958). *The origin of species* (6th ed.). New York: New American Library. (Original work published 1859)

Davison, G. C., & Neale, J. M. (1982). *Abnormal psychology* (3rd ed.). New York: Wiley.

Goldberg, L. R. (1981). Language and individual differences: The search for universals in personality lexicons. In L. Wheeler (Ed.), *Personality and social psychology review* (Vol. 2, pp. 141–165). Beverly Hills: Sage.

Hinde, R. A. (1984). Why do the sexes behave differently in close relationships? *Journal of Social and Personal Relationships, 1*, 471–501.

Hogan, R. (1982). A socioanalytic theory of personality. In M. Page (Ed.), *Nebraska symposium on motivation* (pp. 55–89). Lincoln: University of Nebraska Press.

Kenrick, D. T. (1986). How strong is the case against contemporary social and personality psychology? A response to Carlson. *Journal of Personalia and Social Psychology, 50*, 839–844.

Kenrick, D. T. (1987). Gender, genes, and the social environment: A biosocial interactionist perspective. In P. Shaver & C. Hendrick (Eds.), *Review of personality and social psychology: Sex and gender* (Vol. 7, pp. 14–43). Newbury Park, CA: Sage.

Kenrick, D. T., & Keefe, R. C. (1989). Time to integrate sociobiology and social psychology. *Behavioral and Brain Sciences, 12*, 24–25.

Kenrick, D. T., Montello, D., & MacFarlane, S. (1985). Personality: Social learning, social cognition, or sociobiology? In R. Hogan & W. Jones (Eds.), *Perspectives in personality* (Vol. 1, pp. 201–234). Greenwich, CT: JAI Press.

Kenrick, D. T., Stringfield, D. O., Wagenhals, W. L., Dahl, R. H., & Ransdell, H. J. (1980). Sex differences, androgyny, and approach responses to erotica: A new variation on the old volunteer problem. *Journal of Personality and Social Psychology, 38*, 517–524.

Kenrick, D. T., & Trost, M. R. (1987). A biosocial theory of heterosexual relationships. In K. Kelley (Ed.), *Females, males, and sexuality: Theories and research* (pp. 59–100). Albany: State University of New York Press.

Kenrick, D. T., & Trost, M. R. (1989). Reproductive exchange model of heterosexual relationships: Putting proximate economics in ultimate perspective. In C. Hendrick (Ed.), *Review of personality and social psychology* (Vol. 10, pp. 92–118). Newbury Park, CA: Sage.

Kinsey, A. C., Pomeroy, W. B., & Martin, C. E. (1948). *Sexual behavior in the human male.* Philadelphia: Saunders.

Kinsey, A. C., Pomeroy, W. B., Martin, C. E., & Gebhard, P. H. (1953). *Sexual behavior in the human female.* Philadelphia: Saunders.

McDougall, W. (1908). *Social psychology: An introduction.* London: Methuen.

O'Brien, G., & Kaiser, M. K. (1985). MANOVA method for analyzing repeated measures designs: An extensive primer. *Psychological Bulletin, 97*, 316–333.

Sadalla, E. K., & Fausal, M. (1980). *Dominance and heterosexual attraction: A field study.* Unpublished manuscript, Arizona State University.

Sadalla, E. K., Kenrick, D. T., & Vershure, B. (1987). Dominance and heterosexual attraction. *Journal of Personality and Social Psychology, 52*, 730–738.

Shepher, J., & Reisman, J. (1985). Pornography: A sociobiological attempt at understanding. *Ethology and Sociobiology, 6*, 103–114.

Symons, D. (1979). *The evolution of human sexuality.* New York: Oxford University Press.

Trivers, R. L. (1972). Parental investment and sexual selection. In B. Campbell (Ed.), *Sexual selection and the descent of man* (pp. 136–179). Chicago: Aldine.

Trivers, R. (1985). *Social evolution.* Menio Park, CA: Benjamin/Cummings.

Williams, G. C. (1966). Natural selection, the costs of reproduction, and a refinement of Lack's principle. *American Naturalist, 100*, 687–690.

Williams, J. E., & Best, D. L. (1982). *Measuring sex stereotypes.* Beverly Hills: Sage.

Sociosexuality and Romantic Partner Choice

JEFFRY A. SIMPSON AND STEVEN W. GANGESTAD

In three studies, we explored how individual differences in sociosexual orientation systematically relate to the types of attributes people prefer in romantic partners. In Investigation 1, individuals rated the importance of 15 partner attributes. Two factors emerged: personal/parenting qualities and attractiveness/social visibility. Individuals who possessed a restricted sociosexual orientation rated attributes that loaded highly on the former factor as being more important than those that loaded highly on the second one, whereas the reverse was true for unrestricted individuals. In Investigation 2, individuals evaluated two prospective romantic partners, one who was described as highly attractive and socially visible but less desirable in terms of personal/parenting qualities and one who had the opposite set of attributes. Unrestricted individuals tended to select the former partner, whereas restricted individuals chose the latter one. Investigation 3 examined the attributes actually possessed by their romantic partners. Unrestricted individuals were dating partners who were more socially visible and attractive, whereas restricted individuals were dating partners who were more responsible, faithful/loyal, and affectionate. Results are discussed in terms of an evolutionary model that links sociosexuality to mate selection.

P ast research on mate preference can be classified into three areas of study: consensually desired attributes; attributes on which men and women place differential emphasis; and attributes that certain kinds of people find differentially attractive. Research examining consensually preferred characteristics has revealed that most individuals desire partners who are physically attractive (Buss & Barnes, 1986; Green, Buchanan, & Heuer, 1984; Walster, Aronson, Abrahams, & Rottmann, 1966), possess attitudes, values, and beliefs similar to their own (Byrne, 1971; Hill, Rubin, & Peplau, 1976), and have pleasant personality characterstics (Buss & Barnes, 1986; Kaplan & Anderson, 1973). These findings have been qualified by research on sex differences, which has shown that men tend to place greater emphasis on physical attractiveness, whereas women tend to stress personal characteristics such as kindness, considerateness, and earning capacity (Buss, 1989; Buss & Barnes, 1986; Hill, 1945; Hudson & Henze, 1969; McGinnis, 1958).

Given that men and women should have differed in level of parental investment in offspring during evolutionary history (Trivers, 1972), evolutionary theorists (e.g., Buss, 1985; Kenrick & Trost, 1987; Symons, 1979; Wilson, 1978) have suggested that

From J. A. Simpson and S. W. Gangestad, "Sociosexuality and romantic partner choice," *Journal of Personality*, 60 (1992): 31–51. Reprinted with permission of Blackwell Publishing.

these sex differences may reflect different reproductive strategies. Specifically, males in our ancestral past should have been selected to be more sexually permissive and to prefer mates who possessed attributes presumably indicative of youth and high fertility/reproductive value (e.g., physical attractiveness; see Buss, 1989). Females, on the other hand, should have been selected to be less permissive (demanding considerable paternal investment prior to mating) and to desire mates who possessed abundant resources and/or offered evidence of high paternal investment.

Considerably less theoretical and empirical attention has been devoted to studying *within-sex* individual differences underlying romantic partner preference (for an exception, see Buss & Barnes, 1986). This is surprising for several reasons. First, even though certain characteristics tend to be consensually valued, individuals exhibit substantial variability in the specific attributes they find most and least important when choosing a romantic partner. Second, since most people do not have the kind of attributes necessary to attract a partner who possesses the entire array of consensually desired attributes, individuals typically must place greater importance on some attributes than others. And third, for any given attribute (e.g., physical attractiveness), the variability in responses which exists within the sexes typically is larger than that which exists between them (see Buss & Barnes, 1986).

What individual difference dimension might serve as a good candidate for exploring individual differences in romantic partner preference? One strong candidate is suggested by the newly developed theoretical model (Gangestad & Simpson, 1990a, 1990b; Simpson & Gangestad, 1991a) and measure (Simpson & Gangestad, 1991b) of sociosexuality. Sociosexuality refers to individual differences in willingness to engage in sexual relations without closeness, commitment, and other indicators of emotional bonding. Individuals who have demonstrated an *unrestricted sociosexual orientation* tend to engage in sex in the absence of such indicators, whereas those who have demonstrated a *restricted sociosexual orientation* typically do not.

The origins of mate preference can be considered at proximal as well as distal levels of explanation. Proximal accounts focus on more immediate, contemporaneous influences on behavior (e.g., current or recent environmental influences). Distal explanations seek to understand behavior in terms of events that may have transpired in our more distant past (e.g., evolutionary pressures). Focusing on possible distal influences, Gangestad and Simpson (1990a, 1990b) have proposed that individual differences in sociosexuality may reflect evolutionarily selected alternate sexual strategies (i.e., reproductive orientations that, in past evolutionary environments, enhanced inclusive fitness). At least three features of a mate should influence an individual's inclusive fitness: (*a*) a mate's ability or willingness to invest in one's offspring; (*b*) the extent to which a mate possesses either adaptive traits *or* resources that could be passed on to offspring (either genetically or socially) to enhance their fitness; and (*c*) for males who invest heavily in offspring, a mate's sexual exclusivity (see Trivers, 1972). During evolutionary history, all three features probably were difficult to obtain in a single mate (Buss, 1985). Therefore, individuals could have enhanced their inclusive fitness by preferentially focusing on one feature.

According to this perspective, some women may have come to prefer romantic partners who were willing to invest in their offspring, as revealed by the partner's pronounced faithfulness and proficient caregiving qualities. Other women may have preferred partners who possessed characteristics associated with fitness in our evolutionary past, particularly those that could be genetically or culturally transmitted to their offspring. Although it is not clear precisely what these characteristics were, physical attractiveness (an attribute that might have possessed additive genetic variance associated with fitness in the past; Hamilton & Zuk, 1982) and dominance/social status (Sadalla, Kenrick, & Vershure, 1987) are two viable candidates.

These patterns of mate choice should covary with female sociosexuality. Women who choose mates based on males' willingness to invest in offspring should require relatively greater evidence of paternal investment (and, therefore, more time) before engaging in sex. By definition, such women ought to exhibit a restricted sociosexual orientation. Women who choose mates according to attributes historically associated with male fitness (e.g., attractiveness), however, should require less time to evaluate these features. Consequently, they ought to adopt an unrestricted sociosexual orientation.

Males in evolutionary history who invested heavily in a mate's offspring should have desired long-term partners who demonstrated sexual exclusivity to the relationship, as revealed by resolute faithfulness and commitment. Conversely, men who did not invest exclusively should have preferred partners who possessed attributes associated with better fitness, such as greater physical attractiveness and/or social status. As with women, these choice patterns also should correlate with sociosexuality. Those men who invested exclusively in offspring should have required greater time to demonstrate and evaluate exclusivity to long-term relationships, thereby adopting a restricted sociosexual orientation. On the other hand, men who did not invest exclusively should have exhibited an unrestricted orientation.

Speculations based on evolutionary considerations concern behaviors shaped by and functional in past evolutionary environments (Symons, 1979; Tooby & Cosmides, 1990). Current environments may depart substantially from past ones. For example, while sex and reproduction were inextricably linked with one another during evolutionary history, they are not as closely associated today. Although behavioral propensities shaped in past environments no longer may be relevant to and functional in the current environment, the effects of such propensities still may be witnessed in certain forms of social behavior, particularly behavior pertaining to mate selection (Buss, 1985, 1989).

In view of contemporary social sanctions against sex outside of long-term, committed relationships (e.g., marriages), we examined our evolutionary speculations within premarital romantic relationships across three investigations.[1]

INVESTIGATION 1
METHOD

Participants

Two hundred and twenty-one male and 252 female Texas A&M University undergraduates participated for course credit in introductory psychology.

Procedure

Participants completed an anonymous questionnaire survey in large, same-sex groups. Two indices were embedded in the survey: the Romantic Partner Attribute Index and the Sociosexual Orientation Inventory (SOI). Once participants completed the survey, they were thanked and debriefed.

Measures

Romantic Partner Attribute Index. This index was composed of 15 attributes (listed in Table 1), all of which have been used in previous research (e.g., Buss & Barnes, 1986; Hill, 1945; McGinnis, 1958). Participants rated each attribute from 1 (not at all important) to 9 (extremely important) according to how much it influenced their selection of a romantic partner.

Sociosexual Orientation Inventory. Sociosexual orientation was assessed by the SOI, which consists of five self-report indices (Simpson & Gangestad, 1991b): (*a*) number of different sex partners in the past year; (*b*) number of different sex partners foreseen in the next five years; (*c*) number of times having engaged in sex with someone on one and only one occasion; (*d*) frequency of sexual fantasy involving partners other than the current one (responded to on an 8-point scale, where 1 = never and 8 = at least once a day); and (*e*) three aggregated items tapping attitudes toward engaging in casual, uncommitted sex (e.g., "I can imagine myself being comfortable and enjoying casual sex with different partners"; answered on 9-point scales, where 1 = strongly disagree and 9 = strongly agree). The five indices were standardized (through z-score transformation) separately for men and women and then aggregated (Cronbach α = .74). Higher scores indicate an unrestricted sociosexual orientation.

The SOI has been validated against both Q data (self-reports) and L data (independent reports provided by current romantic partners; Simpson & Gangestad, 1991b). Convergent validation evidence indicates that unrestricted individuals, relative to restricted ones, typically engage in sex earlier in their dating relationships, require less love, investment, commitment, and emotional bonding prior to engaging in sex, and are more likely to engage in concurrent sexual affairs. Discriminant validation evidence reveals that sociosexuality does not correlate highly with sex drive, sexual satisfaction, sex-related anxiety, or sex-related guilt. The SOI correlates approximately .40 with gender, with men typically scoring higher than women.

RESULTS AND DISCUSSION

Past research has shown that men and women emphasize different attributes when evaluating romantic partners (e.g., Buss & Barnes, 1986; Hudson & Henze, 1969). Thus, we first correlated biological sex (coded 1 if male, 0 if female) with each of the 15 attributes. In accord with previous findings, men rated physical attractiveness, $r(219) = .26$, and sex appeal, $r(219) = .18$, higher than did women. Women rated kindness and understanding, $r(250) = -.31$, financial resources, $r(250) = -.23$, responsibility, $r(250) = -.29$, similarity of values, $r(250) = -.23$, faithfulness and loyalty, $r(250) = -.25$, fun and exciting personality, $r(250) = -.17$, and stability of personality, $r(250) =$

−.15, higher than did men. Because we primarily were concerned with examining *within-sex* variation on these attributes, all subsequent analyses were conducted separately on men and women.

To determine whether one or more global dimensions might underlie participants' ratings on the 15 attributes, we first subjected these ratings to principal axis factor analyses (SPSSX PA2) in which communalities were iterated within the subsamples of men and women. Based on eigenvalue scree (Cattell, 1966) and factor interpretability, two factors accounting for over 40% of the variance were extracted in each subsample and rotated according to varimax criteria. Factor loadings are presented in Table 1.

Seven attributes loaded highly (.35 or greater within both subsamples) on the first factor, which we label *personal/parenting qualities:* qualities of a good parent, responsibility, kindness and understanding, sense of humor, stability of personality, similar values and beliefs, and faithfulness/loyalty. Four attributes loaded highly on the second factor, which we label *attractiveness/social visibility:* physical attractiveness, sex appeal, financial resources, and social status. Tucker's (1951) coefficient of factor congruence revealed that men and women had very similar loadings on the two factors (Tucker's coefficient = .96 and .97 for the two factors, respectively).

Factor scores were computed for both factors by summing the 11 respective factor score coefficients (one for each attribute) associated with each factor (see Harman, 1976). Both factors were then correlated with the SOI within each sex. For both men and women, the SOI correlated significantly with the personal/parenting qualities factor, $rs = -.21$ and $-.24$, respectively, $ps < .01$. Furthermore, within both sexes, the SOI correlated significantly with the attractiveness/social visibility factor, $rs = .43$ and .16

TABLE 1   Factor Loadings for the 15 Romantic Partner Attributes

Variable	Females		Males	
	Factor 1	*Factor 2*	*Factor 1*	*Factor 2*
Kindness and understanding	.53	−.09	.65	−.09
Faithfulness and loyalty	.40	−.13	.46	.10
Stable personality	.47	.20	.52	.10
Responsibility	.60	.03	.69	−.10
Sense of humor	.41	.25	.61	.10
Similar values and beliefs	.53	.07	.35	.06
Qualities of a good parent	.73	.10	.64	.03
Sex appeal	−.03	.59	.14	.68
Physical attractiveness	−.15	.73	.07	.59
Social status	.09	.56	.11	.51
Financial resources	.00	.62	−.15	.55
Fun and exciting personality	.31	.35	.43	.13
Desire for children	.46	.06	.28	.05
Quality of health	.28	.42	.37	.33
Intelligence	.32	.33	.32	.27

Note. $N = 252$ females and 221 males. For both sexes, Factor 1 corresponds to personal/parenting qualities; Factor 2 corresponds to attractiveness/social status.

respectively, $ps < .001$ and .05. As predicted, unrestricted individuals rated attributes pertaining to attractiveness and social visibility as relatively more important than did restricted individuals, whereas restricted individuals rated attributes dealing with personal/parenting qualities as more important than did unrestricted ones.

As reported in Table 2, correlations between the SOI and individual attributes revealed that most of the seven attributes which loaded on the personal/parenting qualities factor were reliably associated with the SOI within each sex. All four attributes loading on the attractiveness/social visibility factor significantly correlated with the SOI among men. Among women, two attributes carried the overall effect for the attractiveness/social visibility factor: physical attractiveness and sex appeal. That is, unrestricted females, relative to restricted ones, did not indicate a stronger preference for men possessing higher social status or greater financial resources. These results suggest that unrestricted women may place greater emphasis on potentially adaptive traits than partner resources when choosing romantic partners, at least during the college years.[2]

INVESTIGATION 2

Based on these preliminary findings, we next developed two vignettes. The first vignette depicted a potential romantic partner who possessed attributes that loaded highly on the attractiveness/social visibility factor as well as attributes that were the

TABLE 2   Correlations between Individuals' Sociosexual Orientation and Self-Rated Attributes

Attribute	Females	Males
Physical attractiveness	.18**	.36***
Social status	−.01	.16*
Kindness and understanding	−.17*	−.16*
Faithfulness and loyalty	−.16*	−.12+
Financial resources	.06	.19**
Responsibility	−.07	−.19**
Fun and exciting personality	−.10	.12+
Sense of humor	−.12+	−.03
Similar values and beliefs	−.26***	−.16*
Intelligence	.05	.10
Qualities of a good parent	−.18**	−.20**
Sex appeal	.22***	.43***
Stable personality	−.15*	−.01
Desire for children	−.17*	−.12+
Quality of health	.04	.10

Note. Ns = 252 females and 221 males. All tests are two-tailed.
$+p < .10$
$*p < .05$
$**p < .01$
$***p < .001$.

opposite of those that loaded highly on the personal/parenting factor. The second vignette described a potential partner who possessed the reverse pattern of attributes. Restricted and unrestricted individuals were asked to indicate which partner (*a*) most closely resembled their most recent one; (*b*) represented the type of individual they ideally would prefer to date; and (*c*) was most attractive to them. We hypothesized that unrestricted individuals would be more likely to select the romantic partner represented in the first vignette, while restricted individuals would choose the partner represented in the second.

METHOD

Participants

One hundred and ninety-eight male and 200 female Texas A&M University undergraduates participated for course credit in introductory psychology.

Procedure

Participants were recruited to complete a questionnaire survey in which the SOI was embedded. A purportedly ancillary part of the survey involved reading and evaluating two vignettes. The first vignette depicted a potential romantic partner who exhibited attributes that defined the attractiveness/social visibility factor as well as the *opposite* of those that characterized the personal/parenting factor:

> *Description/Person A:* Person A is considered physically attractive and "sexy." He/she has a sort of charisma that attracts the attention of those around him/her. Although some might consider him/her arrogant, A possesses a kind of self-confidence that others admire. A is not known, however, for living a responsible life-style. In the past, he/she has had a series of relatively short-term relationships. Some have ended because of questionable faithfulness on the part of A.

The second vignette described a potential partner who displayed the opposite set of attributes:

> *Description/Person B:* Person B is an average-looking person, someone most people wouldn't consider "sexy." He/she is sufficiently socially skilled but does not possess the kind of magnetic personality that draws the attention of others. Rather, B has a stable and responsible personality. In a relationship, B is caring, dependable, and faithful. He/she would like very much to have a family, likes children, and would probably be good with them.

After reading both vignettes, participants responded to three dependent measures: (*a*) "Which of these two descriptions is more similar to the sort of person you are currently involved with (or have been involved with in the past)?" (*b*) "Which of these descriptions represents the sort of person you would ideally prefer (either now or in the future) to be involved with?" and (*c*) "Which of the persons just described (Person A or Person B) do you typically find yourself attracted to, regardless of what kind of person you believe is best for you?" Participants were then thanked and debriefed.

RESULTS AND DISCUSSION

To determine whether restricted and unrestricted individuals expressed a differential preference for one of the two prospective romantic partners, we constructed an index reflecting the total number of choices allotted to each vignette. For each dependent measure, choice of the first vignette was coded as 1 and choice of the second was coded as 0. Participants' answers to all three dependent measures were aggregated to form a global partner choice index. We then conducted a hierarchical regression analysis, treating the partner choice index as the criterion measure and participants' gender, sociosexuality, and their interaction as predictors (entered in this order). This order of entry was chosen for two reasons. First, we wanted to partial out the effects of gender from scores on the SOI. Second, we needed to partial out main effects associated with gender and sociosexuality prior to testing for their interaction (see Cohen & Cohen, 1983).

Gender was not reliably associated with scores on this index, $\beta = .07$, $t < 1.5$, ns. However, after controlling for the effects of gender, the SOI was associated with scores on this index, $\beta = -.30$, $t = -6.43$, $p < .001$. Unrestricted individuals, relative to restricted ones, allotted a significantly larger number of their total choices to the attractive, charismatic, less dependable partner, whereas restricted individuals, compared to unrestricted ones, allotted a reliably larger number of their choices to the less attractive, less charismatic, more dependable one. A reliable Gender × SOI interaction did not emerge, $\beta = -.07$, $t < 1$, ns.[3]

INVESTIGATION 3

Investigation 3 examined the attributes actually possessed by the romantic partners of restricted and unrestricted individuals. Based on the results of Investigations 1 and 2, we identified three attributes that broadly tapped the personal/parenting factor (faithfulness/loyalty, kindness/understanding, and responsibility) and three that tapped the attractiveness/social visibility factor (social visibility, physical attractiveness, and sex appeal).[4] Faithfulness/loyalty was assessed by an index that measured partners' expectations of remaining in or leaving the current relationship (see Kelley, 1983). Kindness/understanding was indexed by Rubin's Love Scale (Rubin, 1970), given that the amount of kindness, understanding, and affection one displays toward one's partner should be reflected in higher scores on this index (Rubin, 1973). Responsibility was tapped by Zuckerman's Disinhibition Scale (Zuckerman, 1971) in view of the fact that disinhibited persons are known to behave in less dependable ways than inhibited ones (Zuckerman, 1983). Social visibility was tapped by Eysenck's Introversion/Extraversion Scale (S. G. B. Eysenck & H. J. Eysenck, 1975) since extraverts tend to be more socially visible than introverts (see H. J. Eysenck, 1967).[5] Physical and sexual attractiveness were assessed by ratings made by three independent observers.

We hypothesized that unrestricted individuals, relative to restricted ones, would be dating partners who (a) did not expect the relationship to last; (b) possessed lower scores (indicative of less love for the partner) on Rubin's Love Scale; (c) possessed higher scores (indicative of greater disinhibition) on Zuckerman's Disinhibition Scale; (d) possessed higher scores (indicative of greater extraversion) on Eysenck's

Introversion/Extraversion Scale; and (*e*) were more physically and sexually attractive, as rated by independent judges.

Factors other than sociosexuality could generate these hypothesized effects. Two alternate explanations seem most viable. First, these effects might stem from assortative dating/mating processes whereby individuals are attracted to similar others independent of their standing on sociosexuality. Unrestricted individuals, for instance, may value attractiveness because they themselves are more attractive. Second, individual differences in general risk tolerance or harm avoidance might underlie these effects. If restricted individuals are more inclined to avoid risky or potentially threatening situations, whereas unrestricted individuals are more disposed to seek them out, these different inclinations might explain their contrasting patterns of romantic partner preferences. To address these alternate interpretations, we conducted partial correlations controlling for these potential confounds.

METHOD

Participants

Ninety-seven dating couples (97 men and 97 women), all of whom were Texas A&M University undergraduates, participated for course credit.

Procedure

Couples reported to a large experimental room in groups of 10 to 20. Upon arrival, the experimenter distributed number-coded questionnaire packets to each couple so that partners could respond anonymously yet both could be later identified as a couple for data analysis. The experimenter physically separated couples to ensure that partners could not communicate during the study. Participants then completed the questionnaire survey. As they returned their questionnaire packet, three raters, blind to who was dating whom, unobtrusively rated them on measures of physical and sexual attractiveness. When participants left the room, they were debriefed.

Measures

Participants completed the SOI, Rubin's Love Scale, Eysenck's extraversion measure (the EPQ; S. B. G. Eysenck & H. J. Eysenck, 1975), the Disinhibition Scale, and the MPQ Harm Avoidance Scale (Tellegen, 1982). They also responded to a three-item index that assessed the likelihood their current relationship would endure over time (e.g., "What is the likelihood that you will be dating your current dating partner 1 year from now?"). All three items were answered on 7-point Likert-type scales (where 1 = very low likelihood and 7 = very high likelihood) and aggregated to form a single index (Cronbach $\alpha = .90$).

Participants then rated their partner on 33 attributes that tap the 11 traits underlying the MPQ (Tellegen & Waller, in press). Three attributes assessed their partner's level of harm avoidance: safety-conscious, thrill-seeking (reverse keyed), and adventurous (reverse keyed). All attributes were rated on 5-point Likert-type scales and aggregated.

As participants returned their packets, three independent observers rated them according to their physical and sexual attractiveness. Evaluations were made on two 7-point scales, where 1 = very unattractive and 7 = very attractive. Raters' evaluations for each item were then aggregated, resulting in a three-item physical attractiveness index and a three-item sexual attractiveness index. Because the two indices were highly correlated ($rs = .72$ and $.80$ for females and males, respectively), they were combined to form a global index of physical/sexual attractiveness (Cronbach α's = .68 and .78 for ratings of females and males across the three judges, respectively).

RESULTS AND DISCUSSION

To perform an overall test of our predictions, we first transformed the five attributes into z scores separately for each sex. Each attribute was keyed so that higher scores should have correlated positively with partner SOI. Following this, the five attributes were aggregated within each sex. We then correlated each male's SOI with his female partner's composite of the five attributes, and each female's SOI with her male partner's composite. As revealed in Table 3, each correlation was substantial, $rs = .40$ and $.46$, respectively, $ps < .001$. Follow-up analyses on individual attributes revealed that the SOI correlated significantly with all but two partner attributes (absolute rs ranged from .15 to .38 and averaged .25). The two nonsignificant correlations (between female SOI and male attractiveness and male extraversion) were marginally significant.

To ascertain whether these effects might be attributable to assortative dating or harm avoidance, partial correlations were performed. Specifically, we correlated each female's SOI with her male partner's composite, partialling out her self-reported standing on each attribute, her self-reported harm avoidance, and her harm avoidance as reported by her partner. We then conducted a parallel set of analyses for males. Results revealed that when each female's standing on these dimensions was partialled out, a significant relation between female SOI and the composite of her male partner's

TABLE 3   Correlation Analyses: Partner's Attributes Correlated with Sociosexual Orientation

Attribute	Male Partner Attributes with Female SOI	Female Partner Attributes with Male SOI
Composite	.46***	.40***
Disinhibition	.36***	.30**
Likelihood of Remaining in Relationship Index	−.38***	−.22*
Physical and Sexual Attractiveness Index	.15+	.26**
Extraversion	.15+	.17*
Love Scale	−.34***	−.18*

Note. N = 93 to 97. Tests on all effects are one-tailed. SOI = Sociosexual Orientation Inventory.
+$p < .10$
*$p < .05$
**$p < .01$
***$p < .001$.

attributes still emerged, partial $r = .30$, $p < .01$. Once the effects of each male's standing on all attributes were partialled out, a marginally significant relation emerged between male SOI and the composite of his female partner's attributes, partial $r = .15$, $p < .10$. Generally speaking, then, systematic differences in assortative mating and harm avoidance do not appear to account for these effects, particularly among women.

GENERAL DISCUSSION

These three investigations provide converging evidence that restricted and unrestricted individuals desire (Investigation 1), choose (Investigation 2), and actually acquire (Investigation 3) romantic partners who manifest different sets of attributes. Unrestricted individuals seek out romantic partners who are more physically and sexually attractive and who possess higher social visibility. Restricted individuals prefer romantic partners who are more kind/affectionate, responsible, and loyal/faithful.

One major issue that many researchers who adopt evolutionary perspectives have not addressed is how to account for *why* more variability typically exists within the sexes than between them on most mate choice attributes. To date, theoretical and empirical attention has been devoted mainly to examining sex differences in mate selection. Yet sex differences explain only a portion of the variance underlying mate preferences. Many of the sociosexuality effects reported in these studies, in fact, were larger than gender effects. Given the present findings, how might one arrive at a more comprehensive evolutionary understanding of mate selection phenomena?

Gangestad and Simpson (1990a, 1990b) have suggested that variation in both mate choice preferences and sociosexual orientation might exist for two reasons. First, intrasexual competition should have produced differential reproductive success. Individuals who were not successful at an "all else equal" preferred strategy may have reproduced more successfully by adopting an *alternate* one. Selection, therefore, could have generated more than one reproductive strategy within each sex. Second, paternal investment is not all a male can offer a female; he also can offer "good genes" (Trivers, 1972).

Consider first the case of females. All else being equal, females should have been selected to mate with males who (*a*) possessed adaptive attributes or resources that could have been transmitted—either genetically or socially—to their offspring (e.g., adaptive traits with additive genetic variance); and (*b*) invested heavily in their offspring. All else should not have been equal, however. Those males most sought after for their adaptive attributes could have afforded to invest less in any one female's offspring. Hence, males should have been selected to invest less exclusively when they possessed adaptive attributes or resources (Gangestad & Simpson, 1990a, 1990b; Simpson & Gangestad, 1991a). As a result, the genetic fitness of a male should have covaried negatively with his willingness to invest exclusively. Given these circumstances, both a female strategy geared toward mating with males who had high fitness (and, by default, relatively unrestricted sociosexuality) *and* a female strategy geared toward mating with males who would invest exclusively (and, therefore, who demonstrated relatively restricted sociosexuality) could have been maintained through frequency-dependent selection (see Gangestad & Simpson, 1990a, 1990b; Simpson & Gangestad, 1991a).

Now consider males. Certain males—most likely those who possessed either adaptive traits (e.g., physical attractiveness) or important resources that would confer a reproductive advantage to their offspring—may have been able to enact an unrestricted strategy more successfully than others. By possessing valued attributes and/or resources, these males may have been able to attract mates without having to grant high paternal investment (see Gangestad & Simpson, 1990a, 1990b; Simpson & Gangestad, 1991a). Such males, therefore, might have been selected to adopt an unrestricted sociosexual orientation and seek out attractive mates who, at the same time, did not require pronounced commitment, loyalty, and investment prior to mating. Males who did not possess adaptive traits or resources may have been unable to successfully compete for mates without granting paternal investment. Hence, selection pressures may have produced a mechanism whereby these males switched to a restricted sociosexual orientation, offering long-term investment, commitment, and loyalty to their romantic partners and expecting the same in return (see Gangestad & Simpson, 1990a, 1990b; Simpson & Gangestad, 1991a).

What characteristics should have been related to male fitness in past environments? Recent analyses suggest that physical attractiveness ought to have been one. Hamilton and Zuk (1982) have argued that attractive features should have been related to pathogen resistance during evolutionary history. Through host-parasite co-evolution, heritable differences in pathogen resistance (and, hence, male fitness) could have been maintained. Female choice based on male attractiveness, therefore, could have been selected for in view of the advantages it conferred to her offspring (Trivers, 1972).

According to our model, then, individual differences in male and female sociosexuality might reflect genetically influenced or ecologically contingent reproductive strategies that fostered inclusive fitness in *both* restricted and unrestricted individuals during evolutionary history (see Tooby & Cosmides, 1990). Needless to say, this model is speculative. Empirical evidence from several different sources, however, supports some of its major premises. First, as anticipated by the model, scores on the SOI are positively and significantly correlated within romantic dyads (Simpson & Gangestad, 1991b). Second, as revealed by ratings of independent observers in Investigation 3, unrestricted males are significantly more physically attractive than their restricted counterparts.

Perhaps the most compelling evidence, however, comes from a study examining offspring sex ratios (Gangestad & Simpson, 1990a). In evolutionary history, male and female offspring should have been of differential reproductive value to restricted and unrestricted females. Unrestricted females should have been selected to mate with attractive males whose evolutionarily adaptive characteristics would have been passed on to their own offspring. Sons, however, should have profited more by possessing these characteristics than daughters since men probably varied more than did women in total number of offspring produced during our evolutionary past (Alexander, Hoogland, Howard, Noonan, & Sherman, 1979; Clutton-Brock & Iason, 1986). As a result, unrestricted females should have been selected to have relatively more sons (Weatherhead & Robertson, 1979). Restricted females, on the other hand, should have been selected to have relatively more daughters because their sons would have been at a disadvantage competing with the reproductively successful sons of unrestricted females.

A new analysis of the original Kinsey data (Kinsey, Pomeroy, Martin, & Gebhard, 1953) has, in fact, revealed that the number of premarital sexual partners significantly predicts offspring sex ratio (see Gangestad & Simpson, 1990a). Women who have engaged in sex with a larger number of premarital partners tend to have more sons, relative to their more restricted counterparts. Conversely, women who have had fewer premarital partners are more likely to have daughters, compared to more unrestricted women.

Additional support for this evolutionary perspective is provided by the present findings. Both unrestricted men and women prefer partners who are attractive, while restricted men and women desire partners who are more likely to demonstrate exclusivity and investment. Although the results of Investigation 3 suggest that female preferences may have a stronger impact on actual behavior than male preferences, even this finding is consistent with an evolutionary account. Women tend to be the "choosier" sex in most mammalian species (Trivers, 1972). Hence, female preference patterns should exert more influence over actual mate choice outcomes than male preference patterns.

It might be suggested that individual differences in sociosexuality reflect differences in r- versus K-selected reproductive strategies (see Rushton, 1985; Kenrick & Trost, 1987). According to the r-K model, more promiscuous people have adopted an r-strategy characterized by early and plentiful reproduction coupled with less parental care for offspring. Less promiscuous people subscribe to a K-strategy in which reproduction is delayed and less frequent but greater parental care is provided. A variety of disparate physical and reproductive attributes purportedly differentiate these two strategies. For example, r-strategists should mature more rapidly, reproduce earlier, have more offspring, exhibit less parental care, have a shorter life span, be smaller in size, have higher metabolisms, and have higher rates of infant mortality (see Rushton, 1990). K-strategists should display the opposite tendencies.

The r-K model does share one major feature in common with ours: Both models suggest that restricted individuals—and particularly restricted women—may have been selected for gaining paternal investment. However, the two models differ in several critical respects. Our model does *not* predict that sociosexuality should covary with the entire constellation of physical and reproductive attributes presumed to underlie r- and K-strategies. Within our model, for instance, there is no reason to expect that restricted individuals, relative to unrestricted ones, should necessarily mature more slowly, reproduce later, have a longer life span, be larger in size, have lower metabolisms, produce less offspring, or have lower rates of infant mortality. In accord with this position, recent evidence indicates that unrestricted women reproduce neither earlier nor at a higher rate than do restricted ones (Gangestad & Simpson, 1990a). Moreover, neither unrestricted men nor women become sexually active at an earlier age than their restricted counterparts (Simpson & Gangestad, 1989).

The two models also differ with respect to what types of selection pressures might have generated unrestricted sociosexuality. The r-K model assumes that unrestricted sociosexuality was selected to promote early and plentiful reproduction as a result of prolonged exposure to variable or unstable environments. By contrast, our model suggests that—at least for women—unrestricted sociosexuality may have evolved to secure mates who possessed attributes or resources that would enhance the inclusive fitness of subsequent offspring, particularly sons. Moreover, both restricted and unrestricted sociosexuality could have emerged and been maintained by frequency-dependent selection (see Gangestad & Simpson, 1990a, 1990b). r-K theory does not address these novel aspects of our model.

Perspectives other than evolutionary ones, of course, may account for the mate choice patterns discovered in these investigations. Two important points, however, must be kept in mind. First, any explanation must account for the total pattern of evidence we have marshaled, including the offspring sex ratio findings. Second, if evolutionary forces have operated on *any* form of human social behavior, they should have operated on behaviors pertaining to sociosexuality and the patterns of mate preference that covary with it. Future research should examine this model in the context of committed marital relationships.

ENDNOTES

1. Among college students, attributes deemed important in dating partners and marital partners tend to be very similar within individuals (Simpson & Gangestad, 1988). Thus, even though these investigations focus on what kinds of attributes individuals seek in dating partners, they should be a fairly accurate reflection of what they look for in marital ones.

2. Additional analyses revealed reliable or marginally reliable sex differences in correlations between the SOI and four attributes—physical attractiveness ($z = 2.10$, $p < .05$), sex appeal ($z = 2.54$, $p < .05$), fun and exciting personality ($z = 2.38$, $p < .05$), and social status ($z = 1.84$, $p < .10$). Although physical attractiveness and sex appeal correlated reliably with sociosexuality for both men and women, the relations between these two attributes and sociosexuality were significantly stronger among males.

3. We also conducted three Probit analyses, one for each dichotomous dependent measure. Reliable effects for sociosexuality emerged on each dependent measure: "Which . . . description is more similar to the sort of person you are currently involved with . . . ?" ($\beta = -.19$, $t = -3.52$, $p < .001$); "Which . . . description represents the sort of person you would ideally prefer . . . ?" ($\beta = -.31$, $t = -5.95$, $p < .001$); and "Which of the persons . . . do you typically find yourself attracted to . . . ?" ($\beta = -.27$, $t = -5.13$, $p < .001$).

4. The attribute "qualities of a good parent" was not included for two reasons. First, it does not reflect a single attribute but rather a conglomeration of several different attributes. Second, some features of good parental qualities should be reflected in the three attributes chosen to assess the personal/parenting factor.

5. We used extraversion as a marker of social visibility because it is a widely used, highly reliable, and well-validated measure that assesses individual differences in social visibility (see Tellegen, 1982). Extraverted persons typically are the center of attention in social settings, often assuming roles (e.g., leadership) that heighten their social prominence and visibility (see H. J. Eysenck, 1967).

REFERENCES

Alexander, R. D., Hoogland, J. L., Howard, R. D., Noonan, K. M., & Sherman, P. W. (1979). Sexual dimorphisms and breeding systems in pinnipeds, ungulates, primates, and humans. In N. Chagnon & W. Irons (Eds.), *Evolutionary biology and human social behavior: An anthropological perspective* (pp. 402–435). North Scituate, MA: Duxbury.

Buss, D. M. (1985). Human mate selection. *American Scientist, 73*, 47–51.

Buss, D. M. (1989). Sex differences in human mate preferences: Evolutionary hypotheses tested in 37 cultures. *Behavioral and Brain Sciences, 12*, 1–14.

Buss, D. M., & Barnes, M. (1986). Preferences in human mate selection. *Journal of Personality and Social Psychology, 50*, 559–570.

Byrne, D. (1971). *The attraction paradigm*. New York: Academic Press.

Cattell, R. B. (1966). The scree test for the number of factors. *Multivariate Behavioral Research, 1*, 245–276.

Clutton-Brock, T. H., & Iason, G. R. (1986). Sex ratio variation in mammals. *Quarterly Review of Biology, 61*, 339–374.

Cohen, J., & Cohen, P. (1983). *Applied multiple regression/correlation analysis for the behavioral sciences*. Hillsdale, NJ: Lawrence Erlbaum.

Eysenck, H. J. (1967). *The biological basis of personality.* Springfield, IL: Thomas.

Eysenck, S. B. G., & Eysenck, H. J. (1975). *Manual of the Eysenck Personality Questionnaire.* London: Hodder & Stoughton.

Gangestad, S. W., & Simpson, J. A. (1990a). Toward an evolutionary history of female sociosexual variation. *Journal of Personality, 58,* 69–96.

Gangestad, S. W., & Simpson, J. A. (1990b). *On human sociosexual variation: An evolutionary model of mating propensities.* Manuscript submitted for publication.

Green, S. K., Buchanan, D. R., & Heuer, S. K. (1984). Winners, losers, and choosers: A field investigation of dating initiation. *Personality and Social Psychology Bulletin,* 10, 502–511.

Hamilton, W. D., & Zuk, M. (1982). Heritable true fitness and bright birds: A role for parasites. *Science,* 218, 384–387.

Harman, H. H. (1976). *Modern factor analysis* (3rd ed.). Chicago: University of Chicago Press.

Hill, C. T., Rubin, Z., & Peplau, L. A. (1976). Break-ups before marriage: The end of 103 affairs. *Journal of Social Issues, 32,* 147–167.

Hill, R. (1945). Campus values in mate selection. *Journal of Home Economics, 37,* 554–558.

Hudson, J. W., & Henze, L. P. (1969). Campus values in mate selection: A replication. *Journal of Marriage and the Family, 31,* 772–778.

Kaplan, M. R., & Anderson, N. H. (1973). Information integration theory and reinforcement theory as approaches to interpersonal attraction. *Journal of Personality and Social Psychology, 28,* 301–312.

Kelley, H. H. (1983). Love and commitment. In H. H. Kelley, E. Berscheid, A. Christensen, J. H. Harvey, T. L. Huston, G. Levinger, E. McClintock, L. A. Peplau, & D. R. Peterson (Eds.), *Close relationships* (pp. 265–314). San Francisco: Freeman.

Kenrick, D. T., & Trost, M. R. (1987). A biosocial theory of heterosexual relationships. In K. Kelley (Ed.), *Females, males, and sexuality: Theories and research* (pp. 59–100). Albany: SUNY Press.

Kinsey, A. C., Pomeroy, W. B., Martin, C. E., & Gebhard, P. H. (1953). *Sexual behavior in the human female.* Philadelphia: Saunders.

McGinnis, R. (1958). Campus values and mate selection. *Social Forces, 36,* 368–373.

Rubin, Z. (1970). Measurement of romantic love. *Journal of Personality and Social Psychology, 16,* 265–273.

Rubin, Z. (1973). *Liking and loving: An invitation to social psychology.* New York: Holt, Rinehart, & Winston.

Rushton, J. P. (1985). Differential K theory: The sociobiology of individual and group differences. *Personality and Individual Differences, 6,* 441–452.

Rushton, J. P. (1990). Sir Francis Galton, epigenetic rules, genetic similarity theory, and human life-history analysis. *Journal of Personality, 58,* 117–140.

Sadalla, E. K., Kenrick, D. T., & Vershure, B. (1987). Dominance and heterosexual attraction. *Journal of Personality and Social Psychology,* 52, 730–738.

Simpson, J. A., & Gangestad, S. W. (1988). [Date versus mate preferences]. Unpublished raw data, Texas A&M University.

Simpson, J. A., & Gangestad, S. W. (1989). [Correlates of sociosexuality]. Unpublished raw data, Texas A&M University.

Simpson, J. A., & Gangestad, S. W. (1991a). Personality and sexuality: Empirical relations and an integrative theoretical model. In K. McKinney & S. Sprecher (Eds.), *Sexuality in close relationships* (pp. 71–92). Hillsdale, NJ: Lawrence Erlbaum.

Simpson, J. A., & Gangestad, S. W. (1991b). Individual differences in sociosexuality: Evidence for convergent and discriminant validity. *Journal of Personality and Social Psychology, 60,* 870–883.

Symons, D. (1979). *The evolution of human sexuality.* New York: Oxford University Press.

Tellegen, A. (1982). *A short manual for the Differential Personality Questionnaire.* Unpublished manuscript, University of Minnesota.

Tellegen, A., & Waller, N. (in press). Exploring personality through test construction: Development of the Multidimensional Personality Questionnaire. In S.R. Briggs & J. M. Cheek (Eds.), *Personality measures: Development and evaluation* (Vol. 1). Greenwich, CT: JAI Press.

Tooby, J., & Cosmides, L. (1990). On the universality of human nature and the uniqueness of the individual: The role of genetics and adaptation. *Journal of Personality, 58,* 17–67.

Trivers, R. (1972). Parental investment and sexual selection. In B. Campbell (Ed.), *Sexual selection and the descent of man, 1871–1971* (pp. 136–179). Chicago: Aldine.

Tucker, L. R. (1951). A method for synthesis of factor analysis studies (Personnel Research Section Report No. 984). Washington, DC: Department of the Army.

Walster, E., Aronson, V., Abrahams, D., &Rottmann, L. (1966). Importance of physical attractiveness in dating behavior. *Journal of Personality and Social Psychology, 4,* 508–516.

Weatherhead, P. J., & Robertson, R. J. (1979). Offspring quality and the polygyny threshold: The "sexy son" hypothesis. *American Naturalist, 113,* 201–208.

Wilson, E. O. (1978). *On human nature.* Cambridge, MA: Harvard University Press.

Zuckerman, M. (1971). Dimensions of sensation seeking. *Journal of Consulting and Clinical Psychology, 36,* 45–52.

Zuckerman, M. (1983). A biological theory of sensation seeking. In M. Zuckerman (Ed.), *Biological bases of sensation seeking, impulsivity, and anxiety* (pp. 37–76). Hillsdale, NJ: Lawrence Erlbaum.

Sex Differences in Jealousy
Evolution, Physiology, and Psychology

DAVIS M. BUSS, RANDY J. LARSEN,
DREW WESTEN, AND JENNIFER SEMMELROTH

In species with internal female fertilization, males risk both lowered paternity proba-bility and investment in rival gametes if their mates have sexual contact with other males. Females of such species do not risk lowered maternity probability through partner infidelity, but they do risk the diversion of their mates' commitment and re-sources to rival females. Three studies tested the hypothesis that sex differences in jealousy emerged in humans as solutions to the respective adaptive problems faced by each sex. In Study 1, men and women selected which event would upset them more—a partner's sexual infidelity or emotional infidelity. Study 2 recorded physio-logical responses (heart rate, electrodermal response, corrugator supercilii contrac-tion) while subjects imagined separately the two types of partner infidelity. Study 3 tested the effect of being in a committed sexual relationship on the activation of jeal-ousy. All studies showed large sex differences, confirming hypothesized sex linkages in jealousy activation.

In species with internal female fertilization and gestation, features of reproduc-tive biology characteristic of all 4,000 species of mammals, including hu-mans, males face an adaptive problem not confronted by females—uncertainty in their paternity of offspring. Maternity probability in mammals rarely or never devi-ates from 100%. Compromises in paternity probability come at substantial reproduc-tive cost to the male—the loss of mating effort expended, including time, energy, risk, nuptial gifts, and mating opportunity costs. A cuckolded male also loses the female's parental effort, which becomes channeled to a competitor's gametes. The adaptive problem of paternity uncertainty is exacerbated in species in which males engage in some postzygotic parental investment (Trivers, 1972). Males risk investing resources in putative offspring that are genetically unrelated.

These multiple and severe reproductive costs should have imposed strong selec-tion pressure on males to defend against cuckoldry. Indeed, the literature is replete with examples of evolved anticuckoldry mechanisms in lions (Bertram, 1975), blue-birds (Power, 1975), doves (Erickson & Zenone, 1976), numerous insect species (Thornhill & Alcock, 1983), and nonhuman primates (Hrdy, 1979). Since humans ar-guably show more paternal investment than any other of the 200 species of primates (Alexander & Noonan, 1979), this selection pressure should have operated especially

From D. M. Buss, R. J. Larsen, D. Westen, and J. Semmelroth, "Sex differences in jealousy: Evolu-tion, physiology, and psychology," *Psychological Science, 3* (1992): 251–255. Reprinted with per-mission of Blackwell Publishing.

intensely on human males. Symons (1979); Daly, Wilson, and Weghorst (1982); and Wilson and Daly (in press) have hypothesized that male sexual jealousy evolved as a solution to this adaptive problem (but see Hupka, 1991, for an alternative view). Men who were indifferent to sexual contact between their mates and other men presumably experienced lower paternity certainty, greater investment in competitors' gametes, and lower reproductive success than did men who were motivated to attend to cues of infidelity and to act on those cues to increase paternity probability.

Although females do not risk maternity uncertainty, in species with biparental care they do risk the potential loss of time, resources, and commitment from a male if he deserts or channels investment to alternative mates (Buss, 1988; Thornhill & Alcock, 1983; Trivers, 1972). The redirection of a mate's investment to another female and her offspring is reproductively costly for a female, especially in environments where offspring suffer in survival and reproductive currencies without investment from both parents.

In human evolutionary history, there were likely to have been at least two situations in which a woman risked losing a man's investment. First, in a monogamous marriage, a woman risked having her mate invest in an alternative woman with whom he was having an affair (partial loss of investment) or risked his departure for an alternative woman (large or total loss of investment). Second, in polygynous marriages, a woman was at risk of having her mate invest to a larger degree in other wives and their offspring at the expense of his investment in her and her offspring. Following Buss (1988) and Mellon (1981), we hypothesize that cues to the development of a deep emotional attachment have been reliable leading indicators to women of potential reduction or loss of their mate's investment.

Jealousy is defined as an emotional "state that is aroused by a perceived threat to a valued relationship or position and motivates behavior aimed at countering the threat. Jealousy is 'sexual' if the valued relationship is sexual" (Daly et al., 1982, p. 11; see also Salovey, 1991; White & Mullen, 1989). It is reasonable to hypothesize that jealousy involves physiological reactions (autonomic arousal) to perceived threat and motivated action to reduce the threat, although this hypothesis has not been examined. Following Symons (1979) and Daly et al. (1982), our central hypothesis is that the events that activate jealousy physiologically and psychologically differ for men and women because of the different adaptive problems they have faced over human evolutionary history in mating contexts. Both sexes are hypothesized to be distressed over both sexual and emotional infidelity, and previous findings bear this out (Buss, 1989). However, these two kinds of infidelity should be weighted differently by men and women. Despite the importance of these hypothesized sex differences, no systematic scientific work has been directed toward verifying or falsifying their existence (but for suggestive data, see Francis, 1977; Teismann & Mosher, 1978; White & Mullen, 1989).

STUDY 1: SUBJECTIVE DISTRESS OVER A PARTNER'S EXTERNAL INVOLVEMENT

This study was designed to test the hypothesis that men and women differ in which form of infidelity—sexual versus emotional—triggers more upset and subjective distress, following the adaptive logic just described.

Method

After reporting age and sex, subjects (N = 202 undergraduate students) were presented with the following dilemma:

> Please think of a serious committed romantic relationship that you have had in the past, that you currently have, or that you would like to have. Imagine that you discover that the person with whom you've been seriously involved became interested in someone else. What would distress or upset you more (*please circle only one*):
>
> **(A) Imagining your partner forming a deep emotional attachment to that person.**
>
> **(B) Imagining your partner enjoying passionate sexual intercourse with that other person.**

Subjects completed additional questions, and then encountered the next dilemma, with the same instructional set, but followed by a different, but parallel, choice:

> **(A) Imagining your partner trying different sexual positions with that other person.**
>
> **(B) Imagining your partner falling in love with that other person.**

Results

Shown in Figure 1 (upper panel) are the percentages of men and women reporting more distress in response to sexual infidelity than emotional infidelity. The first empirical probe, contrasting distress over a partner's sexual involvement with distress over a partner's deep emotional attachment, yielded a large and highly significant sex difference (χ^2 = 47.56, df = 3, p < .001). Fully 60% of the male sample reported greater distress over their partner's potential sexual infidelity; in contrast, only 17% of the female sample chose that option, with 83% reporting that they would experience greater distress over a partner's emotional attachment to a rival.

This pattern was replicated with the contrast between sex and love. The magnitude of the sex difference was large, with 32% more men than women reporting greater distress over a partner's sexual involvement with someone else, and the majority of women reporting greater distress over a partner's falling in love with a rival (χ^2 = 59.20, df = 3, p < .001).

STUDY 2: PHYSIOLOGICAL RESPONSES TO
A PARTNER'S EXTERNAL INVOLVEMENT

Given the strong confirmation of jealousy sex linkage from Study 1, we sought next to test the hypotheses using physiological measures. Our central measures of autonomic arousal were electrodermal activity (EDA), assessed via skin conductance, and pulse rate (PR). Electrodermal activity and pulse rate are indicators of autonomic nervous system activation (Levenson, 1988). Because distress is an unpleasant subjective state, we also included a measure of muscle activity in the brow region of the face—electromyographic (EMG) activity of the *corrugator supercilii* muscle. This muscle is responsible for the furrowing of the brow often seen in facial displays of unpleasant

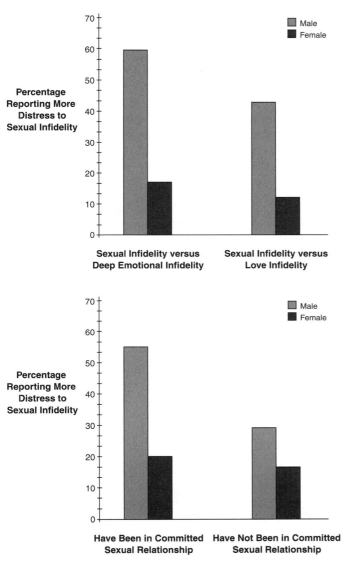

FIGURE 1 Reported comparisons of distress in response to imagining a partner's sexual or emotional infidelity. The upper panel shows results of Study 1—the percentage of subjects reporting more distress to the sexual infidelity scenario than to the emotional infidelity (left) and the love infidelity (right) scenarios. The lower panel shows the results of Study 3—the percentage of subjects reporting more distress to the sexual infidelity scenario than to the emotional infidelity scenario, presented separately for those who have experienced a committed sexual relationship (left) and those who have not experienced a committed sexual relationship (right).

emotion or affect (Fridlund, Ekman, & Oster, 1987). Subjects were asked to image two scenarios in which a partner became involved with someone else—one sexual intercourse scenario and one emotional attachment scenario. Physiological responses were recorded during the imagery trials.

Subjects

Subjects were 55 undergraduate students, 32 males and 23 females, each completing a 2-hr laboratory session.

Physiological Measures

Physiological activity was monitored on the running strip chart of a Grass Model 7D polygraph and digitized on a laboratory computer at a 10-Hz rate, following principles recommended in Cacioppo and Tassinary (1990).

Electrodermal Activity. Standard Beckman Ag/AgCl surface electrodes, filled with a .05 molar NaCl solution in a Unibase paste, were placed over the middle segments of the first and third fingers of the right hand. A Wheatstone bridge applied a 0.5-V voltage to one electrode.

Pulse Rate. A photoplethysmograph was attached to the subject's right thumb to monitor the pulse wave. The signal from this pulse transducer was fed into a Grass Model 7P4 cardiotachometer to detect the rising slope of each pulse wave, with the internal circuitry of the Schmitt trigger individually adjusted for each subject to output PR in beats per minute.

Electromyographic Activity. Bipolar EMG recordings were obtained over the *corrugator supercilii* muscle. The EMG signal was relayed to a wide-band AC-preamplifier (Grass Model 7P3), where it was band-pass filtered, full-wave rectified, and integrated with a time constant of 0.2 s.

Procedure

After electrode attachment, the subject was made comfortable in a reclining chair and asked to relax. After a 5-min waiting period, the experiment began. The subject was alone in the room during the imagery session, with an intercom on for verbal communication. The instructions for the imagery task were written on a form which the subject was requested to read and follow.

Each subject was instructed to engage in three separate images. The first image was designed to be emotionally neutral: "Imagine a time when you were walking to class, feeling neither good nor bad, just neutral." The subject was instructed to press a button when he or she had the image clearly in mind, and to sustain the image until the experimenter said to stop. The button triggered the computer to begin collecting physiological data for 20 s, after which the experimenter instructed the subject to "stop and relax."

The next two images were infidelity images, one sexual and one emotional. The order of presentation of these two images was counterbalanced. The instructions for sexual jealousy imagery were as follows: "Please think of a serious romantic relationship that you have had in the past, that you currently have, or that you would like to have. Now imagine that the person with whom you're seriously involved becomes interested in someone else. *Imagine you find out that your partner is having sexual intercourse with this other person.* Try to feel the feelings you would have if this happened to you."

The instructions for emotional infidelity imagery were identical to the above, except the italicized sentence was replaced with *"Imagine that your partner is falling in love and forming an emotional attachment to that person."* Physiological data were collected for 20 s following the subject's button press indicating that he or she had achieved the image. Subjects were told to "stop and relax" for 30 s between imagery trials.

Results

Physiological Scores. The following scores were obtained: (a) the amplitude of the largest EDA response occurring during each 20-s trial; (b) PR in beats per minute averaged over each 20-s trial; and (c) amplitude of EMG activity over the *corrugator supercilii* averaged over each 20-s trial. Difference scores were computed between the neutral imagery trial and the jealousy induction trials. Within-sex *t* tests revealed no effects for order of presentation of the sexual jealousy image, so data were collapsed over this factor.

Jealousy Induction Effects. Table 1 shows the mean scores for the physiological measures for men and women in each of the two imagery conditions. Differences in physiological responses to the two jealousy images were examined using paired-comparison *t* tests for each sex separately for EDA, PR, and EMG. The men showed significant increases in EDA during the sexual imagery compared with the emotional imagery ($t = 2.00$, $df = 29$, $p < .05$). Women showed significantly greater EDA to the emotional infidelity image than to the sexual infidelity image ($t = 2.42$, $df = 19$, $p < .05$). A similar pattern was observed with PR. Men showed a substantial increase in PR to both images, but significantly more so in response to the sexual infidelity image ($t = 2.29$, $df = 31$, $p < .05$). Women showed elevated PR to both images, but not

TABLE 1 Means and standard deviations on physiological measures during two imagery conditions

Measure	Imagery Type	Mean	*SD*
		Males	
EDA	Sexual	1.30	3.64
	Emotional	−0.11	0.76
Pulse rate	Sexual	4.76	7.80
	Emotional	3.00	5.24
Brow EMG	Sexual	6.75	32.96
	Emotional	1.16	6.60
		Females	
EDA	Sexual	−0.07	0.49
	Emotional	0.21	0.78
Pulse rate	Sexual	2.25	4.68
	Emotional	2.57	4.37
Brow EMG	Sexual	3.03	8.38
	Emotional	8.12	25.60

Note. Measures are expressed as changes from the neutral image condition. EDA is in microsiemen units, pulse rate is in beats per minute, and EMG is in microvolt units.

differentially so. The results of the *corrugator* EMG were similar, although less strong. Men showed greater brow contraction to the sexual infidelity image, and women showed the opposite pattern, although results with this nonautonomic measure did not reach significance ($t = 1.12$, $df = 30$, $p < .14$, for males; $t = -1.24$, $df = 22$, $p < .12$, for females). The elevated EMG contractions for both jealousy induction trials in both sexes support the hypothesis that the effect experienced is negative.

STUDY 3: CONTEXTS THAT ACTIVATE THE JEALOUSY MECHANISM

The goal of Study 3 was to replicate and extend the results of Studies 1 and 2 using a larger sample. Specifically, we sought to examine the effects of having been in a committed sexual relationship versus not having been in such a relationship on the activation of jealousy. We hypothesized that men who had actually experienced a committed sexual relationship would report greater subjective distress in response to the sexual infidelity imagery than would men who had not experienced a high-investing sexual relationship, and that women who had experienced a committed sexual relationship would report greater distress to the emotional infidelity image than women who had not been in a committed sexual relationship. The rationale was that direct experience of the relevant context during development may be necessary for the activation of the sex-linked weighting of jealousy activation.

Subjects

Subjects for Study 3 were 309 undergraduate students, 133 men and 176 women.

Procedure

Subjects read the following instructions:

> Please think of a serious or committed romantic relationship that you have had in the past, that you currently have, or that you would like to have. Imagine that you discover that the person with whom you've been seriously involved became interested in someone else. What would distress or upset you more (*please circle only one*):
>
> **(A) Imagining your partner falling in love and forming a deep emotional attachment to that person.**
>
> **(B) Imagining your partner having sexual intercourse with that other person.**

Alternatives were presented in standard forced-choice format, with the order counterbalanced across subjects. Following their responses, subjects were asked: "Have you ever been in a serious or committed romantic relationship? (yes or no)" and "If yes, was this a sexual relationship? (yes or no)."

Results

The results for the total sample replicate closely the results of Study 1. A much larger proportion of men (49%) than women (19%) reported that they would be more distressed by their partner's sexual involvement with someone else than by their partner's emotional attachment to, or love for, someone else ($\chi^2 = 38.48$, $df = 3$, $p < .001$).

The two pairs of columns in the bottom panel of Figure 1 show the results separately for those subjects who had experienced a committed sexual relationship in the past and those who had not. For women, the difference is small and not significant: Women reported that they would experience more distress about a partner's emotional infidelity than a partner's sexual infidelity, regardless of whether or not they had experienced a committed sexual relationship ($\chi^2 = 0.80$, $df = 1$, ns).

For men, the difference between those who had been in a sexual relationship and those who had not is large and highly significant. Whereas 55% of the men who had experienced committed sexual relationships reported that they would be more distressed by a partner's sexual than emotional infidelity, this figure drops to 29% for men who had never experienced a committed sexual relationship ($\chi^2 = 12.29$, $df = 1$, $p < .001$). Sexual jealousy in men apparently becomes increasingly activated upon experience of the relevant relationship.

DISCUSSION

The results of the three empirical studies support the hypothesized sex linkages in the activators of jealousy. Study 1 found large sex differences in reports of the subjective distress individuals would experience upon exposure to a partner's sexual infidelity versus emotional infidelity. Study 2 found a sex linkage in autonomic arousal to imagined sexual infidelity versus emotional infidelity; the results were particularly strong for the EDA and PR. Study 3 replicated the large sex differences in reported distress to sexual versus emotional infidelity, and found a strong effect for men of actually having experienced a committed sexual relationship.

These studies are limited in ways that call for additional research. First, they pertain to a single age group and culture. Future studies could explore the degree to which these sex differences transcend different cultures and age groups. Two clear evolutionary psychological predictions are (a) that male sexual jealousy and female commitment jealousy will be greater in cultures where males invest heavily in children, and (b) that male sexual jealousy will diminish as the age of the male's mate increases because her reproductive value decreases. Second, future studies could test the alternative hypotheses that the current findings reflect (a) domain-specific psychological adaptations to cuckoldry versus potential investment loss or (b) a more domain-general mechanism such that any thoughts of sex are more interesting, arousing, and perhaps disturbing to men whereas any thoughts of love are more interesting, arousing, and perhaps disturbing to women, and hence that such responses are not specific to jealousy or infidelity. Third, emotional and sexual infidelity are clearly correlated, albeit imperfectly, and a sizable percentage of men in Studies 1 and 3 reported greater distress to a partner's emotional infidelity. Emotional infidelity may signal sexual infidelity and vice versa, and hence both sexes should become distressed at both forms (see Buss, 1989). Future research could profitably explore in greater detail the correlation of these forms of infidelity as well as the sources of within-sex variation. Finally, the intriguing finding that men who have experienced a committed sexual relationship differ dramatically from those who have not, whereas for women such experiences appear to be irrelevant to their selection of emotional infidelity as the more distressing event, should be examined. Why do such ontogenetic experiences matter for men, and why do they appear to be irrelevant for women?

Within the constraints of the current studies, we can conclude that the sex differences found here generalize across both psychological and physiological methods—demonstrating an empirical robustness in the observed effect. The degree to which these sex-linked elicitors correspond to the hypothesized sex-linked adaptive problems lends support to the evolutionary psychological framework from which they were derived. Alternative theoretical frameworks, including those that invoke culture, social construction, deconstruction, arbitrary parental socialization, and structural powerlessness, undoubtedly could be molded post hoc to fit the findings—something perhaps true of any set of findings. None but the Symons (1979) and Daly et al. (1982) evolutionary psychological frameworks, however, generated the sex-differentiated predictions in advance and on the basis of sound evolutionary reasoning. The recent finding that male sexual jealousy is the leading cause of spouse battering and homicide across cultures worldwide (Daly & Wilson, 1988a, 1988b) offers suggestive evidence that these sex differences have large social import and may be species-wide.

REFERENCES

Alexander, R.D., & Noonan, K.M. (1979). Concealment of ovulation, parental care, and human social evolution. In N. Chagnon & W. Irons (Eds.), *Evolutionary biology and human social behavior* (pp. 436–453). North Scituate, MA: Duxbury.

Bertram, B.C.R. (1975). Social factors influencing reproduction in wild lions. *Journal of Zoology, 177*, 463–482.

Buss, D.M. (1988). From vigilance to violence: Tactics of mate retention. *Ethology and Sociobiology, 9*, 291–317.

Buss, D.M. (1989). Conflict between the sexes: Strategic interference and the evocation of anger and upset. *Journal of Personality and Social Psychology, 56*, 735–747.

Cacioppo, J.T., & Tassinary, L.G. (Eds.). (1990). *Principles of psychophysiology: Physical, social, and inferential elements.* Cambridge, England: Cambridge University Press.

Daly, M., & Wilson, M. (1988a). Evolutionary social psychology and family violence. *Science, 242*, 519–524.

Daly, M., & Wilson, M. (1988b). *Homicide.* Hawthorne, NY: Aldine.

Daly, M., Wilson, M. & Weghorst, S.J. (1982). Male sexual jealousy. *Ethology and Sociobiology, 3*, 11–27.

Erickson, C.J., & Zenone, P.G. (1976). Courtship differences in male ring doves: Avoidance of cuckoldry? *Science, 192*, 1353–1354.

Francis, J.L. (1977). Toward the management of heterosexual jealousy. *Journal of Marriage and Family Counseling, 10*, 61–69.

Fridlund, A., Ekman, P., & Oster, J. (1987). Facial expressions of emotion. In A. Siegman & S. Feldstein (Eds.), *Nonverbal behavior and communication* (pp. 143–224). Hillsdalc, NJ: Erlbaum.

Hrdy, S.B.G. (1979). Infanticide among animals: A review, classification, and examination of the implications for the reproductive strategies of females. *Ethology and Sociobiology, 1*, 14–40.

Hupka, R.B. (1991). The motive for the arousal of romantic jealousy: Its cultural origin. In P. Salovey (Ed.), *The psychology of jealousy and envy* (pp. 252–270). New York: Guilford Press.

Levenson, R.W. (1988). Emotion and the autonomic nervous system: A prospectus for research on autonomic specificity. In H. Wagner (Ed.), *Social psychophysiology: Theory and clinical applications* (pp. 17–42). London: Wiley.

Mellon, L.W. (1981). *The evolution of love.* San Francisco: W.H. Freeman.

Power, H.W. (1975). Mountain bluebirds: Experimental evidence against altruism. *Science, 189*, 142–143.

Salovey, P. (Ed.). (1991). *The psychology of jealousy and envy.* New York: Guilford Press.

Symons, D. (1979). *The evolution of human sexuality.* New York: Oxford University Press.

Teismann, M.W., & Mosher, D.L. (1978). Jealous conflict in dating couples. *Psychological Reports, 42*, 1211–1216.

Thornhill, R., & Alcock, J. (1983). *The evolution of insect mating systems.* Cambridge, MA: Harvard University Press.

Trivers, R. (1972). Parental investment and sexual selection. In B. Campbell (Ed.), *Sexual selection and the descent of man, 1871–1971* (pp. 136–179). Chicago: Aldine.

White, G.L., & Mullen, P.E. (1989). *Jealousy: Theory, research, and clinical strategies.* New York: Guilford Press.

Wilson, M., & Daly, M. (in press). The man who mistook his wife for a chattel. In J. Barkow, L. Cosmides, & J. Tooby (Eds.), *The adapted mind: Evolutionary psychology and the generation of culture.* New York: Oxford University Press.

Evolution and Social Cognition
Contrast Effects as a Function of Sex, Dominance, and Physical Attractiveness

DOUGLAS T. KENRICK, STEVEN L. NEUBERG,
KRISTIN L. ZIERK, AND JACQUELYN M. KRONES

Previous research indicates that males, compared with females, evaluate their rela-
tionships less favorably after exposure to physically attractive members of the other
sex. An evolutionary model predicts a converse effect after exposure to opposite-sex
individuals high in dominance, which should lead females to evaluate their current
relationships less favorably than males. Women and men rated their current relation-
ships after being exposed to opposite-sex targets varying in both dominance and
physical attractiveness. Consistent with earlier research, males exposed to physi-
cally attractive, as compared with average, targets rated their current relationships
less favorably. Males' relationship evaluations were not directly influenced by the
targets' dominance, although the effect of physical attractiveness was significant
only for men exposed to women low in dominance. However, females' evaluations of
their relationships were unaffected by exposure to physically attractive males but
were lower after exposure to targets high in dominance. These data support predic-
tions derived from an evolutionary model and suggest that such models can be used
to generate testable hypotheses about ongoing social cognition.

D oes exposure to attractive members of the other sex undermine satisfaction with a person's current relationship? The answer may depend on how one defines *attractive* and on whether the person in question is male or female. Research and theory arising from an evolutionary perspective suggest that exposure to a physically attractive woman might have a selective effect on men's judgments of their wives or girlfriends. In contrast, that same literature suggests that physical attractiveness will have less effect on women's judgments but that their judgments may be undermined by exposure to men who are highly dominant. We briefly review relevant theory and research below and then present a study examining the possibility of sex-differentiated contrast effects.

From D. T. Kenrick, S. L. Neuberg, K. L. Zierk, and J. M. Krones, "Evolution and social cognition: Contrast effects as a function of sex, dominance, and physical attractiveness," *Personality and Social Psychology Bulletin, 20,* pp. 210–217, copyright © 1994 by Sage Publications, Inc. Reprinted by Permission of Sage Publications, Inc.

SEX DIFFERENCES IN REPRODUCTIVE STRATEGIES

Evolutionary biologists have noted that animals vary widely in their reproductive patterns and that such variation is found within, as well as between, species (Daly & Wilson, 1983; Trivers, 1985). The most important division of reproductive strategy within a species is often related to sex. Darwin (1859) noted that, within a species, the two sexes might differ because of the process of *sexual selection*. As part of that process, the members of one sex mate differentially with members of the other sex who possess certain characteristics (such as the brilliant feathers of the male peacock). Presumably, the more an animal invests in the offspring, the more selective that animal will be about its partners (Trivers, 1972), because a careless choice is more costly.

As human males and females both invest heavily in their offspring, they will both be selective (Daly & Wilson, 1983; Kenrick & Keefe, 1992). However, males and females invest different resources and are therefore expected to value different characteristics in a mate (Kenrick, Groth, Trost, & Sadalla, 1993). Females invest relatively more direct physiological resources (contributing their own bodily nutrients to the fetus and nursing child), whereas males invest relatively more indirect resources (such as food, money, protection, and security). For this reason, females who are choosing mates are assumed to pay particular attention to a male's level of social dominance, which is presumably related to his ability to provide indirect resources. Males, in contrast, are assumed to pay special attention to signs of a female's apparent health and reproductive potential (Buss, 1989; Symons, 1979).

A number of researchers have found support for the assumption that women value men who show characteristics related to status or resource acquisition. For instance, Sadalla, Kenrick, and Vershure (1987) manipulated a target person's social dominance in several ways across several experiments. In each case, dominance enhanced a man's attractiveness to women but had no influence on a woman's attractiveness to men. In a similar vein, Buss (1989) found that a potential mate's social status was more important to women than to men across a number of cultures (see also Hill, 1984; Mealey, 1985; Turke & Betzig, 1985). Likewise, Kenrick, Sadalla, Groth, and Trost (1990) found that characteristics related to dominance were more central criteria in a woman's than in a man's choice of dates, sexual partners, and long-term mates. However, both Buss and Barnes (1986) and Kenrick et al. (1990) found that males valued a potential partner's physical attractiveness more highly than females. Several authors have suggested that physical attractiveness might be important to males as an indirect means of assessing age and physical condition (e.g., Buss & Barnes, 1986; Kenrick & Keefe, 1992; Symons, 1979), and there is some evidence supporting this reasoning (Cunningham, 1986; Mathes, Brennan, Haugen, & Rice, 1985). Presumably, age and physical condition are related to fertility (Kenrick & Keefe, 1992; Symons, 1979).

Females also report that physical attractiveness is important to them (Kenrick et al., 1993). However, it is important to note that females' and males' judgments of "attractiveness" are linked to different features. Females base their judgments on physical characteristics linked to dominance (such as a large jaw and a few day's growth of beard), not to the same complex of youthful prettiness and smooth skin that males find attractive in females (Cunningham, Barbee, & Pike, 1990; Keating, 1985). Further, when Townsend and Levy (1990) gave subjects a choice between photographically depicted males varying in physical attractiveness and clothing status, females were more interested in a high-status, low-attractiveness male than in a low-status, high-attractiveness male, whereas males showed the reverse pattern of preferences.

Findings such as these, it might be argued, could be explained in terms of theoretical models based on the sex role norms of American or Western society. The predictions tested in the following pages were *derived* from work done within an evolutionary framework but not intended to test the entire nexus of "evolutionary theory" against the idea that humans are socialized. For reasons we discuss below, however, we believe that there is abundant evidence suggesting the utility of considering the comparative and evolutionary bases of gender differences in human mating behavior. In sum, evolutionary theorists assume that human females will select males on the basis of their position in a dominance hierarchy. Human males are also expected to be selective but to choose females on the basis of physical attractiveness. Extrapolating from these findings, a woman's satisfaction in a relationship with a man might be expected to depend on the dominance of the other men with whom she compares him, whereas a man's satisfaction in a relationship with a woman might be influenced less by dominance and more by the physical attractiveness of the women with whom he compares her.

PREVIOUS STUDIES OF CONTRAST AND ATTRACTIVENESS

Several studies have indicated that exposure to physically attractive people results in diminished ratings of the attractiveness of a target person of the same sex (Kenrick & Gutierres, 1980; Kenrick, Gutierres, & Goldberg, 1989; Kernis & Wheeler, 1981). A similar effect has been found in several studies in which subjects were asked to rate their attraction to their partners (Kenrick et al., 1989; Weaver, Masland, & Zillman, 1984). After exposure to physically attractive centerfold photographs, men rated themselves as less attracted to their partners. However, a parallel effect was not found for women exposed to male centerfolds—those women did not show significant decreases in attraction to their male partners (Kenrick et al., 1989). This sex difference is consistent with the theory and research discussed above. As we noted, women's judgments of their partners are, compared with men's, based less on facial and bodily attractiveness and more on features related to social status and dominance. Although men and women depicted in centerfolds are undoubtedly chosen for their attractiveness, it is unclear that males who pose for nude photographs are perceived as especially high in social status or social dominance.

A PREDICTION

Given the findings that females, compared with males, place greater emphasis on dominance when evaluating a member of the other sex and that males place greater emphasis on physical attractiveness, we predict a sex-differentiated pattern of contrast effects. Consistent with previous findings, we would expect that males, compared with females, will show lower ratings of their relationships with a particular woman after exposure to physically attractive members of the other sex. Consistent with findings indicating that females value dominance more than physical attractiveness in a partner, we expect that females will rate their current relationships less favorably after exposure to dominant members of the other sex and will show less influence of exposure to physically attractive males. Males are expected to be uninfluenced by the dominance of the females to whom they are exposed.

METHOD

Overview

Men and women involved in heterosexual relationships were exposed to profiles of opposite-sex others, ostensibly as part of an attempt to develop a university-sponsored dating service. The profiles depicted individuals of either high or average physical attractiveness and of either high or low dominance. After perusing the profiles, subjects rated both their present relationships and their partners.

Subjects

Subjects were 407 Arizona State University undergraduate students, 217 women and 190 men, who completed the study in partial fulfillment of an introductory psychology class requirement. The sign-up sheets specified the requirement that subjects be in a heterosexual relationship, and all subjects used in the experiment reported being currently involved in a relationship, ranging from dating to marriage. Subjects participated in mixed-sex group sessions of 10 or fewer and were run by one of two female experimenters (who were dressed in lab coats and glasses and had their hair pulled back, in an attempt to minimize any differences in attractiveness). Forty-four subjects were discarded either because of possible suspicions regarding the cover story or because of missing data, leaving 363 remaining subjects (198 women and 165 men).

Design

The experiment followed a 2 (Subject Sex: male/female) × 2 (Target Physical Attractiveness: high/average) × 2 (Target Dominance: high/low) between-subjects design. Male and female subjects were randomly assigned to the four target profile conditions.

Target Profiles

Each subject received a folder containing seven bogus target profiles. Four such profile sets were created, each representing one cell of the Target Physical Attractiveness × Target Dominance design. Thus, each subject viewed seven opposite-sex targets who were either (a) highly physically attractive and highly dominant, (b) highly physically attractive and low in dominance, (c) average in physical attractiveness and highly dominant, or (d) average in physical attractiveness and low in dominance.

Each profile contained the following target information: a name, a 3-in. × 4.5-in. photograph, home town, several hobbies (e.g., "tennis, being with friends, reading novels," "travel, camping"), and three bogus personality scores ("Social Facility/ Likability," "Conscientiousness/ Task Orientation," and "Dominance/Ascendance").

Each of the personality scores was represented in the profiles both as a percentile score and as a point on a scale continuum, with the continuum anchored at each end by traits descriptive of people at that extreme. The profiles varied slightly, and randomly, in hobbies and Social Facility and Conscientiousness scores (i.e., all targets were presented as likable and of average conscientiousness); profiles differed substantially only in the physical attractiveness of the photographs and the targets' scores on the Dominance scale.

In the high-physical-attractiveness conditions, photographs were of professional models; in the average-physical-attractiveness conditions, photographs were of average-looking students taken from a yearbook of a large midwestern university. In the high-dominance conditions, dominance scores varied within the high range (ostensibly from the 80th to the 99th percentile of the student population); in the low-dominance conditions, dominance scores varied within the low range (from the 1st to the 20th percentile).

Procedure

Subjects were recruited for a study allegedly researching ways to implement a university-run dating service. They were informed that they were participating in the second phase of the study. In the initial phase, they were told, romantically unattached students interested in meeting others had completed a variety of personality questionnaires and had provided background information and photographs of themselves. The purpose of the phase in which they were involved, subjects were led to believe, was to determine the best format for presenting the information provided. Because romantically unattached students "did not tend to focus on the kind of information that will help them develop and sustain a relationship" and "were often too anxious about meeting others to provide reliable and valid data," subjects were told that the second phase of the study required the feedback of students who were already romantically involved and who had demonstrated the ability to relate to members of the opposite sex.

Subjects were further informed that they would view profiles—containing photographs and personality descriptions of several romantically unattached students who were interested in meeting others through this program—and subsequently evaluate the information in them. The experimenter then described the three personality dimensions present in the profiles and discussed how to interpret the percentile scores derived from them. For example, the Dominance/Ascendance scale was said to assess one's natural leadership abilities. High scores on this scale indicated that the respondent was powerful, authoritative, high in control, and masterful. The experimenter stressed that high scores indicated a natural leader, *not* someone who is hostile, domineering, dictatorial, or arrogant. Someone who would score low on this scale was described as obedient, yielding, and submissive.

After subjects indicated that they understood how to interpret the profile information, they were given a folder containing profiles of seven members of the other sex who had ostensibly participated in the first phase of the study. Subjects were given 7 min to look through the profiles carefully.

After perusing the profiles, subjects were given a questionnaire asking them to evaluate the proposed "dating program." It was noted that because the nature of their current relationship could affect these types of judgments, they would also be asked several questions about their current relationship. Subjects were reminded that all the information they provided would be kept strictly confidential.

Subjects then completed the dependent measures (see below). Finally, they were probed for suspicion, thoroughly debriefed, and dismissed.

Dependent Measures

Subjects rated their present relationship on 15 dimensions. The items assessed, on 7-point Likert-type scales, the following dimensions: permanence, satisfaction, stability, supportiveness, goodness, closeness, emotional intimacy, excitement, seriousness, commitment, importance, passion, how personally inspiring and how rewarding the relationship was, and how happy subjects were with the relationship.

Additionally, subjects rated their partners on the following 20 dimensions, again on 7-point scales: interesting, romantic, dominant, intelligent, physically attractive, warm, commanding, understanding, likable, passionate, powerful, desirable to the opposite sex, conscientiousness, masterful, sexually attractive, high in control, pleasant, emotionally expressive, natural leader, and sociable. Most of these items were selected because of their conceptual relevance to the dimensions of attractiveness, dominance, and likability.

Finally, subjects provided demographic information regarding their present relationship status, completed three open-ended questions dealing with their opinions about the profile format (in keeping with the cover story), and completed a manipulation check assessing the average attractiveness, sociability, conscientiousness, and dominance of the seven targets whose profiles they had seen.

RESULTS

Manipulation Checks

A Subject Sex × Target Physical Attractiveness × Target Dominance ANOVA on the dominance manipulation check revealed only the predicted main effect of target dominance, indicating that subjects viewed targets as more dominant in the high-dominance condition (average recalled percentile score = 83.42%) than in the low-dominance condition (average recalled percentile score = 12.87%), $F(1, 357) = 7656.90, p < .0001$. A similar ANOVA on the attractiveness manipulation check revealed the expected main effect of target physical attractiveness, indicating that subjects viewed targets as more physically attractive in the high-attractiveness condition (mean rating on a 7-point scale = 6.04) than in the average-attractiveness condition ($M = 3.51$), $F(1, 357) = 568.02, p < .0001$. There was also an interaction of Subject Sex × Target Physical Attractiveness, $F(1, 357) = 15.84, p < .001$, indicating that the attractiveness manipulation had a somewhat larger influence on male subjects (6.17 vs. 3.19) than on female subjects (5.93 vs. 3.79). However, simple effects tests indicated that the physical attractiveness manipulations worked powerfully for *both* female ($p < .0001$) and male ($p < .0001$) subjects. These data thus indicate that both the dominance and physical attractiveness manipulations worked sufficiently well to warrant investigation of our hypotheses of interest.

Evaluations of Own Relationship

We created a composite measure of relationship evaluation by averaging the 15 relationship items (alpha = .95). As predicted, there was a significant main effect of target physical attractiveness on the male subjects' evaluations of their present relationships, $F(1, 161) = 4.85, p < .05$. This effect was somewhat qualified, however, by an unexpected trend toward a Target Physical Attractiveness × Target Dominance interaction, $F(1, 161) = 3.11, p < .08$ (see Figure 1).

Specifically, as the means presented in Figure 1 indicate, the physical attractiveness of the female targets influenced male subjects' evaluations only when the women were of low dominance, $F(1, 84) = 8.47, p < .005$. When the women were of high dominance, no significant effect of physical attractiveness was found ($F < 1$). Finally, there was no main effect of target dominance on male subjects' ratings of their relationships ($F < 1$).

In contrast, women were, as expected, somewhat more influenced by the manipulated dominance of the male targets than by physical attractiveness (see Figure 1). Women exposed to highly dominant men tended to evaluate their present relationships less favorably ($M = 5.74$) than women exposed to low-dominance men ($M = 6.00$), $F(1, 194) = 3.54, p = .061$. There were no effects on women's relationship evaluation for either target physical attractiveness or the Target Dominance × Target Physical Attractiveness interaction ($Fs < .14$, n.s.).

Thus, with respect to the relationship evaluation composite measure, our hypotheses received generally favorable support. First, as predicted, females' judgments were more influenced by the dominance of the male targets than by their physical attractiveness (which had no effect). Second, also as predicted, male subjects were influenced by the physical attractiveness of the female targets. Third, and unexpectedly, male subjects were influenced by female physical attractiveness only when the women were of low dominance.[1]

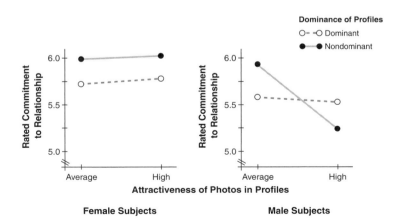

FIGURE 1   Evaluation of present relationship as a function of subject sex and the dominance and physical attractiveness of opposite-sex targets.

Evaluations of Present Partner

We created a composite measure of partner evaluation by averaging the 20 partner items (alpha = .86). For female subjects, unlike the pattern present for the relationship evaluation measure, there were no significant effects of the manipulated variables (all $Fs < .20$, n.s.). For male subjects, however, there was a marginally significant Target Physical Attractiveness × Target Dominance interaction, $F(1, 161) = 3.19, p < .08$. Simple effects tests revealed that male subjects rated their present partners less favorably when the female targets were highly attractive, but again the effect of attractiveness obtained *only* when the women were of low dominance, $F(1, 84) = 6.33, p < .02$; when the female targets were highly dominant, target physical attractiveness had no such influence.[2]

To explore the possible effects of the manipulations on specific partner ratings, we created two other composite partner ratings. *Partner physical desirability* was composed of the items physically attractive, desirable to the opposite sex, and sexually attractive. *Partner dominance* was composed of the items dominant, commanding, powerful, masterful, high in control, and natural leader. These analyses did not suggest that differences in relationship evaluations could be explained as due to changes in the perceived dominance or sexual attractiveness of the partner. Both males and females showed a similar nonsignificant tendency to rate their partners as less physically desirable after being exposed to attractive targets, $F(1, 162) = 2.62, p < .11$, for males, and $F(1, 196) = 1.98, p < .17$, for females.[3] All other effects yielded Fs less than 1 on ratings of partner physical attractiveness, except for a similarly weak tendency for males to show the same Attractiveness × Dominance interaction shown for ratings of relationship commitment, $F(1, 162) = 1.81, p < .18$. On the partner dominance composite, the partner ratings were quite different from ratings of commitment. The effect of the dominance manipulation was significant only for males, $F(1, 162) = 4.47, p < .05$, and it indicated that males exposed to high dominant females rated their partners as more dominant (suggesting an assimilation effect here, opposite to the contrast pattern obtained for females' ratings of commitment). No other effects for either sex approached significance ($Fs < 1$), with the exception of the Dominance × Attractiveness effect for male subjects, which yielded an $F(1, 162) = 2.22, p < .14$. The direction of that interaction was that the dominance effect was more pronounced among males exposed to high-attractive targets. That is, male subjects perceived their partners as least dominant after being exposed to the low-dominance, high-attractive targets.[4]

DISCUSSION

The findings of the present investigation provided reasonable support for our predictions. Women's judgments of their relationships with a particular man did appear to depend more on comparisons with other men who were dominant than with men who were good-looking—women who were exposed to dominant men, but not to physically attractive men, tended to rate themselves as less satisfied with their current relationships. Conversely, there was no main effect of dominance on men's evaluations of their relationships. For the men, physical attractiveness did make a difference—men evaluated their present relationships less favorably after viewing highly physically attractive women. Unexpectedly, that effect occurred only when the target females were low in dominance. Note that these findings were obtained despite the likely existence of psychological pressures to evaluate one's relationship and partner in a favorable manner.

Implications of the Current Findings

These main findings are generally consistent with a number of prior studies of mate evaluation criteria, which suggest that (a) women value dominance in a potential partner more than men (Buss, 1989; Kenrick et al., 1990; Sadalla et al., 1987; Townsend, 1989) and (b) men value physical attractiveness in a potential mate more than women (Buss, 1989; Kenrick et al., 1989; Kenrick et al., 1990). The results of these previous studies, however, could conceivably be explained as due to differential social desirability of males' and females' *self-reports*. That is, it could be argued that subjects who are asked directly about their criteria for a mate simply say the socially appropriate thing: Women report more interest in dominance than men do, and men report relatively more interest in physical attractiveness (while their implicit reactions to actual members of the other sex may be unrelated to such reports). The advantage of the current method is that the indirect undermining of relationship satisfaction suggests a process much less directly amenable to normative self-presentation demands. Our results therefore suggest that males and females may indeed process different information when evaluating different features of partners. Manipulation checks indicated that men registered the dominance levels of the women in the profiles and that women registered the attractiveness of the men. However, those features did not directly affect their satisfaction with their current relationships.

What specific cognitive processes underlie the findings of sex-differentiated contrast in the present investigation? One possibility would parallel findings of color contrast, in which, for instance, a white circle appears red after exposure to a green circle. Analogously, the males' female partners might have actually appeared less attractive in contrast to the attractive women in the profiles, or the females' partners might have actually appeared less dominant in contrast to the dominant men. Such an explanation does not seem to apply well here. For females, the dominance manipulation influenced their relationship evaluations but did not influence their ratings of partner dominance. For males, their judgments of partner desirability did parallel their relationship evaluations, but the partner ratings were decidedly weaker than the relationship ratings. Thus, the changes in relationship ratings did not appear to be caused by the mediating effects of domain-specific decrements in partner ratings.

Alternatively, the ratings of relationships might have been mediated by perceptions of the availability of other desirable members of the other sex. That is, females exposed to a series of highly dominant men could have left their estimations of their current partner's dominance unchanged but reduced their commitment to him in the face of a seemingly abundant population of desirable alternatives who were more dominant. Likewise, males exposed to a series of highly attractive nondominant females might rate themselves as less committed to their partners, not because their partners suddenly appeared unattractive and domineering, but simply because they might have inferred that the population of available attractive submissive alternative partners was higher than they would otherwise have estimated. Future research to examine the specific proximate mechanisms for these findings would be of some interest. In particular, it would be of interest to conduct research examining how exposure to attractive and dominant targets affects subjective estimates of the population of available alternatives and of the partner's position in that distribution.

The tendency for men's ratings of relationship satisfaction to be lowest after exposure to attractive females who were also submissive might indicate a more complicated relationship between dominance and attractiveness than found in previous research. Sadalla and his colleagues (1987) found, in a series of three studies, that dominance was irrelevant to males' judgments of females. However, Sadalla et al. did not examine physical attractiveness as a variable. The present research raises the possibility that dominance may have effects on males' ratings of the attractiveness of females but that those effects interact with the target's attractiveness. In particular, females who are both dominant and attractive may be regarded as inaccessible to most males.

Heuristic Value of Evolutionary Models of Social Cognition

We view the specific empirical findings of this investigation as somewhat secondary to their general value as an indication that evolutionary models can serve as a useful heuristic, suggesting interesting hypotheses about ongoing processes of social cognition. Most experimental social psychologists are not directly interested in conducting gene-mapping studies, in digging up stone implements from the Paleolithic Age, or in tracking baboons across the plains of the Serengeti. However, the modern multidisciplinary evolutionary approach, incorporating findings from anthropology, ethology, behavior genetics, and psychology, has already proved useful in understanding and expanding on a number of existing phenomena in social psychology (Kenrick & Keefe, 1992; Kenrick & Trost, 1989). More important, the perspective has a number of implications for ongoing cognitive processes (Hansen & Hansen, 1988; Kenrick & Hogan, 1991; Lumsden & Wilson, 1981; Tooby & Cosmides, 1989). A consideration of human evolutionary history, in fact, suggests that the evolution of the human brain has been driven at least as much by the need to solve problems in social group living as by the sorts of problems with which modern cognitive scientists concern themselves (such as letter recognition).

Cognitive approaches to behavior have tended to focus on processes and have often ignored content (cf. Baron & Boudreau, 1987; McArthur & Baron, 1983). From an evolutionary perspective, the content of cognition is crucial, and it is, moreover, social content about which some of the most interesting hypotheses can be advanced. From an evolutionary perspective, the choice of a reproductive partner was a crucial one for our ancestors. The importance of such a decision leads to specific expectations about processes of social cognition ranging from attention and perception to memory and retrieval. For instance, our discussion above would lead to the expectation that males are likely to selectively attend to, encode, and recall information about a woman's youth and physical attractiveness whereas women are likely to selectively attend to, encode, and recall information about a man's dominance. Thus, the preliminary findings of the present investigation suggest that an evolutionary perspective can yield a wealth of testable hypotheses about ongoing social cognition.

To what extent is an evolutionary framework necessary to explain these and other findings on gender differences in mating strategies? As we indicated earlier, sex differences in mate preferences and related behaviors are commonly explained in terms of the norms of American or Western society. However, such explanations are often advanced without the necessary evidence that other societies possess different norms and correspondingly different behaviors. Recent findings suggest that an evolutionary model can explain a number of gender differences in mate selection that are difficult to explain with a "tabula rasa" cultural relativist position. For instance, a similar relative female preference for characteristics related to social dominance and a similar relative male preference for characteristics related to youth and attractiveness are found across widely divergent societies in widely divergent geographical areas (Buss, 1989; Kenrick & Keefe, 1992). Regarding dominance, research conducted with numerous other animal species suggests that when one sex shows a preference for dominance, it is females that more strongly prefer dominance in males (Daly & Wilson, 1983; Trivers, 1985). Other findings suggest that these differences are not parsimoniously explained in terms of differential social power of males and females, as even females who attain high levels of social power and wealth continue to indicate a preference for men who are older and more socially powerful than themselves (Kenrick & Keefe, 1992; Townsend, 1989; Wiederman & Allgeier, 1992). Of course, social norms do not operate outside the domain of human evolutionary history, and one would expect social norms to reflect and interact with biological constraints (Lumsden & Wilson, 1981). Models based solely on cultural norms can explain isolated findings but have difficulty incorporating the emerging nomological network of findings. Such models also have difficulty explaining where the cultural norms came from or why the norms are so similar across different societies. An evolutionary perspective is useful in placing current norms and ongoing social behavior in a wider context of cross-cultural, comparative, and physiological findings.

NOTES

1. Given the nature of our predictions, our analyses are appropriately focused. We should note, however, that the three-way Subject Sex × Target Physical Attractiveness × Target Dominance ANOVA on relationship evaluation revealed several overall effects of interest. First, there was a main effect of subject sex, revealing that our female subjects were generally more satisfied with their present relationships than our male subjects, $F(1, 355) = 9.26$, $p < .005$. Second, there was an interaction between subject sex and target physical attractiveness, $F(1, 355) = 3.56$, $p < .06$, such that our male subjects evaluated their present relationships less favorably when exposed to the highly attractive female targets whereas our female subjects showed no such influence of target physical attractiveness. This interaction is reflected in the more focused analyses above.

2. In addition, the overall three-way Subject Sex × Target Physical Attractiveness × Target Dominance ANOVA revealed a significant subject sex main effect, $F(1, 355) = 7.72$, $p < .006$: female subjects evaluated their partners more favorably than male subjects.

3. When subject sex was included as a factor in a 2 × 2 × 2 ANOVA on physical desirability, there was only a main effect of the attractiveness of the target stimuli, $F(1, 358) = 4.68$, $p < .05$. There were no effects of dominance and no significant interactions involving the partner physical desirability ratings.

4. Analyzing the partner dominance composite with the 2 × 2 × 2 ANOVA, there was a significant effect of subject sex, $F(1, 358) = 13.63$, $p < .001$, indicating that females rated their partners as more dominant than males did. There was also a marginal effect of the dominance manipulation, $F(1, 358) = 3.35$, $p < .07$—partners were rated as more dominant when subjects had been exposed to the high-dominance targets. No interactions approached significance.

REFERENCES

Baron, R. M., & Boudreau, L. A. (1987). An ecological perspective on integrating personality and social psychology. *Journal of Personality and Social Psychology, 53,* 1222–1228.

Buss, D. M. (1989). Sex differences in human mate preferences: Evolutionary hypotheses tested in 37 cultures. *Behavioral and Brain Sciences, 12,* 1–49.

Buss, D. M., & Barnes, M. F. (1986). Preferences in human mate selection. *Journal of Personality and Social Psychology, 50,* 559–570.

Cunningham, M. R. (1986). Measuring the physical in physical attractiveness: Quasi-experiments on the sociobiology of female beauty. *Journal of Personality and Social Psychology, 50,* 925–935.

Cunningham, M. R., Barbee, A. P., & Pike, C. L. (1990). What do women want? Facial metric assessment of multiple motives in the perception of male physical attractiveness. *Journal of Personality and Social Psychology, 59,* 61–72.

Daly, M., & Wilson, M. (1983). *Sex, evolution, and human behavior* (2nd ed.). Boston: Willard Grant.

Darwin, C. (1859). *On the origin of species.* London: Murray.

Hansen, C. H., & Hansen, R. D. (1988). Finding the face in the crowd: The anger superiority effect. *Journal of Personality and Social Psychology, 54,* 917–924.

Hill, J. (1984). Prestige and reproductive success in man. *Ethology and Sociobiology, 5,* 77–95.

Keating, C. F. (1985). Gender and the physiognomy of dominance and attractiveness. *Social Psychology Quarterly, 48,* 61–70.

Kenrick, D. T., Groth, G. R., Trost, M. R., & Sadalla, E. K. (1993). Integrating evolutionary and social exchange perspectives on relationships: Effects of gender, self-appraisal, and involvement level on mate selection. *Journal of Personality and Social Psychology, 64,* 951–969.

Kenrick, D. T., & Gutierres, S. E. (1980). Contrast effects and judgments of physical attractiveness: When beauty becomes a social problem. *Journal of Personality and Social Psychology, 38,* 131–140.

Kenrick, D. T., Gutierres, S. E., & Goldberg, L. (1989). Influence of erotica on ratings of strangers and mates. *Journal of Experimental Social Psychology, 25,* 159–167.

Kenrick, D. T., & Hogan, R. (1991). Cognitive psychology. In M. Maxwell (Ed.), *The sociobiological imagination.* Albany: State University of New York.

Kenrick, D. T., & Keefe, R. C. (1992). Age preferences in mates reflect sex differences in human reproductive strategies. *Behavioral and Brain Sciences, 15,* 75–133.

Kenrick, D. T., Sadalla, E. K., Groth, G., & Trost, M. R. (1990). Evolution, traits, and the stages of human courtship: Qualifying the parental investment model. *Journal of Personality, 58,* 97–117.

Kenrick, D. T., & Trost, M. R. (1989). A reproductive exchange model of heterosexual relationships: Putting proximate economics in ultimate perspective. *Review of Personality and Social Psychology, 10,* 92–118.

Kernis, M. H., & Wheeler, L. (1981). Beautiful friends and ugly strangers: Radiation and contrast effects in perceptions of same-sex pairs. *Personality and Social Psychology Bulletin, 7,* 617–620.

Lumsden C. J., & Wilson, E. O. (1981). *Genes, mind, and culture: The coevolutionary process.* Cambridge, MA: Harvard University Press.

Mathes, E. W., Brennan, S. M., Haugen, P. M., & Rice, H. B. (1985). Ratings of physical attractiveness as a function of age. *Journal of Social Psychology, 125,* 157–168.

McArthur, L. Z., & Baron, R. M. (1983). Toward an ecological theory of social perception. *Psychological Review, 90,* 215–238.

Mealey, L. (1985). The relationship between social status and biological success: A case study of the Mormon religious hierarchy. *Ethology and Sociobiology, 6,* 249–257.

Sadalla, E. K., Kenrick, D. T., & Vershure, B. (1987). Dominance and heterosexual attraction. *Journal of Personality and Social Psychology, 52,* 730–738.

Symons, D. (1979). *The evolution of human sexuality.* New York: Oxford University Press.

Tooby J., & Cosmides, L. (1989). Evolutionary psychology and the generation of culture. *Ethology and Sociobiology, 10,* 29–49.

Townsend, J. M. (1989). Mate-selection criteria: A pilot study. *Ethology and Sociobiology, 10,* 241–252.

Townsend, J. M., & Levy, G. D. (1990). Effects of potential partner's costume and physical attractiveness on sexuality and partner selection: Sex differences in reported preferences of university students. *Journal of Psychology, 124,* 371–376.

Trivers, R. L. (1985). *Social evolution.* Menlo Park, CA: Benjamin/Cummings.

Turke, P. W., & Betzig, L. L. (1985). Those who can do: Wealth, status, and reproductive success on Ifaluk. *Ethology and Sociobiology, 6,* 79–87

Weaver, J. B., Masland, J. L., & Zillman, D. (1984). Effect of erotica on young men's aesthetic perception of their female sexual partners. *Perceptual and Motor Skills, 58,* 929–930.

Wiederman, M.W., & Allgeier, E.R. (1992). Gender differences in mate selection criteria: Sociobiological or socioeconomic explanation? *Ethology and Sociobiology, 13,* 115–124.

What Is a Good Mother?
Adaptive Variation in Maternal Behavior of Primates

LYNN A. FAIRBANKS

Understanding and preventing infant abuse and neglect and inadequate maternal behavior is an important goal for everyone concerned with child welfare. This report describes a program of research that focuses on understanding variation in the mothering behavior of primates from the perspective of evolutionary biology. According to this view, maternal care toward individual infants cannot be understood fully without reference to competing demands on the mother for her own maintenance and survival as well as for care of her other offspring, both past and future.[1] Parental investment theory provides a theoretical basis for understanding that there are times when it is in the mother's best interest to reduce the amount of care she gives to a particular infant, and that imperfect or nonresponsive mothering can be seen not simply as a defect that needs to be corrected, but as part of a parenting strategy that has evolved to maximize the lifetime reproductive success of the mother.

PARENTAL INVESTMENT THEORY

The theory of natural selection predicts the evolution of parenting strategies that maximize the number of infants a female can produce in a lifetime that are likely to survive to adulthood and reproduce successfully.[2] Life history strategies involve trade-offs between energy allocated for self-maintenance, growth, and reproduction. If one assumes that a female is limited in the amount of effort she can devote to reproduction without jeopardizing her own survival, then it follows that the energy she spends in caring for one infant will take away from what she has available for producing and caring for other offspring. The dilemma that each female faces is how best to allocate her energy and resources across all the infants that she could have in her lifetime.

Parental investment theory predicts that a mother should shift the effort devoted to infant care from her current infant to her next infant at the point when the fitness gains to her lifetime reproductive success from investing the same amount of effort in the next infant exceed the gains from investing in the current infant.[3] An interesting corollary of this model of parental investment is that the point at which it is optimal

From L. A. Fairbanks, "What is a good mother? Adaptive variation in maternal behavior of primates," *Current Directions in Psychological Science, 2* (1993): 179–183. Reprinted with permission of Blackwell Publishing.

for the mother to shift her reproductive energy to her next infant is earlier than the optimal point for the infant.[4] Thus, although mothers and their infants share common interests and goals, the exact amount of care that it is in the mother's best interest to give is generally less than the amount of care that it is in the infant's best interest to receive. This point is fundamentally important for understanding variation in maternal care.

EVIDENCE OF MATERNAL INVESTMENT IN PRIMATES

Primate mothers typically produce one infant at a time, and in an infant's first year of life, they provide intensive care involving feeding, holding, carrying, cleaning, and protection. Field studies have demonstrated the heavy burden that infant care places on primate mothers, who have to increase the time they spend foraging for food and yet still have a hard time maintaining their body weight.[5] If conditions are favorable, most primate mothers will produce a new infant every year. For monkey species with an average gestation length of 5 to 6 months this means that the mother begins physiologically preparing for the birth of her next infant when her current infant is about 6 months old. Maternal investment theory predicts that the energy a mother gives to her current infant should compromise her ability to invest in her next infant, and vice versa.

Data from several field studies of undisturbed primate populations have verified that infant mortality shortens the time to a female's next conception, thus supporting the hypothesis that caring for one infant influences a mother's ability to invest in the next.[6] Unfortunately, field data verifying the influence of more subtle variation in maternal care on a mother's ability to invest in other infants are hard to come by. Uncontrolled variation in factors such as food quality, ecological conditions, and access to resources make it difficult to separate variance due to maternal investment from variance caused by these other factors.[7] For detailed studies of the consequences of variation in maternal behavior, researchers have turned to provisioned free-ranging and captive populations.

A colony of vervet monkeys has been maintained in naturally composed social groups at the Nonhuman Primate Research Center in Sepulveda, California, since 1975 for observational research on social behavior and development. The animals have been monitored continuously since the colony's inception, and behavioral data on mother–infant relationships have been collected on all infants born in the colony for the past 12 years. A consistent and uniform behavioral sampling system has provided robust measures of maternal and infant behavior over the first 6 months of life for a large sample of infants. We have used these data to test specific hypotheses about the factors that influence maternal care and about the consequences of variation in maternal care for both the mother and the infant. The results generally support the propositions that mothers adjust their maternal care according to factors associated with infant need and that the more care a mother gives to one infant, the less she has available to invest in other infants.

INCREASING MATERNAL CARE

Parental investment theory predicts that maternal care is influenced by the fitness benefits that the infant receives from that care. Ideally, a mother should be sensitive not only to her infant's needs, but also to the likely effect that her care will have on offspring fitness. One of the ways that a mother can evaluate the effectiveness of her caregiving is through past experience.

Research at our colony suggests that primate mothers are able to fine-tune their maternal behavior according to their past experience of success or failure. In a comparison of the maternal behavior of females who had lost their last infant with those who had produced surviving infants, the mothers with a history of failure gave more care and attention to their infants, encouraged contact, were more restrictive of their infants' movements, and played a greater part in keeping their infants near.[8] Figure 1 illustrates this difference for the frequency with which mothers initiated ventral contact with their infants over the first 6 months of life. Mothers who failed in their last pregnancy initiated ventral contact significantly more often than mothers who had succeeded. The differences found suggest that mothers adjusted the level of maternal care they gave to their infants based on their past experience, and that the experience of past failure led to an increase in the level of care given to the next infant. Research is currently under way in the colony to verify these relationships experimentally.

Did the increased care that mothers with a history of failure gave to their infants reduce the mothers' ability to invest in other offspring, as predicted by parental investment theory? The results from the colony suggest that it did. The mothers who had higher levels of maternal care in response to past failure also had significantly longer intervals to the birth of their next infant. Forty-three percent of the mothers in the past-success group gave birth again in less than 12 months, whereas none of the mothers in the past-failure group conceived and delivered again that soon. These results are consistent with the hypothesis that by investing more care in one infant to ensure its survival, a female sacrifices some of her future reproductive potential.

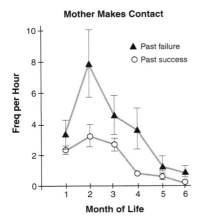

FIGURE 1 Mean (±s.e.m.) frequency per hour that vervet monkey mothers initiated ventral contact with their infants by infant's month of life for mothers who had failed in their last pregnancy and those who had succeeded.

TAKING ADVANTAGE OF OPPORTUNITIES
TO REDUCE MATERNAL CARE

Parental investment theory predicts that mothers have been designed not only to give good-quality, nurturant care to their offspring, but also to judiciously and appropriately withhold care when doing so will increase their lifetime reproductive success. Mothers should take advantage of circumstances that allow them to reduce the time and energy they devote to maternal care, particularly when they can do so at minimal risk to their infants' welfare.

Using Alternative Caretakers

One of the features of vervet monkey society that provides opportunities for mothers to reduce their level of care is the high degree of interest in infants shown by other group members. Infant caretaking by nonmothers is observed frequently in vervet monkey groups.[9] In the first few months of life, infants are particularly attractive to other group members. Juvenile and adult females crowd around new mothers and compete for opportunities to hold and carry the young infants. In our captive vervet monkey groups, the average infant is carried by nonmothers 10% of the time during the first 2 months of life (Figure 2), but there is considerable variability across infants. Some mothers appear reluctant to let their infants go, but others allow caretakers to carry their infants a substantial proportion of the time (up to 40% of instantaneous observations). There are risks associated with leaving infants with relatively inexperienced allomothers, who may not be as concerned as the mothers with the infants' well-being. Compared with low-ranking mothers, high-ranking mothers, who are more able to retrieve their infants when they want to, are more likely to allow caretaking of their infants by others.

In our colony, vervet monkey mothers who allowed caretakers to carry their infants were able to reduce the amount of time they spent in ventral contact without leaving their infants alone.[10] Figure 2 shows the percentage of time that mothers were observed more than a meter away from their infants and the percentage of time that their infants were observed alone over the first 6 months of life. Comparison of infants who were carried by allomothers more than average and less than average showed that

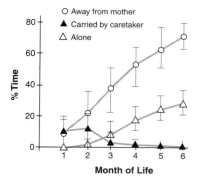

FIGURE 2   Mean percentage of time that vervet monkey infants were observed more than 1 m away from their mothers, carried by allomothers, and alone (more than 1 m away from any other group member), by month of life. Error bars represent 1 standard deviation.

the infants in the high-caretaking group spent significantly more time away from their mothers in the first few months of life, but they were virtually never alone. There was no association between time carried by caretakers and infant mortality in the 1st month of life, indicating that the mothers who used caretakers were not markedly reducing their infants' chances of survival.

As predicted by parental investment theory, mothers who reduced the amount of care they gave to their current infants were able to redirect their energy to other activities that promoted their own welfare and readiness for future reproduction. In the colony, there was a significant inverse relationship between the amount of time a mother's current infant was carried by caretakers and the interval to the birth of her next infant.[10] When circumstances allowed mothers to reduce the level of maternal care without affecting the survival and welfare of their infants, they did so, and this reduction in care was associated with an increase in lifetime reproductive success.

Cross-Generational Social Stability and Support: Grandmothers

The young adult years are an important period of transition in the life history of a female primate, a time when she must simultaneously establish and defend her position in the adult dominance hierarchy and prepare for reproduction. Young mothers generally have a higher rate of pregnancy failure and a more difficult time rearing their infants than older mothers. One of the factors that buffers a young mother during this period is the presence and support of the matriline, particularly the young mother's own mother. Vervet monkeys, like the majority of primates, live in matrilineally based societies, and females grow up in close association with their mothers and female relatives. Female matrilines not only provide social support to developing family members, but also assure a young adult female's social position, or dominance rank, in the group. When a young female's mother dies, she loses her most reliable ally, aggression against her from other matrilines increases, and she is likely to drop in rank and fail to attain the social position that her mother held in the group.[11]

Does the social support and stability provided by the presence of a young mother's mother influence the care she gives to her infant? Research in our colony suggests that young mothers with stable matrilines can invest less energy in caring for their infants compared with young mothers who have lost their own mothers.[12] When infants' grandmothers were available, young mothers were less protective, spent less time in contact with their infants, and were less restrictive of their infants' movements. Infants with grandmothers spent more time at a distance from their mothers and began their forays out of close proximity at an earlier age.

When grandmothers were present, young mothers were able to reduce the time and energy they devoted to infant care without jeopardizing the health and safety of their infants. A comparison of the survival rate of infants with and without grandmothers demonstrated that the presence of the grandmother was positively associated with infant survival. Young mothers with their own mothers in group had higher rates of fecundity and lower rates of infant mortality, and they produced significantly more surviving infants compared with similar young mothers without mothers.[11] These results have recently been verified following experimental removal of older females, providing further support for the hypothesis that young females are able to take advantage of the social support and safety provided by a stable matriline to increase their fecundity and relax the level of care they give to individual infants.

ADJUSTING MATERNAL CARE OVER TIME

Primate mothers not only can increase or decrease the level of care they give to their infants overall, but can also adjust care over time in response to changing risk to their infants. Vervet monkey natural history is characterized by female philopatry and male immigration; that is, females typically remain in their natal group for life, whereas males emigrate at puberty and immigrate into neighboring groups. Immigration of new males generates conflict with resident males and with females and their young. New males are known to pose a threat to infants in many primate species, and their victims are generally young infants who are still dependent on their mothers.[13]

Do mothers respond to the risk presented by new males by adjusting the care they give to their infants? A study of maternal behavior toward infants born after new males had been introduced into the group indicates that they do, but their response was complex.[14] The mothers in groups with new males were more protective than the mothers in groups with no new males when their infants were very young and vulnerable. Figure 3a shows the frequency per hour that mothers restrained their infants and prevented them from breaking contact over the first 6 months of life. In groups with new males, mothers were much more restrictive, particularly during Months 2 and 3, when infants were beginning to make forays away from their mothers. These mothers also initiated contact more often, spent more time in contact, and spent less time at a

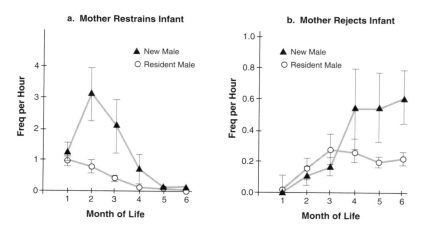

FIGURE 3 Mean (±s.e.m.) frequency per hour that vervet monkey mothers (**a**) restrained and (**b**) rejected their infants, by infant's month of life, in social groups with new adult males versus long-term resident adult males.

distance from their infants in the first 3 months compared with mothers in groups with long-term resident males. All these behaviors would be likely to protect infants from the increased possibility of injury from an adult male stranger.

In Months 5 and 6, mothers shifted their reproductive strategy away from increased protection and toward preparation for breeding. At this age, infants are in contact with their mothers only about 20% of the time, and they spend more than 60% of the time more than a meter away from their mothers. Infant mortality in the colony is extremely low at this point, and the hypothetical risk to infants from new males is minimal. This reduction in risk allowed the mothers to take advantage of the opportunity to increase the genetic diversity of their offspring. Inbreeding is a potential problem in species that live in relatively small matrilineal groups, and females are generally less sexually responsive to males they have known for many years and are more responsive to unfamiliar males. In the colony, mothers in groups with new males prepared for conception by increasing the rate at which they broke contact with their infants and rejected their attempts to gain access to the nipple in Months 5 and 6 (Figure 3b). This effectively timed increase in rejection was associated with shortening the interval to the births of their next infants.

Vervet monkey mothers were able to respond to the presence of new adult males with a mixed strategy that protected infants when they were most at risk and yet allowed the mothers to come into estrous and mate with the new males as soon as possible. Data from other research sites also support the idea that maternal rejection of nipple contact is associated with shortening the interbirth interval.[15] Mothers who are more rejecting are more likely to produce an infant in the next year compared with less rejecting mothers.

CONCLUDING COMMENTS

Research on the life history consequences of subtle variations in maternal care of primates is still in its infancy, but the data that are available suggest there are trade-offs between care given to one infant and the resources and energy that a female has available for other offspring. Primate mothers adjust the level of care they give to their infants in ways that are consistent with attempting to maximize their lifetime reproductive success. When past experience or current circumstances suggest that a female needs to increase her level of maternal care to promote offspring survival, she does so. When conditions allow her to reduce the level of care she gives without unduly jeopardizing her infant's welfare, she does so also. These care decisions have implications not only for a current infant's welfare and survival, however. They also influence the energy a mother has left to invest in other offspring. An increase in care to one offspring lengthens the time it takes for a female to produce another, and a reduction in care shortens the interval to the delivery of her next infant. Evolutionary biological theories of life history strategies and parental investment provide a framework for understanding variability in maternal behavior in terms of its consequences not only for the infant, but also for the mother and for her other offspring.

NOTES

1. T.H. Clutton-Brock, *The Evolution of Parental Care* (Princeton University Press, Princeton, NJ, 1991).
2. E.R. Pianka, Natural selection of optimal reproductive tactics, *American Zoologist, 16,* 775–784 (1976).
3. R.L. Trivers, Parental investment and sexual selection, in *Sexual Selection and the Descent of Man,* B. Campbell, Ed. (Aldine, Chicago, 1972).
4. R.L. Trivers, Parent-offspring conflict, *American Zoologist, 11,* 249–264 (1974).
5. J. Altmann, *Baboon Mothers and Infants* (Harvard University Press, Cambridge, MA, 1980); F.B. Bercovitch, Female weight and reproductive condition in a population of olive baboons [*Papio anubis*], *American Journal of Primatology, 12,* 189–195 (1987); R.I.M. Dunbar, Maternal time budgets in gelada baboons. *Animal Behaviour, 36,* 970–980 (1988).
6. D.L. Cheney, R.M. Seyfarth, S.J. Andelman, and P.C. Lee, Reproductive success in vervet monkeys, and J. Altmann, G. Hausfater, and S.A. Altmann, Determinants of reproductive success in savannah baboons, *Papio cynocephalus,* in *Reproductive Success,* T.H. Clutton-Brock, Ed. (University of Chicago Press, Chicago, 1988); D.P. Watts, Mountain gorilla reproduction and sexual behavior, *American Journal of Primatology, 24,* 211–225 (1991).
7. P. Muruthi, J. Altmann, and S.A. Altmann, Resource base, parity, and reproductive condition affect feeding time and nutrient intake within and between groups in a baboon population, *Oecologia, 87,* 467–472 (1991); I. Malik, R.L. Johnson, and C.M. Berman, Control of post-partum mating behavior in free-ranging rhesus monkeys, *American Journal of Primatology, 26,* 89–95 (1992).
8. L.A. Fairbanks, Mother-infant behavior in vervet monkeys: Response to failure of last pregnancy, *Behavioral Ecology & Sociobiology, 23,* 157–165 (1988).
9. J.B. Lancaster, Play-mothering: The relations between juvenile females and young infants among free-ranging vervet monkeys, in *Primate Socialization,* F.E. Poirier, Ed. (Random House, New York, 1972).
10. L.A. Fairbanks, Reciprocal benefits of allomothering for female vervet monkeys, *Animal Behaviour, 40,* 553–562 (1990).
11. L.A. Fairbanks and M.T. McGuire, Age, reproductive value, and dominance-related behaviour in vervet monkey females: Cross generational influences on social relationships and reproduction, *Animal Behaviour, 34,* 1710–1721 (1986).
12. L.A. Fairbanks, Vervet monkey grandmothers: Effects on mother–infant relationships, *Behaviour, 104,* 176–188 (1989).
13. G. Hausfater and S.B. Hrdy, *Infanticide: Comparative and Evolutionary Perspectives* (Aldine de Gruyter, Hawthorne, NY, 1984).
14. L.A. Fairbanks and M.T. McGuire, Mother-infant relationships in vervet monkeys: Response to new adult males, *International Journal of Primatology, 8,* 351–366 (1987).
15. M.D. Hauser and L.A. Fairbanks, Mother-infant conflict in vervet monkeys: Variation in response to ecological conditions, *Animal Behaviour, 36,* 802–813 (1988); M. Gomendio, Parent/offspring conflict and maternal investment in rhesus macaques, *Animal Behaviour, 42,* 993–1005 (1991); L. Johnson, C.M. Berman, and I. Malik, An integrative model of the lactational and environmental control of mating in female rhesus monkeys, *Animal Behaviour, 46,* 63–98 (1993); C.M. Berman, K.L.R. Rasmussen, and S.J. Suomi, Reproductive consequences of maternal care patterns during estrus among free-ranging rhesus monkeys, *Behavioral Ecology and Sociobiology, 32,* 391–399 (1993).

RECOMMENDED READING

Altmann, J. (1980). *Baboon Mothers and Infants* (Harvard University Press, Cambridge, MA).

Clutton-Brock, T.H. (1991). *The Evolution of Parental Care* (Princeton University Press, Princeton, NJ).

Trivers, R.L. (1985). *Social Evolution* (Benjamin Cummings, Menlo Park, CA).

Evolution and Developmental Sex Differences

DAVID C. GEARY

From an evolutionary perspective, childhood is the portion of the life span during which individuals practice and refine those competencies that facilitate survival and reproduction in adulthood. Although the skeletal structure of these competencies appears to be inherent, social interaction and play flesh them out during childhood so that they are adapted to local conditions. Darwin's principles of sexual selection, including male-male competition over mates and female choice of mating partners, successfully explain the acquisition and expression of reproductive competencies in hundreds of species. When this perspective is applied to humans, it predicts sex differences that are, in fact, found in the childhood activities of boys and girls and that reflect sex differences in reproductive strategies in adulthood. A few of these differences are described, along with cultural factors that modify their expression. The article closes with a brief discussion of the social and scientific implications.

Keywords: sex differences; sexual selection; development; childhood; culture

S ex differences are inherently interesting to the scientist and layperson alike. They always have been and always will be. Although the existence of such differences has been debated in the past, the scientific issue today concerns the source of these differences. The prevailing view in psychology is that most sex differences result from children's adoption of gender roles, roles that reflect society-wide differences in the daily activities of men and women (Eagly, 1987). The goal here is not to provide a review or appraisal of this position, but rather to offer an alternative view of developmental sex differences, a view based on the principles of evolution (Darwin, 1871).

From an evolutionary perspective, cultural and ecological factors are expected to influence the expression of developmental sex differences, and a few of these influences are described in the final section. Before they are discussed, though, a basic evolutionary framework for understanding sex differences in general and developmental sex differences in particular is provided in the first section, and the second provides a few examples of the usefulness of this approach for understanding human developmental sex differences.

From D. C. Geary, "Evolution and developmental sex differences," *Current Directions in Psychological Science,* 8 (1999): 115–119. Reprinted with permission of Blackwell Publishing.

EVOLUTION AND DEVELOPMENT

Sexual Selection

One of Darwin's (1871) seminal contributions was the observation that evolutionary pressures often differ for males and females and that many of these differences center around the dynamics of reproduction. These pressures are termed sexual selection and typically result from males competing with one another for social status, resources, or territory—whatever is needed to attract mates—and from females' choice of mating partners (Andersson, 1994). Although the dynamics of male-male competition can vary across species and social and ecological conditions, one common result is the evolution of physical (see Figure 1), cognitive, and behavioral sex differences. Females' choice of mates has been studied most extensively in birds, although it is also evident in insects, fish, reptiles, and mammals, including humans (Andersson, 1994;

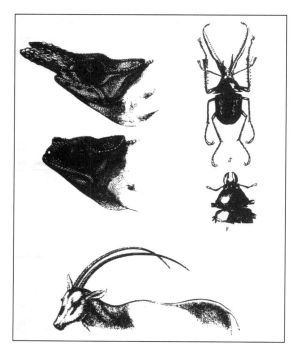

FIGURE 1   Examples of sexually selected characteristics used in physical male-male competition. The pair in the upper left are the male (top) and female (bottom) of the *Chamaeleon bifurcus;* the pair in the upper right are the male and female of the beetle *Chiasognathus grantii;* at the bottom is a male *Oryx leucoryx,* a species of antelope (females do not have horns). From Darwin (1871, Vol. II, p. 35; Vol. I, p. 377; and Vol. II, p. 251, respectively). These exaggerated male characteristics are used in male-on-male aggression. For instance, two male *Oryx leucoryx* will compete by kneeling in front of each other, each then trying to maneuver the points of his horns under the body of his competitor. "If one succeeds in doing this, he suddenly springs up, throwing up his head at the same time, and can thus wound or perhaps even transfix his antagonist" (Darwin, 1871, Vol. II, pp. 251–252).

Buss, 1994). Females typically choose mates on the basis of indicators of physical, genetic, or behavioral fitness, that is, on the basis of traits that signal a benefit to them (e.g., provisioning) or their offspring (e.g., good genes). One example of the evolutionary result of female choice is shown in Figure 2; the long and symmetric tail feathers of the male hummingbird are an indicator of his physical and genetic health.

Male-male competition and female choice are most evident in species in which males devote most of their reproductive energies to attracting mates, and females provide most or all of the parental care (Trivers, 1972), a pattern found in nearly 97% of mammalian species (Clutton-Brock, 1991). As is the case with other mammals, women throughout the world invest more time and resources in the well-being of their children than men do (Geary, 1998). Nonetheless, many men do provide some investment in the well-being of their children, unlike most other mammalian males. Paternal care, in turn, results in female-female competition and male choice of mates, along with male-male competition and female choice of mates.

The sex difference in the level of parental investment, along with other features (see Geary, 1998), results in differences in the nature of male-male versus female-female competition, and in the criteria used in mate choice (Geary, 1998). Throughout the world, men compete with one another for the control of culturally prized resources

FIGURE 2   Female (left) and male (right) hummingbirds (*Spathura underwoodi*). From Darwin (1871, Vol. II, p. 77). The long and symmetric tail feathers of the male appear to signal to the female that he has immune-system genes that can confer resistance to local parasites (e.g., worms). If she mates with this male, then her offspring will also be resistant to local parasites.

(e.g., status, money, or cows), and they often do so through physical contests (Keeley, 1996). Women compete with one another by means of relational aggression. They gossip, shun, and backbite their competitors (Crick, Casas, & Mosher, 1997). Both men and women want intelligent and cooperative spouses, but women more than men focus on the cultural success (e.g., control of money or cows) of suitors and men more than women focus on physical attractiveness (indicators of fertility; Buss, 1994).

Development

Biologists study development by documenting species' life history and by discerning the function of childhood. Life history refers to the typical ages associated with developmental milestones, such as age of weaning and length of childhood. The function of childhood is to refine the competencies that will be needed to survive and reproduce in adulthood (Mayr, 1974). It appears that many cognitive and behavioral systems are initially skeletal in structure—the basic framework is inborn—but are fleshed out as juveniles play, explore the environment, and interact socially (Gelman, 1990). Fleshing out these competencies results in the refinement of those skills needed to survive and reproduce in the local ecology and social group.

Developmental sex differences are expected to the degree that reproductive demands differ for males and females in adulthood. In species in which male-male competition is more intense than female-female competition, the juvenile period is longer for males than for females. Male satin bowerbirds (*Ptilonorhynchus violaceus*), for instance, mature many years after females have matured. Although there is some physical competition, males largely compete behaviorally, through the construction of complex stick structures called bowers. (Females make their mate choices, in part, on the basis of the complexity of these bowers.) During development, "young males spend a great deal of time observing older males at their bower, and practice bower building and display behaviors when the owner is absent from the bower site" (Collis & Borgia, 1992, p. 422). Young males also engage in play fighting, which provides the experience needed for dominance-related encounters in adulthood. Thus, delayed maturation and associated play allow for the refinement of those physical, cognitive, and behavioral skills associated with reproductive demands in adulthood.

HUMAN DEVELOPMENTAL SEX DIFFERENCES

Play Patterns

Play, in one form or another, is found in most mammalian species. "The consensus that emerges from the scores of definitions is that play incorporates many physical components of adult behavior patterns, such as those used in aggression, but without their immediate functional consequences" (Walters, 1987, p. 360). Play provides delayed benefits because the individual practices those behaviors that are important for survival and reproduction in adulthood, as described earlier. Sex differences in play patterns are found in many species and mirror sex differences found in adulthood.

Like juveniles of other mammalian species, boys and girls exhibit sex differences in their play patterns, and these differences in play are a reflection of sex differences found in adulthood (Geary, 1998). One of the most consistently found differences is in the frequency and nature of rough-and-tumble play. Beginning at about 3 years of age, groups of boys engage in various forms of play fighting, such as wrestling, three to six times more frequently than groups of girls do. Boys also engage in group-level competitive play (e.g., football) more frequently than girls do. These patterns are found in every culture in which play has been studied, are related to prenatal exposure to male hormones, and mirror the activities associated with primitive warfare (Keeley, 1996). The one-on-one and group-level play fighting of boys can be viewed as an evolved tendency to practice the competencies that were associated with male-male competition during human evolution (Geary, 1998).

Another sex difference, this one favoring girls, is in the frequency of play parenting (e.g., doll play): Play parenting is the norm in female primates and has been shown to significantly reduce the mortality rates of their first-born offspring. Again, this sex difference is found in all cultures in which play has been studied, is related to prenatal exposure to sex hormones, and mirrors the adult sex difference in investment in children. Play parenting can thus be understood as an evolved tendency to seek out activities that will enhance later parenting skills.

Social Development

Beginning in the preschool years and extending throughout the life span, girls and boys and women and men tend to segregate themselves into same-sex groups. One result is that boys and girls grow up in different social cultures. The tendency of boys to play fight and to organize themselves into competing groups is manifested in the context of the boys' culture. Social relationships among girls, in contrast, are more consistently communal: They manifest greater empathy; more concern for the well-being of other girls; and more nurturing, intimacy, and social and emotional support. In short, the social behavior of boys is focused on achieving status and dominance and developing coalitions for competing against groups of other boys. The social behavior of girls is focused on developing and maintaining a network of personal relationships and social support. Similar sex differences have been found in our closest relative, the chimpanzee, suggesting that these are indeed evolved tendencies in humans (de Waal, 1993).

Nonetheless, girls and women can be quite competitive with one another. As noted earlier, this competition takes the form of relational aggression—attempting to disrupt the personal networks that are important to girls and women—and in adulthood, it is often associated with competition over resources (e.g., job promotion) and mates. As is the case with play fighting in boys, relational aggression emerges in the preschool years for girls and appears to be especially intense during early adolescence. It is likely, although not certain, that relational aggression has been shaped by sexual selection and in childhood is practice for later female-female competition.

CULTURAL AND ECOLOGICAL INFLUENCES

If the function of childhood is to adapt inherent skeletal competencies to local conditions, then cultural and ecological factors should influence the expression of developmental sex differences (Gelman, 1990; Mayr, 1974). Although research conducted within Western countries suggests that parents do not influence children's development as strongly as many people assume, cross-cultural studies suggest that there are important socialization influences on the expression (not creation) of developmental sex differences.

Although boys throughout the world engage in one-on-one and group-level competitive play, the nature and intensity of this play varies across cultures. The play fighting of boys tends to be rougher in societies where male-on-male physical aggression is common in adulthood than in other societies. For instance, intergroup aggression occurs frequently among the Yanomamö Indians of South America, and young Yanomamö boys often play fight with clubs or bows and arrows, practices that are typically discouraged in suburban America. In such societies, boys' play fighting often involves inflicting physical pain and sometimes injury, and there are often social rules that discourage boys from expressing this pain. In other words, boys' play fighting is encouraged and channeled to increase the aggressiveness and physical endurance of boys, and decrease their sensitivity to the distress of other people. These practices prepare boys for the life-and-death male-male competition that they will experience as adults. In other societies, such as our own, boys also play fight, but this behavior is relatively subdued and symbolic, as in competitive sports.

In a study of 93 cultures. Low (1989) found that the socialization of girls and boys was systematically related to the cultures' social structures (e.g., stratified vs. nonstratified societies) and marriage systems (i.e., polygynous vs. monogamous). In nonstratified polygynous societies—where men could improve their social status and thus increase the number of women they could marry—the socialization of boys focused on fortitude, aggression, and industriousness, traits that would influence their cultural and reproductive success in adulthood. For these societies, there was a strong linear relation between the socialization of competitiveness in boys and the maximum harem size allowed within the society. The larger the maximum harem size, the more the competitiveness of boys was emphasized in parental socialization.

For girls, there was a relation between the amount of economic and political power held by women in the society and socialization practices. In societies where women could inherit property and hold political office, girls were socialized to be less obedient, more aggressive, and more achievement oriented than were girls who lived in societies in which men had control over economic and political resources. On the basis of these and other patterns, Low (1989) concluded that "there is thus some evidence that patterns of child training across cultures vary in ways predictable from evolutionary theory, differing in specifiable ways between the sexes, and varying with group size, marriage system, and stratification" (p. 318).

CONCLUSION

From an evolutionary perspective, early biases in the ways in which boys and girls orient themselves to other people, in their play patterns, and in how they interact with and explore the wider ecology are expected, and, in fact, such biases are found (Geary, 1998). They lead girls and boys to create different cultures for themselves, and within these cultures to engage in activities that prepare them for the adult life of our ancestors. At the same time, a long childhood and the associated sensitivity to environmental influences ensure that the differences between boys and girls and men and women are not fixed, but rather are responsive to changing social and ecological conditions.

The combination of biological biases and sensitivity to early environmental conditions has important scientific and social implications. For instance, although boys and men are biologically destined to compete, this competition need not be deadly nor even physical, even if the evolutionary history of male-male competition was both physical and deadly (Keeley, 1996). One goal of psychological research, then, is to understand the social and ecological conditions that can push boys and men into deadly physical competition or to compete in ways that are socially beneficial (e.g., that lead to economic development). An evolutionary perspective on development highlights the importance of social and ecological factors in the expression of developmental sex differences and will provide an important theoretical framework for the study of the social and psychological aspects of these differences.

RECOMMENDED READING

Buss, D.M. (1994). (See References)
Darwin, C. (1871). (See References)
Geary, D.C. (1998). (See References)

Morebeck, M.E., Galloway, A., & Zihlman, A.L. (Eds.). (1997). *The evolving female: A life-history perspective.* Princeton, NJ: Princeton University Press.

REFERENCES

Andersson, M. (1994). *Sexual selection.* Princeton, NJ: Princeton University Press.
Buss, D.M. (1994). *The evolution of desire: Strategies of human mating.* New York: Basic Books.
Clutton-Brock, T.H. (1991). *The evolution of parental care.* Princeton, NJ: Princeton University Press.
Collis, K., & Borgia, G. (1992). Age-related effects of testosterone, plumage, and experience on aggression and social dominance in juvenile male satin bowerbirds (*Ptilonorhynchus violaceus*). *Auk, 109,* 422–434.
Crick, N.R., Casas, J.F., & Mosher, M. (1997). Relational and overt aggression in preschool. *Developmental Psychology, 33,* 579–588.
Darwin, C. (1871). *The descent of man and selection in relation to sex* (2 vols.). London: J. Murray.
de Waal, F.B.M. (1993). Sex differences in chimpanzee (and human) behavior: A matter of social values? In M. Hechter, L. Nadel, & R.E. Michod (Eds.), *The origin of values* (pp. 285–303). New York: Aldine de Gruyter.
Eagly, A.H. (1987). *Sex differences in social behavior: A social-role interpretation.* Hillsdale, NJ: Erlbaum.

Geary, D.C. (1998). *Male, female: The evolution of human sex differences.* Washington, DC: American Psychological Association.
Gelman, R. (1990). First principles organize attention to and learning about relevant data: Number and animate-inanimate distinction as examples. *Cognitive Science, 14,* 79–106.
Keeley, L.H. (1996). *War before civilization: The myth of the peaceful savage.* New York: Oxford University Press.
Low, B.S. (1989). Cross-cultural patterns in the training of children: An evolutionary perspective. *Journal of Comparative Psychology, 103,* 311–319.
Mayr, E. (1974). Behavior programs and evolutionary strategies. *American Scientist, 62,* 650–659.
Trivers, R.L. (1972). Parental investment and sexual selection. In B. Campbell (Ed.), *Sexual selection and the descent of man 1871–1971* (pp. 136–179). Chicago: Aldine Publishing.
Walters, J.R. (1987). Transition to adulthood. In B.B. Smuts, D.L. Cheney, R.M. Seyfarth, R.W. Wrangham, & T.T. Struhsaker (Eds.), *Primate societies* (pp. 358–369). Chicago: University of Chicago Press.

On the Importance of Kin Relations to Canadian Women and Men

CATHERINE A. SALMON AND MARTIN DALY

Sex differences in the salience and meaning of kin relations for contemporary Canadians were examined in two studies. In study 1, 24 opposite-sex adult sibling pairs were asked to reconstruct their kindreds as fully as possible, following a computerized menu. Sisters almost invariably recalled more relatives than did their brothers, especially living and matrilateral relatives. In study 2, a questionnaire administered to 150 female and 150 male undergraduates explored the relevance of kinship to characterizations of the self ("Who are you?") and to nominations of one's closest social relationships. Women were much more likely than men to refer to their kinship statuses in characterizing themselves (I am a daughter, a sister, etc.), whereas 28% of men and only 8% of women mentioned their surnames (I am a Smith, Jones, etc.). Women and men were about equally likely to name a relative, as opposed to a mate or friend, as the person to whom they feel closest, but women more often nominated a parent (especially mother) and men a sibling (especially an older sister). These sex differences are discussed in relation to possible differences in how women and men make use of family ties.

Key Words: Close relationships; Family relations; Genealogical knowledge; Kinship; Self-concept; Sex differences; Sibling relations.

> *For there is no friend like a sister*
> *In calm or stormy weather.*
> —Christina Rossetti, 1991

Ever since Hamilton (1964), kinship has been of central importance to evolutionary thinking about social perceptions, motives, and action. Inclusive fitness theory implies that relatedness imparts a commonality of interests that is likely to be manifested in solidarity of feeling and behavior. In Alexander's (1979, p. 46) words, "we should have evolved to be exceedingly effective nepotists, and we should have *evolved* to be nothing else at all."

The expectation of a close connection between kinship and solidarity gains credence from the prominence of kinship in human affairs. Anthropologists find that

Reprinted from *Ethology and Sociobiology,* vol. 17, C. A. Salmon and M. Daly, "On the importance of kin relations to Canadian women and men," pp. 289–297, Copyright 1996, with permission from Elsevier.

ties of kinship exert a dominant influence on all social phenomena in relatively un-stratified, face-to-face societies, and that they remain extremely salient in more com-plex societies despite the emergence of social structures that are ostensibly independ-ent of kinship (Brown 1991; Fox 1967). According to Leach (1966), "Human beings, wherever we meet them, display an almost obsessional interest in matters of sex and kinship."

It is often maintained that the relevance of kinship to social life and personal iden-tity has been greatly diminished in modern western society (e.g., Leibowitz 1978; Cousins 1989). However, rumors of the demise of familial ties are premature. The no-tion that one attains immortality through one's descendants remains potent (e.g., Tim-berlake and Chipungu 1992), and the thousands of daily visitors to the Mormon Ge-nealogical Library in Salt Lake City attest to the continuing appeal of tracing one's ancestry (Shoumatoff 1985). Family reunions and genealogical reconstruction "open the flood gates of time gone by, reminding us who we are and where we have been . . . establishing pride in self and kin and transmitting a family's awareness of self from the youngest to the oldest" (Taylor 1986, p. 31). And family ties are not just sentimental, but practical. Adult Americans still turn to blood relatives for help, and as the required assistance increases in magnitude, they rely on kin more and on unrelated friends less (e.g., Essock-Vitale and McGuire 1985; Hogan and Eggebeen 1995; Stack 1974).

Granting that kinship networks are of psychological and behavioral significance, even in the modern west, there are several reasons for suggesting that the salience and meaning of kinship may differ for women vs. men. Although ours is a society with bi-lateral descent reckoning, it derives from a European tradition of named patricians, and a biased emphasis on patrilineage persists in our surnaming practices. Moreover, the contemporary United States retains a degree of virilocality: as in most human pop-ulations, women disperse greater distances between birth and first reproduction than do men (Koenig 1989). Nevertheless, American women see their relatives more often than men and exchange more help with them, apparently investing more effort in the maintenance of kin ties (Brody 1965; Hogan and Eggebeen 1995; Oliveri and Reiss 1987; Schneider and Cottrell 1975; Troll 1987). Similarly, Smith (1988) found that Canadian couples with young children saw more of the wife's parents (the children's maternal grandparents) than of the father's parents, despite the fact that the wife's par-ents tended to live farther away.

To compare the subjective kinship universes of American women vs. men, Schneider and Cottrell (1975) interviewed married couples and found that the wives both enumerated more relatives and professed to keep in touch with more relatives than did their husbands. Of course, spouses may differ in their actual numbers of rela-tives of any given degree, so that if a particular wife is cognizant of third cousins whereas her husband is not, we cannot be certain that the difference is one of ge-nealogical awareness. However, we can probably assume that the average woman and man have comparable kindreds and hence that Schneider and Cottrell's method would reveal average sex differences. What it cannot reveal is how consistent those differ-ences might be. A more precise way to assess any such sex differences is to ask full siblings, whose genealogies are identical except for descendants, to reconstruct their shared kindreds as best they can. This is the approach taken in study 1.

In study 2, we investigated the salience of kinship by means of a questionnaire. In addition to questions about the respondent's familial and other relationships, we elicited a series of self-characterizations in response to the question "Who are you?" This technique, adapted from Hartley (1970), has been widely used to study aspects of the self, such as the salience of ethnic identity and sex roles, but the many studies using it have paid scant attention to responses indicative of one's place in a kinship system. [A partial exception is McGuire and Padawer-Singer (1986), who at least distinguished familial from other responses in tabulating young children's answers to this question.]

METHOD

Study 1

Subjects were 24 Canadian opposite-sex sibling pairs. In 12 pairs, the brother was older, and in 12, the sister. All were native speakers of English, of predominantly European descent, with 73% having some level of university education. This availability sample, recruited through links of acquaintanceship, had a mean age of 32.6 (±18.5, SD), with a range of 15 to 91.

Each of the 48 subjects completed a structured computer menu–driven interview concerning their known relatives, without consulting the paired sibling or anyone else. The path that subjects were instructed to take through their genealogy was by generation. Parents were considered first, followed by parents' siblings and their children (i.e., the subject's cousins); the next step was grandparents and their siblings, etc. A relative was counted as having been recalled if the subject could provide a personal name other than the surname, and for each such relative, subjects were asked to provide the first and last (natal) name, relationship to the subject, parents' names, number of siblings, spouse's names, and children's names, if known.

Data from all subjects' self-reported genealogies were summarized to allow between-sex comparisons of genealogical knowledge. Differences between sibling pairs in the numbers of relatives reported in various categories, such as living vs. deceased relatives and matrilineal vs. patrilineal, were subjected to two-tailed, pairwise Wilcoxon signed rank tests, with an absence of sex differences as the null hypothesis.

Study 2

Three hundred McMaster University undergraduate students (150 female, 150 male) were asked to complete a questionnaire concerning "identity and family relationships" as partial fulfillment of a requirement (participation as a research subject or a library research paper) for an introductory course in psychology. Ages ranged from 18 to 30 with most subjects under 21 years of age. Subjects were drawn from two predominantly freshman cohorts in successive years. The questionnaire completed by the second set of 160 subjects (80 female, 80 male) included several new questions in addition to those completed by the first set of 140 subjects (70 female, 70 male), but this report concerns only items that were common to both questionnaires.

In addition to such demographic information as the subject's age, birthplace, and number and ages of siblings, subjects were asked to identify the person to whom they felt closest, how far away that individual lived, and how often they saw him/her. Subjects were also asked the following question:

> In the 10 blanks below, please make 10 different statements in response to the question "Who are you?" Write your answers in the order that they occur to you. Go fairly quickly.

The questionnaire took between 30 minutes and 1 hour to complete.

RESULTS

Study 1

Although sister-brother pairs have identical kindreds, sisters recalled more relatives (mean ± SE: 31.9 ± 2.8) than their brothers (27.5 ± 2.5) (see Table 1). This difference was highly consistent, with 20 women and only two men enumerating more relatives than did the opposite-sex sibling (Wilcoxon test: $p < .001$); in two pairs, sister and brother reported identical numbers of kin. Women performed significantly better than their brothers in recall of both ascendant and collateral kin. The female advantage was almost unanimous with respect to the naming of living relatives and was less consistent but still significant with respect to deceased kin. (Only two subjects named more deceased relatives than living ones, and these two were the oldest sibling pair in the study.) Sisters recalled maternal relatives significantly better than brothers, and also tended to recall more paternal relatives although the difference on this side was not significant. Fourteen sisters knew more natal ("maiden") surnames of their female ascendant kin than did their brothers, whereas no brother knew more than his sister ($p < .001$); 10 sibling pairs tied on this measure. Sisters' superior knowledge of these maiden names was concentrated on maternal relatives.

TABLE 1   Sex Differences in 24 Opposite-Sex Sibling Pairs' Recall of Their Shared Kindreds in Study 1

	Number of Sibships in Which Sisters Named . . .			Difference: # Named by Sister Minus # by Brother (Mean ± SE)
	More Kin Than Brothers	*Same Number as Brothers*	*Fewer Kin Than Brothers*	
All named kin	20	2	2	4.33 ± 1.38
Matrilateral	17	5	2	2.83 ± 0.70
Patrilateral	12	8	4	1.17 ± 1.01
Living	20	3	1	3.38 ± 1.13
Dead	13	9	2	0.96 ± 0.67

Female superiority of performance with respect to one kinship category was not strongly predictive of superiority with respect to another. For example, the sister-minus-brother difference in recall of maternal kin was not significantly correlated with the difference in recall of paternal kin across sibling pairs ($r = 0.243, p = .275$), and neither was the greater female recall of living relatives significantly correlated with the degree of greater female recall of deceased relatives ($r = 0.368, p = .092$).

There were no apparent influences of being the elder (29.6 ± 2.3 relatives recalled) vs. the younger (29.8 ± 2.9) sibling.

Study 2

Women and men were equally likely to make some sort of reference to familial or kinship status in answering the "Who are you?" question: 53% of women and 51% of men mentioned a family role (mother, brother, etc.), a family name, or both. However, the sexes differed significantly in the particular aspects of kinship status mentioned (Table 2), with women more likely to mention family roles and men more likely to mention their surnames as aspects of their identity ($\chi^2_{2df} = 14.4, p < .001$). In addition, considering only those who labeled themselves with a relationship term, 44% of women characterized themselves as a "daughter," whereas just 12.5% of men mentioned being a "son" ($\chi^2_{1df} = 7.2, p < .01$).

TABLE 2   Numbers of Respondents Who Mentioned Familial Roles (e.g., "I Am a Daughter") and Surnames (e.g., "I Am a Smith") When Asked to "Make 10 Different Statements in Response to the Question "Who Are You?" in Study 2

	Family Role	Family Name	Both	Neither
Women	67	0	12	71
Men	35	28	14	73

TABLE 3   Numbers of Respondents Who Nominated Relatives, Mates, or Friends in Response to the Question "Of All the People You Know Who Do You Feel Closest to?" in Study 2

Responses	Female Respondents	Male Respondents
Parent	58	40
Mother	49	28
Father	9	12
Sibling	12	22
Sister	10	15
Brother	2	7
Other genetic relative	4	4
Mate	37	40
Unrelated friend	39	44

When subjects were asked which individual they felt closest to, 83 (27.7%) nominated an unrelated friend, with mothers and mates each nominated by an additional 77 (25.7% of respondents in each case), and only 21 (7%) nominating father (Table 3). Women and men distributed their responses similarly among the three categories of relatives, mates, and unrelated friends; among those who nominated relatives, however, women were significantly likelier to nominate their mothers and men their siblings ($\chi^2_{1df} = 15.3, p < .001$). Both women and men were more likely to nominate a sister than a brother. And when sisters were nominated as the respondent's closest intimates, it was overwhelmingly older sisters: this was the case for 14 of the 15 men and eight of the 10 women who nominated sisters.

DISCUSSION

Genealogical Recall (Study 1)

Contemporary North Americans, like other people, continue to rely on relatives, feeling both some entitlement to ask kin for help and some expectation that it will be willingly provided. Women tend to keep in touch with more relatives than do men, especially maternal relatives (e.g., Schneider and Cottrell 1975), and they apparently rely on kin somewhat more than men, who are relatively likely to turn to unrelated friends instead (e.g., Hogan and Eggebeen 1995). In particular, matrilateral kin are a woman's primary social resources, providing child care, economic assistance, and emotional support (e.g., Stack 1974; Essock-Vitale and McGuire 1985), so it is not surprising that women are highly knowledgeable about them. In this study, women exhibited greater interest in and/or recall of kin than their brothers, especially matrilateral kin. One interpretation is that people who rely heavily on relatives invest the most cognitive resources in keeping track of relatives, and especially relatives in those lineages and subfamilies most relied upon.

Alternatively, the women's superior performance in study 1 might be one manifestation of a sex difference in processing or retrieving social information, rather than being specific to kin. One way to address this hypothesis would be to assess whether sisters can name more unrelated family friends, neighbours, or public figures in various categories than their brothers, perhaps restricting the study to coresiding siblings. It is unlikely that the differential performance reflects an even more domain-general female advantage in this sort of task, since the evidence on sex differences in episodic (as opposed to semantic) memory is mixed, with men doing better on some tasks (e.g., Clifford and Scott 1978), women on others (e.g., Ellis, Shephard, and Bruce 1973), and the sexes performing equally well on still others (e.g., Cunningham and Bringmann 1986). But although there is no general superiority of women in memory tasks, sex differences may emerge when the content to be recalled is of sex-differential salience. Geer and McGlone (1990) investigated sex differences in memory for elements of sexual stories containing romantic, erotic, and neutral elements, for example, finding that whereas the sexes did not differ in responding to the "neutral" sentences, women were quicker and more accurate on romantic elements, whereas men were quicker and more accurate on erotic ones.

If kinship is cognitively distinct, one might hypothesize that women's and men's minds are fundamentally different in this domain. Just as there appear to be distinct female and male sexualities as a result of the different selective pressures faced by women vs. men during human evolution, there could be evolved sex differences in human kinship cognition, as a result of the different social ecologies encountered by the sexes. However, female superiority in genealogical recall is not necessarily cross-culturally universal or even usual. Chagnon (1988) has reported that among the Yanomamö Indians of Venezuela, men, for whom the reconstruction of lineages is crucial for negotiating both marital entitlement and alliance in warfare, are apparently more adept at classifying kin than are women. In a modern nation state like Canada, men are presumably much less dependent on kinsmen, and they may rely more on non-kin reciprocal relationships than women largely because local sex roles afford them more opportunities for interaction with non-relatives. To the extent that sexually differentiated benefits of kinship ties and knowledge vary in relation to locale-specific sex roles and practices in domains such as marriage and intergroup conflict, it appears from the Canada-Yanomamö contrast that sex differences in genealogical abilities and interest vary in parallel. Nevertheless, cross-culturally general evolved sex differences in aspects of interests or abilities remain a possibility worthy of investigation, and more detailed comparison of genealogical recall by women and men in societies with different patterns of kin association could be enlightening.

Identity and Closeness (Study 2)

In responding to the question "Who are you?", many subjects did not refer to their kinship statuses at all, lending some support to claims (e.g., Cousins 1989) that the modern American sense of identity is more concerned with personal physical or attributive traits than with social roles. However, it should be noted that these young adults, 96% single and 99% childless, may represent a life stage in which sociality has an especially strong extrafamilial focus. Testing a wider age range could be of interest, as it is certainly possible that salient aspects of identity change in systematic ways over the lifecourse. For example, the presence of children who could benefit from collateral kin investment may make family especially salient to parents. But be that as it may, just over half of the present respondents of both sexes did mention family roles or surnames in answering "Who are you?" (Table 2), and almost half nominated a genetic relative when asked to name the one person to whom they felt closest (Table 3).

Women were more likely than men to mention their family role(s), such as daughter or sister, whereas men were more likely to mention their surnames (Table 2). Most strikingly, in response to "Who are you?", 28 men but not a single woman provided a "clan" name without any additional reference to the respondent's individual familial relationship status(es). It is perhaps unsurprising that patrilineally derived surnames should be of little salience to female identity, both because women derive so much of their social support from maternal relatives and because most still relinquish their natal surnames at marriage (although it should again be noted that these women were almost all single). It may be somewhat more surprising that a named patrilineage is still a significant element in the identity of Canadian males.

Differential emphasis on one's place within a kinship structure was particularly evident in the relative importance attached to being a daughter vs. a son. Thirty-five women used the word "daughter" in responding to "Who are you?", whereas only six men used the word "son," a much larger sex difference than the 58 women vs. 40 men who nominated a parent as the one person to whom they felt "closest." It has been suggested that mothers actively influence and shape the relationships of all family members with extended kin and that this may be based on an enduring, intimate tie between mother and daughter (Oliveri and Reiss 1987). Under such circumstances, a woman's role in her family may be particularly salient.

If young men tend to break away from family ties and invest themselves in male-male alliances, we might expect them to emphasize friendships, whereas women, who value family responsibility and relationships more highly, would place greater emphasis on closeness to parents, particularly their mothers (Char and McDermott 1987). Women in our study 2 were indeed more likely than men to name parents (especially mothers) as their closest interactants, but men were only slightly more likely than women to nominate unrelated friends. A larger difference was in the frequency of nominating siblings (Table 3). One might propose that fraternal solidarity derives from the fact that brothers have long been a man's most valuable allies, but the men in this study nominated sisters as their closest interactants ($n = 15$) substantially more often than brothers ($n = 7$). This perception of cross-sex sibling closeness is apparently not reciprocated, since only two women nominated a brother as their closest interactant, whereas 10 nominated a sister. Without responses from both members of sibling pairs, it remains unclear to what extent these professions of closeness may be systematically asymmetrical, but some light may be shed by the fact that 88% of respondents who named sisters as their closest interactants named older sisters. The question apparently evoked thoughts of asymmetrical relationships, perhaps with more experienced persons in whom the respondents feel able to confide. Asking respondents from broods of three or more to nominate the sibling to whom they feel closest might further clarify these sibling attachments.

In sum, sisters recalled more relatives than their brothers; men stressed patrilineal surnames as identity features more than women; women stressed specific kin roles more than men; and although respondents of both sexes nominated mother above all other relatives in naming their closest interactants, men were more likely than women to name a sibling instead. These results may be interpreted as reflecting a female kinship psychology that is relatively focused on specific genealogical links between generations and a male psychology that is somewhat more concerned with patrilineal group identity and same-generation alliances. Such sex differences in the meaning or salience of various aspects of kinship could reflect naturally selected responses to consistent differences in the ways in which women and men have made use of their kin, but the contrast between these Canadian results and Chagnon's (1988) Yanomamö data indicates that sex differences in genealogical interest and expertise are labile. Only further study can clarify whether the phenomena reported here are in any way reflections of a sexually differentiated kinship cognition as a result of a history of selection, or are instead the manifestations of a sexually monomorphic psychology responding to the somewhat different social demands and opportunities facing contemporary Canadian women and men.

REFERENCES

Alexander, R.D. *Darwinism and Human Affairs,* Seattle. WA: University of Washington Press, 1979.

Brody, E. Parent care as a normative family stress. *Gerontologist* 25:19–29, 1965.

Brown, D.E. *Human Universals,* New York: McGraw-Hill, 1991.

Chagnon, N.A. Male Yanomamö manipulations of kinship classifications of female kin for reproductive advantage. In *Human Reproductive Behavior: A Darwinian Perspective,* L. Betzig. M. Borgerhoff Mulder, and P. Turke (Eds.). New York: Cambridge University Press, 1988.

Char, W.F., and McDermott, J.F. Family relationships: different attitudes of adolescent boys and girls. *Medical Aspects of Human Sexuality* August 36–43, 1987.

Clifford, B.R., and Scott, J. Individual and situational factors in eyewitness testimony. *Journal of Applied Psychology* 63:352–359, 1978.

Cousins, S.D. Culture and self-perception in Japan and the United States. *Journal of Personality and Social Psychology* 56:124–131, 1989.

Cunningham, J.L., and Bringmann, W.G. A re-examination of William Stem's classic eyewitness research. *Perceptual and Motor Skills* 63:565–566, 1986.

Ellis, H., Shephard, J., and Bruce, A. The effect of age and sex upon adolescents recognition of faces. *Journal of Genetic Psychology* 123:173–174, 1973.

Essock-Vitale, S.M., and McGuire, M.T. Women's lives viewed from an evolutionary perspective. II. Patterns of helping. *Ethology and Sociobiology* 6:155–173, 1985.

Fox, R. *Kinship and Marriage: An Anthropological Perspective,* New York: Penguin, 1967.

Geer, J.H., and McGlone, M.S. Sex differences in memory for erotica. *Cognition and Emotion* 4: 71–78, 1990.

Hamilton, W.D. The genetical evolution of social behaviour I and II. *Journal of Theoretical Biology* 7:1–52, 1964.

Hartley, W.S. *Manual for the Twenty Statements Problem,* Kansas City. MO: Greater Kansas City Mental Health Foundation Department of Research, 1970.

Hogan, D.P., and Eggebeen, D.J. Sources of emergency help and routine assistance in old age. *Social Forces* 73:917–936, 1995.

Koenig, W.D. Sex-biased dispersal in the contemporary United States. *Ethology and Sociobiology* 10: 263–278, 1989.

Leach, E. Virgin birth. *Proceedings of the Royal Anthropological Institute of Great Britain and Ireland,* pp. 39–49, 1966.

Leibowitz, L. *Females, Males, Families: A Biosocial Approach,* North Scituate, MA: Duxbury, 1978.

McGuire, W.J., and Padawer-Singer, A. Trait salience in the spontaneous self-concept. *Journal of Personality and Social Psychology* 53:743–754, 1986.

Oliveri, M.E., and Reiss, D. Social networks of family members: distinctive roles of mothers and fathers. *Sex Roles* 17:719–739, 1987.

Rossetti, C. Goblin market. In *The Penguin Dictionary of Quotations,* J.M. Cohen and M. J. Cohen (Eds.). London: Bloomsbury Press, 1991.

Schneider, D.M., and Cottrell, C.B. *The American Kin Universe: A Genealogical Study,* Chicago: University of Chicago Press, 1975.

Shoumatoff, A. *The Mountain of Names: A History of the Human Family,* New York: Simon and Schuster, 1985.

Smith, M.S. Research in developmental sociobiology: parenting and family behavior. In *Sociological Perspectives on Human Development,* K. MacDonald (Ed.). New York: Springer, 1988.

Stack, C.B. *All Our Kin,* New York: Harper and Row, 1974.

Taylor, R.M. *Generations and Change: Genealogical Perspectives in Social History,* Macon, GA, Mercer Press, 1986.

Timberlake, E. M., and Chipungu, S.S. Grandmotherhood: contemporary meaning among African American middle-class grandmothers. *Social Work* 37:216–222, 1992.

Troll, L.E. Gender differences in cross-generation networks. *Sex Roles* 17:751–763, 1987.